Macroeconomics

Macroeconomics

William Boyes
Arizona State University

Michael Melvin
Arizona State University

HOUGHTON MIFFLIN COMPANY　　BOSTON
Dallas　Geneva, Illinois　Palo Alto　Princeton, New Jersey

To Susan, Katie, and my father, and in memory of my mother and my first economics instructor, John Merriam

W.B.

To Cathy, Jason, Jeremy, and Flo

M.M.

CREDITS

Cover photograph by Ralph Mercer, Boston, MA.

Part and chapter opener photos: Part I, Lisl Dennis/The Image Bank; Part II, Courtesy Matthaes Verlag GMBH, Stuttgart; Part III, H. Mark Weidman; Part IV, Brett Froomer/The Image Bank; Part V, Walter Bibikow/The Image Bank.

Text credits: Appendix to Chapter 1, "The One Who Has the Most Toys When He Dies, Wins." Reprinted with permission from PSYCHOLOGY TODAY MAGAZINE Copyright © 1987 (PT Partners, L.P.).

Printed in the U.S.A.

Library of Congress Catalog Card Number: 90-83022

ISBN: 0-395-48276-3

ABCDEFGHIJ-VH-9543210

Preface

When we looked at today's students and the world they will enter on graduation, we saw a gap: we felt that students would increasingly expect their courses to prepare them to live in a global economy. When we looked at the traditional principles texts and the information our students will need, we saw a gap: the current economic world is vastly different from the one described in most textbooks. We set out to close that gap by writing a textbook that would give students the tools they need to understand the world they face.

Today's economic environment is a global environment. The decisions made by a firm or a government in one part of the world will have far-reaching effects. The coming together of Germany and the vitality of the European Community; the freeing of restraints in Eastern Europe, Russia, and other parts of the communist world; the struggles in Latin America and the Middle East—all affect the U.S. economy and the lives of U.S. citizens. In a like manner, actions taken by the United States and by its citizens alter economic patterns around the globe. ECONOMICS gives students the tools they need to make connections between the principles they learn and the world they live in.

ECONOMICS is the only book designed from the beginning with the intention of presenting a global perspective. By fully integrating international topics throughout the text *from the very beginning,* we have internationalized the study of economics without increasing the difficulty for students or faculty. The basic macroeconomic material is highly readable and accessible even to those who have had no training in international issues.

Throughout the writing process we were continually reminded by our reviewers that we must approach this challenge with care. We are thankful for their good advice, for it became apparent that there were many good reasons why instructors had experienced difficulty as they tried to incorporate international factors into their courses. For this reason we meticulously constructed our core chapters so that they appropriately serve a traditional course structure. For those less willing to dedicate class time to international concerns and variables, you will find our overall structure very accessible.

Throughout each phase of the development, we kept in mind that this text *must* adhere to a few basic principles.

☐ Stress the fundamental concepts.

☐ Connect them to the real world through applications and examples.

☐ Note and explain the deviations and departures from the outcomes predicted in models.

☐ Provide a framework for understanding and critiquing rather than a prescription for answers.

☐ Motivate students to engage in further observation and critical thinking.

Our intention, then, was that by adhering to these basic principles of good authorship, we would expand the traditional scope of the principles course and provide an arena in which economics educators could present and students could absorb the principles of the global economy.

We hope that this text well serves all the students who use it—those who major in business, psychology, education, engineering, English, and other fields, as well as those who choose to pursue economics. All of these readers will inevitably be faced with new issues and questions as the world's economic story continues to unfold.

OVERALL ORGANIZATION AND CONTENT — FLEXIBILITY AND CONNECTIONS

Flexibility and connections are key to the organization of this text. Parts II and IV, the specifically macroeconomic chapters, are self-contained and independent, yet each builds on the introductory concepts presented in the first five chapters and prepares students for the international material at the end of the text. Because this text contains international as well as introductory chapters, it is equally suitable for macro-first or micro-first course sequences.

Flexibility and connections underlie the organization within parts and within chapters as well. The introductory chapters are followed by an IDEA MAP that helps students visualize the relationship of ideas to be covered. We purposely structure Parts II through IV so that they progress from descriptions of basic concepts and analytical tools to policy issues and applications. Within each chapter this same structure exists. We identify key points through our fundamental question system and then go on to explain, exemplify, and apply these fundamentals. Color and photographs on part openers and chapter openers reinforce the interrelatedness of chapters within a part. Numbered headings within each chapter make it easy to point students to specific sections and to reinforce a hierarchy of ideas. By using section references in end-of-chapter summaries and lists of key terms, students are encouraged to group related concepts and terms. Readers are less likely to memorize terms and models in isolation and more likely to see how they fit together to make a whole. Our text will provide ample support for all instructors who are striving to teach their students to think economically rather than merely to memorize isolated facts and figures.

We wanted to provide additional flexibility in our approach to the quantitative side of economics. Appendixes allow instructors to tailor their course to their objectives and their students' abilities. The appendix to Chapter 1 is essential. Students must understand how to read and construct graphs. This appendix tells them what they need to know. Appendixes to the macroeconomic chapters provide algebraic models of aggregate expenditures and macroeconomic equilibrium. Thus, instructors can rely solely on description and graphical analysis by assigning the main chapter only, or they can incorporate algebraic solutions into their course by assigning the appendixes as well. The appendix to Chapter 20 presents indifference analysis, a topic that many instructors cover either to augment their micro coverage or to give students a natural lead-in to the intermediate course.

THOROUGHLY INTEGRATED INTERNATIONAL COVERAGE

Students understand that they live in a global economy—they can hardly shop, or watch the news, or read a major newspaper without understanding this basic fact. International examples are presented in almost every chapter. By introducing, in a descriptive and nontechnical manner, the basics of the foreign exchange market and the balance of payments in Chapter 7, we are able to incorporate the international sector into the theoretical models wherever appropriate thereafter. Because the international content is incorporated from the beginning, students will develop a far more realistic picture of the economy; they will not have to later alter their thinking to allow for international factors. Recognizing that some instructors may wish to reserve international concerns for the last section of their course, we provide international trade and finance chapters in the traditional place. These instructors can follow a very traditional pattern by skipping certain early chapters and treating the international material in detail at the end of their course. In either case, the instructor is in no danger of omitting international coverage. This text offers the optimal opportunity for business programs to better answer the American Assembly of Collegiate Schools of Business (AACSB) call to prepare the student "for imaginative and responsible citizenship and leadership roles in business and society—domestic and worldwide."

Uniquely international elements of the macroeconomic coverage include

☐ Treatment of the international sector as one of the economic participants and inclusion of net exports as early as Chapter 5

☐ Early description of the foreign exchange market and the balance of payments in Chapter 7

☐ Inclusion of international elements in Chapters 9 and 10, including the integration of international effects into the examination of the multiplier

☐ Extended treatment of macroeconomic links between countries in Chapter 17

☐ Examination of foreign exchange risk and international lending in Chapter 23

MODERN MACROECONOMIC ORGANIZATION AND CONTENT

Macroeconomics is changing and textbooks must reflect that change. We begin with the basics—GNP, unemployment, and inflation. These are the ongoing concerns of any economy, for they have a significant influence on how people feel. These are the issues that don't go away. Added to these core basics is an easy-to-understand, descriptive introduction to the foreign exchange market and the balance of payments. We provide a critical alternative for those instructors who believe that it is no longer reasonable to relegate this material to the final chapters, where coverage may be rushed. Instructors today cannot afford *not* to get to this material. The basics covered here present the world as students experience it.

Armed with these basics, students are ready to delve into the richness of macroeconomic thought. Macro models and approaches have evolved over the years, and they continue to invite exciting theoretical and policy debates. The majority of instructors we asked voiced frustration with the challenge of pulling this rich and varied material together in class and stressed that a coherent picture of the aggregate demand and supply model was critical. We have structured the macro portion to allow for many teaching preferences while assuring a clear delineation of the aggregate demand/aggregate supply model.

To help instructors successfully build up to and present a single coherent model, we provide a carefully paced discussion of the logical, rather than the strictly historical, foundations of the aggregate demand/aggregate supply model in Chapters 9 and 10. Instructors may decide for themselves how much time they wish to spend on this material. Chapter 11 then presents a readily understood and complete picture of aggregate supply and aggregate demand. This clear progression is much more easily grasped than a brief introduction of aggregate demand and aggregate supply followed by a lengthy explanation of the foundations and then a return to the AD/AS model. We deliberately avoid the distracting and often confusing habit of continually contrasting different schools of thought. In our experience (and our reviewers concur), students want to know where macroeconomics is today. By structuring the core macro chapters as we do, we offer an extraordinarily teachable and flexible layout that presents a careful and logical base leading toward a single model.

The macroeconomic policy chapters begin with a fairly traditional presentation of fiscal policy, money and banking, and monetary policy—with international elements included. Chapter 15 covers contemporary policy issues, and various schools of thought are treated in Chapter 16, when students are ready to appreciate the differences and can benefit from a discussion of new Keynesian and new classical models as well as of their precursors. Chapter 17 develops macroeconomic links between countries. This chapter helps students understand why economies cannot function in isolation from each other and clearly demonstrates why policy actions undertaken by one government affect not only that government's own citizens but citizens and businesses in other countries as well.

Part IV, Economic Growth and Development, brings together the concepts and issues presented in the core macro chapters to explain how economies grow and what factors encourage or discourage growth. Most of Eastern Europe has embarked on a journey from a planned economy to a market economy. Growth and development are critical to them, as well as to countries that are beset by unchecked inflation and crippling international debt. These chapters build on macro foundations to permit informed analysis of today's world.

ABUNDANT TEACHING AND LEARNING AIDS

This text is designed to make teaching easier by enhancing student learning. Tested pedagogy motivates students, emphasizes clarity, reinforces relationships, simplifies review, and fosters critical thinking.

Fundamental Questions

These questions help to organize the chapter and highlight those issues that are critical to understanding. Students can preview chapters with these questions in mind, reading actively for understanding and retention. The Fundamental Questions reappear in the margin by the text discussion that helps students to answer the question. Fundamental Questions also serve to organize the chapter summaries. Brief paragraphs answering each of these questions are found in the *Study Guides* available as supplements to this text. They also serve as one of several criteria used to categorize questions in the *Test Bank*.

In-text Referencing System

Sections are numbered for easy reference and to reinforce hierarchies of ideas. The key term list and summary at the end of the chapter refer students back to the appropriate *section*. If students can't recall a term or don't understand a point in the summary, they cannot merely turn to a page to memorize a definition or a sentence. The implicit message in this referencing system is that students must try to understand and draw connections between the concepts.

The numbering system also makes it easy to clearly assign portions of a chapter, enhancing the flexibility of the text.

In-text Study System

Pedagogical elements were designed to work together to simplify the task of understanding and retaining the material.

Preview. This motivating lead-in sets the stage for the chapter. Much more than a road map, it helps students identify real issues that relate to the concepts that will be presented.

Recaps. Briefly listing the main points covered, a recap appears at the end of each major section within a chapter. Students are reminded to quickly review what they have just read before going on to the next section.

Summary. The summary at the end of each chapter is organized along two dimensions. The primary organizational device is the list of Fundamental Questions. A brief synopsis of the discussion that helps students to answer those questions is arranged by section below each of the questions. Students are encouraged to create their own links between material as they keep in mind the connections between the "big picture" and the details that comprise it.

Margin Notes

Student Annotations. These hints and comments highlight especially important concepts, point out common mistakes, and warn students of common pitfalls. They alert students to parts of the discussion that they should read with particular care.

Key Terms. Key terms appear in bold type in the text. They also appear with their definition in the margin and are listed at the end of the chapter for easy review. All key terms are included in the glossary at the end of the text.

Fundamental Questions. The fundamental questions presented at the beginning of the chapter appear again next to the discussion that helps students formulate answers to these questions.

Exercises

These exercises provide excellent self-checks for students whose instructors do not assign the exercises as homework.

Basic Terms and Concepts. The exercises rely generally on recognition and recall: Do students remember what they read?

Extended Concepts. The exercises in this group ask students to work with the ideas presented in the chapter: Do they know how to apply the concepts? Can they perform necessary computations? Can they draw conclusions about the real world based on the theories presented?

FULL-COLOR ART PROGRAM

Over 200 figures rely on well-developed pedagogy and consistent use of color to reinforce understanding. Striking colors were chosen to enhance readability and provide visual interest. Experienced art editors developed a color palette that would help students recognize curves and grasp relationships. Specific curves were assigned specific colors. Each time a particular curve appears, it is shown in the same color. Families of curves were assigned related colors. Once again, the pedagogy emphasizes connections.

Because some students have difficulty seeing changes in color intensity or recognizing that related colors refer to the same curve, we have shown curve shifts through the use of slashed lines for the first shift and dotted lines for a subsequent shift. Where a curve may shift either in or out and there is no reference to time sequence (it is an either/or situation), both shifts are shown with dashes to emphasize that one shift is not dependent on or subsequent to the other. One very substantial benefit of this system is the ease with which it can be used at the chalkboard or in notetaking. We chose to illustrate complex sequences of shifts with a series of side-by-side graphs where relying on a single graph would be confusing.

Annotations on the art point out areas of particular concern or importance. Students can see exactly what parts of the graph illustrate a shortage or a surplus, a change in consumption or consumer surplus. The art annotations are the same color as the margin statements. Students know in each case that here is material they should look at carefully to be sure they understand it.

Tables that provide data from which graphs are plotted are paired with their graphs. Where appropriate, color is used to show correlations between the art and the table, as can be seen in Figure 8 in Chapter 3. There the pale yellow screen in the area that shows a surplus echoes the screen over the top two rows of the table, which also show a surplus. The light blue screen designating the area of shortage in the graph echoes the screen over the bottom two rows of the table, which show shortage values.

Extensive captions clearly explain what is shown in the figures and draw explicit connections between the art and the text discussion. Because the critical information is contained in the caption, students can find it easily and have no need to hunt for it in the text.

ENHANCED STUDENT RELEVANCE

With all the demands on today's students, it's no wonder that they resist spending time on a subject unless they see how the material relates to them and how they will benefit from mastering it. We worked hard to incorporate features throughout the text that would show economics as the relevant and necessary subject we know it to be.

Photo Essays

The photo essay—Making Sense of Macroeconomics—engages student interest. Through the use of visually arresting photographs and highly readable text, we show students just how directly macroeconomics affects them. Students can see at a glance that the material they will be studying makes a difference in their own lives.

Idea Maps

The idea map portrays significant interconnections between topics and encourages students to find their own paths through the material. This overview helps them keep the "big picture" in focus while they are concentrating on the details presented in individual topics. These cognitive "hooks" allow for superior retention, comprehension, and synthesis.

Real-world Examples

Students are rarely intrigued by a large manufacturer or a service company. Our text talks about people and firms that students recognize. We describe business decisions made by McDonald's and Pizza Hut, by General Motors and Shearson Lehman Hutton. We talk about the war on drugs and the results of rent control in New York City. These examples grab students' interest. Reviewers have repeatedly praised the use of novel examples to convey economic concepts.

Economic Insight

These short boxes bring in contemporary material from current periodicals and journals to illustrate or extend the discussion in the chapter. By reserving interesting but more technical sidelights for boxes, we lessen the likelihood that students will be confused or distracted by issues that are not critical to understanding the chapter. By including excerpts from articles we help students learn to move from theory to real-world example. And by including plenty of contemporary issues, we guarantee that students will see how economics relates to their own lives.

Economically Speaking

The objective of the principles course is to teach students how to translate the predictions that come out of economic models to the real world and to translate real-world events into an economic model in order to analyze and understand what lies behind the events. The Economically Speaking boxes present students with a model of this kind of analysis. First they read an article which appears on the left-hand page of a two-page spread at the end of each chapter. The commentary on the right-hand page shows how the facts and events in the article translate into a specific economic model or idea, thereby moving the student from reality back to theory.

Carefully Selected Photographs

Vibrant photos that tell a story and illustrate a concept appear throughout the text. Captions explain what is in the photo and draw connections between these images and the discussion in the text. Careful coordination between text, photograph, and caption help students make concepts concrete, enhancing retention of the material and increasing the relevance of the material.

FULLY INTEGRATED TEACHING AND LEARNING PACKAGE

In today's market no book is complete without a full complement of ancillaries. Our package provides the breadth and depth of support for both instructors and students that the market has a right to demand. The ancillary package for ECONOMICS is second to none. Throughout its development, we have kept today's economics instructor in mind. Those instructors who face huge classes find good transparencies (acetates) and transparency masters critical instructional tools. Others, who teach small classes, may find that computer simulations and tutorials are invaluable. ECONOMICS meets both challenges. And to foster the development of consistent teaching and study strategies, the ancillaries pick up pedagogical features of the text—like the fundamental questions—wherever appropriate.

Transparencies   Available to adopters are 164 color acetates showing the most important figures in the text. Over 10 percent of these figures have one to three overlays, which in addition to adding clarity and flexibility to the discussion, allow instructors to visually demonstrate the dynamic nature of economics.

Instructor's Resource Manual   Edward T. Merkel and Paul S. Estenson, two experienced and highly talented economists with a wealth of classroom experience, have collaborated to produce a manual that will streamline preparation for both new and experienced faculty. Preliminary sections cover class administration and alternative syllabi. Each chapter contains

☐ Teaching Objectives. *What are the critical points to cover if your students are to succeed with later chapters?* You can ensure that the foundations are laid and that students see connections between topics.

What concepts are traditionally difficult for students to master? You can concentrate on these topics and develop classroom exercises to bring these topics into clearer focus.

What are the unique features of this chapter? You may wish to augment your lectures and treat these topics differently than you have in the past.

☐ Fundamental Questions listed.

☐ Key Terms listed.

☐ Lecture Outline. The in-text reference system comes into play again in the lecture outline. The numbered heads are picked up from the main text. The authors have identified primary points to cover each section and have suggested examples and classroom activities that have worked well for them or that have been suggested by instructors who reviewed the text.

☐ Teaching Tips. More general techniques and guidelines, essay topics, and other hints to enliven your classes are presented.

☐ Answers to End-of-Chapter Questions. Every exercise in this text is answered here.

☐ Transparency Masters. Significant figures that do not appear in the transparency package are included here.

Study Guides Janet L. Wolcutt and James E. Clark of the Center for Economic Education at Wichita State University have written study guides for MACROECONOMICS and MICROECONOMICS that give students the practice they need to master this course. These two dynamic teachers have come up with an abundance of exercises that reinforce classroom learning and that build student confidence. Written in a warm and lively style, the study guides should keep students on the right track. In each chapter

☐ Fundamental Questions are answered in one or several paragraphs. For students who have trouble formulating their own answers to these questions after reading the text, the study guides provide an invaluable model.

☐ Key terms are listed.

☐ Quick Check Quiz is organized by section, so any wrong answers send the student directly to the relevant material in the text. These questions focus on vocabulary and basic concepts. They alert students to sections of the chapter that they forgot or didn't understand.

☐ Practice Questions and Problems, which is also organized by section, includes a variety of question formats—multiple choice, true/false, matching, and fill-in-the-blank. They test understanding of the concepts and ask students to construct or perform computations.

☐ Thinking About and Applying . . . use the Economically Speaking boxes as a springboard for applications or present new situations for students to think about.

☐ Answers are provided to every question in the study guides. Students are referred back to relevant pages in the main text. Rejoinders are provided where appropriate to alert students to common mistakes or likely reasons for an incorrect answer.

Test Bank Over 5,000 test items provide a wealth of material for classroom testing. All items are identified by topic, question type (factual, interpretative, or applied), level of difficulty, and applicable fundamental question. In addition, the page on which the answer is found is shown for the complete volume and for macro and micro splits. Each chapter includes 5 test items taken directly from the study guide and 5 test items that parallel study guide questions. Instructors who wish to ensure very high similarity between the study guide and classroom tests are able to do so.

FOR THE COMPUTER

PC Test Bank Plus

This innovative test-assembly program renders precise, preprogrammed graphs on the computer quickly, easily, and accurately. You can select from among more than 5,000 questions, edit nongraphic items, peruse items in order, add your own questions to customize tests, and print out alternate versions using a number of variables. Individual items or tests in their entirety can be previewed before printing. The sophisticated data retrieval capabilities of the computerized test bank allow instructors to generate multiple versions of a test automatically and assure comparability of tests consisting of different test items. Available for IBM-PC®, PS/2, and compatible microcomputers.

LXR Test

This state-of-the-art graphic test generator combines text-editing tools for creating or editing test questions with powerful layout features, graphic printing capabilities, and more. Multiple versions of a test can be generated quickly. Available for Macintosh® microcomputers.

Computerized Macroeconomics and Microeconomics Tutorial Package

This easy-to-use software exploits the dynamic capabilities of the computer to create a highly interactive environment for learning. Each of the more than 35 modules reviews a major concept, then asks questions that require students to change variables and work with graphs. For questions answered incorrectly, page numbers refer students back to the appropriate text discussion. Scores are displayed at the end of each module. Available for IBM-PC®, PS/2, and compatible microcomputers.

Computerized Macroeconomics® and Macroeconomics Simulation Package

The simulation builds on the tutorial program by asking students to apply concepts to real-world situations and evaluate the consequences. Unlike most simulation packages, Boyes/Melvin's is highly graphical, thereby promoting analytical skills. If students encounter problems with a particular decision, they are referred back to both the appropriate text page and tutorial module for further review. Available for IBM-PC®, PS/2, and compatible microcomputers.

ACKNOWLEDGMENTS

Writing a text of this scope is a challenge that requires the expertise and efforts of many. We are grateful to our friends and colleagues who have so generously given their time, creativity, and insight to help us create a text that best meets the needs of today's classroom.

We especially want to thank the panel of instructors who reviewed our entire manuscript. In many respects, they were our collaborators—offering suggestions for improvement and innovation, redirecting us when we lost focus, and patiently awaiting new sections of manuscript. Their criticisms and encouragement were invaluable. Now they can see their contributions in print rather than on the manuscript page.

Throughout the development of the text, there were many instructors who reviewed sections of the manuscript, sometimes more than once and often, many sections. We thank them for their candor and diligence in pointing out problems and offering solutions.

We also want to thank our colleagues at Arizona State who have supported us through this entire process. Sometimes a quick answer to a question or a bit of advice provided the new direction we needed to overcome a particularly critical challenge.

During two focus group sessions, one in Atlanta and another in Orlando, we uncovered many ways to improve our manuscript. We very much appreciate the focus group members for their willingness to talk frankly about their course and our manuscript.

Special thanks also go to Michael Klein, who not only reviewed much of this manuscript, but devoted an enormous effort to the Economically Speaking feature. Michael selected many of the articles and developed the commentary for these pieces. We are most grateful for his ability to give concrete form to our objective—showing students how to think like an economist and translate reality back into theory.

We owe a special debt to Tom Oberhofer of Eckerd College for his vision for the idea maps. We met Tom at a focus group in Atlanta where we first proposed the idea of linking the major macroeconomic and microeconomic concepts and issues in a visual way for the students. Tom saw our idea as an exciting opportunity to provide students with an Idea Map and generously provided the time and energy to get it accomplished.

We extend special thanks to Jay Sultan of Bentley College, who patiently reviewed every graph and caption to assure accuracy throughout. His painstaking and thorough approach, combined with the proofreading efforts of many dedicated individuals, has resulted in a text instructors and students can be sure of.

We also want to thank the many people at Houghton Mifflin who devoted countless hours to make this text the best it could be. From the beginning, we have been impressed with their expertise and energy. Through the mail, computer systems, phone, and sometimes by plane, we have managed to join forces continually for the last three years. We could not have completed this book without their enthusiasm and devotion.

Finally, we wish to thank our families and friends. The inspiration they provided through the conception and development of this book cannot be measured, but certainly was essential.

Our students at Arizona State University have helped us along the way: their many questions have given us invaluable insight into how best to present this intriguing subject. It is our hope that this textbook will bring a clear understanding of economic thought to many other students as well. We welcome any feedback for improvements.

W.B.
M.M.

Reviewers

Shahid Alam
Northeastern University

Lori Alden
California State University,
   Sacramento

Maurice Ballabon
City University of New York—
   Baruch College

Mark Berger
University of Kentucky

Donna Bialik
Indiana–Purdue University

Mary Bone
Pensacola Junior College

Bradley Braun
University of Central Florida

Jacqueline Brux
University of Wisconsin

Joan Buccino
Florida Southern College

Conrad Caligaris
Northeastern University

Michael Couvillion
Plymouth State College

Andy Dane
Angelo State University

Elynor Davis
Georgia Southern College

Gary Dymski
University of Southern California

Ana Eapen
William Paterson College

John Eckalbar
California State University, Chico

Paul Estenson
Gustavus Adolphus College

Paul Fahy
Eastern Illinois University

Joel Feiner
State University of New York at
   Old Westbury

Peter Garlick
State University of New York at
   New Paltz

John Gemello
San Francisco State University

Morton Hirsch
Kingsboro Community College

Beth Ingram
University of Iowa

David Jobson
Keystone Junior College

George Kelley
Worcester State College

Dick Kennedy
Odessa College

Barbara Killen
University of Minnesota

Michael Klein
Clark University

Keith Leeseberg
Manatee Community College

James Marchand
Radford University

James Mason
San Diego Mesa College

Edward Merkel
Troy State University

Irving Morrissett
University of Colorado

Denny Myers
Oklahoma City College

Joseph Nieb
Embry-Riddle Aeronautical
   University

Thomas Oberhofer
Eckerd College

Gerard O'Boyle
St. John's University

Erin O'Brien
San Diego Mesa College

Albert Okunade
Memphis State University

Paul Reali
Bryant & Stratton Business
  Institute

Robert Reinke
University of South Dakota

James Rigterink
Polk Community College

Randell Routt
Elizabethtown Community
  College

Gerald Sazama
University of Connecticut

Paul Schmitt
St. Clair County Community
  College

Carole Scott
West Georgia College

William Doyle Smith
University of Texas at El Paso

W.R. Smith
Georgia Southern College

Todd Steen
Hope College

Andrew Stern
California State University,
  Long Beach

Thomas Tacker
Embry-Riddle Aeronautical
  University

Eugenia Toma
University of Kentucky

William Trumbull
West Virginia University

Thomas Watkins
Eastern Kentucky University

Marc Zagara
Community College of the Finger
  Lakes

Brief Contents

Contents

Contents

Contents

Macroeconomics

Introduction to the Price System

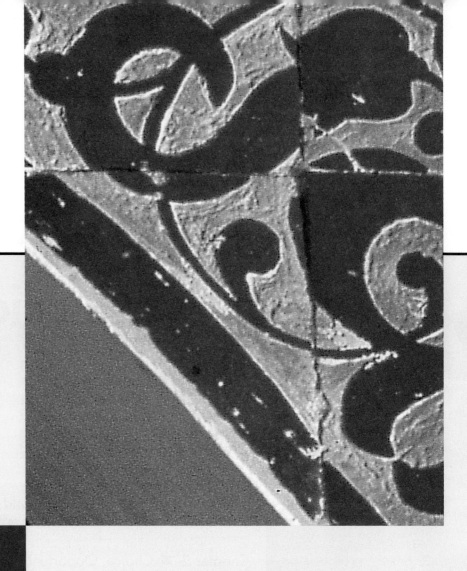

Economics: The World Around You

1. What is economics?

2. What is scarcity?

3. What is rational self-interest?

4. What is the difference between positive and normative analysis?

PREVIEW   Economics has been called "the dismal science," and to many students it does seem dismal. Some have found it dull, abstract, and irrelevant. To the public, economics seems like a house in chaos because economists so frequently argue among themselves. "If all economists were laid end to end," goes one old joke, "they would never reach a conclusion." Yet there seems no end to the number of economists quoted in the newspapers and on television, and virtually everyone thinks of himself or herself as an expert, despite economics' "dismal" status. The reason for such opinionatedness, it seems, is that economics touches every aspect of people's lives and is thus a subject about which everyone has something to say. Because economics does affect every aspect of life, it is anything but dismal. It is, you will find, an exciting subject to study, and one which is very relevant to your life.

Religion, sports, politics, history, sociology, sex, marriage, divorce, crime, anthropology, medicine, and health—what do these topics have to do with economics? You may be surprised to learn that economists study many everyday concerns as well as topics such as inflation, unemployment, the stock market, and international trade. In this book we focus on subjects that you probably already associate with economics, but you will learn to ask questions about subjects that you might never have associated with the study of economics. Asking and answering such questions will help you understand how the economy functions.

If economics is so useful and so insightful, why aren't economists rich? Some are. Some earn $50,000 per lecture appearance and are in such demand that they turn down more offers than they accept. Others earn thousands per day as consultants, as television commentators, or as spokespeople for certain firms. Some are involved in the corporate world as chief executive officers or chief financial officers. Economists are involved in governments at all levels. The president of Mexico has a Ph.D. in economics; reform leaders in Czechoslavakia are economists; the members of the President's Council of Economic Advisers are economists; economists are routinely appointed to high positions in the U.S. government, such as secretary of commerce, treasury, labor, defense, and even state; the Federal Reserve Board consists mainly of economists. Economics is the only business discipline and the only social science to be awarded the Nobel Prize.

Not all economists are rich or powerful, nor is the acquisition of wealth the primary objective of the discipline. Understanding, not wealth, is the objective. Nevertheless, an economist's income is part of economics, as is income earned from any occupation or activity. The Association of Accredited Colleges and Schools of Business (AACSB) reports that in 1989, the average starting salary for graduates with a B.A. or B.S. in economics exceeded starting salaries in most of the other business disciplines and was significantly higher than salaries in the social sciences and humanities.

In the first part of this chapter we present some of the terminology of economics. We then provide an example of how economics is used.

1. WHAT IS ECONOMICS?

Economics is a way of thinking about social issues and problems. It is the application of specific principles in a consistent manner. To understand economics it is necessary to discover these principles and to practice applying them. In this section, we define important terms and concepts; we then turn to the principles of economics.

▼ What is economics? ▲

1.a. The Definition of Economics

People want more *goods* and *services* than they have or can purchase with their incomes. Whether they are wealthy or poor, what they have is never enough. Neither the poor nor the wealthy have unlimited resources. Both have only so much income and time, and both must make choices to allocate these limited resources in ways that best satisfy their wants.

▼ What is scarcity? ▲

Because wants are unlimited and incomes, goods, time, and other items are not, scarcity exists everywhere. **Scarcity** exists when people want more of an item than is available when the price of the item is zero.

scarcity:
the shortage that exists when less of something is available than is wanted at a zero price

Each time you purchase a compact disk (CD), even on sale for $11.99, you give up whatever else that $11.99 could purchase. For $11.99 you could have a pizza and two soft drinks; you could purchase 2 novels; you could see two movies; you could purchase a ticket to one concert; or you could buy one tank of gas. You must make a choice. You can't have everything you want because resources are scarce; your income is limited. If you buy the CD, you have determined that it provides you more enjoyment for that $11.99 than any other use of the money.

economic good:
any good that is scarce

free good:
a good for which there is no scarcity

bad:
any item for which we would pay to have less

unlimited wants:
boundless desires for goods and services

▼ What is rational self-interest? ▲

rational self-interest:
the term economists use to describe how people make choices

land:
all natural resources, such as minerals, timber, and water, as well as the land itself

labor:
the physical and intellectual services of people, including the training, education, and abilities of the individuals in a society

capital:
products such as machinery and equipment that are used in production

Scarcity means that at a zero price the quantity of a good or resource is not sufficient to satisfy people's unlimited wants. Any good for which this holds is called an **economic good**. If there is enough of a good available at a zero price to satisfy wants, the good is said to be a **free good**. If people would pay to have less of a good, that good is called a **bad**. It is difficult to think of examples of free goods. At one time people referred to air as free, but with air pollution so prevalent, it is difficult to consider air a free good. It is not so hard to think of examples of bads: pollution, garbage, and disease fit the description.

Because people's wants are unlimited and the things they want and the income they have are scarce, individuals must make choices. But when they choose some things, they must give up or forgo other things. Economics is the study of how people choose to use their scarce resources to attempt to satisfy their **unlimited wants**.

The choices people make are those they believe to be in their self-interest—that is, they believe they will receive more satisfaction from their choice than they would receive if they selected something else. **Rational self-interest** is the term economists use to describe how people make choices. It means that people will make the choices that, at the time and with the information they have at their disposal, will give them the greatest amount of satisfaction.

As illustrated in Figure 1, there are four categories of resources used to produce goods and services: land, labor, capital, and entrepreneurial ability. **Land** includes all natural resources, such as minerals, timber, and water, as well as the land itself. **Labor** refers to the physical and intellectual services of people and includes the training, education, and abilities of the individuals in a society.

Capital refers to products such as machinery and equipment that are used in production. Capital is a manufactured or created product used solely to produce goods and services. For example, tractors, milling machines, and cotton gins are capital; automobiles and food are goods; and haircuts and manicures are services. The word *capital* is often used to

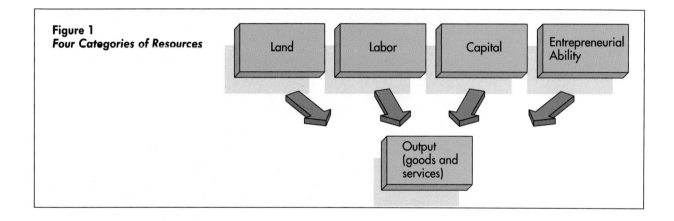

Figure 1
Four Categories of Resources

Land · Labor · Capital · Entrepreneurial Ability

Output (goods and services)

describe financial backing or the dollars used to finance a business. *Financial capital* refers to the money value of capital, as represented by stocks and bonds. In economics, *capital* refers to a physical entity—machinery and equipment and offices, warehouses, and factories.

Entrepreneurial ability is the ability to recognize a profitable opportunity and the willingness and ability to organize land, labor, and capital and assume the risk associated with the opportunity. A special talent that only a few individuals have, entrepreneurial ability plays such an important role in the economy that it is considered to be a separate resource rather than just an aspect of labor. People who demonstrate entrepreneurial abilities are called **entrepreneurs**.

People obtain income by selling the services of their resources. Owners of land receive *rent*. People who provide labor services are paid *wages* and *salaries*. Owners of capital receive *interest,* and people with entrepreneurial ability receive the *profits* from starting, running, and operating businesses. Because land, labor, capital, and entrepreneurial ability are scarce, income is limited.

Income is used to purchase goods and services. Goods that are used over a period of one or more years, such as an automobile, are referred to as **durables**. Those that are used over a short period of time, such as donuts, are **nondurables**. **Services** are work that is done for others that does not involve the production of goods, such as swimming lessons, haircuts, or the use of your telephone, as purchased from the telephone company.

1.b. Macroeconomics and Microeconomics

Economics is usually separated into two general areas, microeconomics and macroeconomics. **Microeconomics** is the study of economics at the level of the individual economic entity: the individual firm, the individual consumer, and the individual worker. **Macroeconomics** is the study of the economy at an aggregate level. Rather than analyzing the behavior of an individual consumer or firm, macroeconomists look at the sum of the behaviors of all consumers (the *consumer sector*) and all firms (the *business sector*) as well as the government and international sectors.

entrepreneurial ability:
the ability to recognize a profitable opportunity and the willingness and ability to organize land, labor, and capital and assume the risk associated with the opportunity

entrepreneur:
an individual who has the ability to organize resources in order to produce a product and the willingness to take the risk to pursue a profitable opportunity

durables:
goods that are used over a period of one or more years

nondurables:
goods that are used over a short period of time

services:
work done for others that does not involve the production of goods

microeconomics:
the study of economics at the level of the individual

macroeconomics:
the study of the economy as a whole

RECAP

1. Economics is the study of how people choose to use their scarce resources to satisfy their unlimited wants.

2. Resources are classified into four general groups: land, labor, capital, and entrepreneurial ability.

3. Scarce resources are used to produce goods and services.

4. The two main branches of economics are macroeconomics and micro-economics. Macroeconomics is the study of the economy as a whole—the consumer sector, the business sector, the government sector, and the international sector. Microeconomics is the study of economics at the level of the individual—individual consumers, individual workers, and individual business firms.

2. THE ECONOMIC APPROACH

In many colleges, economics is considered part of the social sciences or liberal arts; in some, it is taught in the business school. Economics belongs in both. Because economics is a way of thinking about problems and issues, it is useful to historians and sociologists as well as accountants and marketeers. Economics can provide the historian with a logical way to examine historical problems, and it can form the basis of marketing, management, and accounting studies. Of course, economists believe that studying economics is a good idea for everyone— whether a person is interested in the social sciences, business, physics, music, or poetry— because economics is a part of human life. The following brief history lesson provides an example of how economics can shed light on problems not usually considered to be economic topics.

2.a. Positive and Normative Analysis

What is the difference between positive and normative analysis?

Were you taught that the Americans who fought in the Revolutionary War were a ragtag, ill-trained bunch of farmers, merchants, and militiamen who ultimately were victorious because the powerful, well-financed, well-trained British Army rather stupidly wore bright red uniforms and marched in close ranks along wide open paths with drums and bugles playing? Of course, the idea that the British simply made a mistake or were not very intelligent is not supported by what was occurring in warfare in the years preceding and following the American Revolution. The British Army was powerful and successful. It had won decisive victories throughout the world and continued to do so for more than forty years after 1776. Is it likely that the British military machine was less intelligently commanded than were the Americans? If so, then why didn't armies fighting after 1776 use the Americans' tactics rather than those of the British? Only a few years after the American Revolution, Napoleon conquered much of Europe, the Middle East, and Asia using but the formations and approaches employed by the British against the Americans.

Neither an economist nor any other scientist would be satisfied with the conclusion that lack of intelligence explains the behavior of the British Army in the Revolutionary War. The reason is that conclusions based on opinion or value judgments ("the British were stupid") do not advance one's understanding of events.

Before returning to the British Army example, let's consider some important features of economic analysis. Analysis that does not impose the value judgments of one individual on the decisions of others is called **positive analysis**. If you demonstrate that unemployment in the United States rises when people purchase goods produced in other countries instead of goods produced in the United States, you are undertaking positive analysis. However, if you claim that there ought to be a law to stop people from buying foreign-made cars, you are imposing your value judgments on others and are undertaking **normative analysis**.

positive analysis:
analysis of what is

normative analysis:
analysis of what ought to be

In most circumstances, the economic approach is to rely on positive analyses. However, normative analysis plays an important role in the formation of economic policy. It is the basis for evaluating government programs and policies. A norm is defined and then a program is judged in terms of that norm. Suppose the norm is that a program is beneficial if it helps more people than it hurts. A program that taxes the richest 30 percent more than it taxes the rest of the population might meet this norm. However, if the norm is changed, the evaluation of the program could change. Suppose the norm is that a program, to be judged beneficial, must make at least one person better off without harming anyone else. The tax-the-rich program would not measure up because the rich are made worse off by it. The point to be grasped here is that the outcome of normative analysis depends on the norms or value judgments being applied; positive analysis, in contrast, is free of value judgments, so its outcome does not vary as norms change.

The outcome of normative analysis depends on the norm being applied; the outcome of positive analysis does not vary as norms change.

Why do economists disagree? Suppose that one economist, Milton, believes that government programs should not reallocate income from the rich to the poor and another economist, John, believes that incomes should be equalized. Clearly, Milton and John will disagree about most government programs. It is when normative analysis becomes part of the discussion that economists are most likely to disagree.

Now let's return to the analysis of the British Army's behavior. If lack of intelligence does not explain the British Army's behavior, then what does? Economists develop theories, or models, to help explain events. A **theory**, or **model**, is a simplified, logical story based on positive analysis that is used to explain an event. In athletic events, uniforms identify the teams. Perhaps that was the purpose of the British Army's red uniform. Why would the army want to ensure easy identification of its soldiers? If each soldier had little to gain or lose from a victory or a defeat but faced death in either event, then each soldier had an incentive to desert or run and hide at the first sign of trouble. Hiding or running away would be much more difficult for British soldiers wearing red uniforms than it would be for American soldiers who were spread out in the forest and were wearing inconspicuous clothes. Not only could the British commander watch over the behavior of his soldiers, but each soldier could easily monitor the behavior of the others.

theory or model:
a simplified, logical story based on positive analysis that is used to explain an event

The theory, then, is that the British Army used uniforms and formations to identify and monitor the troops. Is this model valid—does it make sense? To answer this question, we must conduct a **test**, using trials or measurements to see whether the model is consistent with the facts.

Perhaps the British had to worry about desertion more than the Americans did, and this concern accounts for their bright uniforms and different tactics. The British were 3,000 miles from home, but the Americans were, at most, only several hundred miles from home. Fighting in one's own country means that a loss is much more costly than a loss incurred while fighting in a foreign land, and a victory won in a foreign land means little to troops who do not share in the spoils of war. Whether the British soldiers won or lost, they received wages and did not share in any property gained by victory. Thus they had much less incentive to fight than did the Americans. As a result, the behavior of the British soldiers had to be monitored closely to ensure that they behaved as their superiors wanted.

The monitoring explanation makes sense in other contexts as well. There are many circumstances where one group must watch over or monitor the behavior of another group but can't watch every move the group makes. In other words, there are many situations where information is scarce and costly. For instance, the owners (stockholders) of large corporations are often not the same people as the managers of those corporations, and the owners can't monitor the behavior of the managers on a minute-to-minute or even a day-to-day basis. What, then, is to ensure that managers guide firms in ways that benefit the owners rather than in ways that benefit only the managers?

The problem faced by the owners of large corporations is not too dissimilar from that faced by the commanders of the British Army. How do owners ensure that managers behave in a desired way? They pay them with both wages and shares of stock. Just as the uniforms and marching formations created an incentive for the British soldiers to behave in the desired manner, the managers' compensation gives the managers the incentive to behave in a desired way. Because shares of stock are shares of ownership, the manager becomes a part-owner and therefore shares with the other owners the desire for the firm to maximize profit.

2.b. Scientific Method

The discussion of the British Army illustrates how economists analyze any issue, by using the **scientific method**. There are five steps in the scientific method: (1) recognize the problem, (2) make assumptions in order to cut away unnecessary detail, (3) develop a model of the problem, (4) present a hypothesis, and (5) test the hypothesis (see Figure 2).

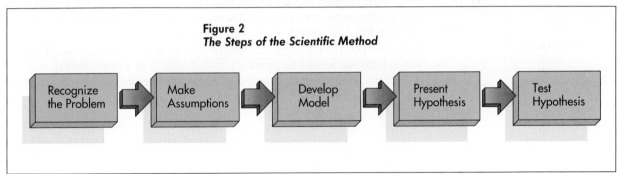

Figure 2
The Steps of the Scientific Method

Recognize the Problem → Make Assumptions → Develop Model → Present Hypothesis → Test Hypothesis

We focused on the problem of why the British Army wore red uniforms and marched in formation with drums and bugles playing. We then attempted to cut away unnecessary detail. We assumed that we didn't need to examine the personal lives of the soldiers or their commanders or look at whether they were draftees or volunteers, even though these might have affected the behavior of the soldiers. Such complexities are too numerous to be taken into account. Moreover, they aren't directly relevant to the issue, so we assume they aren't important. The role of **assumptions** is to reduce the complexity of a problem. We want to cut to the heart of the issue; thus, we use assumptions to cut away unnecessary detail.

One of the most commonly used assumptions in economics is **ceteris paribus**. This is a Latin phrase meaning "other things being equal," or everything else held constant. Thus, we might say that, ceteris paribus, the opportunity to run from battle decreases as tight marching formations are used. This means that if the opportunity to run and the marching formation are the only factors allowed to change, then a tighter formation reduces the opportunity to run. In a different context, we might say that the quantity of any good that is demanded declines as the price of the good rises, ceteris paribus. This means that if only the price and quantity demanded of the good are allowed to change, then as the price rises the quantity demanded falls.

According to the theory that we developed, the British soldiers had an incentive to desert or to hide, and thus a means of monitoring their behavior had to be developed. Remember that a model is nothing more than a logical story. Often when people hear the words *model* or *theory,* they think of complex mathematical formulas. Economic models may be complex equations, but they are more likely to be simple stories that relate the main aspects of the issue at hand.

A model enables us to develop a **hypothesis**, an explanation that accounts for a set of facts and allows us to make predictions in similar situations. For instance, the statement that red uniforms and orderly marching formations were a means of monitoring the behavior of individual British soldiers is a hypothesis. The validity of a hypothesis must be tested to see if the model is substantiated by the facts. If the hypothesis explains the behavior being studied and allows us to make accurate predictions in similar circumstances, then the hypothesis is valid.

2.c. Common Mistakes

Many errors can be made in scientific analysis. Two common mistakes in economics are the fallacy of composition and the fallacy of interpreting association as causation. The **fallacy of composition** is the error of attributing what applies to one to the case of many. If one person in a theater realizes that a fire has begun and races to the exit, that one person is better off than the theatergoers who remain in their seats. If we assume that a thousand people in a crowded theater should behave exactly like the single individual, we would be committing the fallacy of composition.

The mistaken interpretation of **association as causation** occurs when unrelated or coincidental events that occur at about the same time are

assumptions:
statements that are taken for granted without justification

ceteris paribus:
other things being equal, or everything else held constant

hypothesis:
an explanation that accounts for a set of facts

fallacy of composition:
the mistaken assumption that what applies in the case of one applies to the case of many

association as causation:
the mistaken assumption that because two events seem to occur together, one causes the other

The Super Bowl Predictor

The football Giants and the U.S. equity market had much in common in 1987: Both looked as though they had long-lasting vigor last January, and both were near extinction in October–November. Also, they both finished out December on a muted upbeat note.

This came as no surprise to fans of the Super Bowl Predictor, which has proven uncannily accurate in foretelling the stock market's direction for the year in which the game is played. Since Super Bowl I in 1967, whenever a team from the original National Football League (which would include old NFL teams now in the American Football Conference such as the Colts, Steelers and Browns) wins the Super Bowl, the stock market usually has an up year. Conversely, the market tends to go down during years when an American Football Conference team is the winner in the January playoff. The Super Bowl Predictor has been accurate in 19 out

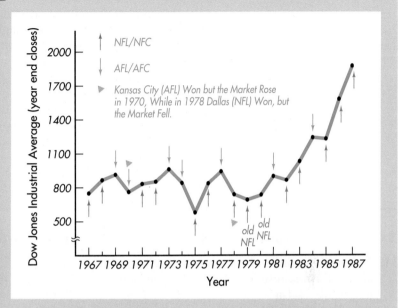

of the 21 Super Bowls played to date, when measured against the Dow or the S&P 500, for a performance percentage of 86% accuracy; when measured against the NYSE Composite, the results, over time, are exactly the same, but that index

ended 1987 out of line with the prediction.

■ Source: Robert H. Stovall, "The Super Bowl Predictor," *Financial World*, January 26, 1988, p. 72.

believed to have a cause-and-effect relationship. The result of the Super Bowl game is often jokingly said to be a predictor of stock market performance in the year in which the game is played, as noted in Economic Insight: "The Super Bowl Predictor." The conference champions from the National Football Conference (NFC) and the American Football Conference (AFC) play in the Super Bowl each January. According to conventional wisdom, if the NFC team wins, the stock market will go up in the new year, but if the AFC team wins, the market will go down. This bit of folklore is a clear example of confusion between causation and association. Simply because two events seem to occur together does not mean that one causes the other.

RECAP

1. Positive analysis is not based on value judgments. Normative analysis is based on value judgments.
2. Economists follow the scientific method when analyzing problems. There are five steps in the scientific method: recognizing the problem, making assumptions, developing a model, presenting a hypothesis, and testing the hypothesis.
3. Two common errors of analysis are fallacy of composition and confusing causation with association.

SUMMARY

▼▲ What is economics?

1. Economics is the study of how people choose to allocate scarce resources to satisfy their unlimited wants. § 1.a

▼▲ What is scarcity?

2. Scarcity is universal. Because of scarcity, choices must be made, and choices are made in a way that is in the decisionmaker's self-interest. § 1.a
3. The resources that go into the production of goods and services are land, labor, capital, and entrepreneurial ability. § 1.a
4. Goods and services are the items that consumers use to satisfy their unlimited wants. § 1.a

▼▲ What is rational self-interest?

5. People make choices that, at the time and with the information at hand, will give them the greatest satisfaction. § 1.a
6. Microeconomics is the study of economics at the level of the individual economic entity: the individual firm, the individual consumer, and the individual worker. Macroeconomics is the study of the overall economy: the consumer sector, the business sector, the government sector, and the international sector. § 1.b

▼▲ What is the difference between positive and normative analysis?

7. Positive analysis is analysis of what is; normative analysis is analysis of what ought to be. § 2.a
8. Economists tend to disagree over the normative aspects of economics, not the positive aspects. § 2.a
9. Economists use theories, or models, to explain economic events. § 2.a
10. The scientific method consists of five steps: recognizing the problem, making assumptions, developing a model, presenting a hypothesis, and testing the hypothesis. § 2.b
11. *Ceteris paribus,* a Latin phrase meaning "other things being equal," or everything else held constant, is a common assumption in economics. § 2.b
12. Two common errors in economics are the fallacy of composition and mistaking association as causation. § 2.c

KEY TERMS

scarcity § 1.a	entrepreneurial ability § 1.a	theory § 2.a
economic good § 1.a	entrepreneur § 1.a	model § 2.a
free good § 1.a	durables § 1.a	test § 2.a
bad § 1.a	nondurables § 1.a	scientific method § 2.b
unlimited wants § 1.a	services § 1.a	assumptions § 2.b
rational self-interest § 1.a	microeconomics § 1.b	ceteris paribus § 2.b
land § 1.a	macroeconomics § 1.b	hypothesis § 2.b
labor § 1.a	positive analysis § 2.a	fallacy of composition § 2.c
capital § 1.a	normative analysis § 2.a	association as causation § 2.c

EXERCISES

Basic Terms and Concepts

1. Define the following terms:

    a. resources

    b. goods and services

    c. economics

    d. scarcity

    e. macroeconomics

    f. land

    g. capital

    h. entrepreneurial ability

    i. positive analysis

2. Are the following statements normative or positive? If they are normative, how could they be changed to positive statements?

    a. The authors of *A New Guide to Rational Living* state that "The main barriers to effective thinking and emoting include these: (1) Some people have too much stupidity to think clearly. Or (2) they possess sufficient intelligence to think straight but just do not know how to do so."[1]

    b. Peter Drucker, a well-known management consultant, states that "the peasants of China are untrained and unskilled people unable to exploit the opportunities of a free economy."[2]

    c. In an editorial in *The Wall Street Journal* (January 8, 1988), Frank Goble notes that "schools can and should teach character development."

3. Make two statements that you consider to be normative. Change them into positive statements.

4. What is the scientific method? Is economics a science? Explain.

5. Explain how the principles of scarcity, choice, and self-interest are related.

Extended Concepts

6. Why do public television stations and the United Way and other charitable organizations give buttons, mugs, and bumper stickers to donors? (Consider the British Army case.)

7. Why were pirates allowed to share the booty? Why have so many armies throughout history allowed their soldiers to plunder and pillage?

---

[1]Albert Ellis, Robert A. Harper, *A New Guide to Rational Living*, (N. Hollywood: Wilshire Book Co.).

[2]Peter F. Drucker, *The New Realities* (New York: Harper & Row Publishers) 1989.

Economically Speaking

Putting the Pedal to the Metal

Sure, it's fun to go fast. But several lawmakers complained last week that matters were whizzing by out of control when Congress agreed to allow states to raise the speed limit to 65 m.p.h. on local highways. In a feat of legislative legerdemain, proponents of the higher speed limit attached an amendment to the $600 billion 1988 spending bill, bypassing the safety-minded House Public Works and Transportation Committee.

Once the long-delayed spending bill reached the full Congress on Dec. 21, few legislators noticed the amendment, which permits as many as 20 states to lift the 55-m.p.h. limit on divided highways in rural areas that meet interstate safety standards. Those who knew of the provision feared that further debate might threaten other, more delicate compromises contained in the spending bill. That infuriated Transportation Committee Chairman James Howard of New Jersey, who wrote the 1974 legislation that slowed down the national speed limit to 55 m.p.h. "What outrages me," he says, "is that this major policy change happened in an appropriations bill. It sort of got buried."

For more than a year, lower fines and selective enforcement of speeding laws had been gaining favor in many states. In April, when Congress permitted all states to raise the speed limit on rural interstate highways to 65 m.p.h., 38 states chose to do so.

The results thus far have been ominous. The National Highway Traffic Safety Administration reports that in 22 of those states, highway deaths jumped 46% between May and July over the same three months in 1986. "Because of a few macho Westerners," says Howard, "more people are going to be killed." Neither the Reagan Administration nor Senator Don Nickles, the Oklahoma Republican who sponsored the latest bill, attaches much significance to these early fatality figures. Observes Nickles: "I don't think it is the speed limit that kills people so much as the behavior of the people driving." He argues that it is illogical for state roads to be bound by lower speed limits if they are comparable with interstates.

"People are voting with their gas pedals," says Gene Berthelsen of the California department of transportation. He points out that the average speed on rural interstates before the limit was raised was 62 m.p.h.; the average speed on 65-m.p.h. interstates in California is now 64.5 m.p.h. Says Berthelsen: "We feel it's wiser to post speeds that people are already going."

The insurance industry is reserving judgment. Traffic accidents cost the U.S. an estimated $80 billion a year, and if collisions, injuries and claims increase, so will premiums. "The fatality count will be a good barometer," says Harvey Seymour of the Insurance Information Institute, an industry public relations organization. "If it continues to increase, someone is going to pay. Sixty-five miles per hour has a price."

Although the new measure is supposed to last for only a four-year "experimental" period, traffic experts are afraid that once the 65-m.p.h. limit is in place, it will be difficult to put on the brakes, no matter what the death rates show. Already, permission to lift the 55-m.p.h. limit has been requested by 14 states: Arkansas, California, Florida, Illinois, Iowa, Kansas, Kentucky, Minnesota, Oklahoma, Michigan, Nevada, Idaho, Texas and West Virginia.

Once the maximum of 20 states is reached, some of those who were left out will undoubtedly start clamoring for 65-m.p.h. eligibility. That may teach speedy lawmakers another lesson of the open road: no one likes to be passed.

■ Source: Amy Wilentz, "Putting the Pedal to the Metal," *Time*, January 11, 1988, p. 29. COPYRIGHT Time Inc. 1988.

Commentary

Why is there a speed limit on highways? This may strike you as a strange question, but in fact some highways, like the autobahn in West Germany, have no speed limit. Does this mean that people drive as fast as possible on the autobahn? Alternatively, why don't people drive within the legal speed limit on interstate highways in the United States? Even if the speed limit is often violated, does the limit have any effect on people's driving habits? Should the government try to influence the manner in which people drive by posting speed limits?

Economics is concerned with the manner in which people choose among different alternatives and with the implications of these choices. Economic analysis of an issue first considers how people select one option over another by focusing on the relative costs and benefits of different choices. The analysis may then look at the implications of these choices for the individual or for society as a whole. We can apply this type of analysis to the issue of the 55-m.p.h. speed limit.

What determines the speed at which you drive on an interstate highway? You probably weigh the benefits as well as the costs of driving within the speed limit. An obvious benefit of staying within the speed limit is that you avoid the risk of receiving a speeding ticket. Another benefit is that driving more slowly saves gas; in fact, one of the primary motivations for the initial imposition of the 55-m.p.h. limit in 1974, which came in the wake of the Organization of Petroleum Exporting Countries (OPEC) oil price increase, was to reduce the consumption of gasoline (and therefore imported oil) in the United States. Other benefits are that driving more slowly reduces the wear and tear on your car and lowers your chances of having an accident. The main cost to driving more slowly is time: the slower you travel, the longer your trip will take. Some people may also simply enjoy driving fast.

The actual speed that people travel on an interstate reflects their weighing of the benefits and costs of different speeds. As the costs or benefits of driving no faster than 55 m.p.h. change, we may expect to see a change in the average speed on the interstate. For example, if the fine for speeding increases, the cost of violating the speed limit rises and we would expect to see a decrease in the average speed on the interstate. If there is an increase in the number of police patrolling the highway, the likelihood of being caught speeding rises and this too would tend to decrease the average speed on the interstate. On the other hand, if the price of gas falls, the comparative cost of driving faster falls and the average speed on the interstate might very well increase.

Thus we would not expect to see every car on the autobahn traveling at full speed, even though there is no posted speed limit, since there are also other costs associated with driving fast. Nor would we expect to see every car on a U.S. interstate traveling at or below the speed limit since, for some drivers, the benefits associated with driving above the speed limit exceed the costs. Policies that attempt to increase the costs of driving above the speed limit, such as by increasing fines, or that increase the likelihood of getting caught, for instance by outlawing radar detectors, would tend to make people drive more slowly on average.

A policy of raising the speed limit to reflect the "speeds that people are already going" would tend to increase the speed at which people travel since the cost of driving faster would decrease. But, as the article states, "sixty-five miles per hour has a price"—specifically, a cost in terms of higher accident rates and more fatalities. No one is in favor of more highway deaths, but a basic principle at work here, as in many policy debates, is that there often exists a trade-off. In this case, the trade-off is between people's desire to drive at a certain speed and the reduction of highway deaths. One way to reduce highway deaths is to lower the speed limit to 25 m.p.h., but few people would be willing to accept this drastic measure. Likewise, one alternative to posting a speed limit is to allow people to drive at whatever speed they wish, but few people may be willing to accept the increase in highway accidents and deaths that would accompany this policy.

Speed limits, like other laws and public policies, carry costs and benefits to individuals and to society. Economic analysis helps us identify these costs and benefits and understand how people may react to them. Thus, economic analysis serves as a useful tool in deciding among different policies and courses of action.

Working with Graphs

According to an old saying, "One picture is worth a thousand words." If that maxim is correct, and, in addition, if producing a thousand words takes more time and effort than producing one picture, it is no wonder that economists rely so extensively on pictures. The pictures that economists use to explain concepts are called *graphs*. The purpose of this appendix is to explain how graphs are constructed and how to interpret them.

1. READING GRAPHS

The three kinds of graphs used by economists are shown in Figures 1, 2, and 3. Figure 1 is a *line graph*. It is the most commonly used type of graph in economics. Figure 2 is a *bar graph*. It is probably used more often in popular magazines than any other kind of graph. Figure 3 is a *pie graph*, or *pie chart*. Although it is less popular than the bar and line graphs, it appears often enough that you need to be familiar with it.

1.a. Relationships Between Variables

Figure 1 is a line graph created by *Psychology Today* from information gathered in annual surveys of college freshmen. The freshmen were asked to identify their essential goals in life. *Psychology Today* calculated the

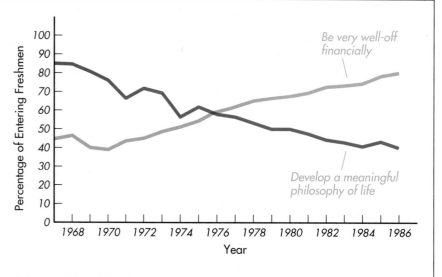

Figure 1
The One Who Has the Most Toys When He Dies, Wins
An annual survey of the goals of college freshmen reports that an increasing percentage of the freshmen has been choosing being "very well-off financially" as one of their goals and a decreasing percentage has been choosing developing "a meaningful philosophy of life." Source: *Psychology Today*, May 1987, p. 54. Data from *The American Freshman: Twenty-Year Trends* (Los Angeles: Higher Education Research Institute at UCLA, 1987).

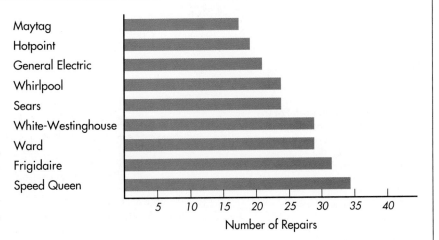

Figure 2
Which Have Been Most Reliable?
The repair information comes from 177,000 responses to the annual questionnaire sent out by Consumers Union. Owners of each brand indicated the number of repairs each washing machine had over a 10-year period.
Source: *Consumer Reports,* February 1988, p. 82. Copyright 1988 by Consumers Union of United States, Inc., Mount Vernon, NY 10553. Reprinted by permission from Consumer Reports, February 1988.

percentage of freshmen answering the question in a particular way each year. This percentage is measured on the vertical axis (the axis going up and down). The year of the survey is measured on the horizontal axis (the axis running from left to right). The line labeled ''Develop a meaningful philosophy of life'' represents the percentage of freshmen who declared that finding a meaningful philosophy of life was one of their essential goals. The line labeled ''Be very well-off financially'' represents the percentage who declared that financial well-being was one of their essential goals.

The freshmen could select both developing a meaningful philosophy of life and financial well-being as their goals, and several did so. Thus the percentage who selected at least one of the goals could add to more than 100 percent.

The lines show the relationship between the year of the survey and the percentage of freshmen who answered the survey question in a certain manner. It shows that the answer to the question depends on the year the survey was conducted. In 1986, for example, 42 percent chose as their primary goal a meaningful philosophy of life, while nearly 80 percent chose to be very well-off financially. Many freshmen, therefore, have been deciding that a meaningful philosophy of life does not rule out financial well-being.

Figure 2, from *Consumer Reports,* is a bar graph rating the reliability of washing machines. The frequency of repairs over the life of a washing machine is measured on the horizontal axis, and the brand of the washing machine is indicated on the vertical axis. The longer the bar, the less reliable the washing machine is.

Notice that the brands are arranged in order from the least repaired brand, at the top, to the brand requiring the most repairs, at the bottom. This arrangement makes the graph easier to read than if, for instance, the washing machines were listed in alphabetical order.

Figure 3 is a pie chart showing the types of goods that are traded between the United States and Canada. Unlike line and bar graphs, a pie chart is not actually a picture of a relationship between two variables. Instead, the pie represents the whole, and the pieces of the pie represent

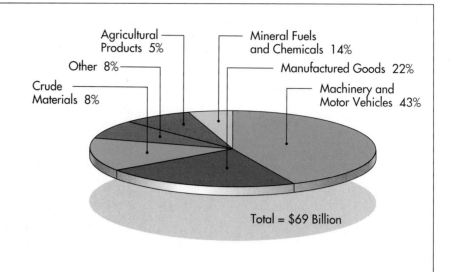

Figure 3
Border Traffic
The pie chart represents the total amount of trade between the United States and Canada, and each slice of the pie indicates the percentage of total trade in a particular type of product. For instance, machinery and motor vehicles constituted 43 percent of the trade between the countries in 1986. Source: U.S. Department of Commerce.

Agricultural Products 5%
Other 8%
Crude Materials 8%
Mineral Fuels and Chemicals 14%
Manufactured Goods 22%
Machinery and Motor Vehicles 43%
Total = $69 Billion

parts of the whole. In Figure 3, the pie is the total value of trade between the United States and Canada. The pieces of the pie represent the percentage of total United States–Canada trade accounted for by specific types of goods and services.

Because a pie chart does not show the relationship between variables, it is not as useful for explaining economic concepts as line and bar graphs. Line graphs are used more often than bar graphs to explain economic concepts.

1.b. Independent and Dependent Variables

independent variable:
the variable whose value does not depend on the value of other variables

dependent variable:
the variable whose value depends on the value of the independent variable

Most line and bar graphs involve just two variables, an **independent variable** and a **dependent variable**. The value of the dependent variable is determined after the value of the independent variable is determined. In Figure 2, the *independent* variable is the brand of washing machine, and the *dependent* variable is the frequency of repair. The number of repairs depends on the brand of the washing machine.

1.c. Direct and Inverse Relationships

direct or positive relationship:
the relationship that exists when the values of related variables move in the same direction

inverse or negative relationship:
the relationship that exists when the values of related variables move in opposite directions

If the value of the dependent variable increases as the value of the independent variable increases, the relationship between the two types of variables is called a **direct**, or **positive**, **relationship**. If the value of the dependent variable decreases as the value of the independent variable increases, the relationship between the two types of variables is called an **inverse**, or **negative, relationship**. In Figure 1, the "well-off financially" line represents a direct relationship because the percentage of freshmen who indicate that financial well-being is one of their essential goals increases over the years. The "philosophy of life" line represents an inverse relationship because the percentage of freshmen noting that a meaningful philosophy of life is their primary goal decreases over the years.

2. CONSTRUCTING A GRAPH

Let's now construct a graph. We will begin with a consideration of the horizontal and vertical axes, and then we will put the axes together.

2.a. The Axes

It is important to understand how the *axes* (the horizontal and vertical lines) are used and what they measure. Let's begin with the horizontal axis. Notice in Figure 4 that the line is divided into equal segments. Each point on the line represents a quantity or the value of the variables being measured. For example, each segment could represent one year or 10,000 pounds of diamonds or some other value. Whatever is measured, the value increases from left to right, beginning with negative values, going on to zero, which is called the *origin,* and then moving on to positive numbers, which increase as they move to the right, away from the origin.

A number line in the vertical direction can be constructed as well, also shown in Figure 4. Zero is the origin, and the numbers increase from bottom to top. Like the horizontal axis, the vertical axis is divided into equal segments; the distance between 0 and 10 is the same as the distance between 0 and -10, between 10 and 20, and so on.

In most cases, the variable measured along the horizontal axis is the independent variable. This isn't always true in economics, however. Economists often measure the independent variable on the vertical axis. Do not assume that the variable on the horizontal axis is independent and the variable on the vertical axis is dependent.

Putting the horizontal and vertical lines together lets us express relationships between two variables graphically. The axes cross, or intersect, at their origins, as shown in Figure 4. From the common origin, move-

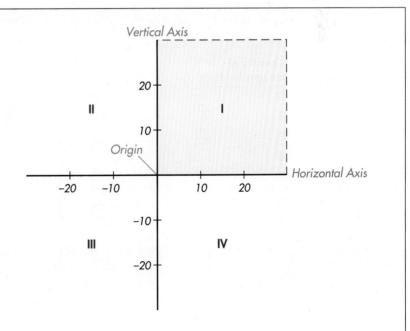

Figure 4
The Axes, the Coordinate System, and the Positive Quadrant
Figure 4 shows a horizontal axis. It has an origin, measured as zero, in the middle. Negative numbers are to the left of zero, positive numbers to the right. Also shown is a vertical axis. Again, the origin is in the middle. Positive numbers are above the origin, negative numbers below. The horizontal and vertical axes together show the entire coordinate system. Because most economic data are positive, often only the upper right quadrant, the positive quadrant, of the coordinate system is used.

ments to the right and up, in the area marked I, are combinations of positive numbers; movements to the left and down, in area III, are combinations of negative numbers; movements to the right and down, in area II, are negative values on the vertical axis and positive values on the horizontal axis; and movements to the left and up, in area IV, are positive values on the vertical axis and negative values on the horizontal axis.

Economic data are typically positive numbers: the unemployment rate, the inflation rate, the price of something, the quantity of something produced or sold, and so on. Because economic data are usually positive numbers, the only part of the coordinate system that usually comes into play in economics is the upper right portion, area I. That is why economists may simply sketch a vertical line down to the origin and then extend a horizontal line out to the right, as shown in Figure 4. Once in a while, economic data are negative—for instance, profit is negative when costs exceed revenues. When data are negative, areas II, III, and IV of the coordinate system would be used.

2.b. A Graph of the Demand for M&M's

Now that you are familiar with axes, you are ready to construct a graph using the data in the table in Figure 5. The table, called a *demand schedule*, lists the prices and the corresponding quantities of M&M's sold by the ABC store each day. In column 1 is a list of possible prices for packages of plain M&M candies. In column 2 is the number of packages of M&M's sold by the ABC store at each price.

Figure 5
The Demand Curve for M&M's
The number of packages of M&M's that the ABC store sells at each price is listed in the demand schedule. The graph shows the relationship between the price of a package of M&M's and the quantity of M&M's sold at the ABC store. The price of M&M's is measured on the vertical axis. The quantity of M&M's sold is measured on the horizontal axis. According to the information given in the table, if the price is $1.00 per package, the ABC store sells no M&M's. When all combinations of price and quantity sold are plotted, the points are connected and a demand curve (Demand₁) is drawn.

(1) Price per Package	(2) Quantity of Packages Sold
$1.00	0
.90	10
.80	20
.70	30
.60	40
.50	50
.40	60
.30	70
.20	80
.10	90

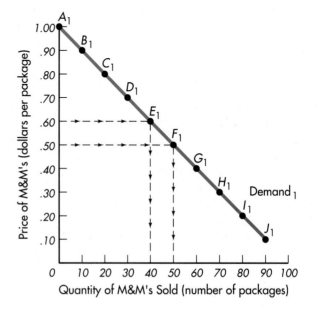

The information given in the table is graphed in Figure 5. Price is measured on the vertical axis; the quantity of packages sold, on the horizontal axis. According to the information presented in the table, if the price is $1.00 per package, no M&M's are sold. The combination of a $1.00 price and 0 packages sold is point A_1 on the graph. To plot this point, find the quantity zero on the horizontal axis (it is at the origin), and then move up the vertical axis from zero to a price of $1.00.

To plot the sale of 10 packages of M&M's at a price of $.90 each, find 10 units on the horizontal axis and then measure up from there to a price of $.90. This is point B_1. Point C_1 represents a price of $.80 and a quantity sold of 20 packages. Point D_1 represents a price of $.70 and a quantity sold of 30 packages. Each combination of price and quantity sold is plotted in Figure 5. The last combination, point J_1, is $.10 and 90 packages.

The final step in constructing a line graph is to connect the points that are plotted. When the points are connected, the straight line slanting downward from left to right in Figure 5 is obtained. It is called a *demand curve* and is labeled "Demand$_1$." It shows the quantity of a good that is sold at each possible price.

3. INTERPRETING POINTS ON A GRAPH

Let's use the Demand$_1$ curve in Figure 5 to demonstrate how points on a graph may be interpreted.

3.a. Points on a Curve

We first consider points on the curve. Suppose the current price of M&M's in the ABC store is $.60 per package. By tracing that price from the vertical axis over to the demand curve and then down to the horizontal axis, you find that 40 packages are sold. You can also find what happens to the sales of M&M's if the price falls from $.60 to $.50. By tracing the price from $.50 to the demand curve and then down to the horizontal axis, you discover that 50 packages are sold. Thus, a change in the price from $.60 to $.50 results in an increase in the quantity of M&M's sold from 40 packages per day to 50 packages.

3.b. Shifts of Curves

Along the Demand$_1$ curve of the graph in Figure 5, the combinations of all the prices and quantities sold at the ABC store each day, ceteris paribus, are shown. If a new housing development near the ABC store increases the number of people shopping at ABC, then the Demand$_1$ curve is no longer relevant.

The table in Figure 6 lists the quantities of M&M's sold after the housing development emerged. The quantities sold before the new housing development opened are listed in column 2 of the table in Figure 5.

The graph in Figure 6 shows two demand curves. The Demand$_1$ curve is based on the information given in Figure 5. The Demand$_2$ curve is based on column 2 of Figure 6. The graph shows the shift in demand that resulted from the opening of new housing near the ABC store. The first new com-

(1) Price per Package	(2) Quantity of Packages Sold
$1.00	10
.90	20
.80	30
.70	40
.60	50
.50	60
.40	70
.30	80
.20	90
.10	100

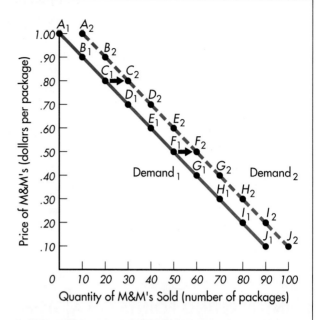

Figure 6
A Shift of the Demand Curve
A curve shifts when the value of the variable measured on one axis changes while the value of the variable measured on the other axis remains constant at every combination of the two variables. In this case, the number of customers shopping at the ABC store each day increased because of a new housing development, and a larger quantity of M&M's was sold at each price (Demand₂).

bination of price and quantity sold, point A_2, is $1.00 and 10 packages of M&M's. Notice that point A_2 lies 10 packages to the right of point A_1 on the Demand₁ curve. The second point, B_2, is a combination of $.90 and 20 packages of M&M's. It lies 10 packages to the right of point B_1. When all other combinations of price and quantity sold are plotted and the points connected, a new demand curve, Demand₂, is created.

The new demand curve shows that the ABC store is able to sell 10 more packages of M&M's at each price after the opening of the new housing development than it sold before the development was completed. The change is shown by the **shift** from Demand₁ to Demand₂. A curve is said to "shift" when for each combination of the variables measured on the horizontal and vertical axes one of the variables changes by a certain amount while the other variable remains the same. A curve shifts either in a horizontal direction, to the right or to the left, or in a vertical direction, up or down. Demand₂ in Figure 6 shows a shift to the right—at each price, the quantity sold increases by 10 packages.

shift:
the movement of a curve left or right that occurs when for all combinations of the variables measured on the horizontal and vertical axes, the value of one variable changes by a certain amount and the value of the other variable remains the same

4. COMPARING GRAPHS

It is often necessary to compare the curves in one graph to those in another graph. This can be done quite easily when the units of measurement along either the vertical or horizontal axes are the same.

4.a. Comparison Along the Horizontal Axis

In Figure 7(a), the top curve shows the net profits of American corporations. Interest payments as a percentage of net profits is shown by the lower curve. The diagram actually consists of two separate graphs. Billions of dollars is measured along the vertical axis on the left side, and percent is measured along the vertical axis on the right side. The horizontal axis shows the years 1962 to 1988. The two graphs were placed together to compare the curves and to suggest that net profits and interest payments might be related. Alternatively, this comparison could be made by two separate diagrams placed one above the other, as shown in Figures 7(b) and 7(c). Whenever the horizontal axes of two or more graphs are the same, comparison along the horizontal axis is possible.

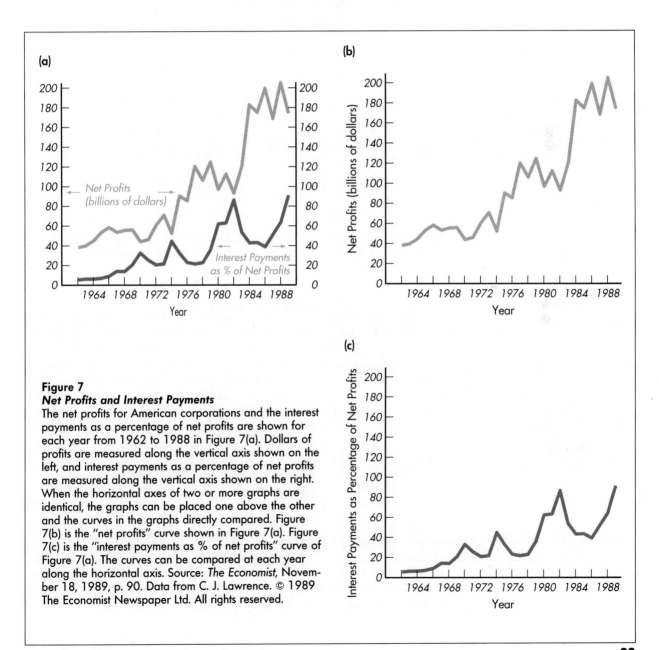

Figure 7
Net Profits and Interest Payments
The net profits for American corporations and the interest payments as a percentage of net profits are shown for each year from 1962 to 1988 in Figure 7(a). Dollars of profits are measured along the vertical axis shown on the left, and interest payments as a percentage of net profits are measured along the vertical axis shown on the right. When the horizontal axes of two or more graphs are identical, the graphs can be placed one above the other and the curves in the graphs directly compared. Figure 7(b) is the "net profits" curve shown in Figure 7(a). Figure 7(c) is the "interest payments as % of net profits" curve of Figure 7(a). The curves can be compared at each year along the horizontal axis. Source: *The Economist,* November 18, 1989, p. 90. Data from C. J. Lawrence. © 1989 The Economist Newspaper Ltd. All rights reserved.

4.b. Comparison Along the Vertical Axis

In some cases you may wish to base a comparison on the variable measured on the vertical axis. You would place the two graphs side by side. Then, because the vertical axes are the same, you can measure across horizontally from one graph to the other.

Figure 8 consists of two graphs placed side by side. In each, interest rates are measured along the vertical axis. Figure 8(a) shows a hypothetical household spending curve that indicates the amount of household spending at each rate of interest. Household spending increases as interest rates decline. Figure 8(b) shows a hypothetical business spending curve that indicates the amount of spending that businesses undertake at each interest rate. Interest rates are denoted as i. Business spending increases as interest rates decline. At an interest rate of 15 percent, the amount of household spending is $100 million. Taking $i_1 = .15$ from Figure 8(a) across to Figure 8(b), you can see how much business spending will occur at i_1—$50 million. The two graphs can be compared because their vertical axes are the same.

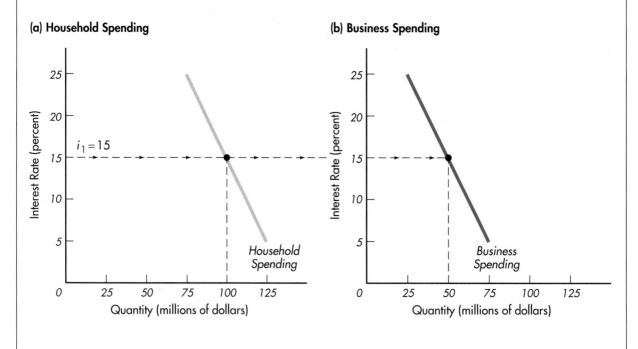

Figure 8
Comparison Along the Vertical Axis
When two or more graphs have identical vertical axes, the curves in the graphs can be directly compared by placing the graphs side by side. In Figure 8(a), the interest rate is measured along the vertical axis, quantity of household spending along the horizontal axis. At an interest rate of 15 percent, household spending is $100 million. Tracing that 15 percent over to Figure 8(b) lets us determine the quantity of business spending at an interest rate of 15 percent. Figure 8(b) has the same vertical axis as Figure 8(a). The horizontal axis in Figure 8(b) is the quantity of business spending. At an interest rate of 15 percent, business spending is $50 million.

(a) Household Spending

(b) Business Spending

5. SLOPES

A curve may represent an inverse, or negative, relationship or a direct, or positive, relationship. The slope of the curve reveals the kind of relationship that exists between two variables.

5.a. Positive and Negative Slopes

slope:
the steepness of a curve, measured as the ratio of the rise to the run

The **slope** of a curve is the rate at which the value of a variable on the vertical axis changes with respect to a given change in the value of a variable on the horizontal axis. If the value of a variable on one axis goes up when the value of the variable on the other axis goes down, the variables have an inverse (or negative) relationship. If the values of the variables on both axes rise or fall together, the variables have a direct (or positive) relationship. Inverse relationships are represented by curves that run downward from left to right; direct relationships, by curves that run upward from left to right.

Slope is calculated by measuring the amount by which the variable on the vertical axis changes and dividing that figure by the amount by which the variable on the horizontal axis changes. The vertical change is called the *rise,* and the horizontal change is called the *run.* Slope is referred to as the "rise over the run":

$$\text{Slope} = \frac{\text{rise}}{\text{run}}$$

The slope of any inverse relationship is negative. The slope of any direct relationship is positive.

In Figure 9(a) price (P) is measured on the vertical axis, and quantity sold (Q) is measured on the horizontal axis. The rise is the change in price (ΔP), the change in the value of the variable measured on the vertical axis. The run is the change in quantity sold (ΔQ), the change in the value of the variable measured on the horizontal axis. The symbol Δ means "change in"; it is the Greek letter delta, so ΔP means "change in P" and ΔQ means "change in Q." Remember that slope equals the rise over the run. Thus the equation for the slope of the straight-line demand curve running downward from left to right in Figure 9(a) is

$$\text{Slope} = \frac{\Delta P}{\Delta Q}$$

As the price (P) declines, the quantity of units sold (Q) increases. The rise is negative, and the run is positive. Thus, the slope is a negative value. From 0 to 90 on the horizontal axis, the vertical change is a negative 90 cents (from $1.00 down to $.10). From $1.00 to $.10 on the vertical axis, the horizontal change is a positive 90 units (from 0 up to 90). Thus, the rise over the run is −.90/90, or −.01. Similarly, from 50 to 90 in the horizontal direction, the rise is $.50 to $.10, or −$.40, so that the rise over the run is −.40/40, or −.01.

Remember that direct, or positive, relationships between variables are represented by lines that run upward from left to right. These lines have positive slopes. Figure 9(b) is a graph showing dollars of spending on the vertical axis and dollars of income on the horizontal axis. The spending curve represents the relationship between the two variables, spending and income. It shows that as income rises, so does spending. The slope of the spending curve is positive. The change in the rise (the vertical direction) that comes with an increase in the run (the horizontal direction) is positive. It doesn't matter whether you measure from 0 to 100 or from 100 to 200, the slope is the same. From 0 to 100 the rise is 75. The rise over the run is 75/100, or .75. From 100 to 200, the rise is 75, so the rise over the run is 75/100, or .75. The slope of a straight line is the same at all points.

Figure 9
The Slope of a Straight Line
In Figure 9(a), the slope of a straight-line inverse relationship is shown. A curve that slopes downward from left to right represents an inverse relationship. As the value of the variable measured on the horizontal axis increases, the value of the variable measured on the vertical axis decreases. An increase in quantity of 40 units (from 50 up to 90) means that the price falls by 40 cents (from $.50 down to $.10). The rise is $-.40; the run is 40; and the slope of the demand curve is -.01. In Figure 9(b), the slope of a straight-line positive relationship is shown. As the value of the variable measured on the horizontal axis increases, the value of the variable measured on the vertical axis also increases. Spending increases as income rises. An increase in income of $100 means an increase in spending of three-fourths of the amount of the increase in income.

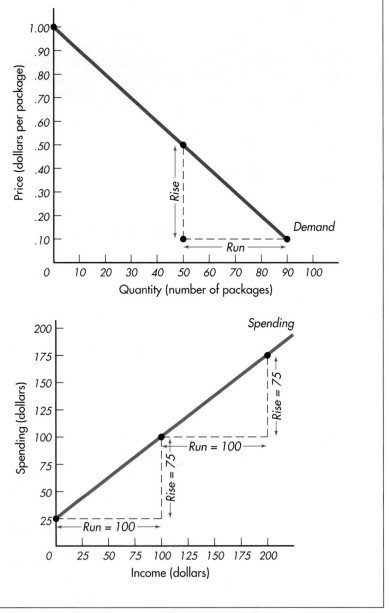

Figure 10
The 45-Degree Line
In Figure 10(a) the 45-degree line bisects the right angle formed at the intersection of the vertical and horizontal axes. Any point on the 45-degree line is equidistant from the axes. Thus the value of the variable on the one axis is equal to the value of the variable on the other axis at all points on the line. At an income level of 25, spending is 25; at an income level of 100, spending is 100; and so on. The slope of the 45-degree line is 1. In Figure 10(b) the 45-degree line appears with the spending curve shown in Figure 9(b). At every point on the 45-degree line, spending equals income. When the spending line rises above the 45-degree line, spending exceeds income. Conversely, when the spending line lies below the 45-degree line, income exceeds spending. At an income level of $50, spending exceeds income by $12.50. At an income level of $150, spending is $12.50 less than income.

(a) The Slope of a 45 – Degree Line

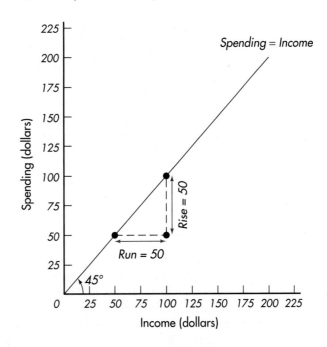

(b) Spending and the 45 – Degree Line

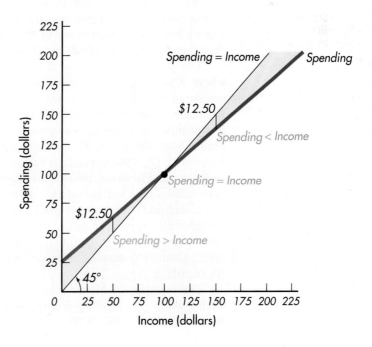

5.b. The 45-Degree Line

In Figure 10(a) spending is measured on the vertical axis, and income is measured on the horizontal axis. We have plotted all combinations of spending and income in which spending equals income. The resulting curve is labeled "spending = income." The slope of this curve is 1. No matter how much the run is, the rise is the same as the run. A curve that has a slope of 1 and begins at the origin is called a **45-degree line.** The reason for this name is that the line divides the right angle formed by the horizontal and vertical axes into two equal angles of 45 degrees each. On a 45-degree line, each variable on the vertical axis is equal in value to the variable measured on the horizontal axis.

45-degree line:
a line that bisects the right angle formed by the vertical and horizontal axes; a line on which any point is equidistant from the vertical and horizontal axes

The 45-degree line can be a useful tool. It allows us to compare spending and income in a relatively easy manner. Figure 10(b) consists of a 45-degree line and the spending curve shown in Figure 9(b). The spending curve lies above the 45-degree line until an income of $100 is reached. At $100, the spending line crosses the 45-degree line and from then on lies below it. At every point on the 45-degree line, spending and income are equal. Thus when the spending line rises above the 45-degree line, spending is greater than income; and when the spending line falls below the 45-degree line, spending is less than income. The vertical distance between the 45-degree line and the spending line measures the amount by which spending either exceeds or is less than income at a particular level of income. With the spending line above the 45-degree line, we know, for example, that spending is more than $50 at an income level of $50 and less than $150 at an income of $150. In both cases, the vertical distance between the 45-degree line and the spending line is $12.50.

5.c. Equations

Graphs and equations can be used to illustrate the same topics. Some people prefer to use equations rather than graphs to explain a concept. Since a few equations are used in this book, we need to briefly discuss how they demonstrate the same things as a graph.

The general equation of a straight line has the form: $Y = a + bX$, where Y is the variable measured on the vertical axis, X is the variable measured on the horizontal axis, a defines the intercept, the value of Y when $X = 0$ and b is the slope. If b is negative, the line slopes downward. If b is positive, the line slopes upward. In the case of the demand curve in Figure 9(a), the price, P, is the independent variable and the quantity demanded, Q, is the dependent variable. The quantity demanded depends on the price. However, price is measured on the vertical axis and quantity demanded on the horizontal axis. In equation form, X represents quantity demanded and Y represents price. When the price is $1.00, the quantity demanded is zero. The intercept, a, is $1.00. The slope, b, is negative, since when price falls, quantity demanded rises. For each $.10 decline in price, quantity demanded increases by 10 packages. The slope, b, is $.10/10, or .01.

The equation of Figure 9(a) is $P = \$1.00 - \$.01Q$. This equation tells us that when Q is 10, the price will be $P = \$1.00 - \$.10 = \$.90$. When Q is 50, $P = \$1.00 - \$.50 = \$.50$.

The equation for the 45-degree line shown in Figure 10(a) is $C = a + bY$, where $a = 0$ and $b = 1$, so that $C = Y$. The equations can be used to illustrate the income levels at which spending is less than, equal to, and greater than income. For instance, comparing the equation for the spending line and the equation for the 45-degree line, we can define where the two are the same, as in Figure 10(b):

$$C = Y$$
$$C = 25 + .75Y$$

Therefore,

$$Y = 25 + .75Y$$
$$Y - .75Y = 25$$
$$.25Y = 25$$
$$Y = 100$$

At any income level less than 100, spending exceeds income; at any income level greater than 100, spending is less than income.

5.d. Maximum and Minimum Points on a Curve

Slopes of curves can be very useful tools. They can be used to describe the relationship between two variables. They can be used to discover the value of one variable at which the other reaches a maximum or minimum value. We might want to know the output level at which profit is a maximum or cost is a minimum. We can use the slope of a curve to discover these output levels.

The slope of a straight line is the same at all points on the line. The slope of a curve changes at every point on the curve. Because the slope changes, it can be used to discover the maximum or minimum points on a curve. Figure 11(a) shows a total profit curve for a store selling videocassette recorders (VCRs). Total dollars of profit is measured on the vertical axis, and quantity of VCRs sold is measured on the horizontal axis. From 0 to 7 VCRs, the slope is positive; from 7 to 8, the slope is zero (the rise is zero because profit does not change); and from 9 on, the slope is negative. Total profit is at a *maximum* at 7 and 8 VCRs. When the slope is initially positive, then becomes zero, and finally becomes negative when going from smaller to larger numbers along the horizontal axis, we know that the variable measured along the vertical axis has reached a maximum and that the maximum occurs at the point of the zero slope.

Figure 11(b) shows a curve that measures the cost of producing each VCR. This U-shaped curve is called the *average total cost curve*. Cost in dollars is measured on the vertical axis, and quantity of VCRs produced is measured on the horizontal axis. From 0 to 4 VCRs, the curve has a negative slope. The slope is zero from 4 to 5 VCRs, and beyond 5 it is positive. The *minimum* average total cost occurs at 4 and 5 VCRs. When a curve has a negative slope followed by a zero slope and then a positive slope, the minimum point of the variable measured along the vertical axis occurs at the point where the slope is zero.

Figure 11
Maximum and Minimum Points on a Curve

In Figure 11(a), a total profit curve for a VCR producer is drawn that relates sales of VCRs to total profit. The curve has a positive slope until 7 units are produced. From 7 to 8 units, the curve has a zero slope; and from 8 units on, the curve has a negative slope. The maximum occurs at the point where the slope is zero. Whenever a curve has a positive slope followed by a zero slope and then a negative slope, a maximum of the variable measured on the vertical axis occurs at the point of the zero slope. In Figure 11(b), the average total cost curve is drawn. It has a negative slope followed by a zero slope and then a positive slope. The minimum point occurs at the zero slope. Whenever a curve has a negative slope followed by a zero slope and then a positive slope, a minimum of the variable measured on the vertical axis occurs at the point of the zero slope.

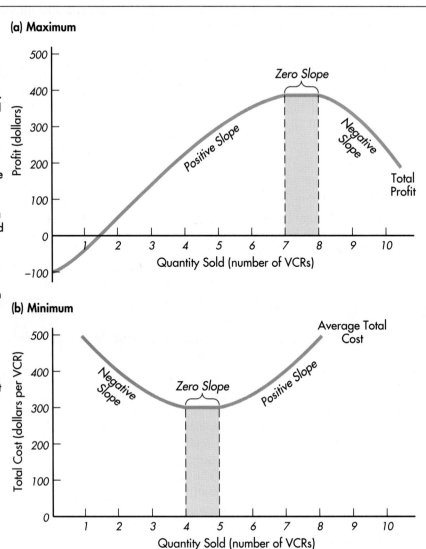

(a) Maximum

(b) Minimum

SUMMARY

1. There are three commonly used types of graphs: the line graph, the bar graph, and the pie chart. § 1

2. An independent variable is a variable whose value does not depend on the values of other variables. The values of a dependent variable do depend on the values of other variables. § 1.b

3. A direct, or positive, relationship occurs when the value of the dependent variable increases as the value of the independent variable increases. An indirect, or negative, relationship occurs when the value of the dependent variable decreases as the value of the independent variable increases. § 1.c

4. Most economic data are positive numbers, so often only the upper right quadrant of the coordinate system is used in economics. § 2.a

5. When the ceteris paribus assumption is relaxed, the demand curve shifts. § 3.b

6. When the horizontal axes of two graphs are the same, the graphs can be placed one above the other and directly compared. § 4.a

7. When the vertical axes of two graphs are the same, the graphs can be placed side by side and directly compared. § 4.b

8. The slope of a line or curve is the rise over the run: the change in the variable measured on the vertical axis that corresponds to a change in the variable measured on the horizontal axis. § 5.a

9. The 45-degree line is a line that bisects the right angle formed by the vertical and horizontal axes. It has a slope of 1. At every point on the 45-degree line, the value of the variable measured on the vertical axis equals the value of the variable measured on the horizontal axis. § 5.b

10. A maximum or minimum occurs when the slope is zero. If the slope goes from positive to zero to negative, a maximum occurs. If the slope goes from negative to zero to positive, a minimum occurs. § 5.d

KEY TERMS

independent variable § 1.b
dependent variable § 1.b
direct relationship § 1.c
positive relationship § 1.c
inverse relationship § 1.c

negative relationship § 1.c
shift § 3.b
slope § 5.a
45-degree line § 5.b

EXERCISES

1. Listed below are two sets of figures: the total quantity of Mexican pesos in circulation (the total amount of Mexican money available) and the peso price of a dollar (how many pesos are needed to purchase one dollar). Figures are given for the years 1980 through 1986.

   a. Plot each set of figures.

   b. What are the dependent and independent variables?

   c. Is the relationship between the dependent and independent variables direct or inverse?

   d. Calculate the slope between 1980 and 1981 and between 1985 and 1986.

Year	Pesos in Circulation (billions)	Peso Price of a Dollar
1980	477	23.26
1981	635	26.23
1982	1,031	96.48
1983	1,447	143.93
1984	2,315	192.56
1985	3,462	371.70
1986	5,790	923.50

2. Make up two sets of figures for 1987, 1988, and 1989. One set should show that a maximum occurs in 1987. The second set should show that a minimum occurs in 1987.

2

Choice, Opportunity Costs, and Specialization

1. What are opportunity costs?

2. What is the full cost of any purchase?

3. What is the production possibilities curve?

4. What accounts for increasing marginal opportunity costs?

5. What accounts for specialization?

6. What is comparative advantage?

PREVIEW

In the previous chapter, you discovered that choices must be made because of scarcity. You also learned that a particular choice is made because that choice provides the individual making the choice the greatest satisfaction. Who is to judge whether the option chosen by each person is, in fact, in that person's best self-interest? A 1987 study claimed that 52 percent of drivers in the United States still do not buckle up even though the probability of death in an automobile accident is nearly 20 percent less if seat belts are worn.[1] Clearly, it was not in the best interest of those who were killed to have gone without seat belts, yet those people decided not to buckle up.

The judge of whether a choice is in an individual's self-interest is the individual faced with the decision. Thus, when economists study choices, they ask not whether a decision was in someone's best interest but rather what factors led the individual to decide that a particular choice was in his or her best interest. An important factor influencing decision making is opportunity costs.

---

[1]Seat-Belt Laws Effective If Enforced," *The Arizona Republic*, December 14, 1987, p. A6.

1. OPPORTUNITY COSTS

What are opportunity costs?

opportunity costs:
the highest-valued alternative that must be forgone when a choice is made

An individual compares the benefits expected from one option with the benefits expected from all other options and selects the option that offers the greatest *anticipated* benefits. Of course, when one option is chosen, the benefits of the other options are forgone. Economists refer to forgone opportunities or forgone benefits as **opportunity costs.** Because every choice involves opportunity costs, you can best understand how choices are made and, thus, best understand economics by studying opportunity costs.

Opportunity costs affect every decision and activity. Your opportunity costs of reading this book are whatever else you could be doing—perhaps watching TV, talking with friends, working, or listening to music. Your opportunity costs of attending college are whatever else you could be doing—perhaps working full time or traveling around the world. Each choice means giving up something else (see Economic Insight: "The Opportunity Cost of Waiting").

1.a. The Opportunity Cost of Going to College

The cost of any item or activity includes the opportunity cost involved in its purchase.

The tuition, room and board charged by five colleges and universities in 1989 are shown in Table 1. Suppose you decide to attend a college where tuition and other expenses add up to $4,290 per year. Are those your total costs of attending college? If you answer yes, you are ignoring opportunity costs. Remember that you must account for forfeited opportunities. Rather than attend college, you could get a full-time job or travel around the world. If your second-best alternative to college is full-time employment, then that's your opportunity cost. If you could obtain a position paying $10 per hour and work 52 weeks a year for 40 hours per week, your annual income would be $20,800. The actual cost of your decision to attend college would be the $4,290 of direct expenses plus the $20,800 of forgone salary, or $25,090.

The cost of an item or activity is not the money price, or what you pay for it. The cost includes the opportunities you sacrifice because of your purchase. The more you value those alternatives, the higher is your opportunity cost.

What is the full cost of any purchase?

Unfortunately, or perhaps fortunately, choices are not quite as straightforward as the simple question "Do I attend college or not?"

Table 1 Tuition at a Few Colleges and Universities

College Costs	
Brandeis University	$20,101
Bennington College (Vermont)	$19,975
UCLA (resident)	$5,212
Purdue (resident)	$4,826
Auburn University (resident)	$3,293

Source: "College Costs still Outrace Inflation Rate", by Pat Ordovensky, *USA Today,* 1990, pp. 1A, 10A.

The Opportunity Cost of Waiting

Standing in line has never been a popular activity, but today it seems that Americans are likely to be more impatient about waiting in line than they have been in 20 years. According to a recent Louis Harris survey, Americans' leisure time has shrunk by 37 percent in the last two decades. With leisure time more valuable, the opportunity cost of waiting in lines is much higher.

Businesses recognize that people choose their products on the basis of the full opportunity cost, not just the price of the good or service. By keeping customers waiting, businesses may be losing customers. They are finding that people will choose one establishment over another because of shorter lines. As a result, businesses are focusing their marketing efforts on what marketers call time utility — providing products and services in ways that do not consume valuable time or providing values to offset the time losses. When the multiple-line approach is used in banks and stores, people get

frustrated because they often find themselves in the slowest line. Single lines do not move any quicker, but they reduce the variance of the wait and thus reduce frustrations. Customers can line up behind the teller or clerk of their choice, or in one line that allows the first person in line to go to the next available server — called a single-server line. As a result, most types of businesses in which several service people handle customers have switched to the single-server line.

Firms have tried several other approaches to dealing with lines. Chemical Bank began a program where any customer who had to wait in a teller line for more than seven minutes was given $5. Hospital emergency rooms in Los Gatos, California now offer a "No waiting" guarantee: If you wait longer than five minutes for emergency-room care, the billing department knocks 25 percent off your bill. The Manhattan Savings Bank offers live entertainment during noontime banking hours.

Some hotels and office buildings have mirrors on their elevator doors in an attempt to distract people while waiting.

Sometimes just telling people how long they have to wait cheers them up. Disneyland has had to learn to comfort those in line, since a popular attraction like Star Tours can attract as many as 1,800 people in a line. Like many amusement parks, Disneyland provides entertainment for those standing in line, but it also gives people updates, in the form of signs, noting "from this point on the wait is 30 minutes." Distractions such as these help people forget how they could be spending their time if they weren't waiting in line.

■ Source: N. R. Kleinfield, "Companies Try a Trick or Two to Conquer Those Killer Queues," *The New York Times*, September 25, 1988, p. F-11. "It'll Only Hurt for a Very Little While", *Business Week*, February 8, 1988, p. 34; Danny N. Bellenger and Pradeep K. Korganokar, "Profiling the Recreational Shopper," *Journal of Retailing*, Vol. 56 (Fall 1980), pp. 77–92.

trade off:
to give up one good or activity in order to obtain some other good or activity

Instead of two options—(1) work full time and not attend college, or (2) not work and attend college—there usually is a range of options. You could work part time and attend college. Clearly, if you do this, the time you devote to studying and other college activities will decrease as you devote more time to work. You **trade off** hours spent at college for hours spent at work. How much time will you devote to work? You will trade off an hour of college for an hour of work as long as the opportunity cost of the forgone hour of college does not exceed the benefits of working. At some point you will probably decide to work no more hours. This will occur when the benefits of the additional hour of work do not offset the opportunity costs of one less hour of college.

1.b. Opportunity Costs and Specialization

The opportunity cost of purchasing some item is the benefit you would have received from items you could have purchased but didn't. The opportunity cost of an activity you participate in is the benefit of the highest-valued alternative activity you could have participated in but chose not to. You will purchase items and participate in activities that minimize opportunity costs. The more you enjoy one type of item or one kind of activity, the more likely you will purchase that type of item and participate in that type of activity. For instance, if you really enjoy Mandarin cooking, you will choose to eat at a Mandarin restaurant. To switch to a Cuban restaurant would create a high opportunity cost for you. Thus, you tend to specialize in eating Mandarin cooking. Similarly, if you really enjoy college, switching from college to working will create high opportunity costs for you. You will tend to specialize in attending college. People, and all resources, tend to specialize in those activities in which their opportunity costs are minimized.

We often think of a specialist as someone who can do only one thing. A specialist may be someone who can do lots of things but enjoys one activity more than others or is relatively better at one activity than others. The stereotype of the "absent-minded professor" is someone who is extremely bright in a narrow field of expertise, say astrophysics, but can not participate in any other activities, such as gourmet cooking or bird-watching, unless they relate to astrophysics. This is also the stereotype of the specialist. Clearly, the professor's opportunity costs of being a professor are very low. It is unlikely this professor would ever do anything other than be a professor.

Dr. Gil Morgan is a specialist in golf. He played for years on the Professional Golf Association tour. Yet, Dr. Morgan had a degree in dentistry and could have been a practicing dentist. The difference between Dr. Morgan and the absent-minded professor is that Dr. Morgan may have switched occupations had the fortunes of golf or of dentistry changed by a small amount. The absent-minded professor would not have switched occupations had the fortunes of professors changed even a great amount. A **specialist** is someone whose opportunity costs of switching to an activity other than the one he or she specializes in is very high relative to the opportunity cost of the activity in which he or she specializes.

1.c. Opportunity Costs and Society's Choices

Societies, like individuals, face scarcity and must make choices. And societies, like individuals, forgo opportunities each time they make a particular choice.

At any given time, a society has a limited amount and quality of resources. If available resources are being used efficiently, a society can increase the production of one good or service only by decreasing the production of some other good or service. Societies make trade-offs just as individuals do.

The trade-offs facing a society can be illustrated in a graph known as the **production possibilities curve (PPC).** Figure 1 shows a production possibilities curve based on information (see table) about the production of

specialist:
someone whose opportunity costs of switching to an activity other than the one he or she specializes in is very high relative to the opportunity cost of the activity in which he or she specializes

Resources are being used efficiently if an increase in the production of one good requires a reduction in the production of other goods.

production possibilities curve (PPC):
a graphical representation showing the maximum quantity of goods and services that can be produced using limited resources to the fullest extent possible

Combination	Defense Goods and Services (millions of units)	Nondefense Goods and Services (millions of units)
A_1	200	0
B_1	175	75
C_1	130	125
D_1	70	150
E_1	0	160
F_1	130	25
G_1	200	75

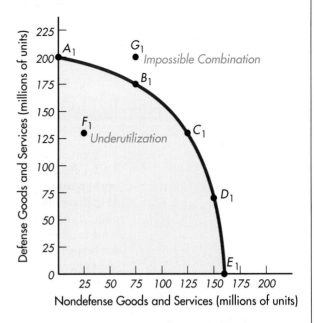

Figure 1
The Production Possibilities Curve
With a limited amount of resources only certain combinations of defense and non-defense goods and services can be produced. The maximum amounts that can be produced, given various trade-offs, are represented by points A_1 through E_1. Point F_1 lies inside the curve and represents the underutilization of resources. More of one type of goods and less of another could be produced, or more of both types could be produced. Point G_1 represents an impossible combination. There are insufficient resources to produce quantities lying beyond the curve.

defense goods and services and nondefense goods and services by a nation such as the United States. Defense goods and services include guns, ships, bombs, and personnel used for national defense. Nondefense goods and services include education, housing, and food that are not used for national defense. All societies allocate their scarce resources to produce some combination of defense and nondefense goods and services. The production possibilities curve shows that more of one product can be produced only by reducing the quantity of other products that are produced.

In Figure 1, units of defense goods and services are measured on the vertical axis; units of nondefense goods and services, on the horizontal axis. If all resources are allocated to producing defense goods, then 200 million units of defense goods can be produced, but the production of nondefense goods and services will cease. The combination of 200 million units of defense goods and 0 units of nondefense goods is point A_1, a point on the vertical axis. At 175 million units of defense goods and services, 75 million units of nondefense goods and services can be produced (point B_1). Point C_1 represents 125 million units of nondefense goods and services and 130 million units of defense goods and services. Point D_1 represents 150 million units of nondefense goods and services and 70 million units of

The production possibilities curve represents the maximum, or the outer limit, of what can be produced.

defense goods and services. Point E_1, a point on the horizontal axis, shows the combination of no production for defense and total production for nondefense goods and services.

The production possibilities curve shows the maximum output that can be produced with a limited amount of resources. The PPC is based on scarcity and shows the opportunity costs of alternative choices. It is a picture of the trade-offs facing society. A nation (or an individual) that chooses to do one thing sacrifices doing others.

1.c.1. Points Inside the Production Possibilities Curve Suppose society chooses to produce 130 million units of defense goods and services and 25 million units of nondefense goods and services. That combination, point F_1 in Figure 1, lies inside the production possibilities curve. A point lying inside the production possibilities curve indicates that resources are not being fully or efficiently used. Because resources are available for use, society can move from point F_1 to a point on the PPC, such as point C_1. The move would mean a gain of 100 million units of nondefense goods and services with no loss of defense goods and services.

1.c.2. Points Outside the Production Possibilities Curve Point G_1 in Figure 1 represents the production of 200 million units of defense goods and services and 75 million units of nondefense goods and services. Point G_1, however, represents more resources than are available—it lies outside the production possibilities curve. Unless more resources can be obtained, or unless new technology allows the production of more goods and services with the same quantity of resources, there is no way the society can produce 200 million units of defense goods and services and 75 million units of nondefense goods.

If the nation obtains more resources, points outside the production possibilities curve become possible. Suppose oil discoveries in several locations significantly increase the world's supplies of oil. What do the discoveries imply for the production possibilities curve? Greater quantities of oil would enable a country to increase production of both defense

Figure 2 shows the production possibilities curves before (PPC$_1$) and after (PPC$_2$) the discovery of oil. PPC$_1$ is based on the data given in Figure 1. PPC$_2$ is based on the data given in Figure 2 (see table). As a result of the increase in oil supplies, the production of goods and services can be increased. The first combination of goods and services on PPC$_2$, point A_2, is 220 million units of defense goods and 0 units of nondefense goods. The second point, point B_2, is a combination of 200 million units of defense goods and 75 million units of nondefense goods. Points C_2 through F_2 reflect the other combinations shown in the table accompanying the graph. Connecting these points yields the bowed-out curve, PPC$_2$. Because of the availability of new supplies of oil, the nation is able to increase production of all goods, as shown by the shift from PPC$_1$ to PPC$_2$. A comparison of the two curves shows clearly that more goods and services for both defense and nondefense are possible along PPC$_2$ than along PPC$_1$.

Combination	Defense Goods and Services (millions of units)	Nondefense Goods and Services (millions of units)
A_2	220	0
B_2	200	75
C_2	175	125
D_2	130	150
E_2	70	160
F_2	0	165

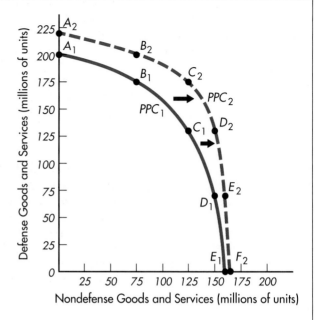

Figure 2
A Shift of the Production Possibilities Curve
Whenever the ceteris paribus conditions change, the curve shifts. In this case, an increase in the quantity of a resource enables the society to produce more of both types of goods. The curve shifts out, away from the origin.

1.c.3. Marginal Opportunity Costs Figure 3 shows three alternative production possibilities curves: a straight line, Figure 3(a); a curve that bows out, Figure 3(b); and a curve that bows in, Figure 3(c).

In each graph in Figure 3, the quantity of defense goods and services is measured on the vertical axis; the quantity of nondefense goods and services, on the horizontal axis. In each graph, both the horizontal and the vertical axes are divided into equal segments of 25 million units each. We will determine what it costs in terms of forgone defense goods and services to increase nondefense goods and services in increments of 50-million units for each of the PPC curves. Each 50-million-unit increase in nondefense goods and services is accompanied by a decrease in defense goods and services. The amount of the decrease varies from curve to curve. To find the amount by which the quantity of defense goods decreases in each graph, we draw a line from points A, B, and C to the vertical axis of each graph. Then we measure the changes along the vertical axis from 200 to the horizontal line at point A, from the horizontal line at point A to the horizontal line at point B, and from the horizontal line at point B to the horizontal line at point C.

marginal opportunity cost:
the amount of one good or service that must be given up to obtain one additional unit of another good or service, no matter how many units are being produced

The amount of one good or service that must be given up to obtain one additional unit of another good or service, no matter how many units are being produced, is called the **marginal opportunity cost.** The term **marginal** means "additional" or "extra." Marginal opportunity costs may remain constant, increase, or decrease as the production of goods and services rises and falls.

Constant Marginal Opportunity Costs   Notice that the distance along the horizontal axis between 0 and 50 million, 50 and 100 million, and 100 and 150 million units on the straight-line PPC curve, Figure 3(a), is associated with equal changes of 50 million units on the vertical axis. A change from 0 to 50 million nondefense units on the horizontal axis causes the defense units on the vertical axis to decrease by 50 million, from 200 million to 150 million; a change from 50 to 100 million nondefense units causes defense units to decrease by 50 million units, from 150 to 100 million; and so on. A change that is a constant amount occurs because the production possibilities curve is a straight line.

The straight-line production possibilities curve shown in Figure 3(a) represents **constant marginal opportunity costs**—unchanging amounts of one good or service that must be given up to obtain one additional unit of another good or service, no matter how many units are being produced.

constant marginal opportunity cost: an unchanging amount of one good or service that must be given up to obtain one additional unit of another good or service, no matter how many units are being produced

Increasing Marginal Opportunity Costs   The bowed-out curve in Figure 3(b) shows that increased production of nondefense goods from 0 to 50 million units causes a 10-million unit decline in the production of defense goods, from 200 million to 190 million. The change from 50 to 100 million units of nondefense goods leads to a 15-million unit decline in defense goods, from 190 to 175 million units. The increase from 100 to 150 million nondefense units leads to a 50-million unit decline in defense goods, from 175 million to 125 million units. The change from 150 to 200 million nondefense units leads to a 125-million unit decline in defense production. The amount of defense goods and services that must be given up in order to produce an additional 50 million units of nondefense goods and services *increases* as nondefense production increases. Thus the bowed-out curve in Figure 3(b) reflects **increasing marginal opportunity costs.**

▼ What accounts for increasing marginal opportunity costs? ▲

Why might marginal opportunity costs rise as more and more nondefense goods and services are produced? Perhaps a nation finds it increasingly difficult to switch scarce resources from military to nondefense production. A specialist in the design of rocket launchers, for instance, might not be very good at designing automobiles. If that specialist is moved from defense production to automobile production, many rocket launchers may be forgone while only a few additional automobiles are produced.

increasing marginal opportunity cost: a rising amount of one good or service that must be given up to obtain one additional unit of any good or service, no matter how many units are being produced

Decreasing Marginal Opportunity Costs   The bowed-in curve in Figure 3(c) represents the opposite situation from the bowed-out curve in Figure 3(b). With the bowed-in curve, marginal opportunity costs are decreasing. For each additional 50 million units of nondefense goods and services produced, fewer and fewer units of defense goods and services must be forgone. To move from 0 to 50 million nondefense units requires a 75-million-unit decline, from 200 to 125 million defense units. An increase in nondefense production from 50 to 100 million units requires a 70-million-unit decline, from 125 to 55 million defense units. An increase from 100 to 150 million nondefense units requires a 35-million-unit decline in the production of defense goods and services, from 55 to 20 million units.

Figure 3
Three Shapes of a Production Possibilities Curve
Production possibilities curves may take one of three shapes. Figure 3(a) shows a straight line that represents constant marginal opportunity costs. For each additional unit of nondefense goods and services produced, society must give up a constant amount of defense goods and services. Figure 3(b) shows a bowed-out curve that represents increasing marginal opportunity costs. For each additional unit of nondefense goods and services produced, society must give up increasing amounts of defense goods and services. Figure 3(c) shows a bowed-in curve that represents decreasing marginal opportunity costs. For each additional unit of nondefense goods and services produced, society must give up decreasing amounts of defense goods and services.

(a) Constant Marginal Opportunity Costs

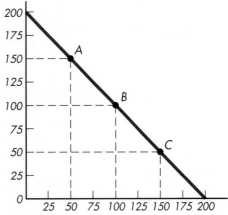

(b) Increasing Marginal Opportunity Costs

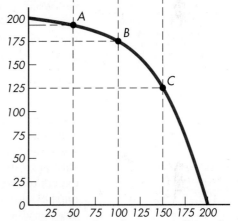

(c) Decreasing Marginal Opportunity Costs

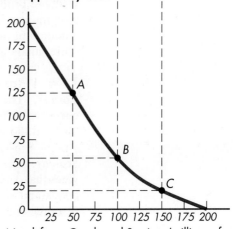

Radar developed by Westinghouse for the military was switched to the detection of drug smuggling when the reduction of tensions between the USSR and the United States allowed the nations to reduce the resources each devoted to military production. The radar was designed for military use and might not be as efficient at detecting the small aircraft of drug smugglers as radar designed specifically for that purpose. Because the radar is a specialized resource, its shift away from the area in which it is specialized may have led to rising marginal opportunity costs or an increasing quantity of military production given up to gain a constant amount of nonmilitary production. For this reason, the PPC is often bowed-out.

decreasing marginal opportunity cost: a falling amount of one good or service that must be given up to obtain one additional unit of another good or service, no matter how many units are being produced

What could explain this relationship, called **decreasing marginal opportunity costs**? Perhaps as more goods and services of one particular type are produced, managers learn to use scarce resources more efficiently. Thus, all resources are used more productively and efficiently.

Which Curve Is the Most Realistic?   Although a society's production possibilities curve could bow in, bow out, or be a straight line, the bowed-out curve showing increasing marginal opportunity costs, Figure 3(b), is the most realistic. The reason is that marginal opportunity costs increase when specialized resources that are productive in their current activity are shifted to an activity in which they are relatively less productive. We expect resources to be used where they are most productive. If resources must be moved from defense to nondefense programs, we might expect the least productive defense resources to be moved first. However, as more and more resources are switched from defense to nondefense uses, the resources that are moved will eventually be those that are highly specialized and productive in providing defense output yet relatively unproductive in providing nondefense goods and services. Larger and larger amounts of defense goods and services will be forgone to obtain nondefense goods and services.

1.c.4. What Can Be Learned from the Production Possibilities Curve?   The production possibilities curve illustrates five basic concepts: scarcity, opportunity costs, specialization, marginal decision making, and the irrelevance of sunk costs.

Scarcity   Resources are limited, and thus the quantity of goods and services that can be produced is limited. The only ways to produce more of all goods and services are to increase the quantity of resources and to use resources more efficiently.

Opportunity Cost   To produce certain amounts of one good means giving up certain amounts of other goods.

Specialization   As a society produces more and more of one type of good, it must give up a constant, an increasing, or a decreasing amount of other types of goods, depending on whether marginal opportunity costs are constant, increasing, or decreasing. Because resources tend to be specialized, the production possibilities curve is most likely to have a bowed-out shape reflecting increasing marginal opportunity costs.

Marginal Decision Making   How does a society choose at which level on the production possibilities curve to produce? In effect, society begins at a point on the defense-goods axis (the vertical axis in Figure 3) and then moves point by point along the PPC toward the nondefense-goods axis (the horizontal axis). At each point society asks, do we want to produce at this point or move on to the next, even though moving on will mean giving up additional units of defense goods? Each move means that society believes the additional benefits it will receive will exceed the marginal opportunity costs it must bear. Society finally says "stop" when it believes that the next move would cost more than the benefits it would create.

Individuals operate in the same way. We all trade off one activity for another until the marginal opportunity cost of an additional amount of the first activity equals the marginal benefits of that additional amount. This is decision making at the margin. When the additional production of defense goods or the additional quantity of some activity is being considered, marginal (additional) opportunity costs come into play.

The United States does not look at the defense budget as a whole each year and decide whether it is appropriate. It looks at the last billion-dollar program and chooses whether to support it. Is the marginal opportunity cost of this last billion dollars worth forgoing whatever else that billion dollars could be spent on? Similarly, you ask whether you should spend the next half-hour watching T.V., or studying. What matters to you is the marginal opportunity cost of that half-hour of watching T.V. or that half-hour of studying, not the total opportunity costs of watching T.V. or of studying. Decision making occurs at the margin.

The Irrelevance of Sunk Costs   The PPC illustrates that choices made and costs borne in the past do not influence current or future choices. Costs borne in the past are known as **sunk costs.** Marginal choices necessarily ignore past choices. Having studied until 10 P.M., you look at the costs and benefits of studying until 11 P.M. You can't reconsider the costs and benefits of studying from 7 to 10 P.M. because that choice and the resulting opportunity costs have already been borne and can't be changed. You can't get to the concert that started at 7:30 P.M., and you can't get to the coffee shop to meet friends at 7 P.M.

Similarly, society, having selected a particular point on the PPC at which to produce, faces the choice (a marginal choice) of whether to move to another point along the curve. Society can't go back to the beginning and produce the goods it decided not to produce before. It has already borne the opportunity costs of moving to its current position.

sunk costs:
costs that occurred in the past

RECAP

1. Opportunity costs are the benefits that are forgone because of a choice. When you choose one thing, you must give up—forgo—others. The full cost of a choice thus includes what is paid for the item or activity chosen and the opportunity cost of this choice.

2. Opportunity cost is a subjective concept. It depends on the individual's attitudes, beliefs, expectations, and knowledge or information regarding an item at the time the choice is made.

3. Opportunity cost is an individual concept but can be used to demonstrate scarcity and choice for a society as a whole.

4. The production possibilities curve represents all combinations of goods and services that can be produced using limited resources to their full capabilities.

5. The production possibilities curve is a picture of opportunity costs. Each choice involves the sacrifice of all other combinations of goods and services.

6. Points inside the production possibilities curve indicate the underutilization of resources—more goods and services could be produced if resources were used more efficiently.

7. Points outside the production possibilities curve indicate combinations of goods and services that are unattainable because of the scarcity of resources. Additional supplies of resources would have to be obtained or a more efficient means of production discovered to produce quantities of goods and services outside the current production possibilities curve.

8. Constant marginal opportunity costs (shown by a straight-line production possibilities curve) indicate that obtaining an additional unit of one good means forgoing a constant amount of other goods.

9. Increasing marginal opportunity costs (shown by a bowed-out production possibilities curve) indicate that obtaining an additional unit of one good means forgoing increasing amounts of other goods.

10. Decreasing marginal opportunity costs (shown by a bowed-in production possibilities curve) indicate that obtaining an additional unit of one good means forgoing decreasing amounts of other goods.

11. The production possibilities curve illustrates five important concepts: scarcity, opportunity cost, specialization, decision making at the margin, and the irrelevance of sunk costs.

2. SPECIALIZATION

Because resources tend to be specialized, a society faces increasing marginal opportunity costs; reallocation of resources tends to result in an increasing number of units of one good being given up as each additional unit of another good is produced. In this section we discuss why resources are specialized and in what activities they are specialized.

2.a. Specialize Where Opportunity Costs Are Lowest

Every coach has a limited number of talented athletes. In order to create the best team, each coach must choose where to play each athlete. People typically have skills or talents in only one or a few areas, and because they lack the time or skill to pursue every activity, they choose where to focus their energy. Firms and nations too have limited amounts of resources and must choose where to use their resources. The problems faced by the coach of an athletic team, by firms, and by whole nations, and the solutions found by each, are fundamentally the same.

You can gain some insight into the behavior of individuals, firms, and nations by looking at the problems of an athletic team. Suppose a football coach has two talented athletes, Sam and Victor, who are excellent runners and passers. What positions will Sam and Victor be assigned to? If Sam becomes a runningback, the team loses his passing ability, but if he becomes the quarterback, the team loses his running ability. Similarly, if Victor plays the quarterback position, the team loses his running, but if he plays runningback, the team loses his passing. How does the coach decide who is quarterback and who is runningback? *He assigns each athlete to the position having the lowest opportunity cost for the team.* In making this choice, the coach behaves no differently from you or even from firms and nations trying to determine what goods and services to produce.

Individuals, firms, and nations select the option with the lowest opportunity cost.

It is in your best interest to specialize where your opportunity costs are lowest. For instance, in most households someone does most of the cooking or cleaning or ironing and someone else fixes leaky faucets or mows the lawn or shovels the sidewalks. If you share an apartment, you and your roommate have probably come to some agreement about responsibilities. One of you cooks and shops for groceries, and the other cleans. Each of you specializes in the activity that produces the lowest opportunity cost. Similarly, fast-food establishments like McDonald's produce hamburgers and fries faster and less expensively than you could. They specialize in cooking certain things. And large corporations have different departments to carry out specific tasks—the accounting department does one thing and marketing does another.

Japan is known for high-tech manufacturing and Saudi Arabia for petroleum. Saudi Arabia's opportunity costs of producing high-tech electronics, like Japan's opportunity costs of producing petroleum, are very high. These nations specialize in producing particular goods and services.

2.b. Comparative and Absolute Advantage

comparative advantage: the ability to produce a good or service at a lower opportunity cost than someone else

The choice of which area or activity to specialize in is made on the basis of relative opportunity costs. Economists refer to relative opportunity costs as **comparative advantage.** Although one person may be better at all activities than someone else, the difference between their performances will not be the same in all activities. The activity in which the differences are smallest is the area in which the person with the lesser ability has the comparative advantage. For instance, although Victor may be worse at both running and passing than Sam, Victor may be only slightly worse than Sam in passing and much worse in running. Thus, Victor has a comparative advantage in passing.

Saffron, that delicious flavoring used in Paella and other rice dishes is quite difficult to obtain and quite expensive to purchase. It is harvested in Spain mostly in family operations. No harvesting machines have yet been developed that speed the process. Because the job of harvesting the saffron is tedious, boring, and requires virtually no skill, the job is filled by those whose opportunity costs are relatively low. Harvesting occurs in the evening when the men aren't at their jobs, the women aren't doing other household tasks and the children aren't attending school. The family has a comparative advantage over a firm. The family members have very low opportunity costs so that labor is cheap and the family home serves as the harvesting station, thereby cutting costs further.

absolute advantage:
the ability to produce a good or service with fewer resources than others use

When one person is more skillful than another person, or when one firm or one nation is better at producing a good than another, that person, firm, or nation has an **absolute advantage.** A person, firm, or nation that has an absolute advantage uses fewer resources to produce a good or service or produces more goods and services with a given amount of resources than does another. If Sam can run faster and pass better than Victor, Sam has an absolute advantage over Victor in both passing and running. However, if Sam's superiority in running is greater than in passing, he has a comparative advantage only in running.

It is comparative advantage, not absolute advantage, that determines specialization. Comparative advantage explains why nations produce what they do and what activities individuals specialize in. Let's focus on the concept of comparative advantage by extending the example of the athletic team.

Assume that on average each time Sam runs with the ball, he runs 5 yards before being tackled. Victor, however, is able to run only 3 yards before being tackled. In addition, assume that Sam passes for an average of 10 yards and Victor passes for an average of 9 yards.

On any given play, Sam averages 5 yards if he runs or 10 yards if he passes; thus, the opportunity cost of Sam's passing is the yards lost by Sam's not running, and the opportunity cost of Sam's running is the yards lost by Sam's not passing. Sam forgoes 5 yards running for each 10 yards he gets passing; his ratio of opportunity costs of passing to running is $5/10 = 1/2$. Victor's ratio of opportunity costs of passing to running is $3/9 = 1/3$, 3 yards running for each 9 yards passing. Victor gives up more by running than does Sam. Sam loses 2 yards passing for each yard he runs; Victor gives up 3 yards passing for each yard he runs. Therefore, the coach should make Victor the quarterback and Sam the runningback. To maximize the total team output, each player will produce in the area in which he has a comparative advantage.

Suppose there are 10 running and 10 passing plays in each game. As shown in Figure 4, with Sam as runningback and Victor as quarterback, the team makes 140 total yards. Sam runs for a total of 50 yards, and Victor passes for a total of 90 yards. With Sam as quarterback and Victor as runningback, the team makes a total of 130 yards. Sam passes for a total of 100 yards, and Victor runs for a total of 30 yards.

Sam is better than Victor at both positions. He has an absolute advantage in each activity. If he could play both positions simultaneously, he would pass 100 yards and run 50 yards, for a total of 150 yards per game. But he can't play both positions simultaneously, so the team is better off if Sam plays the position at which he is comparatively better—runningback. If Victor could play both positions simultaneously, the team would make 30 yards running and 90 yards passing, for a total of 120 yards per game. Victor is poorer than Sam at both positions but comparatively less poor at quarterback; thus, Victor will play quarterback.

The team is better off if the coach assigns players to the position in which their opportunity costs are lowest. Sam and Victor specialized and then exchanged output—yards running for yards passing. As a result, the team got more total yards than if Sam and Victor each played both positions or if Sam was the quarterback.

What would have happened if the two athletes had been free to choose their positions? If each wanted to earn the greatest amount of income (yards) possible, both would have voluntarily decided as the coach did. They would have agreed to divide the total income received (total yards) in such a way that each was better off specializing rather than playing both positions.

If you think of the team as a firm, then you can think of the manager assigning employees to jobs according to their comparative advantage. The employees specialize and then trade or exchange their output. This ensures that the firm gets the greatest output at the lowest cost and more output means more income for the employees.

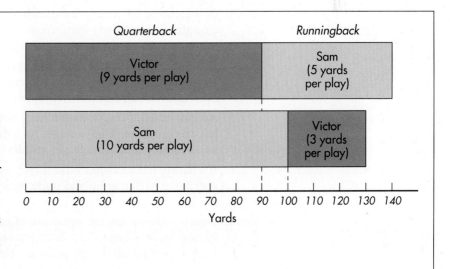

Figure 4
Comparative Advantage in Football
As quarterback, Sam passes 10 yards per play, a total of 100 yards per game. When Victor is quarterback, he passes for 9 yards per play, earning a total of 90 yards. Sam, as runningback, gets 5 yards per play, a total of 50 yards. When Victor is runningback, he gets 3 yards per play, a total of 30 yards. Adding up the total yards, it becomes clear that the team is better off with Sam as runningback and Victor as quarterback, since in this arrangement the total yards gained are highest, and the team's opportunity costs are lowest.

Nations also specialize in the production of goods and services in which they have a comparative advantage and then exchange those goods and services. In this way, each nation is able to obtain more goods and services than each would obtain if it produced all goods and services itself. Just as the football team would be less successful if Sam and Victor each played quarterback and runningback, a nation is less productive if it produces every good and service. A society might prefer to produce a combination of goods and services depicted as a point in the middle of the production possibilities curve. But if the nation has a comparative advantage in producing one type of good, it can specialize in that good and then trade with other countries for the amount of the other type of good it wants. In so doing, the society is able to obtain combinations of the two types of goods that lie beyond its production possibilities curve—beyond what it could produce using its own resources fully if it did not engage in trade with any other nations.

Specializing in the activity that has the lowest opportunity cost is a rule that works for nations just as it does for individuals. Specialization and exchange according to comparative advantage characterize every economy. The more that people can specialize, the greater is the total output that can be produced from given quantities of resources.

RECAP

1. An individual will select the option that has the lowest opportunity cost. Individuals, firms, and nations will specialize in the production of the good or service that has the lowest opportunity cost.

2. Comparative advantage provides the answer to the question of what goods and services to produce. Comparative advantage allows specialization and thus allows individuals, firms, and nations to make the most of limited resources.

3. Comparative advantage exists whenever one person, firm, or nation engaging in an activity incurs fewer opportunity costs than does some other individual, firm, or nation engaging in the same activity.

4. Absolute advantage exists whenever one person, firm, or nation engaging in an activity incurs lower absolute costs than does some other individual, firm, or nation engaging in the same activity.

5. An individual, firm, or nation need not have an absolute advantage to have a comparative advantage. An individual, firm, or nation can be at an absolute disadvantage yet still have a comparative advantage.

6. If a nation has a comparative advantage in producing one good, it can specialize in that good and trade with other countries to obtain other goods.

7. Figure 5 illustrates the structure of economic thinking as we've discussed it in Chapter 2. Scarcity requires that choices be made. Choices are based on self-interest. The option with the lowest opportunity cost is chosen. This means that specialization occurs according to comparative advantage.

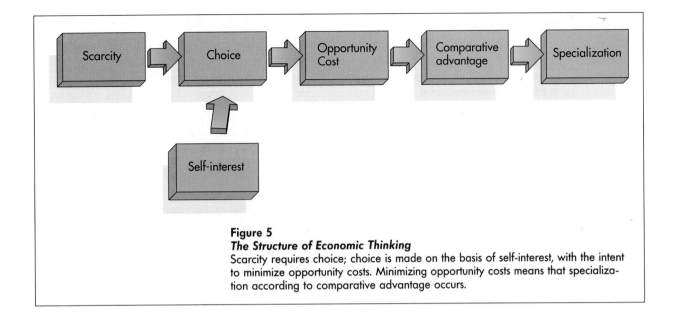

Figure 5
The Structure of Economic Thinking
Scarcity requires choice; choice is made on the basis of self-interest, with the intent to minimize opportunity costs. Minimizing opportunity costs means that specialization according to comparative advantage occurs.

SUMMARY

▼▲ **What are opportunity costs?**

1. Opportunity cost is the highest valued alternative that is forgone when a choice is made. § 1

2. Choice involves both gaining something and giving up something. When you choose one option, you forgo all others. What you forgo is the opportunity cost of your choice. § 1

▼▲ **What is the full cost of any purchase?**

3. Whenever you make a purchase, you forgo whatever else you could have purchased. The full cost of a purchase includes the opportunity cost of the purchase. § 1.a

▼▲ **What is the production possibilities curve?**

4. The production possibilities curve shows all combinations of output that can be produced when a country's resources are fully and efficiently used. § 1.b

5. Points inside the PPC curve represent output combinations where resources are not fully and efficiently used. § 1.c

▼▲ **What accounts for increasing marginal opportunity costs?**

6. Specialization accounts for the bowed out shape of the production possibilities curve, increasing marginal opportunity costs. If two goods are produced using available resources efficiently, then the production of more of the second good means less of the first good. The resources used in the production of the first good must be switched over to production of the second good. Initially, the resources that can be most productive in producing the second good, those that specialize in the production of the second good, are switched, but eventually resources that are specialists in the production of the first good must be switched. § 1.c.3

▼▲ **What accounts for specialization?**

7. Specialization results as resources choose to participate in those activities or produce those goods where their opportunity costs are lowest. § 1.c.4

8. Comparative advantage exists when one person, firm, or nation performing an activity or producing a good incurs fewer opportunity costs than some other person, firm, or nation. § 2.b

9. Comparative advantage accounts for specialization. You specialize in the activities in which you have the lowest opportunity costs—that is, in which you have a comparative advantage. § 2.b

KEY TERMS

opportunity costs § 1

trade off § 1.a

specialist § 1.b

production possibilities curve (PPC) § 1.c

marginal opportunity cost § 1.c.3

marginal § 1.c.3

constant marginal opportunity cost § 1.c.3

increasing marginal opportunity cost § 1.c.3

decreasing marginal opportunity cost § 1.c.3

sunk costs § 1.c.4

comparative advantage § 2.b

absolute advantage § 2.b

EXERCISES

Basic Terms and Concepts

1. Define opportunity costs. Give an example of opportunity costs for an individual, for a firm, and for a nation.

2. Suppose an individual makes the following trade-offs between grades and income:

Total Hours	Hours Studying	GPA	Hours Working	Income
60	60	4.0	0	$ 0
60	40	3.0	20	100
60	30	2.0	30	150
60	10	1.0	50	250
60	0	0.0	60	300

a. Calculate the opportunity cost of an increase in the number of hours spent studying in order to earn a 3.0 grade point average (GPA) rather than a 2.0 GPA.

b. Is the opportunity cost the same for a move from a 0.0 GPA to a 1.0 GPA as it is for a move from a 1.0 GPA to a 2.0 GPA?

c. What is the opportunity cost of an increase in salary from $100 to $150?

3. Suppose a second individual makes the following trade-offs between income and grades:

Total Hours	Hours Studying	GPA	Hours Working	Income
60	50	4.0	10	$ 60
60	40	3.0	20	120
60	20	2.0	40	240
60	10	1.0	50	300
60	0	0.0	60	360

a. Define absolute advantage. Define comparative advantage.

b. Does either the individual in question 2 or the individual in question 3 have an absolute advantage in both activities?

c. Who should specialize in studying, and who should specialize in working?

4. Using the football example in the text, if Sam passed 2 yards farther per attempt than Victor but ran two yards less per attempt, Sam would no longer have an absolute advantage in both positions. To which positions would the coach then assign the players?

5. A doctor earns $250,000 per year, and a professor earns $40,000. They play tennis together each Saturday morning. Compare their opportunity costs of playing tennis.

Extended Concepts

6. A doctor earns $200 per hour, a plumber $40 per hour, and a professor $20 per hour. Everything else the same, who will devote more hours to negotiating the price of a new car?

7. What does the saying "There is no such thing as a free lunch" mean? If someone invites you to lunch and offers to pay, is the meal free to you?

8. You have waited 30 minutes in line for the Star Tours ride at Disneyland. You see a sign that says "from this point on the wait is 45 minutes." You must decide whether to continue waiting in line or to go elsewhere. On what basis do you make the decision? Does the 30 minutes you have already stood in line come into play?

Selling Your Firm May Hike Your Pay

Are you paying for the privilege of working? Is running a business, even a profitable one, costing you money? No successful entrepreneur wants to think that, but there is occasionally some value in thinking the unthinkable.

If your calculations show that selling your company and investing the proceeds would bring you a return that exceeds your current salary and dividends, then you probably should at least entertain the possibility.

Assume, for example, that entrepreneur Smith pays himself $125,000 a year for running his company. A tidy income, but could it be more? If Smith sold the firm for a profit of $5.8 million, he would clear — after payng Uncle Sam a 33 percent tax on the gain — a lump sum of $3,886,000. Because Smith is a conservative investor, he puts all the money into two-year certificates of deposit yielding 8.5 percent, for an annual return of $330,310. By selling his business, Smith would more than double his income.

Put another way, holding on to the company is costing Smith over $200,000 a year. Clearly, he is a prime candidate to sell. Yet he may not do so.

"All too often, entrepreneurs stay at the party too long," says David Hoods, a divisional president of California-based Geneva Corp., investment bankers for small and midsized companies. "They feel that by selling the business they built or founded, they'll be giving up something precious. True, but there's something else to consider. By failing to sell the business when it can fetch a good price, they may be missing out on an opportunity that won't soon repeat itself. If ever!"

How does this happen? Why do smart and sophisticated entrepreneurs let such opportunities slip by? "Because they get lulled into a state of dangerous complacency," Hood says. "Typically, the entrepreneur says to himself, 'Hey, I'm doing great. For running this business, I'm earning a hefty salary.' Hefty? Perhaps. But compared to what?" He cites an example of an entrepreneur who "could sell his electronics-distributing business for $10.5 million, investing the after-tax proceeds for an annual income of $595,000 [based on 8.5 percent]. Suddenly his $300,000 salary doesn't look quite so hefty anymore." . . .

Is selling out right for you? Will you find it to be "the best of both worlds"? The answer depends largely on the company's value and on your ability to invest and live off the proceeds of a sale.

For help in assessing the value of your company, you will need to turn to accountants, valuation consultants, and investment bankers. That's the first step in making the decision. You also will need to assess your own feelings about giving up your company; some entrepreneurs feel they lose their identity if they sell. The value of cash investments can fluctuate over time; after all, someone who wants to buy your company obviously feels the investment will pay off. If you think you can take it to new heights, you are not a candidate for cashing in.

But you may be, and it might be good to think the unthinkable while you have plenty of time to make a considered decision.

■ Source: Mark Stevens, "Selling Your Firm May Hike Your Pay," *Nation's Business,* September, 1989, p. 46.

Commentary

Opportunity costs represent the benefits forgone by choosing one option rather than another. This article illustrates a particular application of the concept of opportunity costs: the choice of whether or not an entrepreneur should sell his or her business. As we will discuss here, an entrepreneur should consider all the benefits—and costs—of selling out when weighing an offer.

Consider the example presented in the article of an entrepreneur who pays himself $125,000 per year as the head of his corporation. While this may seem like a good salary, the article points out that if the company could be sold for $5.8 million, with an after-tax return of $3,886,000, the entrepreneur could earn $330,310 per year in interest (if the interest rate is 8.5 percent). In other words, the entrepreneur is forgoing $205,310 per year in income by not selling his company.

You may have noticed that there are other benefits awaiting the entrepreneur if he sells his company. Besides earning interest payments of $330,310 per year from the proceeds of the sale, the entrepreneur will also "earn" the number of hours per year that he formerly spent working at his business. After selling his company, he could spend these hours at leisure or working in another position.

The opportunity cost to the entrepreneur of retaining ownership of his company is the difference between what he would earn if he sold the company and what he earns as the head of his company. Suppose that the entrepreneur could work at another job that paid $100,000 per year if he sold his company. Then the entrepreneur would earn $330,310 per year in interest plus $100,000 in salary at his new job, for a total yearly income of $430,310. Since his pay if he does not sell the company is $125,000, the opportunity cost of not selling the company is actually $305,310 ($430,310 − $125,000).

What if the entrepreneur chooses to spend his days reading novels rather than finding a new job after he sells his company? Does the $205,310 difference between the interest payments from the proceeds of selling the company and the $125,000 salary he pays himself still understate the opportunity cost of not selling the firm? The answer is yes. The time spent reading novels is valued by the entrepreneur—more highly valued than the next-best opportunity (which may be a position that pays a hefty salary, or may be playing tennis). If the entrepreneur can put a value on this preferred activity, he could figure out the additional opportunity cost, over and above the salary forgone, of not selling the firm. One way for the entrepreneur to put a value on reading novels is to figure out how much a job would have to pay him to entice him out of his literary pursuits.

Our understanding of opportunity cost also suggests a reason that an entrepreneur may not sell his company, even if he is forgoing a higher income. Suppose the entrepreneur enjoys and values running a business he started from scratch, and that it would be very difficult to start another company if he sold the first one. In this case, he might willingly forgo the extra salary he would earn by selling out if the extra income did not compensate him for the satisfaction he receives in running his own company.

Opportunity cost is of central importance in a decision of whether or not to sell a company, or for that matter in any economic decision. The proper application of the principle of opportunity cost considers *all* opportunities forgone by a certain course of action, even though putting an actual dollar value on these opportunities may sometimes pose a challenge.

3

Markets, Demand and Supply, and the Price System

1. What is a market?
2. What is demand?
3. What is supply?
4. How is price determined by demand and supply?
5. What causes price to change?

PREVIEW If you decided to vacation in Phoenix, Arizona, from January 10 through March 15, you could spend $319 per person per night for a first-class resort. If your vacation to Phoenix occurred in August, you could have the same luxurious treatment for less than half that price. During the winter in Vail, Colorado, you could have accommodations for $280 per person; in the summer you would pay $150 per person. For $400 per night per person you could have an ocean view at the Ritz-Carlton in Laguna Niguel, California, any time of the year—but, sorry, the hotel has advance bookings for more than a year.

If you wanted to see *The Phantom of the Opera* on Broadway or in Los Angeles in 1989 or 1990, you could not purchase tickets from the usual places. The show was sold out in advance for more than a year. You could, however, get tickets if you were willing to pay more than ten times the face value and search out those people, called scalpers, who had tickets for sale.

Many restaurants don't take reservations. You simply arrive and wait your turn. If you arrive at 7:30 in the evening, you have at least "an hour wait." Notwithstanding that fact, a few people arrive, speak quietly with the maitre d', hand him some money, and are promptly seated. At some restaurants that do take reservations, you must wait a month for a Saturday evening, three weeks for a Friday evening, two weeks for Tuesday through Thursday, and virtually no time at all for Sunday or Monday.

Do you see any similarities among these examples? Each deals with the allocation of goods and services, with price, and with demand and supply. However, in some of the examples, price changes seem to allocate scarce goods to buyers, but in others, price does not seem to function as an allocating device. Phoenix is a great place in the winter—75 degrees and sunny. Phoenix in August can be an oppressive 108 degrees with humidity of 50 percent. It makes sense that resort prices in Phoenix would be higher in winter than in summer. Why doesn't the same logic apply to rooms at the Ritz-Carlton, to tables at a restaurant, or to tickets to shows?

In this chapter we discuss the role that price plays in allocating goods and services, what economists mean by price, what a market is, and how demand and supply in a market work to determine price.

1. MARKETS

▼ What is a market? ▲

The supermarket, the stock market, the foreign exchange market, the gold market, the labor market, the black market, the underground market, the political market—they are similar in that goods and services are exchanged. The market may be a specific location such as the supermarket or the stock market or it may be the exchange of a particular good or service at many different locations, such as the foreign exchange market and the underground market. In order to understand how price functions, you need to know about markets of all types.

1.a. Market Definition

market:
a place or service that enables buyers and sellers to exchange goods and services

black market:
illegal exchanges

underground market:
unreported exchanges of goods and services

A **market** makes possible the exchange of goods and services between buyers and sellers, and that exchange determines the price of goods and services. Buyers and sellers communicate with each other about the quality and quantity of a product, what the buyers are willing and able to pay, and what the sellers must receive. Food, shares of stock, national currencies, gold, and labor services are bought and sold in, respectively, the supermarket, the stock market, the foreign exchange market, the gold market, and the labor market. **Black market** is the name given to exchanges that violate the law, such as the buying and selling of illegal drugs and counterfeit goods. **Underground market** is the name given to unrecorded transactions, whether legal or illegal. For instance, some people choose not to report their earnings to the Internal Revenue Service in order to avoid paying taxes. Any earnings that go unreported are part of the underground market. And, finally, the political market involves the exchange of votes and political benefits.

Markets may be general or specialized, large or small, local or global. They may consist of one buyer and one seller or many buyers and many sellers. A market may be formally organized, like the New York Stock Exchange, or it may be loosely organized like the market for used bicycles. A market may be confined to one location, like a supermarket, or it may encompass a city, a state, a nation, or the entire world. The market for agricultural products, for instance, is international, but the market for labor services is mostly local or national.

1.b. Barter and Money Exchanges

barter:
the direct exchange of goods and services without the use of money

The purpose of markets is to facilitate the exchange of goods and services between buyers and sellers. In some cases money changes hands; in others only goods and services are exchanged. The exchange of goods and services directly, without money, is called **barter**. Barter occurs when a plumber fixes a leaky pipe for a lawyer in exchange for the lawyer's work on a will; when a Chinese citizen provides fresh vegetables to an American visitor in exchange for a pack of American cigarettes, and when children trade baseball cards.

double coincidence of wants:
the situation that exists when A has what B wants and B has what A wants

transaction costs:
the cost involved in making an exchange

Most markets involve money because goods and services can be exchanged more easily with money than without it. When IBM purchases microchips from Yakamoto of Japan, IBM and Yakamoto do not engage in barter. One firm may not have what the other wants. Barter requires a **double coincidence of wants**: IBM must have what Yakamoto wants, and Yakamoto must have what IBM wants. The **transaction costs** (the costs involved in making an exchange) of finding a double coincidence of wants for barter transactions are typically very high. Money reduces these transaction costs. To obtain the microchips, all IBM has to do is provide dollars to Yakamoto. Yakamoto accepts the money because it can spend the money to obtain the goods that it wants.

The Foreign Exchange Market

Most countries have their own national currency. West Germany has the deutsche mark, France the French franc, England the pound sterling, Japan the yen, the United States the dollar, and so on. The citizens of each country use their national currency to carry out transactions. For transactions among nations to occur, some exchange of foreign currencies is necessary.

Americans buy Toyotas and Nissans from Japan while American computer companies sell pocket calculators to businesses in Mexico. Some Americans open bank accounts in Switzerland while American real-estate companies sell property to citizens in England. These transactions require the acquisition of a foreign currency. An English businessman who wants to buy property in the United States will have to exchange his money, pounds sterling, for dollars. An American car distributor who imports Toyotas will have to

exchange dollars for yen in order to pay the Toyota manufacturer.

The exchange of currency and the determination of the value of national currencies occur in the foreign exchange market. The foreign exchange market is not a tightly organized market operating in a building in New York. Usually people who mention the foreign exchange market are referring to the trading that occurs among large international banks. Such trading is global and is done largely through telephone and computer communication systems. If a foreign exchange trader at First Chicago Bank calls a trader at Bank of Tokyo to buy $1 million worth of Japanese yen, that is a foreign exchange market transaction. Banks buy and sell currencies according to the needs and demands of their customers. Business firms and individuals rely largely on banks to buy and sell foreign exchange for them.

The price of one currency expressed in terms of another currency is called a *foreign exchange rate*. The exchange rate of the dollar is the number of units of other currencies that a dollar can be exchanged for. In July, 1990, 1 U.S. dollar could purchase 151 Japanese yen. The list that follows shows the prices of several currencies relative to the dollar in July, 1990.

Country	Currency Units per Dollar*
Australia	1.24
Belgium	33.86
Canada	1.15
France	5.52
Italy	1,211
Japan	151
Netherlands	1.86
Spain	100
Sweden	5.96
Switzerland	1.39
West Germany	1.65

*(July, 1990)

1.c.   Relative and Nominal Price

relative price:
the price of one good expressed in terms of the price of another good

A price is established when an exchange occurs, whether the exchange is in barter or money terms. That price is called the **relative price**. When you pay $1 for a carton of milk, you are forgoing everything else you could get for that dollar. Thus, the price of milk is, in reality, an opportunity cost. The carton of milk is worth one-third of a $3 box of Quaker Oats 100% Natural cereal, one-two-hundredth of a used Diamond Back mountain bike, 20 sticks of Trident gum at 5 cents per stick, and so on. In a barter exchange, a relative price is established for the goods traded. When the lawyer trades 2 hours of work on the plumber's will for 1 hour of the plumber's work on a leaky pipe, the relative price established is 2/1.

nominal price:
the money price of a good

The **nominal price** is the money price. The nominal price of a $1 carton of milk is $1. The relative price may be expressed as the ratio of the money price of one good to the money prices of other goods. If the price of the carton of milk rises to $2 and no other prices change, the nominal and the relative prices of the milk have risen. After the change in the relative price, the carton of milk is worth two-thirds of a box of cereal, one-one-hundredth of a used bike, and 40 sticks of gum. However, if all prices double so that milk costs $2, the box of cereal $6, the used bike $400, and the gum 10 cents per stick, then the carton of milk is still worth one-third of a box of cereal, one-two-hundredth of a used bike, and 20 sticks of gum. Only the nominal price has changed in this case; the relative price remains the same.

The relative price is the price that affects economic decision making.

Relative prices affect economic behavior. They are a measure of what you must give up to get one unit of a good or service. They are a measure of opportunity costs. The nominal price provides no information about opportunity cost and therefore does not affect economic decisions.

As an illustration, consider the redefinition of Nicaragua's currency in January 1988, when the Sandinista government in effect moved the decimal point on the Nicaraguan cordoba two places to the left. The 100-cordoba coin became a 1-cordoba coin; the 100,000-cordoba bill became a 1,000-cordoba bill. As a result, all prices and incomes dropped by the same percentage—all fell to one-one-hundredth of their previous amounts. Most relative prices were unchanged by the government's action, so the **purchasing power** of incomes did not change. Someone who earned 200,000 cordobas per month and rented an apartment for 100,000 cordobas per month before January 1988 would, after January 1988, have an income of 2,000 (new) cordobas per month and would pay 1,000 (new) cordobas per month for the apartment. The quantities of goods traded remained approximately what they had been before the currency change. If the relative price of the apartment had risen to 2,000 (new) cordobas while the price of everything else stayed the same, the individual earning 2,000 (new) cordobas probably would have rented a different, less expensive apartment.

purchasing power:
the quantity of goods and services that a given quantity of income can buy

August is the time when students start apartment-hunting. Entering the apartment market is not like entering a formal marketplace, like a store, or the building where the New York Stock Exchange is housed; it may only involve looking at a series of index cards tacked up on a bulletin board. Wherever a quantity of apartments is offered for rent, a market will develop. Renters decide how much they are willing and able to pay for various locations and sizes of apartments. Markets simply consist of buyers and sellers. A market enables buyers and sellers to communicate, to exchange information, and to exchange goods and services.

RECAP

1. A market is not necessarily a specific location or store. Instead, the term *market* refers to exchanges between buyers and sellers who communicate with each other about the quality and quantity of a product, what the buyers are willing and able to pay for a product, and what the sellers must receive in order to produce and sell a product.

2. Barter is an exchange of goods or services made without the use of money.

3. With money, the exchange of goods and services is easier and less expensive than it is with barter.

4. The relative price is the nominal price of a good or service expressed in terms of the nominal prices of other goods or services. It is the price that affects economic decision making.

2. DEMAND

▼ **What is demand?** ▲

demand:
the quantities of a well-defined commodity that consumers are willing and able to buy at each possible price during a given period of time, ceteris paribus

Demand and supply determine the price of any good or service. To understand why a price rises or falls and how a price level is determined, it is necessary to know how demand and supply function. We begin by considering demand alone, then supply, and then we put the two together.

Demand refers to the quantities of a well-defined commodity that consumers are willing and able to buy at each possible price during a given period of time, ceteris paribus. Economists distinguish between *demand* and *quantity demanded*. When they refer to the quantity demanded, they are talking about one particular price, whereas when they refer to demand, they are talking about the quantities demanded at every price. Thus, the statement that "the demand for travel to China fell after the violent confrontations between student demonstrators and army troops in Beijing in the spring of 1989" means that fewer people were willing and able to make the trip to China, no matter what the price. And the statement that "the quantity of trips demanded rose as the price of air travel fell in the mid-1970s" means that increasing numbers of people were willing and able to travel by air because the price of flying decreased.

2.a. The Law of Demand

Consumers and merchants know that if you lower the price of a good or service, people will beat a path to your door. This simple truth is referred to as the **law of demand**.

law of demand:
as the price of a good or service rises (falls), the quantity of that good or service that people are willing and able to purchase during a particular period of time falls (rises), ceteris paribus

According to the law of demand, the quantity of an item that people are willing and able to purchase during a particular period of time decreases as the price rises. The law of demand thus dictates that there is an inverse relationship between the quantity demanded and the price of an item. As the price rises, ceteris paribus, the quantity demanded falls.

The definition of the law of demand can be broken down into five phrases:

1. the quantity of a well-defined good or service that
2. people are willing and able to purchase
3. during a particular period of time
4. decreases as the price of that good or service rises
5. ceteris paribus

The first phrase indicates that the good or service must have certain characteristics that are recognized by buyers and sellers. A watch is a commodity defined and distinguished from other goods by several characteristics: quality, color, and design of the watch face, to name a few. The law of demand applies to the well-defined good, in this case, a watch. If one of the characteristics should change, the good would no longer be well-defined—in fact, it would be a different good. A Rolex watch is different than a Timex watch; Polo brand golf shirts are different goods than generic brand golf shirts; Mercedes-Benz automobiles are different goods than Yugo automobiles.

The second phrase indicates that people must not only *want* to purchase some good, but they must be *able* to purchase that good. For example, Sue would love to buy a membership to the Paradise Valley Country Club, but because the membership costs $35,000, she is not able to make the purchase. Though willing, she is not able. At a price of $5,000, however, she is both willing and able to purchase a membership.

The third phrase points out that the demand for any good must be defined for a specific period of time. Without reference to a time period, a demand relationship would not make any sense. For instance, the statement that "at a price of $5 per Happy Meal 13 million Happy Meals are demanded," provides no useful information. Are the 13 million meals sold in one week or one year? Think of demand as a rate of purchase at each possible price over a period of time—2 per month, 1 per day, and so on.

The fourth phrase points out that price and quantity demanded move in opposite directions. There is an inverse relationship between them.

The final phrase, ceteris paribus, is Latin for "other things being equal," or "everything else held constant." In terms of demand, what is "everything else"? It is income, tastes, prices of related goods and services, expectations, and the number of buyers. These are called the **determinants of demand**. Demand is a measure of the relationship between the price and quantity demanded of a particular good or service when the determinants of demand do not change. When one of the determinants does change, the demand relationship also changes.

determinants of demand:
factors other than the price of the good that influence demand—income, tastes, prices of related goods and services, expectations, and number of buyers

2.b. Income and Substitution Effects

The law of demand defines an inverse relationship between the price of an item and the quantity demanded. The demand relationship is inverse because of two tendencies that occur when the price of an item rises relative to all other prices. The tendencies are known as the *substitution effect* and the *income effect*.

The opportunity cost of purchasing one unit of a good whose price has gone up rises because more of other goods and services must be forgone. As a result, many people choose to purchase fewer units of a good whose price has risen and use their limited income to purchase other goods—goods that meet nearly the same wants or needs as the good whose price has risen. This tendency is called the **substitution effect**. For example, due to federal regulations, car manufacturers are currently installing better safety equipment in cars, such as motorized seat belts and air bags, which in some cases is adding as much as $700 to the prices of cars.[1] As a result, some people may choose to avoid buying new cars and substitute continued use of their old cars or the purchase of used cars without the new safety equipment instead. Such decision making is an example of the substitution effect.

When the price of an item increases, people have to allocate their limited incomes among what is now a more expensive set of goods and services. Because they can buy fewer goods and services, the purchasing power of their income has fallen. The change in quantity demanded that occurs when the purchasing power of income is altered as a result of a price change is called the **income effect**. When the price of a good that a consumer typically buys goes up, the purchasing power of that consumer's income goes down. This decline in purchasing power causes the consumer to reduce consumption of all goods, not just the good whose price went up.

Together, the income and substitution effects determine that the quantity demanded of any particular good or service will fall as the price rises and will rise as the price falls, ceteris paribus.

2.c. The Demand Schedule

A **demand schedule** is a table or list of the prices and the corresponding quantities demanded of a particular good. The table in Figure 1 is a demand schedule for bread. It shows the quantity of bread that a consumer named Bob is willing and able to purchase at various prices during the year, ceteris paribus. As the price of bread rises relative to the prices of other goods, Bob will purchase greater quantities of substitute goods and less bread. At the very high price of $5 per loaf, Bob will purchase only 10 loaves of bread, less than one loaf per month. He will switch to beans, rice, and potatoes because those high-carbohydrate foods can serve the same function as bread.

Because Bob has a limited amount of income, as the price of bread rises, the purchasing power of Bob's income falls. If Bob decides to purchase 30 loaves, say, as the price of bread rises from $3 to $5, he will have less income to spend on other goods and services.

At a price of $4 per loaf, Bob will purchase 20 loaves of bread. He will cut back on beans, rice, and potatoes and eat more bread. As the price drops from $4 to $3 to $2 to $1, Bob is willing and able to purchase increasing quantities of bread. At a price of $1, Bob will purchase 50 loaves of bread, giving up almost all of the substitute goods.

---

[1]Melinda Grenier Guiles, "Ford, Chrysler, Lifting Prices, Cite Safety Gear," *The Wall Street Journal,* July 24, 1989, p. A3.

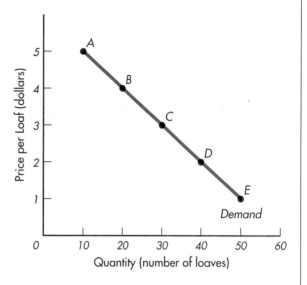

Combination	Price per Loaf (constant-quality units)	Quantity Demanded (constant-quality units)
A	$5	10
B	4	20
C	3	30
D	2	40
E	1	50

Figure 1
Bob's Demand Schedule and Demand Curve for Bread
The quantity of bread that Bob is willing and able to purchase at each price is listed in the table or demand schedule. The demand curve is derived from the combina- tions given in the demand schedule. The price-quantity combination of $5 per loaf and 10 loaves of bread is point A. The combination of $4 per loaf and 20 loaves is point B. Each combination is plotted, and the points are connected to form the demand curve.

2.d. The Demand Curve

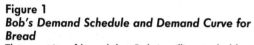
demand curve:
a graph of a demand schedule that measures price on the vertical axis and quantity demanded on the horizontal axis

A **demand curve** is a graph of a demand schedule. The demand curve shown in Figure 1 is plotted from the information given in the demand schedule. Price is measured on the vertical axis; quantity demanded, on the horizontal axis. The demand curve slopes downward because of the inverse relationship between the price of bread and the quantity that Bob is willing and able to purchase. Point *A* on the curve corresponds to combination A in the demand schedule: a price of $5 per loaf and 10 loaves demanded. Similarly, points *B, C, D,* and *E* on the curve represent the corresponding combinations in the demand schedule. The line connecting these points is Bob's demand curve for bread.

All demand curves slope down because of the law of demand: as price falls, quantity demanded increases. The demand curves for bread, elec- tricity, automobiles, colleges, labor services, and all other goods and ser- vices slope down. You might be saying to yourself, ''That's not true. What about the demand for Mercedes-Benz cars or Gucci bags? As their price goes up, they become more prestigious and the quantity demanded actu- ally rises.'' To avoid confusion in such circumstances, we say ''ceteris paribus.'' We assume that tastes do not change and that therefore goods *cannot* become more prestigious as the price changes. Similarly, we do not allow the quality or the brand name to change as we define the demand schedule or demand curve of a product. We concentrate on the one quality or the one brand; so when we say that the price of a good has risen, we are talking about a good that is identical at all prices.

When speaking of the demand curve or demand schedule, we are using constant-quality units. The quality of a good does not change as the price changes along a demand curve.

Figure 2
The Market Demand Schedule and Curve for Bread
The market is defined to consist of three individuals: Bob, Helen, and Art. Their demand schedules are listed in the table and plotted as the individual demand curves shown in Figure 2(a). By adding the quantities that each demands at every price, we obtain the market demand curve shown in Figure 2(b). At a price of $1 we add Bob's quantity demanded of 50 to Helen's quantity demanded of 25 to Art's quantity demanded of 27 to obtain the market quantity demanded of 102. At a price of $2 we add Bob's 40 to Helen's 20 to Art's 24 to obtain the market quantity demanded of 84. To obtain the market demand curve, for every price we sum the quantities demanded by each market participant.

Price per Loaf	Quantities Demanded by			Market Demand
	Bob	Helen	Art	
$5	10	5	15	30
4	20	10	18	48
3	30	15	21	66
2	40	20	24	84
1	50	25	27	102

(a) Individual Demand Curves

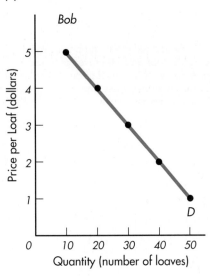

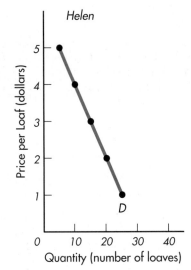

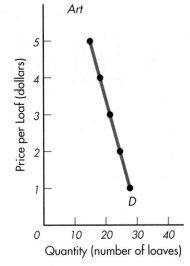

(b) Market Demand Curve

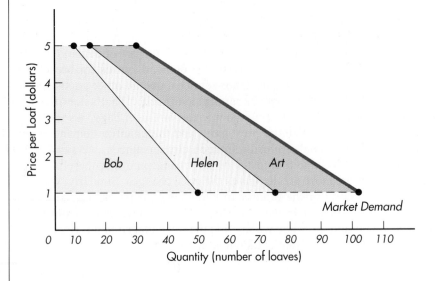

2.e. From Individual Demand Curves to a Market Curve

Bob's demand curve for bread is plotted in Figure 1. Unless Bob is the only purchaser of bread, his demand curve is not the total, or market demand, curve. To derive the market demand curve, the individual demand curves of all consumers in the market must be added together. The table in Figure 2 lists the demand schedules of three individuals: Bob, Helen, and Art. Because in this example the market consists only of Bob, Helen, and Art, their individual demands are added together to derive the market demand. The market demand is shown in the last column of the table.

Bob's, Helen's, and Art's demand schedules are plotted as individual demand curves in Figure 2(a). In Figure 2(b) their individual demand curves have been added together to obtain the market demand curve. (Notice that we add in a horizontal direction—that is, we add quantities at each price, not prices at each quantity.) At a price of $1, we add the quantity Bob would buy, 50, to the quantity Helen would buy, 25, to the quantity Art would buy, 27, to get the market demand, 102. At a price of $2, we add the quantities each consumer is willing and able to buy to get the total quantity demanded in the market—84. Similarly at all prices we add the quantities demanded by each consumer to get the total or market quantity demanded.

2.f. Changes in Demand and Changes in the Quantity Demanded

When the ceteris paribus assumption is relaxed—that is, when one of the determinants of demand (income, tastes, prices of related goods, expectations, number of buyers) is allowed to change—the demand for a good or service changes as well. What does it mean to say that demand changes? Demand is the entire demand schedule or demand curve. When we say that demand changes, we are referring to a change in the quantities demanded at each and every price.

For example, if Bob's income rises, then we expect Bob's demand for bread to rise. At each and every price, the quantity of bread that Bob is willing and able to purchase rises. This increase is shown in the last column of the table in Figure 3. A change in demand is represented by a shift of the demand curve, as shown in Figure 3(a). The shift to the right, from D_1 to D_2, indicates that Bob is willing and able to buy more bread at every price.

A change in the quantity demanded is a movement along the demand curve. A change in demand is a shift of the demand curve.

When the price of a good or service is the only factor that changes, the quantity demanded changes but the demand curve does *not* shift. Instead, as the price falls (rises), ceteris paribus, the quantity that people are willing and able to purchase rises (falls). This change is merely a movement from one point on the demand curve to another point on the same demand curve, not a shift of the demand curve. *Change in the quantity demanded* is the phrase economists use to describe the change in the quantities of a particular good or service that people are willing and able to purchase as the price of that good or service changes. A change in the quantity demanded, from point *A* to point *B* on the demand curve, is shown in Figure 3(b).

Figure 3
A Change in Demand and a Change in the Quantity Demanded
According to the table, Bob's demand for bread has increased by 5 loaves at each price level. In Figure 3(a), this change is shown as a shift of the demand curve from D_1 to D_2. Figure 3(b) shows a change in the quantity demanded. The change is an increase in the quantity that consumers are willing and able to purchase at a lower price.

Price per Loaf	Quantity Demanded Before	Quantity Demanded After
$5	10	15
4	20	25
3	30	35
2	40	45
1	50	55

(a) Change in Demand

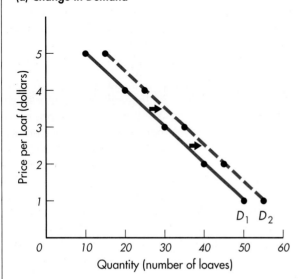

(b) Change in Quantity Demanded

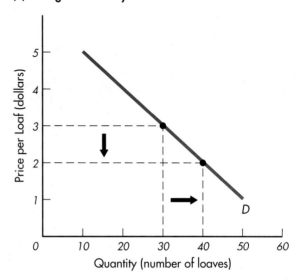

The demand curve shifts when income, tastes, prices of related goods, expectations, or the number of buyers changes. Let's consider how each of these determinants of demand affects the demand curve.

Income   The demand for any good or service depends on income. The higher someone's income is, the more goods and services that person can purchase at any given price. The increase in Bob's income causes his demand to increase. This change is shown in Figure 3(a) by the shift to the right from curve D_1 to the curve D_2. Increased income means a greater ability to purchase goods and services. At every price, more bread is demanded along D_2 than along D_1.

Tastes   The demand for any good or service depends on individuals' tastes and preferences. For decades, the destination of choice for college students in the East and Midwest during spring break was Fort Lauderdale, Florida. In the late 1980s, many students decided that Mexico was a more exciting destination than Fort Lauderdale. Regardless of the prices of the Fort Lauderdale and Mexican vacations, tastes changed and more students went to Mexico. The demand curve for the Mexican vacation shifted to the right, and the demand curve for the Fort Lauderdale vacation shifted to the left.

Prices of Related Goods and Services   Goods and services may be related in two ways: as substitutes and as complements. **Substitute goods** can be used in place of each other, so that as the price of one rises, the demand for the other rises. Bread and crackers, BMWs and Acuras, universities and community colleges, electricity and natural gas are, more or less, pairs of substitute goods. As the price of crackers rises, ceteris paribus, the demand for bread rises and the demand curve for bread shifts to the right.

Complementary goods are used together, and as the price of one rises, the demand for the other falls. Bread and margarine, beer and peanuts, and cameras and film are pairs of complementary goods. If camera prices rise, people tend to purchase fewer cameras, and they also tend to purchase less film. As the price of bread rises, people tend to purchase less bread, and they also demand less margarine. The demand curve for a complementary good shifts to the left when the price of the related good increases.

Expectations   Expectations about the future can have an effect on demand today. People make purchases today because they expect their income to be a certain amount in the future. A change in expected income can have an effect on today's expenditures. For instance, you might purchase a car, some furniture, or a house today thinking that your income will be a certain amount next year. If for some reason you change your expectation of next year's income, you may also change your current expenditures. Expecting more income next year may induce you to buy a higher-priced car or more furniture today. The effect of changed expectations on demand is represented by a shift of the demand curve. The demand for a good or service may rise (fall) and the demand curve may shift to the right (left) because of a change in expectations.

Number of Buyers   Market demand consists of the sum of the demands of all individuals. The more individuals there are with income to spend, the greater the market demand is likely to be. For example, the populations of Florida and Arizona are much larger during the winter than they are during the summer. The demand for any particular good or service in Arizona and Florida rises (the demand curve shifts to the right) during the winter months and falls (the demand curve shifts to the left) during the summer months.

RECAP

1. According to the law of demand, the quantity demanded of any good or service is inversely related to the price of the good or service during a specific period of time, ceteris paribus.

substitute goods:
goods that can be used in place of each other (as the price of one rises, the demand for the other rises)

complementary goods:
goods that are used together (as the price of one rises, the demand for the other falls)

A change in demand is represented by a shift of the demand curve.

2. The substitution effect and the income effect of a price change account for the inverse relation between price and quantity demanded.

3. A demand schedule is a listing of the quantity demanded at each price.

4. The demand curve is a downward-sloping line plotted from the values of the demand schedule.

5. Demand changes when one of the determinants of demand changes. A demand change is a shift of the demand curve.

6. The quantity demanded changes when the price of the good or service changes. This change is a move from one point on the demand curve to another point on the same demand curve.

3. SUPPLY

▼ What is supply? ▲

Why is the price of hotel accommodations in Phoenix higher in the winter than in the summer? Demand *and* supply. Why is the price of beef higher in Japan than in the United States? Demand *and* supply. Why did the price of the dollar in terms of other countries' currencies rise during 1989? Demand *and* supply. Both demand and supply determine price, not demand alone or supply alone. We now discuss supply.

3.a. The Law of Supply

Just as demand is the relation between the price and the quantity demanded of a good or service, supply is a relation between price and quantity supplied. **Supply** is the amount of a good or service that producers are willing and able to offer for sale at each possible price during a period of time, ceteris paribus. According to the **law of supply**, as the price of a good or service rises, the quantity supplied rises, and as the price falls, the quantity supplied falls, ceteris paribus.

A **supply schedule** is a table or list of the prices and the corresponding quantities supplied of a well-defined good or service. The table in Figure 4 presents Orobran's supply schedule for bread. The schedule lists the quantity that Orobran is willing and able to produce at each price, ceteris paribus. As the price increases, ceteris paribus, the quantity that Orobran is willing and able to supply also increases.

A **supply curve** is a graph of a supply schedule. Figure 4 shows Orobran's supply curve for bread. The price and quantity combinations given in the supply schedule correspond to the points on the supply curve. Combination A in the table corresponds to point *A* on the curve, combination B in the supply schedule corresponds to point *B* on the curve, and so on for each price-quantity combination.

Orobran's supply curve slopes upward. This means that the quantity that Orobran is willing and able to supply increases as the price increases. Recall from Chapter 2 that the bowed-out production possibilities curve is the most realistic shape because of increasing marginal opportunity costs.

supply:
the amount of a good or service that producers are willing and able to offer for sale at each possible price during a period of time, ceteris paribus

law of supply:
as the price of a good or service that producers are willing and able to offer for sale at each possible price during a particular period of time rises (falls), the quantity of that good or service rises (falls), ceteris paribus

supply schedule:
a list or table of prices and corresponding quantities supplied of a particular good or service

supply curve:
a graph of a supply schedule that measures price on the vertical axis and quantity supplied on the horizontal axis

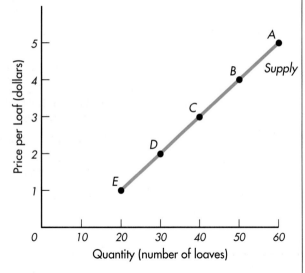

Combination	Price per Loaf (constant-quality units)	Quantity Supplied (constant-quality units)
A	$5	60
B	4	50
C	3	40
D	2	30
E	1	20

Figure 4
Orobran's Supply Schedule and Supply Curve for Bread
The quantity that Orobran is willing and able to offer for sale at each price is listed in the supply schedule and

shown on the supply curve. At point A, the price is $5 per loaf and the quantity supplied is 60 loaves. The combination of $4 per loaf and 50 loaves is point B. Each price-quantity combination is plotted, and the points are connected to form the supply curve.

As a society puts more and more resources into the production of any specific item, the opportunity cost of each additional unit of production rises because more and more specialized resources are transferred to activities in which they are relatively less productive. Orobran, too, finds that as it increases production, the marginal opportunity costs of production rise. Hence, Orobran, or any producer, is willing and able to produce more only if the price rises enough to cover the increasing opportunity costs.

3.b. From Individual Supply Curves to the Market Supply

To derive the market supply, the quantities that each producer supplies at each price must be added together, just as the quantities demanded by each consumer are added together to derive the market demand. The table in Figure 5 lists the supply schedules of three producers: Orobran, Holsom, and Deliteful. Market supply is shown in the last column of the table.

The supply schedules of each producer are plotted as individual supply curves in Figure 5(a). Then in Figure 5(b) the individual supply curves have been added together to obtain the market supply curve. At a price of $5, the quantity supplied by Orobran is 60, the quantity supplied by Holsom is 30, the quantity supplied by Deliteful is 12, and the total quantity supplied in the market is 102 loaves. At a price of $4, the quantities supplied are 50 by Orobran, 25 by Holsom, and 9 by Deliteful, for a total market supply of 84. The sums of the quantities supplied at each price yield the market supply curve plotted in Figure 5(b). The market supply

Figure 5
The Market Supply Schedule and Curve for Bread

The market supply is derived by summing the quantities that each producer is willing and able to offer for sale at each price. In this example, there are three producers: Orobran, Holsom, and Deliteful. The supply schedules of each are listed in the table and plotted as the individual supply curves shown in Figure 5(a). By adding the quantities supplied at each price, we obtain the market supply curve shown in Figure 5(b). For instance, at a price of $5, Orobran offers 60 units, Holsom 30 units, and Deliteful 12 units, for a market quantity of 102. The market supply curve reflects the quantities that each producer is able and willing to supply at each price.

Price per Loaf	Quantities Supplied by			Market Supply
	Orobran	Holsom	Deliteful	
$5	60	30	12	102
4	50	25	9	84
3	40	20	6	66
2	30	15	3	48
1	20	10	0	30

(a) Individual Supply Curves

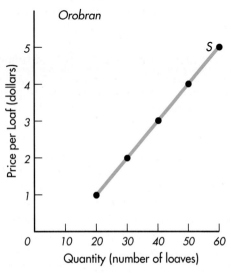

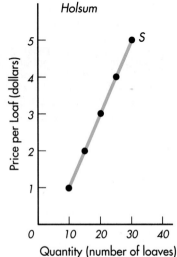

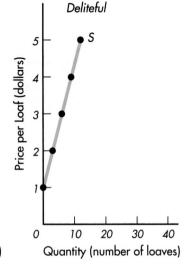

(b) Market Supply Curve

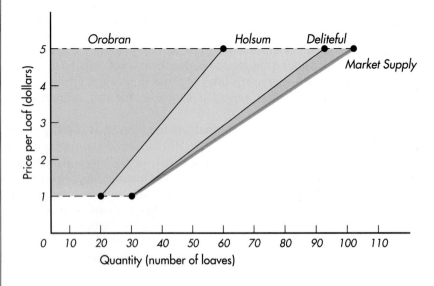

curve slopes up because each of the individual supply curves in Figure 5(a) has a positive slope. The market supply curve indicates that the quantity supplied in the market increases as the price rises.

3.c. The Determinants of Supply

When we draw the supply curve, we allow only the price and quantity supplied to change. Everything else that might affect supply is assumed not to change. The factors held constant are called the **determinants of supply**. They include the prices of resources used to produce the product, technology and productivity, expectations of producers, the number of producers in the market, and the prices of related goods and services. If any one of these changes, the supply schedule changes and the supply curve shifts.

determinants of supply:
factors other than the price of the good that influence supply—prices of resources, technology and productivity, expectations of producers, number of producers, and the prices of related goods and services

Prices of Resources   If the cost of wheat—one of the resources used to produce bread—rises, higher bread prices will be necessary to induce bakers to produce as much bread as they did before the cost of the resource rose. The higher cost of resources causes a decrease in supply, meaning a leftward shift of the supply curve, from S_1 to S_2 in Figure 6(a).

Two interpretations of a leftward shift of the supply curve are possible. One comes from a comparison of the old and new curves in a horizontal direction. The other comes from a comparison of the curves in a vertical direction. In the vertical direction, the decrease in supply means that sellers want a higher price to produce any given quantity. Compare, for example, point A on curve S_1 with point C on curve S_2. Points A and C represent the same quantity but different prices. Sellers will offer 66 units for sale at a price of $3 per loaf, according to supply curve S_1. But if the supply curve shifts to the left, sellers want more ($3.50), for 66 units.

In the horizontal direction, the decrease in supply means that sellers will offer less for sale at any given price. This can be seen by comparing point B on curve S_2 with point A on curve S_1. Both points correspond to a price of $3, but along curve S_1 sellers are willing to offer 56 units for sale, while curve S_2 indicates that sellers will offer only 57 units for sale.

If resource prices declined, then supply would increase. That combination would be illustrated by a rightward shift of the supply curve.

Technology and Productivity   If resources are used more efficiently in the production of a good or service, more of that good or service can be produced for the same cost, or the original quantity can be produced for a lower cost. As a result, the supply curve shifts to the right, as shown in Figure 6(b).

When technology changes, resources typically are used more efficiently and supply increases. For instance, the move from horse-drawn plows to tractors or from mainframe computers to personal computers meant that each worker was able to produce more. The increase in output produced by each unit of resource is called a *productivity increase*. **Productivity** is defined as the quantity of output produced per unit of resource. Improvements in technology cause productivity increases, which lead to an increase in supply.

productivity:
the quantity of output produced per unit of resource

Figure 6
A Shift of the Supply Curve
Figure 6(a) shows a decrease in supply and the shift of the supply curve to the left, from S_1 to S_2. The decrease is caused by a change in one of the determinants of bread supply — an increase in the price of wheat. Because of the increased price of wheat, producers are willing and able to offer less bread for sale at each price than they were before the price of wheat rose. Supply curve S_2 shows that at a price of $3 per loaf, producers will offer 57 loaves. That is 9 units less than the 66 loaves at $3 per loaf indicated by supply curve S_1. Conversely, to offer a given quantity producers must receive a higher price per loaf than they previously were getting: $3.50 per loaf for 66 units (on supply curve S_2) instead of $3 per loaf (on supply curve S_1).

Figure 6(b) shows an increase in supply. A technological improvement or an increase in productivity causes the supply curve to shift to the right, from S_1 to S_2. At each price, a higher quantity is offered for sale. At a price of $3, 66 units were offered, but with the shift of the supply curve, the quantity of units for sale at $3 apiece increases to 84. Conversely, producers can reduce prices for a given quantity — for example, charging $2 per loaf for 66 units.

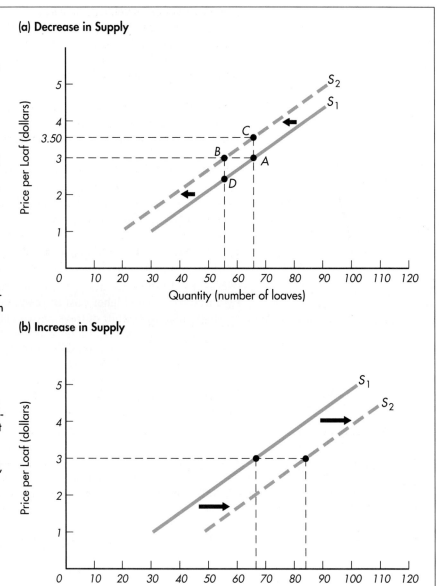

(a) Decrease in Supply

(b) Increase in Supply

Expectations of Producers   Sellers may choose to alter the quantity offered for sale today because of a change in their expectations about future prices or the determinants of supply. If producers change their expectations of the future level of consumer income, they may change the quantities of goods and services they produce today. If producers become pessimistic about future income levels they might expect to sell less in the future and will reduce their production today. This would be shown as a leftward shift of the supply curve.

A change in expectations about the price of a product can also affect a producer's current willingness to supply. For example, during the 1980s, some owners of oil wells in Texas may have kept their wells capped (out of production) because they believed the price of oil was going to rise and they wanted to wait and sell at the higher price. If those owners had been more pessimistic about oil prices, they might have decided to increase the number of wells in operation causing the supply curve to shift to the right.

The Number of Producers When more people decide to produce a good or service, the market supply increases. More is offered for sale at each and every price, resulting in a rightward shift of the supply curve.

The Prices of Related Goods or Services The opportunity cost of producing and selling any good or service is the forgone opportunity to produce any other good or service. If the price of alternative goods changes, then the opportunity cost of producing a particular good changes. This could cause the supply curve to change. For instance, if bakeries can produce muffins or bread with equal ease, an increase in the price of muffins can induce the bakeries to produce muffins rather than bread. The supply curve for bread then shifts to the left.

3.d. Changes in Supply and Changes in the Quantity Supplied

A change in the quantity supplied is a movement along the supply curve. A change in the supply is a shift of the supply curve.

A change in supply occurs when the quantity supplied at each and every price changes or there is a shift in the supply curve—like the shift from S_1 to S_2 in Figure 7(a). A change in one of the determinants of supply brings about a change in supply.

Figure 7
A Change in Supply and a Change in the Quantity Supplied
In Figure 7(a), the quantities that producers are willing and able to offer for sale at every price decrease, caus-ing a leftward shift of the supply curve from S_1 to S_2. In Figure 7(b), the quantities that producers are willing and able to offer for sale increase, due to an increase in the price of the good, causing a movement along the supply curve from point A to point B.

(a) Change in Supply

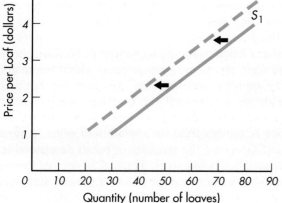

(b) Change in Quantity Supplied

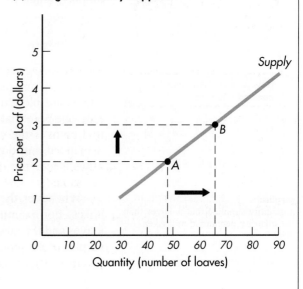

When only the price changes, a greater or smaller quantity is supplied. This is shown as a movement along the supply curve, not as a shift of the supply curve. A change in price is said to cause a change in the quantity supplied. An increase in the quantity supplied is shown in the move from point *A* to point *B* on the supply curve in Figure 7(b).

RECAP

1. According to the law of supply, the quantity supplied of any good or service is directly related to the price of the good or service during a specific period of time, ceteris paribus.

2. Market supply is found by adding together the quantities supplied at each price by every producer in the market.

3. Supply changes if the prices of relevant resources change, if technology or productivity changes, if producers' expectations change, if the number of producers changes, or if the price of related goods and services changes.

4. Changes in supply—that is, changes in the quantity supplied at each price—are reflected in shifts of the supply curve. Changes in the quantity supplied—the result of a change in price—are reflected in movements along the supply curve.

4. EQUILIBRIUM: PUTTING DEMAND AND SUPPLY TOGETHER

equilibrium:
the point at which quantity demanded and quantity supplied are equal at a particular price

The demand curve shows the quantity of a good or service that buyers are willing and able to purchase at each price. The supply curve shows the quantity that producers are willing and able to offer for sale at each price. Only at the point where the two curves intersect is the quantity supplied equal to the quantity demanded. This intersection is the point of **equilibrium**.

4.a. Determination of Equilibrium

▼ How is price determined by demand and supply? ▲

Figure 8 brings together the market demand and market supply for bread. The supply and demand schedules are listed in the table in Figure 8. The curves are plotted in the graph in Figure 8. Notice that they intersect at only one point, labeled *e,* a price of $3 and a quantity of 66. The intersection point is the equilibrium price, the only price at which the quantity demanded and quantity supplied are the same. You can see that at any other price, the quantity demanded and the quantity supplied are not the same.

surplus:
a quantity supplied that is larger than the quantity demanded at a given price

Whenever the price is greater than the equilibrium price, a **surplus** arises. For example, at $4 per loaf the quantity of bread demanded is 48 loaves and the quantity supplied is 84 loaves. Thus, at $4 per loaf there is a surplus of 36—that is, 36 loaves of bread are not sold. Conversely, whenever the price is below the equilibrium price, the quantity demanded is greater than the quantity supplied, and there is a **shortage**. For instance, if the price is $2 per loaf, consumers will want and be able to pay for more loaves of bread than are produced. As shown in the table in Figure 8, the quantity demanded at a price of $2 is 84, but the quantity supplied is only 48. There is a shortage of 36 loaves at the price of $2 per loaf.

Neither a surplus nor a shortage exists for long if the price of the product is free to change. Producers who are stuck with loaves of bread getting stale on their shelves will lower the price and reduce the quantities they are producing to eliminate a surplus. Conversely, producers whose shelves are empty even as consumers demand bread will increase production and raise the price to eliminate a shortage. Surpluses lead to decreases in the price and the quantity supplied and increases in the quantity demanded. Shortages lead to increases in the price and the quantity supplied and decreases in the quantity demanded.

Note that a shortage is not the same thing as scarcity. A shortage exists only when the quantity that people are willing and able to purchase at a particular price is greater than the quantity supplied at that price. Scarcity applies to everything at every price. The only goods that are not scarce are free goods—a greater quantity of them exists than people are willing and able to purchase even when the price is zero.

Figure 8
Equilibrium
Equilibrium is established at the point where the quantity that suppliers are willing and able to offer for sale is the same as the quantity that buyers are willing and able to purchase. Here, equilibrium occurs at the price of $3 per loaf and the quantity of 66 loaves. It is shown as point e at the intersection of the demand and supply curves. At prices above $3, the quantity supplied is greater than the quantity demanded, and the result is a surplus. At prices below $3, the quantity supplied is less than the quantity demanded, and the result is a shortage.

Price per Loaf	Quantity Demanded	Quantity Supplied	Status
$5	30	102	Surplus of 72
4	48	84	Surplus of 36
3	66	66	Equilibrium
2	84	48	Shortage of 36
1	102	30	Shortage of 72

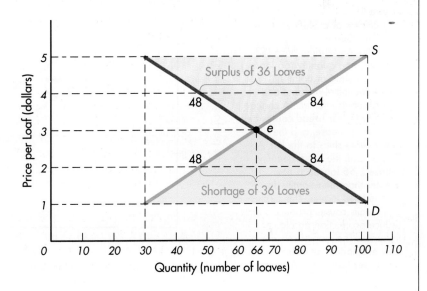

4.b. Changes in the Equilibrium Price: Demand Shifts

What causes price to change?

Equilibrium is the combination of price and quantity at which the quantity demanded and the quantity supplied are the same. Once an equilibrium is achieved, there is no incentive for producers or consumers to move away from it. An equilibrium price changes only when demand or supply changes—that is, when the determinants of demand or the determinants of supply change.

Let's consider a shift in demand and what it means for the equilibrium price. Suppose that experiments on rats show that bread causes cancer. As a result, a large segment of the population decides not to purchase bread. Bakeries find that the demand for bread has decreased, as shown in Figure 9; a leftward shift of the demand curve has occurred, from D_1 to D_2.

Once the demand curve has shifted, the original equilibrium price of $3 per loaf at point e_1 is no longer equilibrium. At a price of $3, the quantity supplied is still 66 loaves, but the quantity demanded declines to 48 (look at curve D_2 at a price of $3). There is, therefore, a surplus of 18 loaves.

With a surplus comes downward pressure on the price. This downward pressure occurs because producers decrease production and reduce the price in an attempt to get rid of the bread sitting on their shelves. Producers continue to reduce the price and the quantity produced until consumers buy all that the sellers offer for sale, or until a new equilibrium is established. That new equilibrium occurs at point e_2 with a price of $2.50 and a quantity of 57.

The decrease in demand is represented by the leftward shift of the demand curve and results in a lower equilibrium price and a lower equilibrium quantity. Conversely, an increase in demand would be represented by a rightward shift of the demand curve and would result in a higher equilibrium price and a higher equilibrium quantity. Thus, whether demand increases or decreases, the change in the equilibrium price and quantity is in the same direction as the change in demand.

Figure 9
The Effects of a Shift of the Demand Curve
The initial equilibrium price ($3 per loaf) and quantity (66 loaves) are established at point e_1, where the initial demand and supply curves intersect. A change in the tastes for bread causes demand to decrease, and the demand curve shifts to the left. At $3 per loaf, the initial quantity supplied, 66 loaves, is now greater than the quantity demanded, 48 loaves. The surplus of 18 units causes producers to reduce production and lower the price. The market reaches a new equilibrium, at point e_2, $2.50 per loaf and 57 loaves.

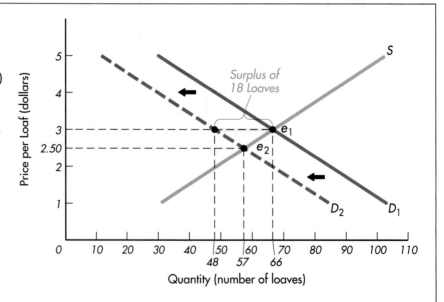

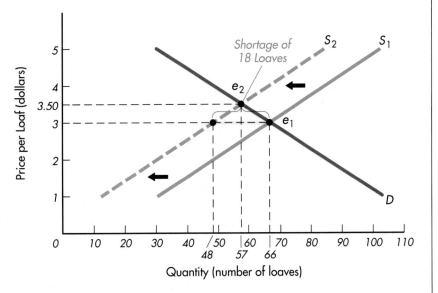

Figure 10
The Effects of a Shift of the Supply Curve
The initial equilibrium price and quantity are $3 and 66 units, at point e_1. When the price of wheat increases, producers are willing and able to offer a smaller number of loaves at each price. The result is a leftward (upward) shift of the supply curve, from S_1 to S_2. At the old price of $3, the quantity demanded is still 66, but the quantity supplied falls to 48. The shortage is 18 loaves. The shortage causes producers to increase production and raise price. The new equilibrium, e_2, the intersection between curves S_2 and D, is $3.50 per loaf and 57 loaves.

4.c. Changes in the Equilibrium Price: Supply Shifts

The equilibrium price and quantity may be altered by a change in supply as well. If the price of relevant resources, technology and productivity, expectations of producers, the number of producers, or the price of related products changes, supply changes. Suppose drought causes the production of wheat to decline by 40 percent, and every bread producer has to pay more for wheat. To cover higher input costs, producers must receive a higher price per loaf. This is represented by the leftward shift of the supply curve in Figure 10.

The leftward shift from curve S_1 to curve S_2 leads to a new equilibrium price and quantity. At the original equilibrium price of $3 at point e_1, 66 loaves of bread are supplied. After the shift in the supply curve, 48 loaves of bread are offered for sale at a price of $3 apiece, and there is a shortage of 18 loaves. The shortage puts upward pressure on price. As the price rises, consumers decrease the quantities that they are willing and able to purchase, and sellers increase the quantities that they are willing and able to supply. Eventually, a new equilibrium price and quantity are established at $3.50 per loaf and 57 loaves, at point e_2.

A decrease in supply causes the price to rise and the quantity to fall. Conversely, an increase in supply leads to a decrease in price and an increase in quantity.

4.d. Equilibrium in Reality

We have examined a hypothetical market for bread in order to represent what goes on in real markets. We have established that the price of a good or service is defined by equilibrium between demand and supply. When not in equilibrium, the price and the quantities demanded or supplied change until equilibrium is established. Looking at last year's sweaters piled up on the sale racks or finding that the VCR rental store never has a copy of the movie you want to rent in stock may make you wonder whether equilibrium is ever established. In fact, it is not uncommon to observe situations where quantities demanded and supplied are not equal. But this observation does not cast doubt on the usefulness of the equilibrium concept. Even if all markets do not clear all the time, we can be assured that market forces are operating so that the market is moving toward an equilibrium.

There are many economic reasons that quantities demanded and supplied are not always equal. Rapid price changes or price changes that occur very often can be costly to producers and consumers. There are also noneconomic reasons that markets are not always in equilibrium. Governments often prevent prices or quantities from changing so that their equilibrium levels cannot be attained. Let's now discuss each of these reasons in turn.

4.d.1. Price Changes Can Be Costly
In some markets it is too costly for producers to change prices rapidly. Consider a restaurant where there are huge crowds on weekends and empty tables during the week. Should the owner of the restaurant raise the price of all foods and beverages on Friday and Saturday evenings and lower the prices on the weekdays? Should separate menus be printed for each day of the week? Even if day-by-day differentials are logical, how should the restaurant owner react when the size of the crowd varies hour by hour? Printing menus or even writing menus on chalkboards and training the staff to report and respond to crowd changes and menu changes can be costly. Perhaps more importantly, steady customers want to have a good idea of what a meal will cost. If they walk into the restaurant and find that prices have doubled because of an unexpected increase in business that day, they may choose to patronize restaurants that have stable prices. Thus, it simply might be too difficult and too expensive for a restaurant to allow prices to change freely in order to equate demands and supplies all the time.

Instead of changing prices instantaneously to reflect all information in the market (the size of crowds, the day of the week), it might be easier and less costly for the restaurant owner to allow the full cost, the opportunity cost of the time spent waiting plus the price, to allocate the tables in the restaurant. In a sense then, the wait imposed on the patrons is an increase in the price they must pay, because it is an increase in their opportunity costs. Although the price of the food and service does not vary as demand conditions change, the full cost—that is, the opportunity cost of going to the restaurant—does. Because the price does not adjust instantaneously to equate customers and places to sit, **disequilibrium** may occur. During the busiest times, lines form because there is a shortage of tables. During slack times, there is a surplus of unoccupied tables. A market experiences disequilibrium when the quantity demanded and the quantity supplied are not equal.

disequilibrium:
a point at which quantity demanded and quantity supplied are not equal at a particular price

4.d.2. Buyers and Sellers May Not Want Price Changes
Business firms often agree to purchase a certain quantity of resources at certain prices for a given period of time. These long-term arrangements with sup-

pliers place a limit on how much prices can change. For example, many labor unions and business firms establish three-year wage agreements that set the hourly wage for each of the next three years. Changes in demand or supply do not alter the wage rates during that three-year period, and neither buyers nor sellers expect changes while the agreement is in effect. In a similar vein, business firms may not want their prices to fluctuate for fear of alienating their customers. A firm with a reputation for quality may not want to cut prices during slow periods for fear of losing its reputation.

Long lines of customers waiting to buy tickets to a concert or an athletic event are not uncommon. One reason is that ticket prices are set, advertising is purchased, and tickets are printed before anyone knows how many people will choose to attend. Most promoters believe that having too high a price for tickets and, consequently, many empty seats is worse than having too low a price and long lines of ticket purchasers.

4.d.3. Government Intervention Affects Prices In some countries, prices are set by government authorities rather than determined in freely functioning markets by demand and supply. Money prices set by government authorities are typically lower than the equilibrium money prices would be because the government believes that artificially low prices will keep citizens happy and maintain popular support for the government. As a result, people stand in long lines to purchase goods and services, and shortages are common.

Even governments that do not control all prices all the time sometimes set the price of particular goods. For instance, in the United States, the federal government defines a minimum wage and a minimum price for many agricultural products; many cities set limits or maximums on apartment rents; and many states define maximum interest rates that may be charged on loans. In addition, at times the U.S. government has decreed that no prices can change or that price changes must be limited to a certain amount. Such policies, called *wage and price controls,* have been used to try to slow down rising prices or to limit the use of price as a rationing device. In each of these cases, the price may not clear the market because of government intervention.

There are many reasons for excess supplies or demands in the real world. Nevertheless, keep in mind that markets, if permitted, do tend to move toward equilibrium.

RECAP

1. Equilibrium occurs when the quantity demanded and the quantity supplied are equal. Equilibrium is the price-quantity combination where the demand and supply curves intersect.
2. A price that is above the equilibrium price creates a surplus, because producers are willing and able to offer more for sale than buyers are willing and able to purchase.
3. A price that is below the equilibrium price leads to a shortage, because buyers are willing and able to purchase more than producers are willing and able to offer for sale.

4. When demand changes, price and quantity change in the same direction. Both rise as demand increases, and both fall as demand decreases.

5. When supply changes, price and quantity change but not in the same direction. When supply increases, price falls and quantity rises. When supply decreases, price rises and quantity falls.

6. When both demand and supply change, the direction of the change in price and quantity depends on the relative sizes of the changes in demand and supply.

7. Markets may not always be in equilibrium because price changes may be costly, buyers and sellers may fix prices for long periods of time, or the government may regulate prices.

SUMMARY

▼▲ **What is a market?**

1. A market is a place or service that allows buyers and sellers to exchange well-defined commodities. § 1.a

▼▲ **What is demand?**

2. Demand is the quantities that buyers are willing and able to buy at alternative prices. § 2

3. The quantity demanded is a specific amount that buyers are willing and able to buy at one price. § 2

4. The law of demand states that as the price of a well-defined commodity rises (falls), the quantity demanded during a given period of time falls (rises), ceteris paribus. § 2.a

5. The determinants of demand are income, tastes, prices of related goods, expectations, and number of buyers. § 2.a

6. Demand changes when one of the determinants of demand changes. A demand change is illustrated as a shift of the demand curve. § 2.f

▼▲ **What is supply?**

7. Supply is the quantities that sellers are able and willing to sell at alternative prices. § 3.a

8. The quantity supplied is a specific amount that sellers are willing and able to offer at one price. § 3.a

9. The law of supply states that as the price of a well-defined commodity rises (falls), the quantity supplied during a given period of time rises (falls), ceteris paribus. § 3.a

10. The determinants of supply are the prices of resources, technology and productivity, expectations of producers, the number of producers, and the prices of related goods or services. § 3.c

11. Supply changes when one of the determinants of supply changes. A supply change is illustrated as a shift of the supply curve. § 3.d

▼▲ **How is price determined by demand and supply?**

12. Together, demand and supply determine the equilibrium price and quantity. § 4.a

13. A price that is above equilibrium creates a surplus, which leads to a lower price. A price that is below equilibrium creates a shortage, which leads to a higher price. § 4.a

▼▲ **What causes price to change?**

14. A change in demand or a change in supply (a shift of either curve) causes the equilibrium price and quantity to change. §§ 4.b and 4.c

15. Markets are not always in equilibrium. There are both economic and noneconomic reasons that some prices do not change in response to changes in demand and supply. § 4.d

KEY TERMS

market § 1.a

black market § 1.a

underground market § 1.a

barter § 1.b

double coincidence of wants § 1.b

transaction costs § 1.b

relative price § 1.c

nominal price § 1.c

purchasing power § 1.c

demand § 2

law of demand § 2.a

determinants of demand § 2.a

substitution effect § 2.b

income effect § 2.b

demand schedule § 2.c

demand curve § 2.d

substitute goods § 2.f

complementary goods § 2.f

supply § 3.a

law of supply § 3.a

supply schedule § 3.a

supply curve § 3.a

determinants of supply § 3.c

productivity § 3.c

equilibrium § 4

surplus § 4.a

shortage § 4.a

disequilibrium § 4.d.1

EXERCISES

Basic Terms and Concepts

1. What is a market?

2. How does a supermarket differ from the labor market?

3. Exchange occurs within markets. Why do buyers and sellers make exchanges?

4. Give some examples of barter.

5. Define demand, quantity demanded, supply, and quantity supplied.

6. Define equilibrium. Describe what occurs when the quantities demanded and the quantities supplied are not equal.

7. What occurs to price when (a) demand increases, (b) supply falls, (c) demand rises and supply falls?

8. List the ceteris paribus conditions for both demand and supply. Explain why a change in one of the conditions changes either the demand or the supply.

9. Explain how price adjusts to changes in demand and supply.

10. Use the following schedules to define the equilibrium price and quantity. Describe the situation at a price of $10. What occurs? Describe the situation at a price of $2. What occurs?

Price	Quantity Demanded	Quantity Supplies
$ 1	500	100
2	400	120
3	350	150
4	320	200
5	300	300
6	275	410
7	260	500
8	230	650
9	200	800
10	150	975

11. Suppose the government imposed a minimum price of $7 in the schedules shown in question 10. What would occur?

Extended Concepts

12. A common feature of skiing is waiting in lift lines. Does the existence of lift lines mean that price is not working to allocate a scarce resource? If so, what should be done?

13. Why are barter systems less common than systems that use currency?

Modern Materials Putting the Ax to Wood in Sports

The crack of a Little League baseball bat today is more likely a dull clang.

Four out of five bats in Little League are now aluminum, says Tim Hughes, director of public relations at Little League national headquarters in Williamsport, Pa.

Indeed, outside the major leagues, aluminum bats have become the norm and those made of wood the exception.

"There's no question about the reason: the economics," says Lee Eilbracht, executive director of the American Baseball Coaches Association in Champaign, Ill. Aluminum bats don't break as often as wooden bats, outlasting them "10 or 20 to 1," he says, which is why they have been generally accepted in the past seven or eight years.

And the trend away from wood has not been limited to baseball.

In the decades since World War II, wood sporting goods have been increasingly harder to find, a fact that has been noted but not studied, says Thomas B. Doyle, director of information and research at the National Sporting Goods Association in Mount Prospect, Ill.

"There aren't a lot of [sporting goods] being made of wood anymore. There is less and less wood."

The exception appears to be at the professional level in sports, where there is still a strong preference for wood. To some extent this may be due to tradition, but some officials say the main reason is that wood is still better than anything else.

Bill Murray, administrative officer at the Baseball Commissioner's office in New York, says studies have shown

that aluminum bats extend the distance a ball is hit, and that if aluminum bats were allowed at the major-league level, it would affect the record standings of players. So American and National League batters are required to stick to wooden bats.

In hockey, "players find they get the greatest performance from sticks made of wood," says Gary Meagher, assistant director of information at the National Hockey League headquarters in Montreal. One manufacturer adds that this is because players prefer the strength and response of wood.

But outside professional sports, wood has been edged out in favor of various new substances, as manufacturers of sporting goods over the years have taken advantage of advances in the aerospace and petrochemical industries.

. . . Fiberglass is widely used for snow skis, fishing rods, and canoes. There are high-strength glass basketball backboards, ping-pong tables made of composite board, polyurethane skateboards, bows and arrows of high-strength metal, backpacks with aluminum frames, and steel tent pegs.

A decrease in experienced woodworkers and the high labor costs of woodworking have been important factors in the shift away from wood.

High-quality wood is "a more costly resource" than the modern alternatives, says Sebastian DiCasoli, director of marketing for the Sporting Goods Manufacturers Association in North Palm Beach, Fla. It has become hard to sell wood at a profit, he says.

Other reasons for wood's lower profile are that sporting goods made from metals and plastics are, as a general rule, easier to shape, cheaper to make, lighter in weight, and better able to withstand the stress of play than their wooden counterparts.

Tennis rackets, for example, come in aluminum these days. Another wood substitute in racket handles is composite board.

Composite board is made by passing fiber, which looks like yarn, through a bath of epoxy. The fiber then "cures," or hardens. (Three commonly used fibers are graphite, boron, and fiberglass.)

To make a tennis handle, a mold is placed around the board. Pressure applied from the inside makes the board into a tube. When this process is completed, the racket handle can then be finished and painted.

Graphite is gaining prominence. Products made from it are prestigious — and expensive. Manufacturers and players say that a graphite tennis racket, golf club, or fishing rod is durable, elastic, lightweight, and stronger than wood.

But graphite sporting goods are also a boon to manufacturers. They are more profitable than wood, Mr. DiCasoli says, and graphite's esoteric quality makes it easy to market in a highly competitive field.

■ Source: Richard L. Wentworth, "Modern Materials Putting the Ax to Wood in Sports," *The Christian Science Monitor,* June 21, 1983. © 1983 The Christian Science Publishing Society.

Commentary

Economics pops up in surprising places. Baseball players are switching from traditional wooden bats to metal bats, and the reason is a matter of supply and demand.

In terms of a supply-and-demand analysis, the supply of wooden bats, labeled S_w in part (a) of the figure below, is lower at any price than is the supply of metal bats, labeled S_m in part (b). We have also drawn the supply curve for wooden bats steeper than the supply curve for metal bats. This indicates that the wooden bats are more expensive to supply than the metal bats. For simplicity, we assume that the demand for wooden bats and metal bats is the same; this last assumption allows us to focus on the issue of the effects of different costs of production on the price of bats and on the number sold.

Our supply-and-demand analysis leads us to predict that more metal bats are sold. The number of wooden bats sold equals Q_{w1} while the number of metal bats sold equals the larger quantity Q_{m1}. Also, the price of wooden bats is higher than that of metal bats. Wooden bats sell for the price P_{w1} and metal bats sell for the lower price P_{m1}. Our predictions are, in fact, true: wooden bats are now mainly used by professional teams while amateurs commonly use metal bats.

What would happen if more people began playing baseball? The demand curve for bats would shift outward from D_1 to D_2 in both part (a) and part (b). The number of metal bats sold would rise from Q_{m1} to Q_{m2} and the number of wooden bats sold would rise from Q_{w1} to Q_{w2}. The increase in the number of metal bats sold, the distance Q_{m1} to Q_{m2}, is greater than the increase in the number of wooden bats sold, the distance Q_{w1} to Q_{w2}. The demand-curve shift would also lead to a smaller increase in the price of metal bats than in the price of wooden bats; the distance P_{m1} to P_{m2} is less than the distance P_{w1} to P_{w2}.

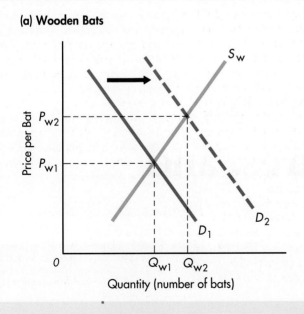

(a) Wooden Bats

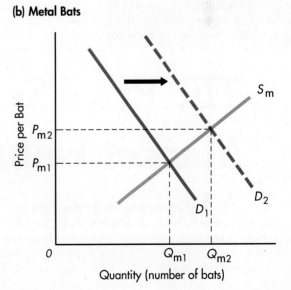

(b) Metal Bats

4

The Price System, Market Failures, and Alternatives

1. In a market system, who decides what goods and services are produced?

2. How are goods and services produced?

3. Who obtains the goods and services that are produced?

4. What is a market failure?

5. How do different economic systems answer the *what*, *how*, and *for whom* questions?

PREVIEW

The years 1970 to 1985 were times of ever-increasing demand for fast-food restaurant services. Wendy's opened an average of 400 new restaurants each year during the period. With the increased demand came increased sales by restaurants, increased numbers of restaurants, and increased prices for franchises. At its peak, the price of an average Wendy's franchise reached nearly $750,000, not including the price of the building.

Since 1985, the industry has changed. In the past, any well-managed franchised fast-food outlet could do very well. Now, a restaurant must be able to lure customers away from competitors. Pizza makers have responded to the challenge by pushing delivery. For years, Pizza Hut had tried to persuade customers to come to its restaurants. But by 1988, Pizza Hut was forced to change its strategy and began to encourage customers to stay at home and phone for a pizza delivery. Executives of Godfather's Pizza point out that consumers today are dollar rich and time poor. Believing that consumers do not want to spend their time in restaurants, pizza makers assert that it is essential to promote, advertise, and market delivery.

Pizza firms are also competing by slashing prices, offering two-for-one deals, and sending out discount coupons by the boxload. They may offer extra drinks or a larger pizza at no extra charge to customers who pick up their own orders. "We have taken the gloves off," stated a marketing executive from the Pizza Hut Division of PepsiCo. "If we have to cut our prices to be competitive, we'll cut our prices. We aren't going to let anybody invade our territory without the fight of their life."[1]

What will be the impact of the changing demand for fast-food restaurant services? Some argue that the quality of food is likely to decline as the chains scramble to cut corners. They predict that the fast-food firms will use cheap, preprocessed cheese and low-quality meats to reduce costs. Others argue that consumers will not stand by and let quality fall.

In the previous chapter you learned that price and quantity are determined by demand and supply. In this chapter, you will see how prices respond to changing market conditions. In addition, you will consider the three fundamental questions of economics, *what, how,* and *for whom:*

1. What is produced?
2. How is it produced?
3. For whom is it produced?

1. WHAT IS PRODUCED

market, or **price system:**
an economic system in which supply and demand determine what goods and services are produced and the prices at which they are sold

centrally planned system:
an economic system in which the government determines what goods and services are produced and the prices at which they are sold

The production possibilities curve represents all possible combinations of goods and services that a society can produce if its resources are used efficiently. Which combination will society choose? In a **market**, or **price**, **system**, in which the production of goods and services and the prices at which they are sold are determined by demand and supply, the answer depends on what goods and services individuals demand. In a **centrally planned system**, in which production and price are determined by the government, the answer depends on what goods and services the government demands. In the first four sections of this chapter, we examine the market system; then we look briefly at centrally planned systems.

1.a. Consumer Sovereignty

After World War II, incomes rose and people began to enjoy more leisure time. Instead of eating three square meals a day at home, families began to go to restaurants once in a while. In the 1950s and 1960s, consumers wanted more and more restaurants and fast-food outlets. As a result, McDonald's, Wendy's, Big Boy, White Castle, Pizza Hut, Godfather's Pizza, and other fast-food outlets flourished. The trend toward eating away from home reached fever pitch in the late 1970s, when the average number of meals per person eaten out (excluding brown-bag lunches and other meals prepared at home but eaten elsewhere) exceeded one per day.

---

[1]David Novak, quoted in Joanne Lipman, "Pizza Makers Slug It Out for Share of Growing Eat-at-Home Market," *The Wall Street Journal*, January 12, 1988, p. B1.

In the 1980s, people chose to spend more time at home with their families; the demand for restaurants decreased and was replaced by a demand for food delivered to the home.

By emphasizing delivery, Little Caesar's Pizza and a few other fast-food outlets became very successful. However, the star of this story is not Little Caesar's, Pizza Hut, or Wendy's. It is the consumer. In a market system, if consumers are willing and able to pay for more restaurant meals, more restaurants appear. If consumers are willing and able to pay for food delivered to their homes, food is delivered to their homes.

Why does the consumer wield such power? The name of the game for business is profit, and the only way business can make a profit is by satisfying consumer wants. The consumer, not the politician or the business firm, ultimately determines what is to be produced. A firm that produces something that no consumers want will not remain in business very long. **Consumer sovereignty**—the authority of consumers to determine what is produced through their purchases of goods and services—dictates what goods and services will be produced.

▼ In a market system, who decides what goods and services are produced? ▲

consumer sovereignty:
the supreme authority of consumers to determine, by means of their purchases, what is produced

1.b. Profit and the Allocation of Resources

When a good or service seems to have the potential to generate a profit, some enterprising person with entrepreneurial ability will be eager to put together the resources needed to produce that good or service. Recall from Chapter 1 that economists classify the resources used to produce goods and services into four general groups: land, labor, capital, and entrepreneurial ability. The returns to the owners of these resources are *rent* for the use of land, *wages* and *salaries* for the use of labor, *interest* for the use of capital, and *profits* for the use of entrepreneurial ability. An individual with entrepreneurial ability aims to earn a profit by renting land, hiring labor, and using capital to produce a good or service that can be sold for more than the sum of rent, wages, and interest. If the potential profit turns into a loss, the entrepreneur stops buying resources and turns to some other occupation or project. The resources used in the losing operation are then available for use in an activity where they are more highly valued.

To illustrate how the allocation of resources works, let's look at the market for fast foods. Figure 1 shows a change in demand for meals eaten in restaurants. The initial demand curve, D_1, and supply curve, S, are shown in Figure 1(a). With these demand and supply curves, the equilibrium price (P_1) is \$8, and the equilibrium quantity (Q_1) is 100 units (meals). At this price-quantity combination, the number of meals demanded equals the number of meals sold, equilibrium is reached, and the market clears.

As already noted, consumer tastes changed during the 1980s. Consumers preferred to have food delivered to their homes instead of eating out. This change in tastes caused the demand for fast-food restaurants to decline and is represented by a leftward shift of the demand curve, from D_1 to D_2, in Figure 1(b). The demand curve shifted to the left because fewer in-restaurant meals were demanded at each price. Consumer tastes, not the price of in-restaurant meals, changed first. (A price change would have led to a change in the quantity demanded and would be represented by a move *along* demand curve D_1.) The change in tastes caused a change in demand and a leftward shift of the demand curve. The shift from D_1 to D_2

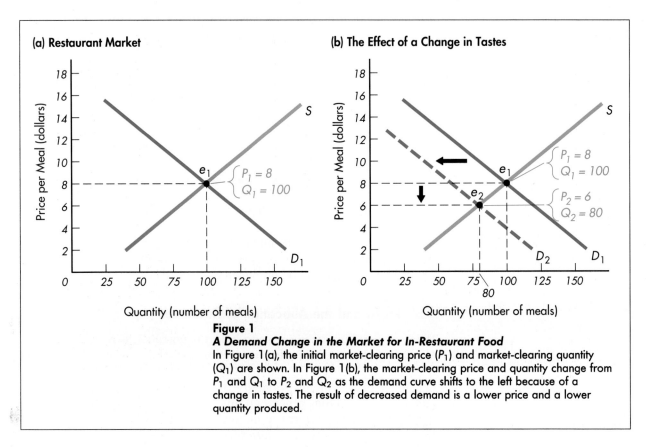

(a) Restaurant Market

(b) The Effect of a Change in Tastes

Figure 1
A Demand Change in the Market for In-Restaurant Food
In Figure 1(a), the initial market-clearing price (P_1) and market-clearing quantity
(Q_1) are shown. In Figure 1(b), the market-clearing price and quantity change from
P_1 and Q_1 to P_2 and Q_2 as the demand curve shifts to the left because of a
change in tastes. The result of decreased demand is a lower price and a lower
quantity produced.

created a new equilibrium point. The equilibrium price (P_2) decreased to
$6, and the equilibrium quantity (Q_2) decreased to 80 units (meals).

While the market for in-restaurant food was changing, so was the market for delivered food. People substituted meals delivered to their homes
for meals eaten in restaurants. Figure 2(a) shows the original demand for
food delivered to the home. Figure 2(b) shows a rightward shift of the
demand curve, from D_1 to D_2, representing increased demand for home
delivery. This demand change resulted in a higher market-clearing price
for food delivered to the home, from $10 to $12.

The changing profit potential of the two markets induced existing
firms to switch from in-restaurant service to home delivery and for new
firms to offer delivery from the start. Domino's Pizza, which is a delivery-
only firm, grew from a one-store operation to become the second largest
pizza chain in the United States, with sales exceeding $2 billion per year.
Little Caesar's, another take-out chain, grew from $63.6 million in sales in
1980 to nearly $1 billion in 1987. Pizza Hut, which at first did not offer
home delivery, had to play catch-up; but by 1990, about half of Pizza Hut's
more than 5,000 restaurants were delivering pizza.[2]

As the market-clearing price of in-restaurant fast food fell (from $8 to
$6 in Figure 1[b]), the quantity of in-restaurant meals sold also declined
(from 100 to 80). The reason was that the decreased demand, lower price,

---

[2]See note 1.

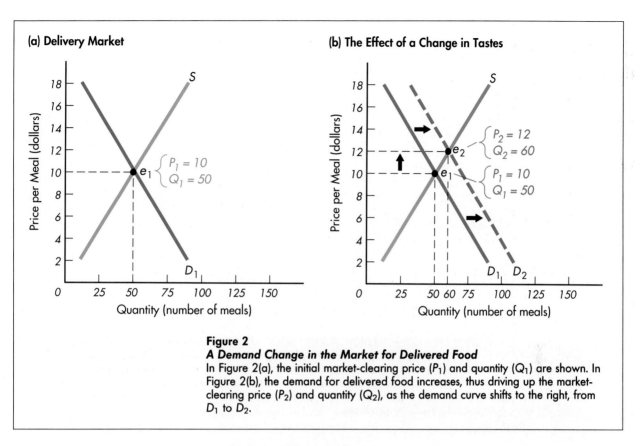

(a) Delivery Market

(b) The Effect of a Change in Tastes

Figure 2
A Demand Change in the Market for Delivered Food
In Figure 2(a), the initial market-clearing price (P_1) and quantity (Q_1) are shown. In Figure 2(b), the demand for delivered food increases, thus driving up the market-clearing price (P_2) and quantity (Q_2), as the demand curve shifts to the right, from D_1 to D_2.

and resulting lower profit induced some firms to decrease production. In the delivery business, the opposite occurred. As the market-clearing price rose (from $10 to $12 in Figure 2[b]), the number of meals delivered also rose (from 50 to 60). The increased demand, higher price, and resulting higher profit induced firms to increase production.

Why did the production of delivered foods increase while the production of meals at restaurants decrease? Not because of government decree. Not because of the desires of the business sector, especially the owners of restaurants. The consumer—consumer sovereignty—made all this happen. Businesses that failed to respond to consumer desires and failed to provide the desired good at the lowest price failed to survive.

1.c. The Flow of Resources

After demand shifted to home-delivered food, the resources that had been used to produce pizzas consumed in the restaurants were available for use elsewhere. A few former waiters, waitresses, and cooks were able to get jobs in the delivery firms. Some of the equipment used in eat-in restaurants—ovens, pots and pans—was purchased by the delivery firms; and some of the ingredients that previously would have gone to the eat-in restaurants was bought by the delivery firms. A few former employees of the eat-in restaurants became employed at department stores, at local pubs, and at hotels. Some of the equipment was sold as scrap; other equipment was sold to other restaurants. In other words, the resources moved

Adam Smith

Economists date the beginning of their discipline from the publication of *The Wealth of Nations* in 1776. In this major treatise, Adam Smith emphasizes the role of self-interest in the functioning of markets, specialization, and division of labor.

According to Smith, the fundamental explanation of human behavior is found in the rational pursuit of self-interest. In a celebrated and often-quoted passage Smith says:

> But man has almost constant occasion for the help of his brethren, and it is in vain for him to expect it from their benevolence only. He will be more likely to prevail if he can interest their self-love in his favour, and show them that it is for their own advantage to do for him what he requires of them . . . It is not from the benevolence of the butcher, the brewer, or the baker, that we can expect our dinner, but from their regard to their own interest.

The self-interest drive is always present in *The Wealth of Nations*. Smith uses it to explain how men choose occupations, how farmers till their lands, and how leaders of the American Revolution were led by it to rebellion. Smith broadened the definition of self-interest, believing that a person is interested "in the fortune of others and renders their happiness necessary to him, though he derives nothing from it, except the pleasure of seeing it." On the basis of self-interest Smith constructed a theory of how markets work: how goods, once produced, are sold to the highest bidders, and how the quantities of the goods that are produced are governed by their costs and selling prices.

Adam Smith was born in 1723 and reared in Kirkaldy, Scotland, near Edinburgh. He went to the University of Glasgow when he was 14 and three years later began studies at Oxford, where he stayed for six years. In 1751, Smith became professor of logic and then moral philosophy at Glasgow. From 1764 to 1766, he tutored the future duke of Buccleuch in France, and then he was given a pension for the remainder of his life. Between 1766 and 1776, Smith completed *The Wealth of Nations*. He became commissioner of customs for Scotland and spent his remaining years in Edinburgh. He died in 1790.

■ Source: *An Inquiry into the Nature and Causes of the Wealth of Nations*, edited and with an Introduction, Notes, Marginal Summary, and Index, by Edwin Cannan, With a Preface by George J. Stigler. (Chicago: The University of Chicago Press, 1976)

from one activity where their value was relatively low to another activity where they were more highly valued. No one commanded the resources to move. They moved because they could earn more in some other activity. It is as if an invisible hand reached out and guided the resources to their most-valued use. That invisible hand is the self-interest that drives firms to provide what consumers want to buy and leads consumers to use their limited incomes to buy the goods and services that bring them the greatest satisfaction.

RECAP

1. Consumers dictate what is to be produced by means of their purchases of goods and services.

2. To make a profit, business firms must react to consumer wants.

3. Resources tend to flow from lower-valued uses to higher-valued uses as firms seek to make a profit.

2. HOW GOODS AND SERVICES ARE PRODUCED

How are goods and services produced?

technical efficiency:
the combination of inputs that results in the lowest cost

economic efficiency:
the employment of resources in their highest-valued use to maximize the value of output

Consumers use their limited incomes to buy the goods and services that give them the greatest satisfaction. Firms produce the goods and services that generate the highest profits. Owners of resources sell the services of their resources to the highest bidders. This is the market system in operation. Whenever consumer sovereignty is coupled with competitive, profit-seeking producers in a market system, resources are used as efficiently as possible.

Two aspects of efficiency concern economists: technical efficiency and economic efficiency. **Technical efficiency** is the combination of inputs that results in the lowest cost. Lack of technical efficiency is reflected in statements such as "This firm is inefficient" and "Employees are not being used efficiently." A manager of a pizza restaurant who schedules 20 delivery people for a shift when only 10 cars are available is not using people efficiently. Assigning two delivery people per car is technically inefficient. The same output could be produced by only 10 delivery people. Similarly, having 20 cars but only 10 delivery people would be technically inefficient. Technical efficiency occurs when appropriate combinations of inputs are used. Technical efficiency for a society occurs when the society is on its production possibilities curve.

Economic efficiency refers to the employment of resources in their most highly valued use. Normally, the manager of a pizza restaurant would not be scheduled to make deliveries because the value of management skills is higher than the value of the skills needed to deliver pizzas.

The market system ensures that both technical and economic efficiency occur. The higher profits go, the more income is earned by people with entrepreneurial ability. In order to earn profits, entrepreneurs have to provide, at the lowest possible cost, the goods and services that consumers want and are able to buy. This means that the least-cost combination of resources is used by each firm. It also means that resources are employed in their most highly valued uses and that the goods and services that consumers want and are able to buy are produced.

RECAP

1. The search for profit induces firms to use resources in their most efficient manner.
2. As a result of the search for profit, resources flow to their most highly valued use.
3. The market system ensures that both technical and economic efficiency result.
4. *Technical efficiency* refers to the manner in which inputs are combined. If a good can be produced with fewer resources or at a lower cost without altering its quality, then production is not technically efficient.
5. *Economic efficiency* refers to the employment of resources in their highest-valued uses.

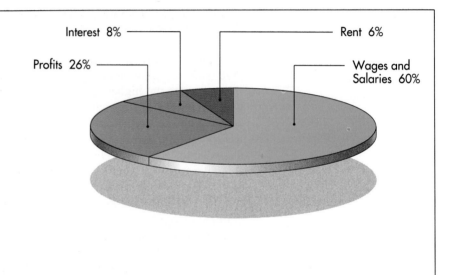

Figure 3
The Sources of Total National Income
As shown in the pie chart, wages and salaries make up the largest percentage of national income, a total of 60 percent. Profits, the return earned by entrepreneurs for their services, are the next largest piece of the pie, accounting for 26 percent of national income. Source: *Economic Report of the President, 1990* (Washington, D.C.: U.S. Government Printing Office, 1990).

3. THE DISTRIBUTION OF GOODS AND SERVICES: FOR WHOM

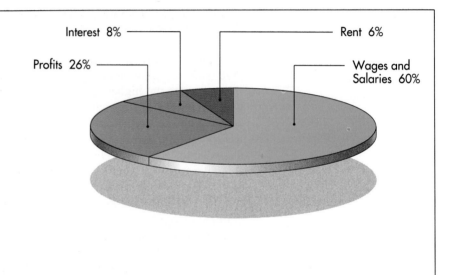

Who obtains the goods and services that are produced?

The consumer reigns supreme in a market, or price, system. Consumer demands dictate *what* is produced, and the search for profit defines *how* goods and services are produced. Prices and income determine *who* gets the goods and services that are produced. Consumers willing and able to pay the equilibrium price for a large pepperoni pizza delivered to their home will get the pizza. Consumers not willing to pay that price will not get the pizza. The price system serves as a rationing device.

3.a. The Determination of Money Income

A consumer's ability to purchase goods and services depends on the size of his or her money income. Where does the income come from? Income is obtained by selling the services of resources. When you sell your labor services, your money income reflects your wage rate or salary level. When you sell the services of the capital you own, you receive interest; and when you sell the services of the land you own, you receive rent. A person with entrepreneurial ability earns profit as a payment for services. As shown in the pie chart in Figure 3, most income, about 60 percent of total national income in the United States, comes from wages and salaries. About 8 percent is derived from selling the services of capital, and about 6 percent comes from rent. The rest, profit, is the return for entrepreneurial ability.

3.b. The Distribution of Income

In a market system, incomes are distributed according to the ownership of resources. Those who own the most highly valued resources have the highest incomes. Thus, in a market system, incomes are unequally distributed—everyone does not receive the same income. The reason is that all abilities are not the same, and the most highly valued abilities or resources receive the highest returns.

Figure 4 indicates how income is distributed in several countries. If the distribution was equal so that each person received the same income, the percentage of income going to each twentieth percentile would be the same in each country. On average, in developed countries, the richest 20 percent of households receive about 40 percent of household income, and the poorest 20 percent receive 5 to 6 percent of household income. Notice that the most unequal distribution of income occurs in less developed countries such as Mexico and Brazil, where the richest 20 percent of the population receives more than 55 percent of total household income while the poorest 20 percent receives less than 3 percent. One reason that income distributions differ among developed and less developed nations is that the developed nations have typically relied more on free markets and less on government-directed answers to the questions of what to produce, how to produce, and for whom to produce. With government-directed answers to these questions special interest groups can gain special favors and higher incomes, as we discuss in detail in later chapters.

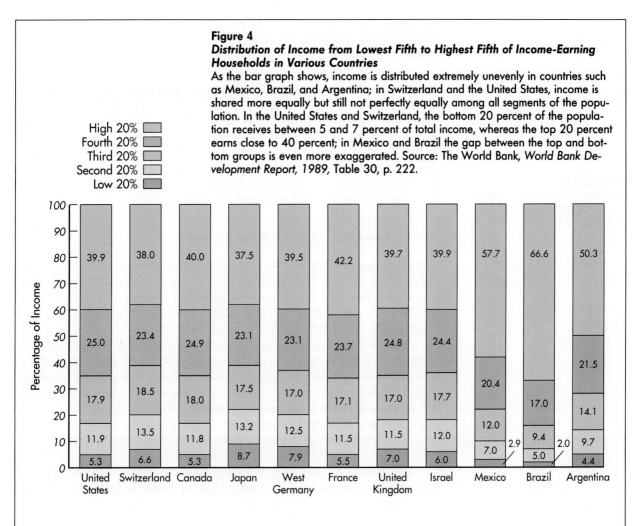

Figure 4
Distribution of Income from Lowest Fifth to Highest Fifth of Income-Earning Households in Various Countries
As the bar graph shows, income is distributed extremely unevenly in countries such as Mexico, Brazil, and Argentina; in Switzerland and the United States, income is shared more equally but still not perfectly equally among all segments of the population. In the United States and Switzerland, the bottom 20 percent of the population receives between 5 and 7 percent of total income, whereas the top 20 percent earns close to 40 percent; in Mexico and Brazil the gap between the top and bottom groups is even more exaggerated. Source: The World Bank, *World Bank Development Report, 1989*, Table 30, p. 222.

RECAP

1. In a market system, those who can afford to buy goods and services receive goods and services.

2. Income and price determine for whom to produce.

3. Money income is created when individuals sell the services of the resources they own. Wages and salaries, rent, interest, and profits are the payments for resource services.

4. A result of a market system is unequal distribution of income.

4. EVALUATING THE PRICE SYSTEM

The market system enables goods and services to be allocated to the uses in which they have the highest value. The market system functions as if an invisible hand is guiding resources to their most highly valued uses and ensuring that consumers get the goods and services they want and are able to pay for. Just because the system functions without someone manipulating aspects of it does not mean that everyone agrees with the outcome or that the system is free of problems.

▼ **What is a market failure?** ▲

As just noted, not everyone has the same income. Often the rich get richer, and the poor get poorer. Many people do not like some of the results of the market system and may try to use the political system to effect a change. For instance, the price of something may be fixed above or below its equilibrium level, thereby creating surpluses or shortages. Or people may conspire or act in some way to alter the outcome of the market system. Sometimes the system simply fails to work. These situations are known collectively as **market failure**, the failure of the market system to achieve economic and technical efficiency.

market failure:
the failure of the market system to achieve economic and technical efficiency

4.a. Information and the Price System

A market is a place or service that allows buyers and sellers to exchange information on what they know about a product, what buyers are willing and able to pay for a product, and what sellers want to receive in order to produce and sell a product. The market price is the summation of this information. The **market price** is the equilibrium price.

market price:
the equilibrium price

A market price is a signal indicating when more or less of a good is desired. When the market price rises, buyers know that the quantity demanded at the prior equilibrium price exceeded the quantity supplied. When the market price falls, buyers know that the quantity demanded at the prior equilibrium price was less than the quantity supplied. The market price also provides other information. Consumers may believe that a rising price is an indication of higher product quality. Conversely, a price that is very low may be taken as a sign of low quality.

The market price is only as good a summary statistic as the information that exists in the market. It takes time for people to gather information about a product. It takes time to go to a market and purchase an item. It takes time for producers to learn what people want and bring together the resources necessary to produce that product. Time, however, is not free. Information gathering is costly; and because it is costly, people are not likely to have complete and perfect information, nor will everyone have the same information. This means that not all markets will adjust instantaneously or even at the same speed to a change in demand or supply. As a result, people may purchase products that they are uninformed about, and producers may produce too much or too little. Some people may be looking for jobs at the same time that some firms are looking for workers. Some people may pay higher prices for a product than others pay. Some people may be swindled by a sharp operator, and some firms may fail to collect debts owed them.

Situations can arise where buyers and sellers have different amounts or types of information about the product. For instance, each worker knows how productive he or she is. A firm, however, may not be able to determine each person's productivity and may have to rely on a statistic that is correct, on average, in predicting productivity. For instance, a college degree is a good indicator of productivity. A person with a college degree is, on average, a more productive worker than a person without a college degree. This relationship does not hold for every person and every job, but it does hold on average. Thus, an employer may choose to hire or to promote or to pay more to a person with a college degree. The result of this action is that workers without college degrees earn less than workers with college degrees even if they are equally productive.

Another illustration of the problem that results when buyers and sellers have different information is given by the used-car market. When you drive a new car off the lot, its value decreases significantly. You can't take that new car directly home from the dealership and sell it for anything close to the amount you paid for it. Why? The reason is lack of information about used cars. Because people are more likely to sell a car that is a lemon than a car that is reliable, buyers of used cars believe there is a good chance that they will get a lemon. As a result, they are willing to pay only a low price for a used car so that they have money left to cover any repairs that are necessary. Pity those people who want to sell a good used car. There is no way for them to prove that their car is not a lemon. They receive the low used-car price even if their car is in excellent shape.

market imperfection:
a lack of efficiency that results from imperfect information in the marketplace

When information is not perfect and complete, **market imperfections**, such as those just discussed, may result. A least-cost combination of resources may not be used, or a resource may not be used where it has the highest value. One solution to the problem is for the government to pass rules and regulations concerning the amount of information that must be provided. The government can require, for example, that information be provided on labels and that used cars be returnable within 30 days. The government can also declare that certain actions by firms or consumers are illegal. Such laws and rules may reduce market imperfections.

long run:
a period of time in which something once believed to be fixed becomes variable

Another solution is to allow the imperfections to remain until the market participants are able to get sufficient information. In the long run, some market imperfections will disappear. The **long run** is a period of time in which something once believed to be fixed becomes variable. Information

Gridlock on the Highways

The health of an economy depends on the quality of its transportation systems. Concern is growing that the transportation system of the United States is failing because of congestion and age. In just ten years, congestion on urban highways nationwide has increased by over 50 percent. The labor loss attributable to congestion delays equals 17 percent of the average workday.

The solution does not seem to be increases in highway capacity. Indeed, highway congestion grew just as rapidly in the United States between 1960 and 1970 as it did between 1970 and 1980, even though spending on highways in the earlier decade was almost double the spending that occurred in the later decade. Moreover, highway construction is very expensive; one new lane-mile for the morning rush-hour commute can cost $40,000 per commuter in an urban area.

Most consumers accept the principle that the prices they pay for goods and services should reflect the full cost of providing those goods and services. If they buy goods in a shop, for example, they understand that the price includes compensation for the salesperson's time and the cost of the premises, in addition to the cost of the goods purchased. Consumers also accept the principle that the price of goods and services varies with the strength of demand relative to the available supply. Virtually everywhere in the economy, prices are highest during periods of peak demand. Neither of these principles, however, has been adopted by transportation policymakers. Indeed, highways usually are not priced directly at all and are financed instead with gasoline or other taxes. The exceptions are toll bridges and toll highways.

Transportation facilities are beleaguered by an externalities problem. The use of a highway by one additional vehicle adversely affects the amount of time that other users must spend to make their trips. Because no driver has to compensate other travelers for their lost time, each trip-making decision ignores the externalities imposed on others. During rush hours, the externalities can be extremely large.

Congestion delays are a cost imposed on others and should be reflected in the price of the facility. Only a few states in the United States have begun to implement this full-cost pricing idea with the use of toll roads that will be built and operated by private investors, but several other countries have had such a pricing scheme in practice for some time. The United Kingdom, Singapore, and Hong Kong have implemented full-cost pricing of some roads by setting tolls at appropriate levels or by issuing license tags that indicate when a car is allowed on the road.

■ Source: "Unlocking Gridlock," Federal Reserve Bank of San Francisco, Weekly Letter, December 9, 1988; "Be Prepared to Pay, *The Economist*, May 20, 1989, p. 63. "States Give Private Toll Roads Green Light," by Wendy White, *Investor's Daily*, January 17, 1990, pp. 1, 32.

that people previously did not have becomes available in the long run. Quantities of resources that previously were not available become available in the long run. A short-term shortage disappears in the long run. There are cases where market failures and market imperfections, may be ongoing, however, which means that the government may have to resolve the problems.

4.b. Externalities

The market system works efficiently only if the market price reflects the full costs of producing and consuming a particular good or service. In some cases, the full costs of a good or service are not borne by the producer and consumers. For instance, when you use air conditioners, you contaminate the ozone layer with freon but you don't pay the costs of that contamination. When you drive, you don't pay for the pollution created by your car. When you throw candy wrappers out of your car window, you don't pay for the garbage along the road. When firms dump wastes or create radioactive by-products, they don't pay the costs. When homeowners allow their properties to become run-down, they reduce the value of neighboring properties but they don't pay for the loss of value. All these side effects, which are not covered by the market price, are called **externalities**.

externalities:
costs or benefits of a transaction that are borne by someone not directly involved in the transaction

Externalities are the costs or benefits of a market activity borne by someone who is not a party to the market transaction. When you drive, you pay only for gasoline and car maintenance. You don't pay for the noise and pollutants that your car emits. You don't pay for the added congestion and delays that you impose on other drivers. The *market* price of driving understates the *full* cost of driving to society; as a result, people drive more frequently than they would if they had to pay the full cost. (See Economically Speaking: "Gridlock on the Highways".)

The government often intervenes in the market to resolve an externality problem. The government establishes agencies, such as the Environmental Protection Agency, to set and enforce air quality standards, and it also imposes taxes to obtain funds to pay for external costs.

Externalities are not always negative. Education enriches not only those going to school but also the entire society. Literacy enables a democracy to function effectively, and higher education may stimulate scientific discoveries that improve the welfare of society. The government intervenes to provide education to society at below-market prices because the positive externality of education benefits everyone.

4.c. Public Goods

public goods:
goods whose consumption cannot be limited only to the person who purchased the good

The market system works efficiently only if the benefits derived from consuming a particular good or service are available only to the consumer who buys the good or service. You buy a pizza, and only you receive the benefits of eating that pizza. What would happen if you weren't allowed to enjoy that pizza all by yourself? Suppose your neighbors have the right to come to your home when you have a pizza delivered and share your pizza. How often would you buy a pizza? There is no way to exclude others from enjoying the benefits of some of the goods you purchase. These types of goods are called **public goods**, and they create a problem for the market system.

Radio broadcasts are public goods. Everyone who tunes in a station enjoys the benefits. National defense is a public good. You could buy a missile to protect your house, but your neighbors, as well as you, would benefit from the protection it provided. A pizza, however, is not a public good. If you pay for it, only you get to enjoy the benefits. Thus you have an incentive to purchase pizza. You don't have that incentive to purchase public goods. If you and I both benefit from the public good, who will buy it? I'd prefer that you buy it so that I receive its benefits at no cost. Conversely, you'd prefer that I buy it. The result may be that no one will buy it.

Fire protection provides a good example of the problem that occurs with public goods. Suppose that as a homeowner you have the choice of subscribing to fire protection services from a private firm or having no fire protection. If you subscribe and your house catches fire, the fire engines will arrive as soon as possible and your house may be saved. If you do not subscribe, your house will burn. Do you choose to subscribe? You might say to yourself that as long as your neighbors subscribe, you need not do so. The fact that your neighbors subscribe means that fires in their houses won't cause a fire in yours, and you do not expect a fire to begin in your house. If many people made decisions in this way, fire protection services would not be available because not enough people would subscribe to make the services profitable.

The problem with a public good is the communal nature of the good. No one has a **private property right** to a public good. If you buy a car, you must pay the seller an acceptable price. Once this price is paid, the car is all yours and no one else can use it without your permission. The car is your private property, and you make the decisions about its use. In other words, you have the private property right to the car. Public goods are available to all because no one individual owns them or has property rights to them.

When goods are public, people have an incentive to try to obtain a **free ride**—the enjoyment of the benefits of a good without paying for the good. Your neighbors would free-ride on your purchases of pizza if you didn't have the private property rights to the pizza. People who enjoy public radio and public television stations without donating money to them are getting free rides from those people who do donate to them. People who benefit from the provision of a good whether they pay for it or not have an incentive not to pay for it. Therefore it is likely that eventually the good will not be provided or, if the good is considered to be important for society, the government must intervene to ensure that the good is provided.

Typically, in the absence of private property rights to a good, the government claims ownership and provides the good. For instance, local governments act as owners of police departments and specify how police services are used. Some goods and services, however, are not so easily managed. Fish in the ocean belong to no one, and no government can claim ownership because no government owns the sea. As a result, fishing ships have an incentive to harvest all they can. If one crew decides to harvest only 80 percent of the fish it sees in order to leave enough for the future, there is no guarantee that the fish will be available in the future. The crew of a ship is not able to claim or harvest at a later time the fish it chooses not to catch today. This creates survival problems for many species of fish. An additional problem is that no government can claim ownership of the oceans and thereby distribute fishing rights.

If one country owned all the oceans and could effectively control their use, a price for fish could be established that would reflect their value. The price would be high enough to provide an incentive to maintain stocks of fish for future years.

The problem with the oceans is one that is shared by commonly owned goods. Common ownership results in overutilization. When common ownership exists, there is an incentive for each individual to use too much of the good or to free-ride.

The market failure problems, their effects, and possible solutions are summarized in Table 1.

private property right:
the limitation of ownership to an individual

free ride:
the enjoyment of the benefits of a good by a producer or consumer without having to pay for it

Table 1 Summary of Market Failures

Failure	Effects	Possible Solutions
Imperfect information	Inefficiencies	Government provides information or requires information to be provided
Negative externality	Too much of the good is produced or consumed	Government ensures that the cost of the externality is part of the cost and price of the good
Positive externality	Too little of the good is produced or consumed	Government provides subsidies
Public goods	Too little of the good is produced or consumed	Government assigns private property rights or produces the good

RECAP

1. In some cases, the price system is not allowed to function. Laws restricting the movement of prices are quite common. When the price system is not allowed to work, the result is shortages, surpluses, and nonprice allocation schemes.

2. The price system does not affect externalities. The cost or benefit is borne by a third party, one not directly involved in the market transaction.

3. The price system does not allocate public goods or goods in which private ownership rights are not well defined. As a result, individuals are able to enjoy the good without paying a market price for it.

5. ALTERNATIVE ECONOMIC SYSTEMS

▼ How do different economic systems answer the *what, how,* and *for whom* questions?

Different economic systems answer the *what, how,* and *for whom* questions differently. The main economic systems today are capitalism, socialism, communism, mixed economies, and traditional economies.

5.a. Capitalism

capitalism:
an economic system in which most economic decisions are made by private owners and most property is privately owned

laissez faire:
total reliance on the market system, with no government intervention

Capitalism is an economic system characterized by private ownership of most resources, goods, and services. Capitalism typically relies on the market system to allocate resources, goods, and services to their most highly valued use. Total reliance on the market system, with no government intervention, is known as **laissez faire**, or "leave alone," in French.

In a capitalist economy, what to produce is determined by consumers, how to produce is determined by profit-seeking entrepreneurs who maximize profit by producing in the most efficient manner, and for whom to produce is determined by income and prices. In a capitalist system, if you can afford it, you can buy it.

5.b. Socialism

Socialism is an economic system characterized by government ownership of resources other than labor and centralized economic decision making. Under socialist systems, government authorities answer the questions *what, how,* and *for whom.* In a capitalist system, workers are generally paid according to how productive they are, and the distribution of income is unequal because people differ in their abilities. In a socialist system, government planners set wages, and although wages are not equal for all workers, incomes tend to be more evenly distributed than in capitalist countries.

In centrally planned economies, government planners decide what goods will be produced and set the prices at which they are sold. Because central planners cannot always know the correct equilibrium price, money prices do not always ration the limited quantities of goods. Nonprice rationing of goods and services—by long waiting lines, for example—is frequently observed.

5.c. Communism

Communism is an economic system in which all resources (including labor) are commonly owned and economic decision making is centrally planned. According to communist theory, people contribute what they are able to the economy but receive what they need. In theory, this means that goods are produced for use rather than to earn profits and that everyone's needs are met. Communist countries have central planning boards that set prices and output quotas and assign workers to alternative tasks. Reliance on the price system occurs only in the black market.

5.d. Mixed Economies

Sections 5.a, 5.b, and 5.c describe pure capitalist, pure socialist, and pure communist economies. The real world, however, is characterized by **mixed economies**—economies that have characteristics of more than one system. There may be both private and public ownership of property. There may also be common ownership of resources that are provided by government.

Faced with declining productivity and steadily worsening economic conditions, Mikhail Gorbachev began to restructure the Soviet system in the late 1980s, allowing in a few instances private ownership of property and free markets. The changes spread beyond the Soviet Union and reverberated throughout Eastern Europe. Restrictions on travel from East to West were relaxed, and central planning became less important. Hungary, Poland, Czechoslovakia, East Germany, Romania, and Yugoslavia embarked on a transformation from communist to capitalist economies characterized by private property rights, free markets, and the free flow of resources. Those nations of Eastern Europe took steps to join the ranks of Western developed nations in becoming mixed economies.

Real-world economies lie on a continuum ranging from pure capitalism to pure socialism. Figure 5 places a few representative countries in their likely spots along the continuum. The United States and Canada are

Figure 5
The Continuum of Economic Systems
The closer a country is to the capitalist end of the continuum, the greater is its reliance on the market system. Countries closer to the socialist end of the continuum rely less on the market system. Source: Raymond D. Gastil, *Freedom in the World* (New York: Greenwood Press, 1986).

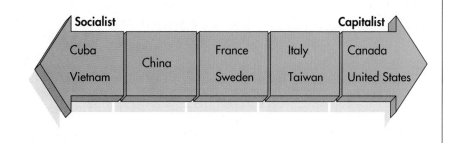

representative of nations that are closest to the pure capitalist form. Cuba and Vietnam are representative of nations that are closest to the pure socialist form. China is closer to socialism than it is to capitalism, and Italy is closer to capitalism than to socialism. The Eastern European and Soviet economies are currently in transition from socialist to capitalist systems and thus do not appear on the continuum.

There is little doubt that the collapse of the Berlin Wall in 1989 marked the beginning of dramatic changes for East Germany and the rest of Europe, but there is great uncertainty about the exact form these changes will take. In Hungary, the move away from socialism toward capitalism began nearly two years before the collapse of the Berlin Wall. On January 1, 1988, Hungarians became the only Soviet-bloc citizens to pay an income tax. That date, according to Hungary's economists, marks the birth of the first true hybrid of socialism and capitalism. Before 1988, Hungary had taxed successful companies in order to provide subsidies for inefficient companies. In a change of policy, the government decided to create banks that would compete with each other and determine which struggling companies deserved loans. Firms judged not worthy are allowed to fail. For the first time, a socialist system is permitting bankruptcy. In addition, profitable companies are allowed to keep a larger share of their profits. Instead of supporting weak companies and artificial prices, the government supports laid-off workers while they look for jobs in healthy industries. Hungary is attempting to make the shift away from pure socialism gradually. Government leaders fear that Hungarians will revolt if the prices of food, clothing, and rent rise too rapidly. The government, therefore, will continue for a while to control the prices of those items.

Signs of capitalism have appeared in the Soviet Union, but they are not widespread. To boost agricultural productivity, Mikhail Gorbachev implemented a system that allows a group of farmers (a collective) or a single family to manage, though not to own, a tract of cropland and some livestock and to keep a share of the profits. The fatter the cows, the more money the cattle raisers make. So far the experiment is doing well. Some couples who used to earn $490 per month now earn $1,800 a month. They work harder, often 15 hours a day, in the expectation that they will be able to buy a country house and a car. Soviet farming has a long way to go to become a truly free market enterprise. Nevertheless, the incentives of the market system are increasingly being recognized and utilized.

Free markets emerge in centrally planned economies just as regulated businesses exist in free-market economies. Solzhenitsyn's "Gulag Archipelago" and a magazine on Rambo are among the books found at this stand in busy Liberation Square, in Budapest, Hungary (left). Much of the literature offered at the stand was once banned. The reform of the Hungarian economy has seen the emergence of many new enterprises. In the United States, private firms are not allowed to compete with the U.S. Post Office for the delivery of first class mail. Here sorters spend time behind machines that sort the mail by zip code (right).

In Poland, the leaders are embracing free market economics. In December 1989, a series of laws were implemented that cut the subsidies to state-run enterprises and laid the groundwork for private enterprise and the decontrol of all prices. The problem that Poland and the other nations of Eastern Europe face is the disruption that will occur during the transition. Forecasts of unemployment of sizable proportions in nations that had no unemployment under communism frighten many. As much as half of the labor force will probably have to find new jobs. In addition, bankruptcies will occur at a large rate in countries that previously had no bankruptcy laws.[3]

The transition from a system of common ownership to a system of private ownership has never occurred before on a wide scale. There are few precedents to provide lessons. How is private property instituted? Which individuals become managers, workers, or unemployed? An interesting small experiment in shifting from communism to capitalism occurred in the United States in Amana, Iowa, on June 1, 1932. Perhaps a look at this experience might provide some clues about how the nations of Eastern Europe could proceed.[4]

The Amana colonies of German Inspirationists existed as a system of almost pure communism from 1859 to 1932. The Amana congregation owned the land, so it could decide how the fruits of its labor and capital investment would be shared. Frustrated by the obvious differences in

[3]Alan Murray, "The Outlook: Polish Economic Plan Is Boldly Capitalistic," *The Wall Street Journal*, December 4, 1989, p. 1.
[4]John F. Stehle, "How Some Communists Became Capitalists Overnight," *The Wall Street Journal*, November 29, 1989, p. A16.

material living standards between Amana and the surrounding community, over 90 percent of the members of Amana voted to change their system. At midnight on June 1, 1932, the Amana colonies shifted from a system of pure collective ownership of their land, factories, and homes to private ownership of shares of stock in the land and factories and private ownership of the houses. The transition occurred with relative ease, and productivity improved significantly. Whether that experience can be replicated on a national scale remains to be seen.

5.e. The Traditional Economy

In many developing countries, long-established custom provides answers to the *what, how,* and *for whom* questions. In these economies, ways of doing things are passed down from generation to generation. If your father was a carpenter, you are likely to be a carpenter. If your parents were poor, you are likely to be poor. Economic and other decisions may be made by a group of elders, who follow the beliefs and practices of previous generations. Such economies are called **traditional economies**.

traditional economies:
economic systems in which economic decisions are based on customs, beliefs, and practices handed down from one generation to another

Developing nations such as Ethiopia, the Sudan, and Bolivia exhibit elements of traditional economies in their tendency to make economic decisions according to how things have been done in the past. The answers to the *what, how,* and *for whom* questions in these countries are: produce what we have always produced; produce the way we have always produced; and distribute income and wealth as they have been distributed in the past. Just as most economies consist of a mixture of capitalism and socialism but are dominated by one or the other, a traditional economy may have elements of capitalism or socialism, but is predominantly traditional in the way economic decisions are made. For instance, in the local economies of large cities within developing countries, such as La Paz, tradition is not the primary determinant of economic questions; the economy of Bolivia as a whole, however, is strongly traditional.

Traditional economies exist because people lack the opportunities or incentives to learn new ways. As children, they learn how to do the job their parents do, and thus their comparative advantage lies in following in their parents' footsteps. People living on subsistence incomes assume a great risk if they choose to try a new technology or change production strategies. Farmers whose families' lives depend directly on the success of their crops assume a great risk if they decide to employ untried "new" techniques in their farming. In addition, new technologies often involve capital expenditures well beyond the cash available to farmers in the less developed countries.

RECAP

A summary of the various systems and how they answer the fundamental questions of economics is presented in Table 2 on the following page.

1. A capitalist or market economy relies on the price system.
2. Socialism is characterized by government ownership of resources other than labor and centralized economic decision making.

Table 2 How Different Economic Systems Answer Fundamental Economic Questions

| Who decides: | Economic Systems | | | |
	Capitalism	Socialism	Communism	Traditional
What is produced?	Consumer	Government	Government	What was produced in the past
How it is produced?	Entrepreneur	Government	Government	How it was produced in the past
For whom it is produced?	Those able to pay	Equitably	According to need	For whom it was produced in the past

3. Communism is characterized by collective ownership of all resources and centrally planned economic decision making.

4. The real world is characterized by mixed economies rather than by pure socialist or pure capitalist systems.

5. In many developing countries, traditional beliefs and practices affect economic decision making.

SUMMARY

▼▲ In a market system, who decides what goods and services are produced?

1. In a market system, consumers are sovereign and decide by means of their purchases what goods and services will be produced. § 1.a

▼▲ How are goods and services produced?

2. In a market system, firms decide how to produce the goods and services that consumers want. In order to earn maximum profits, firms use the least-cost combinations of resources. § 2

▼▲ Who obtains the goods and services that are produced?

3. Income and prices determine who gets what in a market system. Income is determined by the ownership of resources. § 3.a

▼▲ What is a market failure?

4. Market failures occur when information is imperfect, when there are externalities, when public goods are produced, and when common ownership exists. §§ 4.a, 4.b, and 4.c

5. When the market system fails to work, the government usually steps in to deal with the resulting inefficiencies. Governments typically provide public goods and services such as fire protection, police protection, and national defense, because of the inability of the market system to provide them. Governments place limits on what firms and consumers can do in certain types of situations. Governments tax externalities or otherwise attempt to make price reflect the full cost of production and consumption. §§ 4.a, 4.b, and 4.c

▼▲ How do different economic systems answer the *what, how,* and *for whom* questions?

6. Capitalist systems rely on the decisions of individuals. Centrally planned systems rely on a planning board or central committee to answer questions for all individuals. §§ 5.a, 5.b, and 5.c

7. All economic systems have some elements of capitalism and socialism. The degree to which a mixed economy relies on socialism or capitalism tends to define the type of system it is. § 5.d

8. The transition from communism to capitalism requires the establishment of private property rights. § 5.d

9. A traditional economy is a system in which economic decisions are based on customs, beliefs, and practices handed down from one generation to another. § 5.e

KEY TERMS

market system § 1
price system § 1
centrally planned system § 1
consumer sovereignty § 1.a
technical efficiency § 2
economic efficiency § 2
market failure § 4

market price § 4.a
market imperfection § 4.a
long run § 4.a
externalities § 4.b
public goods § 4.c
private property right § 4.c
free ride § 4.c

capitalism § 5.a
laissez faire § 5.a
socialism § 5.b
communism § 5.c
mixed economies § 5.d
traditional economies § 5.e

EXERCISES

Basic Terms and Concepts

1. What is meant by the term *price system?* What is meant by the term *market system?*

2. Why is consumer sovereignty so important in a market system?

3. Define technical efficiency and economic efficiency. How do the two types of efficiency differ? Can one exist without the other?

4. Describe how the questions *what, how,* and *for whom* are answered in capitalism, socialism, communism, and a mixed economy.

5. What is a market failure?

6. What problem do public goods create for the price system?

7. What problem is created by common ownership?

8. What problem is created by externalities?

Extended Concepts

9. During the late 1970s, interest rates rose to double-digit levels. In many states, usury laws restricted banks and other lending institutions from charging interest rates higher than some legal maximum. Demonstrate how a usury law could create a shortage as the demand for credit rises. What would occur if the law prevented interest rates from falling below some level, say 5 percent, instead of restricting the price from rising above some level like 9 percent? Suppose that banks do not know which individuals are the best risks and that the higher the interest rate the greater is the quantity of high-risk people applying for loans. What is the information problem? What might be some of the effects of the information problem? What solutions would you propose to the problem?

10. Porpoises drown when they get caught in the huge nets used by fishing fleets. Many fear that the porpoise will become extinct. Why doesn't the price of fish rise so that the quantity demanded will decline and the number of fish and porpoises caught will decline? What solution is there for this problem?

11. Most highways are "free" ways. There is no toll charge for using them. What problem does free access create? How would you solve this?

12. Many nations of Eastern Europe are undergoing a transition from communism to capitalism. An important step in the process is to define private property rights in countries where they did not exist before. How would you go about doing this? Is it possible to have no private property rights yet still have a capitalist system?

Travel Industry Is Out of Touch, Customers Say

"These guys never seem to know what I want," says the San Mateo, California, resident, vowing never to use Hertz again. Of all things that bug frequent travelers, Mr. Pavisidis's sentiment may well be the most common. A special *Wall Street Journal* "American Way of Buying" survey shows that many believe travel companies often become fixated on services people don't care about, while ignoring many they do consider important.

The survey of 403 of the nation's most frequent travelers found that a large number don't care much about in-room bars, computerized travel directions, or other new gimmicks. What they really want are simple pleasures — quiet hotel rooms, clean rental cars, comfortable airplane seats.

In fact, the travel industry might save a lot just by paying more attention to its customers. Having newspapers delivered to rooms, which many hotels don't bother with, appeals far more to travelers than a health club,

the poll shows. The delivery service costs 10 cents a room; health clubs can cost as much as $50,000 to build.

Three of the fastest-growing services these days are business service centers, airplane telephones, and in-room bars and refrigerators. Airlines have put phones in more than 1,200 planes, in some cases sticking them on every other seat. Sheraton Corp. has built business centers — which offer secretarial services, fax machines, and personal computers — in more than 200 hotels. And hotels have installed 65,000 in-room bars since January 1988. . . . Yet, 73 percent of the poll's respondents don't think bars and refrigerators are important in picking a hotel.

Travelers obviously care about important things like cost and flight cancellations, but 45 percent of the respondents also consider something as innocuous as nonsmoking hotel rooms "extremely" important. Thick hotel room walls are valued, too.

Travel companies say a lot of their

customers' requests aren't so modest as they seem. While many hotel chains now build walls that are supposed to be as noise-resistant as 11 inches of concrete, they say there's little they can do about the walls in older properties. Improving airline food isn't easy either, since the low humidity in airplane cabins dries up meats. The travel industry also takes exception to some of the survey findings. Hertz, for example, says its car phones are widely used. And travel executives say some services that aren't universally popular are nonetheless crucial to some people. "People's demands are not homogeneous," says Michael Ribero, senior vice president of marketing for Hilton Hotels Corp.

■ Source: Jonathan Dahl, "Travel Industry Is Out of Touch, Customers Say," *The Wall Street Journal*, November 30, 1989, p. B1.

Commentary

What lies behind the proliferation of services offered to travelers? Does it represent a case of consumer sovereignty, with firms responding to travelers' desires? Or is it an example of sovereign businesses foisting extra services on an unwilling public?

In a competitive market, additional services are provided if they result in greater profit. These services add to the expenses firms undertake when they supply a product, but may also increase demand. In the diagram below, S_1 represents the supply of rental cars without phones and S_2 represents the supply of rental cars with phones. Likewise, D_1 represents the demand for rental cars without phones and D_2 represents the demand for rental cars with phones. Since D_2 has shifted out farther than S_2 has shifted in, the increase in demand outweighs the additional costs so that firms have an incentive to install car phones.

Of course, not all possible services will be provided to travelers. Some are too expensive and others aren't wanted by consumers. The cost of thick hotel room walls is too high in existing hotels; the upward shift of the supply curve would be much larger than the outward shift of the demand curve resulting from the

quieter rooms. As a result, the hotels would lose money attempting to reconstruct their rooms. In some cases, services aren't offered by firms until the managers of the firms learn that consumers do indeed want the services and that the services are profitable. For instance, daily newspaper delivery to hotel guests may be valued by consumers. As managers learn this, they will begin newspaper delivery. If the newspapers increase the demand more than they increase costs, managers will continue to provide them. Conversely, firms may have carried out surveys or marketing studies indicating that travelers want some service when in fact travelers aren't willing to pay enough extra for their hotel rooms to cover the cost of the services. Managers may think providing in-room bars will increase demand but, in fact, they may not. Once managers learn that consumers do not value the bars, additional bars will not be purchased.

There are some services that are too costly today but might not be in the future. If technological improvements can offer a way to provide better food on airplanes (food that won't dry out), a means to clean the smell of cigarette smoke out of rooms, or a way to provide insulation in existing buildings without significant cost increases, these services might be provided in the future. Technological improvements would mean that the upward shift of the supply curve that occurs when a new service is instituted would be less than would have been the case without the technological change. If the demand curve increase offsets the supply curve shift, the service will be offered.

Profit-maximizing firms will respond to consumer wishes whenever it is profitable to do so. Services that increase demand at low cost, such as newspaper delivery, will be instituted. Services that have little effect on demand, such as in-room bars, will be abandoned. Alas, for the light sleepers of the world, the high cost of providing thick walls in existing hotels will probably keep these from being provided.

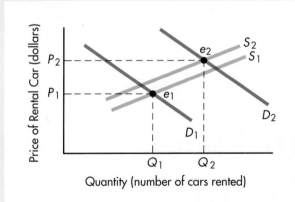

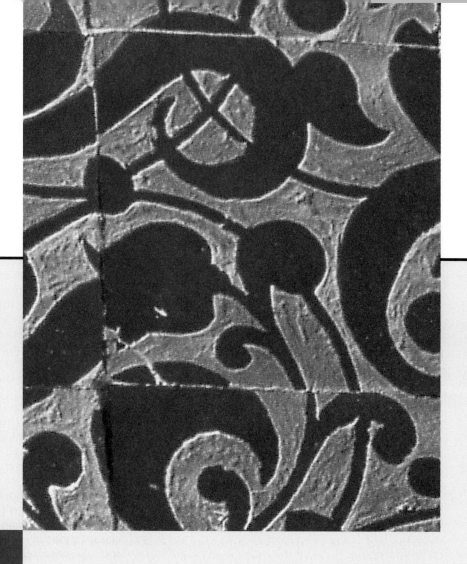

5

Households, Businesses, Government, and the International Sector

1. What is a household, and what is household income and spending?
2. What is a firm, and what is business spending?
3. What is the economic role of government?
4. How does the international sector affect the economy?
5. How do the four sectors interact in the economy?

PREVIEW You decide to buy a new Toyota, so you go to a Toyota dealer and exchange money for the car. The Toyota dealer has rented land and a building and hired workers in order to make cars available to you and other members of the public. The employees earn incomes paid by the Toyota dealer and then use their incomes to buy food from the grocery store. This transaction generates revenue for the grocery store, which hires workers and pays them incomes that they then use to buy groceries and Toyotas. Your expenditures for the Toyota are part of a circular flow. Revenue is received by the Toyota dealer, who pays employees, who, in turn, buy goods and services.

Of course the story is complicated by the fact that the Toyota is originally purchased in Japan and shipped to the United States before it can be sold by the local Toyota dealer. Your purchase of the Toyota creates revenue for the local dealer as well as for the manufacturer in Japan who pays Japanese autoworkers to produce Toyotas. Furthermore, when you buy your Toyota, you must pay a tax to the government, which uses tax revenues to pay for police protection, national defense, the legal system, and other services. Many people in different areas of the economy are involved.

An economy is made up of individual buyers and sellers. Economists could discuss the neighborhood economy that surrounds your university, the economy of the city of Chicago, or the economy of the state of Massachusetts. But typically it is the national economy, the economy of the United States, that is the center of their attention. To clarify the operation of the national economy, economists usually group individual buyers and sellers into three sectors: households, businesses, and government. Omitted from this grouping, however, is an important source of activity, the international sector. Since the U.S. economy affects, and is affected by, the rest of the world, to understand how the economy functions we must include the international sector.

We begin this chapter by examining basic data and information on each individual sector with the objective of answering some general questions: What is a household, and how do households spend their incomes? What is a corporation, and how does a corporation differ from a partnership? What is the federal budget deficit? What does it mean if the United States has a trade deficit?

After describing the four sectors that make up the national economy, we present a simple economic model to illustrate the interrelationships linking all the individual sectors into the national economy.

1. HOUSEHOLDS

household:
one or more persons who occupy a unit of housing

What is a household, and what is household income and spending?

A **household** consists of one or more persons who occupy a unit of housing. The unit of housing may be a house, an apartment, or even a single room, as long as it constitutes separate living quarters. A household may consist of related family members like a father, mother, and children, or it may comprise unrelated individuals like three college students sharing an apartment. The person in whose name the house or apartment is owned or rented is called the *householder*.

Figure 1
Age of Householder, Number of Households, and Median Household Income in the United States
The graph reveals that householders aged 25 to 34 made up the largest number of households, and householders aged 45 to 54 earned the highest median annual income in 1986, when the survey was taken. Source: U.S. Bureau of the Census, *Current Population Reports*, series P-60, no. 162 (Washington, D.C.: U.S. Government Printing Office, 1988), pp. 29–30.

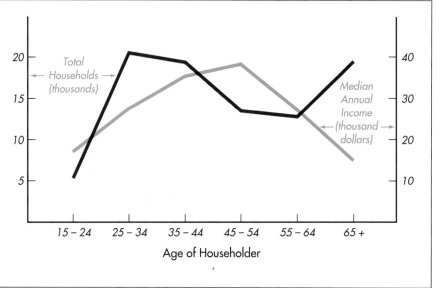

Figure 2
Size Distribution of Households in the United States
As the pie chart illustrates, two-person households made up a larger percentage of the total number of households than any other group in 1986, a total of 32 percent. Large households with seven or more persons are becoming a rarity, accounting for only 1 percent of the total number of households in 1986.
Source: U.S. Bureau of the Census, *Current Population Reports,* series P-90, no. 162 (Washington, D.C.: U.S. Government Printing Office, 1988), pp. 26–28.

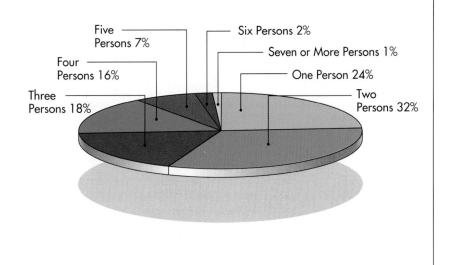

Five Persons 7%

Six Persons 2%

Seven or More Persons 1%

Four Persons 16%

One Person 24%

Three Persons 18%

Two Persons 32%

1.a. Number of Households and Household Income

In 1987, there were 91,066,000 households in the United States. The breakdown of households by age of householder is shown in Figure 1. Householders between 25 and 34 years old make up the largest number of households. Householders between 45 and 54 years old have the largest median income. The *median* is the middle value—half of the households in an age group have an income higher than the median and half have an income lower than the median. Figure 1 shows that households in which the householder is between 45 and 54 years old have a median income of $37,250, substantially higher than the median incomes of other age groups. Typically, workers in this age group are at the peak of their earning power. Younger households are gaining experience and training; older households include retired workers.

The size distribution of households in the United States is shown in Figure 2. Thirty-two percent of all households, or 29,295,000, are two-person households. The stereotypical household of husband, wife, and two children accounts for only 16 percent of all households. There are relatively few large households in the United States. Of the 91,066,000 households in the country, only 1,320,000 (1 percent) have seven or more persons.

1.b. Household Spending

consumption:
household spending

Household spending is called **consumption**. Householders consume housing, transportation, food, entertainment, and other goods and services. The pattern of household spending (also called *consumer spending*) in the United States between 1940 and 1988 is shown in Figure 3. The pattern is one of steady increase. This spending by the household sector is the largest component of total spending in the economy—rising above $3 trillion in 1988.

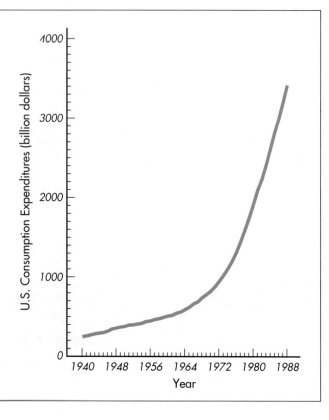

Figure 3
U.S. Consumption Expenditures, 1940–1988
Household expenditures have been rising in a very smooth manner since 1940. Source: *Economic Report of the President, 1989* (Washington, D.C.: U.S. Government Printing Office, 1989), p. 308.

RECAP

1. A household consists of one or more persons who occupy a unit of housing.

2. An apartment or house is rented or owned by a householder.

3. As a group, householders between the ages of 45 and 54 have the highest incomes.

4. Household spending is called *consumption*.

2. BUSINESS FIRMS

business firm:
a business organization controlled by a single management

A **business firm** is a business organization controlled by a single management. The firm's business may be conducted at more than one location. The terms *company, enterprise,* and *business* are used interchangeably with *firm*.

2.a. Forms of Business Organization

sole proprietorship:
a business owned by one person who receives all the profits and is responsible for all the debts incurred by the business

Firms are organized as sole proprietorships, partnerships, or corporations. A **sole proprietorship** is a business owned by one person. This type of firm may be a one-person operation or a large enterprise with many employees.

partnership:
a business with two or more owners who share the firm's profits and losses

corporation:
a legal entity owned by shareholders whose liability for the firm's losses is limited to the value of the stock they own

multinational business:
a firm that owns and operates producing units in foreign countries

In either case, the owner receives all the profits and is responsible for all the debts incurred by the business.

A **partnership** is a business owned by two or more partners who share both the profits of the business and responsibility for the firm's losses. The partners could be individuals, estates, or other businesses.

A **corporation** is a business whose identity in the eyes of the law is distinct from the identity of its owners. State law allows the formation of corporations. A corporation is an economic entity that, like a person, can own property and borrow money in its own name. The owners of a corporation are shareholders. If a corporation cannot pay its debts, creditors cannot seek payment from the shareholders' personal wealth. The corporation itself is responsible for all its actions. Shareholders' liability is limited to the value of the stock they own.

Many firms are global in their operations even though they may have been founded and may be owned by residents of a single country. Firms typically first enter the international market by selling products to foreign countries. As revenues from these sales increase, the firm realizes advantages by locating subsidiaries in foreign countries. A **multinational business** is a firm that owns and operates producing units in foreign countries. The best-known U.S. corporations are multinational firms. Ford, IBM, PepsiCo, and McDonald's all own operating units in many different countries. Ford Motor Company, for instance, is the parent firm of sales organizations and assembly plants located around the world. As transportation and communication technology progresses, multinational business activity will grow.

2.b. Business Statistics

Figure 4 shows that in the United States there are far more sole proprietorships than partnerships or corporations. Figure 4 also compares the revenues earned by each type of business. The great majority of sole proprietorships are small businesses, with revenues under $25,000 a year. Almost half of all partnerships also have revenues under $25,000 a year, but only 21.7 percent of the corporations are in this category.

The second graph in Figure 4 shows that the 69.1 percent of sole proprietorships that earn less than $25,000 a year account for only 10 percent of the revenue earned by proprietorships. The 0.3 percent of proprietorships with revenue of $1 million or more account for 15.7 percent. Even more striking are the figures for partnerships and corporations. The 49 percent of partnerships with the smallest revenue account for only 0.7 percent of the total revenue earned by partnerships. At the other extreme, the 3.3 percent of partnerships with the largest revenue account for 70 percent of total partnership revenue. The 21.7 percent of corporations in the smallest range account for only 0.1 percent of total corporate revenue, while the 16.4 percent of corporations in the largest range account for 92.6 percent of corporate revenue.

The message of Figure 4 is that big business is important in the United States. There are many small firms, but large firms and corporations account for the greatest share of business revenue. Although there are only about one-third as many corporations as sole proprietorships, corporations have more than 15 times the revenue of sole proprietorships.

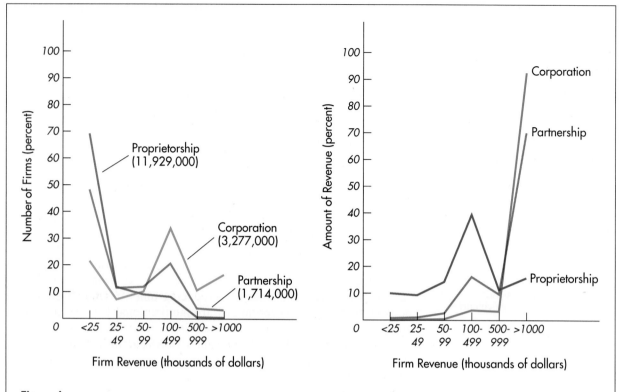

Figure 4
Number and Revenue of Business Firms
As the first graph illustrates, most sole proprietorships and partnerships are small firms, with nearly 70 percent of all proprietorships falling into the less-than-$25,000 category, and nearly 50 percent of all partnerships falling into the same lowest revenue category. Corporations are more likely to be larger — 33 percent fall into the $100,000 to $499,000 category. The second graph shows that most sole proprietorship revenues are earned by the larger proprietorships, those in the $100,000 to $499,000 category. By contrast, the small number of partnerships in the top revenue category is enough to account for 70 percent of all partnership revenues. The same is true of corporations, to a greater degree. Source: Statistical Abstract of the United States, 1989 (Washington, D.C.: U.S. Government Printing Office, 1989, p. 516.

2.c. Firms Around the World

Big business is a dominant force in the United States. Many people believe that because the United States is the world's largest economy, U.S. firms are the largest in the world. Figure 5 shows that this is not true. Of the ten largest corporations in the world, seven are Japanese. Only two, IBM and Exxon Corp., are U.S. firms. Big business is not just an American phenomenon.

2.d. Entrepreneurial Ability

The emphasis on bigness should not hide the fact that many new firms are started each year. Businesses are typically begun as small sole proprietorships. The people who begin new firms are called *risk-taking owners*, or *entrepreneurs*. Entrepreneurs are responsible for many advances in technology and services. Yet many of them are forced to go out of business within a year or two. Businesses survive in the long run only if they pro-

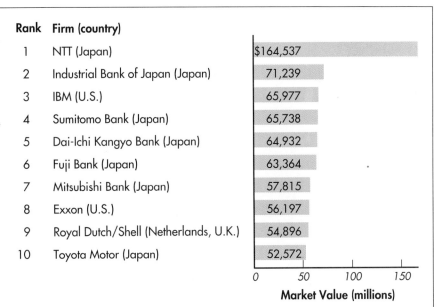

Figure 5
The World's Ten Largest Public Companies
As shown in the chart, the Japanese own seven out of ten of the world's largest companies. Only two U.S.-owned companies appear on the list, though one, IBM, is the third largest company in the world. Source: "The World's Ten Largest Public Companies," *The Wall Street Journal*, September 22, 1989, p. R14.

Rank	Firm (country)	Market Value (millions)
1	NTT (Japan)	$164,537
2	Industrial Bank of Japan (Japan)	71,239
3	IBM (U.S.)	65,977
4	Sumitomo Bank (Japan)	65,738
5	Dai-Ichi Kangyo Bank (Japan)	64,932
6	Fuji Bank (Japan)	63,364
7	Mitsubishi Bank (Japan)	57,815
8	Exxon (U.S.)	56,197
9	Royal Dutch/Shell (Netherlands, U.K.)	54,896
10	Toyota Motor (Japan)	52,572

vide a good or service that people want enough to yield a profit for the entrepreneur. Although there are fabulous success stories, the failure rate among new firms is high.

Regardless of the business they choose, entrepreneurs tend to agree about the incentives and problems associated with starting a business. The results of a survey of entrepreneurs after their first year of business are summarized in Table 1. Several of the responses suggest the small size of the typical new business. That 47 percent of entrepreneurs surveyed could hire employees by "word of mouth" while 15.5 percent used relatives for employees indicates that the firms generally required a small number of employees. It is clear that the entrepreneurs undertook personal risks to begin their businesses: 81 percent used personal assets to finance the business. Relatively few, 6 percent, received **venture capital**—a loan provided by an individual or firm that specializes in lending to new, unproven businesses. (Venture capitalists speculate on the success of the new business.) Only 3 percent received loans from the Small Business Administration (SBA), a government agency that assists small firms.

That many new businesses fail is a fact of economic life. In the U.S. economy, anyone with an idea and sufficient resources has the freedom to open a business. However, if buyers do not respond to the new offering, the business fails. Only firms that satisfy this "market test" survive. Entrepreneurs thus try to ensure that as wants change, goods and services are produced to satisfy those wants.

venture capital:
funds provided by a firm or individual that specializes in lending to new, unproven firms

▼ What is a firm, and what is business spending? ▲

2.e. Business Spending

investment:
spending on capital goods to be used in producing goods and services

Investment is the expenditure by business firms for capital goods— machines, tools, and buildings—that will be used to provide goods and services. The economic meaning of *investment* is different from the everyday meaning, "a financial transaction such as buying bonds or stocks."

Table 1 Results of a Survey of Entrepreneurs

How Entrepreneurs Choose New Business Sites	
Factor	Percentage of entrepreneurs
Near customers	53.9
Reasonable rent	52.6
Near freeway or major street	40.5
Near home	34.5
Near suppliers	9.9
Near similar businesses	8.2

How Entrepreneurs Find Employees	
Method	Percentage of entrepreneurs
Word of mouth	47.0
Newspaper ad	21.1
Other	20.3
Relatives	15.5
Employment agency	4.3
Management consultants	1.3

How Entrepreneurs Financed New Firms	
Method	Percentage of entrepreneurs
Personal assets	81.0
Bank loans	38.4
Relatives	17.7
Forgone wages	15.5
Venture capital	6.0
Friends	3.9
SBA loans	3.0

Most Difficult Problems Facing Entrepreneurs	
Problem	Percentage of entrepreneurs
Financing and cash flow	29.7
Becoming known	19.8
Keeping good employees	14.2
Government (permits, taxes, etc.)	9.5

Source: *Arizona Business,* October 1987, p. 6. From *ARIZONA BUSINESS,* a monthly publication of the Center for Business Research, College of Business, Arizona State University, Tempe, AZ 85287.

In economics, the term *investment* refers to business spending for capital goods.

Investment spending in 1988 was $750.3 billion, an amount equal to roughly one-fourth of consumption, or household spending. Investment spending between 1940 and 1988 is shown in Figure 6. Compare Figures 3 and 6 and notice the different patterns of spending. Investment increases

Figure 6
U.S. Investment Spending 1940–1988
Business expenditures on capital goods have been increasing erratically since 1940. Source: *Economic Report of the President, 1989* (Washington, D.C.: U.S. Government Printing Office, 1989), p. 308.

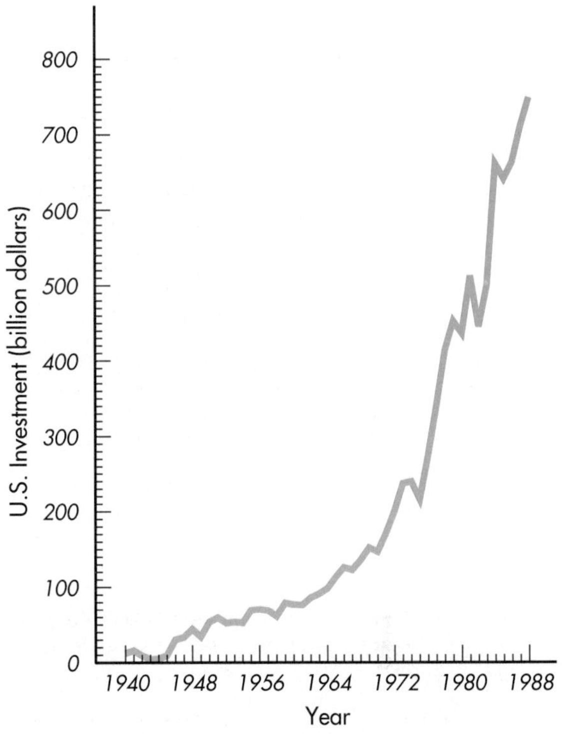

unevenly, actually falling at times and then rising very rapidly. Even though investment spending is much smaller than consumption, the wide swings in investment spending mean that business expenditures are an important factor in determining the economic health of the nation.

RECAP

1. Business firms may be organized as sole proprietorships, partnerships, or corporations.
2. Large corporations account for the largest fraction of total business revenue.
3. Entrepreneurs are business organizers and risk-takers.
4. Business investment spending fluctuates widely over time.

3. GOVERNMENT

Government in the United States exists at the federal, state, and local levels. Local government includes county, regional, and municipal units. Economic discussions tend to focus on the federal government because national economic policy is set at that level. Nevertheless, each level affects us through its taxing and spending decisions, and laws regulating behavior.

The Successful Entrepreneur (Sometimes It's Better to Be Lucky Than Good)

Entrepreneurs do not always develop an abstract idea into reality when starting a new firm. Sometimes people stumble onto a good thing by accident and then are clever enough and willing to take the necessary risk to turn their lucky find into a commercial success.

In 1875, a Philadelphia pharmacist on his honeymoon tasted tea made from an innkeeper's old family recipe. The tea, made from 16 wild roots and berries, was so delicious that the pharmacist asked the innkeeper's wife for the recipe. When he returned to his pharmacy, he created a solid concentrate of the drink that could be sold for home consumption.

The pharmacist was Charles Hires, a devout Quaker, who intended to sell "Hires Herb Tea" to hard-drinking Pennsylvania coal miners as a nonalcoholic alternative to beer and whiskey. A friend of Hires suggested that miners would not drink anything called "tea" and recommended that he call his drink "root beer."

The initial response to Hires Root Beer was so enthusiastic that Hires soon began nationwide distribution. The yellow box of root beer extract was a familiar sight in homes and drugstore fountains across America. By 1895, Hires, who started with a $3,000 loan, was operating a business valued at half a million dollars (a lot of money in 1895) and bottling ready-to-drink root beer across the country.

Hires, of course, is not the only entrepreneur clever enough to turn a lucky discovery into a business success. In 1894, in Battle Creek, Michigan, a sanitarium handyman named Will Kellogg was helping his older brother prepare wheat meal to serve to patients in the sanitarium's dining room. The two men would boil wheat dough and then run it through rollers to produce thin sheets of meal. One day they left a batch of the dough out overnight. The next day, when the dough was run through the rollers, it broke up into flakes instead of forming a sheet.

By letting the dough stand overnight, the Kelloggs had allowed moisture to be distributed evenly to each individual wheat berry. When the dough went through the rollers, the berries formed separate flakes instead of binding together. The Kelloggs toasted the wheat flakes and served them to the patients.

They were an immediate success. In fact, the brothers had to start a mail-order flaked-cereal business because patients wanted flaked cereal for their household.

Will saw the market potential for their discovery and started his own cereal company (his brother refused to join him in the business). Will Kellogg was a great promoter who used innovations like four-color magazine ads and free sample promotions. In New York City, he offered a free box of corn flakes to every woman who winked at her grocer on a specified day. The promotion was considered risqué, but Kellogg's sales in New York increased from two railroad cars of cereal a month to one car a day.

Will Kellogg, a poorly paid sanitarium worker in his mid-40s, became a daring entrepreneur after his mistake with wheat flour led to the discovery of a way to produce flaked cereal. He became one of the richest men in America because of his entrepreneurial ability.

■ Source: Based on Joseph J. Fucini and Suzy Fucini, *Entrepreneurs* (Boston: Hall and Co., 1985).

3.a. Policymakers

What is the economic role of government?

When Americans think of government policies, rules, and regulations, they typically think of Washington, D.C., because their economic lives are regulated and shaped more by policies made there than by policies made at the local and state levels. Who actually is involved in economic policy making? Important government institutions that shape U.S. economic policy are listed in Table 2.

Table 2 U.S. Government Economic Policymakers and Related Agencies

Institution	Role
Fiscal policymakers	
President	Provides leadership in formulating fiscal policy
Congress	Sets government spending and taxes and passes laws related to economic conduct
Monetary policymaker	
Federal Reserve	Controls money supply and credit conditions
Related agencies	
Council of Economic Advisers	Monitors the economy and advises the president
Office of Management and Budget	Prepares and analyzes the federal budget
Treasury Department	Administers the financial affairs of the federal government
Commerce Department	Administers federal policy regulating industry
Justice Department	Enforces legal setting of business
Comptroller of the Currency	Oversees national banks
International Trade Commission	Investigates unfair international trade practices
Federal Trade Commission	Administers laws related to fair business practices and competition

Economic policy involves macroeconomic issues like government spending and control of the money supply and microeconomic issues like the legal restrictions on business and the promotion of a competitive business environment. The microeconomic policy of government is typically aimed at providing public goods like police and military protection, correcting externalities like pollution, maintaining a competitive capitalist economy, and redistributing income from those with relatively high incomes to those with relatively low incomes.

Government provides public goods to avoid the free-rider problem that would occur if private firms provided the goods.

3.a.1 Microeconomic Policy One reason for government's microeconomic role is the free-rider problem associated with the provision of public goods. If an army makes all citizens safer, then all citizens should pay for it. But even if one person does not pay taxes, the army still protects this citizen from foreign attack. To minimize free riding, the government collects mandatory taxes to finance public goods. Congress and the president determine the level of public goods needed and how to finance them.

Microeconomic policy also deals with externalities, or spillover effects. Activities that cause air or water pollution impose costs on everyone. For instance, a steel mill may generate air pollutants that have a negative effect on the surrounding population. A microeconomic function of government is to internalize the externality—that is, to force the steelmaker to bear the full cost to society of producing steel. In addition to assuming the costs of hiring land, labor, and capital, the mill should bear the costs associated with polluting the air. Congress and the president determine which externalities to address and the best way of taxing or subsidizing each activity in order to ensure that the amount of the good produced and its price reflect the true value to society.

Government taxes or subsidizes some activities that create externalities.

A market system works efficiently when competition exists. One of government's microeconomic roles is to promote competition. Antitrust laws are aimed at restricting the ability of business firms to engage in practices that limit competition. Some firms, such as public utilities, naturally face no competition. The cost of generating electricity is so high that to have several firms generating electricity and running several sets of wires through a city would be inefficient. The government regulates industries in which free market competition cannot exist. The Justice Department is a major policymaker and enforcer of the competitiveness of the economy.

Government regulates industries where free market competition cannot exist and polices other industries to promote competition.

Yet another microeconomic area of government policy is income distribution. In a market system, incomes reflect the productivity of resources. Skilled labor earns higher wages than unskilled labor. Because all individuals do not have equal ability, some have higher incomes than others. The least able citizens in an economy typically have the lowest incomes. Governments respond to the unequal distribution of income that results from unequal abilities by taxing citizens with high incomes and transferring this tax revenue to citizens with lower incomes. Congress and the president decide on the appropriate amount of income redistribution.

Government taxes high-income individuals and transfers the tax revenue to lower-income individuals.

3.a.2. Macroeconomic Policy

The focus of the government's macroeconomic policy is monetary policy and fiscal policy. **Monetary policy** is policy directed toward control of money and credit. The major player in this policy arena is the Federal Reserve, commonly called "the Fed." The **Federal Reserve** is the central bank of the United States. It serves as a banker for the U.S. government and regulates the U.S. money supply.

monetary policy:
policy directed toward control of the money supply

Federal Reserve:
the central bank of the United States

The Federal Reserve System is run by a seven-member Board of Governors. The most important member of the Board is the chairman (at the time of this writing, Alan Greenspan). The Fed Board meets regularly (from ten to twelve times a year) with a group of high-level Fed officials to review the current economic situation and set policy for the growth of U.S. money and credit. The Federal Reserve exercises a great deal of influence on U.S. economic policy.

fiscal policy:
policy directed toward government spending and taxation

Fiscal policy, the other area of macroeconomic policy, is policy directed toward government spending and taxation. In the United States, fiscal policy is determined by laws that are passed by Congress and signed by the president. The relative roles of the legislative and executive branches in shaping fiscal policy vary with the political climate, but usually it is the president who initiates major policy changes. Presidents rely on key advisers for fiscal policy information. These advisers include Cabinet officers such as the secretary of the treasury and the secretary of state as well as the director of the Office of Management and Budget. In addition, the president has a Council of Economic Advisers made up of three economists—usually a chairman, a macroeconomist, and a microeconomist—who together with their staff monitor and interpret economic developments for the president. The degree of influence wielded by these advisers depends on their personal relationship with the president.

3.b. Government Spending

Federal, state, and local government spending for goods and services between 1940 and 1988 is shown in Figure 7. Except during times of war in the 1940s and 1950s, federal expenditures were roughly similar in size to state and local expenditures until 1968. Since 1968, state and local spending has been growing more rapidly than federal spending.

Combined government spending on goods and services is larger than investment spending but much smaller than consumption. In 1988, combined government spending was $968.9 billion, investment spending was $750.3 billion, and consumption was $3,235.1 billion. The magnitude of federal government spending relative to federal government revenue from taxes has become an important issue in recent years. Figure 8 shows that the federal budget was roughly balanced until the early 1970s. The budget is a measure of spending and revenue. A balanced budget occurs when federal spending is approximately equal to federal revenue. This was the case through the 1950s and 1960s. If federal government spending is less

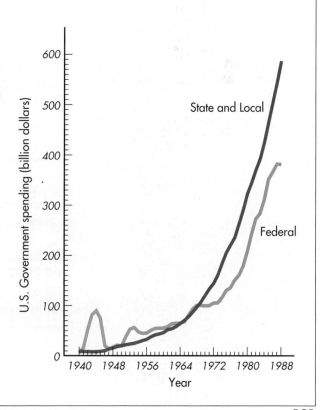

Figure 7
Federal, State, and Local Government Expenditures for Goods and Services, 1940–1988
In the 1940s and 1950s, federal government spending was well above state and local government spending because of war-related expenditures. In the late 1960s, state and local expenditures rose above federal spending and have remained higher ever since. Source: *Economic Report of the President, 1989* (Washington, D.C.: U.S. Government Printing Office, 1989), p. 309.

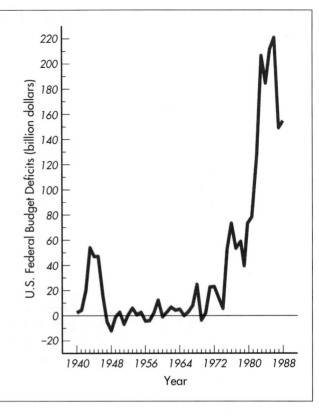

Figure 8
U.S. Federal Budget Deficits, 1940–1988
The budget deficit is equal to the excess of government spending over tax revenue. If taxes are greater than government spending, a budget surplus (shown as a negative deficit) exists. The United States has run a budget deficit for much of the period 1940–1988. Source: *Economic Report of the President, 1989* (Washington, D.C.: U.S. Government Printing Office, 1989), p. 397.

budget surplus (deficit):
the excess (shortage) that results when government spending is less (greater) than revenue

than tax revenue, a **budget surplus** exists. The United States government last had a budget surplus in 1969. By the early 1980s, federal government spending was much larger than revenue, so a large **budget deficit** existed. The federal budget deficit grew very rapidly to around $200 billion by the mid-1980s. When spending is greater than revenue, the excess spending must be covered by borrowing, and this borrowing can have effects on investment and consumption as well as on economic relationships with other countries.

RECAP

1. The microeconomic functions of government include correcting externalities, redistributing income from high-income groups to lower-income groups, enforcing a competitive economy, and providing public goods.

2. Macroeconomic policy attempts to control the economy through monetary and fiscal policy.

3. The Federal Reserve conducts monetary policy. Congress and the president formulate fiscal policy.

4. Government spending is larger than investment spending but much smaller than consumption spending.

5. When government spending exceeds tax revenue, a budget deficit exists. When government spending is less than tax revenue, a budget surplus exists.

4. THE INTERNATIONAL SECTOR

▼ How does the international sector affect the economy? ▲

Years ago, only households, businesses, and government were included in discussions of the participants in the economy because the international aspects of the U.S. economy were so small. Today, however, foreign buyers and sellers have a significant effect on economic conditions in the United States, and developments in the rest of the world often influence U.S. buyers and sellers.

4.a. Types of Countries

The nations of the world may be divided into two categories: industrial countries and developing countries. Developing countries greatly outnumber industrial countries (see Figure 9). The World Bank (an international organization that makes loans to developing countries) groups countries according to per capita income (income per person). Low-income economies are those with per capita incomes of $480 or less. Middle-income economies have per capita incomes of $481 or more. High-income economies—oil exporters and industrial market economies—are distinguished from the middle-income economies. The nations of Eastern Europe are not members of the World Bank and so are not categorized, and information about a few small countries is so limited that the World Bank is unable to classify them.

It is readily apparent from Figure 9 that low-income economies are heavily concentrated in Africa and Asia. Countries in these regions have a low profile in U.S. trade, although they may receive humanitarian aid from the United States. U.S. trade is concentrated with Canada, Mexico, and the other major industrial powers. Nations in each group present different economic challenges to the United States.

4.a.1. The Industrial Countries
The World Bank uses per capita income to classify 19 countries as "industrial market economies." They are listed in the bar chart in Figure 10. The 19 countries listed in Figure 10 are among the wealthiest countries in the world. Not appearing on the list are the high-income oil-exporting nations like Libya, Saudi Arabia, Kuwait, and the United Arab Emirates. The World Bank considers those countries to be "still developing."

The economies of the industrial nations are highly interdependent. As conditions change in one nation, business firms and individuals looking for the best return or interest rate on their funds may shift large sums of money between countries. As the funds flow from one country to another, economic conditions in one country spread to other countries. As a result, the industrial countries, particularly the major economic powers like the United States, West Germany, and Japan, are forced to pay close attention to each other's economic policies.

Figure 9
World Economic Development
The colors on the map identify low-income, middle-income, and high-income economies. Countries have been placed in each group on the basis of GNP per capita and, in some instances, other distinguishing economic characteristics. Source: World Bank, *World Development Report, 1989*, pp. 160–161. From WORLD DEVELOPMENT REPORT 1989 by the World Bank. Copyright © 1989 by The International Bank for Reconstruction and Development/The World Bank. Reprinted by permission of Oxford University Press.

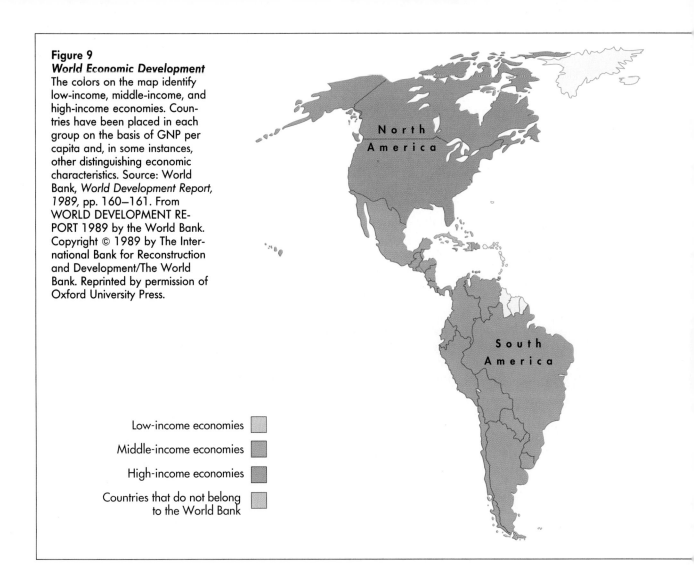

Low-income economies ▢
Middle-income economies ▢
High-income economies ▢
Countries that do not belong to the World Bank ▢

4.a.2. The Developing Countries The developing countries (sometimes referred to as *less developed countries* or *LDCs*) provide a different set of problems for the United States than do the industrial countries. In the 1980s, the debts of the developing countries to the developed nations reached tremendous heights. For instance, at the end of 1987, Brazil owed foreign creditors $106.1 billion, Mexico owed $96.9 billion, and Argentina owed $50.3 billion. In each case, the amounts owed were more than three times the annual sales of goods and services by those countries to the rest of the world. The United States had to arrange loans at special terms and establish special trade arrangements in order for those countries to be able to buy U.S. goods.

The United States tends to buy, or *import*, primary products such as agricultural produce and minerals from the developing countries. Products that a country buys from another country are called **imports**. The United States tends to sell, or *export*, manufactured goods to developing coun-

imports:
products that a country buys from other countries

exports:
products that a country sells to other
countries

tries. Products that a country sells to another country are called **exports**.
The United States is the largest producer and exporter of grains and other
agricultural output in the world. The efficiency of U.S. farming relative to
farming in much of the rest of the world gives the United States a comparative advantage in many agricultural products.

4.b. International Sector Spending

U.S. economic activity with the rest of the world includes U.S. spending
on foreign goods and foreign spending on U.S. goods. Figure 11 shows
how U.S. exports and imports are spread over different countries. Notice
that two countries, Canada and Japan, account for roughly one-third of
U.S. exports and more than one-third of U.S. imports. Trade with the
industrial countries is approximately twice as large as trade with the developing countries, and U.S. trade with Eastern Europe is trivial.

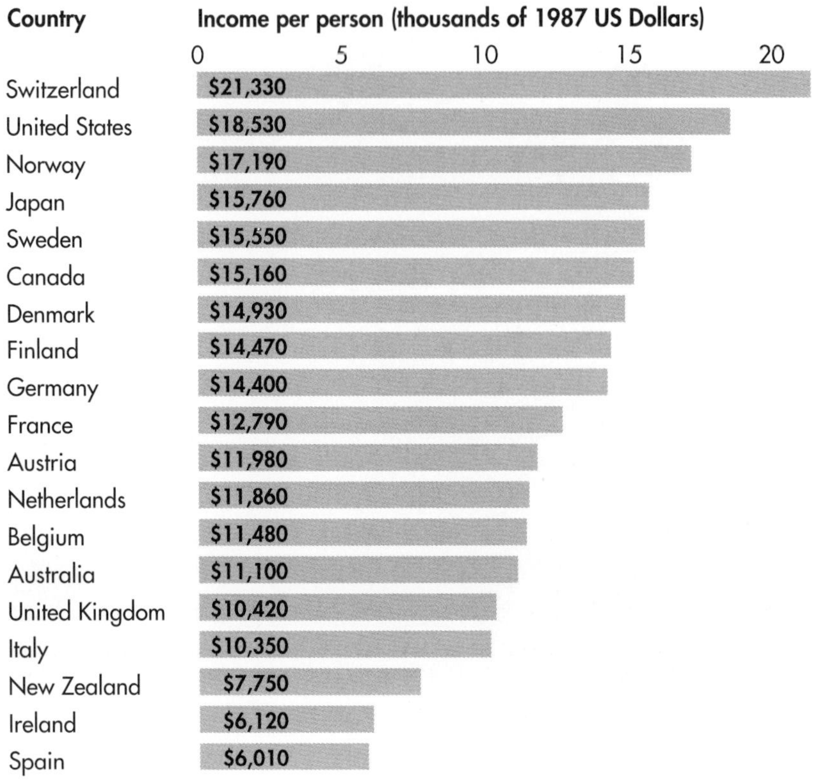

Figure 10
The Industrial Market Economies

The bar chart lists some of the wealthiest countries in the world. Ironically, high-income oil-exporting countries such as Libya, Saudi Arabia, Kuwait, and the United Arab Emirates do not appear on the list because the World Bank still considers them to be developing. Source: Data from World Bank, *World Development Report 1989*.

Country	Income per person (thousands of 1987 US Dollars)
Switzerland	$21,330
United States	$18,530
Norway	$17,190
Japan	$15,760
Sweden	$15,550
Canada	$15,160
Denmark	$14,930
Finland	$14,470
Germany	$14,400
France	$12,790
Austria	$11,980
Netherlands	$11,860
Belgium	$11,480
Australia	$11,100
United Kingdom	$10,420
Italy	$10,350
New Zealand	$7,750
Ireland	$6,120
Spain	$6,010

trade surplus (deficit):
the situation that exists when imports are less than (exceed) exports

net exports:
exports minus imports

When exports exceed imports, a **trade surplus** exists. When imports exceed exports, a **trade deficit** exists. Figure 11 shows that the United States is importing much more than it exports.

The term **net exports** refers to the difference between the value of exports and the value of imports: net exports equals exports minus imports. Figure 12 traces U.S. net exports for the period 1940–1988. Positive net exports represent trade surpluses; negative net exports represent trade deficits. The trade deficits (indicated by negative net exports) of the 1980s are the first since the World War II era. Reasons for this pattern of international trade are discussed in later chapters.

RECAP

1. The majority of U.S. trade is with the industrial market economies.
2. Exports are products sold to foreign countries; imports are products bought from foreign countries.
3. Exports minus imports equals net exports.
4. Positive net exports signal a trade surplus; negative net exports signal a trade deficit.

Figure 11
Direction of U.S. Trade
This chart shows that a trade deficit exists for the United States, since U.S. imports greatly exceed U.S. exports. The chart also shows that trade with Western Europe, Japan, and Canada accounts for most of U.S. trade. Source: *Economic Report of the President, 1989* (Washington, D.C.: U.S. Government Printing Office, 1989), p. 427.

Eastern Europe
Other Countries
 (except Eastern Europe)
 (Oil Exporters)

Industrial Countries:
W. Europe
Japan
Canada
Other

U.S. Exports to:

$249,570

U.S. Imports from:

$409,850

0   50   100   150   200   250   300   350   400   450
Millions of 1987 Dollars

Figure 12
U.S. Net Exports, 1940–1988
Between 1946 and 1982, the United States exported more than it imported and had a trade surplus. Since 1983, net exports have been negative, and the United States has had a trade deficit. Source: *Economic Report of the President, 1989* (Washington, D.C.: U.S. Government Printing Office, 1989), p. 309.

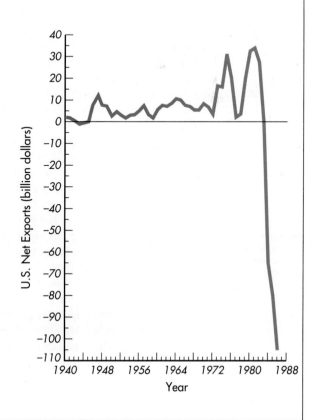

▼ How do the four sectors
interact in the economy? ▲

How are the major players in the economy—households, businesses, government, and the international sector—linked together? We first examine the simplest possible economy, one with only households and firms; then we add government and the international sector. We end up with an economic model that brings together all four sectors.

5.a. Households and Firms

factors of production:
land, labor, capital, and
entrepreneurial activity

Households own all the basic resources, or **factors of production**, in the economy. The factors of production are the land, labor, capital, and entrepreneurial ability that are combined to produce other goods and services. Household members own land and provide labor, and they are the entrepreneurs, stockholders, proprietors, and partners who own business firms. Land includes all natural resources. Labor represents all human resources except for entrepreneurial ability. Capital is manufactured resources, like machines and tools, that can be used to produce other goods and services.

Households and businesses interact with each other by means of buying and selling. Businesses, hoping to earn profits, employ the services of the factors of production in order to produce goods and services. Business firms pay for the use of the factors of production. Because households own the factors of production, firms pay households for the services of the factors of production.

Households sell the services of their factors of production (land, labor, capital, and entrepreneurial ability) to businesses in exchange for money payments. The flow of resources from households to businesses is shown by the blue-green line at the bottom of Figure 13. The flow of money payments from firms to households is shown by the gold line at the bottom of Figure 13. Households use the money payments to buy goods and services from firms. These money payments are the firms' revenues. The flow of money payments from households to firms is shown by the gold line at the top of the diagram. The flow of goods and services from firms to households is shown by the blue-green line at the top of Figure 13. There is, therefore, a flow of money and goods and services from one sector to the other. The payments made by one sector are the receipts taken in by the other sector. Money, goods, and services flow from households to firms and back to households in a circular flow.

circular flow diagram:
a model showing the flow of output
and income from one sector of the
economy to another

The **circular flow diagram** indicates that income is equal to the value of output. Money flows to the household sector are the sum of the payments to the factors of production, including the payments to entrepreneurs. Money flows to firms are the revenue that firms receive when they sell the goods and services they produce. Revenue minus the costs of land, labor, and capital is profit. Profit represents the payment to entrepreneurs and other owners of corporations, partnerships, and sole proprietorships. Thus, household income is equal to business revenue—the value of goods and services produced.

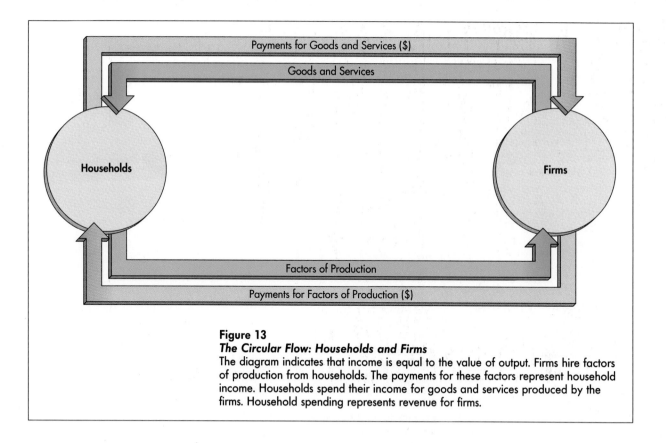

Figure 13
The Circular Flow: Households and Firms
The diagram indicates that income is equal to the value of output. Firms hire factors of production from households. The payments for these factors represent household income. Households spend their income for goods and services produced by the firms. Household spending represents revenue for firms.

5.b. Households, Firms, and Government

Let's now add government to the circular flow model. Government at the federal, state, and local levels interacts with both households and firms. Because the government employs factors of production to produce government services, households receive payments from the government in exchange for the services of the factors of production. The flow of factors of production from households to government is illustrated by the blue-green line flowing from the households to government in Figure 14. The flow of money from government to households is shown by the gold line flowing from government to households.

Households pay taxes to support the provision of government services, such as national defense, education, and police and fire protection. In a sense then, the household sector is purchasing goods and services from the government as well as from private businesses. The flow of tax payments from households and businesses to government is illustrated by the gold lines flowing from households and businesses to government, and the flow of government services to households and businesses is illustrated by the purple lines flowing from government.

The addition of government brings significant changes to the model. Households have an additional place to sell their resources for income, and businesses have an additional market for goods and services. The value of *private* production no longer equals the value of household

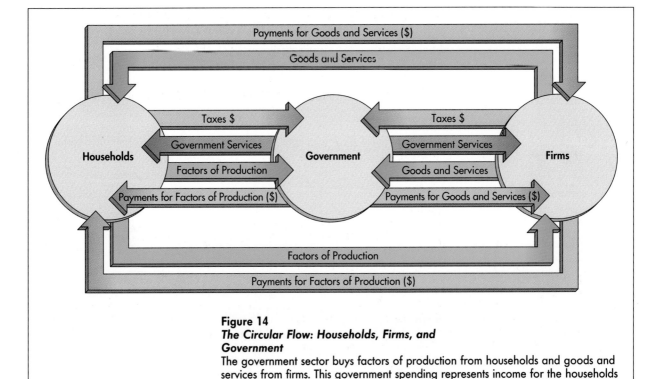

Figure 14
The Circular Flow: Households, Firms, and Government
The government sector buys factors of production from households and goods and services from firms. This government spending represents income for the households and revenue for the firms. The government uses the factors and goods and services to provide government services for households and firms. Households and firms pay taxes to the government to finance government expenditures.

income. Households receive income from government in exchange for providing factor services to government. The total value of output in the economy is equal to the total income received, but government is included as a source of income and a producer of services.

5.c. Households, Firms, Government, and the International Sector

The international sector must be included in order to properly describe the economy. Figure 15 includes foreign countries in the circular flow. To simplify the circular flow diagram, let's assume that households and government are not directly engaged in international trade and that only business firms are buying and selling goods and services across international borders. This assumption is not far from the truth for the industrial countries and for many developing countries.

A line labeled ''net exports'' connects firms and foreign countries in Figure 15, as well as a line labeled ''payments for net exports.'' Notice that neither line has an arrow indicating the direction of flow as do the other lines in the diagram. The reason is that net exports of the home country may be either positive (a trade surplus) or negative (a trade deficit). When net exports are positive, there is a net flow of goods from the firms of the home country to foreign countries and a net flow of money from foreign countries to the firms of the home country. When net exports are negative, the opposite occurs. A trade deficit involves net flows of goods from foreign countries to the firms of the home country and net money flows from the domestic firms to the foreign countries. If exports and imports are equal, net exports are zero because the value of exports is offset by the value of imports.

Figure 15 shows the complete circular flow linking the major sectors of the economy. This model is a simplified view of the world, but it highlights the important interrelationships. The value of output equals income, as always; but spending may be for foreign as well as domestic goods. Domestic firms may also produce for foreign as well as domestic consumption.

Figure 15
The Circular Flow: Households, Firms, Government, and Foreign Countries
The diagram assumes that households and government are not directly engaged in international trade. Domestic firms trade with firms in foreign countries. The flow of goods and services between countries is represented by the line labeled "net exports." Neither the net-exports line nor the line labeled "payments for net exports" has an arrow indicating the direction of the flow. The reason is that the flow can go from the home country to foreign countries or vice versa. When the domestic economy has positive net exports (a trade surplus), goods and services flow out of the domestic firms toward foreign countries and money payments flow from the foreign countries to the domestic firms. With negative net exports (a trade deficit), the reverse is true.

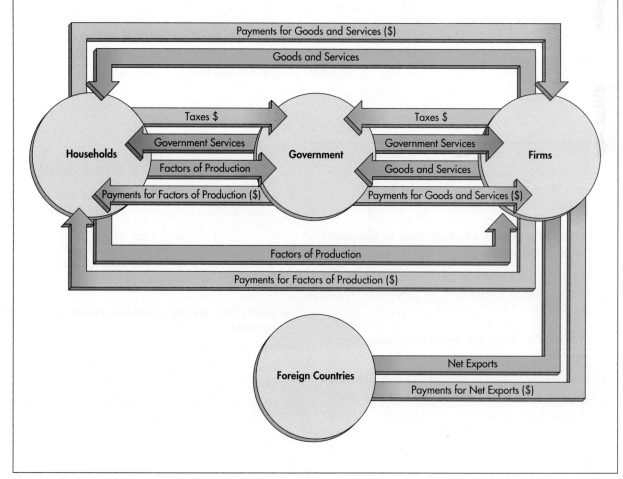

Some symbols of American culture are very popular with young Japanese. The Hard Rock Cafe and Tower Records do a lot of business in Japan, and the movie *Batman* sparked a craze there. Americans also purchase many products from the Japanese. Subway cars used in the New York subway system are made by Kawasaki of

Japan. Over the past 10 years, the United States has spent more on Japanese products than the Japanese have spent on U.S. products. Many observers are concerned that Japan has replaced the United States as the world's leading manufacturer, and that the U.S. economy has become largely a services economy.

RECAP

1. The circular flow diagram illustrates how the main sectors of the economy fit together.
2. The circular flow diagram shows that the value of output is equal to income.

SUMMARY

1. An economy is made up of households, business firms, government, and the international sector. Preview section

▼▲ **What is a household, and what is household income and spending?**

2. Household spending is called *consumption* and is the largest component of spending in the economy. § 1.b

▼▲ **What is a firm, and what is business spending?**

3. Businesses may be organized as sole proprietorships, partnerships, or corporations. § 2.a

4. Business investment spending fluctuates a great deal over time. § 2.e

▼▲ **What is the economic role of government?**

5. Monetary policy is the control of money and credit and is conducted by the Federal Reserve. § 3.a.2

6. Fiscal policy is the control of government spending and taxation and is determined by the president and Congress. § 3.a.2

▼▲ **How does the international sector affect the economy?**

7. The international trade of the United States occurs predominantly with the other industrial economies. § 4.a

8. Exports are products sold to the rest of the world. Imports are products bought from the rest of the world. § 4.a.2

9. Exports minus imports equals net exports. Positive net exports mean that exports are greater than imports and a trade surplus exists. Negative net exports mean that imports exceed exports and a trade deficit exists. § 4.b

▼▲ **How do the four sectors interact in the economy?**

10. The resources combined to produce goods and services are known as *factors of production*. They consist of land, labor, capital, and entrepreneurial ability. § 5.a

11. The total value of output produced by the factors of production is equal to the income received by the owners of the factors of production. § 5.a

KEY TERMS

household § 1
consumption § 1.b
business firm § 2
sole proprietorship § 2.a
partnership § 2.a
corporation § 2.a
multinational business § 2.a

venture capital § 2.d
investment § 2.e
monetary policy § 3.a.2
Federal Reserve § 3.a.2
fiscal policy § 3.a.2
budget surplus (deficit) § 3.b

imports § 4.a.2
exports § 4.a.2
trade surplus (deficit) § 4.b
net exports § 4.b
factors of production § 5.a
circular flow diagram § 5.a

EXERCISES

Basic Terms and Concepts

1. Is a family a household? Is a household a family?

2. What is the median value of the following series:
   4, 6, 8, 3, 9, 10, 10, 1, 5, 7, 12

3. Which sector (households, business, or government) spends the most? Which sector spends the least? Which sector, because of volatility, has importance greater than is warranted by its size?

4. What kind of economic policy is controlled by (a) the Federal Reserve, and (b) Congress and the president?

5. What microeconomic role does government play?

6. What does it mean if net exports are negative?

7. Why does the value of output always equal the income received by the resources that produced the output?

Extended Concepts

8. Total spending in the economy is equal to consumption plus investment plus government spending plus net exports. If households want to save and thus do not use all of their income for consumption, what will happen to total spending? Because total spending in the economy is equal to total income and output, what will happen to the output of goods and services if households want to save more?

9. People sometimes argue that imports should be limited by government policy. Suppose a government quota on the quantity of imports causes net exports to rise. Using the circular flow diagram as a guide, explain why total expenditures and national output may rise after the quota is imposed. Who is likely to benefit from the quota? Who will be hurt?

Student Entrepreneurs Find Road to Riches on Campus

Mark Frank went to Washington University in St. Louis to study finance and accounting. He hasn't graduated yet, but Mr. Frank already qualifies for an advanced degree in entrepreneurship.

While still a freshman, Mr. Frank noticed that fellow students were buying more [VCRs], microwave ovens and computers than ever. Figuring that they hated hauling everything home each summer, he quickly made a profit renting storage space in the basement of his house on campus.

With the earnings from this venture, Mr. Frank bought 100 pricey microwave ovens at a discount for about $90 each, then rented them to students for $95 per academic year. By the end of his second year in . . . business, Mr. Frank, now a senior, had made a profit of $18,000. . . .

Students today are used to having conveniences at home, such as microwave ovens, says Tony Nowak, director of residence life at Washington University. When they come to college, he adds, they want to duplicate these conveniences. . . .

Michael Stein's college business, a laundry service, began in 1984 with a freshman marketing-class project at Skidmore College in Saratoga Springs, N.Y. Mr. Stein initially planned to operate the service until the end of the semester. But it was so successful that he mailed letters to incoming freshmen offering to wash or dry-clean up to 20 pounds of clothes a week for about $300 per school year; the response was so good he eventually hired four employees. . . .

With an ear to the market, the student entrepreneurs find they can even turn campus gripes into good money. After hearing classmates moan about high prices at the university bookstore, Princeton University undergraduate Paul Wong and a couple of friends opened a discount bookstore two years ago.

The all-student staff helped spread word of the bargain prices. In its first year, the Princeton, N.J., store had sales of $125,000. With the recent addition of Gnomon Copy, a copy-shop franchise, Mr. Wong estimates this year's revenue will soar to $300,000.

Raising start-up money can be hard . . . , so student entrepreneurs often must be resourceful. For instance, Mr. Wong and his partners initially opened their bookstore as a book club. The collection of $7,000 in membership fees, coupled with the students' personal savings and credit from publishers, enabled the trio to lease a small store and purchase $80,000 of books. . . .

One of the major problems student entrepreneurs face is successfully balancing schoolwork and business. . . .

"I just squeaked by with graduation," says Harris Tessler, a recent graduate of Tulane University . . . and founder of Gourmet on the Go, a service that delivers dinners from eight New Orleans restaurants. . .

Working evenings, Mr. Tessler sublets — at a low rent — a business office that closes at 5 p.m. His employees, students clad in tuxedo pants and white waiter's jackets, deliver Italian, Chinese, French, Cajun and other types of food from 5:30 p.m. to 9:30 p.m. to downtown areas of New Orleans. More than half of the customers are students at Tulane and other nearby universities. Open since January, Gourmet on the Go is nearly breaking even, says Mr. Tessler. "Our start-up costs have been eliminated now. In the next three months, I expect to start making a couple thousand dollars a month. . ."

Not every student enterprise makes big money, of course, as James Apple and a colleague at Rhodes College in Memphis, Tenn., found out. Figuring that students need cheap furniture, the two went into business making futon beds.

The College Futon Factory started up at an initial cost of $100.

"I borrowed a saw from my dad and then bought a drill and a sander," says Mr. Apple, a recent Rhodes graduate. Evenings and weekends, the two students worked out of the basement of the Sigma Nu Fraternity house, where they spent an average of seven hours constructing each futon frame and mattress.

But after nine months in business, they sold . . . just 10 beds (at $169 to $199 each) and made a profit of only $500. Sales suffered, Mr. Apple says, because the group merely printed a few fliers and didn't focus enough attention on marketing.

Besides, "we spent a lot of money on refreshments during construction," Mr. Apple says. "Unfortunately, most of our profits went toward that." The company was disbanded last month because Mr. Apple graduated and his partner went abroad to study.

■ Source: Suzanne Alexander, "Student Entrepreneurs Find Road to Riches on Campus," *The Wall Street Journal*, June 23, 1989, p. B1.

Commentary

Entrepreneurial activity represents an important factor of production. Entrepreneurs perceive a business opportunity, initiate a response by organizing other factors of production, and attempt to profit from introducing a new good or service or from doing a better job than existing firms. This article presents some actual cases of entrepreneurial activity undertaken by college students who met with varying degrees of success.

Although the article focuses on the special case of the student entrepreneur, the experiences described are not too different from the overall experience of start-up companies described in the chapter. As with most start-up businesses, the ones described in the article began as small sole proprietorships or partnerships. Each of the student businesses had few, if any, employees, which is a common feature of new firms. Mark Frank's appliance storage and rental company and Harris Tessler's Gourmet on the Go provided innovative services; Michael Stein's laundry service provided an unmet need; Paul Wong and his friends saw a service that was not well met and responded with a lower-cost alternative. The experience of James Apple's futon factory, however, is probably more typical of many start-up firms, since most fail to survive.

Successful entrepreneurs introduce new goods and services that the public wants at a cost that makes their products both competitive and profitable. Through this activity, entrepreneurs bring new products to the market and expand the set of goods and services available to consumers (such as microwave rentals or laundry service on campus), or provide existing services (such as selling books) at lower costs. Firms that do not serve the interests of consumers will not survive for long because they incur losses instead of profits. The futon factory lasted for only nine months because the owners were not earning enough to reward their time and effort—they were not covering their opportunity costs. By closing their business, the owners made their labor services available for some other activity in which they would be more highly rewarded.

MACROECONOMICS

Macroeconomics gives you the big picture. It helps you to understand how individuals, business firms, and government units affect each other. In the past, many people concerned themselves only with economic events in their own neighborhood, town, state, or country. But now the "big picture" includes the entire planet. You could lose your job in a computer company because a manager in Tokyo decided to lower prices. Or you could find that your degree in Slavic languages has suddenly become very valuable because American companies are trying to expand their operations into Eastern Europe. Americans cannot afford to ignore the big picture.

▲▲▲▲▲▲▲▲▲▲▲▲▲▲▲

Macroeconomics gives you the big picture. It helps you to understand how individuals, business firms, and government units affect each other.

▼▼▼▼▼▼▼▼▼▼▼▼▼

*V*oters judge candidates on a number of measures—their party affiliation, their political philosophy, their record, their ethics, and their effectiveness. Many of these students waiting to vote for president probably cast their ballots with the hope of improving the financial well-being of themselves and their country. Yet casting a vote to improve the economy is not simply a matter of choosing a candidate who promises to cut taxes or increase government spending.

To make an intelligent choice, you will need to be able to answer questions like these: How can you tell how healthy the economy is? How do changes in gross national product and the inflation rate affect your prospects of getting a job or buying a home? Is a candidate's program of taxation and spending likely to spur economic growth or bring on a recession? Will tax revenues support expanded government spending on environmental programs?

These are difficult questions. But if you want to function effectively as a voter—or as a consumer, investor, businessperson, or manager—you'll need to be able to formulate your own answers to such questions. The study of macroeconomics can help you to reach such answers.

*C*hief among the players in this big picture are the world's governments. A government plays many roles, from providing national defense to issuing money to employing thousands of workers to enacting and administering income support pro-

*O*ne of the American government's responses to the Great Depression was to put more citizens on the government payroll; but even in the best of times, the government hires some citizens to help others. This ranger in Mt. Rushmore National Park has been hired by the government to deal with the summer influx of tourists, not to lower the unem-

grams to overseeing banking systems. Government policies can either work against or contribute to the kind of economic inequalities graphically demonstrated in this picture of Caracas, Venezuela. Even in the United States, homeless people sleep at the foot of the elegant Trump Tower. U.S. foreign aid and banking policies can affect poverty and prosperity in the Philippines or Latin America, just as domestic policy affects poverty and prosperity in Detroit or the Bronx. To influence government policies wisely, you need

an understanding of the interrelationships of macroeconomic variables.

One way that government policies affect citizens is through altering business cycles. Governments generally try to forge policies that keep the economy on an even keel, avoiding recession or wild inflation. Americans don't think much about inflation when it's in the 3 to 5 percent range, as it was in the late 1980s, but when it climbs near 20 percent, as it did in the early 1980s, inflation may be just as frightening as a recession.

ployment rate. In the 1930s, government agencies hired thousands of Americans to build, improve, and maintain parks, roads, and buildings. While the government can in such ways try to prevent and help to smooth out economic and employment downturns, no government has yet found a way to guarantee its citizens both a job and a reasonable living standard.

*A*mericans who feel their jobs are secure often don't concern themselves with economic trends and indicators. They are content to raise a family and pursue their version of the American dream. But no part of that dream is immune from changes in the national economy. The value of your home, that centerpiece of American life, can go

through boom and bust fluctuations totally out of your control. A planned move may turn into a nightmare if you can't find a buyer for your house. If you understand business cycles, you have a better chance of predicting and preparing for such changes.

*A*s Californians learned in 1989, not all disasters are linked to business cycles. The earthquake in October of that year shook the lives of everyone from Santa Cruz to Oakland. After the earthquake, government em-

ployees like these Oakland police provided protection for rescue workers and business owners, while other government workers began sorting out the mess and rebuilding. A prime

concern of state, local, and federal agencies was rebuilding the infrastructure—the highways, railways, and communication links—upon which almost all business depends.

*O*bviously macroeconomics helps us to understand prosperity as well as depressions and disasters. The United States, Japan, Canada, and other developed countries are huge productive machines, churning out goods and services to satisfy the needs of their own citizens and people around the world. Their cities bring together millions of people, offering good jobs and an attractive lifestyle. What causes such growth? Macroeconomics provides some answers, and also some warnings. As Dallas learned in the 1980s, it is

very difficult even for the most technologically advanced areas to sustain growth through the downturns of business cycles.

*O*ne reason for the economic growth of Japan and other Pacific rim nations has been their

reliance on high technology. Modern communications systems can move information from one point on the globe to any other point almost instantaneously, making possible the "global economy." Technological advances, like this Matsushita Electric robot, have helped

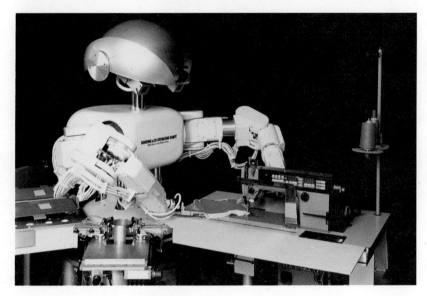

give Japanese goods their reputation for quality. This sewing robot lowered the company's production costs when it replaced a human worker. Do you share the fear of having your job taken over by a robot? In a healthy economy, workers replaced by machines can find jobs elsewhere, or they may be retrained to run the machines that replaced them. In a sluggish economy or a dying industry, however, displaced workers may find themselves on an unemployment line. Again, therefore, it is in the interest of every worker to understand macroeconomics and to identify trends in the economy and in specific industries before those trends change the worker's life.

▲▲▲▲▲▲▲▲▲▲▲▲▲▲

Does the United States as a whole benefit by allowing U.S. consumers to buy what they want, regardless of where goods are made?

▼▼▼▼▼▼▼▼▼▼▼▼▼▼

If robots enable a Japanese manufacturer to reduce its clothing production costs, is that good or bad for Americans? Such questions are not easy to answer, and they require the use of many different kinds of macroeconomic analysis. An American clothing manufacturer might view a Japanese competitor's robot as a threat. But an American company that supplies robot parts may expand production

and hire more workers as a result of the robot's success. Similarly, an American clothing store chain that buys goods made by the robot may pay less for those goods and therefore earn a larger profit. And if you're buying the robot-made clothing, its low price may allow you to spend more on American-made jewelry. It is, therefore, very difficult to generalize about how the success of a foreign company will affect American businesses and citizens.

*T*his South Korean ship being loaded in Seattle illustrates the various factors involved in international trade. The Hanjin ship brought goods from Korea that

American consumers will buy because they feel that the goods represent a better value at the price than comparable American goods. These purchases will frustrate some American manufacturers but please consumers. Now the ship is being loaded with American goods bound for the Far East. The loading process employs people in Seattle, and the sale of the goods not only yields profits for the manufacturers of the goods but also helps the American foreign trade deficit. This example highlights a question that we will explore in the chapters to come: Does the United States as a whole benefit by allowing U.S. consumers to buy what they want, regardless of where goods are made?

*A*lthough we read most about the competition between American and Japanese goods, every nation produces products that can compete internationally. Airlines around the world use the airplanes produced by the French Airbus assembly line in the photograph. The purchase of these planes is not a simple matter. Deals in huge industries like aircraft-making almost always involve political concerns as well as economic ones.

*F*orward-thinking companies like Procter & Gamble take ad-

vantage of the global marketplace. In the past, many American companies tried to expand overseas selling the same goods in the same ways as they sold them in the United States. More recently, American companies have learned that success overseas requires a sensitivity to the unique needs and desires of the overseas market. Procter & Gamble doesn't try to sell just one soap product everywhere. It tests its laundry products in the machines and the waters of the countries it wants to sell in. To sell its soap successfully in Peru, it needs to make sure that the Peruvian households that use the soap in Peruvian washing machines will be satisfied.

*I*n many ways, you are now closer to people in Amsterdam or Hong Kong than your grand-

parents were to people in a neighboring state. If you think that a global economy is just an abstract economic idea, look at the labels in your shirts and see how many countries are represented. Luckily, when you buy a shirt from Malaysia or shoes from Costa Rica, you don't have to pay in the local currency. But international trade does require a constant exchange of currencies—like American dollars, Swiss francs, German marks, and Singapore dollars.

*O*nce, most Americans, like these tourists at the Taj Mahal, viewed foreign countries solely as places to vacation. You might have wanted to visit India, but you did business at home. No businessperson can afford to think that way today. Multinational firms have operations and employees around the world. Foreign countries' goods, needs, and policies affect more and more Americans. Conditions in the United States affect business firms everywhere. As a citizen, an employee, a manager, or a business owner, you will need to understand the global economy.

▲▲▲▲▲▲▲▲▲▲▲▲▲▲▲▲▲▲

Macroeconomics is not just about the economic theories currently popular in Washington and on Wall Street. It is about your life.

▼▼▼▼▼▼▼▼▼▼▼▼▼▼▼▼▼

*A*s you explore the pages of this text, you will learn to use the tools of macroeconomics. You may decide to make economics a major part of your career, but even if this is the last economics book you ever read, you will find that the understanding you gain will enable you to choose a job, buy a house, or move across the country with more certainty that your choice is the right one. And when you go into the voting booth, you should be better able to choose a candidate whose views of America's long-term economic future are most consistent with your own. Macroeconomics is not just about the economic theories currently popular in Washington and on Wall Street. It is about your life. ◆

This text presents all the key concepts of economics. In addition it explains how people use these concepts—in business, in government, and in ordinary households. In both the world of theory and the real world of application, knowing the relationships of ideas is crucial. No one can move about in either world without knowing the pathways that relationships form. When studying, it helps a great deal to have some picture of these pathways. That is why a map to show you the important conceptual and real-world pathways of macroeconomics is presented on the following pages. Using this map will help you

- pull together and manage a large subject
- learn the process of economic thinking
- improve your own critical thinking.

TAKE MORE THAN ONE VIEW

As you work through the chapters of this book, you will examine in close-up each particular concept. Yet to understand the material, and to get a feel for how economists think, you need to have a second point of view too—an overview. Keeping yourself "up above it" at the same time you are "down in it" will help you remember what you are reading much better and also help you understand and use the concepts you learn more easily. Taking more than one view of your subject has another benefit; it is an ingredient of good critical thinking.

MAKE YOUR OWN CONNECTIONS

To understand economics you need to keep track of how one thing changes in response to another, to see relationships more than fixed ideas. And this requires another ingredient of critical thinking, a sense of independence. With the idea map you can get around on your own (just as different classes may follow different sequences of chapters). Use it to get a feel for how ideas connect and then make your own connections as you read, actively asking yourself questions that cause you to evaluate, structure, and personalize the ideas. Work toward finding your own pathways, from idea to idea and from idea to reality.

USE THIS TEXT AS A SYSTEM

The other features of the text also show pathways, but they do it in a verbal way instead of the visual way the map does. The *Fundamental Questions* point to main issues and help you categorize details, examples, and theories accordingly. Colors in the *graphs* help you classify curves and see relationships to data in the *tables*. The *Recaps* reinforce overarching ideas; they orient you before you go on to the next big section. (Using them, in fact, is a lot like pausing to look at a map.) The *system of referencing* sections and headings by number will help you group concepts and also keep track of what level of ideas you are working with. If you use the idea map and the other features of the text, this text can be more than an authoritative source of information—it can be a system for comprehension. ▶

Making Sense of Macroeconomics

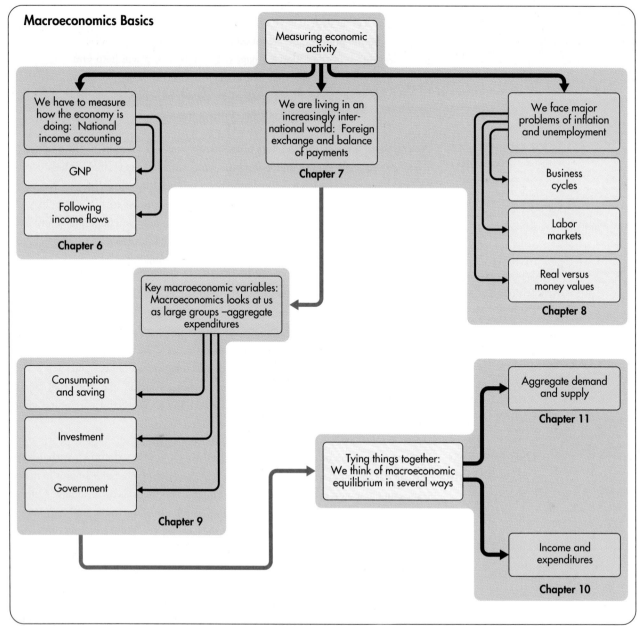

Introduction to the Price System

What is economics and why is it important to you?

Chapter 1

Peaple have to make choices and weigh costs

Chapter 2

Our choices are reflected in markets: supply and demand

Chapter 3

What happens when markets don't or can't work: Market failures and interventions

Chapter 4

We are all particpants in the economic system: Households, business, government, international

Chapter 5

Macroeconomics Basics

Measuring economic activity

We have to measure how the economy is doing: National income accounting

GNP

Following income flows

Chapter 6

We are living in an increasingly inter-national world: Foreign exchange and balance of payments

Chapter 7

We face major problems of inflation and unemployment

Business cycles

Labor markets

Real versus money values

Chapter 8

Key macroeconomic variables: Macroeconomics looks at us as large groups –aggregate expenditures

Consumption and saving

Investment

Government

Chapter 9

Tying things together: We think of macroeconomic equilibrium in several ways

Aggregate demand and supply

Chapter 11

Income and expenditures

Chapter 10

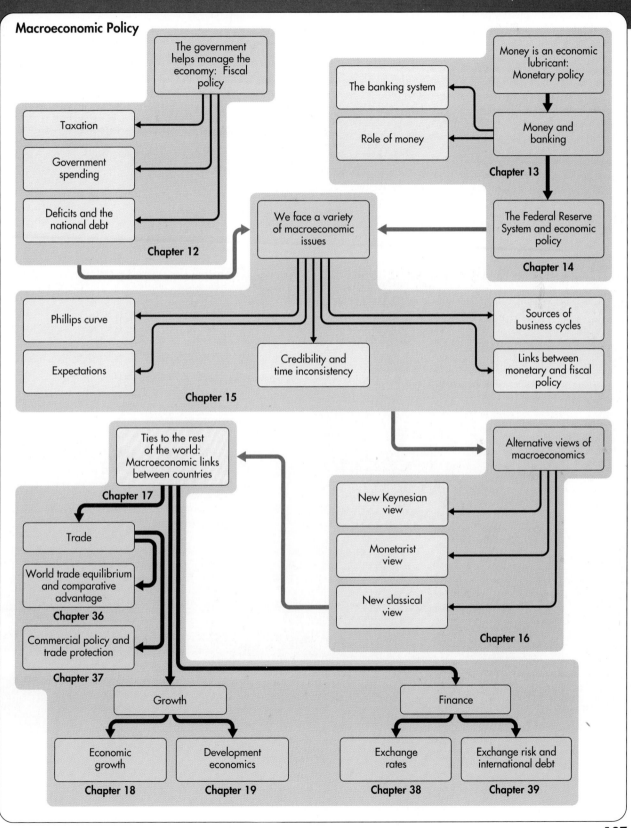

Macroeconomic Policy

The government helps manage the economy: Fiscal policy

Taxation

Government spending

Deficits and the national debt

Chapter 12

Money is an economic lubricant: Monetary policy

The banking system

Role of money

Money and banking

Chapter 13

The Federal Reserve System and economic policy

Chapter 14

We face a variety of macroeconomic issues

Phillips curve

Expectations

Credibility and time inconsistency

Sources of business cycles

Links between monetary and fiscal policy

Chapter 15

Ties to the rest of the world: Macroeconomic links between countries

Chapter 17

Trade

World trade equilibrium and comparative advantage

Chapter 36

Commercial policy and trade protection

Chapter 37

Alternative views of macroeconomics

New Keynesian view

Monetarist view

New classical view

Chapter 16

Growth

Finance

Economic growth

Development economics

Exchange rates

Exchange risk and international debt

Chapter 18

Chapter 19

Chapter 38

Chapter 39

137

Macroeconomic Basics

6

National Income Accounting

1. How is the total output of an economy measured?

2. Who produces the nation's goods and services?

3. Who purchases the goods and services produced?

4. Who receives the income from the production of goods and services?

5. What is the difference between nominal and real GNP?

6. What is a price index?

PREVIEW   The Japanese economy grew at an average rate of 4.4 percent per year from 1970 to 1988. This compares with an average rate of 2.8 percent per year in the United States over the same period. Still, the U.S. economy is twice as large as the Japanese economy and larger than the economies of the fifty largest developing countries combined. The *size* of an economy cannot be compared across countries without common standards of measurement. National income accounting provides these standards. Economists use this system to evaluate the economic condition of a country and to compare conditions across time and countries.

A national economy is a complex arrangement of many different buyers and sellers—of households, businesses, and government units—and of their interactions with the rest of the world. To assess the economic health of a country or to compare the performance of an economy from year to year, economists must be able to measure national output and national income. Without these data, policymakers cannot evaluate their economic policies. For instance, national income fell in the United States in 1980, 1981, and again in 1982. This drop in national income was accompanied by widespread job loss and a general decline in the economic health of the country. As this information became known, political and economic debate centered on economic policies, on what should be done to stimulate the economy. Without national income statistics, policymakers would not have known there were problems, let alone how to go about fixing them.

In this chapter we discuss gross national product, national income, and other measures of national output and income, and national income accounting, the system used to calculate them. National income accounting provides a framework for discussing macroeconomics. That framework is based on the idea that national expenditures equal national income. Figure 1 reproduces the circular flow diagram you saw in Chapter 5. The lines connecting the various sectors of the economy represent flows of goods and services, and money expenditures (income). National income accounting is the process of counting the value of the flows between sectors, and then summing them to find the total value of economic activity in an economy.

Figure 1
The Circular Flow: Households, Firms, Government, and Foreign Countries
The value of national output equals expenditures and income. If the domestic economy has positive net exports (a trade surplus), goods and services flow out of the domestic firms toward the foreign countries and money payments flow from the foreign countries to the domestic firms. If the domestic economy has negative net exports (a trade deficit), just the reverse is true.

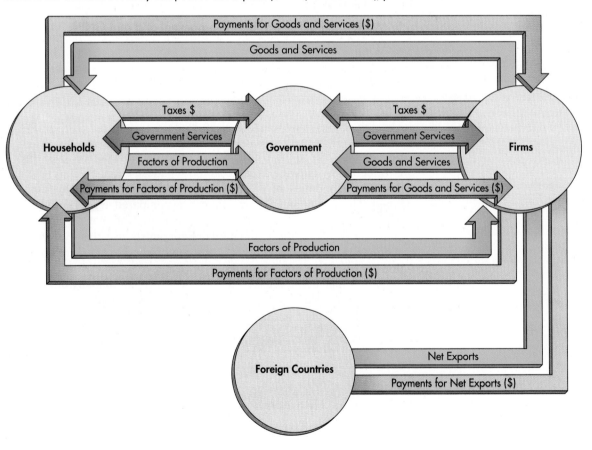

MEASURES OF OUTPUT AND INCOME

national income accounting:
the process that summarizes the level of production in an economy over a specific period of time, typically a year

▼

How is the total output of an economy measured?

▲

National income accounting measures the output of an entire economy as well as the flows between sectors. It summarizes the level of production in an economy over a specific period of time, typically a year. In practice, the process *estimates* the amount of activity that occurs. It is beyond the capability of government officials to count every transaction that takes place in a modern economy. Still, national income accounting generates useful and fairly accurate measures of economic activity in most countries, especially wealthy industrial countries that have comprehensive accounting systems.

1.a. Gross National Product

Modern economies produce an amazing variety of goods and services. To measure an economy's total production, economists combine the quantities of oranges, golf balls, automobiles, and all the other goods and services produced, into a single measure of output. Of course simply adding up the number of things produced—the number of oranges, golf balls, and automobiles—does not reveal the *value* of what is being produced. If a nation produces 1 million more oranges and 1 million fewer automobiles this year than it did last year, the total number of things produced remains the same. But because automobiles are much more valuable than oranges, the value of output has dropped substantially. Prices reflect the value of goods and services in the market, so economists use the money value of things to create a measure of total output, a measure that is more meaningful than the sum of units produced.

The most common measure of a nation's output is GNP.

gross national product (GNP):
the market value of all final goods and services produced in a year by domestic resources

The most common measure of a nation's output is gross national product. **Gross national product (GNP)** is the market value of all final goods and services produced in a year by domestic resources. A closer look at three parts of this definition—*market value, final goods and services,* and *produced in a year*—will make clear what the GNP does and does not include.

Market value The *market value* of final goods and services is their value at market price. The process of determining market value is straightforward where prices are known and transactions are observable. However, there are cases where prices are not known and transactions are not observable. For instance, illegal drug transactions are not reported to the government, which means they are not included in GNP statistics. In fact almost any activity that is not traded in a market is not included. For example, production that takes place in households is not counted (see Economic Insight: "The Value of Homemaker Services"), nor are barter and cash transactions in the underground economy. For instance, if a lawyer has a sick dog and a veterinarian needs some legal advice, by trading services each can avoid taxation on the income that would have been reported had they sold their services to each other. If the value of a transaction is not recorded as taxable income, it generally does not appear in the GNP. There are some exceptions, however. Contributions toward GNP are estimated for *in-kind wages*, nonmonetary compensation like room and board. GNP values also are assigned to the output consumed by a producer—for example, the home consumption of crops by a farmer.

One way GNP underestimates the total value of a nation's output is by failing to record non-market production. A prime example is the work homemakers do. Of course, people are not paid for their work around the house, so it is difficult to measure the value of their output. But notice that we say *difficult,* not impossible. Economists can use several methods to assign value to homemaker services.

One is an opportunity cost approach. This approach measures the value of a homemaker's services by the forgone market salary the homemaker could have earned if he or she worked full-time outside the home. The rationale is that society loses the output the homemaker would have produced in the market job in order to gain the output the homemaker produces in the home.

Another alternative is to estimate what it would cost to hire workers to produce the goods and services that the homemaker produces. For example, what would it cost to hire someone to prepare meals, iron, clean, and take care of the household? It has been estimated that the average homemaker spends almost 8 hours a day, 7 days a week, on household work. This amounts to over 50 hours a week. At a rate of $10 an hour, the value of the homemaker's services is over $500 a week.

Whichever method we use, two things are clear. The value of homemaker services to the household and the economy is substantial. And by failing to account for those services, the GNP substantially underestimates the value of the nation's output.

Final goods and services   The second part of the definition of GNP limits the measure to *final goods and services*, the goods and services available to the ultimate consumer. This limitation avoids double-counting. Suppose a retail store sells a shirt to a consumer for $20. The value of the shirt in the GNP is $20. But the shirt is made of cotton that has been raised by a farmer, woven at a mill, and cut and sewn by a manufacturer. What would happen if we counted the value of the shirt at each of these stages of the production process? We would overstate the market value of the shirt.

intermediate good:
a good that is used in the production of final goods and services

Intermediate goods are goods that are used in the production of a final product. The stages of production of the $20 shirt are shown in Figure 2. The value-of-output axis measures the value of the product at each stage. The cotton produced by the farmer sells for $1. The cloth woven by the textile mill sells for $5. The shirt manufacturer sells the shirt wholesale to the retail store for $12. The retail store sells the shirt—the final good—to the ultimate consumer for $20.

Remember that GNP is based on the market value of final goods and services. In our example, the market value of the shirt is $20. That price already includes the value of the intermediate goods that were used to produce the shirt. If we add to it the value of output at every stage of production, we would be counting the value of the intermediate goods twice, and we would be overstating the GNP.

value added:
the difference between the value of output and the value of the intermediate goods used in the production of that output

It is possible to compute GNP by computing the value added at each stage of production. In fact, value added is used in many countries as a base for taxation. **Value added** is the difference between the value of output and the value of the intermediate goods used in the production of that output. In Figure 2, the value added by each stage of production is listed at the right. The farmer adds $1 to the value of the shirt. The mill takes the cotton worth $1 and produces cloth worth $5, adding $4 to the value of the

Figure 2
Stages of Production and Value Added in Shirt Manufacturing
A cotton farmer sells cotton to a textile mill for $1, adding $1 to the value of the final shirt. The textile mill sells cloth to a shirt manufacturer for $5, adding $4 to the value of the final shirt. The manufacturer sells the shirt wholesale to the retail store for $12, adding $7 to the value of the final shirt. The retail store sells the final shirt to a consumer for $20, adding $8 to the value of the final shirt. The sum of the prices received at each stage of production equals $38, which is greater than the price of the final shirt. The sum of the value added at each stage of production equals $20, which equals the market value of the shirt.

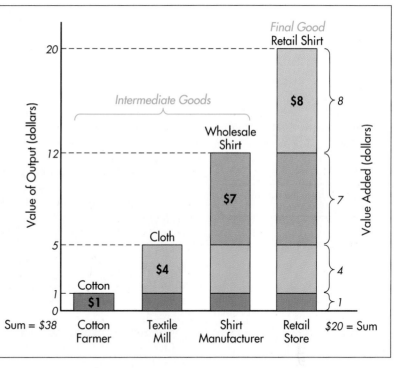

shirt. The manufacturer uses $5 worth of cloth to produce a shirt it sells for $12; so the manufacturer adds $7 to the shirt's value. Finally, the retail store adds $8 to the value of the shirt: it pays the manufacturer $12 for the shirt and sells it to the consumer for $20. The sum of the value added at each stage of production is $20. The total value added, then, is equal to the market value of the final product.

Economists can compute GNP using two methods: the final goods and services method uses the market value of the final good or service; the value-added method uses the value added at each stage of production. Both methods count the value of intermediate goods only once. This is an important distinction: GNP is not based on the market value of *all* goods and services, but on the market value of all *final* goods and services.

Produced in a year   GNP measures the value of output *produced in a year*. The value of goods produced last year is counted in last year's GNP; the value of goods produced this year is counted in this year's GNP. The year of production, not the year of sale, determines allocation to GNP. Although the value of last year's goods is not counted in this year's GNP, the value of services involved in the sale is. This year's GNP does not include the value of a house built last year, but it does include the value of the real-estate broker's fee; it does not include the value of a used car, but it does include the income earned by the used car dealer in the sale of that car.

To determine the value of goods produced in a year but not sold in that year, economists calculate changes in inventory. **Inventory** is a firm's stock of unsold goods. If a shirt that is produced this year remains on the

inventory:
the stock of unsold goods held by a firm

retail store's shelf at the end of the year, it increases the value of the store's inventory. A $20 shirt increases that value by $20. Changes in inventory allow economists to count goods in the year in which they are produced whether or not they are sold.

Changes in inventory can be planned or unplanned. A store may want a cushion above expected sales (*planned inventory*), or it may not be able to sell all the goods it expected to sell when it placed the order (*unplanned inventory*).

Who produces the nation's goods and services?

1.a.1. GNP as Output   GNP is a measure of a nation's total output in a year. Remember that economists divide the economy into four sectors: household, businesses, government, and the international sector. Figure 1 shows how the total value of economic activity equals the sum of the output produced in each sector. Figure 3 indicates where the U.S. GNP was produced in 1989.[1]

Not unexpectedly in a capitalist country, privately owned businesses account for the largest percentage of output: in the United States, 85 percent of the GNP is produced by private firms. Government produces 10.3 percent of the GNP, households 4 percent, and the international sector just .7 percent.

You may be wondering why production in the international sector is included in the U.S. GNP. After all, the U.S. GNP is supposed to reflect the output of domestic resources—that is, factors of production owned by U.S. residents. However, U.S. residents can own factors of production in a foreign country (a U.S. auto parts manufacturer, for example, may own a plant in Germany or Mexico). The value of output produced by these factors is part of the U.S. GNP; the value of output from other factors is not. For instance, the profit the U.S. owner of a foreign plant earns from that plant is counted in the U.S. GNP as the value of the owner's foreign production. But the value of foreign laborers and resources owned by foreign residents is counted in the foreign country's GNP. Another measure of a nation's output, *gross domestic product (GDP),* omits production by foreign factors. We discuss GDP in Section 1.b.5.

---

[1]Due to rounding, percents and dollar amounts in the next three figures will not add exactly to the totals given.

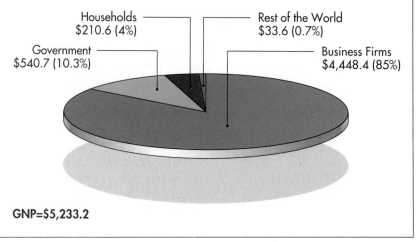

Figure 3
U.S. Gross National Product by Sector, 1989 (billion dollars)
Business firms produce 85 percent of the U.S. GNP. Government produces 10.3 percent; households, 4 percent; the rest of the world, .7 percent. Source: Data from *Economic Report of the President 1990* (Washington, D.C.: U.S. Government Printing Office, 1990).

Households
$210.6 (4%)

Rest of the World
$33.6 (0.7%)

Government
$540.7 (10.3%)

Business Firms
$4,448.4 (85%)

GNP=$5,233.2

GNP is the value of final goods and services produced by domestic households, businesses, government, and domestically owned resources located in the rest of the world.

Figure 3 defines GNP in terms of output: GNP is the value of final goods and services produced by domestic households, businesses, government units, and domestically owned resources located in the rest of the world.

1.a.2. GNP as Expenditures The circular flow in Figure 1 shows not only the output of goods and services from each sector, but also the payment for goods and services. Here we look at GNP in terms of what each sector pays for the goods and services it purchases.

The dollar value of total expenditures—the sum of the amount each sector spends on final goods and services—equals the dollar value of output. In Chapter 5 you learned that household spending is called *consumption*. Households spend their income on goods and services to be consumed. Business spending is called *investment*. Investment is spending on capital goods that will be used to produce other goods and services. The two other components of total spending are *government spending* and *net exports*. Net exports are the value of goods and services exported to the rest of the world minus the value of goods and services imported from the rest of the world.

$$GNP = consumption + investment + government\ spending +\\ net\ exports$$

Or, in the shorter form commonly used by economists,

$$GNP = C + I + G + X$$

where X is net exports.

Figure 4 shows the U.S. GNP in terms of total expenditures. Consumption, or household spending, accounts for 66.3 percent of national expenditures. Government spending represents 19.8 percent of expenditures; and business investment, 14.8 percent. Net exports are negative ($-.9$ percent), which means that imports exceeded exports in 1989. *Imports* are the foreign goods and services purchased by U.S. consumers, businesses, and government units. To determine total national expenditures on domestic output, the value of imports must be subtracted from total expenditures.

$GNP = C + I + G + X$

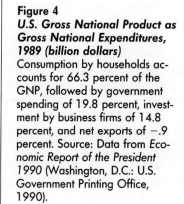

Who purchases the goods and services produced?

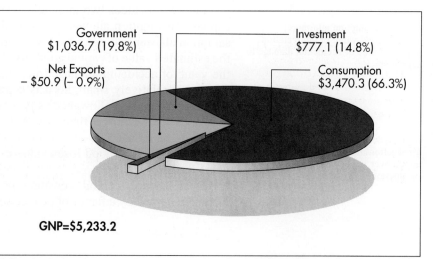

Figure 4
U.S. Gross National Product as Gross National Expenditures, 1989 (billion dollars)
Consumption by households accounts for 66.3 percent of the GNP, followed by government spending of 19.8 percent, investment by business firms of 14.8 percent, and net exports of −.9 percent. Source: Data from *Economic Report of the President 1990* (Washington, D.C.: U.S. Government Printing Office, 1990).

Government $1,036.7 (19.8%)

Investment $777.1 (14.8%)

Net Exports − $50.9 (− 0.9%)

Consumption $3,470.3 (66.3%)

GNP=$5,233.2

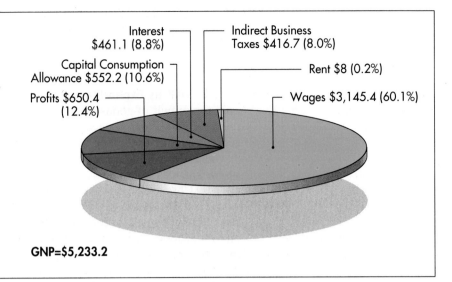

Figure 5
U.S. Gross National Product as Income Received, 1989 (billion dollars)
The largest component of income is wages, at 60.1 percent of the GNP. Profits represent 12.4 percent, interest 8.8 percent, and rent .2 percent. Capital consumption allowance (10.6 percent) and indirect business taxes (8 percent) are not income received but still must be added to the GNP to yield national income. Source: Data from *Economic Report of the President 1990* (Washington, D.C.: U.S. Government Printing Office, 1990).

Interest $461.1 (8.8%)

Indirect Business Taxes $416.7 (8.0%)

Capital Consumption Allowance $552.2 (10.6%)

Rent $8 (0.2%)

Profits $650.4 (12.4%)

Wages $3,145.4 (60.1%)

GNP=$5,233.2

Who receives the income from the production of goods and services?

capital consumption allowance:
the estimated value of depreciation plus the value of accidental damage to capital stock

depreciation:
a reduction in the value of capital goods over time due to their use in production

1.a.3. GNP as Income The total value of output can be calculated by adding up the expenditures of each sector. And because one sector's expenditures are another's income, the total value of output also can be computed by adding up the income of all sectors.

Business firms use factors of production to produce goods and services. Remember that the income earned by factors of production is classified as wages, interest, rent, and profits. *Wages* are payments to labor, including fringe benefits, social security contributions, and retirement payments. *Interest* is the net interest paid by businesses to households plus the net interest received from foreigners (the interest they pay us minus the interest we pay them). *Rent* is income earned from selling the use of real property (houses, shops, farms). Finally, *profits* are the sum of corporate profits plus proprietors' income (income from sole proprietorships and partnerships).

Figure 5 shows the U.S. GNP in terms of income. Notice that wages account for 60.1 percent of the GNP. Interest and profits account for 8.8 percent and 12.4 percent of the GNP, respectively. Rent (0.2 percent) is very small in comparison.

Figure 5 includes two income categories that we have not discussed: capital consumption allowance and indirect business taxes. **Capital consumption allowance** is not a money payment to a factor of production; it is the estimated value of capital goods used up or worn out in production plus the value of accidental damage to capital goods. The value of accidental damage is relatively small, so it is common to hear economists refer to capital consumption allowance as *depreciation*. Machines and other capital goods wear out over time. The reduction in the value of capital stock due to its being used up or worn out over time is called **depreciation**. A depreciating capital good loses value each year of its useful life until its value is zero.

Even though capital consumption allowance does not represent income received by a factor of production, it must be accounted for in the

GNP as income. Otherwise the value of the GNP as output would be higher than the value of the GNP as income. Depreciation is a kind of resource payment, part of the total payment to the owners of capital. All of the income categories—wages, interest, rent, profits, and capital consumption allowance—are expenses incurred in the production of output.

indirect business tax:
a tax that is collected by businesses for a government agency

The last item in Figure 5 is indirect business taxes. **Indirect business taxes**, like capital consumption allowances, are not payments to a factor of production. They are taxes collected by businesses that then are turned over to the government. Both excise taxes and sales taxes are forms of indirect business taxes.

For example, suppose a motel room in Florida costs $80 a night. A consumer would be charged $90. Of that $90, the motel receives $80 as the value of the service sold; the other $10 is an excise tax. The motel cannot keep the $10; it must turn it over to the state government. (In effect, the motel is acting as the government's tax collector.) The consumer spends $90; the motel earns $80. To balance expenditures and income, we have to allocate the $10 difference to indirect business taxes.

GNP as income is equal to the sum of wages, interest, rent, profits, capital consumption allowance, and indirect business taxes.

To summarize, GNP as income includes the four payments to the factors of production: wages, interest, rent, and profits. These income items represent expenses incurred in the production of GNP. Along with these payments are two nonincome items: capital consumption allowance and indirect business taxes.

$$GNP = wages + interest + rent + profits +$$
$$capital\ consumption\ allowance + indirect\ business\ taxes$$

GNP is the total value of output produced in a year, the total value of expenditures made to purchase that output, and the total value of income received by the factors of production. Because all three are measures of the same thing—GNP—all must be equal.

1.b. Other Measures of Output and Income

GNP is the most common measure of a nation's output, but it is not the only measure. Economists rely on a number of others in analyzing the performance of components of an economy.

net national product (NNP):
gross national product minus capital consumption allowance

1.b.1. Net National Product Net national product (**NNP**) equals GNP minus capital consumption allowance. NNP measures the value of goods and services produced in a year less the value of depreciation. Because NNP includes only net additions to a nation's capital, it is a better measure of the expansion or contraction of current output than is GNP.

Remember how we defined GNP in terms of expenditures in Section 1.a.2:

$$GNP = consumption + investment + government\ spending$$
$$+ net\ exports$$

gross investment:
total investment, including investment expenditures required to replace capital goods consumed in current production

The investment measure in GNP is called **gross investment**. Gross investment is total investment, which includes investment expenditures required to replace capital goods consumed in current production. NNP does not include investment expenditures required to replace worn-out capital

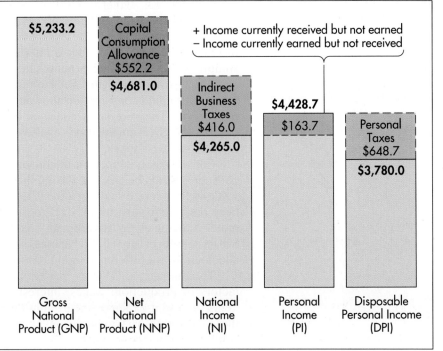

Figure 6
U.S. National Income Accounts, 1989 (billion dollars)
Gross national product minus capital consumption allowance equals net national product. Net national product minus indirect business taxes equals national income. National income plus income currently received but not earned (transfer payments, personal interest, dividend income) minus income currently earned but not received (corporate profits, net interest, social security taxes) equals personal income. Personal income minus personal taxes equals disposable personal income. Source: Data from *Economic Report of the President 1990* (Washington, D.C.: U.S. Government Printing Office, 1990).

net investment:
gross investment minus capital consumption allowance

goods; it includes only net investment. **Net investment** is equal to gross investment minus capital consumption allowance. Net investment measures business spending over and above that required to replace worn-out capital goods.

NNP = consumption + (investment − capital consumption allowance) + government spending + net exports

Figure 6 shows the standard measures of output and income, known as national income *accounts,* in the United States in 1989. The figure begins with the GNP and then shows the calculations necessary to obtain the NNP and other measures of national output. In 1989, the U.S. NNP was $4,681 billion. This means that the U.S. economy produced well over $4 trillion worth of goods and services above those required to replace capital stock that had depreciated. Over $552 billion in capital was "worn out" in 1989.

national income (NI):
net national product minus indirect business taxes

1.b.2. National Income National income (NI) equals the NNP minus indirect business taxes, plus or minus a couple of other small adjustments. NI captures the costs of the factors of production used in producing output. Remember that GNP includes two nonincome expense items: capital consumption allowance and indirect business taxes (Section 1.a.3). Subtracting both of these items from the GNP leaves the income payments that actually go to resources.

Because the NNP equals the GNP minus capital consumption allowance, we can subtract indirect business taxes from the NNP to find NI, as shown in Figure 6. This measure helps economists analyze how the costs of (or payments received by) resources change.

personal income (PI):
national income plus income currently received but not earned, minus income currently earned but not received

transfer payment:
income transferred from one citizen, who is earning income, to another citizen, who may not be

1.b.3. Personal Income Personal income (PI) is national income adjusted for income that is received but not earned in the current year and income that is earned but not received in the current year. Social security and welfare benefits are examples of income that is received but not earned in the current year. They are called **transfer payments**. Transfer payments represent income transferred from one citizen, who is earning income, to another citizen, who may not be. The government transfers income by taxing one group of citizens and using the tax payments to fund the income for another group. An example of income that is currently earned but not received is profits that are retained by a corporation to finance current needs rather than paid out to stockholders. Another is social security (FICA) taxes, which are deducted from workers' paychecks.

disposable personal income (DPI):
personal income minus personal taxes

1.b.4. Disposable Personal Income Disposable personal income (DPI) equals personal income minus personal taxes—income taxes, excise and real estate taxes on personal property, and other personal taxes. DPI is the income that individuals have at their disposal for spending or saving.

gross domestic product (GDP):
gross national product minus net factor income from abroad

1.b.5. Gross Domestic Product Gross domestic product (GDP) measures the purely domestic output of a country. GNP is the total output produced by and total income received by a nation's residents, including income earned from foreign factors of production. The difference between GNP and GDP is *net factor income from abroad,* income received from other nations by domestic residents less income payments made to foreign residents. GDP, then, equals GNP minus net factor income from abroad. It is the market value of the final goods and services produced by factors of production located in the home country.

Table 1 lists GNP and GDP for several countries. In Morocco and the United States, for example, GNP exceeds GDP because the factor income received from abroad exceeds the factor income paid out to foreign countries. In Honduras and South Africa, GDP exceeds GNP because more is paid to foreign factor owners than is received from abroad by domestic factor owners. Some countries report only GDP data, and international organizations often use GDP to measure the output of nations.

Table 1   GNP and GDP for Selected Countries, 1988

Country (and Currency Units)	GNP	GDP
Canada (billion dollars)	580	599
Costa Rica (billion colones)	332	358
Honduras (million lempiras)	8,333	8,799
Kenya (billion shillings)	146	153
Morocco (billion dirhams)	186	180
Philippines (billion pesos)	824	827
South Africa (billion rand)	191	201
Switzerland (billion francs)	283	269
United Kingdom (billion pounds)	468	462
United States (billion dollars)	4,881	4,847

Source: International Monetary Fund, *International Financial Statistics,* February 1990. Used by permission.

How are the sales that occur in this open air market in Moscow counted in Soviet Union national income? The Soviet Union (and other Eastern European nations) has traditionally reported *net material product* (NMP) rather than GNP as a measure of the national income and output. The main difference between NMP and GNP is that NMP does not include a capital consumption allowance or the value added in service industries like medical care. The value of the masks sold in Ismailova Park is counted in NMP.

RECAP

1. Gross national product (GNP) is the market value of all final goods and services produced in an economy in a year.

2. GNP can be calculated by summing the market value of all final goods and services produced in a year, by summing the value added at each stage of production, by adding total expenditures on goods and services (GNP = consumption + investment + government spending + net exports), and by adjusting the total income earned in the production of goods and services (GNP = wages + interest + rent + profits) for depreciation and indirect business taxes.

3. Other measures of output and income include net national product (NNP), national income (NI), personal income (PI), disposable personal income (DPI), and gross domestic product (GDP):

NNP = GNP − capital consumption allowance

NI = NNP − indirect business taxes

PI = NI − income earned but not received + income received but not earned

DPI = PI − personal taxes

GDP = GNP − net factor income from abroad

GNP = consumption + investment + government spending + net exports

GDP = GNP − net factor income from abroad

NNP = GNP − capital consumption allowance

NI = NNP − indirect business taxes

PI = NI − income earned but not received + income received but not earned

DPI = PI − personal taxes

2. NOMINAL AND REAL MEASURES

GNP is the market value of all final goods and services produced in an economy in a year. Value is measured in money terms, so the U.S. GNP is reported in dollars, the German GNP in marks, the Mexican GNP in pesos. Market value is the product of two elements: the money price and the quantity produced.

2.a. Nominal and Real GNP

nominal GNP:
a measure of national output based on the current prices of goods and services

real GNP:
a measure of the quantity of goods and services produced, adjusted for price changes

▼
What is the difference between nominal and real GNP?
▲

Nominal GNP measures output in terms of its current dollar value. **Real GNP** is adjusted for changing price levels. In 1980, the U.S. GNP was $2,732 billion; in 1987, it was $4,526.7 billion—an increase of 66 percent. Does this mean that the United States produced 66 percent more goods and services in 1987 than it did in 1980? If the numbers reported are for nominal GNP, we cannot be sure. Nominal GNP cannot tell us whether the economy produced more goods and services because nominal GNP changes when prices change *and* when quantity changes.

Real GNP measures output in constant prices. This allows economists to identify what portion of a change in GNP is due to a change in prices and what portion is due to a change in quantity. Real GNP measures the quantity of goods and services produced after adjusting for price changes. In 1980, real GNP in the United States was $3,187.1 billion; in 1987, it was $3,847 billion, an increase of just 21 percent. The 66 percent increase in nominal GNP in large part reflects increased prices, not increased output.

Since we prefer more goods and services to higher prices, it is better to have nominal GNP rise because of higher output than higher prices. We want nominal GNP to increase as a result of an increase in real GNP.

Here is a simple example that illustrates the difference between nominal GNP and real GNP. Suppose a hypothetical economy produces just three goods: oranges, coconuts, and pizzas. The dollar value of output in three different years is listed in the table in Figure 7.

As shown in Figure 7, in year 1, 100 oranges were produced at $.50 per orange, 300 coconuts at $1 per coconut, and 2,000 pizzas at $8 per pizza. The total dollar value of output in year 1 is $16,350. In year 2, prices are constant at the year-1 values, but the quantity of each good has increased by 10 percent. The dollar value of output in year 2 is $17,985, 10 percent higher than the value of output in year 1. In year 3, the quantity of each good is back at the year-1 level, but prices have increased by 10 percent. Oranges now cost $.55, coconuts $1.10, and pizzas $8.80. The dollar value of output in year 3 is $17,985.

Notice that in years 2 and 3, the dollar value of output ($17,985) is 10 percent higher than it was in year 1. But there is a difference here. In year 2, the increase in output is due entirely to an increase in the production of the three goods. In year 3, the increase is due entirely to an increase in the prices of the goods.

Because prices did not change between years 1 and 2, the increase in total output is an increase in nominal GNP as well as real output, or real GNP. In years 1 and 3, the actual quantities produced did not change, which means that real GNP was constant; only nominal GNP was higher, a product only of higher prices.

2.b. Price Indexes

The total dollar value of output or income is equal to price multiplied by the quantity of goods and services produced:

$$\text{Dollar value of output} = \text{price} \times \text{quantity}$$

▼ What is a price index? ▲

By dividing the dollar value of output by price, you can determine the quantity of goods and services produced:

$$\text{Quantity} = \frac{\text{dollar value of output}}{\text{price}}$$

In terms of GNP, the equation becomes

$$Real\ GNP = \frac{nominal\ GNP}{price\ level}$$

$$\text{Real GNP} = \frac{\text{nominal GNP}}{\text{price level}}$$

price index:
a measure of the average price level in an economy

In macroeconomics, a **price index** measures the average level of prices in an economy and shows how prices, on average, have changed. Prices of individual goods can rise and fall relative to one another, but a price index shows the general trend in prices across the economy.

base year:
the year against which other years are measured

2.b.1. Base Year The example in Figure 7 provides a simple introduction to price indexes. The first step is to pick a **base year**, the year against which other years are measured. Any year can serve as the base year. Suppose we pick year 1 in Figure 7. The value of the price index in year 1, the base year, is 100. This simply means that prices in year 1 are 100 percent of prices in year 1 (100 percent of 1 is 1). In the example, year-2 prices are equal to year-1 prices, so the price index also is equal to 100 in year 2. In year 3, every price has risen 10 percent relative to the base-year (year-1) prices, so the price index is 10 percent higher in year 3, or 110. The value of the price index in any particular year indicates how prices have changed relative to the base year. A value of 110 indicates that prices are 110 percent of base-year prices, or that the average price level has increased 10 percent.

The value of the price index in any particular year indicates how prices have changed relative to the base year.

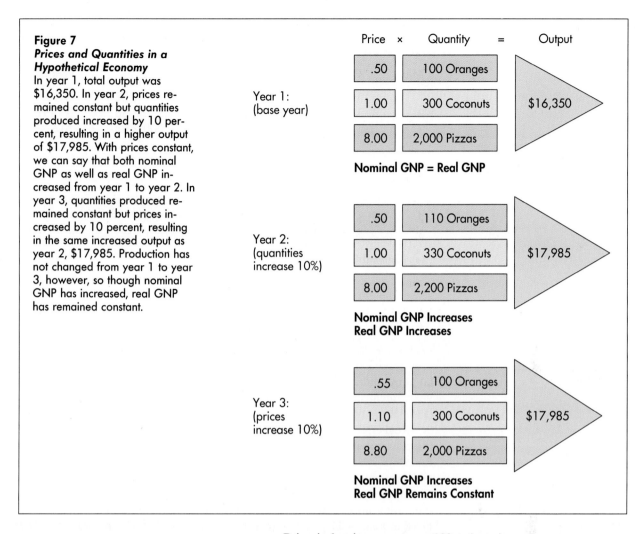

Figure 7
Prices and Quantities in a Hypothetical Economy
In year 1, total output was $16,350. In year 2, prices remained constant but quantities produced increased by 10 percent, resulting in a higher output of $17,985. With prices constant, we can say that both nominal GNP as well as real GNP increased from year 1 to year 2. In year 3, quantities produced remained constant but prices increased by 10 percent, resulting in the same increased output as year 2, $17,985. Production has not changed from year 1 to year 3, however, so though nominal GNP has increased, real GNP has remained constant.

Price × Quantity = Output

Year 1:
(base year)

.50	100 Oranges
1.00	300 Coconuts
8.00	2,000 Pizzas

$16,350

Nominal GNP = Real GNP

Year 2:
(quantities
increase 10%)

.50	110 Oranges
1.00	330 Coconuts
8.00	2,200 Pizzas

$17,985

**Nominal GNP Increases
Real GNP Increases**

Year 3:
(prices
increase 10%)

.55	100 Oranges
1.10	300 Coconuts
8.80	2,000 Pizzas

$17,985

**Nominal GNP Increases
Real GNP Remains Constant**

Price index in any year = 100 + (or −)
percentage change in prices from the base year

In Figure 7, prices in year 3 are 10 percent higher than the base-year prices, so the price index in year 3 is equal to 110 (100 + 10).

Because nominal GNP is measured using current prices in each year and real GNP is measured using base-year prices, the ratio between nominal GNP and real GNP multiplied by 100 is equal to the price index:

$$\frac{\text{Nominal GNP}}{\text{Real GNP}} \times 100 = \text{price index}$$

And the ratio between nominal GNP and the price index multiplied by 100 is equal to real GNP:

$$\frac{\text{Nominal GNP}}{\text{Price index}} \times 100 = \text{real GNP}$$

Table 2 shows the relationship between nominal and real GNP for the hypothetical three-good economy. Part (a) shows how real GNP is calcu-

Table 2   Real and Nominal GNP

(a) Base year price × current year quantity = real GNP

Year	Oranges		Coconuts		Pizzas		Real GNP
1	100 × $.50	+	300 × $1	+	2,000 × $8	=	$16,350
2	110 × $.50	+	330 × $1	+	2,200 × $8	=	$17,985
3	100 × $.50	+	300 × $1	+	2,000 × $8	=	$16,350

(b) Nominal GNP/Real GNP × 100 = price index

Year	
1	$16,350/$16,350 × 100 = 1 × 100 = 100
2	$17,985/$17,985 × 100 = 1 × 100 = 100
3	$17,985/$16,350 × 100 = 1.1 × 100 = 110

(c) Nominal GNP/Price Index × 100 = real GNP

Year	
1	$16,350/100 × 100 = $16,350
2	$17,985/100 × 100 = $17,985
3	$17,985/110 × 100 = $16,350

lated by multiplying the base year prices by the quantities produced each year. Because year 1 is the base year, the nominal GNP shown in Figure 7 ($16,350) is equal to the real GNP.

Real GNP and nominal GNP are always equal in the base year because the prices in the base year and the current prices are the same. In year 2, real GNP is $17,985, or 10 percent higher than year 1. This increase in real GNP reflects a 10 percent increase in the quantities of goods produced. Finally, in year 3, real GNP is the same as it was in year 1 because the quantities produced in year 3 equal those produced in year 1. Nominal GNP increased in year 3 (see Figure 7) simply because prices increased. Once we evaluate year-3 production at base-year prices, we see that real output has not changed compared to the base year.

Part (b) of Table 2 shows how the ratio of nominal GNP to real GNP, multiplied by 100, equals the price index. Remember that the price index always equals 100 in the base year, year 1 in our example. The price index also equals 100 in year 2 and any other year in which prices are equal to base-year prices. The price index equals 110 in year 3 because nominal GNP ($17,985) is 10 percent higher than real GNP ($16,350).

Part (c) of the table shows how to use nominal GNP and the price index to find real GNP. For each year, nominal GNP is divided by the price index; then the quotient is multiplied by 100.

The three parts of Table 2 are based on the same idea. In the real world, both prices and quantities change. To identify real changes in a nation's output, economists have to hold constant the effect of price changes. Increases in nominal GNP may signal nothing more than price increases rather than increases in the amount of goods and services produced.

2.b.2. Types of Price Indexes   The price of a single good is easy to determine. But how do economists determine a single measure of the prices of the millions of goods and services produced in an economy? They construct price indexes. Not all prices rise or fall at the same time or by the same amount. This is why there are several measures of the price level in an economy.

The price index given by the ratio of nominal GNP to real GNP is the **implicit GNP deflator**, a measure of prices across the economy that reflects all of the categories of goods and services included in GNP. The implicit GNP deflator is a very broad measure. Economists use other price indexes to analyze how prices change in more specific categories of goods and services.

Probably the best-known price index is the **consumer price index (CPI)**. The CPI measures the average price of consumer goods and services that a typical household purchases. The CPI is a narrower measure than the implicit GNP deflator because it includes fewer items. However, because of the relevance of consumer prices to the standard of living, news reports on price changes in the economy typically focus on consumer price changes. In addition, many labor contracts include provisions that raise wages as the CPI goes up. Social security payments also are tied to increases in the CPI. These increases are called **cost of living adjustments (COLAs)**, because they are supposed to keep nominal income rising along with the cost of items purchased by the typical household.

The **producer price index (PPI)** measures average prices received by producers. At one time this price index was known as the *wholesale price index (WPI)*. Because the PPI measures price changes at an earlier stage of production than the CPI, it can indicate a coming change in the CPI. If producer input costs are rising, we can expect the price of goods produced to go up as well.

Figure 8 illustrates how the three different measures of prices changed between 1975 and 1989. Notice that the PPI is much more volatile than

implicit GNP deflator:
a broad measure of the prices of goods and services included in the gross national product

consumer price index (CPI):
a measure of the average price of goods and services purchased by the typical household

cost of living adjustment (COLA):
an increase in wages that is designed to match increases in prices of items purchased by the typical household

producer price index (PPI):
a measure of average prices received by producers

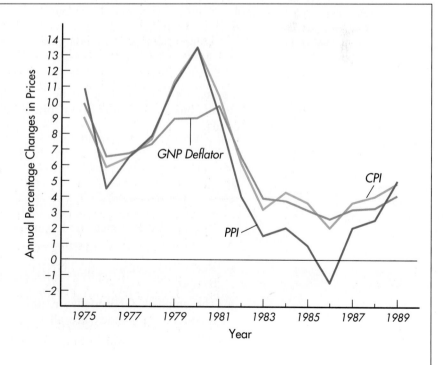

Figure 8
The Implicit GNP Deflator, the CPI, and the PPI
The graph plots the annual percentage change in the implicit GNP deflator, the consumer price index (CPI), and the producer price index (PPI). The implicit GNP deflator is the ratio of nominal GNP to real GNP. The CPI measures the average price of consumer goods and services that a typical household purchases. The PPI measures the average price received by producers; it is the most variable of the three because fluctuations in equilibrium prices of intermediate goods are much greater than for final goods. Source: Various pages of the *Economic Report of the President 1990* (Washington, D.C.: U.S. Government Printing Office, 1990).

The Consumer Price Index

The CPI is calculated by the Department of Commerce using price surveys taken in 91 American cities. Although the CPI often is called a *cost of living index*, it is not. The CPI represents the cost of a fixed market basket of goods purchased by a hypothetical household, not a real one.

In fact, no household consumes the market basket used to estimate the CPI. As relative prices change, households alter their spending patterns. But the CPI market basket changes only every 10 years. This is due in part to the high cost of surveying the public to determine spending patterns. Then, too, individual households have different tastes and spend a different portion of their budgets on the various components of household spending (housing, food, clothing, transportation, medical care). Only a household that spends exactly the same portion of its income on each item counted in the CPI would find the CPI representative of its cost of living.

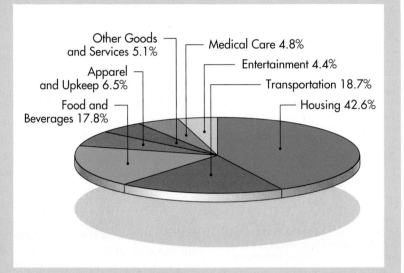

The current CPI market basket is based on spending patterns in the period between 1982 and 1984. The Department of Commerce surveys spending in seven major areas. The figure shows the areas and the percentage of the typical household budget devoted to each area. If you kept track of your spending over the course of several months, you probably would find that you spend much more than the "typical" household on some items and much less on others. In other words, the CPI is not a very good measure of *your* cost of living.

■ Source: Data from Bureau of Labor Statistics

the implicit GNP deflator or the CPI. This is because there are smaller fluctuations in the equilibrium prices of final goods than intermediate goods.

RECAP

1. Nominal GNP is measured using current dollars.
2. Real GNP is measured using constant base-year dollars.
3. Real GNP equals nominal GNP divided by the price index, multiplied by 100.
4. The implicit GNP deflator, the consumer price index, and the producer price index are all measures of the level of prices in an economy.

3. FLOWS OF INCOME AND EXPENDITURES

GNP is both a measure of total expenditures on final goods and services and a measure of the total income earned in the production of those goods and services. The idea that total expenditures equal total income is clearly illustrated in Figure 1.

The figure links the four sectors of the economy: households, firms, government, and foreign countries. The arrows between the sectors indicate the direction of the flows. Gold arrows with dollar signs represent money flows; blue-green arrows without dollar signs represent flows of real goods and services. The money flows are both income and expenditures. For instance, household expenditures for goods and services from business firms are represented by the gold arrow at the top of the diagram. Household income from firms is represented by the gold arrow flowing from firms to households at the bottom of the diagram. Because one sector's expenditures represent another sector's income, the total expenditures on goods and services must be the same as the total income from selling goods and services, and those must both be equal to the total value of the goods and services produced.

RECAP

1. Total spending on final goods and services equals the total income received in producing those goods and services.

2. The circular flow model shows that one sector's expenditures represent the income of other sectors.

SUMMARY

▼▲ **How is the total output of an economy measured?**

1. National income accounting is the system economists use to measure both the output of an economy and the flows between sectors of that economy. § 1

2. Gross national product (GNP) is the market value of all final goods and services produced in a year by domestic resources. § 1.a

3. GNP also equals the value added at each stage of production. § 1.a

▼▲ **Who produces the nation's goods and services?**

4. GNP as output equals the sum of the output of households, business firms, government, and the international sector. Business firms produce 85 percent of the U.S. GNP. § 1.a.1

▼▲ **Who purchases the goods and services produced?**

5. GNP as expenditures equals the sum of consumption plus investment plus government spending plus net exports. In the United States, consumption accounts for roughly two-thirds of total expenditures. § 1.a.2

▼▲ **Who receives the income from the production of goods and services?**

6. GNP as income equals the sum of wages, interest, rent, profits, capital consumption allowance, and indirect business taxes. Wages account for 60.1 percent of the total. § 1.a.3

7. Capital consumption allowance is the estimated value of depreciation plus the value of accidental damage to capital stock. § 1.a.3

8. Other measures of national output include net national product (NNP), national income (NI), personal income (PI), disposable personal income (DPI), and gross domestic product (GDP). § 1.b

▼▲ **What is the difference between nominal and real GNP?**

9. Nominal GNP measures output in terms of its current dollar value; real GNP measures output in terms of base-year dollar values. § 2.a

▼▲ **What is a price index?**

10. A price index measures the average level of prices across an economy. § 2.b

11. The implicit GNP deflator is a measure of the prices of all the goods and services included in the GNP. § 2.b.2

12. The consumer price index (CPI) measures the average price of goods and services consumed by the typical household. § 2.b.2

13. The producer price index (PPI) measures average prices received by producers (wholesale prices). § 2.b.2

14. Total expenditures on final goods and services equal total income. § 3

KEY TERMS

national income accounting § 1

gross national product (GNP) § 1.a

intermediate good § 1.a

value added § 1.a

inventory § 1.a

capital consumption allowance § 1.a.3

depreciation § 1.a.3

indirect business tax § 1.a.3

net national product (NNP) § 1.b.1

gross investment § 1.b.1

net investment § 1.b.1

national income (NI) § 1.b.2

personal income (PI) § 1.b.3

transfer payment § 1.b.3

disposable personal income (DPI) § 1.b.4

gross domestic product (GDP) § 1.b.5

nominal GNP § 2.a

real GNP § 2.a

price index § 2.b

base year § 2.b.1

implicit GNP deflator § 2.b.2

consumer price index (CPI) § 2.b.2

cost of living adjustment (COLA) § 2.b.2

producer price index (PPI) § 2.b.2

EXERCISES

Basic Terms and Concepts

1. The table lists the stages required in the production of a personal computer. What is the value of the computer in the GNP?

Stage	Value Added
Components manufacture	$50
Assembly	$250
Wholesaler	$500
Retailer	$1,500

2. What is the difference between GNP and each of the following?

   a. Net national product

   b. National income

   c. Personal income

   d. Disposable personal income

   e. Gross domestic product

3. In a given year, nominal GNP equals $3,500 billion and real GNP equals $2,800 billion.

   a. What is the value of the price index in the base year?

   b. How much has the price level changed since the base year?

   c. What is the value of the implicit GNP deflator?

4. Why do total expenditures on final goods and services equal total income in the economy?

Extended Concepts

5. Why don't we measure national output by simply counting the total number of goods and services produced each year?

6. Why isn't the CPI a useful measure of *your* cost of living?

Shaky Numbers: U.S. Statistics Mills Grind Out More Data That Are Then Revised

... This year, the Labor Department has repeatedly issued reports on the sluggish growth of the nation's employment — only to say "never mind" within a month. In April, the growth in new jobs was estimated at a mere 117,000; after the statistics mills had gathered more information, however, the figure was nearly doubled to 206,000. Similarly, the May total was raised from 101,000 initially to 207,000, and June's from 180,000 to 250,000.

There's more. While Wall Street bet billions, while the Federal Reserve set policy and while corporate boards examined their buying and borrowing plans, the government revised so many statistics so significantly that the forecasts of many economists flipped in only a few weeks. . .

It turns out, for instance, that retail sales, which account for a third of the nation's economic activity, didn't decline in May as the government earlier reported. They *grew* — at a healthy rate. And new orders for big-ticket items such as cars rose 1.4% instead of creeping up at the anemic 0.3% rate reported previously.

The spate of revisions "almost makes a mockery out of trying to interpret what's going on," says Gary Ciminero, the chief economist at Fleet/Norstar Financial Group in Providence, R.I.

All of this confusion culminated [Tuesday] in a new report on the bottom-line performance of the economy, the nation's total output of goods and services. The annual rate of growth in gross national product was revised upward a full percentage

point, to 2.7% from 1.7%. The second quarter makeover spelled the difference between an economy that some experts thought on the brink of recession and one capable of meeting the Bush administration's rosy 1989 growth forecast. . .

The statistics concern rank-and-file citizens as well as economists. Half the U.S. population lives in a household where someone's income is affected by the consumer price index. Some federal grants for community projects are tied to regional unemployment rates. The Labor Department's earnings data are used to index hundreds of billions of dollars of defense contracts.

The Labor Department dislikes the epidemic of big revisions. "I certainly hope it doesn't continue," says Janet Norwood, the commissioner of labor statistics. "It's not unusual from time to time to have a revision as we've had for the past few months, but if it continued over a very long period, it would be a real cause for concern."

Does she know why the revisions are so wide? "I really do not," she says.

Private economists and some government officials offer some theories. The recent run of big revisions at this critical stage in the business cycle, they suggest, may stem partly from shifts in the economy and from growing difficulties in collecting information. . . .

. . . Statistical agencies, like virtually every office in the government, have been squeezed in the federal budget crunch. Some officials complain that the widening gap between

government and private salaries has made it difficult to attract top-notch Ph.D. economists to analyze the data — and every statistic involves some degree of judgment and analysis beyond merely crunching numbers.

For the most part, the government is frank about the shortcomings of its economic numbers, issuing them with warning labels printed plainly on the front of most reports. One widely reported series of statistics, which measures the monthly change in sales of new homes, reported a huge 5.5% increase in June. But in the fine print, the authors of the report cautioned that the margin of error was so great that it was actually "unclear whether there was an increase or decrease." Indeed, a revision issued [this week] said there hadn't been any increase in June at all.

While the Fed and the financial markets scrutinize the latest economic data, people such as Martin Zimmerman, the chief economist at Ford Motor Co., use the numbers to formulate long-term forecasts that guide the auto maker's major business decisions. Mr. Zimmerman says the revisions so far have helped confirm a view he held all along — that the economy was slowing, but not to the point of a recession. But he notes: "In theory, you're trying to find out what the future is going to be like. That's difficult when the past keeps changing."

■ Source: "Shaky Numbers: U.S. Statistics Mills Grind Out More Data That Are Then Revised," *The Wall Street Journal*, August 31, 1989, p. 1.

Commentary

In this chapter we learn about different measures of the performance of the economy. The actual compilation of these statistics is a formidable task in any country, especially in one with an economy as large and complex as that of the United States. This article demonstrates how difficult it is to measure accurately an economy's performance and provides some insight into the manner in which government economists and statisticians attempt to interpret what is occurring. The impression we are left with is that the collection and reporting of economic data, at least in terms of presenting a picture of recent performance, is more of an art than a science.

Most macroeconomic data are estimates. It is simply impossible to count every new final good and service produced in a year to measure GNP exactly. Instead, government economists attempt to construct reasonable estimates of GNP by sampling small amounts of output in the many different sectors of the economy. For example, veterinary services and pet services provided by pet stores are included in GNP. However, the government does not know the exact number and value of services actually provided by every veterinarian and pet store in a given year. The value of pet services is estimated by the number of purebred dogs reported to be in the United States by the American Kennel Club multiplied by a consumer price index for pet services. As the number of dogs increases, the value of pet services in GNP also increases.

As the article indicates, much rides on these short-run estimates of GNP, employment, and prices. The cost of inaccurate data may be large and is borne by many sectors of the economy. For example, it is easy to imagine a case in which managers of a firm, learning that growth in retail sales is sluggish, react accordingly by not hiring new workers or by not undertaking new investment projects. If the retail sales report is too pessimistic, the profits of this firm will be adversely affected. Large and frequent revisions of data may also contribute to volatility in the stock market, where prices reflect the latest economic news. An initial rosy report on GNP growth may drive stock prices up, while the revised, less optimistic data may drive stock prices down again. Finally, government agencies that attempt to stabilize movements of GNP and prices depend upon good data to guide their decisions. Flawed statistics severely limit their ability to make good policy. For example, an inaccurate report on recent movements in prices may prompt the Federal Reserve to undertake policies that it would not choose if more accurate data were available.

Given the difficulties in obtaining accurate data on very recent movements in the economy, a wise course of action is to be cautious when interpreting short-run economic changes. The article indicates that many revisions occur as the government receives new information that alters original estimates. As a result, it is wise to observe several months or even several quarters of a year before concluding that a major change in the economy indicated by the "latest" data is in fact under way.

7

An Introduction to the Foreign Exchange Market and the Balance of Payments

1. How do individuals of one nation trade money with individuals of another nation?

2. How do changes in exchange rates affect international trade?

3. How do nations record their transactions with the rest of the world?

PREVIEW International transactions have grown rapidly in recent years as the economies of the world have become increasingly interrelated. Improvements in transportation and communication, and global markets for goods and services, have created a community of world economies. Products made in one country sell in the world market, where they compete against products from other nations. Europeans purchase stocks listed on the New York Stock Exchange. Americans purchase bonds issued in Japan.

Different countries use different monies. When goods and services are exchanged across international borders, national monies also are traded. To make buying and selling decisions in the global marketplace, people must be able to compare prices across countries, to compare prices quoted in Japanese yen with those quoted in Mexican pesos. This chapter begins with a look at how national monies are priced and traded in the foreign exchange market.

In Chapter 6, you learned that gross national product equals the sum of consumption, investment, government spending, and net exports $(GNP = C + I + G + X)$. Net exports (X) are the measure of a nation's transactions with other countries, a principal link between a nation's GNP and developments in the rest of the world.

1. THE FOREIGN EXCHANGE MARKET

foreign exchange:
foreign currency and bank deposits
that are denominated in foreign
money

foreign exchange market:
a global market in which people trade
one currency for another

▼
How do individuals of one
nation trade money with
individuals of another
nation?
▲

Foreign exchange is foreign money, including paper money and bank deposits like checking accounts that are denominated in foreign currency. When someone with U.S. dollars wants to trade those dollars for Japanese yen, the trade takes place in the **foreign exchange market**, a global market in which people trade one currency for another. Many financial markets are located in a specific geographic location. For instance, the New York Stock Exchange is a specific location in New York City where stocks are bought and sold. The Commodity Exchange is a specific location in New York City where contracts to deliver agricultural and metal commodities are bought and sold. The foreign exchange market is not in a single geographic location. Trading occurs all over the world by telephone. Most of the activity involves large banks in New York, London, and other financial centers. A foreign exchange trader at the First Chicago Bank in Chicago can buy or sell currencies with a trader at Barclays Bank in London by calling the other trader on the telephone.

Only tourism and a few other transactions in the foreign exchange market involve the actual movement of currency. The great majority involve the buying and selling of bank deposits denominated in foreign currency. A bank deposit can be a checking account that a firm or individual writes checks against to make payments to others, or it may be a savings account that exists for a specific amount of time with no check-writing privileges but the owner of the deposit earns interest. Currency notes, like dollar bills, are relatively unimportant. When a large corporation or a government buys foreign currency, it buys a bank deposit denominated in the foreign currency. Still, all exchanges in the market require that monies have a price.

Figure 1
Exchange Rates
The first two columns list U.S. dollars per foreign currency, or how much one unit of foreign currency is worth in U.S. dollars. On February 21, you could get about 83 American cents for one Canadian dollar. The second two columns list foreign currency per U.S. dollars, or how much one U.S. dollar is worth in foreign currency. On the same day, you could get about 1.19 Canadian dollars for one U.S. dollar. Source: *Wall Street Journal*, February 22, 1990, p. C12.

EXCHANGE RATES

Wednesday, February 21, 1990
The New York foreign exchange selling rates below apply to trading among banks in amounts of $1 million and more, as quoted at 3 p.m. Eastern time by Bankers Trust Co. Retail transactions provide fewer units of foreign currency per dollar.

Country	U.S. $ equiv. Wed.	U.S. $ equiv. Tues.	Currency per U.S. $ Wed.	Currency per U.S. $ Tues.
Argentina (Austral) ...	.0002381	.0002381	4200.09	4200.09
Australia (Dollar)	.7665	.7590	1.3046	1.3175
Austria (Schilling)	.08511	.08505	11.75	11.76
Bahrain (Dinar)	2.6522	2.6522	.3771	.3771
Belgium (Franc)				
Commercial rate	.02872	.02867	34.82	34.88
Financial rate	.02872	.02867	34.82	34.88
Brazil (Cruzado)	.03749	.03732	26.68	26.80
Britain (Pound)	1.7130	1.7110	.5838	.5845
30-Day Forward	1.7044	1.7023	.5867	.5874
90-Day Forward	1.6862	1.6840	.5930	.5938
180-Day Forward ...	1.6605	1.6582	.6022	.6031
Canada (Dollar)	.8342	.8330	1.1987	1.2005
30-Day Forward	.8313	.8300	1.2030	1.2048
90-Day Forward	.8250	.8236	1.2121	1.2142
180-Day Forward ...	.8174	.8163	1.2234	1.2251
Chile (Official rate) ...	.003439	.003439	290.80	290.80
China (Yuan)	.211752	.211752	4.7225	4.7225
Colombia (Peso)	.002252	.002252	444.09	444.09
Denmark (Krone)	.1555	.1552	6.4315	6.4440
Ecuador (Sucre)				
Floating rate	.001458	.001458	686.07	686.07
Finland (Markka)	.25419	.25361	3.9340	3.9430
France (Franc)	.17646	.17635	5.6670	5.6704
30-Day Forward	.17616	.17602	5.6767	5.6811
90-Day Forward	.17535	.17510	5.7030	5.7109
180-Day Forward ...	.17402			5.7549

The foreign exchange market is a global market. Traders in the Bank of Tokyo trading room shown here are making deals with other traders all over the world by communicating through electronic mail and telephone.

1.a. Exchange Rates

An **exchange rate** is the price of one country's money in terms of another country's money. Exchange rates are needed to compare prices quoted in two different currencies. Suppose a shirt that has been manufactured in Canada sells for 20 U.S. dollars in Seattle, Washington, and for 25 Canadian dollars in Vancouver, British Columbia. Where would you get the better buy? Unless you know the exchange rate between U.S. and Canadian dollars, you can't tell. The exchange rate allows you to convert the foreign currency price into its domestic currency equivalent, which then can be compared to the domestic price.

Figure 1 reproduces a table of exchange rates that appeared in *The Wall Street Journal*. The table lists exchange rates for two days, Tuesday, February 20, 1990, and Wednesday, February 21, 1990. The rates are quoted in U.S. dollars per foreign currency in the first two columns, and foreign currency per U.S. dollar in the last two columns. For instance, on Wednesday, the Canadian dollar was selling for $.8342, or a little more than 83 U.S. cents. The same day, the U.S. dollar was selling for 1.1987 Canadian dollars (1 U.S. dollar would buy 1.1987 Canadian dollars).

If you know the price in U.S. dollars of a currency, you can find the price of the U.S. dollar in that currency by taking the reciprocal. To find the reciprocal of a number, write it as a fraction and then turn the fraction upside down. Let's say that 1 British pound sells for 2 U.S. dollars. In fraction form, 2 is ⅔₁. The reciprocal of ⅔₁ is ½, or .5. So 1 U.S. dollar sells for .5 British pounds. The figure shows that on Wednesday, the actual dollar price of the pound was 1.7130. The reciprocal of 1.7130 is .5838 (1/1.7130), which was the pound price of 1 dollar that day.

Find the reciprocal of a number by writing it as a fraction and then turning the fraction upside down. In other words, make the numerator the denominator and the denominator the numerator.

Look at the top of Figure 1. Notice that the exchange rates are the values quoted at a specific time, 3:00 P.M. Eastern time. The time is listed because exchange rates fluctuate throughout the day as the supply of and demand for currencies change. At some other time of day, the exchange rates could have had different values than those listed in the figure. Notice also that the exchange rates quoted are based on large trades ($1 million or more) in what is essentially a wholesale market. The smaller the quantity of foreign currency purchased, the higher the price. A British tourist traveling in the United States would find the pound price of a dollar to be greater than .5838 at the front desk of a hotel.

Let's go back to comparing the price of the Canadian shirt in Seattle and Vancouver. The symbol for the U.S. dollar is $. The symbol for the Canadian dollar is C$. (Table 1 lists the symbols for a number of currencies.) The shirt sells for $20 in Seattle and C$25 in Vancouver. Suppose the exchange rate between the U.S. dollar and the Canadian dollar is .8. This means that C$1 costs .8 U.S. dollars, or 80 U.S. cents. To find the domestic currency value of a foreign currency price, multiply the foreign currency price times the exchange rate:

Domestic currency value = foreign currency price × exchange rate

In our example, the U.S. dollar is the domestic currency:

$$\text{U.S. dollar value} = \text{C}\$25 \times .8$$
$$= \$20.$$

If we multiply the price of the shirt in Canadian dollars (C$25) by the exchange rate (.8), we find the U.S. dollar value ($20). After adjusting for the exchange rate, then, we can see that the shirt sells for the same price when the price is measured in a single currency.

1.b. Exchange Rate Changes and International Trade

How do changes in exchange rates affect international trade?

Because exchange rates determine the domestic currency value of foreign goods, changes in those rates affect the demand for and supply of goods traded internationally. Suppose the price of the shirt in Seattle and Vancouver remains the same, but the exchange rate changes from .8 to .9 U.S. dollars per Canadian dollar. What happens? The U.S. dollar price of the shirt in Vancouver increases. At the new rate, the shirt that sells for C$25 in Vancouver costs a U.S. buyer $22.50 (C$25 × .9).

A rise in the value of a currency is called *appreciation*. In our example, as the exchange rate moves from $.8 = C$1 to $.9 = C$1, the Canadian dollar appreciates against the U.S. dollar. As a country's currency appreciates, international demand for its products falls, ceteris paribus.

A currency appreciates in value when its value rises in relation to another currency.

Suppose the exchange rate in our example moves from $.8 = C$1 to $.7 = C$1. Now the shirt that sells for C$25 in Vancouver costs a U.S. buyer $17.50 (C$25 × .7). In this case the Canadian dollar has *depreciated* in value relative to the U.S. dollar. As a country's currency depreciates, its goods sell for lower prices in other countries and the demand for its products increases, ceteris paribus.

A currency depreciates in value when its value falls in relation to another currency.

When the Canadian dollar is appreciating against the U.S. dollar, the U.S. dollar must be depreciating against the Canadian dollar. For instance, when the exchange rate between the U.S. dollar and the Canadian dollar moves from $.8 = C$1 to $.9 = C$1, the *reciprocal exchange rate*—the rate between the Canadian dollar and the U.S. dollar—moves

Table 1 International Currency Symbols, Selected Countries

Country	Currency	Symbol
Australia	Dollar	A$
Austria	Schilling	Sch
Belgium	Franc	BF
Canada	Dollar	C$
China	Yuan	Y
Denmark	Krone	DKr
Finland	Markka	FM
France	Franc	FF
Germany	Deutsche mark	DM
Greece	Drachma	Dr
India	Rupee	Rs
Iran	Rial	RI
Italy	Lira	Lit
Japan	Yen	¥
Kuwait	Dinar	KD
Mexico	Peso	Ps
Netherlands	Guilder	FL
Norway	Krone	NKr
Saudi Arabia	Riyal	SR
Singapore	Dollar	S$
South Africa	Rand	R
Spain	Peseta	Pts
Sweden	Krona	SKr
Switzerland	Franc	SF
United Kingdom	Pound	£
United States	Dollar	$
U.S.S.R.	Ruble	Rub
Venezuela	Bolivar	B

from C$1.25 = $1 (1/.8 = 1.25) to C$1.11 = $1 (1/.9 = 1.11). At the same time that Canadian goods are becoming more expensive to U.S. buyers, U.S. goods are becoming cheaper to Canadian buyers.

In later chapters we look more closely at how changes in exchange rates affect international trade and at how governments use exchange rates to change their net exports.

RECAP

1. The foreign exchange market is a global market in which foreign money, largely bank deposits, is bought and sold.

2. An exchange rate is the price of one money in terms of another.

3. Foreign demand for domestic goods decreases as the domestic currency appreciates, and increases as the domestic currency depreciates.

Many developing countries impose restrictions on foreign currency transactions. These restrictions can take the form of government licensing requirements, under which only the government is allowed to exchange foreign currency for domestic currency; quotas on the amount of foreign currency that can be purchased; or even prohibitions on the use of foreign currency by private concerns. One product of these restrictions is illegal markets, or *black markets*, in foreign exchange. In many countries, the black market exists openly with little or no government intervention. In other countries, foreign exchange laws are strictly enforced.

Government policy creates the black market. The demand stems from the legal restrictions on buying foreign exchange; the supply, from government-mandated exchange rates that offer less than the free market. Ironically, governments cite the need for controls to conserve scarce foreign exchange for high-priority uses. But controls actually reduce the flow of foreign exchange to the government, as traders turn to the black market instead.

During periods of economic hardship, illegal markets allow normal economic activities to continue through a steady supply of foreign exchange. Some governments unofficially acknowledge the benefits of the black market by allowing the market to exist openly. For instance, Guatemala had an artificially low official exchange rate of 1 quetzal per U.S. dollar for more than three decades. But the government allowed a black market to operate openly in front of the country's main post office. There the exchange rate fluctuated daily with market conditions. In many Latin American countries, the post office is a center for black market trading because relatives living in the United States send millions of dollars in checks and money orders home. This sort of government-tolerated alternative to the official exchange market often is called a *parallel market* rather than a black market.

Mexico has had a thriving parallel market whenever the official exchange rate between the peso and the U.S. dollar has diverged greatly from the market rate. For example, in August 1982 the Mexican government banned the sale of U.S. dollars by Mexican banks. The parallel market immediately responded. The official exchange rate was 69.5 pesos per 1 U.S. dollar; the rate on the street ranged from 120 to 150. Private currency trades flourished at the Mexico City airport and other public places.

Black markets or parallel markets are common in developing countries where foreign exchange transactions are restricted. In many countries the official exchange rate bears no relation to current economic reality. Economists often look to the black market to see how the supply of and demand for foreign exchange are changing.

2. THE BALANCE OF PAYMENTS

▼ How do nations record their transactions with the rest of the world? ▲

balance of payments:
a record of a country's trade in goods, services, and financial assets with the rest of the world

The U.S. economy does not operate in a vacuum. It affects and is affected by the economies of other nations. This point was brought home to Americans in the 1980s. Headlines announced the latest trade deficit. Politicians denounced foreign countries for running trade surpluses against the United States. And everywhere there was talk of the balance of payments.

The **balance of payments** is a record of a country's trade in goods, services, and financial assets with the rest of the world. This record is divided into categories, or *accounts*, that summarize the nation's trade.

For example, one category measures transactions in merchandise; another measures transactions involving financial assets (bank deposits, bonds, stocks, loans). These accounts distinguish between private transactions (by individuals and businesses) and official transactions (by governments). Balance of payments data are reported quarterly for most developed countries.

2.a. Accounting for International Transactions

double-entry bookkeeping:
a system of accounting in which every transaction is recorded in at least two accounts and in which the debit total must equal the credit total for the transaction as a whole

The balance of payments is an accounting statement based on **double-entry bookkeeping**, a system in which every transaction is recorded in at least two accounts. Suppose a Canadian store sells a $20 shirt to a U.S. resident. The transaction is recorded twice: once as the shirt going from Canada to the United States, and then again as the payment of $20 going from the United States to Canada.

Double-entry bookkeeping means that for each transaction there is a credit entry and a debit entry. *Credits* record activities that bring payments into a country; *debits* record activities that involve payments to the rest of the world. Table 2 shows the entries in the U.S. balance of payments to record the sale of a $50,000 U.S. tractor to a French importer. The sale of the tractor represents a $50,000 credit entry in the balance of payments because U.S. exports earn foreign exchange for U.S. residents. To complete the record of this transaction, we must know how payment was made for the tractor. Let's assume that the French buyer paid with a $50,000 check drawn on a U.S. bank. Money that is withdrawn from a foreign-owned bank account in the United States is treated as foreign exchange moved out of the country. So we record the payment as a debit entry in the balance of payments. In fact, the money did not leave the country; its ownership was transferred from the French buyer to the U.S. seller.

The tractor sale is recorded on both sides of the balance of payments. There is a credit entry, and there is a debit entry. For every international transaction, there must be both a credit entry and a debit entry. This means that the sum of total credits and the sum of total debits must be equal. Credits always offset, or balance, debits.

The sum of total credits must equal the sum of total debits so that the two columns of the balance of payments always balance.

Table 2 Balance of Payments Entries for the Sale of a U.S. Tractor to a French Buyer

Activity	Credit	Debit
U.S. firm exports tractor and receives $50,000 from French buyer	$50,000	
French buyer imports tractor and transfers $50,000 from U.S. bank account to U.S. firm		$50,000
	$50,000	$50,000

Table 3 Simplified U.S. Balance of Payments, 1989

Account	(million dollars)		Net Balance
	Credit	Debit	
Current account			
Merchandise	$319,251	$446,466	−$127,215
Services	$210,555	$195,232	15,323
GNP net exports			−$111,892
Unilateral transfers			−$ 14,656
Current account			−$126,548
Capital account	$219,299	$82,110	$137,189
Statistical discrepancy			− 10,641
			$ 0

Source: Data from U.S. Department of Commerce, *Survey of Current Business* (Washington, D.C.: U.S. Government Printing Office, March 1990), pp. 48–49.

2.b. Balance of Payments Accounts

The balance of payments uses several different accounts to classify transactions (Table 3). The **current account** is the sum of the balances in the merchandise, services, and unilateral transfers accounts:

current account:
the sum of the merchandise, services, and unilateral transfers accounts in the balance of payments

surplus:
in a balance of payments account, the amount by which credits exceed debits

deficit:
in a balance of payments account, the amount by which debits exceed credits

Merchandise   This account records all transactions involving goods. U.S. exports of goods are merchandise credits; U.S. imports of foreign goods are merchandise debits. When exports (or credits) exceed imports (or debits), the merchandise account shows a **surplus**. When imports exceed exports, the account shows a **deficit**.

In 1989, the merchandise account in the U.S. balance of payments showed a deficit of $127,215 million. This means that the merchandise credits of $319,251 million created by U.S. exports were $127,215 million less than the merchandise debits of $446,466 million created by U.S. imports. In other words, the United States bought more goods from other nations than it sold to them.

Services   This account measures trade involving services. It includes travel and tourism, royalties, transportation costs, and insurance premiums. The largest component of the services account is return on investments. The income earned from investments in foreign countries is a credit; the income paid on foreign-owned investments in the United States is a debit. Investment income is recorded in the services account because it is the value of services provided by capital in foreign countries. If a U.S. firm owns a factory in Mexico, the profits from that factory are counted in the U.S. gross national product. The profits to the U.S. owner are the value of the factory's output that is attributable to U.S. investment. In 1989, there was a surplus of $15,323 million in the services account. The United States traditionally shows a surplus in the services account because of its large investment in the rest of the world.

The sum of the merchandise and services balances is *GNP net exports*. Remember that net exports are a component of gross national product, along with consumption, investment, and government spending. In 1989, GNP net exports equaled −$111,892 million. This means imports exceeded exports by $111,892 million.

Unilateral transfers In a unilateral transfer, one party gives something but gets nothing in return. Gifts and retirement pensions are forms of unilateral transfers. The United States always shows a large deficit in this account, a product of its foreign aid programs and the large number of U.S. residents who send money to relatives living in foreign countries. Only the net balance on unilateral transfers is reported. In 1989, that balance was a deficit of $14,656 million.

capital account:
the record in the balance of payments of the flow of financial assets into and out of a country

The current account is a useful measure of international transactions because it contains all of the activities involving goods and services. The **capital account** is where trade involving financial assets is recorded.[1] In 1989, the current account showed a deficit of $126,548 million. This means that U.S. imports of merchandise, services, and unilateral transfers were $126,548 million greater than exports of these items. All entries below the current account relate to financing the movement of merchandise, services, and unilateral transfers into and out of the country.

In the terminology of the balance of payments, *capital* refers to financial flows—bank deposits, purchases of stocks and bonds, and loans—not factories and equipment. Credits to the capital account reflect foreign purchases of U.S. financial assets, and debits reflect U.S. purchases of foreign financial assets. In 1989, the U.S. capital account showed a surplus of $137,189 million.

The *statistical discrepancy account,* the last account listed in Table 3, could be called *omissions and errors.* Government cannot accurately measure all transactions that take place. Some international shipments of goods and services go uncounted or are miscounted, as are some international flows of capital. The statistical discrepancy account is used to correct for these omissions and errors. In 1989, measured credits exceeded measured debits, so the statistical discrepancy was −$10,641 million.

Over all of the balance of payments account, the sum of credits must equal the sum of debits. The bottom line—the *net balance*—must be zero. It cannot show a surplus or a deficit. When people talk about a surplus or a deficit in the balance of payments, they actually are talking about a surplus or a deficit in one of the balance of payments accounts. The balance of payments itself by definition is always in balance, a function of double-entry bookkeeping.

2.c. The Current Account and the Capital Account

The current account reflects the movement of goods and services into and out of a country. The capital account reflects the flow of financial assets into and out of a country. In Table 3, the current account shows a deficit balance of $126,548 million. Remember that the balance of payments must *balance*. If there is a deficit in the current account, there must be a surplus in the capital account that exactly offsets that deficit.

---

[1]Payments for existing investments are included in the services account.

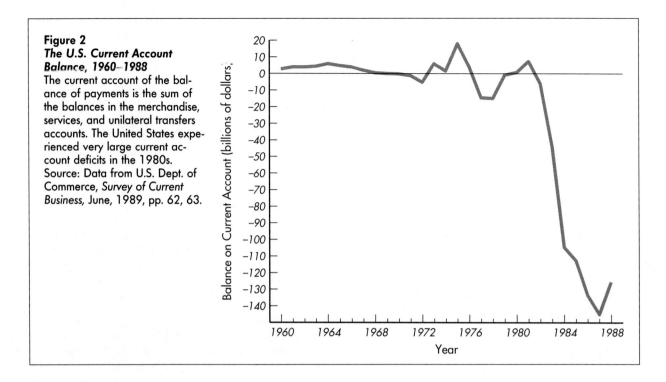

Figure 2
The U.S. Current Account Balance, 1960–1988
The current account of the balance of payments is the sum of the balances in the merchandise, services, and unilateral transfers accounts. The United States experienced very large current account deficits in the 1980s.
Source: Data from U.S. Dept. of Commerce, *Survey of Current Business*, June, 1989, pp. 62, 63.

A net debtor owes more to the rest of the world than it is owed; a net creditor is owed more than it owes.

What is important here is not the bookkeeping process, the concept that the balance of payments must balance, but rather the meaning of deficits and surpluses in the current and capital accounts. These deficits and surpluses tell us whether a country is a net borrower from or lender to the rest of the world.

A deficit in the current account means that a country is running a net surplus in its capital account. And it signals that a country is a net borrower from the rest of the world. A country that is running a current account deficit must borrow from abroad an amount sufficient to finance that deficit. A capital account surplus is achieved by selling more bonds and other debts of the domestic country to the rest of the world than the country buys from the rest of the world.

Figure 2 shows the current account balance in the United States for each year from 1960 to 1988. The United States experienced large current account deficits in the 1980s. This means that the United States sold financial assets and borrowed large amounts of money from foreign residents to finance its current account deficits (see Economic Insight: The World's Largest Debtor Nation). Capital account transactions indicate whether a nation is increasing its net borrowing from or net lending to the rest of the world. A *net debtor* owes more to the rest of the world than it is owed; a *net creditor* is owed more than it owes. The United States was an international net creditor from the end of World War I until the mid-1980s. The country financed its large current account deficits in the 1980s by borrowing from the rest of the world. As a result, in 1985, the United States became an international net debtor for the first time in almost 70 years.

Economic Insight

The World's Largest Debtor Nation

On September 16, 1985, the Department of Commerce announced that the United States was a debtor nation for the first time since World War I. In fact the size of the deficit in the current account in 1985 and 1986 made the United States the largest debtor in the world. Its debts now exceed even those of large developing countries like Brazil and Mexico.

The movement from net creditor to debtor followed a decade in which U.S. bank loans abroad had increased the country's net creditor position. In fact in 1982, with net international investments of $147 billion, the United States was the largest creditor nation in the world. This changed with the current account deficits of the 1980s. In order to consume more at home than it produces (this is what a country does when it is running a current account deficit), a country has to borrow from abroad. In the case of the United States, borrowing was at such a high level that its

record net creditor position of 1982 was eliminated in just three years.

The change in the U.S. current account was the product of several economic factors. First, the world debt crisis reduced U.S. foreign lending, as banks tried to lower their exposure to loan defaults by developing countries. Second, record U.S. federal budget deficits forced the U.S. Treasury to borrow huge sums of money. U.S. banks, which had reduced their foreign lending, replaced those loans with relatively high return loans to the government. Finally, these same high returns, along with the perception of the United States as a safe haven for investment, made U.S. securities more attractive to foreign lenders.

There is nothing wrong with being a net debtor as long as borrowed funds contribute to a more productive economy. Without a large inflow of foreign funds in the late 1980s, U.S. interest rates would have been

higher and investment probably would have been lower. If the borrowing increased the rate of production in the United States, then future generations, who share the burden of repaying the debt, will enjoy a higher standard of living. Furthermore, the fact that the United States changed from a net creditor to a net debtor had no perceptible effect on the life of the typical American. Consumers and producers have continued to live life as usual.

Large current account deficits and capital account surpluses will not continue forever. When foreign portfolios reach the point where dollar-denominated assets are no longer needed or wanted, the dollar will tend to depreciate and interest rates will tend to fall. As the capital account surplus falls, the current account deficit falls. Ultimately, the United States could once again become a net lender, and the title "world's largest debtor" could fall to another nation.

RECAP

1. The balance of payments is a record of a nation's international transactions.

2. Double-entry bookkeeping requires that every transaction be entered in at least two accounts, so that credits and debits are balanced.

3. In the balance of payments, credits record activities that represent payments into the country and debits record activities that represent payments out of the country.

4. The current account is the sum of the balances in the merchandise, services, and unilateral transfers accounts.

5. A surplus exists when credits exceed debits; a deficit exists when credits are less than debits.
6. GNP net exports are the sum of the balances in the merchandise and services accounts.
7. The capital account is where the transactions necessary to finance the movement of merchandise, services, and unilateral transfers into and out of the country are recorded.
8. The net balance in the balance of payments must be zero.
9. A deficit in the current account must be offset by a surplus in the capital account. It also indicates that the nation is a net borrower.

SUMMARY

1. Foreign exchange is foreign currency and bank deposits that are denominated in foreign currency. § 1

▼▲ How do individuals of one nation trade money with individuals of another nation?

2. The foreign exchange market is a global market in which people trade one currency for another. § 1

3. Exchange rates are necessary to compare prices quoted in different currencies. § 1.a

4. The value of a good in a domestic currency equals the foreign currency price times the exchange rate. § 1.a

▼▲ How do changes in exchange rates affect international trade?

5. When a domestic currency appreciates, domestic goods become more expensive to foreigners and foreign goods become cheaper to domestic residents. § 1.b

6. When a domestic currency depreciates, domestic goods become cheaper to foreigners and foreign goods become more expensive to domestic residents. § 1.b

▼▲ How do nations record their transactions with the rest of the world?

7. The balance of payments is a record of a nation's transactions with the rest of the world. § 2

8. The balance of payments is based on double-entry bookkeeping. § 2.a

9. Credits record activities that bring payments into a country; debits record activities that take payments out of a country. § 2.a

10. In the balance of payments, the sum of total credits and the sum of total debits must be equal. § 2.b

11. The current account is the sum of the balances in the merchandise, services, and unilateral transfers accounts. § 2.b

12. In a balance of payments account, a surplus is the amount by which credits exceed debits, and a deficit is the amount by which debits exceed credits. § 2.b

13. The capital account reflects the transactions necessary to finance the movement of merchandise, services, and unilateral transfers into and out of the country. § 2.b

14. The net balance in the balance of payments must be zero. § 2.b

15. A deficit in the current account must be offset by a surplus in the capital account. § 2.c

16. A country that shows a deficit in its current account (or a surplus in its capital account) is a net debtor. § 2.c

foreign exchange § 1

foreign exchange market § 1

exchange rate § 1.a

balance of payments § 2

double-entry bookkeeping § 2.a

current account § 2.b

surplus § 2.b

deficit § 2.b

capital account § 2.b

EXERCISES

Basic Terms and Concepts

1. What is the price of 1 U.S. dollar given the following exchange rates?

   a. 1 Austrian schilling = $.10

   b. 1 Chinese yuan = $.33

   c. 1 Israeli shekel = $.60

   d. 1 Kuwaiti dinar = $4.20

2. A bicycle manufactured in the United States costs $100. Using the exchange rates listed in Figure 1 for Wednesday, what would the bicycle cost in each of the following countries?

   a. Argentina

   b. Brazil

   c. Canada

   d. Hong Kong

   e. Italy

   f. Mexico

   g. Philippines

3. The U.S. dollar price of a Swedish krona changes from $.1572 to $.1730.

   a. Has the dollar depreciated or appreciated against the krona?

   b. Has the krona appreciated or depreciated against the dollar?

4. When U.S. exports of merchandise go up, what happens to the value of the U.S. gross national product?

Extended Concepts

5. How reasonable is it for every country to follow policies aimed at increasing net exports?

6. What does the concept of equilibrium mean in terms of the balance of payments?

7. How did the United States become the world's largest debtor nation in the 1980s?

U.S. Exporters Upbeat as Dollar Comes Down

U.S. companies that export or do business overseas are breathing easier now that the dollar has come down from its spring peaks.

The currency's slide has calmed fears that both exports and earnings made by overseas operations would wither under the effects of a strengthening dollar.

"The rise the dollar went on was surprising and disturbing," says Timothy McKenna, director of financial communications for Union Camp Corp., a Wayne, N.J., maker of paper and chemical products. "We feel a lot better now." About 5% of Union Camp's $2.7 billion in annual sales comes from exports.

"I don't think we were alarmed" by the dollar's rally, "but our eyes certainly opened a little wider," says Alan Hall, production manager at Dynacorp Inc. in Rockford, Ill. The maker of copier parts sends about 15% of its goods overseas. With the dollar edging down, he says, "we've got one less thing to worry about."

The dollar began 1989 at 123.8 Japanese yen and 1.77 West German marks. Then Japan's political scandal, China's upheaval and West Germany's argument with the USA about NATO policies all occurred at roughly the same time.

Result: Investors rushed to the dollar as a "safe haven." The dollar hit peaks of 151.80 yen and 2.05 marks during trading on June 15.

"It was getting tougher to sleep at night," says Robert Stefanko, spokesman for Akron, Ohio-based A. Schulman Inc., a maker of plastic compounds.

As events overseas stabilized and U.S. interest rates fell, the dollar came back to earth. Monday it closed in New York at 141.40 yen and 1.903 marks, from 140.90 yen and 1.912 marks Friday.

Why the drop is good news:

- It keeps our exports price competitive. When the dollar hit its spring peak, a West German firm would need to exchange 1,600 marks into dollars to pay for an $800 piece of electrical testing equipment from Riser-Bond Industries in Aurora, Neb. Now, the equipment is worth 1,500 marks.

- It keeps earnings made in other currencies from deteriorating when they're translated into dollars. At the dollar's peak, every 200 marks that Koss Corp. earned in West Germany for its headphones were worth $100. Now 200 marks equals $109.

■ Source: "U.S. Exporters Upbeat as Dollar Comes Down," *USA Today*, July 18, 1989, p. B1.

Commentary

Firms are very interested in currency movements because the exchange rate serves to translate the price of a good in one currency to a price in another currency. Firms that sell goods across international borders find that changes in exchange rates affect the competitiveness of their products in foreign countries. Even firms that do not export goods must be cognizant of exchange rates because the price of foreign competing products is affected by currency movements. The large movements in currencies of major industrial countries since the present system of floating exchange rates began in 1973 cause concern because they affect competitiveness and make predictions about future prices more uncertain.

This volatility of currencies reflects the fact that many different types of events, political as well as economic, affect exchange rates. Such events have caused wide swings in the value of the dollar over the past few years. Wide swings in the exchange rate of the dollar occur even over periods shorter than one year. For instance, the dollar began 1989 at 123.8 Japanese yen and 1.77 West German marks. The dollar appreciated over the first half of 1989, reaching a peak of 151.80 yen and 2.05 marks in June, which represents a 23-percent appreciation of the dollar against the yen and a 16-percent appreciation of the dollar against the mark. Within a month, the dollar had depreciated over 7 percent against the yen, to 140.90 yen to the dollar, and just under 7 percent against the mark, to 1.912 marks to the dollar. By early 1990, the dollar reversed course against the yen, rising to 146 yen, while it continued to depreciate against the mark, falling to 1.71 marks.

These dollar movements have important consequences for the two manufacturers discussed in the article—and indeed for all manufacturers who sell products overseas or who face international competition. The dollar appreciation hurts exports of U.S. goods and also adversely affects the sale of U.S. products at home since foreign imports become more competitively priced when the dollar appreciates. For example, at the beginning of 1989, an $800 piece of electrical equipment from the Aurora, Nebraska, firm would cost 99,040 yen (at an exchange rate of 123.8 yen to the dollar) and 1,416 marks (at an exchange rate of 1.77 marks to the dollar).

Six months later, when the dollar appreciated to 151.80 yen and 2.05 marks, the same piece of equipment would cost 121,440 yen and 1,640 marks. With such large price changes resulting from exchange-rate movements (a 13-percent rise in Japan and a 6-percent rise in Germany), it is easy to understand why firms that trade internationally are very interested in exchange rates. (As an exercise, calculate the yen and mark price of the $800 piece of equipment in 1990, using the data on exchange rates in the chapter.)

The movements in the dollar also affect the price of foreign-made products sold in the United States. Suppose Union Camp Corporation competes against a German firm that manufactures chemicals at a cost of 1,000 marks. At the exchange rate of 1.77 marks at the beginning of 1989, the dollar cost of the German-made chemicals is $565 (1,000 marks divided by 1.77 marks per dollar equals $565). In June, when the dollar appreciated to 2.05 marks, the same German-made chemicals would be priced more competitively in the United States, at $488. Thus, even though Union Camp Corporation does not export goods, it is concerned about movements in the exchange rate because it faces import competition.

There are two components to the determination of the price of an imported good: its price in terms of its home currency and the exchange rate. Recently, we have seen interactions between the exchange rate of the dollar and the home-currency price of foreign exports that have moderated the effects of exchange-rate movements on the price of imports to the United States. Beginning in early 1985, the dollar depreciated against many currencies. With constant home-currency prices of foreign products, this depreciation would have translated into higher prices for imports to the United States. Many of the companies that exported to the United States, however, mitigated the effect of the falling dollar by decreasing the home-currency price of their goods. Such price reductions offset the extent to which exchange-rate movements were passed on to the price of imports to the United States. As a result, the U.S. trade balance did not improve as rapidly as many had predicted it would after the dollar dropped in value.

8

Unemployment and Inflation

1. What is a business cycle?
2. How is the unemployment rate defined and measured?
3. What is the cost of unemployed resources?
4. What is inflation?
5. Why is inflation a problem?

PREVIEW If you were graduating from college today, what would your job prospects be? In 1932, they would have been bleak. A large number of people were out of work, and a large number of firms had laid off workers or gone out of business. At any time, job opportunities depend not only on the individual's ability and experience, but also on the current state of the economy.

Economies operate in cycles, periods of expansion followed by periods of contraction. These cycles have a major impact on people's income and standard of living. When the economy is growing, the demand for goods and services tends to increase. To produce those goods and services, firms hire more workers. So as the economy expands, the unemployment rate falls. Economic expansion also has an impact on inflation. As the demand for goods and services goes up, the prices of those goods and services also tend to rise. During periods of recession, the unemployment rate goes up and inflation tends to slow. Both unemployment and inflation are affected by business cycles in fairly regular ways. But their effects on individual standards of living, income, and purchasing power are much less predictable.

Why do certain events move in tandem? What are the links between unemployment and inflation? What causes the business cycle to behave as it does? What effect does government activity have on the business cycle—and on unemployment and inflation? Who is harmed by rising unemployment and inflation? Who benefits? Macroeconomics attempts to answer these questions.

In this chapter we describe the business cycle and examine measures of unemployment and inflation. We talk about the ways in which the business cycle, unemployment, and inflation are related. And we describe their effects on the participants in the economy.

1. BUSINESS CYCLES

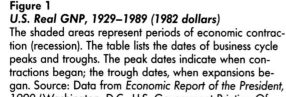

What is a business cycle?

The most widely used measure of a nation's output is gross national product. When we examine the value of real GNP over time, we find periods in which it rises and other periods in which it falls.

1.a. Definitions

business cycle:
the recurrent pattern of rising real GNP followed by falling real GNP

This pattern—real GNP rising then falling—is called a **business cycle**. The pattern occurs over and over again; but as Figure 1 shows, the pattern over time is anything but regular. Historically the duration of business cycles

Figure 1
U.S. Real GNP, 1929–1989 (1982 dollars)
The shaded areas represent periods of economic contraction (recession). The table lists the dates of business cycle peaks and troughs. The peak dates indicate when contractions began; the trough dates, when expansions began. Source: Data from *Economic Report of the President, 1990* (Washington, D.C.: U.S. Government Printing Office, 1990).

Peaks	Troughs
August 1929	March 1933
May 1937	June 1938
February 1945	October 1945
November 1948	October 1949
July 1953	May 1954
August 1957	April 1958
April 1960	February 1961
December 1969	November 1970
November 1973	March 1975
January 1980	July 1980
July 1981	November 1982

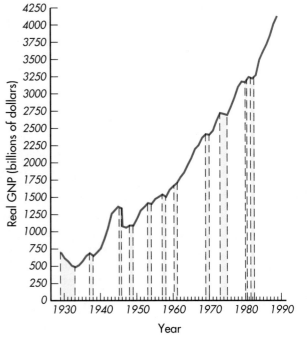

Figure 2
The Business Cycle
The business cycle contains four phases: the expansion (boom), when real GNP is increasing; the peak, which marks the end of an expansion and the beginning of a contraction; the contraction (recession), when real GNP is falling; and the trough, which marks the end of a contraction and the beginning of an expansion.

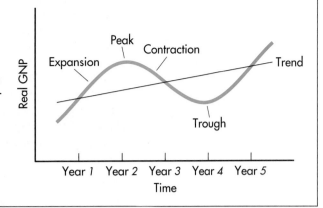

and the rate at which real GNP rises or falls (indicated by the steepness of the line in Figure 1) vary considerably.

Looking at Figure 1, it is clear that the U.S. economy has experienced up and down swings in the years since 1929. Still, real GNP has grown at an average rate of approximately 3 percent per year.

Figure 2 shows how real GNP behaves over a hypothetical business cycle and identifies the stages of the cycle. The vertical axis on the graph measures the level of real GNP; the horizontal axis measures time in years. In year 1, real GNP is growing; the economy is in the *expansion* phase, or *boom* period, of the business cycle. Growth continues until the *peak* is reached, in year 2. Real GNP begins to fall during the *contraction* phase of the cycle, which continues until year 4. The *trough* marks the end of the contraction and the start of a new expansion.

Even though the economy illustrated in Figure 2 is subject to periodic ups and downs, real GNP, the measure of a nation's output, has risen over the long term, as illustrated by the upward-sloping line labeled *trend*. It is important to recognize that periods of economic growth or prosperity are followed by periods of contraction or **recession**. It is also important to recognize long-term economic growth.

recession:
a period in which real GNP falls

If an economy is growing over time, why do economists worry about business cycles? Economists try to understand the causes of business cycles so that they can learn to moderate or avoid recessions and their harmful effects on standards of living.

1.b. Historical Record

The official dating of recessions in the United States is the responsibility of the National Bureau of Economic Research (NBER), an independent research organization. The NBER has identified the shaded areas in the graph in Figure 1 as recessions, the unshaded areas as expansions. Recessions are periods between cyclical peaks and the troughs that follow them. Expansions are periods between cyclical troughs and the peaks that follow them. There have been eleven recessions since 1929. The most severe was the Great Depression. Between 1929 and 1933, national output fell by 25 percent. A **depression** is a prolonged period of severe economic contraction. The fact that people refer to ''the Depression'' when speaking about

depression:
a severe, prolonged economic contraction

As real income falls, living standards go down. This 1937 photo of a depression-era bread line indicates the paradox of the world's richest nation, as emphasized on the billboard in the background, having to offer public support to feed able-bodied workers who are out of work due to the severity of the business-cycle downturn.

the recession that began in 1929 indicates the severity of that contraction relative to others in recent experience. There was widespread suffering during the Depression. Many people were jobless and homeless, and many firms went bankrupt.

1.c. Indicators

We have been talking about the business cycle in terms of real GNP. There are a number of other variables that move in a fairly regular manner over the business cycle. The Department of Commerce classifies these variables in three categories—leading indicators, coincident indicators, and lagging indicators—depending on whether they move up or down before, at the same time as, or following a change in real GNP (Table 1).

Table 1 Indicators of the Business Cycle

Leading Indicators	
Average work week	New building permits
Unemployment claims	Delivery times of goods
Manufacturers' new orders	Inventories
New businesses formed	Materials prices
Stock prices	Money supply
New plant and equipment orders	Outstanding business and consumer credit

Coincident Indicators	Lagging Indicators
Payroll employment	Labor cost per unit of output
Industrial production	Inventories to sales ratio
Personal income	Unemployment duration
Manufacturing and trade sales	Consumer credit to personal income ratio
	Outstanding commercial loans
	Prime interest rate

Remembrances of Recessions Past

It may be 1990 before the Federal Reserve learns if it has managed to cool the economy without causing a recession. Compared with past efforts, however, so far, so good. Interest rates are falling. Bulging inventories and other "imbalances" that precede a downturn are not evident. Still, inflation persists. A sudden surge in oil prices could turn a soft landing into a nose dive.

December, 1969 to November, 1970

The Johnson White House assured Americans they could have both guns and butter. But the rapid run-up in prices prompted largely by the Vietnam War dealt a body blow to the economy. To counter inflation, which had surged from just under 2 percent in 1965 to more than 6 percent during 1969, the Federal Reserve tightened monetary policy. Interest rates headed upward; defense expenditures were cut by 18 percent from their 1968 peak. This de-escalation, plus a strike at General Motors, raised unemployment to over 6 percent, pushed corporate profits down by 12.3 percent and slowed business investment.

November, 1973 to March, 1975

Remember when gas guzzlers ruled the road and driving was fun? The first Arab oil embargo temporarily ended America's love affair with big cars by quadrupling oil prices and putting the U.S. economy through the wringer of double-digit inflation. Purchasing power declined by a full percentage point in 1974 as higher petroleum costs transferred American wealth to oil-producing nations and consumers moved into higher tax brackets. The combination of tightened fiscal and monetary policy pushed unemployment to 8.6 percent. Housing starts plummeted by 40 percent from 1974 to 1975, while auto sales registered a 23 percent decline.

January–July, 1980

The Islamic revolution in Iran could not have come at a more inopportune time for the U.S. economy. America was even more dependent on foreign-oil supplies than it had been in 1973, and the resulting oil shortages and price hikes combined to shoot unemployment to 7.8 percent. Inflation once again soared into the double digits. In March, 1980, the Federal Reserve adopted austere credit-control measures; by April, the prime rate hit 20 percent. Compared with 1979, corporate profits fell 10 percent and industrial production was off 1.9 percent. By July, the shortest but one of the most severe post-World War II recessions had run its course.

July, 1981 to November, 1982

Few figures stir as much *Sturm und Drang* among financial circles as the Federal Reserve's cigar-smoking ex-Chairman Paul Volcker. He is praised for reining in inflation; unfortunately, his vehicle was the deepest recession since World War II. And the 1981–82 downturn was a doozy. The nation was still reeling from the wage-and-price spirals of the late 1970s. To battle back inflation, then running about 13 percent, the Fed squeezed the money supply to a mere trickle, sending interest rates up sharply. The prime interest rate almost doubled to 19.5 percent. While the measures succeeded in wringing high inflation from the economy, the price was high. Unemployment soared to the highest levels since the Great Depression, while industrial production dropped by 9 percent. But recovery from the trauma paved the way for Ronald Reagan's reelection in 1984, and for the current expansion, one of the longest in memory.

■ Source: "Remembrances of Recessions Past," *U.S. News & World Report,* August 14, 1989, pp. 42–43. Copyright, Aug. 14, 1989, *U.S. News & World Report.*

leading indicator:
a variable that changes before real output changes

Leading indicators change before real GNP changes. As a result, economists use them to forecast changes in output. Looking at Table 1, it is easy to see how some of these leading indicators could be used to forecast future output. For instance, new building permits signal new construction. If the number of new permits issued goes up, economists can expect the amount of new construction to increase. Similarly, if manufacturers receive more new orders, economists can expect more goods to be produced.

Leading indicators are not infallible, however. The link between them and future output can be tenuous. For example, leading indicators may fall one month and then rise the next, while real output rises steadily. Economists want to see several consecutive months of a new direction in the leading indicators before forecasting a change in output. Short-run movements in the indicators can be very misleading.

coincident indicator:
a variable that changes at the same time that real output changes

Coincident indicators are economic variables that tend to change at the same time real output changes. For example, as real output increases, economists expect to see employment and sales rise. The coincident indicators listed in Table 1 have demonstrated a strong tendency over time to change along with changes in real GNP.

lagging indicator:
a variable that changes after real output changes

The final group of variables listed in Table 1, **lagging indicators**, do not change their value until after the value of real GNP has changed. For instance, as output increases, jobs are created and more workers are hired. It makes sense, then, to expect the duration of unemployment (the average time workers are unemployed) to fall. The duration of unemployment is a lagging indicator. Lagging indicators are used along with leading and coincident indicators to identify the peaks and troughs in business cycles.

RECAP

1. The business cycle is a recurring pattern of rising and falling real GNP.
2. Although all business cycles move through periods of expansion and contraction, the duration of expansion and recession varies.
3. Real GNP is not the only variable affected by business cycles; leading, lagging, and coincident indicators also feel the effects of economic expansion and contraction.

2. UNEMPLOYMENT

Recurring periods of prosperity and recession are reflected in the nation's labor markets. In fact this is what makes understanding the business cycle so important. If business cycles only signified a little more or a little less profit for businesses, governments would not be so anxious to forecast or to control their swings. It is the human costs of lost jobs and incomes—the inability to maintain standards of living—that make an understanding of business cycles and of the factors that affect unemployment so important.

The news media are very aware of the importance of unemployment to government, to businesses, and to everyday citizens. So they pay a great deal of attention to the monthly unemployment data published by the government. Certainly there are good reasons to be concerned about the unemployment rate, but first we have to understand exactly what the numbers mean.

2.a. Definition and Measurement

unemployment rate:
the percentage of the labor force that
is not working

The **unemployment rate** is the percentage of the labor force that is not working. The rate is calculated by dividing the number of people who are unemployed by the number of people in the labor force:

$$\text{Unemployment rate} = \frac{\text{number unemployed}}{\text{labor force}}$$

This ratio seems simple enough, but there are several subtle issues at work here. First, the unemployment rate does not measure the percentage of the total population that is not working; it measures the percentage of the *labor force* that is not working. Who is in the labor force? Obviously everybody who is employed is part of the labor force. But only some of those who are not currently employed are counted in the labor force.

▼
**How is the unemployment
rate defined and measured?**
▲

The Bureau of Labor Statistics of the Department of Labor compiles labor data each month based on an extensive survey of U.S. households. All U.S. residents are potential members of the labor force. The Labor Department arrives at the size of the actual labor force using this formula:

$$\text{Labor force} = \begin{array}{c}\text{all U.S. residents} - \text{residents under 16} \\ \text{years old} - \text{institutionalized adults} - \text{adults} \\ \text{who are not looking for work}\end{array}$$

*You are in the labor force if you are
working or actively seeking work.*

So the labor force includes those adults (an adult being 17 or older) currently employed or actively seeking work. It is relatively simple to see to it that children and institutionalized adults (for instance, those in prison or long-term care facilities) are not counted in the labor force. It is more difficult to identify and accurately measure adults who are not actively looking for work.

A person is actively seeking work if he or she is available to work, has looked for work in the past four weeks, is waiting for a recall after being laid off, or is starting a job within 30 days. Those who are not working and who meet these criteria are considered unemployed.

2.b. Interpreting the Unemployment Rate

Is the unemployment rate an accurate measure? The fact that the rate does not include those who are not actively looking for work is not necessarily a failing. Many people who are not actively looking for work—homemakers, older citizens, and students, for example—have made a decision to work at home, to retire, or to stay in school. These people rightly are not counted among the unemployed.

But there are people missing from the unemployment statistics who are not working and are not looking for work, yet would take a job if one was offered. **Discouraged workers** have given up looking for work because they believe that no one will hire them. These individuals are ignored by the official unemployment statistics even though they are able to work and may have spent a long time looking for work. Estimates of the number of discouraged workers are hard to make, but it is clear that the reported unemployment rate underestimates the true burden of unemployment in the economy when it ignores discouraged workers.

Discouraged workers are one source of hidden unemployment; under-

discouraged workers:
workers who have stopped looking
for work because they believe no one
will offer them a job

*Activity in the underground economy
is not included in official statistics.*

The Underground Economy

Official unemployment data, like national income data, do not include activity in the underground economy. Obviously drug dealers and prostitutes do not report their earnings. Nor do many of the people who supplement their unemployment benefits with part-time jobs. In addition, people like the waiter who reports a small fraction of his actual tips and the housecleaning person who requests payment in cash in order to avoid reporting taxable income are also part of the underground economy.

Because activity in the underground economy goes unreported, there is no exact way to determine its size. Estimates range from 5 to 33 percent of the gross national product. With the GNP at $5 trillion, this places the value of underground activity between $250 billion and $1.33 trillion.

We will never know the true size of the underground economy, but evidence suggests that it is growing. That evidence has to do with cash. The vast majority of people working in the underground economy are paid in cash. One indicator of the growth of that economy, then, is the rise in currency over time rel-

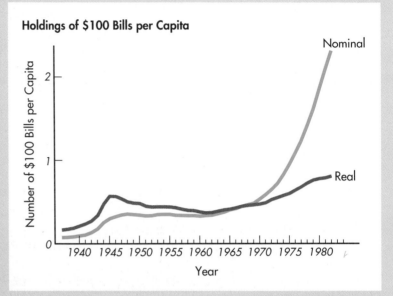

Holdings of $100 Bills per Capita

ative to checking accounts. Also, per capita holdings of $100 bills have increased substantially. The graph shows this increase, from less than half a $100 bill per person in the 1960s to almost 2.5 bills per person by the early 1980s. Certainly, much of the demand for $100 bills is a product of inflation (as the prices of goods and services go up, it is easier to pay for them in larger-denomination bills). But the lower line in the graph shows a substantial rise in real holdings of $100 bills as well.

The underground economy forces us to interpret government statistics carefully. We must remember that

- official income statistics understate the true national income.
- official unemployment data overestimate true unemployment.
- when the underground economy grows more rapidly than the rest of the economy, the true rate of growth is higher than reported.

underemployment:
the employment of workers in jobs that do not utilize their productive potential

employment is another. **Underemployment** is the underutilization of workers, employment in tasks that do not fully utilize their productive potential. Even if every worker has a job, substantial underemployment leaves the economy producing less than its potential GNP.

The effect of discouraged workers and underemployment is an unemployment rate that understates actual unemployment. The effect of the *underground economy* is a rate that overstates actual unemployment. A sizable component of the officially unemployed is actually working. The unemployed construction worker who plays in a band at night may not report that activity because he or she wants to avoid paying taxes on his or her earnings as a musician. This person is officially unemployed but has a source of income. Many officially unemployed individuals have an alternate source of income. This means that official statistics overstate the true magnitude of unemployment. The larger the underground economy, the greater this overstatement.

We have identified two factors, discouraged workers and underemployment, that cause the official unemployment rate to underestimate true unemployment. Another factor, the underground economy, causes the official rate to overestimate the true rate of unemployment. There is no reason to expect these factors to cancel one another out, and there is no way to know for sure which is most important. The point is to remember what the official data on unemployment do and do not measure.

2.c. Types of Unemployment

Economists have identified four basic types of unemployment:

Seasonal unemployment   A product of regular, recurring changes in the hiring needs of certain industries on a monthly or seasonal basis.

Frictional unemployment   A product of the short-term movement of workers between jobs, and of first-time job seekers.

Structural unemployment   A product of technological change and other changes in the structure of the economy.

Cyclical unemployment   A product of business cycle fluctuations.

In certain industries, labor needs to fluctuate throughout the year. When local crops are harvested, farms need lots of workers; the rest of the year, they do not. (Migrant farmworkers move from one region to another, following the harvests, to avoid seasonal unemployment.) Ski resort towns like Park City, Utah, and Aspen, Colorado, are booming during the ski season, when employment peaks, but need fewer workers during the rest of the year. In the nation as a whole, the Christmas season is a time of peak employment and low unemployment rates. To avoid confusing seasonal fluctuations in unemployment with other sources of unemployment, unemployment data are seasonally adjusted.

Frictional and structural unemployment are always present in a dynamic economy.

Frictional and structural unemployment exist in any dynamic economy. In terms of individual workers, frictional unemployment is short term in nature. Workers quit one job and soon find another; students graduate and soon find a job. This kind of unemployment cannot be eliminated in a free society. In fact it is a sign of efficiency in an economy when workers try to increase their income or improve their working conditions by leaving one job for another. Frictional unemployment often is called *search unemployment* because workers take time to search for a job after quitting a job or leaving school.

Unemployment imposes costs on the economy and on society. But it also provides benefits. Both society and the individual worker benefit when a new job makes better use of the worker's skills so that more output is produced.

Frictional unemployment is short term; structural unemployment, on the other hand, can be long term. Workers who are displaced by technological change (assembly line workers who have been replaced by machines, for example) or a permanent reduction in the demand for an industry's output (cigar makers who have been laid off because of a decrease in demand for tobacco) may not have the necessary skills to maintain their level of income in another industry. Rather than accept a much lower salary, these workers tend to prolong their job search. Eventually they adjust their expectations to the realities of the job market, or they enter the pool of discouraged workers.

Cyclical unemployment is a product of recession.

Structural unemployment is very difficult for those who are unemployed. But for society as a whole, the technological advances that cause structural unemployment raise living standards by giving consumers a greater variety of goods at lower cost.

Cyclical unemployment is a product of recession. It is also a primary focus of macroeconomic policy. Economists believe that a greater understanding of business cycles and their causes can contribute to their ability to smooth out those cycles and swings in unemployment. In addition to macroeconomic policy aimed at moderating cyclical unemployment, other policy measures—for example, job training and counseling—are being used to reduce frictional and structural unemployment.

2.d. Costs of Unemployment

▼ What is the cost of unemployed resources? ▲

The cost of being unemployed is more than the obvious loss of income and status suffered by the individual who is not working. In a broader sense, society as a whole loses when resources are unemployed. Unemployed workers produce no output. Economists measure this lost output in terms of the *GNP gap:*

$$\text{GNP gap} = \text{potential GNP} - \text{real GNP}$$

potential GNP:
the output produced at the natural rate of unemployment

natural rate of unemployment:
the unemployment rate that would exist in the absence of cyclical unemployment

Potential GNP is the level of output produced when nonlabor resources are fully utilized and unemployment is at its natural rate. The **natural rate of unemployment** is the unemployment rate that would exist in the absence of cyclical unemployment. The natural rate of unemployment is not fixed; it can change over time. For instance, some economists believe that the natural rate of unemployment has risen in recent decades, a product of the influx of baby boomers and women into the labor force. As more workers move into the labor force (begin looking for jobs), frictional unemployment increases, raising the natural rate of unemployment.

Potential GNP measures what we are capable of producing at the natural rate of unemployment. If we compute potential GNP and then subtract actual real GNP, we have a measure of the output lost as a result of unemployment, or the cost of unemployment.

The GNP gap in the United States from 1975 to 1989 is shown in Figure 3(a). The gap widens during recessions and narrows during expansions. As the gap widens (as the output not produced increases), there are fewer goods and services available, and living standards are lower than they would be at the natural rate of unemployment. Figure 3(b) is a graph of the gap between potential and real GNP, taken from Figure 3(a).

Because frictional and structural unemployment are always present, the term full employment *is misleading. Today economists use the term* natural rate of unemployment *instead.*

Until recently economists used the term *full employment* instead of *natural rate of unemployment.* Today the term is rarely used because it implies a zero unemployment rate. If frictional and structural unemployment are always present, zero unemployment is impossible; there must always be unemployed resources in an economy. *Natural rate of unemployment* describes the labor market when the economy is producing what it realistically can produce.

What is the value of the natural rate of unemployment? In the 1950s and 1960s, economists generally agreed on 4 percent. By the 1970s, that rate had gone up to 5 percent. In the early 1980s, many economists placed the natural rate of unemployment in the United States at 6 to 7 percent. By the late 1980s, some had revised their thinking, placing the rate back at 5 percent. In fact economists do not know exactly what the natural rate of unemployment is. Over time it varies within a range from around 4 percent to around 7 percent.

Figure 3
The GNP Gap (1982 dollars)
The GNP gap is the difference between what the economy can produce at the natural rate of unemployment (potential GNP) and actual output (real GNP). When the unemployment rate is higher than the natural rate, actual GNP is less than potential GNP. The gap between potential and actual GNP is a cost associated with unemployment. Recession years are shaded to highlight how the gap widens around recessions. Source: Data from *Economic Report of the President, 1990* (Washington, D.C.: U.S. Government Printing Office, 1990).

(a) Potential and Real GNP

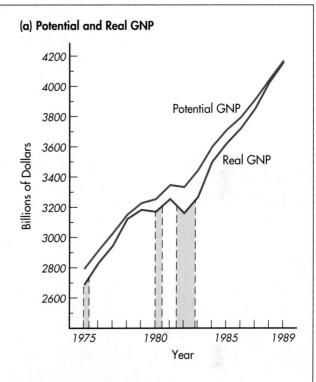

(b) A Graph of the GNP Gap

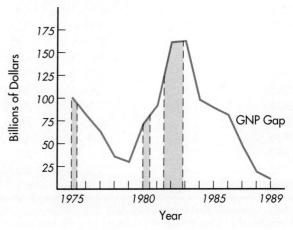

Table 2 Unemployment Rates in the United States, 1948–1989

Year	Unemployment Rate, All Workers*	Unemployment Rate (percent), Civilian Workers†					
		All Civilian Workers	Males	Females	Both sexes 16–19 years	White	Black and Other
1948		3.8	3.6	4.1	9.2	3.5	5.9
1949		5.9	5.9	6.0	13.4	5.6	8.9
1950	5.2	5.3	5.1	5.7	12.2	4.9	9.0
1951	3.2	3.3	2.8	4.4	8.2	3.1	5.3
1952	2.9	3.0	2.8	3.6	8.5	2.8	5.4
1953	2.8	2.9	2.8	3.3	7.6	2.7	4.5
1954	5.4	5.5	5.3	6.0	12.6	5.0	9.9
1955	4.3	4.4	4.2	4.9	11.0	3.9	8.7
1956	4.0	4.1	3.8	4.8	11.1	3.6	8.3
1957	4.2	4.3	4.1	4.7	11.6	3.8	7.9
1958	6.6	6.8	6.8	6.8	15.9	6.1	12.6
1959	5.3	5.5	5.2	5.9	14.6	4.8	10.7
1960	5.4	5.5	5.4	5.9	14.7	5.0	10.2
1961	6.5	6.7	6.4	7.2	16.8	6.0	12.4
1962	5.4	5.5	5.2	6.2	14.7	4.9	10.9
1963	5.5	5.7	5.2	6.5	17.2	5.0	10.8
1964	5.0	5.2	4.6	6.2	16.2	4.6	9.6
1965	4.4	4.5	4.0	5.5	14.8	4.1	8.1
1966	3.7	3.8	3.2	4.8	12.8	3.4	7.3
1967	3.7	3.8	3.1	5.2	12.9	3.4	7.4
1968	3.5	3.6	2.9	4.8	12.7	3.2	6.7
1969	3.4	3.5	2.8	4.7	12.2	3.1	6.4
1970	4.8	4.9	4.4	5.9	15.3	4.5	8.2
1971	5.8	5.9	5.3	6.9	16.9	5.4	9.9
1972	5.5	5.6	5.0	6.6	16.2	5.1	10.0
1973	4.8	4.9	4.2	6.0	14.5	4.3	9.0
1974	5.5	5.6	4.9	6.7	16.0	5.0	9.9
1975	8.3	8.5	7.9	9.3	19.9	7.8	13.8
1976	7.6	7.7	7.1	8.6	19.0	7.0	13.1
1977	6.9	7.1	6.3	8.2	17.8	6.2	13.1
1978	6.0	6.1	5.3	7.2	16.4	5.2	11.9
1979	5.8	5.8	5.1	6.8	16.1	5.1	11.3
1980	7.0	7.1	6.9	7.4	17.8	6.3	13.1
1981	7.5	7.6	7.4	7.9	19.6	6.7	14.2
1982	9.5	9.7	9.9	9.4	23.2	8.6	17.3
1983	9.5	9.6	9.9	9.2	22.4	8.4	17.8
1984	7.4	7.5	7.4	7.6	18.9	6.5	14.4
1985	7.1	7.2	7.0	7.4	18.6	6.2	13.7
1986	6.9	7.0	6.9	7.1	18.3	6.0	13.1
1987	6.1	6.2	6.2	6.2	16.9	5.3	11.6
1988	5.4	5.5	5.5	5.6	15.3	4.7	10.4
1989	5.2	5.3	5.2	5.4	15.0	4.5	10.0

Source: *Economic Report of the President, 1990* (Washington, D.C.: U.S. Government Printing Office, 1990), p. 338.
*Unemployed as a percentage of the labor force including resident armed forces.
†Unemployed as a percentage of the civilian labor force in the group specified.

2.e. The Record of Unemployment

Unemployment rates in the United States from 1948 to 1989 are listed in Table 2. Over this period, the unemployment rate for all workers reached a low of 2.8 percent in 1953 and a high of 9.5 percent in 1982 and 1983. The table shows some general trends in the incidence of unemployment across different demographic groups:

In most years, women have higher unemployment rates than men. Several factors may be at work here. First, during this period, a large number of women entered the labor force for the first time. Second, discrimination against women in the workplace limited job opportunities for women, particularly early in this period. Finally, a large number of women move out of and into the labor force on temporary maternity leaves.

Teenagers have the highest unemployment rates in the economy. This makes sense because teenagers are the least-skilled segment of the labor force.

Whites have lower unemployment rates than nonwhites. Certainly discrimination plays a role here. That discrimination extends beyond hiring practices and job opportunities for minority workers, to the education that is necessary to prepare students to enter the work force. There is evidence that the quality of education provided in many schools with large minority populations is not as good as that provided in schools with large white populations. Equal opportunity programs and legislation are aimed at rectifying this inequality.

Although exact comparisons across countries are difficult to make because countries measure unemployment in different ways, it is interesting to look at the reported unemployment rates of different countries. Table 3 lists unemployment rates for seven major industrial nations. The rates have been adjusted to match as closely as possible the U.S. definition of unemployment. For instance, the official Italian unemployment data include people who have not looked for work in the past 30 days. The data for Italy in Table 3 have been adjusted to remove these people. If the data had not been adjusted, the Italian unemployment rates would be roughly twice as high as those listed.

Countries not only define unemployment differently, they also use different methods to count the unemployed. All major European countries except Sweden use a national unemployment register to identify the unemployed. Only those people who register for unemployment benefits are considered unemployed. A problem with this method is that it excludes those who have not registered because they are not entitled to benefits and it includes those who receive benefits but would not take a job if one was offered. Other countries—among them the United States, Canada, Sweden, and Japan—conduct monthly surveys of households to estimate the unemployment rate. Surveys allow more comprehensive analysis of unemployment and its causes than does the use of a register. The Organization for Economic Cooperation and Development compared annual surveys of the labor force in Europe with the official register unemployment data and found that only 80 to 85 percent of those surveyed as unemployed were registered in Germany, France, and the United Kingdom. In Italy, only 63 percent of those surveyed as unemployed were registered.

Table 3 Unemployment Rates in Major Industrial Countries, 1960–1989

	Civilian Unemployment Rate (percent)						
Year	United States	Canada	France	Italy	Japan	United Kingdom	West Germany
1960	5.5	6.5	1.5	3.7	1.7	2.2	1.1
1961	6.7	6.7	1.2	3.2	1.5	2.0	.6
1962	5.5	5.5	1.4	2.8	1.3	2.7	.6
1963	5.7	5.2	1.6	2.4	1.3	3.3	.5
1964	5.2	4.4	1.2	2.7	1.2	2.5	.4
1965	4.5	3.6	1.6	3.5	1.2	2.1	.3
1966	3.8	3.4	1.6	3.7	1.4	2.3	.3
1967	3.8	3.8	2.1	3.4	1.3	3.3	1.3
1968	3.6	4.5	2.7	3.5	1.2	3.2	1.1
1969	3.5	4.4	2.3	3.5	1.1	3.1	.6
1970	4.9	5.7	2.5	3.2	1.2	3.1	.5
1971	5.9	6.2	2.8	3.3	1.3	3.9	.6
1972	5.6	6.2	2.9	3.8	1.4	4.2	.7
1973	4.9	5.5	2.8	3.7	1.3	3.2	.7
1974	5.6	5.3	2.9	3.1	1.4	3.1	1.6
1975	8.5	6.9	4.1	3.4	1.9	4.6	3.4
1976	7.7	7.1	4.5	3.9	2.0	5.9	3.4
1977	7.1	8.1	5.1	4.1	2.0	6.4	3.5
1978	6.1	8.3	5.3	4.1	2.3	6.3	3.3
1979	5.8	7.4	6.0	4.4	2.1	5.4	3.0
1980	7.1	7.5	6.4	4.4	2.0	7.0	2.9
1981	7.6	7.5	7.6	4.9	2.2	10.5	4.1
1982	9.7	11.0	8.3	5.4	2.4	11.2	5.8
1983	9.6	11.8	8.5	5.9	2.7	11.7	7.1
1984	7.5	11.2	10.0	5.9	2.8	11.7	7.4
1985	7.2	10.5	10.4	6.0	2.6	11.2	7.5
1986	7.0	9.5	10.6	7.5	2.8	11.2	6.9
1987	6.2	8.8	10.8	7.9	2.9	10.2	6.4
1988	5.5	7.8	10.4	7.9	2.5	8.3	6.3
1989	5.3	7.5	10.1	7.8	. . .	6.4	5.7

Source: *Economic Report of the President, 1990* (Washington, D.C.: U.S. Government Printing Office, 1990), p. 417.

Knowing their limitations, we can still identify some important trends from the data in Table 3. Through the 1960s and early 1970s, European unemployment rates generally were lower than U.S. and Canadian rates. Over the next decade, European unemployment rates increased substantially, as did the rates in North America. But in the mid-1980s, while U.S. unemployment began to fall, European unemployment remained high. The issue of high unemployment rates in Europe has become a major topic of discussion at international summit meetings. Japanese unemployment rates, like those in Europe, were much lower than U.S. and Canadian rates in the 1960s and 1970s. However, unlike European rates, Japanese rates remained much lower in the 1980s. We will discuss the reasons for Japan's rapid growth and low unemployment in future chapters.

RECAP

1. The unemployment rate is the number of people unemployed as a percentage of the labor force.

2. To be in the labor force, one must either have or be looking for a job.

3. By its failure to include discouraged workers and the output lost because of underemployment, the unemployment rate understates real unemployment in the United States.

4. By its failure to include activity in the underground economy, the U.S. unemployment rate overstates actual unemployment.

5. Unemployment data are adjusted to eliminate seasonal fluctuations.

6. Frictional and structural unemployment are always present in a dynamic economy.

7. Cyclical unemployment is a product of recession; it can be moderated by controlling the period of contraction in the business cycle.

8. Economists measure the cost of unemployment in terms of lost output.

9. Unemployment data show that women generally have higher unemployment rates than men, that teenagers have the highest unemployment rates in the economy, and that blacks and other minority groups have higher unemployment rates than whites.

3. INFLATION

inflation:
a sustained rise in the average level of prices

What is inflation?

Inflation is a sustained rise in the average level of prices. Notice the word *sustained*. Inflation does not mean a short-term increase in prices; it means prices are rising over a prolonged period of time. Inflation is measured by the percentage change in price level. The inflation rate in the United States was 4.8 percent in 1989. This means that the level of prices increased 4.8 percent over the year.

3.a. Absolute Versus Relative Price Changes

In the modern economy, over any given period, some prices rise faster than others. To evaluate the rate of inflation in a country, then, economists must know what is happening to prices on average. Here it is important to distinguish between *absolute* and *relative* price changes.

Let's look at an example using the prices of fish and beef:

	Year 1	Year 2
1 pound of fish	$1	$2
1 pound of beef	$2	$4

In year 1, beef is twice as expensive as fish. This is the price of beef *relative* to fish. In year 2, beef is still twice as expensive as fish. The relative prices have not changed between years 1 and 2. What has

Table 4 The Real Value of a Dollar, 1946–1988

Year	Average Price Level*	Purchasing Power of a Dollar†
1946	.195	$5.13
1950	.241	4.15
1954	.269	3.72
1958	.289	3.46
1962	.302	3.31
1966	.324	3.09
1970	.388	2.58
1974	.493	2.03
1978	.652	1.53
1982	.965	1.04
1986	1.096	.91
1988	1.184	.85

*Measured by the consumer price index as given in the *Economic Report of the President*, Washington, D.C.: U.S. Government Printing Office, 1990, p. 359.
†Found by taking the reciprocal of the consumer price index (1/CPI).

changed? The prices of both beef and fish have doubled. The *absolute* levels of all prices have gone up, but because they have increased by the same percentage, the relative prices are unchanged.

Inflation measures changes in absolute prices. In our example, all prices doubled, so the inflation rate is 100 percent. There was a 100 percent increase in the prices of beef and fish. Inflation does not proceed evenly through the economy. Prices of some goods rise faster than others, which means that relative prices are changing at the same time that absolute prices are rising. The measured inflation rate records the *average* change in absolute prices.

3.b. Effects of Inflation

The purchasing power of a dollar is the amount of goods and services it can buy.

To understand the effects of inflation, you have to understand what happens to the value of money in an inflationary period. The real value of money is what it can buy, its *purchasing power*:

$$\text{Real value of \$1} = \frac{\$1}{\text{price level}}$$

The higher the price level, the lower the real value (*or purchasing power*) of the dollar.

Table 4 lists the real value of the dollar in selected years from 1946 to 1988. The price level in each year is measured relative to the average level of prices over the 1982–1984 period. For instance, the 1946 value, .195, means that prices in 1946 were, on average, only 19.5 percent of prices in the 1982–1984 period. Notice that as prices go up, the purchasing power of the dollar falls. In 1946 a dollar bought five times more than a dollar bought in the early 1980s. The value $5.13 means that it took $5.13 with prices at their 1982–1984 level to buy what $1 bought in 1946.

Prices have risen steadily in recent decades. By 1988, they had gone up more than 18 percent above the average level of prices in the 1982–1984 period. Consequently, the purchasing power of a 1988 dollar was lower.

Living with Hyperinflation in Argentina

Jose and Eva Furfaro used to see themselves as solidly middle class: an occasional vacation, a color television set, weekend trips to the movies, even a bit of savings.

"Then the hyperinflation grabbed hold of us," Jose Furfaro said. "Now we are just trying to get to the end of the month without being hungry. I'd say that describes the lower class." . . .

Jose Furfaro, 43, has worked for 10 years as an assembly-line supervisor in a tin-can factory in an industrial suburb of Buenos Aires. He is a union member, oversees 20 workers, and his salary as recently as December and January — 9,000 australs — was the equivalent of a respectable $550 per month. He now earns 45,000 australs a month, but the austral has depreciated so dramatically in dollar terms that it is worth just $64.

His salary has plummeted in value not only in dollar terms, with the collapse of the austral from 17 per $1 to more than 700, but in buying power as well. Despite periodic raises,

Furfaro figures his real decline in income to be 50% over the last six months, as hyperinflation overwhelms his paycheck. . . .

Food, traditionally abundant and cheap in this land of grain and cattle, has become the constant preoccupation for the family. With prices rising as often as twice daily, they budget now between 700 and 1,000 australs a day, or 21,000 to 30,000 per month. . . .

"No one was prepared for this; it's like a war — hyperinflation means total destruction. All we lack are the destroyed buildings," Jose said in a conversation at his dinner table, which fills most of the combination kitchen-dining-living room.

"Now we deny ourselves many things that we used to take for granted," he added. "We used to go out to eat; now we don't. We could go to a sports event; now we can't.

"We took a four-day vacation in January to Mar del Plata [a seaside resort], and we thought, 'This is lovely; we'll come back soon.' We didn't know what was coming." . . .

"We worry about reaching the end of the month, but I know that many more are worried about getting to the 10th of the month," he said, adding that the family has so far been able to avoid the need for Eva to go back to work — assuming she could find a job.

Meanwhile, the family goes without its usual weekend desserts, which Eva enjoyed making. At 1,000 australs ($1.42) for the ingredients, a cake or pie is now a once-a-month treat, if that. Coffee, never before a luxury, now is served occasionally, supplanted by cheaper tea and *yerba mate*, an herb-like drink. . . .

"Our dream is to have our own house," Jose said. "But with this constant inflation, when we nearly had enough, the price shot out of our reach. Finally, we managed, and then this disaster fell on top of us."

■ Excerpted from James F. Smith, "Inflation Turns Argentina Family's Life into Daily Struggle for Survival," *Los Angeles Times*, July 23, 1989, p. 1.

In 1988 $1 bought just $.85 of goods and services priced at their 1982–1984 level compared to the 1988 cost of $1 for the same quantity of goods.

If prices and income rise by the same percentage, inflation is not a problem. It doesn't matter if it takes twice as many dollars now to buy fish and beef than it did before, if we have twice as many dollars in income available to buy the products. Obviously inflation is very much a problem when income rises at a slower rate than prices. Inflation hurts those households whose income does not keep up with the prices of the goods they buy.

▼ Why is inflation a problem? ▲

In the 1970s in the United States, the rate of inflation rose to near-record levels. Many workers believed that their incomes were lagging behind the rate of inflation, so they negotiated cost of living raises in their wage contracts. The typical cost of living raise ties salary to changes in the consumer price index. If the CPI rises 8 percent over a year, workers receive an 8 percent raise plus compensation for experience or productivity increases. As the U.S. rate of inflation fell during the 1980s, concern about cost of living raises subsided as well.

It is important to distinguish between expected and unexpected inflation. *Unexpectedly high inflation* redistributes income away from those who receive fixed incomes toward those who make fixed expenditures. For example, consider a simple loan agreement:

> Maria borrows $100 from Ali, promising to repay the loan in one year at 10 percent interest. In one year, Maria will pay Ali $110—principal of $100 plus interest of $10 (10 percent of $100, or $10).

When Maria and Ali agree to the terms of the loan, they do so with some expected rate of inflation in mind. Suppose they both expect 5 percent inflation over the year. In one year it will take 5 percent more money to buy goods than it does now. Ali will need $105 to buy what $100 buys today. Because Ali will receive $110 for the principal and interest on the loan, he will gain purchasing power. However, if the inflation rate over the year turns out to be surprisingly high—say 15 percent—then Ali will need $115 to buy what $100 buys today. He will lose purchasing power.

Economists use nominal and real interest rates to adjust interest rates for inflation. The **nominal interest rate** is the observed interest rate in the market. The **real interest rate** is the nominal rate minus the rate of inflation:

Real interest rate = nominal interest rate − rate of inflation

If Ali charges Maria 10 percent nominal interest and the inflation rate is 5 percent, the real interest rate is 5 percent. This means that Ali will earn a positive real return from the loan. However, if the inflation rate is 10 percent, the real return from a nominal interest rate of 10 percent is zero. The interest Ali will receive from the loan will just compensate him for the rise in prices; he will not realize an increase in purchasing power. If the inflation rate is higher than the nominal interest rate, then the real interest rate is negative—the lender will lose purchasing power by making the loan.

Now you can see how unexpected inflation redistributes income. Borrowers and creditors agree to loan terms based on what they *expect* the rate of inflation to be over the period of the loan. If the *actual* rate of inflation turns out to be different from what was expected, then the real interest rate paid by the borrower and received by the lender will be different from what was expected. If Ali and Maria both expect a 5 percent inflation rate and agree to a 10 percent nominal interest rate for the loan, then they both expect a real interest rate of 5 percent to be paid on the loan. If the actual inflation rate turns out to be greater than 5 percent, then the real interest rate will be less than expected. Maria will get to borrow Ali's money at a lower real cost than she expected, and Ali will earn a lower real return than he expected. Unexpectedly high inflation hurts creditors and benefits borrowers because it lowers real interest rates.

Figure 4 shows the real interest rates on U.S. Treasury bills from 1965 through 1989. You can see a pronounced pattern in the graph. In the late 1970s, there was a period of negative real interest rates, followed by high positive real rates in the 1980s. The evidence suggests that nominal inter-

Unexpectedly high inflation redistributes income away from those who receive fixed incomes toward those who make fixed expenditures.

nominal interest rate:
the observed interest rate in the market

real interest rate:
the nominal interest rate minus the rate of inflation

Real interest rates are lower than expected when inflation is higher than expected.

est rates did not rise fast enough in the 1970s to offset high inflation. This was a time of severe strain on many creditors, including savings and loan associations and banks. These firms had lent funds at fixed nominal rates of interest. When those rates of interest turned out to be lower than the rate of inflation, the financial institutions suffered significant losses. In the early 1980s, the inflation rate dropped sharply. Because nominal interest rates did not drop nearly as fast as the rate of inflation, real interest rates were high. In this period many debtors were hurt by the high costs of borrowing to finance business or household expenditures.

Unexpected inflation affects more than the two parties to a loan. Any contract calling for fixed payments over some long-term period changes in value as the rate of inflation changes. For instance, a long-term contract that provides union members with 5 percent raises each year for five years gives the workers more purchasing power if inflation is low than if it is high. Similarly, a contract that sells a product at a fixed price over a long-term period will change in value as inflation changes. Suppose a lumber company promises to supply a builder with lumber at a fixed price for a two-year period. If the rate of inflation in one year turns out to be higher than expected, the lumber company will end up selling the lumber for less profit than it had planned. Inflation raises costs to the lumber company.

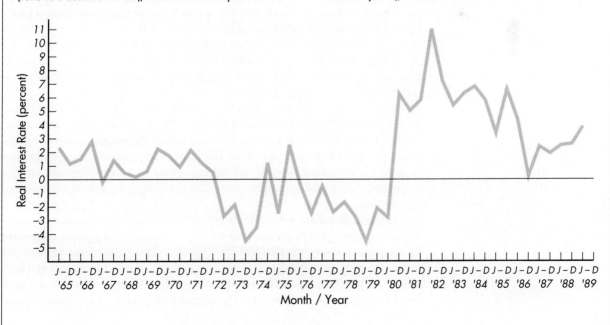

Figure 4
The Real Interest Rate on U.S. Treasury Bills
The real interest rate is the difference between the nominal rate (the rate actually observed) and the rate of inflation over the life of the bond. For instance, in June 1965, a six-month Treasury bill paid the holder 3.87 percent interest. This is the nominal rate of interest. To find the real rate of interest on the bond, we subtract the rate of inflation that existed over the six months of the bond's life (June to December 1965), which was 1.56 percent. The difference between the nominal interest rate (3.87 percent) and the rate of inflation (1.56 percent) is the real interest rate, 2.31 percent. Notice that real interest rates were negative in the middle and late 1970s and then turned highly positive (by historical standards) in the early 1980s. Source: Data from *Federal Reserve Bulletin* (Washington, D.C.: Board of Governors of the Federal Reserve System), various issues.

Usually the company would raise its prices to compensate for higher costs. Because the company contracted to sell its goods at a fixed price to the builder, the builder benefits at the lumber company's expense. Again, unexpectedly high inflation redistributes real income or purchasing power away from those receiving fixed payments to those making fixed payments.

One response to the effects of unexpected inflation is to allow prices, wages, or interest rates to vary with the rate of inflation. Organized labor often negotiates cost of living adjustments as part of new wage contracts. Financial institutions offer variable interest rates on home mortgages to reflect current market conditions. Any contract can be written to adjust dollar amounts over time as the rate of inflation changes.

3.c. Types of Inflation

Economists often classify inflation according to the source of the inflationary pressure. The most straightforward method defines inflation in terms of pressure from the demand side of the market or the supply side of the market:

> *Demand-pull inflation*   Increases in total spending that are not offset by increases in the supply of goods and services cause the average level of prices to rise.

> *Cost-push inflation*   Increases in production costs cause firms to raise prices to avoid losses.

Sometimes inflation is blamed on "too many dollars chasing too few goods." This is a roundabout way of saying that the inflation stems from demand pressures. Because demand-pull inflation is a product of increased spending, it is more likely to occur in an economy that is producing at maximum capacity. If resources are fully employed, in the short run it may not be possible to increase output to meet increased demand. The result: existing goods and services are rationed by rising prices.

Some economists claim that rising prices in the late 1960s were a product of demand-pull inflation. They believe that increased government spending for the Vietnam War caused the level of U.S. prices to rise.

Cost-push inflation can occur in any economy, whatever its output. If prices go up because the costs of resources are rising, the rate of inflation can go up regardless of demand.

For example, some economists argue that the inflation in the United States in the 1970s was largely due to rising oil prices. This means that decreases in the oil supply (a shift to the left in the supply curve) brought about higher oil prices. Because oil is so important in the production of goods, higher oil prices led to increases in prices throughout the economy. Cost-push inflation stems from changes in the supply side of the market.

Cost-push inflation is sometimes attributed to profit-push or wage-push pressures. *Profit-push pressures* are created by suppliers who want to increase their profit margins by raising prices faster than their costs increase. *Wage-push pressures* are created by labor unions and workers who are able to increase their wages faster than their productivity. There have been times when "greedy" businesses and unions have been blamed for periods of inflation in the United States. The problem with these "theories" is that people have always wanted to improve their economic status and always will. In this sense, people have always been greedy. But inflation has not always been a problem. Were people less greedy in the early 1980s when inflation was low than they were in the late 1970s when inflation was high? Obviously we have to look to other reasons to explain inflation. We discuss some of those reasons in later chapters.

3.d. The Inflationary Record

Many of our students, having always lived with inflation, are surprised to learn that inflation is a relatively new problem for the United States. From 1789, when the U.S. Constitution was ratified, until 1940, there was no particular trend in the general price level. At times prices rose, and at times they fell. The average level of prices in 1940 was approximately the same as it was in the late eighteenth century.

Since 1940, prices in the United States have gone up markedly. The price level today is seven times what it was in 1940. But the rate of growth has varied. Figure 5 plots the path of consumer prices in the United States in the post–World War II period. Notice that prices rose rapidly for the first couple of years following the war, and then grew at a relatively slow rate through the 1950s and 1960s. In the early 1970s, the rate of inflation began to accelerate. Prices climbed quickly until the early 1980s, when inflation slowed.

Annual rates of inflation for several industrial and developing nations are shown in Table 5. In 1988, the average rate of inflation across all industrial countries was 3.3 percent; the average across all developing countries was 57.8 percent. Look at the diversity across countries: rates range from 0.7 percent in Japan to 682.3 percent in Brazil.

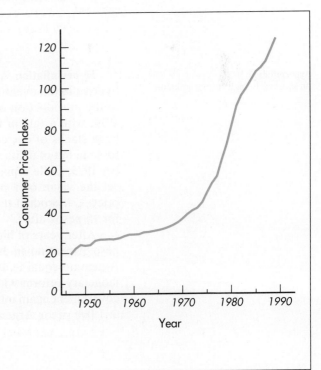

Figure 5
U.S. Consumer Prices, 1946–1989
Prices rose relatively rapidly after World War II, then at a slow rate from the late 1940s until the late 1960s. Prices again rose at a fairly rapid rate through the 1970s. In the early 1980s, price increases moderated. Source: Data from *Economic Report of the President, 1990* (Washington, D.C.: U.S. Government Printing Office, 1990).

Table 5   Rates of Inflation for Selected Countries, 1988

Country	Inflation Rate (percent)
All industrial	3.3
All developing	57.8
Selected industrial:	
Canada	4.0
Germany	1.2
Italy	5.1
Japan	.7
United Kingdom	4.9
United States	4.0
Selected developing:	
Argentina	343.0
Botswana	8.4
Brazil	682.3
Chile	14.7
China	20.7
Egypt	17.7
Hong Kong	7.4
India	9.4
Israel	16.2
Mexico	114.2
Philippines	8.8
Poland	60.0
South Africa	12.8
Uganda	183.6

Source: International Monetary Fund, *International Financial Statistics* (Washington, D.C.), various issues.

hyperinflation:
an extremely high rate of inflation

Hyperinflation is an extremely high rate of inflation. In most cases hyperinflation eventually makes a country's currency worthless and leads to the introduction of a new money. Chile experienced hyperinflation in 1974, with a rate of inflation exceeding 500 percent. People had to carry large stacks of currency for small purchases. Cash registers and calculators ran out of digits as prices reached ridiculously high levels. In September 1975, Chile replaced its money, the escudo, with the Chilean peso. It set the value of 1 peso at 1,000 escudos (striking three zeros from all prices). A product that had sold for 10,000 escudos before the reform sold for 10 pesos after.

After years of high inflation, Argentina replaced the old peso with the peso Argentino in June 1983. The government set the value of 1 peso Argentino equal to 10,000 old pesos. But Argentina did not follow up its monetary reform with a change in economic policy. Two years later the government again introduced a new currency, the austral, setting its value at 1,000 pesos Argentino.

Table 6 German Wholesale Prices, 1914–1924

Year	Price Index
1914	100
1915	126
1916	150
1917	156
1918	204
1919	262
1920	1,260
1921	1,440
1922	3,670
1923	278,500
1924	117,320,000,000,000

Source: J. P. Young, *European Currency and Finance* (Washington, D.C.: U.S. Government Printing Office, 1925).

The most dramatic hyperinflation in modern times occurred in Europe after World War I. Table 6 shows how the price level rose in Germany between 1914 and 1924 in relation to prices in 1914. For instance, the value in 1915, 126, indicates that prices were 26 percent higher that year than in 1914. The value in 1919, 262, indicates that prices were 162 percent higher that year than in 1914. By 1924, German prices were more than 100 trillion times higher than they had been in 1914. At the height of the inflation, the mark was virtually worthless.

As we discuss in later chapters, high rates of inflation generally are caused by rapid growth of the money supply. When a central government wants to spend more than it is capable of funding through taxation or borrowing, it simply issues money to finance its budget deficit. As the money supply increases faster than the demand to hold it, spending increases and prices go up.

RECAP

1. Inflation is a sustained rise in the average level of prices.
2. The higher the price level, the lower the real value (purchasing power) of money.
3. Unexpectedly high inflation redistributes income away from those who receive fixed dollar payments toward those who make fixed dollar payments.
4. The real interest rate is the nominal interest rate minus the rate of inflation.
5. Demand-pull inflation is a product of increased spending; cost-push inflation reflects increased production costs.
6. Hyperinflation is a very high rate of inflation that often results in the introduction of a new currency.

▼▲ **What is a business cycle?**

1. Business cycles are recurring changes in real GNP, in which expansion is followed by contraction. §1.a

2. The four stages of the business cycle are expansion (boom), peak, contraction (recession), and trough. §1.a

3. Leading, coincident, and lagging indicators are variables that change in relation to changes in output. §1.c

▼▲ **How is the unemployment rate defined and measured?**

4. The unemployment rate is the percentage of the labor force that is not working. §2.a

5. To be in the U.S. labor force, an individual must be working or actively seeking work. §2.a

6. Unemployment can be classified as seasonal, frictional, structural, or cyclical. §2.c

7. Frictional and structural unemployment are always present in a dynamic economy; cyclical unemployment is a product of recession. §2.c

▼▲ **What is the cost of unemployed resources?**

8. The GNP gap measures the output lost because of unemployment. §2.d

▼▲ **What is inflation?**

9. Inflation is a sustained rise in the average level of prices. §3

10. The higher the level of prices, the lower the purchasing power of money. §3.b

▼▲ **Why is inflation a problem?**

11. Inflation becomes a problem when income rises at a slower rate than prices. §3.b

12. Unexpectedly high inflation hurts those who receive fixed dollar payments and benefits those who make fixed dollar payments. §3.b

13. Inflation can stem from demand-pull or cost-push pressures. §3.c

14. Hyperinflation—an extremely high rate of inflation—can force a country to introduce a new currency. §3.d

KEY TERMS

business cycle §1.a
recession §1.a
depression §1.b
leading indicator §1.c
coincident indicator §1.c
lagging indicator §1.c

unemployment rate §2.a
discouraged workers §2.b
underemployment §2.b
underground economy §2.b
potential GNP §2.d

natural rate of unemployment §2.d
inflation §3
nominal interest rate §3.b
real interest rate §3.b
hyperinflation §3.d

EXERCISES

Basic Terms and Concepts

1. What is the labor force? Do you believe that the U.S. government's definition of the labor force is a good one—that it includes all the people it should include? Explain your answer.

2. List the reasons why the official unemployment rate may not reflect the true social burden of unemployment. Explain whether the official numbers overstate or understate "true" unemployment in light of each reason you discuss.

3. Suppose you are able-bodied and intelligent but lazy. You'd rather sit home and watch television than work, even though you know you could find an acceptable job if you looked for work.

   a. Are you officially unemployed?

   b. Are you a discouraged worker?

4. Should government try to do anything to reduce the number of people in the following categories?

   a. Frictionally unemployed

   b. Structurally unemployed

   c. Cyclically unemployed

5. Does the GNP gap measure all of the costs of unemployment? Why or why not?

6. Why do teenagers have the highest unemployment rate in the economy?

7. What is a cost of living raise?

8. Define the real interest rate. Use the concept to explain why unexpectedly high inflation redistributes income from creditors to debtors.

Extended Concepts

9. The word *cycle* suggests a regular, recurring pattern of activity. Is there a regular pattern in the business cycle? Support your answer by examining the duration (number of months) of each expansion and contraction in Figure 1.

10. Using the list of leading indicators in Table 1, write a brief paragraph explaining why each variable changes before real output changes. In other words, provide an economic reason why each indicator is expected to lead the business cycle.

When Plant Shuts Down, Retraining Laid-Off Workers Is Toughest Job Yet

CICERO, III.—Spread over miles of fissured asphalt and chain-link fences, blocks beyond the western edge of Chicago, lie the carcasses of once mighty factories.

On March 2, yet another factory expired, one where the General Electric Company made refrigerators. It is making them instead in Decatur, Ala., where it pays nonunion workers $9.50 an hour, $4 less than it paid here...

One of the 1,200 people to lose a job here is Freddie Anderson, 42 years old, divorced and the father of two.... This week Mr. Anderson joined a résumé-writing class in a cheery... room that has been carved into G.E.'s ... administration building...

At the outplacement center here, the ... factory worker confronts the new world of work in the starkest terms possible. Better production technology and tougher competition, much of it against foreign industries that pay workers far less than the men and women here were paid, have driven down the earning power of people who for years made a good living. Good pay now comes with versatility and good education, and few of these people have either.

"That work force is as dysfunctional as you can get," Roberts T. Jones, Assistant Secretary of Labor for Employment and Training, said of the G.E. plant. "You have the anomaly of people coming out of a long successful job history and not able to meet entry-level requirements of other jobs...."

General Electric voluntarily set up the Cicero center ... by using $1.3 million of its own and $2.7 million from the Department of Labor.

Policy makers and labor experts call retraining the antidote to the human dislocations that accompany the demise of old industries. But so far the results have been mixed.

Mr. Anderson had one of the better jobs at the plant ... But even his prospects are not especially bright.

"My last job was repairman," he said. "... It was a very good job. I loved it."

He said he had found only two other jobs so far—one driving a school bus, ... the other as a ... three-month temporary worker at the United States Postal Service....

Many Problems, Few Successes

Drawing firm conclusions about the Cicero program is not possible yet. The program was established two years ago ... and has one more year to run. Problems have cropped up—some because of the attitudes of the workers, some because of company practices, some because of union hostility.

By G.E.'s own measure of success—placing 85 percent of the workers in jobs that pay at least 75 percent of their G.E. wage—the company has a long way to go. ... 187 people had found other jobs through March. But 148 of them were not really retrained; they transferred to Decatur and other G.E. plants. ...

The 39 others who have found new jobs are mostly in manufacturing, jobs that pay an average of $8.50 an hour, or 63 percent of their old wage. About 225 of the plant's 1,200 workers ... have retired with pensions and other benefits. ...

'One of the Best' in Retraining

Still, the dislocated workers here have an edge on most others. Many companies provide no retraining at all, leaving their former employees to fend for themselves. ...

"We don't like closings," said William H. Bywater, president of the International Union of Electronic Workers, G.E.'s biggest union. But in retraining, he said, G.E. is "one of the best. ..."

Adult Education and Job Hunting

The outplacement center provides adult education courses in math, in English as a second language and in preparing for a high school diploma. It provides job-hunting assistance, with help in conducting interviews, filling out applications, writing résumés and negotiating on the telephone.

It also steers workers into on-the-job training with other employers ... Employers who find a worker qualified in most respects but lacking a skill agree to take him on and teach him the skill. In return, the center gives the employer half the worker's wages until the worker is fully trained, up to 26 weeks. ... But few workers sought such jobs in the first two years of the program. About 200 took the adult education and job placement courses, but few were willing to take the final step and commit themselves to another job. ...

■ Source: Peter T. Kilborn, "When Plants Shut Down, Retraining Laid-Off Workers Is Toughest Job Yet," *The New York Times*, April 23, 1990, p. A14.

Commentary

Structural change in an economy forces difficult adjustments. Some of the most dramatic examples of this kind of change have occurred in the so-called rustbelt of the United States. This term refers to the industrial region of the Northeast and the Midwest, where well-paying factory jobs are disappearing in the face of foreign competition and new production techniques. Many workers in this region who once had jobs in automobile manufacturing and steel production have recently been left with fewer job prospects and uncertain futures.

What has caused the reversal in the fortunes of so many industrial workers in the United States? The article mentions that changes in production techniques and foreign competition have driven down manufacturing wages. But this cannot be a complete answer to the question since we expect that well-paid workers are highly valued by their companies. If workers were valuable to their former employers, why are they not considered as valuable to other companies? Is it truly an ''anomaly,'' as stated by a Labor Department official, that laid-off workers with successful job histories are unable to meet entry-level requirements for other jobs, or does economics explain why a situation like this may occur?

We can better understand the causes of the plight of many laid-off industrial workers if we consider the determinants of people's wages. Economic theory suggests that people's wages are tied to the amount they contribute to their firm, which implies that wages increase with people's skills. We can think of two broad categories of skills: general skills that make people valuable to any firm and more specialized skills that make people valuable to certain firms. Examples of general skills include welding, bookkeeping, and an ability to manage people. Skills that are useful to only one firm are those that are specifically tied to the product or structure of that firm. Specific knowledge of this second type is not transferable to other firms.

People who work in a particular firm for an extended period learn both general skills that make them valuable to any similar company and specific skills that make them valuable to their company only. For example, the article mentions Freddie Anderson, who had worked at the General Electric plant in Cicero, Illinios, for almost twenty years and had most recently held a skilled repairman's job. The knowledge Mr. Anderson had acquired in his position may not be transferable to similar positions in other companies since much of his skill may be linked to the particular product line produced at the Cicero plant. Thus, the amount that he was paid at the Cicero plant, reflecting the amount he could contribute to the production of refrigerators there, is greater than the amount he could earn in his next-best job opportunity.

This distinction between general skills and firm-specific skills begins to explain why retraining has not been very successful. Only 39 of the 1,200 workers who lost their jobs at the Cicero plant were successful in finding other manufacturing jobs, and the pay they received was less than two-thirds of their former pay. The skills involved in retraining are very general; the article mentions that the G.E. outplacement center provides courses in math and in English as a second language. To the extent that these skills provide workers with abilities that new employers value, retraining will help the workers earn more. But it is difficult to provide workers with firm-specific skills for new jobs. These skills can only be learned on the job. For this reason, G.E. subsidized the hiring of workers in new jobs.

The distinction between general and firm-specific skills also suggests why workers least likely to benefit from retraining are those within a few years of retirement. Older workers who must undergo on-the-job training will not be able to use their new firm-specific skills for as many years as will younger workers. It is not worthwhile for firms to hire and train workers who are near retirement. That is why many workers at the G.E. plant took early retirement.

Structural change is an integral part of a dynamic, growing economy. Dislocations are probably inevitable when large-scale structural change occurs, and these dislocations benefit some people while hurting others. While retraining helps mitigate some of the effects of the upheaval that accompanies structural change, unfortunately it cannot solve all the problems that will arise.

9

Aggregate Expenditures

1. How are consumption and saving related?
2. What are the determinants of consumption?
3. What are the determinants of investment?
4. What are the determinants of government spending?
5. What are the determinants of net exports?
6. What is the aggregate expenditures function?

PREVIEW

The 1920s were a time of prosperity and economic growth. Real GNP increased by 42 percent between 1920 and 1929. Construction was booming. Stock prices soared. People were optimistic, and that optimism was reflected in their clothes and the popular dance, the Charleston.

The euphoria came to an abrupt end on October 24, 1929, Black Thursday. Stock market speculation turned into panic. Banks failed. The economy collapsed. The recession that began in 1929 and lasted until 1933 was the most severe in recent U.S. history.

The Great Depression had far-reaching effects on economics. Before the Depression, economists believed the economy was self-correcting. Problems of excess demand for or excess supply of goods and services could be solved by the competitive response of a free market. There was no need for the government to intervene in the economy. But the experience of the 1930s seemed to call for a new theory, and that theory was provided by John Maynard Keynes.

During the 1930s, Keynes refined his thinking on output and

employment, offering an alternative to existing economic theory. His ideas were published in 1936, in *The General Theory of Employment, Interest, and Money*. Keynes's theory not only appeared to explain the crash and other economic developments, but also suggested a way in which economic stability could be achieved. Those suggestions initiated and sustained modern interest in macroeconomics. Whether or not economists agree with the philosophy that emerged from Keynes's work, there is no doubt that the study of macroeconomics today is still shaped by the ideas he set forth in the 1930s. More recent economists have developed important alternative macroeconomic theories. Chapter 16 will summarize the differences between the various approaches.

To fully understand why national income, unemployment, and inflation rise and fall over time, we must know what causes the components of spending to change. We cannot understand why the U.S. economy has experienced nine recessions since 1945 or why the 1980s witnessed the longest peace time business cycle expansion in modern times unless we understand why aggregate expenditures change.

In Chapter 6, we said that gross national product is equal to total expenditures. In this chapter we begin an analysis of aggregate spending. We examine each component of spending—consumption, investment, government spending, and net exports—and identify the factors that affect them. In the next chapter we describe how aggregate spending determines the level of national income and how fluctuations in the components of aggregate spending cause fluctuations in national income, unemployment, and inflation.

We begin our examination of aggregate expenditures by discussing consumption, which accounts for approximately 66 percent of total expenditures in the U.S. economy. We then look at investment (15 percent of expenditures), government spending (20 percent of expenditures), and net exports (recently, a small negative percentage of expenditures). Finally we examine the aggregate expenditures function, $C+I+G+X$. We use this model to determine the equilibrium level of income in Chapter 10.

1. CONSUMPTION AND SAVING

▼
How are consumption and saving related?
▲

Households can do three things with their income. They can spend it for the consumption of goods and services, they can save it, or they can pay taxes. Disposable income is what is left after taxes have been paid. It is the sum of consumption and saving:

Disposable income = consumption + saving

or $Yd = C + S$

Disposable income is the income that households actually have available for spending. Whatever disposable income is not spent is saved.

Why are we talking about saving, which is not a component of total spending, in a chapter that sets out to discuss the components of total spending? Saving is simply "not consuming"; it is impossible to separate the incentives to save from the incentives to consume.

1.a. Saving and Savings

Saving occurs over a unit of time; it is a flow concept.

Savings are an amount accumulated at a point in time; they are a stock concept.

Before we go on, you must understand the difference between *saving* and *savings*. *Saving* occurs over a unit of time—a week, a month, a year. For instance, you might save $10 a week or $40 a month. Saving is a *flow* concept. *Savings* are an amount accumulated at a particular point in time—today, December 31, your sixty-fifth birthday. For example, you might have savings of $2,500 on December 31. Savings are a *stock* concept.

Like saving, GNP and its components are flow concepts. They are measured by the year or quarter of the year. Consumption, investment, government spending, and net exports are also flows. Each of them is an amount spent over a period of time.

1.b. The Consumption and Saving Functions

The primary determinant of the level of consumption over any given period is the level of disposable income. The higher disposable income, the more households are willing and able to spend. This relationship between disposable income and consumption is called the **consumption function**. Figure 1(a) shows a hypothetical consumption function. In this economy, when disposable income is zero, consumption is $30. As disposable income rises, consumption rises. For instance, when disposable income is $400, consumption is $390.

consumption function:
the relationship between disposable income and consumption

We use C to represent consumption and Yd to represent disposable income. The line labeled C in Figure 1(a) is the consumption function: it represents the relationship between disposable income and consumption. The other line in the figure creates a 45-degree angle with either axis. (A 45-degree line makes a graph easier to read because every point on the line represents the same value on both axes.) In Figure 1(a), the 45-degree line shows all the points where consumption equals disposable income.

The level of disposable income at which all disposable income is being spent occurs at the point where the consumption function (line C) crosses the 45-degree line. In the graph, C equals Yd when disposable income is $300. What happens if disposable income is more than $300? Consumers save a fraction of any income above $300. You can see this in the graph. The 45-degree line represents all possible points where income equals consumption. Saving occurs at any level of disposable income at which the consumption function lies below the 45-degree line (at which consumption is less than disposable income). The amount of saving is measured by the vertical distance between the 45-degree line and the consumption function. If disposable income is $500, consumption is $480 and saving is $20.

saving function:
the relationship between disposable income and saving

The **saving function** is the relationship between disposable income and saving. Figure 1(b) plots the saving function (S). When the level of disposable income is at $300, consumption equals disposable income, so saving is zero. As disposable income increases beyond $300, saving goes up. In Figure 1(a), saving is the vertical distance between the 45-degree line and the consumption function. In Figure 1(b), we can read the level of saving directly from the saving function.

Notice that at relatively low levels of disposable income, consumption exceeds disposable income. How can consumption be greater than dispos-

Figure 1
Consumption and Saving in a Hypothetical Economy

Figure 1(a) shows that consumption is a positive function of disposable income: it goes up as disposable income rises. The line labeled C = Yd forms a 45-degree angle at the origin. It shows all points where consumption equals disposable income. The point at which the consumption function (line C) crosses the 45-degree line — where disposable income measures $300 — is the point at which consumption equals disposable income. At lower levels of disposable income, consumption is greater than disposable income; at higher levels, consumption is less than disposable income. Figure 1(b) shows the saving function. Saving equals disposable income minus consumption. When consumption equals disposable income, saving is 0. At higher levels of disposable income, we find positive saving; at lower levels, we find negative saving, or dissaving.

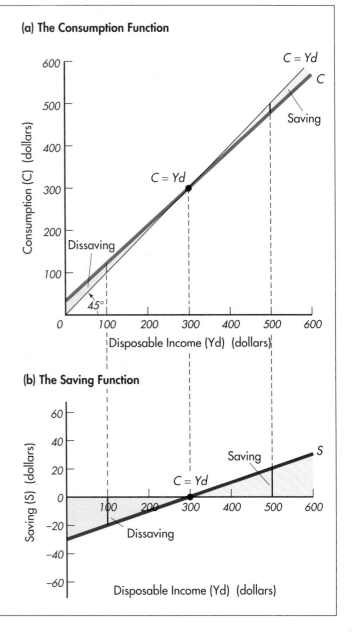

(a) The Consumption Function

(b) The Saving Function

(1) Disposable Income (Yd)	(2) Consumption (C)	(3) Saving (S)
$0	$ 30	$-30
100	120	-20
200	210	-10
300	300	0
400	390	10
500	480	20
600	570	30

dissaving:
spending financed by borrowing or using savings

able income? When a household spends more than it earns in income, the household must finance the spending above income by borrowing or using savings. This is called **dissaving**. In Figure 1(a), dissaving occurs at levels of disposable income between 0 and $300, where the consumption function lies above the 45-degree line. Dissaving, like saving, is measured by the vertical distance between the 45-degree line and the consumption function, but here the consumption function lies *above* the 45-degree line. In Figure 1(b), dissaving occurs where the saving function (line S) lies below the disposable income axis, at disposable income levels between zero and $300. For example, when disposable income is $100, dissaving (negative saving) is $20.

Both the consumption function and the saving function have positive slopes: as disposable income rises, consumption and saving increase. Consumption and saving, then, are positive functions of disposable income. Notice that when disposable income equals zero, consumption is still positive. Even if income falls to zero during a year, families still eat and try as much as possible to maintain their standard of living by borrowing or using their savings.

autonomous consumption:
consumption that is independent of income

There is a level of consumption, called **autonomous consumption**, that does not depend on income. (*Autonomous* here means "independent of income.") In Figure 1(a), consumption equals $30 when disposable income equals zero. This $30 is autonomous consumption; it does not depend on income.

The consumption function consists of two parts: autonomous consumption and consumption that depends on income. The intercept of the consumption function (the value of C when Yd equals zero) measures the amount of autonomous consumption. The intercept in Figure 1(a) is $30, which means that autonomous consumption in this example is $30.

1.c. Marginal Propensity to Consume and Save

Total consumption equals autonomous consumption plus the spending that depends on income. As disposable income rises, consumption rises. This relationship between change in disposable income and change in consumption is the **marginal propensity to consume (MPC)**. The MPC measures change in consumption as a proportion of the change in disposable income:

marginal propensity to consume (MPC):
change in consumption as a proportion of change in disposable income

$$\text{MPC} = \frac{\text{change in consumption}}{\text{change in disposable income}}$$

In Table 1, columns 1 and 2 list the consumption function data we use in Figure 1. The marginal propensity to consume is shown in column 4. In our example, each time that disposable income changes by $100, consumption changes by $90. This means that consumers spend 90 percent of any extra income they receive.

$$\text{MPC} = \frac{\$90}{\$100} = .90$$

Table 1 Marginal Propensity to Consume and Save

(1) Disposable Income (Yd)	(2) Consumption (C)	(3) Saving (S)	(4) Marginal Propensity to Consume (MPC)	(5) Marginal Propensity to Save (MPS)
0	$30	−$30	—	—
$100	$120	−$20	.90	.10
$200	$210	−$10	.90	.10
$300	$300	0	.90	.10
$400	$390	$10	.90	.10
$500	$480	$20	.90	.10
$600	$570	$30	.90	.10

marginal propensity to save (MPS): change in saving as a proportion of change in disposable income

The MPC tells us how much consumption changes when income changes. The **marginal propensity to save (MPS)** defines the relationship between change in saving and change in disposable income. It is the change in saving divided by the change in disposable income:

$$MPS = \frac{\text{change in saving}}{\text{change in disposable income}}$$

The MPS in Table 1 is a constant 10 percent at all levels of income. Each time that disposable income changes by $100, saving changes by $10:

$$MPS = \frac{\$10}{\$100}$$
$$= .10$$

The MPC and the MPS will always be constant at all levels of disposable income in our examples.

The marginal propensity to consume plus the marginal propensity to save must total 1:

$$MPC + MPS = 1$$

Because any change in disposable income is either consumed or saved, the percentage of additional income that is not consumed must be saved. If consumers spend 90 percent of any extra income, they save 10 percent of that income.

The MPC and the MPS determine the rate of consumption and saving as disposable income changes. The MPC is the slope of the consumption function; the MPS is the slope of the saving function. Remember that the slope of a line measures change along the vertical axis that corresponds to change along the horizontal axis. In the case of the consumption function, the slope is the change in consumption (the change on the vertical axis) divided by the change in disposable income (the change on the horizontal axis):

The slope of the consumption function is the same as the MPC; the slope of the saving function is the same as the MPS.

$$\text{Slope of consumption function} = \frac{\text{change in consumption}}{\text{change in disposable income}}$$
$$= MPC$$

If the MPC is higher than .90, consumers want to spend more than 90 percent of any change in disposable income. For example, if the MPC is .95, consumers want to spend 95 percent of any change in disposable income. The consumption function with an MPC of .95 would be a steeper line than the one drawn in Figure 1(a). In general, the steeper the consumption function, the larger the MPC. If the MPC is less than .90, the consumption function would have a flatter slope than the one in the figure.

The slope of the saving function is the MPS:

$$\text{Slope of saving function} = \frac{\text{change in saving}}{\text{change in disposable income}}$$
$$= MPS$$

In general, the steeper the saving function, the greater the slope, and the greater the MPS.

Figure 2(a) shows three consumption functions. All have the same intercept, so autonomous consumption is the same for all. But each has a different slope. C_1 has an MPC of .80. A larger MPC, .90, produces a steeper function (line C_2). A smaller MPC, .70, produces a flatter function (line C_3). The saving functions that correspond to these consumption functions are shown in Figure 2(b). Function S_1, with an MPS of .20, corresponds to consumption function C_1, with an MPC of .80 (remember: MPS = 1 − MPC). Function S_2 corresponds to C_2, and S_3 corresponds to C_3. The higher the MPC (the steeper the consumption function), the lower the MPS (the flatter the saving function). The slope of the consumption function (MPC) measures change in consumption given a change in income. If people spend a greater fraction of extra income, they save a smaller fraction.

Figure 2
Marginal Propensity to Consume and Save
The MPC is the slope of the consumption function. The greater the MPC, the steeper the consumption function. The MPS is the slope of the saving function. The greater the MPS, the steeper the saving function. Because the sum of the MPC and the MPS is 1, the greater the MPC, the smaller the MPS. The steeper the consumption function, then, the flatter the saving function.

(a) Three Consumption Functions

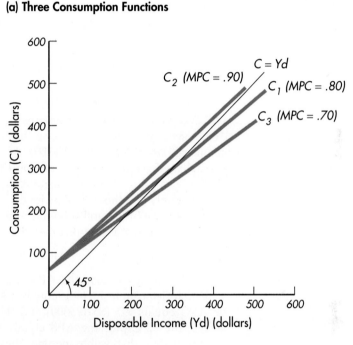

(b) Three Saving Functions

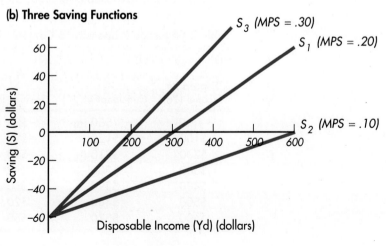

1.d. Average Propensity to Consume and Save

Suppose our interest is not the proportion of change in disposable income that is consumed or saved, but the proportion of disposable income that is consumed or saved. For this we must know the average propensity to consume and the average propensity to save.

average propensity to consume (APC): the proportion of disposable income spent for consumption

The **average propensity to consume (APC)** is that portion of disposable income spent for consumption:

$$APC = \frac{\text{consumption}}{\text{disposable income}}$$

$$\text{or} \quad APC = \frac{C}{Yd}$$

average propensity to save (APS): the proportion of disposable income saved

The **average propensity to save (APS)** is that portion of disposable income that is saved:

$$APS = \frac{\text{saving}}{\text{disposable income}}$$

$$\text{or} \quad APS = \frac{S}{Yd}$$

Table 2 uses the consumption and saving data plotted in Figure 1. The APC and APS are shown in columns 4 and 5. When disposable income is $300, consumption is also $300, so the ratio of consumption to disposable income (C/Yd) equals 1 ($300/$300). At this point, saving equals 0, so the ratio of saving to disposable income (S/Yd) also equals 0 (0/$300). We really do not have to compute the APS because we already know the APC. There are only two things to do with disposable income: spend it or save it. The percentage of income spent plus the percentage saved must add up to 100 percent of disposable income. This means that

$$APC + APS = 1$$

If the APC equals 1, then the APS must equal 0.

When disposable income equals $600, consumption equals $570, so the APC equals .95 ($570/$600) and the APS equals .05 ($30/$600). As always, the APC plus the APS equals 1. If households are spending 95 percent of their disposable income, they must be saving 5 percent.

Table 2 Average Propensity to Consume and Save

(1) Disposable Income (Yd)	(2) Consumption (C)	(3) Saving (S)	(4) Average Propensity to Consume (APC)	(5) Average Propensity to Save (APS)
0	$30	−$30	—	—
$100	$120	−$20	1.20	−.20
$200	$210	−$10	1.05	−.05
$300	$300	0	1.00	.00
$400	$390	$10	.975	.025
$500	$480	$20	.96	.04
$600	$570	$30	.95	.05

Notice in Table 2 how the APC falls as disposable income rises. This is because households spend just a part of any change in income. In Figure 1 (a), the consumption function rises more slowly than the 45-degree line. Remember that consumption equals disposable income along the 45-degree line. The consumption function tells us, then, that consumption rises as disposable income rises, but not by as much as income rises. Because households spend a smaller fraction of disposable income as that income rises, they must be saving a larger fraction. You can see this in Table 2, where the APS rises as disposable income rises. At low levels of income, the APS is negative, a product of dissaving (we are dividing negative saving by disposable income). As disposable income rises, saving rises as a percentage of disposable income, which means that the APS is increasing.

1.e. Determinants of Consumption

▼ What are the determinants of consumption? ▲

Income is just one determinant of household spending. Others include wealth, expectations, demographics, and taxation.

1.e.1. Disposable Income Household income is the primary determinant of consumption, which is why the consumption function is drawn with disposable income on the horizontal axis. Household income usually is measured as current disposable income. By *current* we mean income that is received in the current period—today, this month, this year. Past income and future income certainly can affect household spending, but their effect is through household wealth, not income. Disposable income is after-tax income.

Changes in disposable income are shown by moving along a given consumption function. In the example we have been using, if disposable income rises from $300 to $600, consumption increases from $300 to $570. You can see this by moving along the consumption function from the point where disposable income is $300 to the point, located up and to the right on the consumption function, where disposable income equals $600.

The two-dimensional graphs we have been using relate consumption only to current disposable income. We include the effects of other variables by shifting the consumption function up and down as the values of these other variables change. The slope of the functions does not change, but the intercepts do. All variables except disposable income change autonomous consumption.

Changes in taxation affect disposable income, causing the consumption function to shift. As taxes increase, autonomous consumption falls; as taxes decrease, autonomous consumption rises. We study the effects of taxation in Chapter 12.

wealth:
the value of all assets owned by a household

1.e.2. Wealth Wealth is the value of all the assets owned by a household. Wealth is a stock variable; it includes homes, cars, checking and savings accounts, and stocks and bonds, as well as the value of income expected in the future. (We discuss the role of expectations in the next section.) As household wealth increases, consumption increases at every level of income. You can see this in Figure 3(a) as a shift of the consumption function from C to C_1. The autonomous increase in consumption shifts the intercept of the consumption function from $60 to $100, so consumption increases by $40 at every level of income. If households spend more of their current disposable income as wealth increases, they save less. You can see this as the downward shift of the saving function in Figure 3(b), from S to S_1. The higher level of wealth has households more willing to dissave at each income level than before. Dissaving now occurs at any level of disposable income below $500.

A decrease in wealth has just the opposite effect. Here you would see an autonomous drop in consumption, like the shift from C to C_2, and an autonomous increase in saving, like the shift from S to S_2. Now at every level of disposable income, households spend $40 less than before and save $40 more. The intercept of the consumption function is $20, not $60, and the intercept of the saving function is −$20, not −$60. The new con-

Figure 3
Autonomous Shifts in Consumption and Saving
Autonomous consumption is the amount of consumption that exists when income is 0. It is the intercept of the consumption function. The shift from C to C_1 is an autonomous increase in consumption of $40; it moves the intercept of the consumption function from $60 to $100. The shift from C to C_2 is an autonomous decrease in consumption of $40; it moves the intercept of the consumption function from $60 to $20. Autonomous saving is the amount of saving that exists when income is 0. This is the intercept of the saving function. The shift from S to S_1 is an autonomous decrease in saving of $40; it moves the intercept of the saving function from −$60 to −$100. The shift from S to S_2 is an autonomous increase in saving of $40; it moves the intercept of the saving function from −$60 to −$20. Because disposable income minus consumption equals saving, an autonomous increase in consumption is associated with an autonomous decrease in saving, and an autonomous decrease in consumption is associated with an autonomous increase in saving.

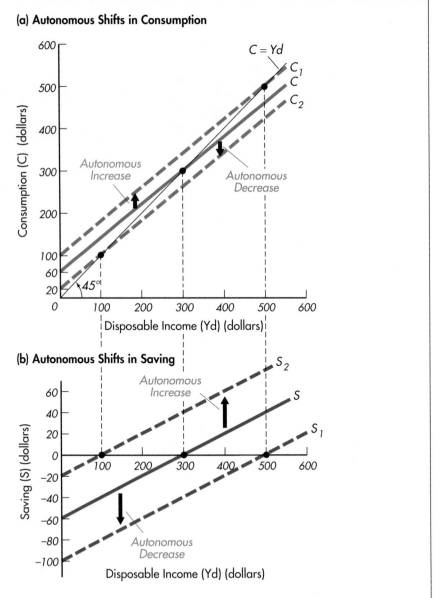

(a) Autonomous Shifts in Consumption

(b) Autonomous Shifts in Saving

sumption function parallels the old one; the curves are the same vertical distance apart at every level of income. So consumption is $40 lower at every level of income. Similarly, the saving functions are parallel because saving is $40 greater at every level of income along S_2 compared to S.

1.e.3. Expectations

Another important determinant of consumption is consumer expectations about future income, prices, and wealth. When consumers expect a recession, when they are worried about losing jobs or cutbacks in hours worked, they tend to spend less and save more. This means an autonomous decrease in consumption and increase in saving. Conversely, when consumers are optimistic, we find an autonomous increase in consumption and decrease in saving.

Expectations are subjective opinions; they are difficult to observe and measure. This creates problems for economists looking to analyze the effect of expectations on consumption. The Conference Board, an independent economic research organization, surveys households to construct its *consumer confidence index,* a measure of consumer opinion regarding the outlook for the economy. Figure 4 plots this index over time. The shaded areas indicate periods of recession in the U.S. economy.

Notice that the index began to fall in mid-1978, foreshadowing the recession of 1980. And the index fell again just before the recessions in the early 1980s, then rose near the end of the recessions. In retrospect, it seems that consumers were predicting both the recessions and the expansions that followed them. But look at the index over the entire period shown in the figure. Notice the many ups and downs that were not followed by expansion or recession.

Clearly the consumer confidence index is not always a reliable indicator of expansion or recession. Still economists' increasing use of this and other measures to better understand fluctuations in consumption underscores the importance of the consumer in the economy.

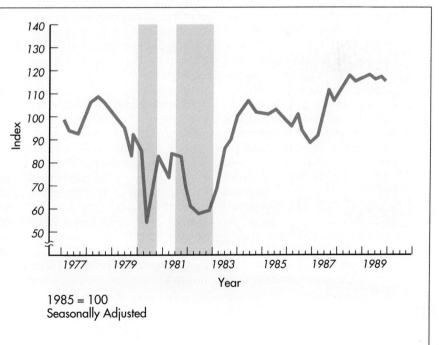

Figure 4
Consumer Confidence Index, 1977–1989
The Conference Board uses surveys to produce an index of consumer confidence in the economy. The index increases with consumers' optimism and decreases with their pessimism. The shaded areas represent recessions. These periods are marked by the low points of consumer confidence in the economy.
Source: *Conference Board Briefing Charts,* February 7, 1990, p. 9. Used by permission.

1985 = 100
Seasonally Adjusted

Permanent Income, Life Cycles, and Consumption

Studies of the consumption function over a long period of time find a function like the one labeled C_L in the graph. This function has a marginal propensity to consume of .90 and an intercept of 0. Consumption functions studied over a shorter period of time have lower MPCs and positive intercepts, like function C_s in the graph, with an MPC of .60. How do we reconcile these two functions?

Economists offer two related explanations for the difference between long-run and short-run consumption behavior: the permanent income hypothesis and the life-cycle hypothesis. The basic idea is that people consume based on their idea of what their long-run or permanent level of income is. A substantial increase in income this month does not affect consumption much in the short run unless it is perceived as a permanent increase.

Let's use point 1 on the graph as our starting point. Here disposable income is $50,000 and consumption is $45,000. Now suppose household income rises to $60,000. Initially consumption increases by 60 percent, the short-run MPC. The household moves from point 1 to point 2 along the short-run consumption function (C_s). The short-run consumption function has a lower MPC than the long-run consumption function because households do not completely adjust their spending and saving habits to short-run fluctuations in income. Once the household is convinced that $60,000 is a permanent level of income, it

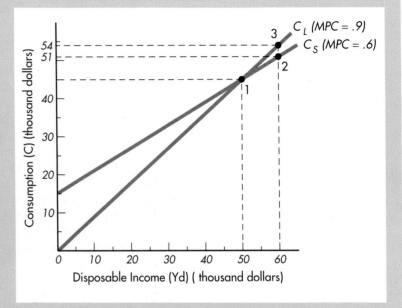

moves from point 2 to point 3 along the long-run consumption function. Here consumption increases by 90 percent, the long-run MPC. In the long run, households adjust fully to changes in income; in the short run, a fluctuation in income does not cause as large a fluctuation in consumption.

When income falls below the permanent income level, the household is willing to dissave or borrow to support its normal level of consumption. When income rises above the permanent income level, the household saves at a higher rate than the long-run MPS. The lower MPC in the short run works to smooth out consumption in the long run. The household does not adjust current consumption

to every up and down in household income.

To maintain a steady rate of consumption over time, households follow a pattern of saving over the life cycle. Saving is low when current income is low relative to permanent income (during school years, periods of unemployment, or retirement). Saving is high when current income is high relative to the lifetime average, typically during middle age.

In the long run, households adjust fully to changes in income. In the short run, in order to smooth consumption over time, they do not. This explains both the difference between the long-run and short-run consumption functions and the stability of consumption over time.

1.e.4. Demographics Other things being equal, economists expect the level of consumption to rise with increases in population. The focus here is on both the number of people in the economy and the composition of that population. The size of the population affects the position of the consumption function; the age of the population affects the slope of the consumption function. The greater the size of the population, ceteris paribus, the higher the intercept of the consumption function. Young households typically are accumulating durable consumer goods (refrigerators, washing machines, automobiles); they have higher MPCs than older households.

RECAP

1. It is impossible to separate the incentives to save from the incentives to consume.
2. Saving is a flow; savings is a stock.
3. Dissaving is spending financed by borrowing or using savings.
4. The marginal propensity to consume measures change in consumption as a proportion of change in disposable income.
5. The marginal propensity to save measures change in saving as a proportion of change in disposable income.
6. The MPC plus the MPS must equal 1.
7. Change in the MPC changes the slope of the consumption function; change in the MPS changes the slope of the saving function.
8. The average propensity to consume measures that portion of disposable income spent for consumption.
9. The average propensity to save measures that portion of disposable income saved.
10. The APC and the APS must equal 1.
11. The determinants of consumption include income, wealth, expectations, demographics, and taxation.
12. Change in disposable income is shown by movement along a consumption function.
13. Change in wealth, expectations, population, or taxation change autonomous consumption, which is shown as a shift of the consumption function.

2. INVESTMENT

Investment is business spending on capital goods and inventories. Investment is the most variable component of total spending. In the next sections we will look at the determinants of investment, and see why investment changes so much over the business cycle.

2.a. Autonomous Investment

In order to simplify our analysis of national income in the next chapter, we assume that investment is autonomous, that it is independent of current income. This does not mean that we assume investment is fixed at a constant amount. There are several factors that cause investment to change, but we assume that current income is not one of them.

As a function of income, autonomous investment is drawn as a horizontal line. This means that investment remains constant as national income changes. In Figure 5, the investment function (the horizontal line labeled I) indicates that investment equals $50 at every level of income. As the determinants of investment change, the investment function shifts autonomously. As investment increases, the function shifts upward (for example, from I to I_1); as investment decreases, the function shifts downward (from I to I_2).

Throughout this text we use graphs that plot income on the horizontal axis in order to analyze how the level of income is determined. Because investment is autonomous, the investment function shows up as a horizontal line. But, investment can and does fluctuate with changes in factors other than income. We look at those factors in the next section.

2.b. Determinants of Investment

What are the determinants of investment?

Investment is business spending on capital goods and inventories. Capital goods are the buildings and equipment businesses need to produce their products. Inventories are final goods that have not been sold. Inventories can be planned or unplanned. For example, in the fall a retail department store wants to have enough sizes and styles of the new clothing lines to attract customers. Without a good-sized inventory, sales will suffer. The goods it buys are planned inventory, based on expected sales. But come February, the store wants to have as few fall clothes left unsold as possible. Goods not sold at this stage are unplanned inventory. They are a sign that sales were not as good as expected and that too much was produced last year.

Both types of inventories—planned and unplanned—are called investment. But only planned investment—capital purchases plus planned inventories—combine with consumer, government, and foreign-sector spending to determine national income. Unplanned investment and unwanted inventories do not. They are simply the leftovers of what has recently gone on in the economy. What economists are interested in are the determinants of planned investment.

2.b.1. The Interest Rate   Business investment is made in the hopes of earning profits. The greater the expected profit, the greater is investment. A primary determinant of whether or not an investment opportunity will be profitable is the rate of interest. The interest rate is the cost of borrowed funds. Much of business spending is financed by borrowing. As the rate of interest goes up, fewer investment projects offer enough profit to warrant their undertaking. In other words, the higher the interest rate, the lower the rate of investment. As the interest rate falls, opportunities for greater profits increase and investment rises.

Figure 5

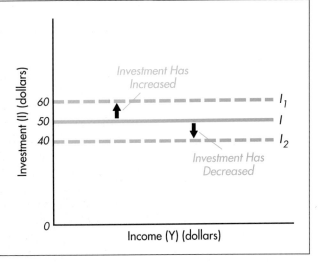

Investment as a Function of Income
Investment is assumed to be autonomous. Because it is independent of current income, it is drawn as a horizontal line. An autonomous increase in investment shifts the function upward, from I to I_1. An increase could be the product of lower interest rates, optimism in business about future sales and revenues, technological change, an investment tax credit that lowers the cost of capital goods, or a need to expand capacity because of a lack of available productive resources. An autonomous decrease in investment moves the function down, from I to I_2. The same factors that cause investment to rise also can cause it to fall as they move in the opposite direction.

rate of return:
profit as a percentage of the cost of an investment

Let's look at a simple example. A firm can acquire a machine for $100 that will yield $120 in output. Whether or not the firm is willing to undertake the investment depends on whether it will earn a sufficient rate of return on its investment. **Rate of return** is the profit from an investment divided by its cost.

If the firm has to borrow $100 for the investment, it will have to pay interest to the lender. Suppose the lender charges 10 percent interest. The firm will have to pay 10 percent of $100, or $10 interest. This raises the cost of the investment to $110, the $100 cost of the machine plus the $10 interest. The firm's rate of return from the investment is 9 percent:

$$\text{Return on investment} = \frac{\$120 - \$110}{\$110}$$
$$= .09$$

As the interest rate rises, the firm's cost of borrowing also rises and the rate of return falls. When the interest rate is 20 percent, the firm must pay $20 in interest, so the total cost of the investment is $120. Here the rate of return is 0 ([$120 − $120]/$120). The higher interest rate reduces the rate of return from the investment and discourages investment spending.

As the interest rate falls, the firm's cost of borrowing falls and the rate of return from the investment rises. If the interest rate is 5 percent, the firm must pay $5 in interest. The total cost of the investment is $105, and the rate of return is 14 percent ([$120 − $105]/$105). The lower interest rate increases the rate of return from the investment and encourages investment spending.

2.b.2. Profit Expectations Firms undertake investment in the expectation of earning a profit. Obviously they cannot know exactly how much profit they will earn. So they use forecasts of revenues and costs to decide on an appropriate level of investment. It is their expected rate of return that actually determines their level of investment.

Many factors affect expectations of profit and, therefore, change the level of investment. Among them are new firms entering the market; political change; new laws, taxes, or subsidies from government; and the overall economic health of the country or world as measured by gross national product.

2.b.3. Other Determinants of Investment

In a sense everything that might affect a firm's expected rate of return determines its level of investment. But three factors—technological change, the cost of capital goods, and capacity utilization—warrant special attention.

Technological change Technological change often is a driving force behind new investment. New products or processes can be crucial to remaining competitive in a technological industry. The computer industry, for example, is driven by technological change. As faster and larger-capacity memory chips are developed, computer manufacturers must utilize them in order to stay competitive.

The impact of technology on investment spending is not new. For example, the invention of the cotton gin stimulated investment spending in the early 1800s, and the introduction of the gasoline-powered tractor in 1905 created an agricultural investment boom in the early 1900s. More recently, the development of integrated circuits stimulated investment spending in the electronics industry.

One measure of the importance of technology is commitment to research and development. Data on spending for research and development across U.S. industries and across countries are listed in Table 3. The industries listed in the table are industries that rely on innovation and the development of new technologies to remain competitive. Research and development is a multi-billion-dollar commitment for these industries. The data on the four industrial countries indicate that these countries spend roughly the same percentage of GNP on research and development. The most obvious trend is the increase in Japanese spending since the mid-1960s. As Japan has grown to be an industrial giant, the role of technological innovation has become increasingly important there.

A commitment to research and development is a sign of the technological progress that marks the industrial nation. The countries listed in Table 3, along with other industrial nations, are the countries where new technology generally originates. New technology developed in any country tends to stimulate investment spending across all nations as firms in similar industries are forced to adopt new production methods to keep up with their competition.

Cost of Capital Goods The cost of capital goods also affects investment spending. As capital goods become more expensive, the rate of return from investment in them drops and the amount of investment falls. One factor that can cause the cost of capital goods to change sharply is government tax policy. The U.S. government has imposed and then removed investment tax credits several times in the past. These credits allow firms to deduct part of the cost of investment from their tax bill. When the cost of investment drops, investment increases. When the cost of investment increases, the level of investment falls.

Table 3 Research and Development Expenditures

Industry	In Selected U.S. Industries, 1986		
	Expenditures (millions of dollars)	*Expenditures as percentage of sales*	*Number of researchers*
Aircraft and missiles	16,240	15.7	100,300
Electrical equipment	18,030	9.1	124,500
Machinery	10,696	7.4	79,900
Chemicals	9,021	5.1	68,100

As a Percentage of GNP, Selected Years, 1965–1987				
Year	*United States*	*France*	*Germany*	*Japan*
1965	2.8	2.0	1.7	1.5
1968	2.8	2.1	2.0	1.6
1971	2.4	1.9	2.2	1.9
1974	2.2	1.8	2.1	2.0
1977	2.2	1.8	2.1	1.9
1980	2.3	1.8	2.4	2.2
1983	2.6	2.2	2.5	2.6
1985	2.7	2.3	2.7	2.9
1986	2.7	2.3	2.7	2.8
1987	2.6	2.3	2.8	n.a.

Source: U.S. Bureau of the Census, *Statistical Abstract of the United States, 1989* (Washington, D.C.: U.S. Government Printing Office, 1989).

Capacity Utilization   If its existing capital stock is being used heavily, a firm has an incentive to buy more. But if much of its capital stock stands idle, the firm has little incentive to increase that stock. Economists sometimes refer to the productive capacity of the economy as the amount of output that can be produced by businesses. In fact the Federal Reserve constructs a measure of capacity utilization that indicates how close to capacity output the economy is.

Figure 6 plots the rate of capacity utilization in the U.S. economy over the 1967–1989 period. During this time, U.S. industry operated at a high rate of 87.9 percent of capacity in 1973 and at a low rate of 72.1 percent of capacity in the recession year of 1982. We never expect to see 100 percent of capacity utilized for the same reasons that we never expect zero unemployment. There are always capital goods that are temporarily moving between jobs or looking for employment as in the case of frictional unemployment of labor and there are always capital goods that are unemployed because of technological change similar to the case of structural unemployment.

When the economy is utilizing its capacity at a high rate, there is pressure to increase the production of capital goods and expand productive capacity. When capacity utilization is low—when factories and machines sit idle—investment tends to fall.

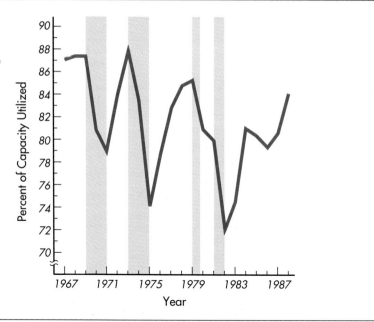

Figure 6
Capacity Utilization Rates for Total U.S. Industry, 1967–1989
The Federal Reserve estimates the rate at which capacity is utilized in U.S. industry. The higher the rate, the greater the pressure for investment to expand productive capacity.

2.c. Volatility

We said that investment is the most variable component of total spending. What role do the determinants of investment play in that volatility?

Figure 7 graphs interest rates on Treasury bills in the 1980s in several industrial countries. Notice that the rates fluctuate widely. They are much more variable than income. Interest rates are a very important determinant of investment. Clearly the fact that they are so variable contributes to the variability of investment.

Expectations are subjective judgments about the future. Expectations can and often do change suddenly with new information. A rumor of a technological breakthrough, a speech by the president or a powerful member of Congress, even a revised weather forecast can cause firms to re-examine their thinking about the expected profitability of an investment. In developing economies, the protection of private property rights can have a large impact on investment spending. If a business expects a change in government policy to increase the likelihood of the government's expropriating its property, obviously it is not going to undertake new investments. Conversely, if a firm believes that the government will protect private property and encourage the accumulation of wealth, it will increase its investment spending. The fact that expectations are subject to large and frequent swings contributes to the volatility of investment.

Technological change proceeds very unevenly, making it difficult to forecast. Historically we find large increases in investment when a new technology is first developed and decreases in investment after the new technology is in place. This causes investment to move up and down unevenly through time.

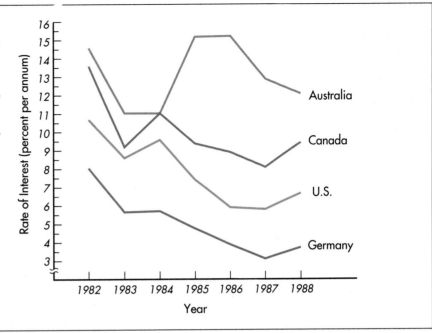

Figure 7
Interest Rates on Treasury Bills, 1982–1989
Treasury bills are government debt. The interest rates on this kind of debt in Australia, Canada, Germany, and the United States over time illustrate how interest rates vary. The variability of interest rates is one reason for the variability of investment. Source: Data from International Monetary Fund, *International Financial Statistics*, Washington, D.C., various issues.

Changes in tax policy occur infrequently, but they can create large incentives to invest or not to invest. U.S. tax laws have swung back and forth on whether or not to offer an investment tax credit. A credit was first introduced in 1962. It was repealed in 1969, then readopted in 1971, and later revised in 1975, 1976, and 1981. In 1986, the investment tax credit was repealed again. Each of these changes had an impact on the cost of capital goods and contributed to the volatility of investment.

Finally, investment generally rises and falls with the rate of capacity utilization over the business cycle. As capacity utilization rises, some firms must add more factories and machines in order to continue increasing output and avoid reaching their maximum output level. As capacity utilization fluctuates, so will investment.

RECAP

1. As a function of income, autonomous investment is drawn as a horizontal line.
2. The primary determinants of investment are the interest rate and profit expectations. Technological change, the cost of capital goods, and the rate of capacity utilization have enormous inpact on those expectations.
3. Investment fluctuates widely over the business cycle because the determinants of investment are so variable.

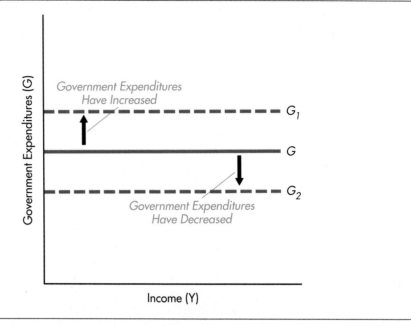

Figure 8
Government Expenditures as a Function of Income
Government spending is assumed to be autonomous and set by government policy. The government spending function is the horizontal line labeled G. Autonomous increases in government spending move the function upward (for example, from G to G_1); decreases move the function downward (for example, from G to G_2).

3. GOVERNMENT SPENDING

▼ What are the determinants of government spending? ▲

Government spending on goods and services is the second largest component of aggregate expenditures in the United States. In later chapters we examine the behavior of government in detail. Here we focus on how the government sector fits into the aggregate expenditures–income relationship. We assume that government spending is set by government authorities at whatever level they choose, independent of current income. In other words, we assume that government spending, like investment, is autonomous.

Figure 8 depicts government expenditures as a function of income. The function, labeled *G,* is a horizontal line. If government officials increase government expenditures, the function shifts upward, parallel to the original curve by an amount equal to the increase in expenditures (for example, from *G* to G_1). If government expenditures are reduced, the function shifts downward by an amount equal to the drop in expenditures (for example, from *G* to G_2).

4. NET EXPORTS

The last component of aggregate expenditures is net exports, spending in the international sector. GNP net exports equal a country's exports (what it sells to the rest of the world) minus its imports (what it buys from the rest of the world) on the merchandise and services accounts. When net exports are positive, there is a surplus on the merchandise and services accounts. When net exports are negative, there is a deficit. The United States has had a net exports deficit since 1983. This is a relatively new phenomenon: the country had run surpluses throughout the post–World War II era.

4.a. Exports

We assume that exports are autonomous. There are many factors that determine the actual value of exports, among them foreign income, tastes, government trade restrictions, and exchange rates. But we assume that exports are not affected by current domestic income. You can see this in the second column of Table 4, where exports are $30 at each level of domestic income.

As foreign income increases, domestic exports increase at every level of domestic income. Decreases in foreign income lower domestic exports at every level of domestic income. Similarly, changes in tastes or government restrictions on international trade or exchange rates can cause the level of exports to shift autonomously. When tastes favor domestic goods, exports go up. When tastes change, exports go down. When governments impose restrictions on international trade, exports fall. When restrictions are lowered, exports rise. Finally, when the domestic currency depreciates on the foreign exchange market (making domestic goods cheaper in foreign countries), exports rise. When the domestic currency appreciates on the foreign exchange market (making domestic goods more expensive in foreign countries), exports fall.

4.b. Imports

Domestic purchases from the rest of the world (imports) also are determined by tastes, trade restrictions, and exchange rates. Here domestic income plays a role too. The greater domestic income, the greater domestic imports. The import data in Table 4 show imports increasing with income. When income is 0, autonomous imports equal $10. As income increases, imports increase.

Table 4   Hypothetical Export and Import Schedule

Domestic Income	Exports	Imports	Net Exports
0	$30	$10	$20
$100	$30	$20	$10
$200	$30	$30	$ 0
$300	$30	$40	−$10
$400	$30	$50	−$20
$500	$30	$60	−$30
$600	$30	$70	−$40

America was deluged by foreign ice cream last year: 576 gallons came in from New Zealand and 12 gallons from Denmark. In other words, foreigners "foisted" almost as much ice cream on "hapless" Americans as a large Safeway sells on a summer Saturday. Obviously, a crisis was imminent.

While many people relish American-made ice cream with deliberately foreign-sounding names, few people realize that the U.S. government restricts ice-cream imports to less than one-tenth of one percent of U.S. consumption. Jamaica, the Netherlands and Belgium are the only other countries allowed to sell ice cream to Americans, and with quotas so low and transportation costs high, they don't bother to ship us any ice cream at all.

The U.S. exports hundreds of thousands of gallons of ice cream to Canada, yet Canadian ice cream is banned from the U.S. Canada expressed its appreciation for this treatment last year by slapping a quota on U.S. ice-cream exports to Canada. (Dairy trade was exempted from last year's Free Trade Agreement.)

Across North America, armies of bureaucrats have mobilized to slug this one out. Officials from the Canadian Embassy met with U.S. State Department officials to raise the ice-cream issue last October. Canada filed a formal complaint with the U.S. government in November. The U.S. Agriculture Department convened a task force that spent months studying ice-cream quotas.

On May 5 of this year, President Bush sent a letter to the U.S. International Trade Commission demanding an ice-cream investigation. The ITC has had as many as 30 people dealing with this project. The ITC made a report on Aug. 28 to the U.S. Trade Representative's Office, which is responsible for forwarding it to the president. According to Claire Buchan, spokeswoman for the trade rep, "The president has not made a decision on this, and there is not a deadline." Doesn't he realize the ice cream is melting?

The U.S. ice-cream quotas date back to Dec. 31, 1970, when President Nixon decreed that future ice-cream imports could not exceed 431,330 gallons a year. Why? That year, according to Deputy Secretary of Agriculture Ann Veneman, testifying this July before the ITC, the U.S. was hit with a "flood of imports." This so-called "flood" amounted to barely 1% of U.S. ice cream consumption.

How did Mr. Nixon decide to limit imports to exactly 431,330 gallons a year? Section 22 of the Agriculture Adjustment Act allows the U.S. government to protect domestic price-support programs by restricting imports to 50% of the annual average

marginal propensity to import (MPI): change in imports as a proportion of change in income

We measure the sensitivity of changes in imports to changes in income by the marginal propensity to import. The **marginal propensity to import (MPI)** is that portion of any extra income spent on imports.

$$\text{MPI} = \frac{\text{change in imports}}{\text{change in income}}$$

In Table 4, the MPI is .10, or 10 percent. Every time income changes by $100, imports change by $10.

How do other factors—tastes, government trade restrictions, and exchange rates—affect imports? When domestic tastes favor foreign goods, imports rise. When they do not, imports fall. When government tightens restrictions on international trade, imports fall. (See Economic Insight: ''The Great Ice Cream War.'') When those restrictions are loosened, imports rise. Finally, when the domestic currency depreciates on the foreign exchange market (making foreign goods more expensive to

imports of a representative period. Ice-cream imports did not begin until 1969 — so the U.S. government chose the years 1967, 1968, and 1969. This allowed the government to slash imports by 95% of their 1970 level and then tell foreigners that the 5% remaining was their "fair" market share.

Under the "free trade" Bush administration, the Agriculture Department still has a phobia about foreign ice cream. Deputy Undersecretary Veneman told the ITC, "We believe that imports above (the current) level would render or tend to render ineffective or materially interfere with the domestic dairy price support program."

The ice-cream controversy illustrates the meaninglessness of some of the central terms in our trade law. In 1983, the Agriculture Department concluded that imports of roughly 160 million pounds of casein, a dairy derivative, did not "materially interfere with domestic dairy (price)

supports," even though the casein imports had far greater impact on the dairy price support program than did ice-cream imports.

This July, when ITC Chairman Anne Brunsdale pushed Agriculture Department official John Mengel to explain what had changed between 1983 and 1989, Mr. Mengel sputtered, "I think, Madam Chairman, that perhaps budget is a stronger consideration now." Yet the Agriculture Department a few weeks later endorsed a $900 million drought bailout to farmers who had failed to protect themselves by buying crop insurance.

Given all this controversy, what was the ITC looking at? Apparently, it looked only at changing the distribution of the quota — allowing more countries to compete to sell the same tiny amount of ice cream to the U.S. Abolishing or increasing the quota apparently was not even seriously considered.

In this mega-investigation, the U.S. government has probably already spent more than a thousand dollars in administrative expenses for each gallon of ice cream imported into the U.S. last year. International trade disputes are rapidly degenerating into a full employment program for government bureaucrats.

Since 1987, the U.S. has been hollering for the abolition of all trade-distorting agricultural subsidies. But how can we tell the Japanese to abolish their rice subsidies or the Europeans to stop dumping wheat when the U.S. is terrified over a few scoops of ice cream?

■ Source: James Bovard, "The Great Ice Cream War," *The Wall Street Journal,* September 6, 1989, p. A18.

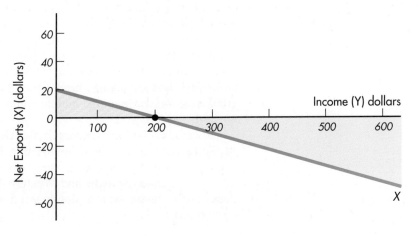

Figure 9
Net Exports as a Function of Income
The net exports function is the downward-sloping line labeled X. Because exports are autonomous and imports increase with income, net exports fall as domestic income rises. Notice that net exports can be positive or negative.

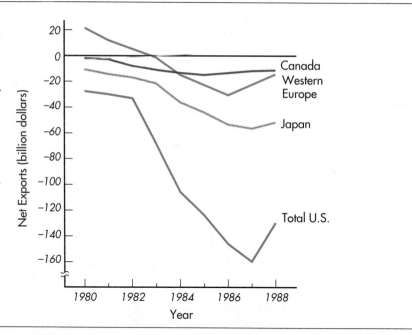

Figure 10
Total U.S. Net Exports and Net Exports with Canada, Japan, and Western Europe, 1980–1988
Total U.S. net exports were negative over the years in the figure, in large part a product of negative net exports with Japan. Net exports with Western European countries were positive in the early 1980s, then turned negative. Net exports with Canada remained relatively stable over the period. Source: Data from *Economic Report of the President, 1990* (Washington, D.C.: U.S. Government Printing Office, 1990), p. 413.

domestic residents), imports fall. And when the domestic currency appreciates on the foreign exchange market (lowering the price of foreign goods), imports rise.

4.c. The Net Export Function

The higher domestic income, the lower net exports.

In our hypothetical economy in Table 4, net exports are listed in the last column. They are the difference between exports and imports. Because imports rise with domestic income, the higher that income, the lower net exports.

The net exports function, labeled *X,* is shown in Figure 9. The downward slope of the function indicates that net exports fall as income increases. Net exports are the only component of aggregate expenditures that can take on a negative value (saving can be negative, but it is not part of spending). Negative net exports mean that the domestic economy is importing more than it exports. The net exports function shifts with changes in income (foreign and domestic), tastes, government trade restrictions, and exchange rates. For example, as foreign income increases, domestic exports increase and the net exports function shifts upward.

Recent levels of net exports in the United States are shown in Figure 10. Total U.S. net exports were negative over the years plotted. The figure also shows the net exports of the United States with its largest trading partners—Canada, Japan, and Western Europe. Clearly the U.S. trade deficit with Japan was a dominant factor in the size of the overall trade deficit.

There are many assembly plants on the Mexican side of the U.S.-Mexico border known as *maquiladoras*, such as this RCA plant in Juarez, Mexico. U.S. firms ship components to these plants where Mexican workers assemble the components into products which are then shipped back to the United States. The value of these assembly operations represent imports for the United States. As U.S. income rises, the value of such imports will also rise and U.S. net exports will fall. Correspondingly, Mexican net exports will rise.

RECAP

1. Net exports equal a country's exports minus its imports.
2. Exports are determined by foreign income, tastes, government trade restrictions, and exchange rates; they are independent of domestic income.
3. Imports are a positive function of domestic income; they also depend on tastes, government trade restrictions, and exchange rates.
4. The marginal propensity to import measures change in imports as a proportion of the change in domestic income.
5. Net exports fall as domestic income rises.

5. THE AGGREGATE EXPENDITURES FUNCTION

What is the aggregate expenditures function?

The aggregate or total expenditures function is the sum of the individual functions for each component of spending. Aggregate expenditures (AE) equal consumption (C), plus investment (I), plus government spending (G), plus net exports (X):

$$AE = C + I + G + X$$

Before we can add the components together, we must account for the fact that the consumption function was drawn with consumption as a function of disposable income (Yd), while investment, government spending,

Figure 11
The Aggregate Expenditures Function

To find the aggregate expenditures function, we begin with the consumption function (labeled C) and add the investment function (I), to create the C+I function. We then add the government spending function (G) to find the C+I+G function. Notice that the C, C+I, and C+I+G functions are all parallel. They have the same slope because investment and government spending are assumed to be autonomous. Because I and G do not change with income, the slope of the C+I and C+I+G functions equals the slope of the consumption function (the MPC). Net exports are added to the C+I+G function to find the aggregate expenditures function, C+I+G+X. The aggregate expenditures function has a smaller slope than the other functions when net exports are negative.

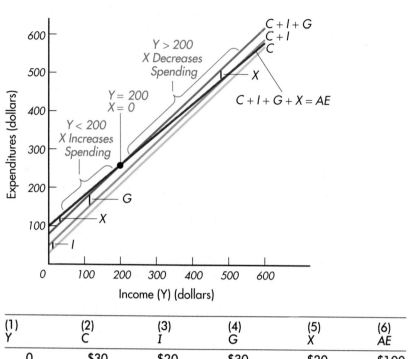

(1) Y	(2) C	(3) I	(4) G	(5) X	(6) AE
0	$30	$20	$30	$20	$100
$100	$120	$20	$30	$10	$180
$200	$210	$20	$30	0	$260
$300	$300	$20	$30	−$10	$340
$400	$390	$20	$30	−$20	$420
$500	$480	$20	$30	−$30	$500
$600	$570	$20	$30	−$40	$580

and net exports were drawn as functions of income (Y), where Y equals net national product or national income. Disposable income is less than national income because of taxes. If we assume that there are no taxes, then Yd equals Y and the consumption function can be drawn as a function of national income. Let's make that assumption for now just to simplify our analysis. In the next chapter we add the effect of taxes on consumption and aggregate expenditures.

The table in Figure 11 lists aggregate expenditures data for a hypothetical economy. Income is in the first column; the individual components of aggregate expenditures are in columns 2 through 5. Aggregate expenditures, listed in column 6, are the sum of the components at each level of income.

The aggregate expenditures function (AE) can be derived graphically by summing the individual expenditure functions (Figure 11). We begin with the consumption function (C) and then add autonomous investment, $20, to the consumption function at every level of income to arrive at the C + I function. To this we add constant government spending, $30, at every level of income to find the C+I+G function. Finally, we add the net exports function to find C+I+G+X, or the AE function.

Notice that the C, C+I, and C+I+G functions are all parallel. They all have the same slope, that determined by the MPC. The AE function has a smaller slope than the other functions because the slope of the net exports function is negative. By adding the X function to the C+I+G function, we are decreasing the slope of the AE function; the C+I+G+X function has a smaller, flatter slope than the C+I+G function.

The X function increases spending for levels of income below $200 and decreases spending for levels of income above $200. At $200, net exports equals 0 (see column 5). Because domestic imports increase as domestic income increases, net exports fall as income rises. At incomes above $200, net exports are negative, so aggregate expenditures are less than C+I+G.

We use the AE function in the next chapter to derive the equilibrium level of income. The concept of macroeconomic equilibrium points out the key role aggregate expenditures play in determining output and national income. As you will see, the equilibrium level of national income is that level toward which the economy automatically tends to move. Once that equilibrium is established, there is no tendency for income to change unless a change in autonomous expenditures occurs.

RECAP

1. Aggregate expenditures are the sum of consumption, investment, government spending, and net exports at every level of income.

2. Assuming that I is autonomous and G is constant, the C, C+I, and C+I+G functions are parallel lines.

3. Net exports increase aggregate expenditures at relatively low levels of domestic income and decrease aggregate expenditures at relatively high levels of domestic income.

SUMMARY

▼▲ How are consumption and saving related?

1. Consumption and saving are the components of disposable income; they are determined by the same variables. § 1

2. Dissaving occurs when consumption exceeds income. § 1.b

3. The marginal propensity to consume (MPC) is change in consumption divided by change in disposable income; the marginal propensity to save (MPS) is change in saving divided by change in disposable income. § 1.c

4. The average propensity to consume (APC) is consumption divided by disposable income; the

average propensity to save (APS) is saving divided by disposable income. § 1.d

▼▲ **What are the determinants of consumption?**

5. The determinants of consumption are income, wealth, expectations, demographics, and taxation. §§ 1.e.1, 1.e.2, 1.e.3, 1.e.4

▼▲ **What are the determinants of investment?**

6. Investment is assumed to be autonomous, independent of current income. § 2.a

7. The determinants of investment are the interest rate, profit expectations, technological change, the cost of capital goods, and the rate at which capacity is utilized. §§ 2.b.1, 2.b.2, 2.b.3

8. Firms use the expected rate of return to determine the expected profitability of an investment project. § 2.b.1

9. Investment is highly variable over the business cycle because the determinants of investment are themselves so variable. § 2.c

▼▲ **What are the determinants of government spending?**

10. Government spending is set by government authorities at whatever level they choose. § 3

▼▲ **What are the determinants of net exports?**

11. Net exports are the difference between what a country exports and what it imports; both exports and imports are a product of foreign or domestic income, tastes, trade restrictions, and exchange rates. §§ 4.a, 4.b

12. Because imports rise with domestic income, the higher that income, the lower net exports. § 4.c

▼▲ **What is the aggregate expenditures function?**

13. The aggregate expenditures function is the sum of the individual functions for each component of spending. § 5

14. The slope of the aggregate expenditures function is flatter than that of the consumption function because it includes the net exports function, which is negative. § 5

KEY TERMS

consumption function § 1.b
saving function § 1.b
dissaving § 1.b
autonomous consumption § 1.b
marginal propensity to consume (MPC) § 1.c
marginal propensity to save (MPS) § 1.c

average propensity to consume (APC) § 1.d
average propensity to save (APS) § 1.d
wealth § 1.e.2
rate of return § 2.b.1
marginal propensity to import (MPI) § 4.b

EXERCISES

Basic Terms and Concepts

1. Why do we study the consumption and saving functions together?

2. Explain the difference between a flow and a stock.

3. Fill in the blanks in the following table:

Income	Consumption	Saving	MPC	MPS	APC	APS
$1,000	$400	————			———	.60
$2,000	$900	$1,100	———	———	———	———
$3,000	$1,400	———	———	.50	———	———
$4,000	———	$2,100	———	———	———	———

4. Why is consumption so much more stable over the business cycle than investment? In your answer, discuss household behavior as well as business behavior.

5. Assuming investment is autonomous, draw an investment function with income on the horizontal axis. Then show how the function shifts if

a. the interest rate falls.

b. an investment tax credit is repealed by Congress.

c. a new president is expected to be a strong advocate of probusiness policies.

d. there is a great deal of excess capacity in the economy.

6. Use the table below to answer the following questions:

a. What is the MPC?

b. What is the MPS?

c. What is the MPI?

d. What is the level of aggregate expenditures at each level of income?

e. Graph the aggregate expenditures function.

Y	C	I	G	X
$500	$500	$10	$20	$60
$600	$590	$10	$20	$40
$700	$680	$10	$20	$20
$800	$770	$10	$20	0
$900	$860	$10	$20	-$20
$1,000	$950	$10	$20	-$40

Extended Concepts

7. Based on the table in exercise 6, what is the linear equation for each of the following functions?

a. Consumption

b. Investment

c. Net exports

d. Aggregate expenditures

Saving: Not the American Way

Can anything persuade spendthrift Americans to put a little more of each week's paycheck into the bank? Plenty of skeptics say nothing will work. . .

Maybe so, but that won't stop Washington from trying. . . Policymakers led by President Bush will release a flurry of proposals designed to push people to squirrel away more money. The president . . . is expected to propose a two-pronged plan to enlarge the pool of capital: one, tentatively called the American Family Savings Plan, would permit families to put up to $5,000 a year into a savings plan, and the interest and dividends would accumulate tax free. Bush is also expected to renew his effort for a cut in the capital-gains tax . . . which failed last year. . . .

The United States is one of the world's lowest savers (chart). In 1988 American households banked only 4.4 percent of their after-tax income, well below Japan and Germany. . . Tax law, which generally benefits borrowing far more than saving, is in part responsible. In addition, the slide in savings is "a by-product of our social progress," says Harvard economics professor Lawrence Summers. The spread of pension plans, health and disability insurance and large increases in social-security benefits have vastly reduced the need felt by many Americans to save. . .

Does the low savings rate matter? Federal Reserve Board chairman Alan Greenspan calls it "the most important long-term issue that has to be addressed." Savings . . . act as a pool of money that businesses can tap for new plants, equipment and employ-ees. Greater savings keep interest rates lower, making it cheaper for businesses to borrow in this country. Because of these advantages, most economists dismiss the commonly held view that curbing consumption would drag the economy into a recession. . . .

The Bush administration concept, the American Family Savings Plan, is a variation on the IRA theme and intended to play to middle-income families. . . . Critics say the plan would eventually cost the Treasury billions of dollars. "What you're really doing is planting a lot of delayed budget deficits that will blossom like fruit trees in half a dozen years," says Henry Aaron of The Brookings Institution.

Critics like Aaron believe that tax incentives are a poor way to attack the low savings rate in any case. They argue that balancing the budget . . . would accomplish the same aims. Other experts think Washington frets too much over savings. John Makin of the American Enterprise Institute says that the rest of the world is saving so much and investing it in this country that the U.S. savings rate isn't as relevant as before. Some economists contend the problem will right itself. . . .

Michael Darby, under-secretary of Commerce for economic affairs, points out that the savings rate can be improved without sweeping changes in consumers' spending habits. He explains that vast as it is, the U.S. trade deficit — in effect, the savings gap — represents only about 2 percent of U.S. annual output. Darby says that if Americans saved just two more pennies out of every dollar they earn, they would close the entire gap — and eliminate any additional borrowing from foreigners. "Even a 1 cent increase in savings would halve the problem," Darby says. On that argument, Bush can expect wide congressional support for this year's saving proposals. The only question then is whether the public will put those two pennies away.

■ Source: Rich Thomas, "Saving: Not the American Way," Newsweek, January 8, 1990, pp. 44–45.

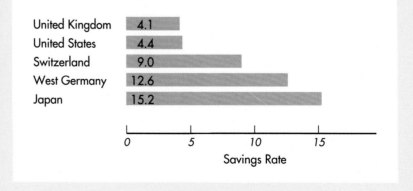

United Kingdom 4.1
United States 4.4
Switzerland 9.0
West Germany 12.6
Japan 15.2

Savings Rate

Commentary

You may remember the fable about the frugal ant who survives because of his thrifty nature and the spend-thrift grasshopper who perishes due to his profligate ways. Does this fable suggest dire consequences for the United States, in which the average household saves only 4.4 percent of its after-tax income? Does it also predict that households in more frugal Germany and Japan, which save 12.6 and 15.2 percent of their after-tax income, respectively, face the brighter future enjoyed by the ant? The article addresses this issue and also discusses reasons for saving, reasons that may help explain why savings rates differ across countries.

To understand the determinants of the savings rate, we need to consider why people save. Savings provide a safety net against economic hardship caused by an accident, illness, or the loss of employment. Another reason people save is to purchase homes and big-ticket durable goods, as well as to finance future educational expenses. People also save in anticipation of their retirement, or to pass on their wealth to their heirs.

The savings rate will be sensitive to conditions related to these motivations. For example, the spread of pension plans, health and disability insurance, and increases in social security payments have reduced the savings rate in the United States by diminishing the motivation for saving. The relatively high savings rate in Japan reflects the influence of another motive: high real-estate prices mean that it takes thirteen years' worth of savings at the national rate from an average salary to accumulate a down payment on a house. The savings rate for an individual also depends upon his or her stage of life, with higher rates of savings occurring when an individual's income is large relative to the average of that person's income over a lifetime. This life-cycle theory of savings helps explain the impact of demographics on a country's savings rate. For example, as a large cohort of people in the United States enter their late thirties and forties during the 1990s, they will begin to save for their retirement, raising the national savings rate. If the middle-age population bulge in the United States exceeds that in Japan or Germany, the U.S. savings rate will tend to rise relative to that of those two countries.

What can the government do to promote savings?

One tool that the government may attempt to use is taxes. In Canada, for example, the creation of a tax-free savings account increased the Canadian savings rate, but in the United States the savings flowing into IRA accounts may simply have come from other savings that were not tax-exempt. The government may also attempt to promote savings by discouraging people from taking on debt. In Germany, in contrast to the United States, interest payments on mortgages and consumer loans are not tax-deductible. A tax deduction on a mortgage lowers its cost and encourages people to take on debt rather than save.

The concern with the low savings rate in the U.S. stems from the fear that a small pool of national savings will make borrowing for investment projects more expensive. As borrowing becomes more expensive, less investment will be undertaken, which adversely affects an economy's prospects for growth. As the world economy becomes more intertwined and U.S. investors are able to borrow from outside the country, a relatively small pool of U.S. savings becomes less constraining to U.S. investors. However, money borrowed from abroad must be paid back with interest to citizens of foreign countries. This represents a transfer of wealth from U.S. borrowers to foreign lenders.

These points help us make sense of two seemingly contradictory statements in the article. The statement by John Makin that the U.S. savings rate is not as relevant as before is true if we focus on the fact that the worldwide pool of savings is available to U.S. borrowers. But it is also true that money borrowed from abroad must be paid back with interest, and this future transfer of wealth may represent, as Alan Greenspan, the chairman of the Federal Reserve, states, "the most important long-term issue that has to be addressed."

The parable of the ant and the grasshopper promotes the virtue of thrift. But is the ant happier than the grasshopper? Does the ant's saving enable it to prosper in the future, while the grasshopper continues to scratch for its life? In terms of this fable, the economist (posing as an entomologist) wants to know why the ant was frugal, why the grasshopper was a spendthrift, and what this behavior meant for the survival and happiness of each species.

An Algebraic Model of Aggregate Expenditures

Aggregate expenditures (AE) equal consumption (C) plus investment (I) plus government spending (G) plus net exports (X). If we can develop an equation for each component of spending, we can put them together in a single model.

Consumption The consumption function can be written in general form

$$as \quad C = C^a + c \ Yd$$

where C^a is autonomous consumption and c is the MPC. The consumption function for the data in Chapter 9 is

$$C = \$30 + .90 \ Yd \text{ as shown in Figure 1.}$$

Saving The corresponding saving function is

$$S = -\$30 + .10 \ Yd \text{ as illustrated in Figure 2.}$$

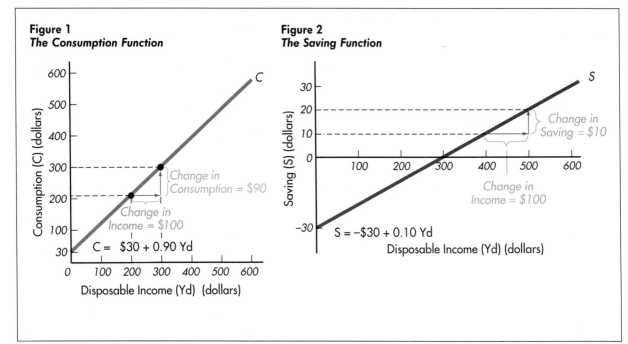

Figure 1
The Consumption Function

Figure 2
The Saving Function

Investment Investment is autonomous at I^a, which is equal to $20.

Government Spending Government spending is autonomous at G^a, which is equal to $30.

Net Exports Exports are autonomous at EX^a and equal to $30. Imports are given by the function:

$$IM = IM^a + im\ Y$$

where im is the MPI. Here, then,

$$IM = \$10 + .10Y$$

Net exports equal exports minus imports, or

$$X = \$30 - \$10 - .10Y$$
$$= \$20 - .10Y$$

as shown in Figure 3.

Aggregate Expenditures Summing the functions for the four components (and ignoring taxes, so that Yd equals Y):

$$AE = C^a + c\ Y + I^a + G^a + EX^a - IM^a - im\ Y$$
$$= \$30 + .90Y + \$20 + \$30 + \$30 - \$10 - .10Y$$
$$= \$100 + .80Y$$

as shown in Figure 4.

In the appendix to Chapter 10 we use the algebraic model of aggregate expenditures presented here to solve for the equilibrium level of national income.

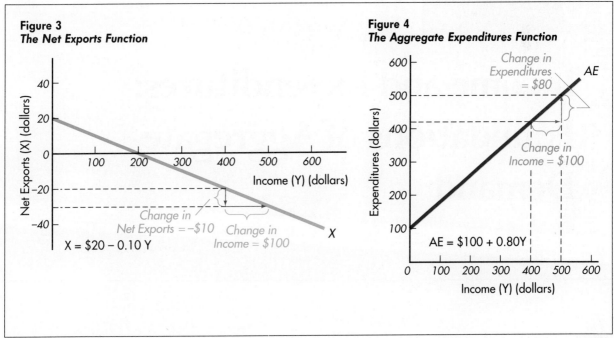

Figure 3
The Net Exports Function

Figure 4
The Aggregate Expenditures Function

10

Income and Expenditures: Foundations of Aggregate Demand

1. How do aggregate expenditures affect income?

2. What does equilibrium mean in macroeconomics?

3. What are the leakages from and injections to spending?

4. Why does equilibrium income change by a multiple of a change in autonomous expenditures?

5. What is the multiplier?

6. What is the relationship between the GNP gap and the recessionary gap?

7. How does international trade affect the size of the multiplier?

PREVIEW   What determines the level of national income? If you know the answer to this question, you are well on your way to understanding business cycles. Sometimes national income is growing and jobs are relatively easy to find; at other times national income is falling and large numbers of people are out of work. Macroeconomists use several models to analyze the causes of business cycles. We discuss some of them in Chapter 16. Underlying all of these models is the concept of macroeconomic equilibrium.

Equilibrium here means what it did when we talked about supply and demand: a point of balance, a point from which there is no tendency to move. In macroeconomics, equilibrium is the level of income and expenditures that the economy tends to move toward and remain at until autonomous spending changes.

Economists have not always agreed on how an economy reaches equilibrium, on the forces that move an economy from one equilibrium to another, or on the effect of equilibrium income on unemployment. This last issue formed the basis of economic debate during the Great Depression. Before the 1930s, classical economists generally believed that the economy always established an equilibrium consistent with a high level of employed resources. John Maynard Keynes did not agree. He believed that an economy can come to rest at a level of income that generates a high level of unemployed resources and that certain actions are necessary to ensure that the economy rises to a level of income consistent with a high level of employment. In particular, Keynes argued that government must intervene in a big way in the economy.

To understand the debate that began during the 1930s and continues on various fronts today, it is necessary to understand how equilibrium income is determined. This is our focus here. In later chapters we examine the relationship between equilibrium and the level of employed resources, and the effect of government policy on both of these elements.

1. EQUILIBRIUM INCOME AND EXPENDITURES

▼ What does equilibrium mean in macroeconomics? ▲

Equilibrium is a point from which there is no tendency to move. People do not change their behavior when everything is consistent with what they expect, with their plans. However, when plans and reality do not match, people adjust their behavior to make them match. Determining a nation's equilibrium level of income and expenditures is the process of defining that level of income and expenditures at which plans and reality are the same.

1.a. Expenditures and Income

We use the aggregate expenditures function we described at the end of Chapter 9 to demonstrate how equilibrium is determined. Keep in mind that the aggregate expenditures function represents *planned* expenditures at different levels of income. We focus on planned expenditures because they represent the level at which households, firms, government, and the foreign sector expect to spend.

Actual expenditures always equal income and output because they reflect changes in inventories. That is, inventories automatically raise or lower investment expenditures so that actual spending equals income, which equals output. However, aggregate expenditures may not equal income. What happens when planned spending and income are not equal? When planned spending on goods and services *exceeds* the current value of output, the production of goods and services increases. Because output equals income, the level of national income also increases. This is the situation for all income levels below $500 in Figure 1. At these levels, total spending is greater than income, which means that more goods and services are being purchased than are being produced. The only way this can

John Maynard Keynes

John Maynard Keynes is considered by many to be the greatest economist of the twentieth century. His major work, *The General Theory of Employment, Interest, and Money,* had a profound impact on macroeconomics, on both thought and policy. Keynes (pronounced *canes*) was born in Cambridge, England, on June 5, 1883. He studied economics at Cambridge University, where he became a lecturer in economics in 1908. During World War I, Keynes worked for the British treasury. At the end of the war, he was the treasury's representative at the Versailles Peace Conference. He resigned from the British delegation at the conference to protest the harsh terms being imposed on the defeated countries. His resignation and publication of the *Economic Consequences of the Peace* (1919) made him an international celebrity.

In 1936, Keynes published *The General Theory.* It was a time of world recession (it has been estimated that around one-quarter of the U.S. labor force was unemployed at the height of the Depression), and policymakers were searching for ways to explain the persistent unemployment. In the book Keynes suggested that an economy could come to equilibrium at less than potential GNP. More important, he argued that government policy could be altered to end recession. His analysis emphasized aggregate expenditures. If private expenditures were not sufficient to create equilibrium at potential GNP, government expenditures could be increased to stimulate income and output. This was a startling concept. Most economists of the time believed that government should not take an active role in the economy. With his *General Theory,* Keynes started a "revolution" in macroeconomics.

happen is for goods produced in the past to be sold. When spending is greater than income, then, business inventories fall. The change in inventories offsets the excess of planned expenditures over income, so that actual expenditures (including the unplanned change in inventories) equal income. You can see this in column 7 of the table, where the change in inventories offsets the excess of aggregate expenditures over income (the difference between columns 6 and 1).

What happens when inventories fall? As inventories fall, manufacturers increase production to meet the demand for products. This increased production increases income. This means that when aggregate expenditures exceed income, income rises.

When aggregate expenditures exceed income, income rises.

At income levels above $500 in the table, aggregate expenditures are less than income. This means that inventories are accumulating above planned levels, that more goods and services are being produced than are being purchased. As inventories rise, businesses begin to lower output. The unplanned increase in inventories is counted as a form of investment spending, so that actual expenditures equal income. For example, when income is $600, aggregate expenditures are only $580. The $20 of produced goods that are not sold are measured as inventory investment. The $580 of aggregate expenditures plus the $20 of unplanned inventories equal $600, the level of income. As inventories increase, firms cut production, which causes income to fall. When aggregate expenditures are less than income, then, income falls.

When aggregate expenditures are less than income, income falls.

There is only one level of income in the table in Figure 1 where income does not change, as is shown in the highlighted bar. When income is $500,

(1) Income (Y)	(2) Consumption (C)	(3) Investment (I)	(4) Government Spending (G)	(5) Net Exports (X)	(6) Aggregate Expenditures (AE)	(7) Unplanned Change in Inventories	(8) Change in National Income
0	$30	$20	$30	$20	$100	−$100	Increase
$100	$120	$20	$30	$10	$180	−$80	Increase
$200	$210	$20	$30	0	$260	−$60	Increase
$300	$300	$20	$30	−$10	$340	−$40	Increase
$400	$390	$20	$30	−$20	$420	−$20	Increase
$500	$480	$20	$30	−$30	$500	0	No change
$600	$570	$20	$30	−$40	$580	$20	Decrease
$700	$660	$20	$30	−$50	$660	$40	Decrease

Figure 1
The Equilibrium Level of National Income

Macroeconomic equilibrium occurs where aggregate expenditures (AE) equal national income (Y). In the graph it is the point where the AE line crosses the 45-degree line, where expenditures and income both equal $500. When aggregate expenditures exceed income (as they do at an income level of $400, for example), income rises to the equilibrium level. When aggregate expenditures are less than income (as they are at an income level of $600, for example), income falls back to the equilibrium level.

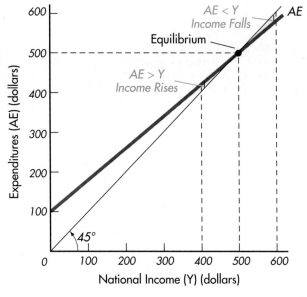

The equilibrium level of income is where aggregate expenditures equal national income.

▼ How do aggregate expenditures affect income? ▲

aggregate expenditures equal $500. The equilibrium level of income (or output) is that point at which aggregate expenditures equal national income (or output).

When aggregate expenditures equal income, planned spending equals the output produced and the income generated from producing that output. As long as planned spending is consistent with income, income does not change. But if planned spending is higher or lower than income, income does change. Equilibrium is that point at which planned spending and income are equal.

The graph in Figure 1 illustrates equilibrium graphically. The 45-degree line shows all possible points where aggregate expenditures (measured on the vertical axis) equal income (measured on the horizontal axis). The equilibrium level of income, then, is simply the point where the aggre-

The Paradox of Thrift

People generally believe that saving is good and that more saving is better. However, if every family increased its saving, the result could be less income for the economy as a whole. In fact increased saving could actually lower savings for all households.

This effect of higher saving is called the *paradox of thrift*. A *paradox* is a true proposition that seems to contradict common beliefs. We believe that we will be better off by increased saving, but in the aggregate, increased saving could cause the economy to be worse off. The paradox of thrift is a *fallacy of composition*: what is true of a part is true of the whole. It often is unsafe to generalize that what is true at the micro level is also true at the macro level.

The graph illustrates the effect of higher saving. Initial equilibrium occurs where the $S+T+IM$ curve intersects the $I+G+EX$ curve, at an income of $500. Suppose saving increases by $20 at every level of income.

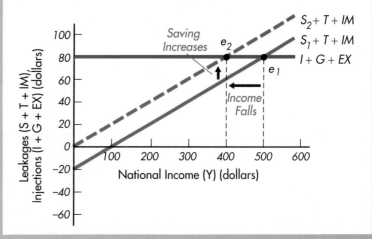

The S_1+T+IM curve shifts up to the S_2+T+IM curve. A new equilibrium is established at an income level of $400. The higher rate of saving causes equilibrium income to fall by $100.

Notice that the graph is drawn with a constant $I+G+EX$ line. If investment increases along with saving, equilibrium income would not necessarily fall. In fact, because saving is necessary before there can be any investment, we would ex-

pect a greater demand for investment funds to induce higher saving. If increased saving is used to fund investment expenditures, the economy should grow over time to higher and higher levels of income. Only if the increased saving is not injected back into the economy is there a paradox of thrift. The fact that governments do not discourage saving suggests that the paradox of thrift generally is not a real-world problem.

gate expenditures line (*AE*) crosses the 45-degree line. In the figure, equilibrium occurs where income and expenditures are $500.

An economy is always somewhere on the *AE* curve. When the *AE* curve lies above the 45-degree line—for example, at an income level of $400—aggregate expenditures are greater than income. What happens? National income rises to the equilibrium level, where it tends to stay. When the *AE* curve lies below the 45-degree line—at an income level of $600, for example—aggregate expenditures are less than income, which pushes income down. Once income falls to the equilibrium level ($500 in our example), it tends to stay there.

The response of business to spending pushes the economy toward equilibrium. Keynes used the interaction of aggregate expenditures and national income to describe the behavior of the economy. Next, we examine another way of looking at macroeconomic equilibrium.

1.b. Leakages and Injections

Investment, government spending, and exports are injections that increase autonomous aggregate expenditures.

Saving, taxes, and imports are leakages that reduce autonomous aggregate expenditures.

The equilibrium level of income occurs where leakages equal injections.

Equilibrium can be determined using aggregate expenditures and income. Another way to determine equilibrium involves leakages from and injections into the income stream, the circular flow of income and expenditures.

Leakages reduce autonomous aggregate expenditures. There are three leakages in the stream from domestic income to spending: saving, taxes, and imports.

The more households save, the less they spend. An increase in autonomous saving means a decrease in autonomous consumption, which could cause the equilibrium level of income to fall.

Taxes are an involuntary reduction in consumption. The government transfers income away from households. Higher taxes lower autonomous consumption, in the process lowering autonomous aggregate expenditures and the equilibrium level of income.

Imports are expenditures for foreign goods and services. They reduce expenditures on domestic goods and services. An autonomous increase in imports reduces net exports, causing autonomous aggregate expenditures and the equilibrium level of income to fall.

For equilibrium to occur, these leakages must be offset by corresponding *injections* of spending into the domestic economy, through investment, government spending, and exports.

☐ Household saving generates funds that businesses can borrow and spend for investment purposes.

☐ The taxes collected by government are used to finance government purchases of goods and services.

☐ Exports bring foreign capital into the domestic economy.

There is no reason to expect that each injection matches its corresponding leakage—that investment equals saving, that government spending equals taxes, or that exports equal imports. But for equilibrium to occur, total injections must equal total leakages.

Figure 2 shows how leakages and injections determine the equilibrium level of income. Column 5 of the table lists the total leakages from aggregate expenditures: saving (S) plus taxes (T) plus imports (IM). Saving and imports both increase when income increases. We assume that there are no taxes so the total amount of leakages ($S + T + IM$) increases as income increases.

Column 9 lists the injections at alternative income levels. Because investment (I), government spending (G), and exports, (EX) are all autonomous, total injections ($I + G + EX$) are constant at all levels of income.

To determine the equilibrium level of income, we compare leakages with injections. As long as injections exceed leakages, national income goes up. In the table in Figure 2, national income increases at every level of income under $500 (see the last column). When leakages exceed injections, which happens at all levels of income above $500, national income falls. When income equals $500, both leakages and injections equal $80, so there is no pressure for income to change. The equilibrium level of income

Figure 2
Leakages, Injections, and Equilibrium Income
Leakages equal saving (S), taxes (T), and imports (IM). Injections equal investment (I), government spending (G), and exports (EX). Equilibrium is that point where leakages equal injections, shown by the highlighted bar in the table. In the graph equilibrium is the point at which the S+T+IM curve intersects the I+G+EX curve, where national income (Y) equals $500. At lower levels of income, injections exceed leakages, so Y rises. At higher levels of income, leakages exceed injections, so Y falls.

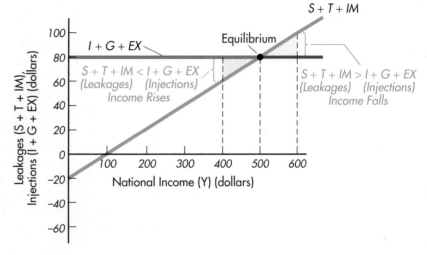

(1) Income (Y)	(2) Saving (S)	(3) Taxes (T)	(4) Imports (IM)	(5) Leakages (S+T+IM)	(6) Investment (I)	(7) Government Spending (G)	(8) Exports (EX)	(9) Injections (I+G+ EX)	(10) Change in National Income
0	−$30	0	$10	−$20	$20	$30	$30	$80	Increase
$100	−$20	0	$20	0	$20	$30	$30	$80	Increase
$200	−$10	0	$30	$20	$20	$30	$30	$80	Increase
$300	0	0	$40	$40	$20	$30	$30	$80	Increase
$400	$10	0	$50	$60	$20	$30	$30	$80	Increase
$500	$20	0	$60	$80	$20	$30	$30	$80	No change
$600	$30	0	$70	$100	$20	$30	$30	$80	Decrease
$700	$40	0	$80	$120	$20	$30	$30	$80	Decrease

occurs where leakages ($S + T + IM$) equal injections ($I + G + EX$).

When leakages exceed injections, planned spending is less than current income or output, so national income and production fall. When injections exceed leakages, planned spending is greater than current income or output, so national income and production rise. Only when leakages equal injections is the equilibrium level of national income established.

The graph in Figure 2 shows the interaction of leakages and injections graphically. The equilibrium point is where the $S+T+IM$ and $I+G+EX$ curves intersect, at an income level of $500. At higher levels of income, leakages are greater than injections (the $S+T+IM$ curve lies above the $I+G+EX$ curve). When leakages are greater than injections, income falls to the equilibrium point. At lower levels of income, injections are greater than leakages (the $I+G+EX$ curve lies above the $S+T+IM$ curve). Here income rises until it reaches $500. Only at $500 is there no pressure for income to change.

If you compare Figures 1 and 2, you can see that it does not matter whether we use aggregate expenditures or leakages and injections—the equilibrium level of income is the same.

As imports rise, spending leakages from the domestic economy increase and the equilibrium level of national income falls. The photo shows a natural gas tanker entering Boston Harbor with a shipment of liquefied natural gas intended for U.S. consumption. The United States is heavily dependent on foreign sources of fuels even though the United States is a large producer of oil and gas.

RECAP

1. Equilibrium is a point from which there is no tendency to move.
2. When aggregate expenditures exceed income, income rises.
3. When aggregate expenditures are less than income, income falls.
4. Saving, taxes, and imports are leakages of planned spending from domestic aggregate expenditures.
5. Investment, government spending, and exports are injections of planned spending into domestic aggregate expenditures.
6. Equilibrium occurs at the level of income at which aggregate expenditures equal income, and leakages equal injections.

2. CHANGES IN EQUILIBRIUM INCOME AND EXPENDITURES

Equilibrium is a point from which there is no tendency to move. But in fact the equilibrium level of income does move. In the last section we described how aggregate expenditures push income and output up or down toward their level of equilibrium. Here we examine how changes in autonomous expenditures affect equilibrium. This becomes very important in understanding macroeconomic policy, the kinds of things government can do to control the business cycle.

2.a. The Multiplier

Any change in autonomous expenditures is multiplied into a larger change in equilibrium income.

▼ Why does equilibrium income change by a multiple of a change in autonomous expenditures? ▲

Remember that equilibrium is that point where aggregate expenditures equal income. If we increase autonomous expenditures, then we raise the equilibrium level of income. But by how much? It seems logical to expect a 1 to 1 ratio: if autonomous spending increases by a dollar, equilibrium income should increase by a dollar. Actually, equilibrium income increases by more than a dollar. The change in autonomous expenditures is multiplied into a larger change in the equilibrium level of income.

In Chapter 6 we used a circular flow diagram to show the relationship of expenditures to income. In that diagram you saw how one sector's expenditures become another sector's income. This concept helps explain the effect of a change in autonomous expenditures on the equilibrium level of income. If A's autonomous spending increases, then B's income rises. B spends part of that income in the domestic economy (the rest is saved or used to buy foreign goods), generating new income for C. C spends part of that income in the domestic economy, generating new income for D. And the rounds of increased spending and income continue. All of this is the product of A's initial autonomous increase in spending. And each round of increased spending and income affects the equilibrium level of income.

We talk here about rounds of increased spending and income. But the process is more of a spiral (see Figure 3) than a circle because in each new round the amount by which spending and income increases grows smaller.

Let's look at an example, using Table 1 and Figure 3. Suppose government spending goes up $20 to improve public parks. What happens to the equilibrium level of income? The autonomous increase in government spending increases the income of park employees by $20. As their income increases, so does the consumption of park employees. For example, let's say they spend more money on hamburgers. In the process, they are increasing the income of the hamburger producers, who in turn increase their consumption.

Table 1 shows how a single change in spending generates further changes. Round 1 is the initial increase in government spending to improve public parks. That $20 expenditure increases the income of park employees by $20 (column 1). As income increases, those components of aggregate expenditures that depend on current income—consumption and net exports—also increase by some fraction of the $20.

Consumpton changes by the marginal propensity to consume multiplied by the change in income; imports change by the marginal propensity to import multiplied by the change in income. To find the total effect of the initial change in spending, we must know the fraction of any change in income that is spent in the domestic economy. In the hypothetical economy we have been using, the MPC is .90 and the MPI is .10. This means that for each $1 of new income, consumption rises by $.90 and imports rise by $.10. Spending on *domestic* goods and services, then, rises by $.80. Because consumption is spending on domestic goods and services, and imports are spending on foreign goods and services, the percentage of a change in income that is spent domestically is the difference between the MPC and the MPI. If the MPC equals .90 and the MPI equals .10, then 80 percent of any change in domestic income ($MPC - MPI = .80$) is spent on domestic goods and services.

The percentage of a change in income that is spent domestically is the difference between the MPC and the MPI.

Table 1 The Multiplier Effect

	(1) Change in Income	(2) Change in Domestic Expenditures	(3) Change in Saving	(4) Change in Imports
Round 1	$ 20.00	$16.00	$ 2.00	$ 2.00
Round 2	16.00	12.80	1.60	1.60
Round 3	12.80	10.24	1.28	1.28
Round 4	10.24	8.20	1.02	1.02
	.	.	.	.
	.	.	.	.
	.	.	.	.
Totals	$100.00	$80.00	$10.00	$10.00

Column 2 = column 1 × (MPC − MPI)

Column 3 = column 1 × MPS

Column 4 = column 1 × MPI

$$\text{Multiplier} = \frac{1}{MPS + MPI}$$

$$= \frac{1}{.1 + .1}$$

$$= \frac{1}{.2}$$

$$= 5$$

In round 1 of Table 1, the initial increase in income of $20 induces an increase in spending on domestic goods and services of $16 (.80 × $20). Out of the $20, $2 is saved because the marginal propensity to save is .10 (1 − *MPC*). The other $2 is spent on imports (*MPI* = .10). The park employees receive $20 more income. They spend $16 on hamburgers at a local restaurant; they save $2; and they spend $2 on imported beer.

Only $16 of the workers' new income is spent on goods produced in the domestic economy, hamburgers. That $16 becomes income to the restaurant's employees and owner. When their income increases by $16, they spend 80 percent of that income ($12.80) on domestic goods (round 2, column 2). The rest of the income is saved and spent on imports.

Each time income increases, expenditures increase. But the increase is smaller and smaller each new round of spending. Why? Because 10 percent of each change in income is saved and another 10 percent is spent on imports. These are leakages out of the income stream. This means just 80 percent of the change in income is spent and passed on to others in the domestic economy as income in the next round.

To find the total effect of the initial change in spending of $20, we could keep on computing the change in income and spending round after round, and then sum the total of all rounds. The change in income and spending never reaches zero, but becomes infinitely small.

Fortunately we do not have to compute each round-by-round increase

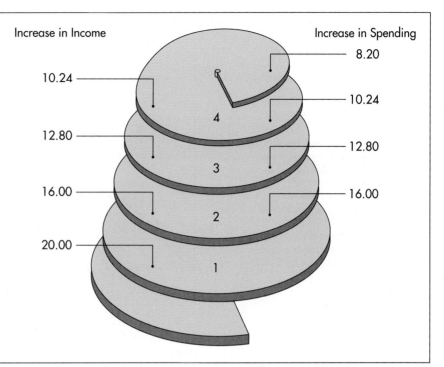

Figure 3
A Diagram of the Multiplier Effect
The initial increase in government spending of $20 increases the incomes of park employees by $20, which then induces them to spend their money. The park employees spend only $16 of the total on domestic goods, or 80 percent; $2 is saved (10 percent), and $2 (10 percent) is spent on imported items. The $16 spent becomes income of $16 for another group of employees, who then spend 80 percent of their $16, or $12.80, on domestic goods, while saving $1.60 (10 percent) and spending $1.60 (10 percent) on imports. With each round of expenditures income increases, but in smaller and smaller amounts, giving the multiplier effect a spiral shape.

Increase in Income

10.24

12.80

16.00

20.00

Increase in Spending

8.20

10.24

12.80

16.00

What is the multiplier?

multiplier:
A measure of the change in income produced by a change in autonomous expenditures.

in spending to find the total increase. If we know the percentage of additional income that "leaks" from domestic consumption at each round, we can determine the total change in income by finding its reciprocal. This measure is called the **multiplier**. The leakages are that portion of the change in income that is saved (the MPS) and that proportion of the change in income that is spent on imports (the MPI).

$$\text{Multiplier} = \frac{1}{\text{MPS} + \text{MPI}}$$

When the MPS is .10 and the MPI is .10, the multiplier equals 5 ($\frac{1}{.20}$). An initial change in expenditures of $20 results in a total change in income of $100, 5 times the original change in expenditures. The greater the leakages, the smaller the multiplier. When the MPS equals .20 and the MPI equals .30, the multiplier equals 2 ($\frac{1}{.50}$). The multiplier is smaller here because less new income is being spent in the domestic economy. The more people save, the smaller the expansionary effect on income of a change in spending. And the more people spend on imports, the smaller the expansionary effect on income of a change in spending. Notice that the multiplier would be larger in a *closed economy*, an economy that does not trade with the rest of the world. Here, because the MPI equals zero, the multiplier is simply equal to the reciprocal of the MPS.

2.b. The Multiplier and Equilibrium

The multiplier is an extremely useful concept. It allows us to calculate how a change in autonomous expenditures affects national income. To better understand how changes in spending can bring about changes in equilib-

Figure 4
A Change in Equilibrium
Expenditures and Income
A change in aggregate expenditures (AE) causes a change in equilibrium national income (Y). Initially equilibrium is $500, the point at which the AE_1 curve intersects the 45-degree line. If autonomous expenditures increase by $20, the aggregate expenditures curve shifts up to AE_2. The new curve intersects the 45-degree line at a new equilibrium level of income, $600. An increase in autonomous expenditures of $20, then, causes equilibrium income to increase by $100.

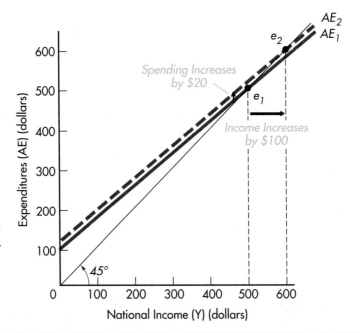

(1) Income (Y)	(2) Consumption (C)	(3) Investment (I)	(4) Government Spending (G)	(5) Net Exports (X)	(6) Aggregate Expenditures (AE)	(7) Unplanned Change in Inventories	(8) Change in National Income
0	$30	$20	$50	$20	$120	−$120	Increase
$100	$120	$20	$50	$10	$200	−$100	Increase
$200	$210	$20	$50	0	$280	−$80	Increase
$300	$300	$20	$50	−$10	$360	−$60	Increase
$400	$390	$20	$50	−$20	$440	−$40	Increase
$500	$480	$20	$50	−$30	$520	−$20	Increase
$600	$570	$20	$50	−$40	$600	0	No change
$700	$660	$20	$50	−$50	$680	$20	Decrease

rium income, let's modify the example we used in Figure 1. In the table in Figure 4 we have increased government spending to $50. The autonomous increase in government spending raises aggregate expenditures by $20 at every level of income. Aggregate expenditures now equal income at $600. The increase in government spending of $20 yields an increase in equilibrium income of $100.

The graph in Figure 4 shows the change in equilibrium income when spending increases by $20. The original aggregate expenditures curve, AE_1, intersects the 45-degree line at an income level of $500. A spending increase of $20 at every level of income creates a new aggregate expenditures curve, AE_2, which lies $20 above the original curve. AE_2 is parallel to AE_1 because the increase is in autonomous spending. The new curve, AE_2, intersects the 45-degree line at an income of $600.

In Chapter 8, we introduced the concept of the natural rate of unemployment—the unemployment rate that exists in the absence of cyclical unemployment. When the economy operates at the natural rate of unemployment, the corresponding level of output (and income) is called potential GNP. However, equilibrium does not necessarily occur at potential GNP. Equilibrium is any level of national income at which planned expenditures equal national income. Suppose that equilibrium income is not at the level of potential GNP and that government policymakers make the achievement of potential GNP an important goal. In this case, government policy is addressed to closing the *GNP gap*, the difference between potential GNP and real GNP. The nature of that policy depends on the value of the multiplier.

If we know the size of the GNP gap and we know the size of the multiplier, we can determine how much spending needs to change to yield equilibrium at potential GNP. Remember that the GNP gap equals potential GNP minus real GNP:

$$\text{GNP gap} = \text{potential GNP} - \text{real GNP}$$

When real GNP is less than potential GNP, the GNP gap is the amount the GNP must rise to reach its potential. Suppose potential GNP is $500, but the economy is in equilibrium at $400. GNP must rise by $100 to reach potential GNP. How much must spending rise? If we know the size of the multiplier, we simply divide the multiplier into the GNP gap to determine how much spending must rise to achieve equilibrium at potential GNP. This required change in spending is called the **recessionary gap**:

▼ What is the relationship between the GNP gap and the recessionary gap? ▲

recessionary gap:
the increase in expenditures required to reach potential GNP

$$\text{Recessionary gap} = \frac{\text{GNP gap}}{\text{multiplier}}$$

Figure 5 shows an economy in which equilibrium income (Y_E) is less than potential income (Y_P). The difference between the two—the GNP gap—is $100. It is the *horizontal* distance between equilibrium income and potential income. The amount that spending must rise in order for income to reach a new equilibrium level of $500 is measured by the recessionary gap. The recessionary gap is the vertical distance between the aggregate expenditures curve and the 45-degree line at the potential income level.

The recessionary gap is the vertical distance between the aggregate expenditures curve and the 45-degree line at the potential income level.

The recessionary gap in Figure 5 is $20.

$$\text{Recessionary gap} = \frac{\$100}{5}$$

$$= \$20$$

With a multiplier of 5, if aggregate expenditures rise by $20, equilibrium rises by the $100 necessary to close the GNP gap. In Chapter 12 we analyze how government policy can bring about this kind of change in aggregate expenditures.

2.c. Real-World Complications

Our definition of the multiplier

$$\frac{1}{\text{MPS} + \text{MPI}}$$

Figure 5
The GNP Gap and the Recessionary Gap

In the graph, the GNP gap is $100, the difference between potential national income (Y_P) of $500 and equilibrium national income (Y_E) of $400. The GNP gap tells us that equilibrium national income must rise by $100 to reach equilibrium at the potential level of income. The recessionary gap indicates the amount autonomous expenditures must rise to close the GNP gap. The recessionary gap is the vertical distance between the 45-degree line and the AE curve at the potential level of national income, or $20. If autonomous expenditures are increased by $20, the AE curve moves up, intersecting with the 45-degree line at $500.

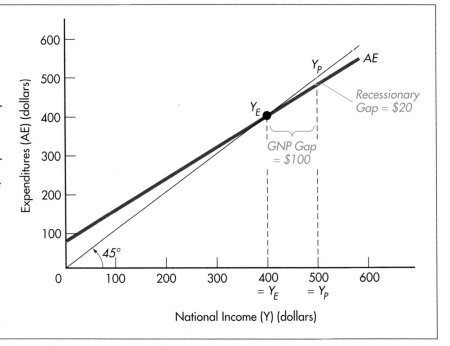

is a simplification of reality. Often other factors besides the MPS and MPI determine the actual multiplier in an economy. One stems from the treatment of imports. We have assumed that whatever is spent on imports is permanently lost to the domestic economy. For a country whose imports are a small fraction of the exports of its trading partners, this is a realistic assumption. But for a country whose imports are very important in determining the volume of exports of the rest of the world, this simple multiplier understates the true value of the multiplier. To see why, let's examine how U.S. imports affect income in the rest of the world.

2.c.1. Foreign Repercussions of Domestic Imports   When a resident of the United States buys goods from another country, that purchase becomes income to foreign residents. If Mike in Miami buys coral jewelry from Victor in the Dominican Republic, Mike's purchase increases Victor's income. So the import of jewelry into the United States increases income in the Dominican Republic.

Imports purchased by one country can have a large effect on the level of income in other countries. Table 2 shows the importance of U.S. imports to many of its trading partners. Column 4 lists the percentage of total exports from each of the countries listed in column 1 to the United States. Obviously Canada and Mexico are very dependent on sales to the United States, with 70 and 73 percent, respectively, of their exports going to the United States. Yugoslavia, on the other hand, sold just 6 percent of its total exports to U.S. buyers in 1988. If U.S. imports from Yugoslavia doubled, the effect on total Yugoslavian exports and income would be small. But if imports from Canada or Mexico doubled, the effect on those countries' exports and income would be substantial.

Table 2 The Importance of Trade with the United States, 1988 (millions of dollars)

(1) Country	(2) Exports to U.S.	(3) Total Exports	(4) Exports to U.S./ Total Exports (2)/(3)	(5) Imports from U.S.	(6) Total Imports	(7) Imports from U.S./Total Imports (5)/(6)
Australia	3,508	33,069	.11	7,228	33,340	.22
Brazil	8,717	33,783	.26	3,347	16,047	.21
Canada	81,990	116,841	.70	70,450	108,742	.65
Chile	1,393	7,046	.20	1,002	4,731	.21
Germany	26,020	323,374	.08	16,583	250,565	.07
India	2,879	13,312	.22	2,748	19,164	.14
Japan	90,245	264,856	.34	42,267	187,378	.23
Korea	21,478	60,697	.35	12,759	51,811	.25
Mexico	21,404	29,373	.73	20,644	27,546	.75
Philippines	2,512	7,032	.36	1,823	8,721	.21
Saudi Arabia	5,670	28,400	.20	3,069	25,619	.12
South Africa	1,445	21,549	.07	1,691	17,350	.10
Sweden	4,897	49,747	.10	3,472	45,627	.08
Turkey	628	10,081	.06	1,160	11,284	.10
U.K.	18,853	145,166	.13	19,351	189,339	.10
Venezuela	5,071	9,629	.53	4,611	11,407	.40
Yugoslavia	767	12,663	.06	723	13,171	.05

Source: International Monetary Fund, *Direction of Trade Yearbook*, Washington, D.C., 1989. Used by permission.

U.S. imports play a key role in determining the national income of its major trading partners. This is important because foreign income is a determinant of U.S. exports. As that income rises, domestic exports rise (see Chapter 9). That is, foreign imports increase with foreign income, and some of those imports come from the United States. Column 7 of Table 2 shows the percentage of purchases from the United States in the total imports of its trading partners. Canada and Mexico, both of which export in large quantities to the United States, are also important markets for U.S. goods. If the income in these countries goes up, it is likely that their purchases of U.S. goods will rise correspondingly. And, of course, when foreign spending on U.S. goods increases, national income in the United States rises.

How does international trade affect the size of the multiplier?

The simple multiplier understates the true multiplier effects of increases in autonomous expenditures because of the foreign repercussions of domestic spending. Some spending on imports comes back to the domestic economy in the form of exports. This means the chain of spending can be different from that assumed in the simple multiplier. Figure 6 illustrates the difference.

Part (a) of the figure shows the sequence of spending when there are no foreign repercussions from domestic imports. In this case, domestic spending rises, which causes domestic income to rise. Higher domestic income leads to increased spending on imports as well as further increases

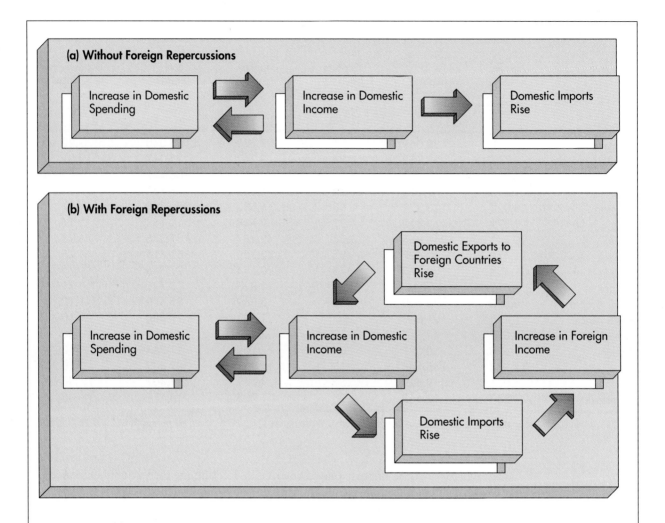

Figure 6
The Sequence of Expenditures
If there are no foreign repercussions from changes in domestic income, the simple multiplier holds. Increases in domestic spending increase domestic income, which causes domestic spending — including spending on foreign goods — to rise further. Here higher expenditures on domestic imports do not have any effect on domestic exports to foreign countries.

If there are foreign repercussions from changes in domestic income, the simple multiplier underestimates the actual effect of a change in autonomous expenditures on the equilibrium level of income. As part (b) shows, increases in domestic spending increase domestic income, which causes domestic spending — including spending on foreign goods — to rise further. Here higher spending on foreign goods causes foreign income to rise and, with it, spending on domestic exports. Higher domestic exports stimulate domestic income further. The actual multiplier effect of an increase in domestic spending, then, is larger than it is when domestic imports have no effect on domestic exports.

in domestic spending, which induce further increases in income, and so on, as the multiplier process works itself out. Notice, however, that the imports are simply a leakage from the spending stream.

In part (b), the sequence of expenditures includes the foreign repercussions of domestic imports. As before, increases in domestic spending cause domestic income to rise, which in turn leads to more domestic

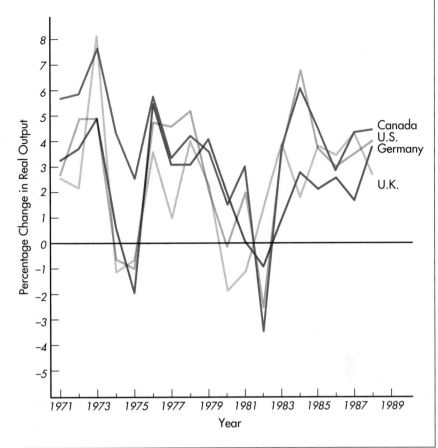

Figure 7
Changes in Real Output Across Countries
The graph plots the percentage change in real output (gross domestic product) for four major industrial countries between 1971 and 1988. Notice the similarity of the business cycles. When output is rising in the United States, it also is rising in the other countries. When the United States has a recession, the other countries also have a recession. Source: Data from International Monetary Fund, *International Financial Statistics Yearbook*, Washington, D.C., 1989.

spending as well as greater domestic imports. Now, however, the greater imports increase foreign income, which increases foreign imports of goods produced in the domestic economy. As domestic exports rise, domestic income rises.

The diagrams in Figure 6 show why the multiplier effect is higher with foreign repercussions than without. Rather than complicate the multiplier definition, we continue to use the simple multiplier. But remember that our definition underestimates the true magnitude of the multiplier's effects in open economies. In fact the foreign repercussions of domestic imports help explain the similarity in business cycles across countries. Figure 7 illustrates the percentage changes in real output (gross domestic product) for four major industrial countries from 1971 through 1988. When the United States is booming, the economies of other countries that depend on exports to the U.S. market also boom. When the United States is in recession, income in these other countries tends to fall.

2.c.2. Multiplier Estimates Many private and public organizations have developed descriptions or models that are used to analyze current economic developments and to forecast future ones. A large number of these

Table 3 Spending Multiplier Estimates

Multiplier effects of U.S. government spending increases	
Country	Multiplier*
United States	2.0
Canada	.5
Germany	.2
Japan	.7
United Kingdom	.2

Multiplier effects in the United States of foreign government spending increases	
Country	Multiplier*
Canada	.2
Germany	.1
Japan	.1
United Kingdom	.1

*Based on first year after increase in spending.
Source: Hali J. Edison, Jaime R. Marquez, and Ralph W. Tryon, *The Structure and Properties of the FRB Multicountry Model*, International Finance Discussion Paper, no. 293 (Washington, D.C.: Board of Governors of the Federal Reserve System, 1986).

models include foreign repercussions. From these models we get a sense of just how much the simple multiplier underestimates the true multiplier.

Table 3 reports multiplier estimates from one well-known model that incorporates foreign repercussions. The numbers listed in the table are the multiplier effects after one year. Because of further rounds of spending in later years, the actual multipliers are larger than those reported in the table.

The first section of the table gives the multiplier effect of an increase in U.S. government spending. The U.S. effect is a multiplier of 2. This means that if autonomous government expenditures increased by $20, U.S. equilibrium national income would be $40 higher after one year.

The income of the other countries in the first part of the table is increased by higher spending in the United States because some of that spending is on imports into the United States. The multipliers for these countries range from .7 for Japan to .2 for Germany and the United Kingdom. If U.S. autonomous government expenditures go up $20, U.K. equilibrium national income would be $4 (.2 × $20) higher after one year. Over time, as income in these foreign countries rises, their spending on U.S. goods and services increases. And as U.S. exports increase, so does U.S. income.

The second part of the table shows the sensitivity of U.S. income to changes in foreign government spending. The largest multiplier is only .2, in the case of Canada. If autonomous government spending increases by $20 in Canada, U.S. equilibrium national income would be $4 higher after one year. Clearly U.S. spending increases have a much larger effect on

This Canadian armed forces helicopter is used in civil search and rescue operations. When the Canadian government purchases a helicopter, Canadian national income rises. Some of the increased income will be spent on foreign goods. In this way, changes in foreign government spending cause changes in U.S. equilibrium national income. In fact, Canadian government spending has the largest multiplier effect in the United States of any foreign government spending.

foreign income than foreign spending increases have on U.S. income. The reason for this is the vast size of the domestic market in the United States relative to that in other countries.

The multiplier examples we use in this chapter show autonomous government spending changing. It is important to realize that the multiplier effects apply to any change in autonomous expenditures in any sector of the economy.

RECAP

1. Any change in autonomous expenditures is multiplied into a larger change in the equilibrium level of income.
2. The multiplier measures the change in income produced by a change in autonomous spending.
3. The multiplier equals

$$\frac{1}{\text{MPS} + \text{MPI}}$$

4. The recessionary gap is the amount spending must increase to achieve equilibrium at the potential level of income; graphically, it is measured by the vertical distance between the 45-degree line and the aggregate expenditures curve at potential income.
5. The true multiplier is larger than the simple multiplier [1/(MPS + MPI)] because of the foreign repercussions of domestic spending.

3. THE KEYNESIAN MODEL REVIEWED

The Keynesian model is a fixed-price model.

The approach to macroeconomic equilibrium presented in this chapter focuses on aggregate expenditures and income. It is called the *Keynesian model*. This model of the economy can be very useful in explaining some real-world events. But it suffers from a serious drawback: the model assumes that the supply of goods and services in the economy always adjusts to aggregate expenditures, that there is no need for price changes. In other words, the Keynesian model is a *fixed-price model*.

In the real world, we find that shortages of goods and services often are met by rising prices, not just increased production. We also find that when supply increases in the face of relatively constant demand, prices may fall. In other words, prices as well as production adjust to differences between demand and supply. We introduce price as a component of macroeconomic equilibrium in the next chapter, in the aggregate demand and supply model.

SUMMARY

▼▲ **How do aggregate expenditures affect income?**

1. When aggregate expenditures exceed income, income rises; when they are less than income, income falls. § 1.a

▼▲ **What does equilibrium mean in macroeconomics?**

2. Macroeconomic equilibrium is that point where aggregate expenditures equal national income. § 1.a

▼▲ **What are the leakages from and injections to spending?**

3. Leakages are saving, taxes, and imports; injections are investment, government spending, and exports. § 1.b

4. Equilibrium income occurs where leakages equal injections. § 1.b

▼▲ **Why does equilibrium income change by a multiple of a change in autonomous expenditures?**

5. The effect of a change in autonomous spending is multiplied by a spiral of increased spending and income. § 2.a

▼▲ **What is the multiplier?**

6. The multiplier equals the reciprocal of the sum of the MPS and the MPI. § 2.a

▼▲ **What is the relationship between the GNP gap and the recessionary gap?**

7. The recessionary gap is the amount autonomous expenditures must change to eliminate the GNP gap and reach potential GNP. § 2.b

▼▲ **How does international trade affect the size of the multiplier?**

8. The actual multiplier may be larger than the reciprocal of the sum of the MPS and the MPI because of the foreign repercussion of changes in domestic spending. § 2.c.1

9. The Keynesian model is a fixed-price model. § 3

multiplier § 2.a

recessionary gap § 2.b

EXERCISES

Basic Terms and Concepts

1. Explain the role of inventories in keeping actual expenditures equal to income.

2. Rework Figure 1 assuming a closed economy (net exports equal zero at all levels of income). What is the equilibrium level of income? (You may have to extend the example beyond the $700 level.) What is the multiplier?

3. Draw a graph representing a hypothetical economy. Carefully label the two axes, the $S+T+IM$ curve, the $I+G+EX$ curve, and the equilibrium level of income. Illustrate the effect of an increase in the level of autonomous saving.

4. Given the following information, what is the multiplier in each case?

   a. MPC = .90, MPI = .10
   b. MPC = .90, MPI = .30
   c. MPC = .80, MPI = .30
   d. MPC = .90, MPI = 0

5. Draw a graph representing a hypothetical economy. Carefully label the two axes, the 45-degree line, the AE curve, and the equilibrium level of income. Indicate and label the GNP gap and the recessionary gap.

6. Explain the effect of foreign repercussions on the value of the multiplier.

Extended Concepts

7. Suppose the MPC is .80, the MPI is .10 and the income tax rate is 10 percent. What is the multiplier in this economy?

Argentina's Painful Path to Efficiency

Argentina is suffering through one of its worst recessions since the 1930's. Thousands of people employed by private companies have lost their jobs, and for the first time in 40 years, the hard times might even result in layoffs among the millions of workers on the public payroll.

Their jobs have so far been safe because government employment is Argentina's social safety net. Rather than unemployment insurance or welfare payments, Juan Perón hired thousands in the late 1940's for his new state-owned enterprises. . . The public payroll has grown to 30 percent of all jobholders. Now the president, Carlos Saúl Menem, is trying to dismantle the system as part of his effort to salvage the economy.

Three developments favor his attempt to trim . . . excess workers from the public payroll. . . . He is a Peronist; until now, the Peronist movement . . . opposed public-sector layoffs. The second is that union opposition to layoffs is losing its clout . . . And finally, the worldwide disenchantment with state-owned companies has reached Argentina, where most of the state enterprises are inefficient, bribery-ridden and profitless. . . .

Numerous public opinion polls find that a majority of Argentines yearn for an efficiently functioning economy, even accepting . . . the anguish that would come from a sharp reduction in the public payroll.

For the moment, however, the anguish is more in the private sector. . . . In January, the Menem Government cut back drastically on spending to shake off a huge budget deficit. Government purchases from private companies have been reduced . . . In addition, the . . . Administration has postponed payment of bills to suppliers and has halted repayment of loans.

The upshot is rising unemployment in the private sector, although no Government workers have been laid off, and fewer services for everyone. . . . To raise revenue, telephone, electric and gas rates have more than tripled. Consumers were forced to cut spending when the Government in January seized bank deposits and converted them into forced 10-year loans to itself, at low interest rates. . .

The Government's various measures have indeed eliminated the budget deficit temporarily. March and April ended with surpluses of more than $100 million each month, rather than the usual $500 million or more in monthly deficits. The surpluses have helped to reduce the inflation rate, which dropped to 11 percent in April from more than 60 percent a month in the first quarter, according to Government statistics.

But the drastic cutback provoked what Juan Fernandez Ansola, the Argentine specialist at DRI/McGraw-Hill, . . . describes as "a big, big recession, a collapse basically."

The gross domestic product . . . has shrunk by more than 10 percent since last summer, and the unemployment rate has almost doubled to more than 10 percent. Virtually all of the rise was a result of layoffs and cutbacks in the private sector.

So far, the Menem Government has skirted the issue of reducing the public payroll. . . The President pushed 70,000 Government workers into early retirement, but with full pay for a year or two, until pensions kick in. . . . Hiring has halted, which has reduced the Federal payroll by about 10,000, says Juan Luis Bour, chief economist of the Foundation for Latin American Economic Studies. "But as the Federal payroll dropped, the provincial governments hired, so the net loss is zero," Mr. Bour said. . .

Public employment is deeply entrenched in the Argentine system. Some 2.3 million people are on Government payrolls in a nation where only about 7 million hold salaried jobs while nearly 3 million are self-employed, mostly . . . doing . . . tasks that produce marginal incomes. As the economy weakens, the number of self-employed rises.

More important, nearly all of the public-sector workers are in urban areas. . . . Among the 6.6 million urban jobholders, the Government payroll accounts for 35 percent of them. . . .

But now Congress has authorized Mr. Menem to auction many of the state enterprises, mostly to foreign companies. The telephone company, for example, is to be sold this year, and the winning bidder will probably want to shrink the staff . . .

Thus the Menem Government would hand over to the private sector the responsibility for reducing the public payroll. But most economists and politicians say that before the new owners can act, the Government must put in place unemployment insurance and other social benefits — in effect, a new safety net.

■ Source: Louis Uchitelle, "Argentina's Painful Path to Efficiency," *The New York Times*, May 14, 1990, pp. D1, D4.

Commentary

The 1980s were a very difficult time for the people of Argentina. Real wages in the country fell during this period, and unemployment and inflation were high. Toward the end of the decade, inflation in Argentina began accelerating, hitting a rate of 197 percent *per month* in 1989. This hyperinflation reflects the government budget deficit that is financed through printing money. Shrinking the government's budget deficit is thus an essential step in bringing Argentina's economy under control, but this cure produces its own set of problems.

The article discusses how government employment serves as a social safety net in Argentina. Government jobs account for about 23 percent of all employment nationwide and about 35 percent of all urban employment. Cutting the government's expenditures involves eliminating some proportion of these jobs, as well as cutting government purchases from privately owned businesses. This policy has been successful in turning around the government's monthly deficits of $500 million to surpluses of more than $100 million in both March and April of 1990. However, this massive reversal of the government's expenditure policies has also dramatically affected economic activity in the country's private sector. According to one economist, the restrictive policies resulted in "a big, big recession, a collapse basically" of the Argentine economy.

Economic theory suggests such an outcome. In the graph below, we plot the aggregate expenditures line AE_1, which incorporates the level of government expenditures before the massive cutbacks. The level of GDP corresponding to this aggregate expenditures line is Y_1. The line AE_2 is the aggregate expenditures line after the cuts in government expenditures, with a corresponding level of GDP equal to Y_2. The vertical distance between AE_1 and AE_2 represents the cut in government spending due to a decrease in government purchases of goods and services from the private sector as well as a lower level of government employment (including the 70,000 government workers pushed into early retirement). The

10 percent fall in GDP, represented by the distance $Y_2 - Y_1$, is greater than the vertical distance between AE_1 and AE_2 because of the multiplier effect. This analysis suggests that cuts in government spending have ripple effects in the private sector that cause GDP to fall by several times the cuts in spending. This is, of course, a basic conclusion of multiplier analysis. Evidence presented in the article suggests that this fall in GDP has in fact occurred in Argentina, since private-sector unemployment rates have been rising.

The ultimate goal of President Menem's policy is to stabilize the Argentine economy and bring inflation under control. The path to this goal has proven to be long and painful. One can only hope that, after a trying decade of failed policies, the most recent attempt at stabilizing inflation in Argentina will be successful.

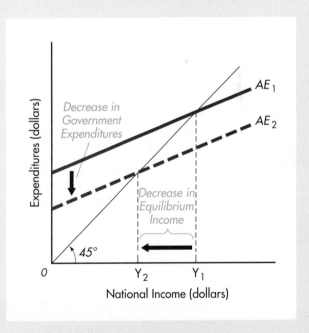

An Algebraic Model of Income and Expenditures Equilibrium

Continuing the example we began in the appendix to Chapter 9, if we know the equations for each component of aggregate expenditures (AE), we can solve for the equilibrium level of national income (Y) for the economy represented in Figure 1:

$$C = \$30 + .90Y$$
$$I = \$20$$
$$G = \$30$$
$$X = \$20 - .10Y$$

Summing these components, we can find the aggregate expenditures function:

$$AE = \$30 + .90Y + \$20 + \$30 + \$20 - .10Y$$
$$= \$100 + .80Y$$

Given the AE function, we can solve for the equilibrium level of Y where

$$Y = AE$$

or $Y = \$100 + .80Y$

or $Y - .80Y = \$100$
$$.20Y = \$100$$

If we divide both sides of the equation by .20, we find equilibrium where Y equals \$500.

The Multiplier   It is also possible to solve for the multiplier algebraically. We start by writing the general equations for each function where C^a, I^a, G^a, EX^a, and IM^a represent autonomous consumption, investment, government spending, exports, and imports, respectively, and where c represents the MPC and im represents the MPI:

$$C = C^a + cY$$
$$I = I^a$$
$$G = G^a$$
$$X = EX^a - IM^a - imY$$

Now we sum the individual equations for the components of aggregate expenditures to get the aggregate expenditures function:

$$AE = C + I + G + X$$
$$= C^a + cY + I^a + G^a + EX^a - IM^a - imY$$
$$= (C^a + I^a + G^a + EX^a - IM^a) + cY - imY$$

We know that aggregate expenditures equal income. So

$$Y = (C^a + I^a + G^a + EX^a - IM^a) + cY - imY$$

Solving for Y, we first gather all of the terms involving Y on the left side of the equation:

$$Y[1 - (c - im)] = C^a + I^a + G^a + EX^a - IM^a$$

Next we divide each side of the equation by $[1 - (c - im)]$ to get an equation for Y:

$$Y = \frac{1}{1 - (c - im)} (C^a + I^a + G^a + EX^a - IM^a)$$

A change in autonomous expenditures causes Y to change by

$$\frac{1}{1 - (c - im)}$$

times the change in expenditures. Because c is the MPC and im is the MPI, the multiplier can be written

$$\frac{1}{1 - (\text{MPC} - \text{MPI})}$$

$$\text{or} \quad \frac{1}{\text{MPS} + \text{MPI}}$$

11

Macroeconomic Equilibrium: Aggregate Demand and Supply

1. Why does the aggregate expenditures curve shift with changes in the price level?

2. What is the aggregate demand curve?

3. What causes the aggregate demand curve to shift?

4. What is the aggregate supply curve?

5. What causes the aggregate supply curve to shift?

6. Why does the short-run aggregate supply curve become steeper as national income increases?

7. Why is the long-run aggregate supply curve vertical?

8. What determines the equilibrium price level and national income?

PREVIEW The Keynesian approach to equilibrium that we presented in Chapter 10 has a limitation: it assumes that the level of prices is fixed. Changes in aggregate expenditures cause changes in the equilibrium level of national income, but this is real national income that changes with no change in the price level. Remember that nominal income could increase due to real income or the price level increasing, but the Keynesian model is a fixed-price model. This may have been a useful characterization of the real world during the Great Depression, when output and employment fell without a corresponding change in the level of prices. But prices have been rising since the 1940s. Realistically, changes in aggregate expenditures generate changes in the price level as well as changes in the output of goods and services. In some instances we find that business cycle expansions go hand in hand with rising prices. In others recessions are marked by a rising price level. It was this combination of contraction and price level increase—called *stagflation*—that led economists to develop models of macroeconomic equilibrium that are alternatives to the Keynesian model.

We did not learn the Keynesian income-expenditures model in Chapter 10 as an end in itself. The income-expenditures equilibrium developed in that chapter is the foundation that allows a simple derivation of the aggregate demand curve. This curve, together with the aggregate supply curve, will be the basic tool of analysis used in our study of macroeconomic policy and its effects.

In this chapter we show how the aggregate expenditures function is converted into the aggregate demand function when the price level is allowed to vary, and we introduce the supply side of the economy. We then have a model that allows changes in the equilibrium level of national income to come from either the demand side or the supply side of the economy. We also have a model that generates changes in the equilibrium level of real output and income as well as changes in the equilibrium price level. That model allows us to analyze a wide range of real-world developments and to explain how recession and inflation can coexist.

1. AGGREGATE DEMAND

The aggregate expenditures curve we saw in Chapter 10 was drawn assuming a fixed price level. Once we allow the level of prices to vary, the *AE* curve shifts each time prices change.

1.a. Aggregate Expenditures and the Price Level

▼ Why does the aggregate expenditures curve shift with changes in the level of prices?

The *AE* curve shifts with changes in the level of prices due to the wealth effect, the interest rate effect, and the international trade effect.

1.a.1. The Wealth Effect Individuals and businesses own money, bonds, and other financial assets. The value of these assets is one of the determinants of expenditures in a world where prices change. When the level of prices falls, the purchasing power of money increases. As the value of their assets increases, households and businesses spend more. When prices go up, the purchasing power of money falls. As the value of their assets decreases, households and businesses spend less. This is the **wealth effect** of a price change: a change in the real value of wealth that causes spending to change when the level of prices changes.

wealth effect:
a change in the real value of wealth that causes spending to change when the level of prices changes

When the price level changes, the purchasing power of financial assets changes.

The wealth effect sometimes is called the *real-balance effect*. *Real values* are values that have been adjusted for price level changes. Here *real value* means "purchasing power." When the price level changes, the purchasing power of financial assets also changes. When prices rise, the real value of assets and wealth falls, and aggregate expenditures tend to fall. When prices fall, the real value of assets and wealth rises, and aggregate expenditures tend to rise.

1.a.2. The Interest Rate Effect When the price level rises, the purchasing power of each dollar falls, which means more money is required to buy any particular quantity of goods and services (see Figure 1). Suppose that a family of three needs $100 each week to buy food. If the price level doubles, the same quantity of food costs $200. The household must have twice as much money to buy the same amount of food. Conversely, when prices fall, the family needs less money to buy food because the purchasing power of each dollar is greater.

When prices go up, people need more money. So they sell their other financial assets, like bonds, to get that money. The increase in supply of bonds lowers bond prices and raises interest rates. The rise in interest rates is necessary to sell the larger quantity of bonds, but it causes investment expenditures to fall, which causes aggregate expenditures to fall.

When prices fall, people need less money to purchase the same quantity of goods. So they use their money holdings to buy bonds and other financial assets. The increased demand for bonds increases bond prices and causes interest rates to fall. So lower interest rates increase investment expenditures, pushing aggregate expenditures up.

interest rate effect:
a change in interest rates that causes investment and therefore aggregate expenditures to change as the level of prices changes

Figure 1 shows the **interest rate effect**, the relationship among price level, interest rates, and aggregate expenditures. As the price level rises, interest rates rise and aggregate expenditures fall. As the price level falls, interest rates fall and aggregate expenditures rise.

1.a.3. The International Trade Effect Net exports is one of the components of aggregate expenditures, along with consumption, investment, and government spending. In Chapter 9 we stated that net exports are a function of domestic income. A change in the level of domestic prices also can cause net exports to change. If domestic prices rise while foreign prices and the foreign exchange rate remain constant, domestic goods become more expensive in relation to foreign goods.

Suppose the United States sells oranges to Japan. If the oranges sell for $1 per pound and the yen-dollar exchange rate is 200 yen = $1, a pound of U.S. oranges costs a Japanese buyer 200 yen. What happens if the level of prices in the United States goes up 10 percent? All prices, including the price of oranges, increase 10 percent. U.S. oranges now sell for $1.10 a pound. If the exchange rate is still 200 yen = $1, a pound of oranges now costs the Japanese buyer 220 yen (200 × 1.10). If orange prices in other countries do not change, the Japanese buyer is going to buy oranges from those countries. The increase in the level of U.S. prices causes U.S. net exports to fall; a decrease in the level of U.S. prices makes U.S. goods cheaper in relation to foreign goods, which increases U.S. net exports.

international trade effect:
the change in aggregate expenditures resulting from a change in the domestic price level that changes the price of domestic goods in relation to foreign goods

When the price of domestic goods increases in relation to the price of foreign goods, net exports fall, causing aggregate expenditures to fall. When the price of domestic goods falls in relation to the price of foreign goods, net exports rise, causing aggregate expenditures to rise. The **inter-**

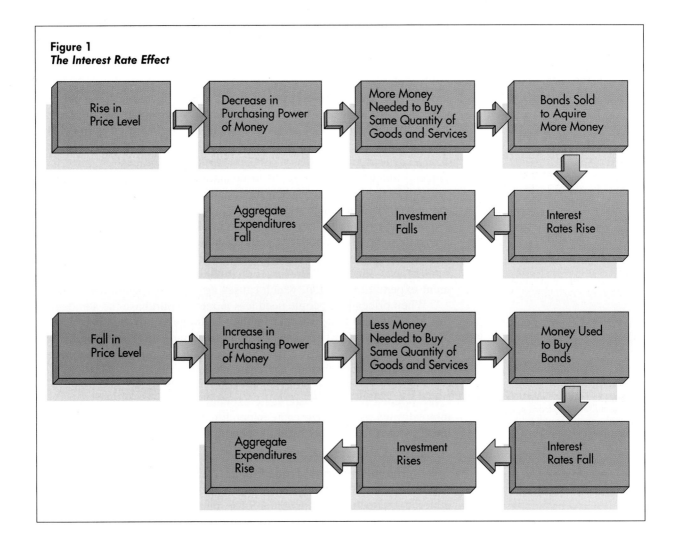

Figure 1
The Interest Rate Effect

national trade effect of a change in the level of domestic prices causes
aggregate expenditures to change in the opposite direction.

1.a.4. The Sum of the Price Level Effects A lower price increases
autonomous consumption (the wealth effect), antonomous investment (the
interest rate effect), and autonomous net exports (the international trade
effect). As the price level drops, aggregate expenditures rise. You can see
this in the shift from AE_0 to AE_1 in part (a) of Figure 2.

A higher price reduces autonomous consumption (the wealth effect),
autonomous investment (the interest rate effect), and autonomous net
exports (the international trade effect). As prices rise, aggregate expenditures fall, like the shift from AE_0 to AE_2 in the graph.

1.b. Deriving the Aggregate Demand Curve

aggregate demand curve:
a curve that shows the different
equilibrium levels of expenditures at
different levels of prices

The **aggregate demand curve** (*AD*) shows how the equilibrium level of
expenditures changes as the price level changes. In other words, the curve
shows the amount people spend at different price levels. Let's use the

Figure 2
Aggregate Expenditures and Aggregate Demand
Part (a) shows how changes in the price level cause the *AE* curve to shift. The initial curve, AE_0, is drawn at the initial level of prices, P_0. On this curve, the equilibrium level of aggregate expenditures (where expenditures equal income) is $500. If the price level falls to P_1, autonomous expenditures increase, shifting the curve up to AE_1 and moving the equilibrium level of aggregate expenditures to $700. If the price level rises to P_2, autonomous expenditures fall, shifting the curve down to AE_2 and moving the equilibrium level of aggregate expenditures to $300.

The aggregate demand curve (*AD*) in part (b) is derived from the aggregate expenditures curves. The *AD* curve shows the equilibrium level of aggregate expenditures at different price levels. At price level P_0, equilibrium aggregate expenditures are $500; at P_1, $700; and at P_2, $300.

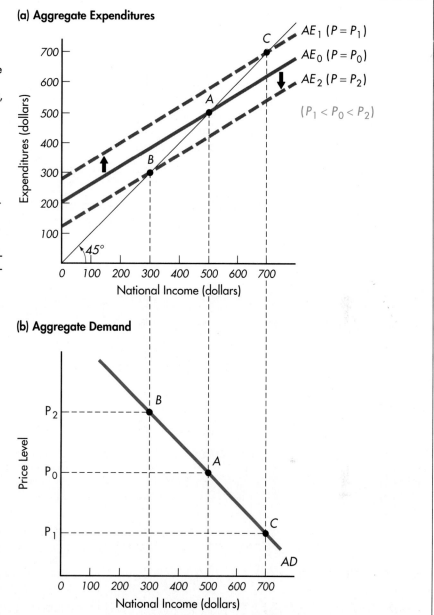

(a) Aggregate Expenditures

(b) Aggregate Demand

What is the aggregate demand curve?

example of Figure 2(a) to show how aggregate demand is derived from the shifting aggregate expenditures curve.

The aggregate demand curve is derived from the *AE* curve. Part (a) of Figure 2 shows three *AE* curves, each drawn for a different price level. Suppose that the initial equilibrium occurs at point *A* on curve AE_0 with prices at P_0. At this point, equilibrium income and expenditures are $500. If prices fall to P_1, the *AE* curve shifts up to AE_1. Here equilibrium is at point *C*, where income equals $700. If prices rise from P_0 to P_2, the *AE* curve falls to AE_2. Here equilibrium is at point *B*, where income equals $300.

In part (b) of Figure 2, price level is plotted on the vertical axis and national income is plotted on the horizontal axis. If you move vertically down from points *A, B,* and *C* in the top figure, you find corresponding points along the aggregate demand curve in the lower figure. The *AD* curve shows all of the combinations of price levels and corresponding equilibrium levels of income and aggregate expenditures.

Because aggregate expenditures increase when the price level decreases, and decrease when the price level increases, the aggregate demand curve slopes down. Although the demand curves for individual goods also slope down, different factors are at work here. Along the

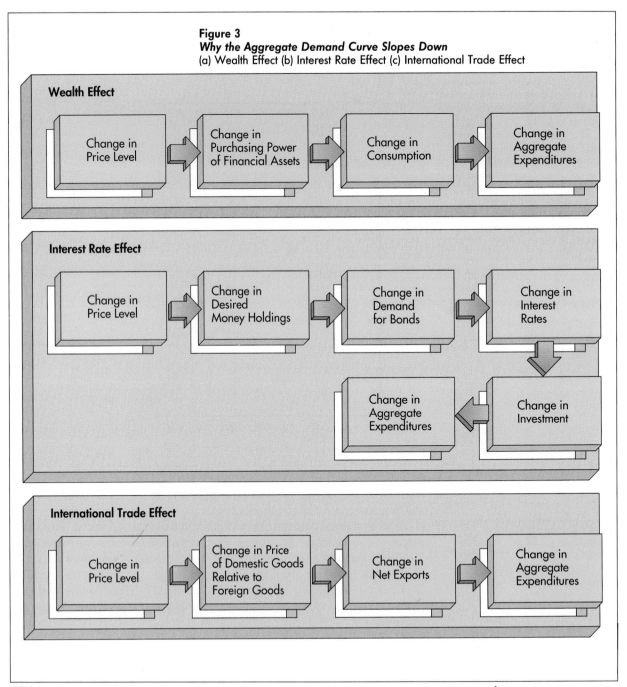

Figure 3
Why the Aggregate Demand Curve Slopes Down
(a) Wealth Effect (b) Interest Rate Effect (c) International Trade Effect

Wealth Effect

Change in Price Level → Change in Purchasing Power of Financial Assets → Change in Consumption → Change in Aggregate Expenditures

Interest Rate Effect

Change in Price Level → Change in Desired Money Holdings → Change in Demand for Bonds → Change in Interest Rates → Change in Investment → Change in Aggregate Expenditures

International Trade Effect

Change in Price Level → Change in Price of Domestic Goods Relative to Foreign Goods → Change in Net Exports → Change in Aggregate Expenditures

demand curve for an individual good, the price of that good changes while the prices of all other goods remain constant. This means that the good in question becomes relatively more or less expensive compared to all other goods in the economy. Consumers tend to substitute a less expensive good for a more expensive good. The effect of this substitution is an inverse relationship between price and quantity demanded. As the price of a good rises, quantity demanded falls.

The aggregate demand curve is drawn with the price level for the *entire economy* on the vertical axis. A price level change here means that, on average, all prices in the economy change; there is no relative price change and no substitution effect among domestic goods. The negative slope of the aggregate demand curve, then, is a product of the wealth effect, the interest rate effect, and the international trade effect (Figure 3).

1.c. Shifts in Aggregate Demand

What causes the aggregate demand curve to shift?

The aggregate demand curve shows equilibrium aggregate expenditures at alternative price levels. We draw the curve holding all other things equal. As those "other things" change, the aggregate demand curve shifts. Those other things—the nonprice determinants of aggregate demand—include expectations, foreign income and price levels, and government policy.

1.c.1. Expectations Consumption and business spending are affected by expectations. Consumption is sensitive to people's expectations of future income, prices, and wealth. For example, when people expect the economy to do well in the future, they increase consumption today. This is reflected in a shift of the aggregate demand curve to the right, from AD_0 to AD_1, as shown in Figure 4. When aggregate demand increases, equilibrium aggregate expenditures increase at every price level.

On the other hand, if people expect a recession in the near future, they tend to reduce consumption and increase saving in order to protect them-

Figure 4
Shifting the Aggregate Demand Curve
The aggregate demand curve shifts with changes in expectations, foreign income and foreign price levels, and government policy. As aggregate demand increases, the AD curve shifts to the right, like the shift from AD_0 to AD_1. At every price level, the quantity of output demanded increases. As aggregate demand falls, the AD curve shifts to the left, like the shift from AD_0 to AD_2. At every price level, the quantity of output demanded falls.

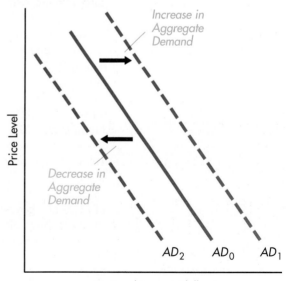

selves against a greater likelihood of losing a job or a forced cutback in hours worked. As consumption drops, aggregate demand decreases. The AD curve shifts to the left, from AD_0 to AD_2. At every price level along AD_2, planned expenditures are less than they are along AD_0.

Expectations also play an important role in investment decisions. Before undertaking a particular project, businesses forecast the likely revenues and costs associated with that project. When the profit outlook is good—say a tax cut is on the horizon—investment and therefore aggregate demand increase. When profits are expected to fall, investment and aggregate demand decrease.

1.c.2. Foreign Income and Price Levels

In Chapter 9 we said that domestic exports are autonomous but shift with changes in foreign income. Above we analyzed how changes in the domestic price level can change the price of domestic goods in relation to foreign goods, in the process changing net exports. Here we look at the effect of changes in the level of foreign prices, the impact of prices in the rest of the world on the net exports of the domestic economy.

When foreign income increases, so does foreign spending. Some of this increased spending is for goods produced in the domestic economy. As domestic exports increase, aggregate demand rises. Lower foreign income has just the opposite effect. As foreign income falls, foreign spending falls, including foreign spending on the exports of the domestic economy. Lower foreign income, then, causes domestic net exports and domestic aggregate demand to fall.

Higher foreign income increases net exports and aggregate demand; lower foreign income reduces net exports and aggregate demand.

Remember the international trade effect on the slope of the aggregate demand curve. As domestic prices rise, domestic goods become more expensive in relation to foreign goods, reducing domestic exports. As the level of domestic prices increases, then, domestic net exports fall. The same logic applies to changes in the level of foreign prices. If foreign prices rise in relation to domestic prices, domestic goods become less expensive than foreign goods and domestic net exports increase. So domestic aggregate demand rises as the level of foreign prices rises. When the level of foreign prices falls, domestic goods become more expensive than foreign goods, causing domestic net exports and aggregate demand to fall.

Change in the level of foreign prices changes domestic net exports and aggregate demand in the same direction.

Let's go back to the market for oranges. Suppose U.S. growers compete with Brazilian growers for the Japanese orange market. If the level of prices in Brazil rises while the level of prices in the United States remains stable, the price of Brazilian oranges to the Japanese buyer rises in relation to the price of U.S. oranges. What happens? U.S. exports of oranges to Japan should rise while Brazilian exports of oranges to Japan fall.[1]

1.c.3. Government Policy

In addition to changes in expectations and foreign income and price levels, government economic policy causes the aggregate demand curve to shift. In the next chapter we examine the effect of taxes and government spending on aggregate demand. In Chapter 14 we describe how changes in the money supply can cause the aggregate demand curve to shift.

---

[1] This assumes no change in exchange rates. We consider the link between price levels and exchange rates in Chapter 17.

RECAP

1. The aggregate demand curve shows the equilibrium level of expenditures at different levels of price.

2. The wealth effect, the interest rate effect, and the international trade effect are three reasons why the aggregate expenditures curve shifts with changes in prices; they also explain the downward slope of the aggregate demand curve.

3. The aggregate demand curve shifts with changes in expectations, foreign income and price levels, and government policy.

2. AGGREGATE SUPPLY

aggregate supply curve:
a curve that shows the amount of production at different price levels

---

▼ What is the aggregate supply curve?

▲

The **aggregate supply curve** shows the quantity of national output (or income) produced at different price levels. Like the supply curve for an individual good, the aggregate supply curve (*AS*) slopes up. Here, too, different factors are at work. The positive relationship between price and quantity supplied of an individual good is based on the price of that good changing in relation to all other goods. As the price of a single good rises relative to the prices of other goods, sellers are willing to offer more of the good for sale. With aggregate supply, we are analyzing how the amount of all goods and services produced changes as the level of prices changes. The direct relationship between prices and national output is explained by the effect of changing prices on profits, not by relative price changes.

2.a. Aggregate Production and the Price Level

Along the aggregate supply curve, everything is held fixed except price level and output. The price level is the price of output. We assume that the costs of production—wages, rent, and interest—are constant. We do not assume that those costs never change, only that they do not change for a short time following a change in prices.

If the level of prices rises while the costs of production remain fixed, business profits go up. As profits rise, firms are willing to produce more output. As prices rise, then, supply increases. The result is the positively sloped aggregate supply curve shown in Figure 5.

We use the word *profit* to mean revenue (output price times quantity of output sold) minus costs. Remember that profit is also the return to the entrepreneur, a reward for effort expended. Businesses react to changes in profits by altering the quantity of output they produce. Rising profits are a sign that output should increase. Falling profits are a sign that output should be reduced.

As the price level rises from P_0 to P_1 in Figure 5, the amount of output increases from $300 to $500. The higher the price level, the higher the profits, ceteris paribus, and the greater the production in the economy. Conversely, as the price level falls, production falls.

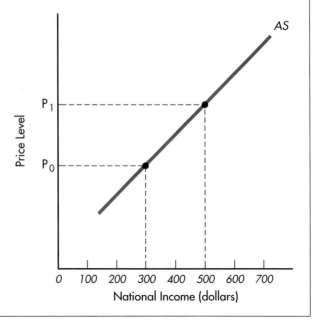

Figure 5
Aggregate Supply
The aggregate supply curve shows the amount of output
produced and income generated at different price levels.
The AS curve slopes up, indicating that the higher the
price level, the greater the quantity of output produced.

Because in the real world the costs of production change over time,
the curve in Figure 5 is a *short-run* aggregate supply curve. Although production costs may not rise immediately when prices rise, eventually they
will. Labor will demand higher wages to compensate for the higher cost of
living. Suppliers will charge more for materials. The positive slope of the
AS curve, then, is a short-run phenomenon. How short is the short run? It
is the period of time over which production costs remain constant. The
long run is the time when all costs change or are variable. For the economy
as a whole, the short run can be months, or at most, a few years.

2.b. Shifts in Aggregate Supply

The aggregate supply curve is drawn with everything but the price level
and national income held constant. There are several things that can
change and cause the aggregate supply curve to shift. The shift from AS_0 to
AS_1 in Figure 6 represents an increase in aggregate supply. AS_1 lies to the
right of AS_0, which means that at every price level, production is higher on
AS_1 than on AS_0. The shift from AS_0 to AS_2 represents a decrease
in aggregate supply. AS_2 lies to the left of AS_0, which means that at every
price level, production along AS_2 is less than along AS_0. The nonprice
determinants of aggregate supply are resource prices, technology, and
expectations.

> What causes the aggregate
> supply curve to shift?

*The aggregate supply curve shifts in
response to changes in the price of
resources, in technology, and in
expectations.*

2.b.1. Resource Prices When the prices of output change, the costs of
production do not change immediately. At first, then, a change in profits
induces a change in production. Costs eventually change in response to the
change in prices. When they do, the aggregate supply curve shifts. When
the cost of resources—labor, capital goods, materials—falls, the aggregate supply curve shifts to the right, from AS_0 to AS_1. This means firms are

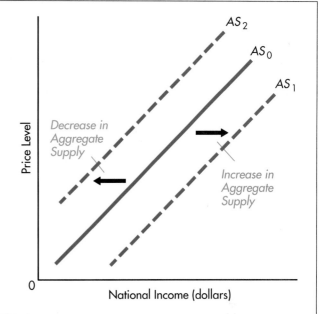

Figure 6
Shifting the Aggregate Supply Curve
The aggregate supply curve shifts with changes in resource prices, technology, and expectations. When aggregate supply increases, the curve shifts to the right, like the shift from AS_0 to AS_1, so that at every price level more is being produced. When aggregate supply falls, the curve shifts to the left, like the shift from AS_0 to AS_2, so that at every price level less is being produced.

willing to produce more output at any given price level. When the cost of resources goes up, the aggregate supply curve shifts to the left, from AS_0 to AS_2. Here, at any given level of price, firms produce less output.

Remember that the vertical axis of the aggregate supply graph plots the price level for the whole economy. Only those changes in resource prices that raise the costs of production across the economy have an impact on the aggregate supply curve. For example, oil is an important raw material. If a new source of oil is discovered, the price of oil falls and aggregate supply increases. Of course if the price of oil increases substantially, aggregate supply decreases.

2.b.2. Technology Technological innovations allow businesses to increase the productivity of their existing resources. As new technology is adopted, the amount of output that can be produced by each unit of input increases, moving the aggregate supply curve to the right.

2.b.3. Expectations Expectations in the business community play an important role in aggregate supply. The short-run aggregate supply curve is drawn as an upward-sloping line because we assume that higher prices increase profits, creating an incentive for more production. The curve is drawn holding technology and resource prices, including wages, constant.

To understand how expectations can affect aggregate supply, consider the case of labor contracts. Workers typically contract for a nominal wage based on what they and their employers expect the future level of prices to be. Because wages typically are set for at least a year, any unexpected increase in the price level during the year lowers real wages. Firms receive higher prices for their output, but the cost of labor stays the same. So profits and production go up.

If wages rise in anticipation of higher prices but prices do not go up, the cost of labor rises. Higher real wages reduce profits and production, moving the aggregate supply curve to the left. Ceteris paribus, anticipated higher prices cause aggregate supply to fall; anticipated lower prices cause aggregate supply to rise.

If real wages increase because the future price is expected to increase, aggregate supply falls.

2.c. The Shape of the Aggregate Supply Curve

The aggregate supply curve does not really look like the lines shown in Figures 5 and 6. Figure 7 shows the actual shape of the short-run aggregate supply curve. Notice that there are three distinct regions on the curve.

When the price level is P_0, the aggregate supply curve is flat over relatively low levels of national income. This horizontal segment of the AS curve is the product of substantial unemployment and excess capacity. Here output could be increased without any pressure on the level of prices from the supply side of the market since the unemployed resources may be put to work.

The horizontal section of the short-run aggregate supply curve often is called the **Keynesian region**. This shape is consistent with the fixed-price model of equilibrium. If prices are constant at all levels of income, the aggregate supply curve is horizontal.

Keynesian region:
the portion of the aggregate supply curve at which prices are fixed because of unemployment and excess capacity

The AS curve in Figure 7 is horizontal only to an income level of Y_1, where aggregate supply begins to slope upward. Once income reaches this point, some areas of the economy begin to approach capacity. The costs of production rise as output increases, which means the level of prices must rise to induce suppliers to produce more. The region between Y_1 and Y_2 is the *intermediate range* of aggregate supply. This is the normal range of the curve—the area that typically is depicted in straight-line aggregate supply curves like those in Figures 5 and 6.

Figure 7
The Shape of the Short-Run Aggregate Supply Curve
At relatively low levels of national income (below Y_1) the AS curve is horizontal. Unemployment and excess capacity at these levels mean output can be expanded with no increase in the price level. As output moves past Y_1, *the* AS curve begins to slope up. In this intermediate range, the price level must rise to induce further increases in output. Eventually, at the potential level of output (Y_2), the economy is producing at capacity; increased prices have no effect on output. Here the AS curve is a vertical line.

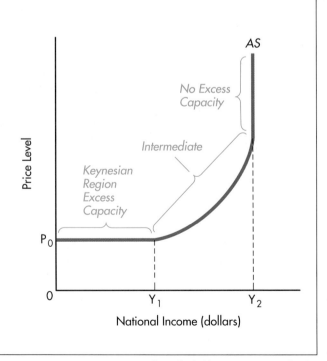

Why does the short-run aggregate supply curve become steeper as national income increases?

Notice that as the level of national income increases in Figure 7, the *AS* curve becomes steeper. As the economy pushes closer and closer toward capacity output (where no resources are unemployed), the price level must keep rising to induce further increases in output. Where the capacity level of output is reached, at Y_2, the aggregate supply curve becomes a vertical line. At this level of national income, no more output can be produced no matter how much the price level rises unless the productive capacity or potential GNP of the economy increases.

In the long run, the quantity of resources can increase and new technology can be developed so that potential GNP increases and the short-run aggregate supply curve shifts to the right. Again, the long run is the time in which the economy adjusts to change in the cost of resources and technological change; it is not an exact period of time on the calendar. The speed with which the cost of resources adjusts to price level changes and the length of time it takes economies to increase potential GNP vary across time and country.

2.d. The Long-Run Aggregate Supply Curve

Why is the long-run aggregate supply curve vertical?

Aggregate supply in the short run is different from aggregate supply in the long run (see Figure 8). That difference stems from the fact that resources and the costs of resources are not fixed in the long run. The short-run *AS* curve slopes upward because resource prices, especially wages, do not change in the short run. Approximately half of all workers in the United States sign wage contracts that last one or more years. Fixed wages allow real wages to move in the opposite direction of a change in price level. When the price level rises, real wages fall and firms expand production. When the price level falls, real wages rise and firms reduce production.

Figure 8
Long-Run Aggregate Supply
In the long run, the AS curve is a vertical line, which indicates that there is no relationship between price level changes and the quantity of output produced. Changes in technology and the availability and quality of resources can shift the LRAS curve. For instance, a new technology that increases productivity would move the curve to the right, from LRAS to LRAS₁.

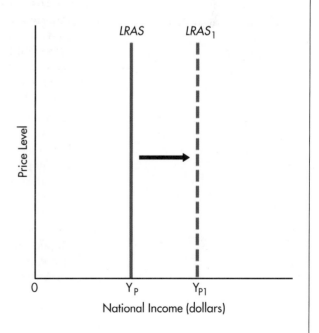

How Lack of Information in the Short Run Affects Wages in the Long Run

Workers do not have perfect information. In other words, they do not know everything that occurs. This lack of information includes information about the price level. If workers form incorrect expectations regarding the price level in the short run, they may be willing to work for a different wage in the short run than in the long run. For example, if workers thought that the inflation rate would be 3 percent over the next year, they would want a smaller wage raise than if they believed that the inflation rate would be 6 percent. If, in fact, they base their wage negotiations on 3 percent inflation and accept a wage based on that inflation rate, but it turns out that the price level has increased by 6 percent, workers will then seek higher wages. In the long run, wages will reflect price level changes.

If it cost nothing to obtain information, everyone who was interested would always know the current economic conditions. However, since there are costs of obtaining and understanding information about the economy, people will make mistakes in the short run. Both managers and employees make mistakes due to lack of information. Such mistakes are not due to stupidity but to ignorance—ignorance of future as well as current economic conditions. In the long run, mistakes about the price level are realized and wages adjust to the known price level.

We now have two reasons why wages will be more flexible in the long run than in the short run: long-term contracts and lack of information in the short run. The same arguments could be made for other resources as well. Because of these two reasons, the short-run aggregate supply curve is generally upward sloping.

Over time, labor contracts expire and wages adjust to current conditions. The increased flexibility of wages in the long run changes the shape of the aggregate supply curve (see Economic Insight: "How Lack of Information in the Short Run Affects Wages in the Long Run").

long-run aggregate supply curve (LRAS):
a vertical line at potential level of national income

The **long-run aggregate supply curve** (LRAS) is a vertical line at the potential level of national income (Y_p), as shown in Figure 8. In the long run there is no relationship between changes in price level and changes in output because wages and other resource costs fully adjust to price changes over time. The short-run *AS* curve slopes up because we assume that the costs of production, particularly wages, do not change to offset changing prices. In the short run, then, higher prices increase producers' profits and stimulate production. In the long run, because the costs of production adjust completely to the change in prices, neither profits nor production increase. What we find here are higher wages and other costs of production to match the higher level of prices.

The fact that the long-run aggregate supply curve is vertical does not mean that the economy is forever fixed at the current level of potential national income or gross national product. Over time, as new technologies are developed and the quantity and quality of the factors of production increase, potential output also increases, shifting the long-run aggregate supply curve to the right. Figure 8 shows long-run economic growth by the shift in the aggregate supply curve from *LRAS* to *LRAS₁*. The movement of the long-run aggregate supply curve to the right reflects the increase in

New technology will increase aggregate supply. The robotic welders shown in the photo allow General Motors to produce more cars at a lower price than would otherwise be possible. As industries develop new, more efficient ways to produce output, the productive capacity of nations increases.

potential national income from Y_p to Y_{p1}. Even though price level has no effect on the level of output in the long run, changes in the determinants of the supply of real output in the economy do.

RECAP

1. The aggregate supply curve shows the quantity of output (income) produced at alternative price levels.

2. The aggregate supply curve slopes up because, ceteris paribus, higher prices increase producers' profits, creating an incentive to increase output.

3. The aggregate supply curve shifts with changes in the price of resources, in technology, and in expectations.

4. The short-run aggregate supply curve has three distinct regions: the horizontal Keynesian region, where unemployment and excess capacity are high; an upward-sloping intermediate region, where the price level changes production; and a vertical region, where no excess capacity exists.

5. The long-run aggregate supply curve is vertical at potential national income because eventually wages and the costs of other resources adjust fully to price level changes.

3. AGGREGATE DEMAND AND SUPPLY EQUILIBRIUM

▼
What determines the equilibrium price level and national income?
▲

Now that we have defined the aggregate demand and aggregate supply curves separately, we can put them together to determine the equilibrium level of price and national income.

3.a. Short-Run Equilibrium

Figure 9 shows the level of equilibrium in a hypothetical economy. In the figure, we use the intermediate range of the short-run aggregate supply curve, where aggregate supply slopes upward.

Initially the economy is in equilibrium at point 1, where AD_1 and AS_1 intersect. At this point, the equilibrium price is P_1 and the equilibrium income is $500. At price P_1, the amount of output demanded is equal to the amount supplied. Suppose aggregate demand increases from AD_1 to AD_2. In the short run, aggregate supply does not change, so the new equilibrium is at the intersection of the new aggregate demand curve, AD_2, and the same aggregate supply curve, AS_1, at point 2. The new equilibrium price is P_2, and the new equilibrium income is $600.

3.b. Long-Run Equilibrium

Point 2 is not a permanent equilibrium because aggregate supply falls to AS_2 once the costs of production rise in response to higher prices. Final equilibrium is at point 3, where the price level is P_3 and national income is $500. Notice that equilibrium income here is the same as the initial equilibrium at point 1. Points 1 and 3 both lie along the long-run aggregate supply curve (*LRAS*).

In the long run, there is no relationship between the level of prices and the level of output. The initial shock to or change in the economy is an increase in aggregate demand. The change in aggregate expenditures initially leads to higher output and higher prices. Over time, however, output falls back to its original value while prices continue to rise. This is a major difference between the aggregate expenditures and income model of the economy and the aggregate demand and supply model. When prices are fixed, as they are in the Keynesian model, an increase in aggregate expenditures increases national income by a multiple of the initial increase in

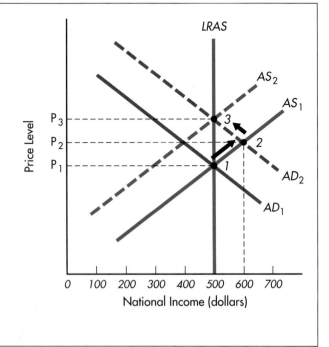

Figure 9
Aggregate Demand and Supply Equilibrium
The equilibrium level of price and income is at the intersection of the *AD* and *AS* curves. Initially equilibrium occurs at point 1, where the AD_1 and AS_1 curves intersect. Here the price level is P_1 and national income is $500. If aggregate demand increases, moving from AD_1 to AD_2, in the short run there is a new equilibrium at point 2, where AD_2 intersects AS_1. The price level rises to P_2, and the equilibrium level of national income increases to $600. Over time, as the costs of wages and other resources rise in response to higher prices, aggregate supply falls, moving AS_1 to AS_2. Final equilibrium occurs at point 3, where the AS_2 curve intersects the AD_2 curve. The price level rises to P_3, but the equilibrium level of national income returns to its initial level, $500. In the long run, there is no relationship between prices and the equilibrium level of national income because the costs of resources adjust to changes in the level of prices.

284

OPEC and Aggregate Supply

In 1973 and 1974 and again in 1979 and 1980, the Organization of Petroleum Exporting Countries (OPEC) reduced the supply of oil, driving the price of oil up dramatically. For example, the price of Saudi Arabian crude oil more than tripled between 1973 and 1974, and more than doubled between 1979 and 1980. Researchers estimate that the rapid jump in oil prices reduced output by 17 percent in Japan, by 7 percent in the United States, and by 1.9 percent in Germany.[1]

Oil is an important resource in many industries. When the price of oil increases, aggregate supply falls. You can see this in the graph. When the price of oil goes up, the aggregate supply curve falls from AS_1 to AS_2. When aggregate supply falls, the equilibrium level of income (the intersection of the AS curve and the AD curve) falls from Y_1 to Y_2.

Notice that each aggregate supply curve is drawn with a vertical region at potential national income (Y_p). A decrease in aggregate supply reduces not only current equilibrium income, but also potential equilibrium in-

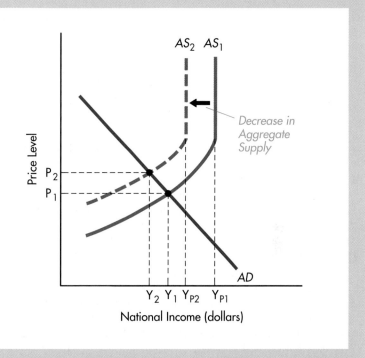

come. When the aggregate supply curve moves from AS_1 to AS_2, potential income falls from Y_{p1} to Y_{p2}. When this happens, there is no price level at which the economy can reach its previous level of potential income. The higher resource (oil) price reduces the productive capacity of the economy.

■ [1]These estimates were taken from Robert H. Rasche and John A. Tatom, "Energy Price Shocks, Aggregate Supply, and Monetary Policy: The Theory and the International Evidence," in Karl Brunner and Allan H. Meltzer, eds., *Carnegie-Rochester Conference Series on Public Policy* 14 (Spring 1981): 9–93.

In the flexible-price model, an increase in aggregate expenditures increases national income only temporarily.

expenditures. When prices are flexible, as they are in the aggregate demand and supply model, an increase in aggregate expenditures increases national income only temporarily. Ultimately the model produces higher prices at the same level of national income.

Remember that we are not saying that the level of output never changes. The long-run aggregate supply curve shifts as technology changes and new supplies of resources are obtained. But in comparison to the fixed-price model, the output change that results from a change in aggregate expenditures is a temporary phenomenon. The price level eventually adjusts, and output eventually returns to the potential level (see Economic Insight: "OPEC and Aggregate Supply").

RECAP

1. The equilibrium level of price and income is at the point where the aggregate demand and aggregate supply curves intersect.

2. In the short run, a shift in aggregate demand establishes a temporary equilibrium along the short-run aggregate supply curve.

3. In the long run, the short-run aggregate supply curve shifts so that changes in aggregate demand determine the price level, not the equilibrium level of output or national income.

SUMMARY

1. The aggregate demand and supply model allows prices to move; it expands the fixed-price aggregate expenditures and income model. Preview section

▼▲ **Why does the aggregate expenditures curve shift with changes in the price level?**

2. The *AE* curve shifts with changes in the price level because of the wealth effect, the interest rate effect, and the international trade effect. §§ 1.a.1, 1.a.2., and 1.a.3

▼▲ **What is the aggregate demand curve?**

3. The aggregate demand curve shows the equilibrium level of expenditures at different price levels. § 1.b

4. Because expenditures and prices move in opposite directions, the *AD* curve is negative. § 1.b

▼▲ **What causes the aggregate demand curve to shift?**

5. The nonprice determinants of aggregate demand are expectations, foreign income and price levels, and government policy. §§ 1.c.1, 1.c.2, and 1.c.3

▼▲ **What is the aggregate supply curve?**

6. The aggregate supply curve shows the quantity of national output (or income) produced at different price levels. § 2

▼▲ **What causes the aggregate supply curve to shift?**

7. The aggregate supply curve shifts with changes in resource prices, technology, and expectations. §§ 2.b.1, 2.b.2, and 2.b.3

▼▲ **Why does the short-run aggregate supply curve become steeper as national income increases?**

8. As the economy pushes closer to potential national income, it moves closer to capacity output. The level of prices must rise here to induce increased production. § 2.c

▼▲ **Why is the long-run aggregate supply curve vertical?**

9. The long-run aggregate supply curve is a vertical line at the potential level of national income. The shape of the curve indicates that there is no relationship between higher prices and output when an economy is producing at capacity. § 2.d

▼▲ **What determines the equilibrium price level and national income?**

10. The equilibrium level of price and income is at the intersection of the aggregate demand and aggregate supply curves. § 3.a

11. In the short run, a shift in aggregate demand establishes a temporary equilibrium along the short-run aggregate supply curve. § 3.a

12. In the long run, the short-run aggregate supply curve shifts so that changes in aggregate demand determine the price level, not the equilibrium level of output or national income. § 3.b

KEY TERMS

wealth effect § 1.a.1

interest rate effect § 1.a.2

international trade effect § 1.a.3

aggregate demand curve § 1.b

aggregate supply curve § 2

Keynesian region § 2.c

long-run aggregate supply curve (LRAS) § 2.d

EXERCISES

Basic Terms and Concepts

1. Derive the aggregate demand curve from an aggregate expenditures diagram. Explain how aggregate demand relates to aggregate expenditures.

2. How is the aggregate demand curve different from the demand curve for a single good, like hamburgers?

3. Why does the aggregate demand curve slope down? Give real-world examples of the three effects that explain the slope of the curve.

4. How does an increase in foreign income affect domestic aggregate expenditures and demand?

5. How does a decrease in foreign price levels affect domestic aggregate expenditures and demand?

6. How is the aggregate supply curve different from the supply curve for a single good, like pizza?

7. There are several determinants of aggregate supply that can cause the aggregate supply curve to shift.

   a. Describe those determinants and give an example of a change in each.

   b. Draw and label an aggregate supply diagram that illustrates the effect of the change in each determinant.

Extended Concepts

8. Draw a short-run aggregate supply curve, with a horizontal region at low levels of national in-come, an upward-sloping region at higher levels of national income, and a vertical region at potential national income.

   a. Explain why the curve has this shape.

   b. Which region do you think best describes the condition of the U.S. economy today? Explain your answer.

9. Draw and carefully label an aggregate demand and supply diagram with initial equilibrium at P_0 and Y_0.

   a. Using the diagram, explain what happens when aggregate demand falls.

   b. How is the short run different from the long run?

10. Draw a graph with an aggregate expenditures curve and 45-degree line, and show equilibrium.

    a. Directly below the graph, draw an aggregate demand and supply diagram with the price level on the vertical axis, and show equilibrium on the new graph.

    b. Show what happens in both diagrams when aggregate expenditures increase.

11. Draw an aggregate demand and supply diagram for Japan. In the diagram show how each of the following affects aggregate demand and supply.

    a. U.S. gross national product falls.

    b. The level of prices in Korea falls.

    c. Labor receives a large wage increase.

    d. Economists predict higher prices next year.

The Economic Scene

Shaken by the latest jeremiads from economists? Wait a while; they are bound to change their minds. The latest target for revisionism is the productivity crisis, the declining rate of growth in output per worker that, some argue, is transforming America into a nation of poorly paid burger flippers and Toyota salesmen.

Productivity and American Leadership (M.I.T. Press, $29.95), a reassessment by William Baumol and Sue Anne Batey Blackman of Princeton University and Edward Wolff of New York University, musters impressive evidence suggesting that the lag in productivity is temporary and that Japan's challenge to American supremacy will run out of steam.

The depressing numbers are real enough. Productivity growth has indeed slumped since the mid-1960's. But the authors say the figures have been bouncing around a trend of about 2.2 percent annual growth for the last century. And a half-dozen previous slumps were deeper, if not longer. It is thus plausible, though not provable, that this latest bad patch is a rebound from a productivity boom after World War II.

The downturn in productivity would probably not have drawn so much attention if it had not been accompanied by more direct signs of economic senescence — the rusting of the steel belt, the rise of low-wage service industries, the invasion of high-technology markets by the Japanese. But here, too, the three economists assert, there is less to worry about than meets the eye.

Sectors of the economy that had traditionally led in productivity are still leading, and still doing well. Paradoxically, it is the spectacular growth in output per worker in manufacturing in the 1980's that generated the sense of malaise.

Pressed by foreign competition, American industry plowed tens of billions of dollars into new machinery and technology. Manufacturing employment fell as companies automated, but total output rose. Manufacturing productivity actually gained more in America between 1979 to 1986 than it did in West Germany.

What, then, explains the huge shift of jobs into service industries, or the loss of world market share in high technology? Unlike manufacturing, productivity gains in services come slowly, or not at all. As the authors point out, it takes as much labor today to play a Scarlatti sonata on the harpsichord as it did in the 18th century.

Thus, while the share of services in total output has not changed, the service sector has absorbed almost all the growth in labor supply since World War II. Japan's parallel shift toward service jobs started later. But between 1965 and 1980 the proportion of the work force in services rose by 30 percent — three times the rate in the United States.

Japan, the authors concede, has done spectacularly well in increasing its world market share of technology-based exports from 7 percent in 1965 to 20 percent in 1984. But most of Japan's gains did not come at America's expense. The United States slipped from 27 to 25 percent, while the combined share of West Germany, Britain and France fell from 35 to 29 percent.

The most soothing argument offered by the three authors is the convergence theory. It is only natural, they claim, that once-poor economies are catching up with America. They are in the best position to exploit technology invented elsewhere. Moreover, their citizens have far more pressing reasons for thrift, creating the pool of cheap capital needed to use the imported technology. Once these countries achieve affluence, it is argued, the worm will turn.

What the three economists do not say is that the economic pessimism that has infected Americans has little to do with productivity statistics and a lot to do with their own experiences. And here, one suspects, much of the personal malaise comes from the failure to protect the losers from the consequences of rapid economic change.

The drop in manufacturing employment may, for example, be a healthy consequence of overdue automation. But that is no consolation to a rubber worker who ends up driving a delivery van at half the pay. The return to technical training may have gone up. But that is no consolation to a 19-year-old who lacks the money — and perhaps the intelligence — to become an engineer.

Does America have a productivity problem? As the three economists convincingly argue, no one really knows. But many Americans certainly do have a problem making ends meet, and they are only too willing to look for scapegoats.

■ Source: Peter Passell, "Economic Scene," *The New York Times*, Nov. 1, 1989, p. D2.

Commentary

Productivity growth is essential for the long-term growth of an economy and for steady improvement in a country's standard of living. Productivity growth also has beneficial consequences for shorter-run macroeconomic factors such as inflation and movements of GNP around trend. The accompanying article discusses recent trends in productivity growth in the United States. But what are the specific implications of these trends for the long-term health of the U.S. economy? And exactly how does productivity growth affect prices and GNP over the shorter term?

In the long run, the level of GNP is determined by supply-side factors. These include the stock of capital in an economy, the number and skill level of workers, and technological factors. Productivity measures the average amount of output each worker produces. An increase in productivity may be caused by an increase in workers' skills, a growth in the capital available for production, or the development of new production techniques or technologies. The standard of living of workers rises as productivity increases. Even a small slowdown in productivity growth is alarming because it implies a large reduction in the future standard of living.

The study cited in the article finds that yearly U.S. productivity growth varies around a long-run growth rate of 2.2 percent. While productivity growth has slumped since the mid-1960s, this may reflect a slowdown after the rapid growth in productivity immediately following World War II. In historical perspective, the latest productivity slump is no worse nor any more protracted than other slumps during the past century.

While this historical perspective is valuable, there are important shorter-term consequences of the poor performance in productivity growth. These can be analyzed by using a macroeconomic model incorporating aggregate supply and aggregate demand. An increase in productivity shifts out the aggregate supply function since it represents an increase in the amount that any given work force can produce. An increase in productivity is depicted as an outward shift in the aggregate supply line from AS_1 to AS_2 with no change in the aggregate demand line (see graph). This results in a change in the equilibrium from e_1 to e_2, representing an increase in output and a decrease in the price level. Thus, an increase in the growth of productivity is im-

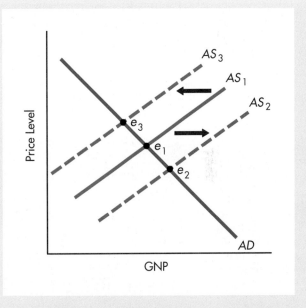

portant both for increasing the growth rate of GNP and for keeping inflation low.

The reason that GNP rises in this example is that firms are willing to hire more workers at any real wage if the productivity of workers rises. Because of the rise in productivity, workers may demand and receive higher wages. If the increase in wages received by workers just matches the increase in productivity, the aggregate supply line does not shift. In this case, where equilibrium remains at point e_1, prices are stable, GNP is stable, and workers are better off because they receive higher wages than before. If, however, the increase in productivity fails to match wage demands, the aggregate supply curve shifts back to AS_3. The new equilibrium, e_3 in the graph, has higher prices and lower output than the original equilibrium point e_1.

Our analysis complements the article, which focuses on the importance of productivity growth for improving a country's long-run standard of living. Our discussion points out the shorter-term macroeconomic consequences of the relationship between productivity growth and wage increases. Both the long-run and short-run approaches point out the importance of productivity growth for the well-being of an economy.

Macroeconomic Policy

12

Fiscal Policy

1. How can fiscal policy eliminate a recessionary gap?

2. What happens to equilibrium national income when government spending and taxes both increase by the same amount?

3. How has U.S. fiscal policy changed over time?

4. What are the effects of budget deficits?

5. How does fiscal policy differ across countries?

PREVIEW   Macroeconomics plays a key role in national politics. When Jimmy Carter ran for the presidency against Gerald Ford in 1976, he created a "misery index" to measure the state of the economy. The index was the sum of the inflation rate and the unemployment rate, and Carter showed that it had risen during Ford's term in office. When Ronald Reagan challenged Carter in 1980, he used the misery index to show that inflation and unemployment had gone up during the Carter years. The implication is that presidents are responsible for the condition of the economy. If the inflation rate or the unemployment rate is relatively high coming into an election year, incumbent presidents are open to criticism by their opponents.

The idea that government is responsible for the macroeconomic health of the nation became the official policy of the United States with passage of the Employment Act of 1946. The act states:

It is the continuing policy and responsibility of the Federal Government to use all practical means consistent with its needs and obligations and other essential considerations of national policy to coordinate and utilize all its plans, functions, and resources for the purpose of creating and maintaining, in a manner calculated to foster and promote free competitive enterprise and the general welfare conditions under which there will be afforded useful employment opportunities, including self-employment for those able, willing, and seeking to work, and to promote maximum employment, production and purchasing power.

The act gave the national government responsibility for creating and maintaining low inflation and unemployment. *Fiscal policy* is the tool the government uses to guide the economy along an expansionary path.

In this chapter we examine the role of fiscal policy—government spending and taxation—in determining the equilibrium level of income. Then we review the budget process and the history of fiscal policy in the United States. Finally we describe the difference in fiscal policy between industrial and developing countries.

1. FISCAL POLICY AND AGGREGATE EXPENDITURES

Fiscal policy is the government's policy toward spending and taxation. Remember that aggregate expenditures include consumption, investment, net exports, and government spending. What the government spends on goods and services affects the level of aggregate expenditures directly. Taxes affect aggregate expenditures indirectly by changing the disposable income of households, which alters consumption.

1.a. Closing the Recessionary Gap

In Chapter 10 we defined the GNP gap as the difference between potential national income and the equilibrium level of national income. Figure 1 (see table) lists aggregate expenditures and income data for a hypothetical economy. Equilibrium income—the level at which aggregate expenditures equal income—is $500. Suppose that potential national income—the level of income at which resources are fully employed—is $600. The GNP gap—the difference between potential income ($600) and equilibrium income ($500)—is $100.

To close the GNP gap, to reach potential GNP, aggregate expenditures must go up. The recessionary gap is the amount by which aggregate expenditures must rise in order for equilibrium national income to reach the level of potential national income. The table in Figure 1 indicates that at the potential income level of $600, aggregate expenditures are $580. The recessionary gap, measured as the difference between aggregate expenditures and national income at the potential level of national income, is $20. Spending must increase by $20 to raise equilibrium income to potential income. If aggregate expenditures increased by $20, national income would increase by $100, telling us that the multiplier must be 5.

You can see the recessionary gap in the graph in Figure 1. The gap is the vertical distance between the 45-degree line and the aggregate expenditures line at the level of potential income ($600). In the figure the vertical distance is $20. If aggregate expenditures increase by $20, the *AE* curve shifts up, intersecting the 45-degree line at the level of potential income. At this point equilibrium income equals potential income.

Figure 1
The Recessionary Gap and the GNP Gap
The GNP gap is the difference between potential national income (Y_p = $600) and equilibrium national income (Y_e = $500). Here the GNP gap equals $100. The recessionary gap is the amount aggregate expenditures must rise to bring equilibrium national income up to potential national income. It is the vertical distance between the AE line and the 45-degree line at Y_p. In this economy, the recessionary gap equals $20.

(1) Income (Y)	(2) Consumption (C)	(3) Investment (I)	(4) Government Spending (G)	(5) Net Exports (X)	(6) Aggregate Expenditures (AE)
0	$30	$20	$30	$20	$100
$100	$120	$20	$30	$10	$180
$200	$210	$20	$30	0	$260
$300	$300	$20	$30	−$10	$340
$400	$390	$20	$30	−$20	$420
$500	$480	$20	$30	−$30	$500
$600	$570	$20	$30	−$40	$580

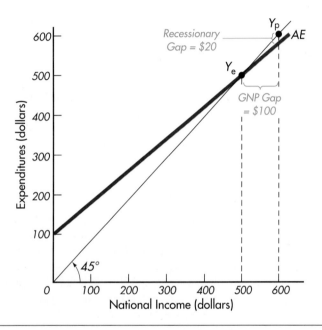

1.a.1. Government Spending

A recessionary gap can be closed by increasing government spending. Look at the table in Figure 2. If we increase government spending by $20, we directly increase aggregate expenditures by $20. The $20 increase in aggregate expenditures pushes the equilibrium level of income up $100, to $600. The multiplier is 5: a $20 increase in expenditures produces a $100 increase in equilibrium income.

Figure 2 shows the effect of increased government spending graphically. The $20 increase in government spending shifts the AE curve up to AE_1. The AE_1 curve and the 45-degree line intersect at the level of potential income, $600. The $20 increase in government spending pushes equilibrium income up $100.

When a government increases spending, it stimulates the economy, raising aggregate expenditures and income. When a government decreases spending, it depresses the economy, reducing aggregate expenditures and income. By varying the level of government spending, policymakers can affect the level of income in the economy. Of course government spending

How can fiscal policy eliminate a recessionary gap?

By varying the level of government spending, policymakers can affect the level of income in the economy.

Figure 2
Eliminating the Recessionary Gap by Increasing Government Spending
On the original aggregate expenditures curve (*AE*), equilibrium national income is $500. Potential national income is $600. The GNP gap ($100) can be eliminated by increasing autonomous government spending by an amount equal to the recessionary gap ($20). This increase in autonomous government spending shifts the *AE* curve up by $20 at every level of national income, to *AE₁*. The *AE₁* curve intersects the 45-degree line at potential national income, raising equilibrium national income to $600.

(1) Income (Y)	(2) Consumption (C)	(3) Investment (I)	(4) Government Spending (G)	(5) Net Exports (X)	(6) Aggregate Expenditures (AE₁)
0	$30	$20	$50	$20	$120
$100	$120	$20	$50	$10	$200
$200	$210	$20	$50	0	$280
$300	$300	$20	$50	−$10	$360
$400	$390	$20	$50	−$20	$440
$500	$480	$20	$50	−$30	$520
$600	$570	$20	$50	−$40	$600

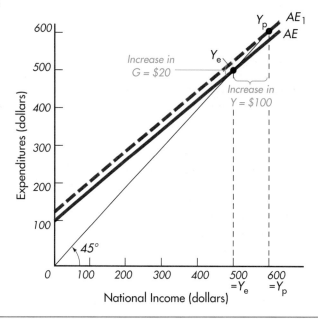

is only part of fiscal policy. Changes in taxes also have an effect on macroeconomic equilibrium.

1.a.2. Taxation Government policymakers can eliminate a recessionary gap, not only by increasing government spending on goods and services, but also by reducing taxes. A recessionary gap is the product of aggregate expenditures that are too low to achieve equilibrium at potential income. To close the gap, aggregate expenditures must go up. Cutting taxes does not increase expenditures directly; it works indirectly, through its effect on disposable income and consumption.

In our example the multiplier is 5: a government spending increase of $20 generates a $100 increase in equilibrium income. What happens if taxes are cut by $20? Initially disposable income increases by $20. How much does household spending increase? Not by $20. Remember that consumption is only a fraction of disposable income. In the example we have been using, the marginal propensity to save (MPS) is .10, as is the marginal propensity to import (MPI). Any time income changes, people save 10 percent of the change and spend 10 percent of the change on imports. This means aggregate expenditures do not change by the full amount of a change in taxes. In fact we can think in terms of two multipliers—one for expenditures and one for taxes.

The **spending multiplier** is the simple multiplier we defined in Chapter 10:

spending multiplier:
the reciprocal of the sum of the MPS
and the MPI

$$\text{Spending multiplier} = \frac{1}{\text{MPS} + \text{MPI}}$$

In our example, because the MPS and the MPI both equal .10, the spending multiplier equals 5:

$$\text{Spending multiplier} = \frac{1}{.10 + .10}$$

$$= \frac{1}{.20}$$

$$= 5$$

When government spending increases by \$20, the equilibrium level of income increases by 5 times \$20, or \$100.

tax multiplier:
a measure of the effect of a change in taxes on the equilibrium level of income

We also can define a **tax multiplier**, a measure of the effect of a change in taxes on equilibrium income. Because a percentage of any change in income is saved and spent on imports, we know that a tax cut increases expenditures by less than the amount of the cut. The percentage of the tax cut that actually is spent is the marginal propensity to consume (MPC) less the MPI. If consumers save 10 percent of any extra income, they spend 90 percent, the MPC. But the domestic economy does not realize 90 percent of the extra income because 10 percent of the extra income is spent on imports. The percentage of any extra income that actually is spent at home is the MPC minus the MPI. In our example, 80 percent (.90 − .10) of any extra income is spent in the domestic economy.

With this information, we can define the tax multiplier like this:

$$\text{Tax multiplier} = -(\text{MPC} - \text{MPI})\left(\frac{1}{\text{MPS} + \text{MPI}}\right)$$

In our example the tax multiplier is −4:

$$\text{Tax multiplier} = -(.90 - .10)\left(\frac{1}{.10 + .10}\right)$$

$$= -(.80)(5)$$

$$= -4$$

A tax cut increases equilibrium income by 4 times the amount of the cut.

Notice that the tax multiplier is always a *negative* number because a change in taxes moves income and expenditures in the opposite direction. Higher taxes lower income and expenditures; lower taxes raise income and expenditures.

Higher taxes lower income and expenditures; lower taxes raise income and expenditures.

The tax multiplier tells us how much taxes must fall to increase equilibrium income to potential income, to close the recessionary gap. We divide the multiplier into the GNP gap to find the required change in taxes.

With a tax multiplier of −4, taxes have to fall $25 to increase income $100. The $20 recessionary gap can be eliminated with a tax cut of $25.

A $25 cut in taxes, then, functions like a $20 increase in government spending. The *AE* curve shifts up to AE_1, intersecting the 45-degree line at $600, the level of potential income.

1.b. The Balanced-Budget Multiplier

▼
What happens to equilibrium national income when government spending and taxes both increase by the same amount?
▲

If government spending increases by the same amount as taxes, the net effect is expansionary. Why? Because government spending increases aggregate expenditures directly, while taxes work indirectly through changes in income (and only part of a change in income is spent in the domestic economy). A change in government spending changes equilibrium income by the spending multiplier. A change in taxes changes equilibrium income by the tax multiplier. The two multipliers give us a measure of the effect on equilibrium income if government spending and taxes both increase or decrease by the same amount. This measure is called the **balanced-budget multiplier**:

balanced-budget multiplier:
a measure of how much equilibrium income changes if government spending and taxes both increase or decrease by the same amount

Balanced-budget multiplier = spending multiplier + tax multiplier

$$= \frac{1}{MPS + MPI} + -(MPC - MPI)\left(\frac{1}{MPS + MPI}\right)$$

$$= \frac{1 - MPC + MPI}{MPS + MPI}$$

Because

$$MPS = 1 - MPC$$

the balanced-budget multiplier is simply 1:

$$= \frac{MPS + MPI}{MPS + MPI}$$

$$= 1$$

A balanced-budget multiplier of 1 means that when government spending and taxes change by the same amount, equilibrium income changes by the amount of the change in government spending. In our example, if government spending and taxes both increase by $20, equilibrium income increases by $20. The $20 increase in government spending increases aggregate expenditures by $20; the $20 increase in taxes lowers aggregate expenditures by $16 (.80 × $20). The net change in aggregate expenditures is $4 ($20 − $16). A net increase in aggregate expenditures of $4 increases equilibrium income by the spending multiplier (5) times $4, or $20.

1.c. Shifting the Aggregate Demand Curve

The aggregate expenditures model assumes that prices are fixed. Once we allow the price level to vary, the multiplier effects of changes in expenditures are modified. To understand the impact of fiscal policy on price and quantity, we must turn to aggregate demand. Changes in government spending and taxes shift the aggregate demand curve (see Figure 3).

Remember that the aggregate demand curve represents combinations of equilibrium aggregate expenditures and alternative price levels. An increase in government spending or a decrease in taxes raises autonomous aggregate expenditures, raising the level of expenditures at every level of prices and moving the aggregate demand curve to the right.

In Figure 3(a), the recessionary gap is eliminated by an increase in government spending. If government spending goes up by the amount of the recessionary gap, aggregate expenditures increase from AE to AE_1, equilibrium national income increases from Y_e to Y_p.

The aggregate demand and supply diagram that corresponds to the shift in the AE curve is shown in Figure 3(b). Remember that the Keynesian model assumes that prices are fixed. Only if the aggregate supply curve is horizontal do prices remain fixed as aggregate expenditures change. In Figure 3(b), equilibrium occurs along the horizontal segment (the Keynesian region) of the AS curve. If government spending increases and the price level remains constant, aggregate demand shifts from AD to AD_1; it increases by the horizontal distance from point A to point B. Once aggregate demand shifts, the AD_1 and AS curves intersect at potential income, Y_p.

But Figure 3(b) is not realistic. The AS curve is horizontal all the way to the level of potential income; it should begin sloping up well before Y_p. And because potential income represents capacity output in the economy, the AS curve should become a vertical line at Y_p, as shown in Figure 3(c).

If the AS curve slopes up in the area of equilibrium, as it does in part (c) of the figure, expenditures have to go up by more than the amount suggested in parts (a) and (b) for the economy to reach Y_p. Why? Because the spending multiplier we use, which assumes constant prices, overestimates the expansionary effect of increases in spending when prices rise. When prices go up, the multiplier effect of spending on real income is reduced. This effect is shown in Figure 3(c). To increase the equilibrium level of national income from Y_e to Y_p, aggregate demand must shift by the amount from point A to C, a larger increase than that shown in Figure 3(b), where the price level is fixed.

If the price level rises as national income increases, the multiplier effects of any given change in aggregate expenditures are smaller than they would be if the price remains constant.

If the price level rises as national income increases, the multiplier effects of any given change in aggregate expenditures are smaller than they would be if the price level remains constant. This means that the spending and tax multipliers overstate the effect of a change in aggregate expenditures. They apply only to an economy in which prices are fixed and aggregate supply curves are horizontal. In the real world, because prices change and aggregate supply curves slope up, the spending and tax multipliers underestimate the actual change in expenditures needed to close a recessionary gap.

1.d. Limitations of the Multiplier Analysis

We have just discussed one reason why the spending and tax multipliers do not accurately measure the change in equilibrium national income that results from a change in fiscal policy: as real income rises, prices tend to rise. There are other reasons too. One is that the expansionary effect of government spending on national income depends on how the government pays for or finances its spending.

Figure 3
Eliminating the Recessionary Gap: Higher Prices Mean Greater Spending

Part (a) shows the Keynesian model. When prices are fixed, an increase in autonomous aggregate expenditures shifts the *AE* curve up to *AE₁*, eliminating the recessionary gap. Part (b) of the figure shows the aggregate demand and supply curve that corresponds to the aggregate expenditures model. When aggregate demand increases from *AD* to *AD₁*, equilibrium national income increases by the full amount of the shift in demand. This is because the aggregate supply curve is horizontal over the area of the shift in aggregate demand. In order for equilibrium national income to rise from Y_e to Y_p, aggregate demand must shift by more than it does in part (b). In reality, the aggregate supply curve begins to slope up before potential national income (Y_p) is reached, as shown in part (c) of the figure.

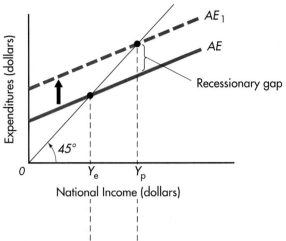

(a) Income-Expenditures Model
(Assumes constant prices)

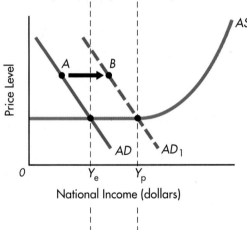

(b) Aggregate Demand and Supply
(constant prices in Keynesian range of AS curve)

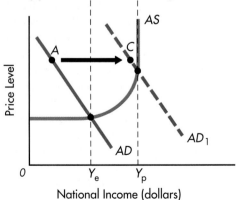

(c) Aggregate Demand and Supply
(rising prices in intermediate range of AS curve)

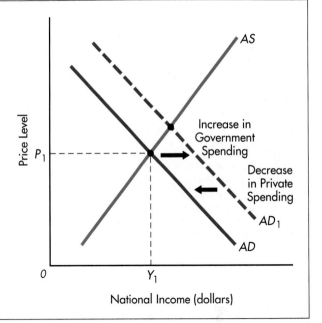

Figure 4
The Effect of Taxation on Aggregate Supply
An increase in government spending shifts the aggregate demand curve from *AD* to *AD₁*, moving equilibrium from point *A* to point *B*, and equilibrium national income from *Y₁* to *Yₚ*. If higher taxes reduce the incentive to work, aggregate supply could fall from *AS* to *AS₁*, moving equilibrium to point *C* and equilibrium national income to *Y₂*, a level below potential national income.

Government spending must be financed by some combination of taxing, borrowing, or creating money:

Government spending = taxes + change in government debt
+ change in government-issued money

In Chapter 14 we discuss the effect of financing government spending by creating money. As you will see, this source of government financing is most important in developing countries. Here we talk about the more practical problem in industrial countries: how taxes and government debt can modify the multiplier analysis.

1.d.1. Government Spending Financed by Tax Increases Suppose that government spending rises by $100 billion and that this expenditure is financed by a tax increase of $100 billion. The balanced-budget multiplier (1) means that equilibrium income rises by the amount of the increase in government spending, $100 billion. However, the multiplier assumes that the only thing that changes is aggregate demand. In fact an increase in taxes can affect aggregate supply.

Aggregate supply measures the output that producers offer for sale at different levels of prices. When taxes go up, workers have less incentive to work because their after-tax income is lower. The cost of taking a day off or extending a vacation for a few extra days is less than it is when taxes are lower and after-tax income is higher. When taxes go up, then, output can fall, causing the aggregate supply curve to shift to the left.

Figure 4 shows the possible effects of an increase in government spending financed by taxes. The economy is initially in equilibrium at point *A*, with prices at *P₁* and national income at *Y₁*. The increase in government spending shifts the aggregate demand curve from *AD* to *AD₁*. If

The large budget deficits incurred by the U.S. government in the 1980s were in part a product of lower tax rates engineered by the Reagan administration. President Reagan's economic team took office in January 1981 apparently believing that lower taxes would stimulate the supply of goods and services to a level that would raise tax revenues even though tax rates as a percentage of income had been cut. This emphasis on greater incentives to produce created by lower taxes came to be known as *supply-side economics*.

The most widely publicized element of supply-side economics was the *Laffer curve*. The curve is drawn with the tax rate on the vertical axis and tax revenue on the horizontal axis. When the rate of taxation is zero, there is no tax revenue. As the tax rate increases, tax revenue increases up to a point. The assumption here is that there is some rate of taxation that is so high that it discourages work. Once this rate is reached, tax revenue begins to fall as the rate

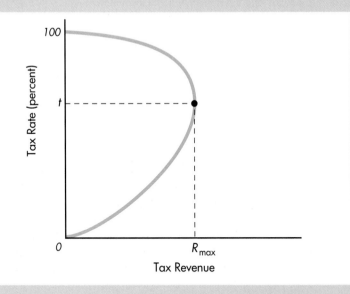

of taxation goes up. In the graph, tax revenue is maximized at R_{max} with a tax rate of t percent. Any increase in the rate of taxation above t percent produces lower tax revenues. In the extreme case — a 100 percent tax rate — no one is willing to work because the government taxes away all income.

Critics of the supply-side tax cuts proposed by the Reagan administration argued that lower taxes would increase the budget deficit. Supply-side advocates insisted that if the United States was in the backward-bending region of the Laffer curve (above t percent in the graph), tax cuts would actually raise, not lower, tax revenue. The evidence following the tax cuts shows they were wrong. The tax cuts did contribute to a larger budget deficit.

this was the only change, the economy would be in equilibrium at point B. But if the increase in taxes reduces output, the aggregate supply curve moves back from AS to AS_1, and output does not expand all the way to Y_p. The decrease in aggregate supply creates a new equilibrium at point C. Here income is at Y_2 (less than Y_p) and the price level is P_3 (higher than P_2). The standard multiplier analysis of government spending and taxation assumes that aggregate supply is not affected by the change in fiscal policy, leading us to expect a greater change in national income than may actually occur.

If tax changes do affect aggregate supply, the expansionary effects of government spending financed by tax increases are moderated. The actual magnitude of the effect is the subject of debate among economists. Most argue that the evidence in the United States indicates that tax increases have a fairly small effect on aggregate supply.

1.d.2. Government Spending Financed by Borrowing The standard multiplier analysis of government spending does not differentiate among the different methods of financing that spending. Yet you just saw how taxation can offset at least part of the expansionary effect of higher government spending so that the multiplier overstates the change in income produced by that spending. Government spending financed by borrowing also can modify the effect of the simple multiplier.

A government borrows funds by selling bonds to the public. These bonds represent debt that must be repaid at a future date. Debt is a kind of substitute for current taxes. Instead of increasing current taxes to finance higher spending, the government borrows the savings of households and businesses. Of course the debt will mature and have to be repaid. This means that taxes will have to be higher in the future in order to provide the government with the funds to pay off the debt.

Current government borrowing, then, implies higher future taxes. This can limit the expansionary effect of increased government spending. If households and businesses take higher future taxes into account, they tend to save more today so that they will be able to pay those taxes in the future. And as saving today increases, consumption today falls.

The idea that current government borrowing can reduce current nongovernment expenditures was suggested originally by early-nineteenth-century English economist David Ricardo. Ricardo recognized that government borrowing could function like increased current taxes, reducing *Ricardian equivalence holds if* current household and business expenditures. *Ricardian equivalence* is *taxation and government borrowing* the principle that taxation and government budget deficits financed by *have the same effect on spending in* borrowing have the same effect on the economy. If Ricardian equivalence *the private sector.* holds, it doesn't matter whether the government raises taxes or borrows more to finance increased spending. The effect is the same: private-sector spending falls by the same amount today.

If Ricardian equivalence holds, the increase in government spending moves the aggregate demand curve out to AD_1 (see Figure 5). But this

---

Figure 5
Ricardian Equivalence
An increase in government spending shifts the aggregate demand curve from AD to AD_1. However, if that spending is financed by government borrowing and if individuals and firms reduce their spending because they expect future taxes to go up to pay for the government debt, the aggregate demand curve shifts back to the left, offsetting at least part of the expansionary effect of higher government spending.

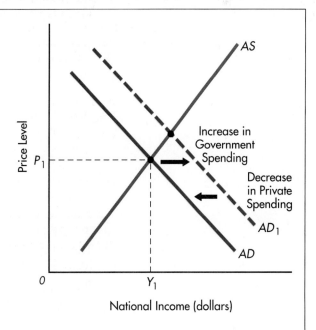

increase in aggregate demand is offset in part by a reduction in private spending as saving increases in anticipation of future tax increases. The reduction in household and business spending shifts the aggregate demand curve back to the left. Just how much private spending drops (and how far to the left the aggregate demand curve shifts) depends on the degree to which current saving increases in response to expected higher taxes. The less that people respond to the future tax liabilities arising from current government debt, the smaller the reduction in private spending.

There is substantial disagreement among economists about the extent to which current government borrowing acts like an increase in taxes. Some argue that it makes no difference whether the government raises current taxes or borrows. Others insist that the public does not base current spending on future tax liabilities. If the first group is correct, we would expect government spending financed by borrowing to have a smaller effect than if the second group is correct. Research on the issue continues, with most economists questioning the relevance of Ricardian equivalence and a small but influential group arguing its importance.

crowd out:
a drop in consumption or investment spending caused by government spending

1.d.3. Crowding Out Expansionary fiscal policy can **crowd out** private-sector spending; that is, an increase in government spending can reduce consumption and investment. Crowding out usually is discussed in the context of government spending financed by borrowing rather than by taxing. Though we have just seen how future taxes can cause consumption to fall today, investment can also be affected. Increases in government borrowing drive up interest rates. As interest rates go up, investment falls. This sort of indirect crowding out works through the bond market. The U.S. government borrows by selling Treasury bonds or bills. Because the government is not a profit-making institution, it does not have to earn a return from the money it raises by selling bonds. A corporation does. When interest rates rise, fewer corporations offer new bonds to raise investment funds because the cost of repaying the bond debt may exceed the rate of return on the investment.

Crowding out, like Ricardian equivalence, is important in principle, but economists have never demonstrated conclusively that its effects can substantially alter spending in the private sector. Still you should be aware of the possibility to understand the shortcomings of the simple multiplier analysis applied to changes in government spending and taxation.

RECAP

1. Fiscal policy refers to government spending and taxation.
2. By increasing spending or cutting taxes, a government can close the recessionary gap.
3. The spending multiplier is the reciprocal of the sum of the MPS and the MPI.
4. The tax multiplier is the negative of the MPC minus the MPI, times the reciprocal of the sum of the MPS and the MPI.
5. If government spending and taxes increase by the same amount, equilibrium income rises by the amount of the spending increase.

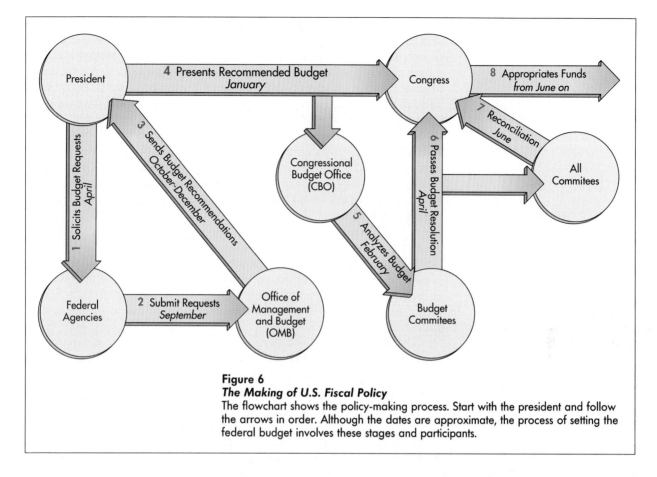

Figure 6
The Making of U.S. Fiscal Policy
The flowchart shows the policy-making process. Start with the president and follow the arrows in order. Although the dates are approximate, the process of setting the federal budget involves these stages and participants.

6. Because it assumes that prices are fixed and the aggregate supply curve is horizontal, the spending multiplier overstates the effect of a change in aggregate demand.

7. If a tax increase affects aggregate supply, the tax multiplier overestimates its effect on equilibrium income.

8. Current government borrowing reduces current spending in the private sector if people increase current saving in order to pay future tax liabilities.

9. Ricardian equivalence holds when taxation and government borrowing have the same effect on current spending in the private sector.

10. Increased government borrowing can crowd private borrowers out of the bond market.

2. FISCAL POLICY IN THE UNITED STATES

2.a. The Budget Process

Fiscal policy in the United States is the product of the budget process, a complex process that involves both the executive and legislative branches of government (Figure 6). The fiscal year for the U.S. government begins

October 1 of one year and ends September 30 of the next. The budget process begins each spring, when the president directs the federal agencies to prepare their budgets for the fiscal year that starts almost eighteen months later. The agencies submit their budget requests to the Office of Management and Budget (OMB) by early September. The OMB reviews and modifies each agency's request and consolidates all of the proposals into a budget that the president presents to Congress in January.

Once Congress receives the president's budget, the Congressional Budget Office (CBO) studies it and committees modify it before funds are appropriated. The budget is evaluated in Budget Committee hearings in both the House of Representatives and the Senate. In addition, the CBO reports to Congress on the validity of the economic assumptions made in the president's budget. A budget resolution is passed by April 15 that sets out major expenditures and estimated revenues. (Revenues are estimated because future tax payments can never be known exactly.) The resolution is followed by *reconciliation*, a process in which each committee of Congress must make relevant tax and spending decisions. Once the reconciliation process is completed, funds are appropriated. The process is supposed to end before Congress recesses for the summer, at the end of June.

The federal budget is determined as much by politics as economics. Politicians respond to different groups of voters by supporting different government programs. It is the political response to constituents that tends to drive up federal budget deficits (the difference between government expenditures and tax revenues). One response to the problem of rising deficits is the Gramm-Rudman-Hollings Act (1985). This act limits federal deficits and requires cuts in spending when the OMB and CBO determine that deficit targets are being exceeded.

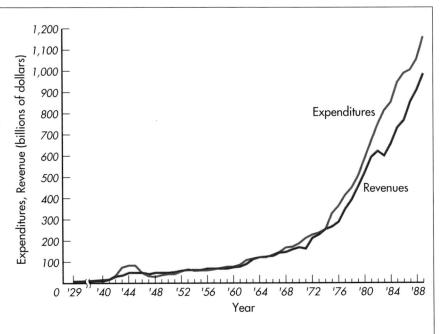

Figure 7
U.S. Government Revenues and Expenditures, 1929–1989
Revenues are total revenues of the U.S. government in each fiscal year. Expenditures are total spending of the U.S. government in each fiscal year. The difference between the two curves equals the U.S. budget deficit (when expenditures exceed revenues) or surplus (when revenues exceed expenditures). Source: Department of the Treasury, Office of Management and Budget, and Department of Commerce.

Part III / Macroeconomic Policy

Our discussion of fiscal policy assumes that policy is made at the federal level. In the modern economy this is a reasonable assumption. This was not the case before the 1930s, however. Before the Depression, the federal government limited its activities largely to national defense and foreign policy, and left other areas of government policy to the individual states.

2.b. The Historical Record

How has U.S. fiscal policy changed over time?

The U.S. government has grown dramatically since the early part of the century. Figure 7 shows federal revenues and expenditures over time. Figure 8 places the growth of government in perspective by plotting U.S. government spending as a percentage of gross national product over time. Before the Great Depression, federal spending was approximately 3 percent of the GNP; by the end of the Depression, it had risen to almost 10 percent. The ratio of spending to GNP reached its peak during World War II, when federal spending hit 45 percent of the GNP. After the war, the ratio fell dramatically and then slowly increased to around 23 percent in the 1980s.

Fiscal policy has two components: discretionary fiscal policy and automatic stabilizers. **Discretionary fiscal policy** refers to changes in government spending and taxation aimed at achieving a policy goal. **Automatic stabilizers** are elements of fiscal policy that automatically change in value as national income changes. Figures 7 and 8 suggest that government spending is dominated by growth over time. There is no indication here of discretionary changes in fiscal policy, changes in government spending and taxation aimed at meeting specific policy goals. Perhaps a better way

discretionary fiscal policy:
changes in government spending and taxation aimed at achieving a policy goal

automatic stabilizer:
an element of fiscal policy that changes automatically as income changes

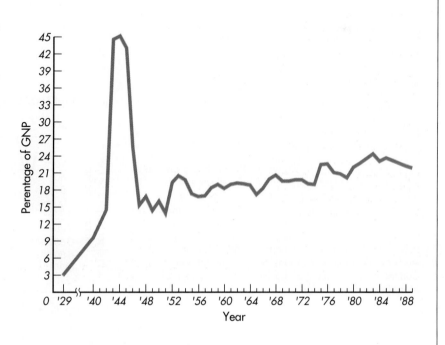

Figure 8
U.S. Government Expenditures as a Percentage of Gross National Product, 1929–1989
U.S. federal government spending as a percentage of the GNP reached a high of 45.2 percent in 1944. Discounting wartime spending and cutbacks after the war, you can see the upward trend in U.S. government spending, which has constituted a larger and larger share of the GNP over time. Source: Department of the Treasury, Office of Management and Budget, and Department of Commerce.

U.S. fiscal policymaking involves many steps. The process begins when federal agencies submit their budget requests to the Office of Management and Budget. The OMB has great power since it reviews each budget request and presents the president with a budget recommendation.

to evaluate the fiscal policy record is in terms of the budget deficit. Government expenditures can rise, but the effect on aggregate demand could be offset by a simultaneous increase in taxes, so that there is no expansionary effect on the equilibrium level of national income. By looking at the deficit, we see the combined spending and tax policy results that are missing if only government expenditures are considered.

Figure 9 illustrates the pattern of the U.S. federal deficit over time, the deficit as a percentage of GNP, and the growth of real GNP. Part (a) shows that the United States ran close to a balanced budget for much of the 1950s and 1960s. There were large deficits associated with financing World War II, and then large deficits resulting from fiscal policy decisions in the 1970s

Through their effect on investment, deficits can lower the level of output in the economy.

Figure 9
The U.S. Deficit and the Business Cycle
As part (a) shows, since 1940 the U.S. government has rarely shown a surplus. For much of the 1950s and 1960s, the United States was close to a balanced budget. Part (b) shows the federal deficit as a percentage of GNP. The deficits during the 1950s and 1960s generally were small. The early 1980s were a time of rapid growth in the federal budget deficit, and this is reflected in the growth of the deficit as a percentage of GNP. The growth of the budget deficit is related to the business cycle (part [c]). The deficit tends to grow during recessions, when real GNP growth is negative and tax revenues are falling in relation to government expenditures. The deficit tends to fall during expansions. Source: Department of Commerce, Department of the Treasury, and Office of Management and Budget.

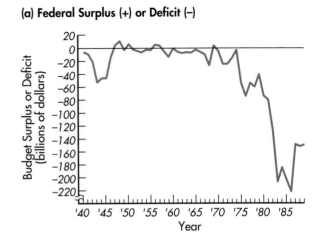

(a) Federal Surplus (+) or Deficit (−)

Part III / Macroeconomic Policy

and 1980s. Figure 9(b) shows that the deficit as a percentage of GNP was much larger during World War II than in recent years.

The deficit increase in the mid-1970s was a product of a recession that cut tax revenues. Historically, aside from wartime, budget deficits increase the most during recessions. Figure 9(c) shows how real GNP has changed over time. When income falls, tax revenues go down and government spending on unemployment and welfare benefits goes up. The figure makes clear that the rapid growth of the deficit in the 1980s involved more than the recessions in 1980 and 1982. As Figure 9(c) shows, the economy grew rapidly after the 1982 recession ended, but so did the fiscal deficit. The increase in the deficit was the product of a rapid increase in government spending to fund new programs and enlarge existing programs while holding taxes constant.

2.c. Deficits and the National Debt

The recent increase in the federal deficit has led many observers to question whether a deficit can harm the economy. Figure 9 shows how the fiscal deficit has changed over time. One major implication of a large deficit is the resulting increase in the national debt, the total stock of government bonds outstanding. Table 1 lists data on the debt of the United States. Notice that the total debt doubled between 1981 ($1,003.9 billion) and 1986 ($2,130.0 billion). Column 3 shows debt as a percentage of GNP. In recent years, the debt has been approximately 50 percent of the GNP, which is in line with the size of the debt in the 1950s and early 1960s. During World War II, the debt was greater than the GNP for five years. Despite the talk of "unprecedented" federal deficits in the 1980s, clearly the ratio of the debt to GNP was by no means unprecedented.

We still have not answered the question of whether deficits are bad. To do so, we have to consider their potential effects.

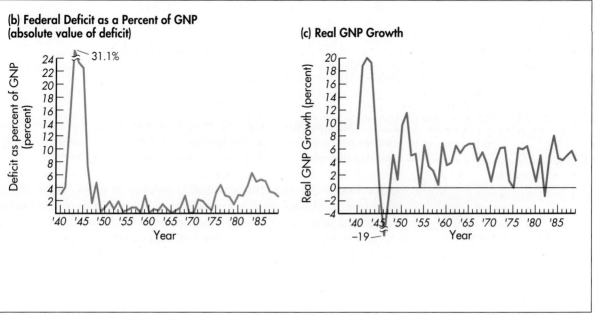

(b) Federal Deficit as a Percent of GNP (absolute value of deficit)

(c) Real GNP Growth

Table 1   Debt of the U.S. Government (dollar amounts in billions)

(1) Year	(2) Total Debt	(3) Debt/GNP (percent)	(4) Net Interest	(5) Interest/Government Spending (percent)
1958	$276.3	62.0	$5.6	6.8
1959	$284.7	60.9	$5.8	6.3
1960	$286.3	57.7	$6.9	7.5
1961	$289.0	56.1	$6.7	6.9
1962	$298.2	54.9	$6.9	6.5
1963	$305.9	52.8	$7.7	6.9
1964	$311.7	50.7	$8.2	6.9
1965	$317.3	47.9	$8.6	7.3
1966	$329.5	45.5	$9.4	7.0
1967	$341.3	43.9	$10.3	6.5
1968	$369.8	44.5	$11.1	6.2
1969	$367.1	40.3	$12.7	6.9
1970	$382.6	39.5	$14.4	7.4
1971	$409.5	39.7	$14.8	7.0
1972	$437.3	38.7	$15.5	6.7
1973	$468.4	37.4	$17.3	7.0
1974	$486.2	35.3	$21.4	8.0
1975	$544.1	36.8	$23.2	7.2
1976	$631.9	38.3	$26.7	7.3
1977	$709.1	38.1	$29.9	7.5
1978	$780.4	37.3	$35.4	7.9
1979	$833.8	35.4	$42.6	8.7
1980	$914.3	35.5	$52.5	9.1
1981	$1,003.9	34.9	$68.7	10.5
1982	$1,147.0	37.5	$85.0	11.6
1983	$1,381.9	42.8	$89.8	11.2
1984	$1,576.7	44.0	$111.1	13.2
1985	$1,827.0	47.7	$129.1	13.6
1986	$2,130.0	50.8	$136.0	13.7
1987	$2,335.2	53.4	$138.6	13.8
1988	$2,600.7	53.3	$151.7	14.3
1989	$2,866.2	54.8	$169.1	14.8

Source: Data are from *Economic Report of the President, 1989* and *Economic Report of the President, 1990* (Washington, D.C.: U.S. Government Printing Office).

2.c.1.   Deficits, Interest Rates, and Investment   Because government deficits mean government borrowing and debt, many economists argue that deficits raise interest rates. Increased government borrowing raises interest rates, which in turn can depress investment. (Remember that as interest rates rise, the rate of return on investment drops, along with the incentive to invest.) What happens when government borrowing crowds out private investment? Lower investment means fewer capital goods in the future. So deficits lower the level of output in the economy both today and in the future.

▼ What are the effects of budget deficits?

2.c.2. Deficits and International Trade

If government deficits raise real interest rates, they also may have an effect on international trade. A higher real return on U.S. securities makes those securities more attractive to foreign investors. As the foreign demand for U.S. securities increases, so does the demand for U.S. dollars in exchange for Japanese yen, British pounds, and other foreign currencies. As the demand for dollars increases, the dollar *appreciates* in value on the foreign exchange market. This means that the dollar becomes more expensive to foreigners while foreign currency becomes cheaper to U.S. residents. This kind of change in the exchange rate encourages U.S. residents to buy more foreign goods and foreign residents to buy fewer domestic goods. Ultimately, then, as deficits and government debt increase, U.S. net exports fall. Many economists believe that the growing fiscal deficits of the 1980s were responsible for the record decline in U.S. net exports during that period.

Remember the leakages and injections model from Chapter 10. Equilibrium is that point where leakages (saving plus taxes plus imports) equal injections (investment plus government spending plus exports:

$$S + T + IM = I + G + EX$$

When the fiscal deficit increases, G goes up in relation to T. We can rearrange the equilibrium condition with the deficit on the left-hand side:

$$G - T = S - I + IM - EX$$

Equilibrium requires that something else must change to offset an increase in the fiscal deficit $(G - T)$. That something could be an increase in S and a drop in I, or an increase in IM and a drop in EX. The typical crowding-out story has saving rising and investment falling to finance the higher fiscal deficit. However, a higher international trade deficit could finance the fiscal deficit with no change in saving or investment. (The international trade deficit is the difference between imports and exports.) Realistically, we would expect saving and investment to be affected by changes in the government deficit; we would not expect a fiscal deficit to be financed completely or even largely by an international trade deficit.

2.c.3. Interest Payments on the National Debt

The national debt is the stock of government bonds outstanding. It is the product of past and current budget deficits. As the size of the debt increases, the interest that must be paid on the debt tends to rise. Column 4 of Table 1 lists the amount of interest paid on the debt; column 5 lists the interest as a percentage of government expenditures. The numbers in both columns have risen steadily over time. The federal government has been paying a higher dollar amount of interest each year, and this interest has been rising as a percentage of total government expenditures. This means that interest payments have been rising faster than total government spending.

The steady increase in the interest cost of the national debt is an aspect of fiscal deficits that worries some people. However, to the extent that U.S. citizens hold government bonds, we owe the debt to ourselves. The tax liability of funding the interest payments is offset by the interest income bondholders earn. In this case there is no net change in national wealth when the national debt changes.

Of course we do not owe the national debt just to ourselves. The United States is the world's largest national financial market, and many U.S. securities, including government bonds, are held by foreign residents. In late 1989, foreign holdings of the U.S. national debt amounted to 14 percent of the outstanding debt. Because the tax liability for paying the interest on the debt falls on U.S. taxpayers, the greater the payments made to foreigners, the lower the wealth of U.S. residents, other things being equal.

Of course other things are not equal. To understand the real impact of foreign holdings on the economy, we have to evaluate what the economy would have been like if the debt had not been sold to foreign investors. If the foreign savings placed in U.S. bonds allowed the United States to increase investment and its productive capacity beyond what would have been possible in the absence of foreign lending, then the country could very well be better off for selling government bonds to foreigners. The presence of foreign funds may keep interest rates lower than they would otherwise be, preventing the substantial crowding out associated with an increase in the national debt and relieving the burden of the debt.

2.d. Automatic Stabilizers

We have been talking about discretionary fiscal policy, the changes in government spending and taxing that policymakers make consciously. *Automatic stabilizers* are the elements of fiscal policy that change automatically as income changes. Automatic stabilizers offset changes in income: as income falls, automatic stabilizers increase spending; as income rises, automatic stabilizers decrease spending. Any program that responds to fluctuations in the business cycle in a way that moderates the effect of those fluctuations is an automatic stabilizer. Examples are progressive income taxes and transfer payments.

In our examples of tax changes, we have been using *lump-sum taxes*—taxes that are a flat dollar amount regardless of income. However, income taxes are determined as a percentage of income. In the United States, the federal income tax is a **progressive tax**: as income rises, so does the rate of taxation. A person with a very low income pays no income tax, while a person with a high income can pay as much as a third of that income in taxes. Countries use different rates of taxation on income. Taxes can be *regressive* (the tax rate falls as income rises) or *proportional* (the tax rate is constant as income rises). But most countries, including the United States, use a progressive tax, the percentage of income paid as taxes rising with taxable income.

Progressive income taxes act as an automatic stabilizer. As income falls, so does the average tax rate. Suppose a household earning $60,000 must pay 30 percent of its income ($18,000) in taxes, leaving 70 percent of its income ($42,000) for spending. If that household's income drops to $40,000 and the tax rate falls to 25 percent, the household has 75 percent of its income ($30,000) available for spending. But if the tax rate is 30 percent at all levels of income, the household earning $40,000 would have only 70 percent of its income ($28,000) to spend. By allowing a greater percentage of earned income to be spent, progressive taxes help offset the effect of lower income on spending.

progressive tax:
a tax whose rate rises as income rises

transfer payment:
a payment to one person that is
funded by taxing others

A **transfer payment** is a payment to one person that is funded by taxing others. Food stamps, welfare benefits, and unemployment benefits are all government transfer payments: current taxpayers provide the funds to pay those who qualify for the programs. Transfer payments that use income to establish eligibility act as automatic stabilizers. In a recession, as income falls, more people qualify for food stamps or welfare benefits, raising the level of government spending.

Unemployment insurance is also an automatic stabilizer. As unemployment rises, more workers receive unemployment benefits. Unemployment benefits tend to rise in a recession and fall during an expansion. This countercyclical pattern of benefit payments offsets the effect of business cycle fluctuations on consumption.

RECAP

1. Fiscal policy in the United States is a product of the budget process.

2. Federal spending in the United States has grown rapidly over time, from just 3 percent of the GNP before the Great Depression to approximately 23 percent of the GNP in the late 1980s.

3. Government budget deficits can hurt the economy through their effect on interest rates and private investment, net exports, and the tax burden on current and future taxpayers.

4. Automatic stabilizers are government programs that are already in place and that respond automatically to fluctuations in the business cycle, moderating the effect of those fluctuations.

3. FISCAL POLICY IN DIFFERENT COUNTRIES

Each country's fiscal policy reflects its philosophy toward government spending and taxation. In this section we present comparative data that demonstrate the variety of fiscal policies in the world (see Table 2).

Table 2 Share of Government Spending in GNP or GDP in Selected Industrial Countries, 1880, 1929, 1960, and 1985 (percent)*

Year	France	Germany	Japan	Sweden	United Kingdom	United States
1880	15	10†	11‡	6	10	8
1929	19	31	19	8	24	10
1960	35	32	18	31	32	28
1985	52	47	33	65	48	37

*For 1880 and 1929, data are the share of GNP; for 1960 and 1985, the share of GDP.
†1881.
‡1885.
Source: World Bank, *World Development Report 1988* (Washington, D.C.), 1988, p. 44.

3.a. Government Spending

How does fiscal policy differ across countries?

Government spending has grown over time as a fraction of GNP in all industrial countries.

Our discussion to this point has centered on U.S. fiscal policy. But fiscal policy and the role of government in the economy can be very different across countries. Government has played an increasingly larger role in the major industrial countries over time. Table 2 shows how government spending has gone up as a percentage of output in six industrial nations. In every case, government spending accounted for a larger percentage of output in 1985 than it did 100 years earlier. For instance, in 1880, government spending was only 10 percent of the GNP in the United Kingdom. By 1929 it had risen to 24 percent; by 1960, to 32 percent; and by 1985, to 48 percent.

Historically in industrial countries, the growth of government spending has been matched by growth in revenues. But in the 1960s, government spending began to grow faster than revenues, creating increasingly large debtor nations.

Developing countries have not shown the uniform growth in government spending found in industrial countries. In fact in some developing countries (Burma, Chile, the Dominican Republic, Peru, and Yugoslavia), government spending was a smaller percentage of GNP in 1985 than it was in 1972. And we find a greater variation in the role of government in developing countries.

One important difference between the typical developed country and the typical developing country is that government plays a larger role in investment spending in the developing country. Table 3 shows government investment as a percentage of total investment in twelve developing countries. In these countries, government investment made up 43 percent of all investment. In thirteen industrial countries, it represented just 30 percent of all investment. One reason for this difference is that state-owned enterprises account for a larger percentage of economic activity in developing countries than they do in developed countries. Also devel-

Table 3 Public-Sector Investment as a Percentage of Total Investment for Selected Developing Countries, Averages for 1980 to 1985

Turkey	68
Egypt	65
Côte d'Ivoire	61
Argentina	58
Botswana	45
Colombia	40
Korea	35
Thailand	33
Mexico	31
Peru	29
Philippines	26
Dominican Republic	24
Average (unweighted):	
Twelve developing countries	43
Thirteen industrial countries	30

Source: World Bank, *World Development Report, 1988* (Washington, D.C.), 1988, p. 47.

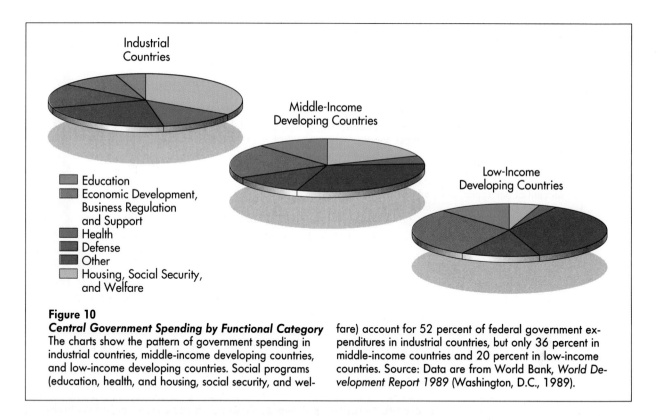

Figure 10
Central Government Spending by Functional Category
The charts show the pattern of government spending in industrial countries, middle-income developing countries, and low-income developing countries. Social programs (education, health, and housing, social security, and wel- fare) account for 52 percent of federal government expenditures in industrial countries, but only 36 percent in middle-income countries and 20 percent in low-income countries. Source: Data are from World Bank, *World Development Report 1989* (Washington, D.C., 1989).

oping countries usually rely more on government than the private sector to build their infrastructure—schools, roads, hospitals—than do developed countries.

How a government spends its money is a function of its income. Here we find differences, not only between industrial and developing countries, but also among developing countries. Figure 10 divides developing countries into low-income (the poorest) and middle-income (not as poor) groups. It clearly illustrates the relative importance of social welfare spending in industrial and developing countries. Although standards of living are lowest in the poorest countries, these countries do not have the resources to spend on social services (education, health, housing, social security, welfare). The industrial countries, on average, spend 52 percent of their budgets on social programs. Middle-income developing countries spend 36 percent of their budgets on social programs. Low-income countries spend only 20 percent of their budgets on these programs.

The labor forces in industrial countries are much better educated than those in developing countries. Figure 11 shows why. The figure measures the cost of educating a student for a year as a percentage of per capita GNP. On average it costs 49 percent of per capita GNP to educate a college student in an industrial country. It costs 370 percent of per capita GNP to provide a year of college education in the average developing country. In the poorest region of the world, Sub-Saharan Africa, a year of college costs 800 percent of per capita GNP. Governments in the poorest countries simply cannot afford to provide a comprehensive system of higher education.

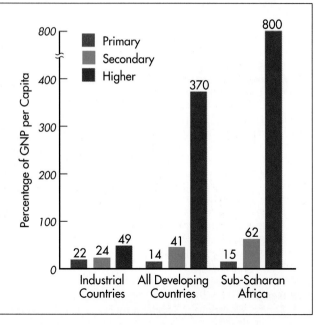

Figure 11
Cost per Student of Public Education as a Percentage of GNP per Capita in Three Country Groups
Industrial countries have much better educated populations than do poor countries. One reason is the higher cost of education in poor countries in terms of percentage of per capita GNP. A year of college education for one student costs an average of 49 percent of per capita GNP in industrial countries; it costs 370 percent on average in developing countries. In the poorest region in the world, Sub-Saharan Africa, one year of higher education costs 800 percent of per capita GNP. Source: *World Bank, World Development Report 1988* (Washington, D.C., 1988), p. 135.

3.b. Taxation

There are two different types of taxes: *direct taxes* (on individuals and firms) and *indirect taxes* (on goods and services). Figure 12 compares the importance of different sources of tax revenue across industrial, middle-income developing, and low-income developing countries. The most obvious difference is that personal income taxes are much more important in industrial countries than in developing countries. Why? Because personal taxes are hard to collect in agricultural nations, where a large percentage of household production is for personal consumption. Taxes on businesses are easier to collect, and thus are more important in developing countries.

That industrial countries are better able to afford social programs is reflected in the great disparity in social security taxes between industrial countries and developing countries. With so many workers living near the subsistence level in the poorest countries, their governments simply cannot tax workers for retirement and health security programs.

Figure 12 also shows that taxes on international trade are very important in developing countries. Because goods arriving or leaving a country must pass through customs inspection, export and import taxes are relatively easy to collect compared to income taxes. In general, developing countries depend more heavily on indirect taxes on goods and services than do developed countries.

Figure 12 lists VAT among the commodity taxes. *VAT* stands for **value-added tax**, an indirect tax imposed on each sale at each stage of production. Each seller from the first stage of production on collects the VAT from the buyer, and then deducts any VATs it has paid in buying its inputs. The difference is remitted to the government. From time to time, Congress has debated the merits of a VAT in the United States, but has never approved this kind of tax.

value-added tax (VAT):
a general sales tax collected at each stage of production

Figure 12
Variations in Tax Composition by Income Group, 1985

When we group countries by income level, the importance of different sources of tax revenue is obvious. Domestic income taxes account for roughly a third of government revenue in industrial and middle-income developing countries and a quarter of government revenue in low-income developing countries. However, personal income taxes are most important in industrial countries, while business income taxes are most important in developing countries. Social security taxes are a major source of government revenue in industrial countries; they are less important in middle-income developing countries; and they are of negligible importance in low-income developing countries, which cannot afford social programs. International trade taxes represent just 2 percent of tax revenues in industrial countries; developing countries rely heavily on these taxes. Source: International Monetary Fund, *Government Finance Statistics* (Washington, D.C., 1987), and World Bank data.

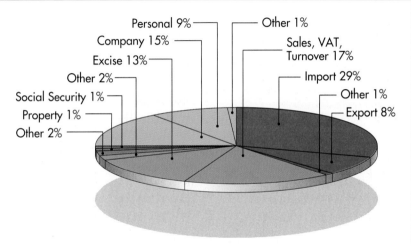

Low-Income Countries

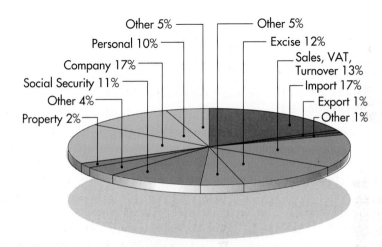

Middle-Income Countries

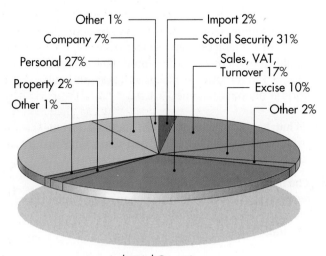

Industrial Countries

Domestic Income Taxes

Other Direct Taxes

Domestic Commodity Taxes

International Trade Taxes

RECAP

1. Over time, government spending has become more important in industrial countries.

2. Governments in developing countries typically account for a larger percentage of investment expenditures in their economies than do the governments of developed countries.

3. Developing countries depend more on indirect taxes on goods and services as a source of revenue than on direct taxes on individuals and businesses.

4. Value-added taxes are general sales taxes that are collected at every stage of production.

SUMMARY

1. Government spending affects aggregate expenditures directly; taxes affect aggregate expenditures indirectly, through their effect on consumption. § 1

2. A recessionary gap is the amount that aggregate expenditures must rise to bring equilibrium national income up to potential national income, to eliminate the GNP gap. § 1.a

▼▲ **How can fiscal policy eliminate a recessionary gap?**

3. A recessionary gap can be closed by increasing government spending or by cutting taxes. §§ 1.a.1 and 1.a.2

4. The spending multiplier is a measure of the effect of a change in government spending on equilibrium income; the tax multiplier is a measure of the effect of a change in taxes on equilibrium national income. § 1.a.2

▼▲ **What happens to equilibrium national income when government spending and taxes both increase by the same amount?**

5. The balanced-budget multiplier measures the effect on equilibrium income when government spending and taxes both change by the same amount. § 1.b

6. The balanced-budget multiplier equals 1, which means that an increase in government spending matched by an increase in taxes raises equilibrium national income by the amount of the increase in government spending. § 1.b

7. Because they assume that prices are fixed and the aggregate supply curve is horizontal, the spending and tax multipliers overstate the actual effect on equilibrium income of a change in spending or taxation. § 1.c

▼▲ **How has U.S. fiscal policy changed over time?**

8. Fiscal policy in the United States is a product of the budget process. § 2.a

9. Federal government spending in the United States has increased from just 3 percent of the GNP before the Great Depression to approximately 23 percent of the GNP today. § 2.b

10. Fiscal policy has two components: discretionary fiscal policy and automatic stabilizers. § 2.b

▼▲ **What are the effects of budget deficits?**

11. Budget deficits, through their effect on interest rates, international trade, and the national debt, can reduce investment, output, net exports, and national wealth. §§ 2.c.1, 2.c.2, and 2.c.3

12. Progressive taxes and transfer payments are automatic stabilizers, elements of fiscal policy that change automatically as national income changes. § 2.d

▼▲ **How does fiscal policy differ across countries?**

13. Industrial countries spend a much larger percentage of their government budget for social programs than do developing countries. § 3.a

14. Industrial countries depend more on direct taxes and less on indirect taxes than do developing countries. § 3.b

KEY TERMS

spending multiplier § 1.a.2
tax multiplier § 1.a.2
balanced-budget multiplier § 1.b
crowd out § 1.d.3
discretionary fiscal policy § 2.b

automatic stabilizers § 2.b
progressive tax § 2.d
transfer payment § 2.d
value-added tax (VAT) § 3.b

EXERCISES

Basic Terms and Concepts

1. Assume that equilibrium income is $800 billion, potential income is $900 billion, the MPC is .80, and the MPI is .40.

   a. What is the size of the GNP gap?

   b. What is the size of the recessionary gap?

   c. How much must government spending increase to eliminate the recessionary gap?

   d. How much must taxes fall to eliminate the recessionary gap?

   e. If government spending and taxes both change by the same amount, how much must they change to eliminate the recessionary gap?

2. Suppose the MPC is .90 and the MPI is .10. If government expenditures go up $100 billion while taxes fall $10 billion, what happens to the equilibrium level of national income?

3. Briefly describe the process of setting the federal budget in the United States. What is the time lag between the start of the process and the point at which the money is actually spent?

4. In what ways are government deficits harmful to the economy?

5. Define and give three examples of automatic stabilizers.

6. Briefly describe the major differences between fiscal policy in industrial countries and those in developing countries.

Extended Concepts

7. What is the balanced-budget multiplier? Show how we find the numerical value of this multiplier using the formulas for the spending and tax multipliers.

8. Discuss the limitations of the spending and tax multipliers and how they overstate or understate the effect on equilibrium income of a given change in government spending or taxes.

Economically Speaking

Fantasy and Facts About the Budget Deficit

Hope, not experience, is shaping [the 1990] budget debate in Washington. The collapse of Communism and evidence that the U.S. economy has skirted a recession are fueling heady talk of peace dividends, tax cuts and repaying the $3 trillion national debt. The administration . . . insists the deficit will disappear by 1993. Reality isn't likely to cooperate.

The good news is that Washington already has made big strides. The deficit is down dramatically from its peak in 1986 and is headed lower. [In 1990] the gap between spending and revenue should narrow to an estimated $138 billion, from $152 billion in 1989. At 2.5 percent of GNP, the deficit is a smaller drain on the nation's savings than in any year since 1979.

Then there is the budget cutter's newest ally, the peace dividend. The Bush team is leading the charge for Pentagon cuts these days, with Congress fighting a rear-guard action to save favorite weapons programs. Defense outlays probably will fall about 2 percent a year, after inflation. Those savings would equal one third of the budget deficit projected for 1995, but [the 1990] reduction is just $4 billion.

But a host of other trends will make squeezing the deficit much harder. For starters, the urge to splurge will become tough to contain, as demand builds for new projects like road repairs. Polls show that 97 percent of Americans would rather spend the peace dividend on domestic programs than use it to trim the deficit.

The biggest threat comes from the swelling ranks of would-be tax cutters. The hottest proposal: A $62 billion Social Security tax giveback over the next two years. Its sponsor, Senator Daniel Patrick Moynihan (D-N.Y.), argues the plan is needed to prevent Washington from "misusing" the growing surplus in the retirement fund to finance the government's budget deficit. . . . President Bush, who still wants a lower capital-gains tax, is on the defensive. As a riposte to Moynihan, the administration has a wildly optimistic plan to "save" Social Security funds by running a budget surplus after 1993 and retiring the national debt by 2010. . . .

Tepid economic growth . . . also will make paring the deficit difficult. As long as the economy was advancing at a 3 percent to 4 percent clip, Washington could count on rapid increases in wages and profits to fatten the tax kitty. Now, revenue growth will be slower. . . .

Don't expect Washington to get within a mile of the Gramm-Rudman spending targets [in 1991 or 1992]. To reach [the 1991] $64 billion goal,

Congress would have to slash the deficit by $75 billion, three times as much as . . . [some] forecasters . . . expect. More important, overly aggressive cutting would likely knock the economy into a recession, ballooning the deficit in the process. . . .

The wild card is interest rates. [February, 1990] jitters in bond markets from Tokyo to New York fanned fears that investors around the globe would dump the dollar. If that happens, the Federal Reserve would be forced to raise rates to keep crucial foreign capital flowing to the U.S. Apart from increasing the odds of a recession, higher rates would swell government interest payments, now one sixth of outlays. Spending would soar by about $10 billion for each 1 percent rise in rates.

Neither the administration nor Congress has a real plan for eliminating the deficit. Until they adopt one, talk of future budget surpluses is pure fantasy.

■ Source: Sylvia Nasar, "Fantasy and Facts About the Budget Deficit," *U.S. News & World Report*, February 5, 1990, p. 61.

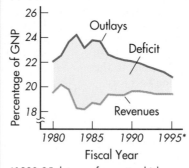

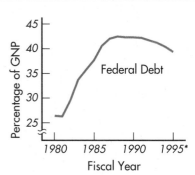

*1990-95 data are forecasts which assume no policy changes.

Commentary

The U.S. budget deficit captured the attention of the nation in the 1980s. While the extent, causes, and political impact of the massive deficit have been extensively covered by the media, there has been relatively less reporting on the deficit's precise effects on the economy. An implicit message in many reports is that budget deficits are harmful. Other reports suggest that budget deficits are either helpful (at least in moderation) or have no effect. Careful economic reasoning provides us with insight into the consequences of the budget deficit for the U.S. economy.

You may have heard arguments concerning the effects of the budget deficit that proceed by means of an analogy between the government's budget and a family's budget. Just as a family cannot spend more than it earns, so the argument goes, the government cannot follow this practice without bringing itself to ruin. The problem with this analogy is that the government has the ability to raise money through taxes and bond sales, options not open to a family.

A more appropriate analogy is to compare the government's budget to that of a large corporation. Large corporations run persistent deficits that are never paid back. Instead, when corporate debt comes due, the corporations "roll over" their debt by selling new debt. Corporations are able to do this because they use their debt to finance investment that enables the corporations to increase their worth. To the extent that the government is investing in projects like road repairs and building the nation's infrastructure, it is increasing the productive capacity of the economy, which widens the tax base and increases potential future tax receipts. Spending the "peace dividend" on certain domestic programs, an option preferred by an overwhelming number of Americans, may actually work in favor of the long-run resolution of the budget deficit if incomes and tax receipts increase as a result.

There are, of course, legitimate problems associated with the budget deficit. The government has two options if it cannot pay for its expenditures with tax receipts. One method of financing the budget deficit is by printing money. This is an unattractive option because it leads to inflation. Another method is to borrow funds by selling government bonds. A problem with this option is that the government must compete for scarce loanable funds and, unless saving increases at the same time, interest rates rise and government borrowing "crowds out" private investment. This results in a lower capital stock and diminished prospects for future economic growth (although the effect of lower economic growth due to reduced levels of private investment must be weighed against the effect on economic growth of increased public investment).

The debt sold by the government will be purchased by both domestic and foreign investors. An increase in the demand for dollar-denominated debt by foreign investors causes the dollar to appreciate in value against other currencies. This makes U.S. products more expensive on the world market and foreign products cheaper in the United States. With fewer U.S. exports being sold and more foreign imports being purchased, the U.S. trade deficit worsens. It is therefore not a coincidence that the period during which the budget deficit was growing was also the period during which the U.S. trade deficit was increasing.

Who benefits and who loses from the budget deficit? The debt that the government incurs is mostly owed to ourselves; that is, U.S. citizens purchase the debt and will receive the interest and principal payments in the future. Future generations will pay back the interest and principal, but this may not be as unfair as it initially sounds since productivity and living standards will be higher in the future because of technological progress. Government debt held by foreign citizens is not, however, "owed to ourselves," and the repayment of this debt represents a transfer of income from citizens of the United States to citizens of other countries.

A balanced federal budget is still many years away. Thus, stories focusing on the budget deficit, which were a mainstay of the economic news of the 1980s, will most likely retain their prominence in the 1990s. An informed reading of these stories requires a knowledge of the effects, not just the causes, of the U.S. budget deficit.

An Algebraic Examination of the Balanced-Budget Change in Fiscal Policy

In Chapter 12 we saw how fiscal policy affects income when government spending and taxes both change by the same amount. A balanced-budget change in policy causes income to change by the amount of the change in spending and taxes. We can use the algebraic model presented in the appendix to Chapter 10 to illustrate the effect of a balanced-budget change in government spending. Here are the model equations:

$$C = \$30 + .90Y$$
$$I = \$20$$
$$G = \$30$$
$$X = \$20 - .10Y$$

Solving for the equilibrium level of Y (as we did in the appendix to Chapter 10), Y equals \$500 where Y equals aggregate expenditures.

Now suppose that G increases by \$10 and that this increase is funded by taxes of \$10. The increase in G changes autonomous government spending to \$40. The increase in taxes affect the autonomous levels of C and X. The new model equations are:

$$C = \$30 + .90(Y - \$10)$$
$$= \$21 + .90Y$$

$$X = \$20 - .10(Y - \$10)$$
$$= \$21 - .10Y$$

Using the new G, C, and X functions, we can find the new equilibrium level of national income by setting Y equal to AE $(C + I + G + X)$:

$$Y = C + I + G + X$$
$$= \$21 + .90Y + \$20 + \$40 + \$21 - .10Y$$
$$= \$102 + .80Y$$

Or

$$Y - .80Y = \$102$$
$$.20Y = \$102$$

then

$$Y = \$510$$

Increasing government spending and taxes by $10 each raises the equilibrium level of national income by $10. A balanced-budget change in G increases Y by the change in G. If government spending and taxes both fall by the same amount, then income will also fall by an amount equal to the change in government spending and taxes.

13

Money and Banking

1. What is money?

2. How is the U.S. money supply defined?

3. How do countries pay for international transactions?

4. Why are banks considered intermediaries?

5. How does international banking differ from domestic banking?

6. How do banks create money?

PREVIEW   We have been talking about aggregate expenditures, aggregate demand and supply, and fiscal policy without explicitly discussing money. Money is used by every sector of the economy in all nations. It plays a crucial role in the economy. In this chapter we discuss money and banking. In the next, we examine the role of money in determining the equilibrium level of national income in the aggregate demand and supply model.

Most people believe they know what money is and how it is used. In this chapter you will see that the question—What is money?—is not as simple as it seems. And you will learn that money serves several functions beyond allowing us to buy goods and services.

After we define money and its functions, we turn to banking. We begin with banking in the United States, and then discuss international banking. And we describe how banks expand the money supply. Someone once joked that banks follow the rule of 3–6–3. They borrow at 3 percent interest, lend at 6 percent interest, and close at

3:00 P.M. If those days ever existed, clearly they do not today. The banking industry in the United States and the rest of the world has undergone tremendous change in recent years. New technology and government deregulation are allowing banks to respond to changing economic conditions in ways that were unthinkable only a few years ago.

1. WHAT IS MONEY?

▼
  What is money?
                              ▲

money:
anything that is generally acceptable to sellers in exchange for goods and services

liquid asset:
an asset that can easily be exchanged for goods and services

Money is anything that is generally acceptable to sellers in exchange for goods and services. The cash in your wallet can be used to buy groceries or a movie ticket. You simply present your cash to the cashier, who readily accepts it. If you want to use your car to buy groceries or a movie ticket, the exchange is more complicated. You would probably have to sell the car before you can use it to buy other goods and services. Cars are seldom exchanged directly for goods and services (except for other cars). Because cars are not a generally acceptable means of paying for other goods and services, we don't consider them to be money.

Money is the most liquid asset. A **liquid asset** is an asset that can easily be exchanged for goods and services. Cash is a liquid asset; a car is not. How liquid must an asset be before we consider it money? To answer this question, we first must consider the functions of money.

1.a. Functions of Money

Money serves four basic functions: it is a *medium of exchange,* a *unit of account,* a *store of value,* and a *standard of deferred payment.* Not all monies serve all of these functions equally well, but to be money, an item must perform enough of these functions to induce people to use it.

1.a.1. Medium of Exchange

Money is a medium of exchange; it is used in exchange for goods and services. Sellers willingly accept money in payment for the products and services they produce. Without money, we would have to resort to *barter,* the direct exchange of goods and services for other goods and services.

For a barter system to work, there must be a *double coincidence of wants.* Suppose Bill is a carpenter and Jane is a plumber. In a monetary economy, when Bill needs plumbing repairs in his home, he simply pays Jane for the repairs using money. Because everyone wants money, money is an acceptable means of payment. In a barter economy, Bill must offer his services as a carpenter in exchange for Jane's work. If Jane does not want any carpentry work done, Bill and Jane cannot enter into a mutually beneficial transaction. Bill has to find a person who can do what he wants and also wants what he can do—there must be a double coincidence of wants.

The use of money as a medium of exchange lowers transaction costs.

Obviously barter is a lot less efficient than money, which means that the cost of a transaction in a barter economy is higher than the cost of a transaction in a monetary economy. The use of money as a medium of exchange lowers transaction costs.

Yap Island Money

Yap Island is one of the three Federated States of Micronesia. The citizens of Yap Island have been using giant doughnut-shaped stones as money for approximately 1,500 years. Some of the stones are 12 feet in diameter and weigh hundreds of pounds. The ancient Yapese quarried the stones on the island of Palau, over 250 nautical miles from Yap. The stones were towed back to Yap on rafts pulled by canoes. The value of each stone is determined by its history. The larger and more perfect the stone, and the greater the effort to bring the stone to Yap, the higher its value

The stones lie around the island, propped up along roads and beside houses. The stones do not have to be moved because ownership is transferred by verbal agreement. Each stone is distinct, and the Yapese acknowledge the current and past owners of each stone. The stones serve as a form of large-denomination money. For instance, a few years ago, the lieutenant governor of the island at the time, Hilary Tacheliol, was quoted as saying, "I recently bought a house that would have cost $12,000 cash. I got it for $2,000 cash and stone money."

Yap stones point out the importance of consumer confidence in determining the value of money. The stones have value because the Yapese believe they are valuable. Norman Angell, in *The Story of Money*, described a Yapese family whose ownership of a very valuable stone was acknowledged by everyone even though no one currently living had ever seen it.[1] For generations, the stone had been lying at the bottom of the sea. An ancestor was bringing the stone back from Palau when a violent storm forced him to cut his stone-carrying raft loose. When he arrived back on Yap, the other men who had been on the voyage testified to the great size and perfection of the lost stone. The islanders accepted the value of the stone and the family's increased wealth as though the stone was leaning against the family home. Over time, ownership of the stone lying at the bottom of the ocean passed from person to person by verbal agreement.

A money is acceptable if people believe that it has value. It is not necessary to physically possess the money or for the money to be backed by any promise of redemption in gold or other precious objects. As long as people believe something is money, it functions as money.

[1] Norman Angell, *The Story of Money*, New York: Garden City Publishing, 1929.

For money to be an effective medium of exchange it must be *portable*—a property the stone money of Yap Island clearly lacks. (See Economic Insight: "Yap Island Money.") Another important property of money is *divisibility*. Money must be measurable in both small units (for low-value goods and services) and large units (for high-value goods and services). Yap stone money is not divisible; so it is not a good medium of exchange for the majority of goods bought and sold.

1.a.2. Unit of Account   Money is a unit of account: we price goods and services in terms of money. This common unit of measurement allows us to compare relative values easily. If whole-wheat bread sells for a dollar a loaf and white bread sells for 50 cents, we know that whole-wheat bread is twice as expensive as white bread.

The use of money as a unit of account lowers information costs.

Using money as a unit of account is efficient. Money is a standard of value that reduces the costs of gathering information on what things are worth. The use of money as a unit of account lowers information costs. In a barter economy, people constantly have to evaluate the worth of the goods and services being offered. When money prices are placed on goods and services, their relative value is obvious.

1.a.3. Store of Value

Money functions as a store of value or purchasing power. If you are paid today, you do not have to hurry out to spend your money. It will still have value next week or next month. Some monies retain their value better than others. In colonial New England, fish and furs both served as money. But because fish do not store as well as furs, their usefulness as a store of value was limited. An important property of a money is its *durability*, its ability to retain its value over time.

Today inflation plays a major role in determining the effectiveness of a money as a store of value. The higher the rate of inflation, the faster the purchasing power of money falls. In high-inflation countries, workers spend their pay as fast as possible because the purchasing power of their money is falling rapidly. It makes no sense to hold on to a money that is quickly losing value. In countries where the domestic money does not serve as a good store of value, people substitute other monies. For instance, U.S. dollars have long been a favorite store of value in Latin American countries that have experienced high inflation. This phenomenon—**currency substitution**—has been documented in Argentina, Bolivia, Mexico, and other countries during times of high inflation.

1.a.4. Standard of Deferred Payment

Finally, money is a standard of deferred payment. Debt obligations are written in terms of money values. If you owe a bill that is due in 90 days, the value you owe is stated in monetary units—for example, dollars in the United States and yen in Japan. It is interesting that many debts around the world that do not involve a U.S. borrower or lender are denominated in U.S. dollars. This is due in large part to the relative stability of the dollar.

We should make a distinction here between money and credit. Money is what we use to pay for goods and services. **Credit** is available savings that are lent to borrowers to spend. If you use your Visa or MasterCard to buy a shirt, you are not buying the shirt with your money. You are taking out a loan from the bank that issued the credit card in order to buy the shirt. Credit and money are different.

1.b. The U.S. Money Supply

The quantity of money available for spending is an important determinant of many key macroeconomic variables. Changes in the money supply affect interest rates, inflation, and other indicators of economic health. When economists measure the money supply, they measure spendable assets. But identifying those assets can be difficult. For example, it would seem that all bank deposits are money. Certainly some bank deposits are held for spending, but others are held for saving. In defining the money supply, economists must differentiate among deposits on the basis of their "moneyness," the likelihood of their being used for spending.

The problem of distinguishing among assets has produced several definitions of the money supply: M1, M2, and M3. Economists and policymakers use all three definitions to evaluate the availability of funds for spending. Although economists have tried to identify a single definition that best explains the business cycle and changes in interest rates and inflation, research indicates that different definitions work better to explain changes in macroeconomic variables at different times.

currency substitution:
the use of foreign money as a substitute for domestic money when the domestic money has a high rate of inflation

credit:
available savings that are lent to borrowers to spend

▼ How is the U.S. money supply defined? ▲

M1 money supply:
financial assets that are immediately available for spending

transactions account:
a checking account at a bank or other financial institution that can be drawn on to make payments

1.b.1. M1 Money Supply

The narrowest measure of the money supply is the **M1 money supply**, the financial assets that are immediately available for spending. This definition emphasizes the use of money as a medium of exchange. The M1 money supply consists of currency, travelers' checks, demand deposits, and other checkable deposits. Demand and other checkable deposits are **transactions accounts**; they can be used to make direct payments to a third party.

Currency Currency includes coins and paper money. In 1989, currency represented 28 percent of the M1 money supply. A common misconception about currency today is that it is backed by gold or silver. This is not true. There is nothing backing the U.S. dollar except the confidence of the public. This kind of monetary system is called a *fiduciary monetary system. Fiduciary* comes from the Latin *fiducia,* which means "trust." Our monetary system is based on trust. As long as we believe that our money is an acceptable form of payment for goods and services, the system works.

The United States has not always operated under a fiduciary monetary system. At one time the U.S. government issued gold and silver coins. Coins with an intrinsic value are known as *commodity money;* they have value as a commodity in addition to their face value. The problem with commodity money is that as the value of the commodity increases, the money stops being circulated. People hoard coins when their commodity value exceeds their face value. For example, no one would take an old $20 gold piece to the grocery store to buy $20 worth of groceries because the gold is worth much more than $20 today.

Thomas Gresham was a successful businessman and financial adviser to Queen Elizabeth I. He insisted that if two coins have the same face value but different intrinsic values—perhaps one is silver and the other brass—the cheaper coin will be used in exchange while the more expensive coin will be hoarded. Today the tendency to hoard currency as its commodity value increases is called *Gresham's Law.*[1]

According to Gresham's Law, bad money drives out good money.

Travelers' checks Outstanding U.S. dollar–denominated travelers' checks issued by nonbank institutions are counted as part of the M1 money supply. There are several nonbank issuers, among them American Express and Cook's. (Travelers' checks issued by banks are included in demand deposits. When a bank issues its own travelers' checks, it deposits the amount paid by the purchaser in a special account that is used to redeem the checks. Because this amount is counted as a part of demand deposits, it is not counted again as part of outstanding travelers' checks.) Travelers' checks accounted for just 1 percent of the M1 money supply in 1989.

Demand deposits Demand deposits are checking account deposits at a commercial bank. These deposits pay no interest. They are called *demand*

---

[1]Actually Gresham was not the first to recognize that bad money drives out good money. A fourteenth-century French theologian, Nicholas Oresme, made the same argument in his book *A Treatise on the Origin, Nature, Law, and Alterations of Money,* written almost 200 years before Gresham was born.

Using Transactions Money

In 1986 the Federal Reserve Board commissioned a survey to determine how U.S. families pay for their goods and services. It found that families use their main checking account for 39 percent of purchases. (The *main checking account* is the one a household uses most frequently.) Cash transactions account for 34 percent of purchases. Other checking accounts are used for 9 percent of expenditures. Credit cards account for 8 percent, as do savings accounts and money market accounts (part of the M2 money supply). Finally, money orders are used for 2 percent of family expenditures.

If you subtract credit cards,

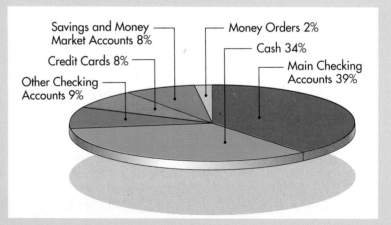

Savings and Money Market Accounts 8%
Credit Cards 8%
Other Checking Accounts 9%
Money Orders 2%
Cash 34%
Main Checking Accounts 39%

savings and money market accounts, and money orders from total household expenditures, you can see that the components of the M1 money supply

are used for 82 percent of family purchases. This is one reason why the M1 money supply is such an important variable in macroeconomic policy.

deposits because the bank must pay the amount of the check immediately on the demand of the depositor. Demand deposits accounted for 35 percent of the M1 money supply in 1989.

Other checkable deposits   Until the 1980s, demand deposits were the only kind of checking account. Today there are many different kinds of checking accounts, known as *other checkable deposits (OCDs)*. OCDs are accounts at financial institutions that pay interest and give the depositor check-writing privileges. Among the OCDs included in the M1 money supply are the following:

Negotiable orders of withdrawal (NOW) accounts   These are interest-bearing checking accounts offered by savings and loan institutions.

Automatic transfer system (ATS) accounts   These are accounts at commercial banks that combine an interest-bearing savings account with a non–interest bearing checking account. The depositor keeps a small balance in the checking account; any time the checking account balance is overdrawn, funds automatically are transferred from the savings account.

Credit union share draft accounts   Credit unions offer their members interest-bearing checking accounts called *share drafts*.

Demand deposits at mutual savings banks   Mutual savings banks are nonprofit savings and loan organizations. Any profits after operating expenses have been paid may be distributed to depositors.

1.b.2. M2 Money Supply The components of the M1 money supply are liquid assets, they are most likely to be used for transactions. M2 is a broader definition of the money supply that includes money in somewhat less liquid forms. The M2 money supply includes the M1 money supply plus overnight repurchase agreements, overnight Eurodollar deposits, money market deposit accounts, savings and small-denomination time deposits, and balances in individual money market mutual funds.

☐ An *overnight repurchase agreement (RP)* is an agreement between a bank and a customer under which the customer buys U.S. government securities from the bank one day and sells them back to the bank the next day at a price that includes the interest earned overnight. Overnight RPs are used by firms that have excess cash one day that may be needed the next.

☐ *Overnight Eurodollar deposits* are deposits denominated in dollars but held outside the U.S. domestic bank market. They mature the day after they are deposited.

☐ *Money market deposit accounts* are accounts at commercial banks and savings and loan institutions. They require a minimum balance and place limits on the number of transactions allowed per month.

☐ *Savings deposits* are accounts at banks and savings and loans that earn interest but offer no check-writing privileges.

☐ *Small-denomination time deposits* often are called *certificates of deposit*. Funds in these accounts must be deposited for a specified period of time. (*Small* means less than $100,000.)

☐ *Individual money market mutual fund balances* combine the deposits of many individuals and invest them in government Treasury bills and other short-term securities. Many money market mutual funds grant check-writing privileges but limit the size and number of checks.

1.b.3. M3 Money Supply The M3 money supply equals the M2 money supply plus *large time deposits* (deposits in amounts of $100,000 or more), *term RPs* and *term Eurodollar deposits* (deposits held by banks for a specified period), and *institution-only money market mutual fund balances* (balances that do not include the balances of individuals). These additional assets are less liquid than those found in the M1 or M2 money supply.

Figure 1 summarizes the three definitions of the money supply.

1.c. Global Money

Every nation has its own monetary unit of account. Japan has the yen, Mexico the peso, Canada, the Canadian dollar. But how do countries pay for international transactions? The foreign exchange market links national monies together, so that transactions can be made across national borders. If a U.S. importer buys an electronic component from a Japanese exporter, the importer can exchange dollars for yen in order to pay the exporter in yen. The exchange rate between the dollar and yen determines how many dollars are needed to purchase the required number of yen. For instance, if the exporter wants 1,000,000 yen for the component and the exchange rate is ¥250 = $1, the U.S. importer needs $4,000 (1,000,000/250) to buy the yen.

How do countries pay for international transactions?

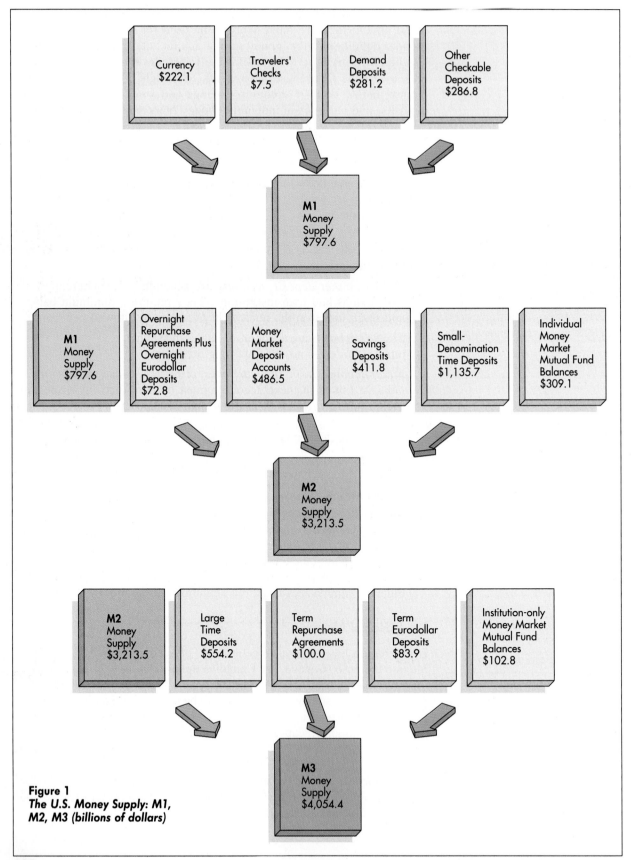

Figure 1
The U.S. Money Supply: M1, M2, M3 (billions of dollars)

Sales contracts between developed countries usually are written (invoiced) in the national currency of the exporter. To complete the transaction, the importer buys the exporter's currency on the foreign exchange market. Trade between developing and developed nations typically is invoiced in the currency of the developed country, whether the developed country is the exporter or importer. The currency of the developed country usually is more stable and more widely traded on the foreign exchange market than the currency of the developing country. As a result, the currencies of the major developed countries tend to dominate the international medium-of-exchange and unit-of-account functions of money.

1.c.1. International Reserve Currencies Governments hold monies as a temporary store of value until they are needed to settle international debts. At one time gold was the primary **international reserve asset**, an asset used to settle debts between governments. Today national currencies function as international reserves. The currencies that are held for this purpose are called **international reserve currencies**.

Table 1 shows the importance of the major international reserve currencies over time. In the mid-1970s, the U.S. dollar comprised almost 80 percent of international reserve holdings. By 1986 its share had fallen to less than 57 percent. One reason for this change was the adoption by the Western European nations of a new unit of currency as their official reserve asset.

1.c.2. Composite Currencies The industrial nations of Western Europe introduced a new unit of account, the **European currency unit (ECU)**, in March 1979. These nations use ECUs to settle debts between them. The ECU is a **composite currency**; its value is an average of the values of several different national currencies. An official organization, the European Monetary System, determines the amount of each currency that is used to make up the ECU, and regularly publishes its value.

The ECU is not an actual currency. ECUs are accounting entries; they are transferred between nations by changing the financial statements of the governments that use them. The ultimate goal of the European nations is a common money. The ECU is a step in that direction. When the ECU was created, the international reserve holdings of Western European nations shifted from the dollar to the ECU. However, the dollar still dominates as an international reserve asset.

international reserve asset:
an asset used to settle debts between governments

international reserve currency:
a currency held by a government to settle international debts

composite currency:
an artificial unit of account that is an average of the values of several national currencies

Table 1 International Reserve Currencies (Percentage Shares of National Currencies in Total Official Holdings of Foreign Exchange)

Year	U.S. Dollar	Pound Sterling	Deutsche Mark	French Franc	Japanese Yen	Swiss Franc	Netherlands Guilder	ECUs	Unspecified Currencies
1976	78.8	1.0	8.7	1.5	1.9	2.1	0.8	0.0	5.2
1978	76.1	1.5	10.8	1.2	2.8	1.7	0.8	0.0	5.1
1980	56.6	2.5	12.8	1.5	3.7	2.8	1.1	16.4	2.7
1982	59.7	2.2	11.1	1.1	4.2	2.5	1.0	13.7	4.5
1984	60.5	2.7	11.3	1.0	5.2	1.9	0.7	11.4	5.3
1986	56.5	2.5	13.6	1.1	7.0	1.8	1.0	12.3	4.1

Source: International Monetary Fund, *International Financial Statistics, Supplement on International Liquidity* (Washington, D.C.), 1987, p. 172. Used by permission.

Table 2 An Example of ECU Transactions

Date of Transaction	Transaction		Exchange Rate	ECU Value
	Bank deposit	*Bank withdrawal*		
September 25	FF1,000,000	—	ECU1 = FF7	ECU142,857
November 25	—	FF1,028,570	ECU1 = FF7.2	ECU142,857

Note: "FF" = French francs

The value of the ECU is an average of the values of these individual European currencies: the Belgian franc, the Danish krone, the French franc, the German mark, the Greek drachma, the Irish pound, the Italian lira, the Luxembourg franc, the Netherlands guilder, the Spanish peseta, and the U.K. pound. Because the value of the ECU is an average of these currencies, an investor who wants to hold a mix of investments in the various European currencies might find an ECU-denominated investment attractive.

How does it work? Let's say that on September 25 a firm deposits 1,000,000 French francs in a European bank to open an ECU time deposit. The value of the deposit in ECUs is determined by the franc value of the ECU on that day (Table 2). Suppose the franc value of the ECU on September 25 is 7 (ECU1 = FF7). To convert the francs into ECUs, we divide 7 into 1,000,000. The beginning balance is ECU142,857. To keep things simple, let's assume that the deposit earns no interest. On November 25, the firm wants to withdraw its ECU142,857 from the bank. On that day, the exchange rate is ECU1 = FF7.2. To find the franc value of ECU142,857, we multiply 142,857 by 7.2. ECU142,857 now equals FF1,028,570. This is the amount the firm withdraws from the bank.

Notice that the deposit and withdrawal are made in an actual currency. ECUs are simply artificial units of account that change in value as the values of the European currencies that comprise them change. ECUs cannot be spent; they are used to denominate bank deposits and other financial transactions. In our example, the franc value of the ECU increased between the time of the deposit and the time of the withdrawal. There is no guarantee that this will happen. Foreign exchange rates change all the time, up and down. But if a firm transacts business in several different European currencies, it may find ECU deposits to be more useful than deposits denominated in any single currency.

Another composite currency used to denominate financial transactions is the **special drawing right (SDR)**. The value of the SDR is an average of the values of the currencies of the five major industrial countries: the U.S. dollar, the French franc, the German mark, the Japanese yen, and the U.K. pound. This currency was created by the International Monetary Fund, an international organization that oversees the monetary relationships among countries. SDRs, like ECUs, are an international reserve asset; they are used to settle international debts by transferring governments' accounts held at the International Monetary Fund. We discuss the SDR and the role of the International Monetary Fund in later chapters.

special drawing right (SDR): a composite currency whose value is the average of the value of the U.S. dollar, the French franc, the German mark, the Japanese yen, and the U.K. pound

Part III / Macroeconomic Policy

RECAP

1. Money is the most liquid asset.

2. Money serves as a medium of exchange, a unit of account, a store of value, and a standard of deferred payment.

3. The use of money lowers transaction and information costs.

4. Money should be portable, divisible, and durable.

5. The M1 money supply equals the sum of currency, travelers' checks, demand deposits, and other checkable deposits.

6. The M2 money supply equals the sum of the M1 money supply, overnight repurchase agreements, overnight Eurodollar deposits, money market deposit accounts, savings and small-denomination time deposits, and individual money market mutual fund balances.

7. The M3 money supply equals the sum of the M2 money supply, large time deposits, term repurchase agreements, term Eurodollar deposits, and institution-only money market mutual fund balances.

8. International reserve currencies are held by governments to settle international debts.

9. ECUs and SDRs are composite currencies; their value is an average of the values of several national currencies.

2. BANKING

Commercial banks are financial institutions that offer deposits on which checks can be written. In the United States and most other countries, commercial banks are privately owned. *Thrift institutions* are financial institutions that historically offered just savings accounts, no checking accounts. Savings and loan associations, credit unions, and mutual savings banks are all thrift institutions. At one time the differences between commercial banks and thrift institutions were much greater than they are today. For example, only commercial banks could offer checking accounts, and those accounts earned no interest. The law also regulated maximum interest rates. In 1980 Congress passed the Depository Institutions Deregulation and Monetary Control Act, in part to stimulate competition among financial institutions. Now thrift institutions and even brokerage houses offer many of the same services as commercial banks.

2.a. Financial Intermediaries

Why are banks considered intermediaries?

Both commercial banks and thrift institutions are *financial intermediaries,* middlemen between savers and borrowers. Banks accept deposits from individuals and firms, then use those deposits to make loans to individuals and firms. The borrowers are likely to be different individuals or firms than the depositors, although it is not uncommon for a household or business to be both a depositor and a borrower at the same institution. Of course depositors and borrowers have very different interests. For instance, depositors typically prefer short-term deposits; they don't want to tie their money up for a long time. Borrowers, on the other hand, usually want more time for repayment. Banks package short-term deposits into longer-term loans. To function as intermediaries, banks must serve the interests of both depositors and borrowers.

A bank is willing to serve as an intermediary because it hopes to earn a profit from this activity. It pays a lower interest rate on deposits than it charges on loans; the difference is a source of profit for the bank. Islamic banks are prohibited by holy law from charging interest on loans; Islamic banks use a different system for making a profit (see Economic Insight: "Islamic Banking").

2.b. U.S. Banking

2.b.1. Current Structure Banking in the United States went through many changes in the 1980s. The Depository Institutions Deregulation and Monetary Control Act narrowed the distinction between commercial banks and thrift institutions. The act also narrowed the distinctions among commercial banks. If you add together all the pieces of the pie chart in Figure 2, you see that there were 59,431 banking offices operating in the United States in 1987. Roughly half of these offices were operated by *national banks*, banks chartered by the federal government; the other half, by *state banks*, banks chartered under state laws. Before the deregulation act was passed, national banks came under Federal Reserve regulations, which were more stringent than the regulations placed on state banks.

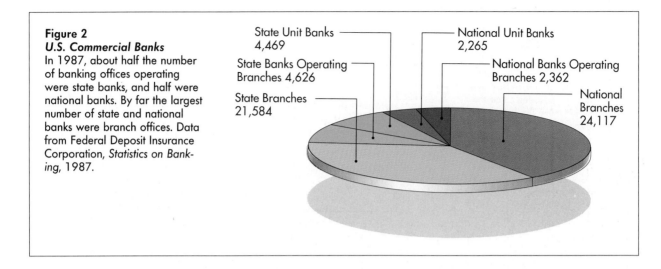

Figure 2
U.S. Commercial Banks
In 1987, about half the number of banking offices operating were state banks, and half were national banks. By far the largest number of state and national banks were branch offices. Data from Federal Deposit Insurance Corporation, *Statistics on Banking*, 1987.

State Unit Banks 4,469

State Banks Operating Branches 4,626

State Branches 21,584

National Unit Banks 2,265

National Banks Operating Branches 2,362

National Branches 24,117

Today these regulatory differences are much smaller than they used to be, and the historical cost advantages of being a state bank effectively have disappeared.

Another change that has taken place in the U.S. bank market is the growth of interstate banking. Historically, banks were allowed to operate in just one state. In fact in some states, banks are allowed to operate in just one location. This is known as *unit banking*. Figure 2 shows that in 1987 approximately half of all state banks (4,469) as well as half of all national banks (2,265) operated as unit banks; the rest operated 21,584 state branch offices and 24,117 national branch offices.

Over time, legal barriers have been reduced so that today almost all states permit entry to banks located out of state. In the future, banking is likely to be done on a national rather than a local scale. The growth of automated teller machines (ATMs) is a big step in this direction. ATM networks give bank customers access to services over a much wider geographic area than any single bank's branches cover. These national networks allow a bank customer from Dallas to withdraw cash in Seattle, Boston, or anywhere in the country. Today more than one-fourth of ATM transactions occur at banks that are not the customer's own bank.

A bank panic occurs when depositors become frightened and rush to withdraw their funds.

2.b.2. Bank Failures Banking in the United States has had a colorful history of booms and panics. A bank panic occurs when depositors, fearing a bank's closing, rush to withdraw their funds. Because banks keep only a fraction of their deposits on reserve, bank panics often result in bank closings.

Banking is like any other business. Banks that are poorly managed can fail; banks that are properly managed tend to prosper. Circumstances are also very important. In the mid-1980s, the circumstances in parts of this country destroyed hundreds of banks. Low oil prices resulted in an enormous number of loan defaults in states with large oil industries, like Texas and Oklahoma. At the same time, banks in Kansas, Nebraska, and other farming states could not collect many of their loans. Table 3 lists the number of banks that failed in the United States between 1985 and 1988. Those states that are heavily dependent on the oil industry and farming had sig-

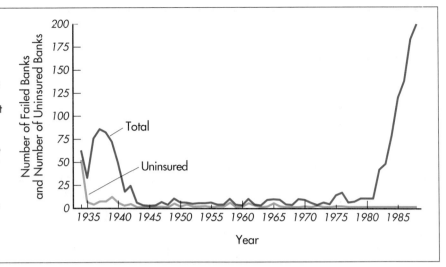

Figure 3
Number of Failed and Uninsured Banks, 1934–1988
The number of banks that went out of business in the 1980s was the highest it had been since the Depression. Unlike the banks that failed in the 1930s, the banks that closed in the 1980s were covered by deposit insurance, so that depositors did not lose their money. Source: Federal Deposit Insurance Corporation, *Annual Report*, 1988 (Washington, D.C., 1989), Table 122.

nificantly more banks fail than did other states. The problem was not so much bad management as it was a matter of unexpectedly bad business conditions. The lesson here is simple: commercial banks, like other profit-making enterprises, are not exempt from failure.

At one time a bank panic could close a bank; in the United States today, this is no longer true. The **Federal Deposit Insurance Corporation (FDIC)** was created in 1933. The FDIC is a federal agency that insures bank deposits in commercial banks so that depositors do not lose their deposits when a bank fails. Figure 3 shows the number of failed banks and

Federal Deposit Insurance Corporation (FDIC):
a federal agency that insures deposits in commercial banks

Table 3 Failed Banks by State, 1985–1988

State	Number of Failed Banks	State	Number of Failed Banks
Alabama	4	Mississippi	1
Alaska	4	Missouri	24
Arizona	1	Montana	5
Arkansas	1	Nebraska	26
California	26	New Mexico	5
Colorado	36	New York	4
Delaware	1	North Dakota	3
Florida	11	Ohio	2
Idaho	1	Oklahoma	83
Illinois	6	Oregon	4
Indiana	6	Pennsylvania	1
Iowa	33	South Dakota	4
Kansas	41	Tennessee	7
Kentucky	3	Texas	201
Louisiana	33	Utah	9
Massachusetts	2	Wisconsin	2
Michigan	1	Wyoming	17
Minnesota	28		

Source: Federal Deposit Insurance Corporation, *Annual Report, 1988* (Washington, D.C., 1989).

Table 4 The Ten Largest Bank Failures in U.S. History (by asset size)

Bank	Assets	Deposits	Year
Franklin National Bank New York, New York	$3,655,662,000	$1,444,981,606	1974
First National Bank and Trust Company Oklahoma City, Oklahoma	$1,419,445,375	$1,006,657,507	1986
The First National Bank of Midland Midland, Texas	$1,404,092,000	$1,076,217,000	1983
United States National Bank San Diego, California	$1,265,868,099	$931,954,458	1973
United American Bank in Knoxville Knoxville, Tennessee	$778,434,000	$584,619,000	1983
Banco Credito y Ahorro Ponceno Ponce, Puerto Rico	$712,540,000	$607,610,000	1978
Park Bank of Florida St. Petersburg, Florida	$592,900,000	$543,900,000	1986
Yankee Bank for Finance and Savings, FSB Boston, Massachusetts	$521,700,000	$474,800,000	1987
Penn Square Bank, N.A. Oklahoma City, Oklahoma	$516,799,000	$470,445,000	1982
The Hamilton National Bank of Chattanooga Chattanooga, Tennessee	$412,107,000	$336,292,000	1974

Source: Federal Deposit Insurance Corporation, *Annual Report, 1987* (Washington, D.C.: 1988).

the number of banks without deposit insurance between 1934 and 1988. In the 1930s, many of the banks that failed were not insured by the FDIC. In this environment, it made sense for depositors to worry about losing their money. In the 1980s, the number of bank failures increased dramatically, but none of the failed banks was uninsured. Deposits in those banks were protected by the federal government. Even though large banks have failed in recent times, as shown in Table 4, the banking system has been able to absorb the shock of those failures for depositors.

2.c. International Banking

> How does international banking differ from domestic banking?

Large banks today are truly transnational enterprises. International banks, like domestic banks, act as financial intermediaries. But they operate in a different legal environment. The laws regulating domestic banking in each nation are typically very restrictive, yet many nations allow international banking to operate largely unregulated. Because they are not hampered by regulations, international banks typically can offer depositors and borrowers better terms than could be negotiated at a domestic bank.

Eurocurrency market:
the market for deposits and loans generally denominated in a currency other than the currency of the country in which the transaction occurs; also called **offshore banking**

2.c.1. Eurocurrency Market   There is a large market for deposits and loans denominated in different currencies. For instance, a bank in London, Tokyo, or the Bahamas may accept deposits and make loans denominated in U.S. dollars. The international deposit and loan market often is called the **Eurocurrency market** or **offshore banking**. In the Eurocurrency market, the currency used in a banking transaction generally is not the domestic currency of the country in which the bank is located. (The prefix *Euro* is misleading here. The Eurocurrency market operates with different foreign currencies; it is in no way limited to European currencies or European banks.)

In those countries that allow offshore banking, we find two sets of banking rules: restrictive regulations for banking in the domestic market and little or no regulation of offshore-banking activities. Domestic banks are required to hold reserves against deposits and to carry deposit insurance; and they often face government-mandated credit or interest rate restrictions. The Eurocurrency market operates with few or no costly restrictions, and international banks generally pay lower taxes than domestic banks. Because offshore banks operate with lower costs, they are able to offer better terms to their customers than can domestic banks.

Figure 4 compares U.S. domestic deposit and loan rates with Eurodollar deposit and loan rates. (A U.S. dollar–denominated deposit outside the domestic U.S. banking industry is called a *Eurodollar deposit*; a U.S. dollar-denominated loan outside the domestic U.S. banking industry is called a *Eurodollar loan*.)

Offshore banks are able to offer a higher rate on dollar deposits and a lower rate on dollar loans than their domestic competitors. Without these differences, the Eurodollar market probably would not exist because Eurodollar transactions are riskier than domestic transactions in the United States, due to the lack of government regulation and deposit insurance.

There are always risks involved in international banking. Funds are subject to control both by the country in which the bank is located and the country in whose currency the deposit or loan is denominated. Suppose a Canadian firm wants to withdraw funds from a U.S. dollar–denominated bank deposit in Hong Kong. The transaction is subject to control in Hong Kong. For example, the government may not allow foreign exchange to leave the country freely. It is also subject to U.S. control. If the United States reduces its outflow of dollars, for instance, the Hong Kong bank may have difficulty paying the Canadian firm with U.S. dollars.

Modern technological innovations like automated teller machines have allowed banks to offer customers 24-hour banking. This technology is available in many countries as shown here by this photo of a teller machine in Puerto Rico.

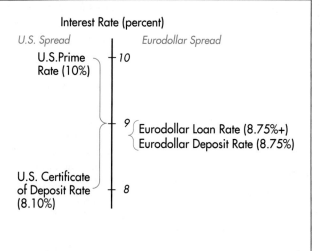

Figure 4
U.S. and Eurodollar Interest Rate Spreads, Nov. 9, 1988
The U.S. deposit rate is the average rate paid on certificates of deposit by major New York banks. The U.S. loan rate is the *prime rate,* the rate banks charge their best corporate customers. The Eurodollar deposit rate is the rate offered on three-month deposits. The Eurodollar loan rate is the *London interbank offer rate,* the rate London banks charge for interbank deposits plus an additional amount based on the credit worthiness of the borrower.

The *spread* is the difference between the interest rate for a deposit and the interest rate on a loan. Eurodollar spreads are narrower than U.S. spreads. This means that Eurodollar deposits offer a higher interest rate than U.S. bank deposits and that Eurodollar loans charge a lower interest rate than U.S. bank loans. Data from The Wall Street Journal, November 10, 1988, p. C–21.

The Eurocurrency market exists for all of the major international currencies, but the value of activity in Eurodollars dwarfs the rest. As Table 5 indicates, between 1981 and 1987, Eurodollars accounted for 61 to 79 percent of deposit and loan activity in the Eurocurrency market. This emphasizes the important role the U.S. dollar plays in global finance. Even deposits and loans that do not involve a U.S. lender or borrower often are denominated in U.S. dollars.

International banking today is dominated by Japanese and U.S. banks, which control almost 50 percent of total international banking assets. Table 6 lists the 25 largest banks in the world as of December 31, 1988. These banks have branches all over the world. Citicorp is headquartered in New York City, but it has foreign branches in every major city, many of which handle a large volume of Eurocurrency transactions.

2.c.2. International Banking Facilities The term *offshore banking* is somewhat misleading in the United States today. At one time U.S. banks were forced to process international deposits and loans through their off-

Table 5 Eurodollars and the Eurocurrency Market, 1981–1987

Year	Gross Size of Eurocurrency Market (billion dollars)	Eurodollars as a Percentage of Gross Market
1981	2,217	75
1982	2,418	77
1983	2,538	78
1984	2,666	79
1985	3,223	72
1986	4,172	68
1987	5,246	61

Source: Morgan Guaranty Trust Company, *World Financial Markets* (New York), various issues.

Table 6 The World's 25 Largest Banks, December 31, 1988

Rank	Company (country)	Assets (billion dollars)
1	Dai-Ichi Kangyo Bank (Japan)	352,368
2	Sumitomo Bank (Japan)	333,334
3	Fuji Bank (Japan)	327,323
4	Mitsubishi Bank (Japan)	317,566
5	Sanwa Bank (Japan)	307,275
6	Industrial Bank of Japan (Japan)	248,855
7	Norinchukin Bank (Japan)	231,946
8	Tokai Bank (Japan)	213,067
9	Citicorp (U.S.)	203,827
10	Banque Nationale de Paris (France)	196,950
11	Mitsubishi Trust & Banking (Japan)	195,225
12	Mitsui Bank (Japan)	194,247
13	Barclays Bank (U.K.)	189,250
14	Credit Lyonnais (France)	178,874
15	National Westminster Bank (U.K.)	178,394
16	Sumitomo Trust & Banking (Japan)	177,621
17	Mitsui Trust & Banking (Japan)	174,599
18	Credit Agricole (France)	173,522
19	Deutsche Bank (West Germany)	170,509
20	Taiyo Kobe Bank (Japan)	166,516
21	Long-Term Credit Bank of Japan (Japan)	166,209
22	Bank of Tokyo (Japan)	161,802
23	Societe Generale (France)	155,479
24	Yasuda Trust & Banking (Japan)	147,392
25	Daiwa Bank (Japan)	143,882

Source: World Business Supplement, *Wall Street Journal*, September 22, 1989.

shore branches. Many of the branches in places like the Cayman Islands and the Bahamas were little more than "shells," small offices with a telephone. Yet these branches allowed U.S. banks to avoid the reserve requirements and interest rate regulations that restricted domestic banking activities.

In December 1981, the Federal Reserve Board legalized **international banking facilities (IBFs)**, allowing domestic banks to take part in international banking on U.S. soil. IBFs are not a physical entity; they are a bookkeeping system set up in existing bank offices to record international banking transactions. IBFs can receive deposits from and make loans to nonresidents of the United States or other IBFs. These deposits and loans must be kept separate from other transactions because IBFs are not subject to the reserve requirements, interest rate regulations, or FDIC deposit insurance premiums that apply to domestic U.S. banking.

international banking facility (IBF): a division of a U.S. bank that is allowed to receive deposits from and make loans to nonresidents of the United States without the restrictions that apply to domestic U.S. banks

Table 7 International Banking Facilities by Jurisdiction

Jurisdiction	Number of Facilities	Jurisdiction	Number of Facilities
New York	254	Washington	7
California	100	Georgia	6
Florida	79	Massachusetts	6
Illinois	28	Ohio	6
Texas	14	New Jersey	5
District of Columbia	11	Others	19
Pennsylvania	8	Total	543

Source: Federal Reserve Board

The goal of the IBF plan was to allow banking offices in the United States to compete with offshore banks without having to use offshore banking offices. The location of IBFs reflects the location of banking activity in general. Table 7 lists the number of IBFs by jurisdiction. It is not surprising that 47 percent of IBFs are located and over 75 percent of IBF deposits are made in New York State, the financial center of the country. Outside New York, few states do significant IBF business. After IBFs were legalized, several states encouraged their formation by reducing or eliminating taxes on IBF transactions. The volume of IBF business these concessions produced mirrored the preexisting volume of international banking activity, with New York outstripping the level of activity in other jurisdictions.

IBFs have grown rapidly since their creation. Where has this growth come from? Although IBFs stimulated a certain amount of new business, most of their business shifted from Caribbean shell branches. After the first month in operation, IBFs held $29.1 billion in claims on foreign residents. During this same period, the claims existing at Caribbean branches of U.S. banks fell $23.3 billion. Since the early 1980s, IBF growth has paralleled the growth of Eurodollar banking in general. Today U.S. international banking facilities have emerged as a major source of offshore banking activity.

RECAP

1. The Depository Institutions Deregulation and Monetary Control Act (1980) eliminated many of the differences between commercial banks and thrift institutions.

2. Banks are financial intermediaries.

3. The deregulation act also eliminated many of the differences between national and state banks.

4. Since the FDIC began insuring bank deposits in commercial banks, bank panics are no longer a threat to the banking system.

5. The international deposit and loan market is called the Eurocurrency market or offshore banking.

6. With the legalization in 1981 of international banking facilities, the Federal Reserve allowed international banking activities on U.S. soil.

3. BANKS AND THE MONEY SUPPLY

fractional reserve banking system:
a system in which banks keep less than 100 percent of the deposits available for withdrawal

Banks create money by lending money. They take deposits, then lend a portion of those deposits in order to earn interest income. The portion of deposits that banks keep on hand is a *reserve* to meet the demand for withdrawals. In a **fractional reserve banking system**, banks keep less than 100 percent of their deposits on reserve. If all banks hold 10 percent of their deposits as a reserve, then 90 percent of their deposits are available for loans.

3.a. Balance Sheet Analysis

Figure 5 shows a simple balance sheet for First National Bank. A *balance sheet* is a financial statement that records a firm's assets (what the firm owns) and liabilities (what the firm owes). The bank has cash assets, ($100,000) and loan assets ($900,000). The deposits placed in the bank ($1,000,000) are a liability (they are an asset of the depositors).[2] Total assets always equal total liabilities on a balance sheet.

required reserves:
the cash reserves (a percentage of deposits) a bank must keep on hand or on deposit with the Federal Reserve

excess reserves:
the cash reserves beyond those required, which can be loaned

Banks keep a percentage of their deposits on reserve. In the United States the reserve requirement is set by the Federal Reserve Board. Banks can keep more than the minimum reserve if they choose. Let's assume that the reserve requirement is set at 10 percent and that banks always hold actual reserves equal to 10 percent of deposits. With deposits of $1,000,000, the bank must keep $100,000 (.10 × $1,000,000) in cash reserves. This $100,000 is the bank's **required reserves**. This is exactly what First National Bank has on hand in Figure 5. Any cash held in excess of $100,000 would represent **excess reserves**. Excess reserves can be loaned by the bank. A bank is *loaned up* when it has zero excess reserves.

---

[2]In our simplified balance sheet, we assume no net worth or owners' equity.

Figure 5
First National Bank Balance Sheet, Initial Position
The bank has cash totaling $100,000 and loans totaling $900,000, for total assets of $1,000,000. Deposits of $1,000,000 make up its total liabilities. With a reserve requirement of 10 percent, the bank must hold required reserves of 10 percent of its deposits, or $100,000. Because the bank is holding cash of $100,000, its total reserves equal its required reserves. Because it has no excess reserves, the bank cannot make new loans.

First National Bank

Assets		Liabilities	
Cash	$100,000	Deposits	$1,000,000
Loans	900,000		
Total	$1,000,000	Total	$1,000,000

Total reserves = $100,000
Required reserves = 0.1 ($1,000,000) = $100,000
Excess reserves = 0

Figure 6
First National Bank Balance Sheet, After $100,000 Deposit
A $100,000 deposit increases the bank's cash reserves to $200,000 and deposits to $1,100,000. The bank must hold 10 percent of deposits, $110,000, on reserve. The difference between total reserves ($200,000) and required reserves ($110,000) is excess reserves ($90,000). The bank now has $90,000 available for lending.

First National Bank

Assets		Liabilities	
Cash	$200,000	Deposits	$1,100,000
Loans	900,000		
Total	$1,100,000	Total	$1,100,000

Total reserves = $200,000
Required reserves = 0.1 ($1,100,000) = $110,000
Excess reserves = $90,000

Because its total reserves equal its required reserves, First National Bank has no excess reserves.

$$\text{Excess reserves} = \text{total reserves} - \text{required reserves}$$
$$= \$100,000 - \$100,000$$
$$= 0$$

The bank cannot make any new loans.

What happens if the bank receives a new deposit of $100,000? Figure 6 shows the bank's balance sheet right after the deposit is made. Its cash reserves are now $200,000, its deposits, $1,100,000. The bank's total reserves equal $200,000. Its required reserves are $110,000 (.10 × $1,100,000). So its excess reserves are $90,000 ($200,000 − $110,000). Given its current reserve position, First National Bank can loan an additional $90,000 (see Table 8).

Suppose the bank lends someone $90,000 by depositing $90,000 in the borrower's First National account. At the time the loan is made, the money supply increases by the amount of the loan, $90,000. But this is not the end of the story. The borrower spends the $90,000, and it winds up being deposited in the Second National Bank. Figure 7 shows the balance

Table 8 The Effect on Bank Deposits of an Initial Bank Deposit of $100,000

Bank	New Deposit	Required Reserves	Excess Reserves (new loans)
First National	$ 100,000	$ 10,000	$ 90,000
Second National	90,000	9,000	81,000
Third National	81,000	8,100	72,900
Fourth National	72,900	7,290	65,610
Fifth National	65,610	6,561	59,049
Sixth National	59,049	5,905	53,144
⋮	⋮	⋮	⋮
Total	$1,000,000	$100,000	$900,000

First National Bank				Second National Bank			
Assets		Liabilities		Assets		Liabilities	
Cash	$110,000	Deposits	$1,100,000	Cash	$90,000	Deposits	$90,000
Loans	990,000						
Total	$1,100,000	Total	$1,100,000	Total	$90,000	Total	$90,000

Total reserves = $110,000
Required reserves = 0.1 ($1,100,000) = $110,000
Excess reserves = 0

Total reserves = $90,000
Required reserves = 0.1 ($90,000) = $9,000
Excess reserves = $81,000

Figure 7
Balance Sheets After a $90,000 Loan Made by First National Bank Is Spent and Deposited at Second National Bank
Once First National Bank makes the $90,000 loan, its cash reserves fall to $110,000 and its loans increase to $990,000. At this point the bank's total reserves ($110,000) equal its required reserves (10 percent of de-posits). Because it has no excess reserves, the bank cannot make new loans.

Second National Bank receives a deposit of $90,000. It must hold 10 percent, or $9,000, on reserve. Its excess reserves equal total reserves ($90,000) minus required reserves ($9,000), or $81,000. Second National Bank can make a maximum loan of $81,000.

sheets of both banks after the loan is made and the money is spent and deposited at Second National Bank. First National Bank now has loans of $990,000 and no excess reserves (the required reserves of $110,000 equal total reserves). So First National Bank can make no more loans until a new deposit is made. Second National Bank has a new deposit of $90,000 (to simplify the analysis, we assume that this is the first transaction at Second National Bank). Its required reserves are 10 percent of $90,000, or $9,000. With total reserves of $90,000, Second National Bank has excess reserves of $81,000. It can make loans up to $81,000.

Notice what has happened to the banks' deposits as a result of the initial $100,000 deposit in First National Bank. Deposits at First National Bank have increased by $100,000. Second National Bank has a new deposit of $90,000, and the loans it makes will increase the money supply even more. Table 8 shows how the initial deposit of $100,000 is multiplied through the banking system. Each time a new loan is made, the money is spent and redeposited in the banking system. But each bank keeps 10 percent of the deposit on reserve, lending only 90 percent. So the amount of money loaned decreases by 10 percent each time it goes through another bank. If we carried the calculations out, you would see that the total increase in deposits associated with the initial $100,000 deposit is $1,000,000. Required reserves would increase by $100,000, and new loans would increase by $900,000.

3.b. Deposit Expansion Multiplier

deposit expansion multiplier: the reciprocal of the reserve requirement

Rather than calculate the excess reserves at each bank, as we did in Table 8, we can use a simple formula to find the maximum increase in deposits given a new deposit. The **deposit expansion multiplier** equals the reciprocal of the reserve requirement:

$$\text{Deposit expansion multiplier} = \frac{1}{\text{reserve requirement}}$$

In our example, the reserve requirement is 10 percent, or .10. So the deposit expansion multiplier equals 10 (1/.10). An initial increase in deposits of $100,000 expands deposits in the banking system by 10 times $100,000, or $1,000,000.

The deposit expansion multiplier indicates the *maximum* possible change in total deposits when a new deposit is made. For the effect to be that large, all excess reserves must be loaned out and all of the money that is deposited must stay in the banking system.

If banks hold more reserves than the minimum required, they lend a smaller fraction of any new deposits, which reduces the effect of the deposit expansion multiplier. For instance, if the reserve requirement is 10 percent, we know that the deposit expansion multiplier is 10. If a bank chooses to hold 20 percent of its deposits on reserve, the deposit expansion multiplier equals 5 (1/.20).

If money (currency and coin) is withdrawn from the banking system and kept as cash, deposits are smaller, as are loans. This *currency drain* reduces the deposit expansion multiplier. The greater the currency drain, the smaller the multiplier.

Remember that the deposit expansion multiplier measures the maximum expansion of the money supply by the banking system. Any single bank can lend only its excess reserves. The whole banking system can expand the money supply only by a multiple of the initial excess reserves. If First National Bank holds no excess reserves, it cannot make new loans. And if it cannot make new loans, it cannot increase the money supply. If the bank receives a new deposit, however, it can loan a percentage of that deposit (a percentage must be held in cash reserves). The bank can only lend its excess reserves; it can only expand the money supply by its excess reserves.

Any single bank can only increase the money supply by lending its excess reserves. The banking system as a whole can increase the money supply by the deposit expansion multiplier times the excess reserves of the system. The initial bank is limited to its initial loan; the banking system generates loan after loan based on that initial loan.

In the next chapter we discuss how changes in the reserve requirement affect the money supply and the economy. This area of policy making is controlled by the Federal Reserve.

▼ How do banks create money?

A single bank increases the money supply by lending its excess reserves; the banking system increases the money supply by the deposit expansion multiplier times the excess reserves of the system.

RECAP

1. The fractional reserve banking system allows banks to expand the money supply by making loans.
2. Banks must keep a fraction of their deposits on reserve; their excess reserves are available for lending.
3. The deposit expansion multiplier measures the maximum increase in the money supply given a new deposit; it is the reciprocal of the reserve requirement.

4. A single bank can increase the money supply by lending its excess reserves.

5. The banking system can increase the money supply by the deposit expansion multiplier times the excess reserves in the banking system.

SUMMARY

▼▲ What is money?

1. Money is anything that is generally acceptable to sellers in exchange for goods and services. § 1

2. Money serves as a medium of exchange, a unit of account, a store of value, and a standard of deferred payment. § 1.a

3. Money, because it is more efficient than barter, lowers transaction costs. § 1.a.1

4. Money should be portable, divisible, and durable. §§ 1.a.1 and 1.a.3

▼▲ How is the U.S. money supply defined?

5. There are three definitions of money based on its availability for spending. § 1.b

6. The M1 money supply equals the sum of currency plus travelers' checks plus demand deposits plus other checkable deposits. § 1.b.1

7. The M2 money supply equals the sum of the M1 money supply plus overnight repurchase agreements, overnight Eurodollar deposits, money market deposit accounts, savings and small-denomination time deposits, and individual money market mutual fund balances. § 1.b.2

8. The M3 money supply equals the M2 money supply plus large time deposits, term repurchase agreements, term Eurodollar deposits, and institution-only money market mutual fund balances. § 1.b.3

▼▲ How do countries pay for international transactions?

9. Using the foreign exchange market, governments are able to convert national currencies to pay for trade. § 1.c

10. The U.S. dollar is the world's major international reserve currency. § 1.c.1

11. The European currency unit (ECU) is a composite currency whose value is an average of the values of several Western European currencies. § 1.c.2

▼▲ Why are banks considered intermediaries?

12. Banks serve as middlemen between savers and borrowers. § 2.a

▼▲ How does international banking differ from domestic banking?

13. Domestic banking in most nations is strictly regulated; international banking is not. § 2.c

14. The Eurocurrency market is the international deposit and loan market. § 2.c.1

15. International banking facilities (IBFs) allow U.S. domestic banks to carry on international banking activities on U.S. soil. § 2.c.2

16. Banks can make loans up to the amount of their excess reserves, their total reserves minus their required reserves. § 3.a

17. The deposit expansion multiplier is the reciprocal of the reserve requirement. § 3.b

▼▲ How do banks create money?

18. A single bank expands the money supply by lending its excess reserves. § 3.b

19. The banking system can increase the money supply by the deposit expansion multiplier times the excess reserves in the system. § 3.b

money § 1

liquid asset § 1

currency substitution § 1.a.3

credit § 1.a.4

M1 money supply § 1.b.1

transactions account § 1.b.1

international reserve asset § 1.c.1

international reserve currency § 1.c.1

European currency unit (ECU) § 1.c.2

composite currency § 1.c.2

special drawing right (SDR) § 1.c.2

Federal Deposit Insurance Corporation (FDIC) § 2.b.2

Eurocurrency market (offshore banking) § 2.c.1

international banking facility (IBF) § 2.c.2

fractional reserve banking system § 3

required reserves § 3.a

excess reserves § 3.a

deposit expansion multiplier § 3.b

EXERCISES

Basic Terms and Concepts

1. Describe the four functions of money.

2. Discuss how the following serve the functions of money.
   a. Gold
   b. Yap stone money
   c. Cigarettes
   d. Diamonds

3. Define the following terms.
   a. Composite currency
   b. International reserve asset
   c. ECU
   d. FDIC
   e. M2 money supply

4. What is a financial intermediary?

5. How is banking in the Eurocurrency market different from domestic banking?

6. What are IBFs? Why do you think they were legalized?

7. First Bank has cash reserves of $200,000, loans of $800,000, and deposits of $1,000,000.
   a. Prepare a balance sheet for the bank.
   b. If the bank maintains a reserve requirement of 12 percent, what is the largest loan it can make?

   c. What is the maximum amount the money supply or deposits of the banking system can be increased by First Bank's new loan?

8. Yesterday Bank A had no excess reserves. Today it received a new deposit of $5,000.
   a. If the bank maintains a reserve requirement of 2 percent, what is the maximum loan Bank A can make?
   b. What is the maximum amount the money supply can be increased as a result of Bank A's new loan?

Extended Concepts

9. "M2 is a better definition of the money supply than M1." Agree or disagree with this statement. In your argument, clearly state the criteria on which you are basing your decision.

10. The deposit expansion multiplier measures the maximum possible expansion of the money supply in the banking system. What factors could cause the actual expansion of the money supply to differ from that given by the deposit expansion multiplier?

Things That Go Bump in The Night

Think of the worst nightmare there has ever been, one that leaves the sleeper breathless and sweating on the edge of the bed staring into the darkness. However belatedly, that's how most of official Washington now feels about what has come to be called the "Thrift Crisis of 1990."

"It is a greater scandal than Teapot Dome by several factors; it may dwarf Teapot Dome, Watergate, Abscam and some others altogether before it is all through," says William S. Sessions, director of the Federal Bureau of Investigation and a man not known for hyperbole. Sessions says his agents currently are probing criminal fraud charges at no less than 234 failed savings and loan institutions, with no end in sight. In all, there are more than 2,300 separate prosecutions stacked up at the Justice Department awaiting grand jury indictments and trial dates, and the lawmen say the scandal is spreading daily.

Consider that the Federal Deposit Insurance Corp. and its Resolution Trust Corp. arm already have 400 thrifts under receivership and perhaps another 1,000 or so teetering on the brink.

Note also that FDIC Chairman William Siedman has conceded to [this magazine] and others that there may be serious fraud in 60% of the cases under examination. Scandal aside, we're talking about serious money — not only scores of billions of dollars that have evaporated in the failures of hundreds of savings and loans over the past five years, but also the possibility of having to come up with *hundreds* of billions more to prevent what could be a repeat of the Depression-era collapse of part of our financial system. . . .

Like a cancer, the crisis keeps getting worse as it spreads. Now the vital deposit base is starting to erode. According to the Federal Reserve Board, at the end of 1989 the entire industry had $945 billion in deposits, down from $971 billion a year earlier. Those deposits are now shrinking at an annual rate of $200 billion. This is in addition to the loss rate, which was running at $3 million an *hour* according to the latest estimates. . . .

Fat chance. Last year the federal courts in Texas were able to issue judgment orders against guilty officials of failed S&Ls there for restitution of a paltry $2.6 million. But only $29,000 was collected by year-end. The rest, according to one former thrift supervisor for the region ". . . is in Switzerland and other places, and you'll never see it." This is out of $10.8 billion that Texas courts have judged to have been swindled from just 38 thrifts in the state. Nationwide, court-ordered paybacks from fraud-killed thrifts totaled $361.5 million last year but very little of that will ever find its way into the coffers of the U.S. Treasury.

All of this means that the American taxpayer will have to come up with the money not only to keep the failed thrifts operating while buyers are found, but also to sweeten the accounts of the associations that are sold and to carry the "bad assets" that the government has to keep in a separate corral in order to sell the "good assets" that the new buyers are taking away.

The bad news is that the price tag on that part of Washington's bid to rescue the S&Ls just increased by scores of billions of dollars more than had originally been anticipated.

Charles Bowsher, head of the General Accounting Office arm of Congress, struck a chilled note throughout the city when he uttered the dreaded warning, "If we had a strong economy working against us, with interest rates going up much faster, the cost of paying off the problem could go as high as half a trillion dollars," in a crisis that could take a full 40 years to work through.

The GAO now estimates the true cost of taking over just the 400 already sunk thrifts (and perhaps 200 more) will be at least $63 billion. Then the government finds itself $5 billion short on the interest it will have to pay for the RTC to borrow the $50 billion it supposedly needed to do the job. Also unbudgeted was the estimated $10 billion the RTC will need to pay its bills and the salaries of the 2,000 or so examiners, liquidators and attorneys it is hiring. Then there is an additional $28 billion for still more interest on the money the RTC is borrowing . . . And, there is a further $12 billion in costs that turned up after the 1988 rescue of 200 previously failed S&Ls.

Add it all up and the final GAO price tag totals $325 billion, which is equal to one year's Defense Department appropriation. It's also approximately the sum many congressmen had hoped to save as the "peace dividend" that could be achieved by 1992 with *glasnost*-era military manpower reductions in Europe and Asia and major military base closings at home. That was supposed to balance the budget and provide extra money for a lot of popular new domestic programs. Forget all of them.

■ Source: James Srodes, "Things That Go Bump in the Night," *Financial World*, May 15, 1990, pp. 46–48.

Commentary

You may have noticed signs in banks that proclaim, "Deposits insured by the Federal Deposit Insurance Corporation." The FDIC insures up to $100,000 for individual depositors in the event that their bank fails. A similar institution insured deposits at savings and loans institutions (S&Ls), which was called the Federal Savings and Loan Insurance Corporation (FSLIC). Both agencies were created in the 1930s in order to protect depositors. This protection helps prevent bank runs because deposit insurance removes the incentive for withdrawing funds from an ailing bank or thrift. While these agencies had been successful in stabilizing the banking industry until the 1980s, recent banking failures, especially among S&Ls, have created a financial crisis whereby the government faces a bailout bill of over $160 billion. The most likely source of funding for this bailout will be U.S. taxpayers.

The background to this crisis begins in the late 1970s and early 1980s when interest rates were very high. The assets of S&Ls were long-term and fixed-rate mortgages that yielded low returns compared to the interest payments the S&Ls had to pay to attract funds. In response to this situation, Congress and several state governments relaxed the rules governing the borrowing and lending practices of these institutions, in effect allowing S&Ls to undertake riskier investments. While some S&Ls maintained prudent policies that kept them solvent at the end of the 1980s, others experienced a combination of bad judgment and bad luck that lowered the value of their assets below the value of their liabilities. The $160 billion bailout figure represents the difference between the assets of the S&Ls and their federally insured deposits.

Was there an incentive in place for managers of S&Ls to undertake risky lending? If risky loans were in fact repaid, the S&Ls stood to make a lot of money, since borrowers who represented a high risk had to pay a premium in order to get financing. If these loans turned out to be bad business decisions, however, S&L managers did not face a downside risk comparable to their possible gains if the loans were repaid because their losses would be absorbed by the FSLIC. This situation of distorted incentives, where a risk-taker potentially enjoys all the gains of a possible outcome but faces only some fraction of the potential losses, is called a situation of *moral hazard*.

In August 1989, the Financial Institutions Reform, Recovery and Enforcement Act abolished the FSLIC and gave its insurance role to the FDIC. A new agency, the Resolution Trust Corporation (RTC), was created to deal with failed savings institutions. Part of its role is to sell the $300 billion worth of real estate held by these institutions in order to help finance the claims made on deposit insurance. It must also sell the so-called junk bonds (bonds that pay a high yield because they are risky) that were held by S&Ls. The sale of these assets has proceeded slowly.

Time is not on the side of the regulators. Attempts to salvage thrift institutions that are technically insolvent may represent throwing good money after bad. These thrifts may be forced to make risky loans in order to regain enough capital to make them solvent. If these risky loans are not repaid, the situation will only get worse.

While there are no easy solutions to the present crisis, government regulators have learned lessons that will help them avoid a repetition of their past mistakes. This lesson has not been cheap, however, and its hefty tuition will be paid by all of us for some time into the future.

14

Monetary Policy

1. What are the determinants of the demand for money?

2. How does monetary policy affect the equilibrium level of national income?

3. What does the Federal Reserve do?

4. How is monetary policy set?

5. What are the tools of monetary policy?

6. What role do central banks play in the foreign exchange market?

PREVIEW

In March 1990 the new president of Brazil, Fernando Collor de Mello, froze most of the deposits in the country's banks. This meant that people could not spend the money they were holding in banks. The immediate effect was a dramatic cut in spending. Shops were almost empty. More important, the prices of many goods fell. This was the reason behind the new president's radical policy move. Inflation in Brazil was very high. The price level had gone up 73 percent in the month before Collor took office. Freezing deposits was the first step in implementing a new monetary policy, an ambitious attempt to cut inflation. Monetary policy (directed toward control of the money supply) in industrial countries does not change as dramatically as it did in Brazil, but what happened in Brazil is a good indicator of the importance of sound monetary policy.

Most of us never think about how money enters the economy. All we worry about is having money available when we need it. In the last chapter, you learned about money and how banks create money by making loans. The quantity of money is a measure of what individuals and businesses have available for spending. So money affects prices, interest rates, foreign exchange rates, and the level of income in the economy. Because money is so important, every government controls the size of its money supply. In the United States, the Federal Reserve System (the Fed) is responsible for monetary policy.

Wanting to hold more money is not the same as wanting more income. You can decide to carry more cash or keep more dollars in your checking account even though your income has not changed. The quantity of dollars you want to hold is your demand for money. By summing the quantity of money demanded by each individual, we find the money demand for the entire economy.

The demand for money is a function of several determinants. Once we explain what determines money demand, we can put that demand together with the money supply and examine how money influences the interest rate and the equilibrium level of income. The interest rate and level of income are critical factors in determining how an economy performs, which is why every government has some means of effecting monetary policy. In the United States, the Federal Reserve System sets and thus implements monetary policy by raising or lowering bank reserves and intervening in the foreign exchange market to control the money supply.

1. MONETARY POLICY AND EQUILIBRIUM INCOME

To see how changes in the money supply affect the equilibrium level of national income, we incorporate monetary policy in the aggregate demand and supply model. The first step in understanding monetary policy is understanding the demand for money. If you know what determines money demand, you can see how monetary policy is used to shift aggregate demand and change the equilibrium level of national income.

1.a. Money Demand

In Chapter 13 we discussed the functions of money. People use money as a unit of account, a medium of exchange, a store of value, and a standard of deferred payment. The last three functions help explain the demand for money.

People use money for transactions, to buy goods and services. The **transactions demand for money** is a demand to hold money in order to spend it on goods and services. Holding money in your pocket or checking account is a demand for money. Spending money is not demanding it; by spending it you are getting rid of it.

If your boss paid you every time you wanted to buy something, the timing of your receipts and expenditures would match perfectly. You would not have to hold money for transactions. But because receipts typically occur much less often than expenditures, money is necessary to cover transactions between paychecks.

What are the determinants of the demand for money?

transactions demand for money: the demand to hold money to buy goods and services

People also hold money to take care of emergencies. The **precautionary demand for money** exists because emergencies happen. People never know when an unexpected expense will crop up or when actual expenditures will exceed planned expenditures. So they hold money as a precaution.

Finally, there is a **speculative demand for money**, a demand created by uncertainty about the value of other assets. This demand exists because money is the most liquid store of value. If you want to buy a stock, but you believe the price is going to fall in the next few days, you hold the money until you are ready to buy the stock.

The speculative demand for money is not necessarily tied to a particular use of funds. People hold money because they expect the price of any asset to fall. Holding money is less risky than buying the asset today if the price of the asset seems likely to fall. For example, suppose you buy and sell fine art. The price of art fluctuates over time. You try to buy when prices are low and sell when prices are high. If you expect prices to fall in the short term, you hold money rather than art until the prices do fall. Then you use money to buy art for resale when the prices go up again.

1.a.1. The Money Demand Function If you understand why people hold money, you can understand what changes the amount of money they hold. That amount depends on the interest rate and nominal income (income measured in current dollars).

The interest rate is the opportunity cost of holding money.

The interest rate There is an inverse relationship between the interest rate and the quantity of money demanded (see Figure 1). The interest rate is the *opportunity cost* of holding money. If you bury a thousand dollar bills in your backyard, that currency is earning no interest. At a low interest rate, the cost of forgone interest is small. At a higher interest rate, the cost of

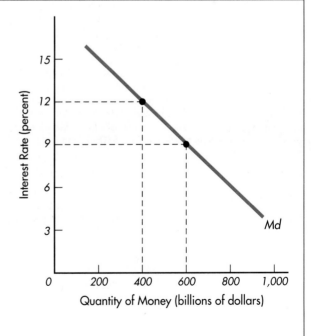

Figure 1
The Money Demand Function
Money demand (Md) is a negative function of the rate of interest. The interest rate is the opportunity cost of holding money. The higher the interest rate, the lower the quantity of money demanded. At an interest rate of 9 percent, the quantity of money demanded is $600 billion. At an interest rate of 12 percent, the quantity of money demanded falls to $400 billion.

holding wealth in the form of money means giving up more interest. The higher the rate of interest, the greater the interest forgone by holding money, so the less money held. The costs of holding money limit the amount of money held.

Some components of the money supply pay interest to the depositor. Here the opportunity cost of holding money is the difference between the interest rate on a bond or some other nonmonetary asset and the interest rate on money. If a bond pays 9 percent interest a year and a bank deposit pays 5 percent, the opportunity cost of holding the deposit is 4 percent.

Figure 1 shows a money demand function where the demand for money depends on the interest rate. The downward slope of the money demand curve (Md) shows the inverse relation between the interest rate and the quantity of money demanded. For instance, at an interest rate of 12 percent, the quantity of money demanded is $400 billion. If the interest rate falls to 9 percent, the quantity of money demanded increases to $600 billion.

The transactions demand for money rises with nominal income.

Nominal income   The demand for money also depends on nominal income. Money demand varies directly with nominal income because as income increases, more transactions are carried out and more money is required for those transactions.

The greater nominal income, the greater the demand for money. This is true whether the increase in nominal income is a product of a higher price level or an increase in real income. Both generate a greater dollar volume of transactions. If the prices of all goods increase, then more money must be used to purchase goods and services. And as real income increases, more goods and services are being produced and sold, which means more money is being demanded.

A change in nominal income changes the demand for money at any given interest rate. Figure 2 shows the effect of changes in nominal income on the money demand curve. If income rises from Y_0 to Y_1, money demand

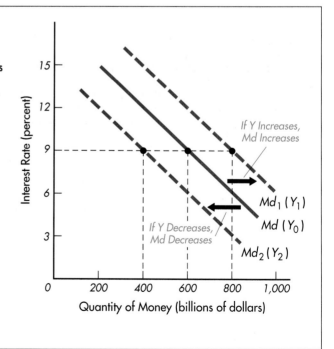

Figure 2
The Effect of a Change in Income or Money Demand
A change in national income, whatever the interest rate, shifts the money demand curve. Initially national income is Y_0; the money demand curve at that level of income is Md. At an interest rate of 9 percent, the quantity of money demanded is $600 billion. If income increases to Y_1, the money demand shifts to Md_1. Here $800 billion is demanded at 9 percent. If income falls to Y_2, the money demand curve falls to Md_2, where $400 billion is demanded at 9 percent.

Part III / Macroeconomic Policy

increases from Md to Md_1. If income falls from Y_0 to Y_2, money demand falls from Md to Md_2. When the money demand function shifts from Md to Md_1, the quantity of money demanded at an interest rate of 9 percent increases from $600 billion to $800 billion. When the money demand function shifts from Md to Md_2, the quantity of money demanded at 9 percent interest falls from $600 billion to $400 billion.

1.a.2. The Money Supply Function
The Federal Reserve is responsible for setting the money supply. The fact that the Fed can choose the money supply means that the money supply function is independent of the current interest rate and income. Figure 3 illustrates the money supply function (Ms). In the figure, the money supply is $600 billion at all interest rate levels. If the Fed increases the money supply, the vertical money supply function shifts to the right. If the Fed decreases the money supply, the function shifts to the left.

1.a.3. Equilibrium in the Money Market
To find the equilibrium interest rate and quantity of money, we have to combine the money demand and money supply functions in one diagram. Figure 4 graphs equilibrium in the money market. Equilibrium, point e, is at the intersection of the money demand and money supply functions. In the figure the equilibrium interest rate is 9 percent and the quantity of money is $600 billion.

The money supply is set by the Federal Reserve. As the supply of money changes, the equilibrium interest rate changes. Why? Look at Figure 4 again. If the interest rate falls below 9 percent, there would be an excess demand for money. People would want more money than the Fed is supplying. But because the supply of money does not change, the demand for more money just forces the interest rate to rise. How? Suppose people try to increase their money holdings by converting bonds into money. As bonds and other nonmonetary assets are sold for money, the interest rate goes up.

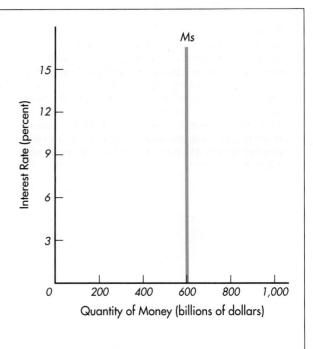

Figure 3
The Money Supply Function
The money supply function is a vertical line. This indicates that the Fed can choose any money supply it wants independent of the interest rate (and national income). In the Figure, the money supply is set at $600 billion at all interest rates. The Fed can increase or decrease the money supply, shifting the curve to the right or left, but the curve remains vertical.

To understand the connection between the rate of interest and buying and selling bonds, you must realize that the current interest rate (yield) on a bond is determined by the bond price:

$$\text{Current interest rate} = \frac{\text{annual interest payment}}{\text{bond price}}$$

The numerator, the annual interest payment, is fixed for the life of the bond. The denominator, the bond price, fluctuates with supply and demand. As the bond price changes, the interest rate changes.

Suppose a bond pays $100 a year in interest and sells for $1,000. The interest rate is 10 percent ($100/$1,000). If the supply of bonds increases because people want to convert bonds to money, the price of bonds falls. Suppose the price drops to $800. At that price the interest rate equals 12.5 percent ($100/$800). This is the mechanism by which an excess demand for money changes the interest rate. As the interest rate goes up, the excess demand for money disappears.

Just the opposite occurs at interest rates above equilibrium. In Figure 4, any rate of interest above 9 percent creates an excess supply of money. Now people are holding more of their wealth in the form of money than they would like. What happens? They want to convert some of their money balances into nonmonetary assets, like bonds. As the demand for bonds rises, bond prices increase. And as bond prices go up, interest rates fall. This drop in interest rates restores equilibrium in the money market.

1.b. Money and Equilibrium Income

How does monetary policy affect the equilibrium level of national income?

Now we are ready to relate monetary policy to the equilibrium level of national income. We use Figure 5 to show how a change in the money supply affects national income. In part (a), as the money supply increases from Ms_1 to Ms_2, the equilibrium rate of interest falls from i_1 to i_2.

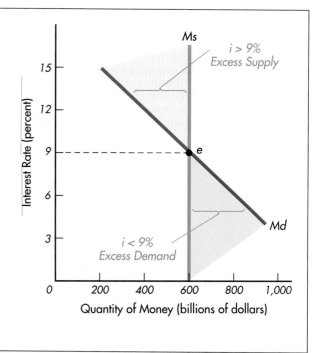

Figure 4
Equilibrium in the Money Market
Equilibrium is at point e, where the money demand and money supply curves intersect. At equilibrium, the interest rate is 9 percent and the money supply is $600 billion. An interest rate above 9 percent would create an excess supply of money because the quantity of money demanded falls as the interest rate rises. An interest rate below 9 percent would create an excess demand for money because the quantity of money demanded rises as the interest rate falls.

Part III / Macroeconomic Policy

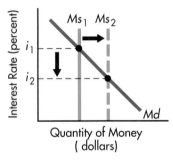

(a) Money Supply Increases and Interest Rate Falls

(b) Investment Spending Increases

(c) Aggregate Demand and Equilibrium Income Increase

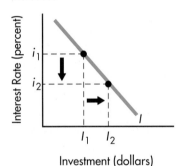

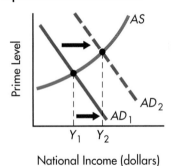

Figure 5
Monetary Policy and Equilibrium Income
The three diagrams show the sequence of events by which a change in the money supply affects the equilibrium level of national income. In part (a), the money supply increases, lowering the equilibrium interest rate. In part (b), the lower interest rate pushes the equilibrium level of investment up. In part (c), the increase in investment increases aggregate demand and equilibrium national income.

An excess supply of (demand for) money can increase (decrease) consumption as well as investment.

Remember that investment is a negative function of the rate of interest (Chapter 9). The interest rate is the cost of borrowed funds. As the interest rate rises, the return on investment falls and with it the level of investment. As the interest rate falls, the return on investment rises and with it the level of investment. In part (a) of Figure 5, the interest rate falls. In part (b) of the figure you can see the effect of the lower interest rate on investment spending. As the interest rate falls from i_1 to i_2, investment increases from I_1 to I_2.

Figure 5(c) is the aggregate demand and supply equilibrium diagram. When investment spending increases, aggregate expenditures are higher at every price level, so the aggregate demand curve shifts to the right, from AD_1 to AD_2. The increase in aggregate demand increases equilibrium income from Y_1 to Y_2.

How does monetary policy affect equilibrium income? As the money supply increases, the equilibrium interest rate falls. As the interest rate falls, the equilibrium level of investment rises. Increased investment increases aggregate demand and equilibrium income. A decrease in the money supply works in reverse: as the interest rate rises, investment falls; as investment falls, aggregate demand and equilibrium income go down.

The mechanism we have just described is an oversimplification because the only element of aggregate expenditures that changes is investment. An excess demand for or supply of money involves more than simply selling or buying bonds. An excess supply of money probably would be reflected in increased consumption as well. If households are holding more money than they want to hold, they buy not only bonds but also goods and services. If they are holding less money than they want to hold, they will sell bonds and consume less. So the effect of monetary policy on aggregate demand is a product of a change in both investment and consumption. We discuss this in Chapter 15, where we also examine the important role expected policy changes can play.

RECAP

1. The transactions demand for money is a demand to hold money to buy goods and services.

2. The precautionary demand for money exists because all expenditures cannot be planned.

3. The speculative demand for money is created by uncertainty about the value of other assets.

4. There is an inverse relationship between the interest rate and the quantity of money demanded.

5. The greater nominal income, the greater the demand for money.

6. Because the Federal Reserve sets the money supply, the money supply function is independent of the interest rate and nominal income.

7. The current yield on a bond equals the annual interest payment divided by the price of the bond.

8. An increase in the money supply lowers the interest rate, which raises the level of investment, which in turn increases aggregate demand and equilibrium income. A decrease in the money supply works in reverse.

2. THE FEDERAL RESERVE SYSTEM

The Federal Reserve is the central bank of the United States. A *central bank* performs several functions: accepting deposits from and making loans to commercial banks, acting as a banker for the federal government, and controlling the money supply. We discuss these functions in greater detail below, but first we look at the structure of the Federal Reserve System, or the Fed.

2.a. Structure of the Fed

Congress created the Federal Reserve System in 1913, with the Federal Reserve Act. Bank panics and failures had convinced lawmakers that the United States needed an agency to control the money supply and make loans to commercial banks when those banks found themselves without sufficient reserves. Because Americans tended to distrust large banking interests, Congress called for a decentralized central bank. The Federal Reserve System divides the nation into 12 districts, each with its own Federal Reserve bank (Figure 6).

2.a.1. Board of Governors
Although Congress created a decentralized system so that each district bank would represent the special interests of its own region, in practice the Fed is much more centralized than its creators intended. Monetary policy is largely set by the Board of Governors in Washington, D.C. The board is made up of seven members, who are appointed by the president and confirmed by the Senate.

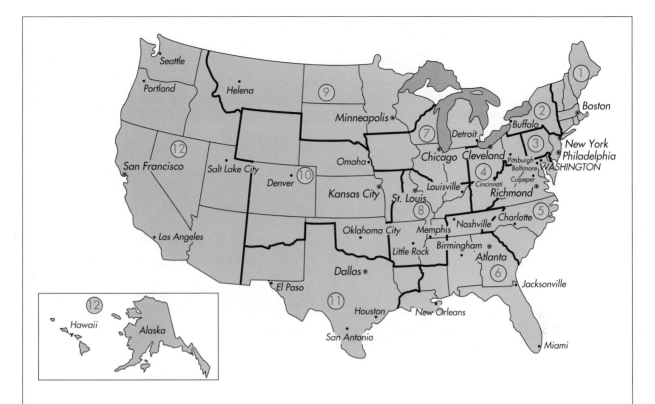

Figure 6
The Federal Reserve System
The Federal Reserve System divides the country into 12 districts. Each district has its own Federal Reserve bank, headquarters for Fed operations in that district. For example, the First District bank is in Boston; the Twelfth is in San Francisco. There also are branch banks in Los Angeles, Miami, and other cities. Source: *Federal Reserve Bulletin* (Washington, D.C.)

The most visible and powerful member of the board is the chairman. In fact the chairman of the Board of Governors has been called *the second most powerful person in the United States*. This individual serves as a leader and spokesperson for the board, and typically exercises more authority in determining the course of monetary policy than do the other governors.

The chairman is appointed by the president to a four-year term, although in recent years most chairmen have been reappointed (Table 1).

Table 1 Recent Chairmen of the Federal Reserve Board

Name	Age at Appointment	Term Begins	Term Ends	Years of Tenure
William McChesney Martin	44	4/2/51	1/31/70	18.8
Arthur Burns	65	1/31/70	2/1/78	8.0
G. William Miller	52	3/8/78	8/6/79	1.4
Paul Volcker	51	8/6/79	8/5/87	8.0
Alan Greenspan	61	8/11/87		

The chairman of the Federal Reserve Board of Governors is sometimes referred to as the second most powerful person in the United States. At the time this book was written, Alan Greenspan was the Fed Chairman. His leadership of the Fed has important implications for money and credit conditions in the United States.

The governors serve fourteen-year terms, the terms staggered so that every two years a new position comes up for appointment. This system allows continuity in the policy-making process and places the board above politics. Congress created the Fed as an independent agency. Monetary policy is supposed to be formulated independent of Congress and the president. Of course this is impossible in practice because the president appoints and the Senate approves the members of the board. But because the governors serve fourteen-year terms, once appointed, they outlast the president who appointed them.

2.a.2. District Banks Each of the Fed's 12 district banks is formally directed by a nine-person board of directors. Three directors represent commercial banks in the district, and three represent nonbanking business interests. These six individuals are elected by the Federal Reserve System member banks in the district. The three remaining directors are appointed by the Fed's Board of Governors. District bank directors are not involved in the day-to-day operations of the district banks. Their primary function is choosing the president of the bank. The president, who is in charge of operations, participates in monetary policy making with the Board of Governors in Washington, D.C.

Federal Open Market Committee (FOMC):
the official policy-making body of the Federal Reserve System

2.a.3. The Federal Open Market Committee The **Federal Open Market Committee (FOMC)** is the official policy-making body of the Federal Reserve System. The committee is made up of the seven members of the Board of Governors plus five of the twelve district bank presidents. All of the district bank presidents, except for the president of the Federal Reserve Bank of New York, take turns serving on the FOMC. Because the New York Fed actually carries out monetary policy, that bank's president is always on the committee. In Section 3 we talk more about the FOMC's role and the tactics it uses.

What's on a Dollar Bill?

The figure shows both sides of a dollar bill. We've numbered several elements for identification.

1. Currency is issued by the Federal Reserve System. The top of a dollar bill used to say "SILVER CERTIFICATE" where it now says "FEDERAL RESERVE NOTE." Silver certificates could be exchanged for silver dollars or silver bullion at the U.S. Treasury. In 1967 Congress authorized the Treasury to stop redeeming silver certificates.

2. Every dollar bill indicates which Federal Reserve bank issued it. The stamp with the *F* in the middle reads "FEDERAL RESERVE BANK OF ATLANTA GEORGIA." *F* is the sixth letter of the alphabet, and the Atlanta Fed is headquarters for the sixth Federal Reserve District. Also the serial number begins with an *F*. Finally, there is a number 6 in each corner, again indicating that the bill was issued by the Sixth District bank.

3. The dollar is the legal money of the United States. Debts and tax obligations can be legally discharged with dollars.

4. *D231* is the number of the engraving plate used to print this dollar bill.

5. *D2*, which stands for row D, column 2, is the position on the sheet where this dollar was printed. Money is printed in large sheets, which are then cut to make individual bills.

6. There are several interesting features in the great seal. ANNUIT COEPTIS means "he has favored our undertakings." The eye represents an all-seeing deity. The pyramid stands for strength. NOVUS ORDO SECLORUM means a "new order of the ages." The Roman numerals at the bottom of the pyramid equal 1776.

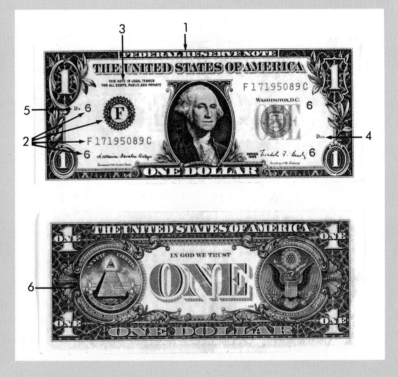

2.b. Functions of the Fed

> What does the Federal Reserve do?

The Federal Reserve System offers banking services to the banking community and the U.S. Treasury, and supervises the nation's banking system. The Fed also regulates the U.S. money supply.

2.b.1. Banking Services and Supervision The Fed provides several basic services to the banking community: it supplies currency to banks, holds their reserves, and clears checks. The Fed supplies U.S. currency

(Federal Reserve notes) to the banking community through its 12 district banks. Commercial banks in each district also hold reserves in the form of deposits at their district bank. In this sense, the Fed is a *banker's bank*. And the Fed clears checks, transferring funds to the banks where checks are deposited from the banks on which the checks are drawn.

The Fed also supervises the nation's banks, ensuring that they operate in a sound and prudent manner. And it acts as the banker for the U.S. government, selling U.S. government securities when the Treasury wants to borrow money to finance government spending.

2.b.2. Controlling the Money Supply All of the functions the Federal Reserve carries out are important, but none is more important than controlling the nation's money supply. Before the Fed was created, the money supply did not change to meet fluctuations in the demand for money. These fluctuations can stem from changes in income or seasonal patterns of demand. For example, every year during the Christmas season, the demand for currency rises because people carry more money to buy gifts. During the holiday season, the Fed increases the supply of currency to meet the demand for cash withdrawals from banks. After the holiday season, the demand for currency drops and the public deposits currency in banks, which then return the currency to the Fed.

The Fed controls the money supply to achieve the policy goals set by the FOMC. It does this largely through its reserve requirements and the money-creating power of commercial banks that we talked about in Chapter 13.

RECAP

1. As the central bank of the United States, the Fed accepts deposits from and makes loans to commercial banks, acts as a banker for the federal government, and controls the money supply.
2. The Federal Reserve System is made up of 12 district banks and the Board of Governors in Washington, D.C.
3. The most visible and powerful member of the Board of Governors is the chairman.
4. The governors are appointed by the president and confirmed by the Senate to serve fourteen-year terms.
5. Monetary policy is made by the FOMC, whose members include the seven governors and five district bank presidents.
6. The Fed provides currency, holds reserves, and clears checks; supervises commercial banks; and acts as the banker for the federal government.
7. The most important function the Fed performs is controlling the U.S. money supply.

3. IMPLEMENTING MONETARY POLICY

Changes in the amount of money in an economy affect the inflation rate, the interest rate, and the equilibrium level of national income. Monetary policy has made currencies worthless and toppled governments. This is why controlling the money supply is so important.

3.a. Policy Goals

The objective of monetary policy is economic growth with stable prices.

The ultimate goal of monetary policy is much like that of fiscal policy: economic growth with stable prices. *Economic growth* means greater output and consumption; *stable prices* means a low, steady rate of inflation, to reduce the uncertainty consumers face.

3.a.1. Intermediate Targets

The Fed does not control gross national product or the price level directly. Instead it controls the money supply, which in turn affects GNP and the level of prices. The money supply or the growth of the money supply is an **intermediate target**; it helps the Fed achieve its ultimate policy objective—economic growth with stable prices.

intermediate target:
an objective used to achieve some ultimate policy goal

Using the growth of the money supply as an intermediate target assumes there is a fairly stable relationship between changes in money and changes in income and prices. The bases for this assumption are the equation of exchange and the quantity theory of money. The **equation of exchange** relates the quantity of money to nominal GNP:

equation of exchange:
an equation that relates the quantity of money to nominal GNP

$$MV = PY$$

where

$$M = \text{the quantity of money}$$
$$V = \text{the velocity of money}$$
$$P = \text{the price level}$$
$$Y = \text{real income or real GNP}$$

velocity of money:
the average number of times each dollar is spent on final goods and services in a year

In Chapter 13 we said there are several definitions of the money supply: M1, M2, and M3. The **velocity of money** is the average number of times each dollar is spent on final goods and services in a year. If P is the price level and Y is real GNP (the quantity of goods and services produced in the economy), then PY equals nominal GNP. If

$$MV = PY$$

then

$$V = \frac{PY}{M}$$

Suppose the price level is 2 and real GNP is $500; *PY,* or nominal GNP, is $1,000. If the money supply is $200, then velocity is 5 ($1,000/$200). A velocity of 5 means that each dollar must be spent an average of 5 times during the year if a money supply of $200 is going to support the purchase of $1,000 worth of new goods and services.

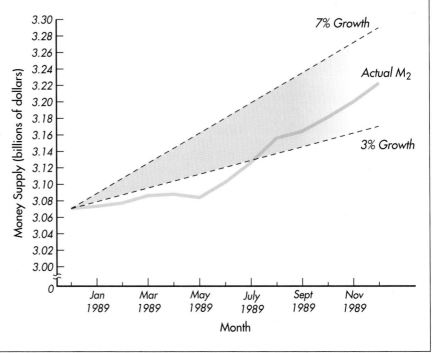

Figure 7
Targeted Versus Actual Growth in the M2 Money Supply, 1989
The Fed defines targeted growth in the money supply in terms of upper and lower bounds. These bounds define a region of acceptable growth shaped like a cone. In 1989 the M2 money supply moved from the bottom of the cone to below the cone, before heading back to the middle of the cone by the end of the year.

quantity theory of money:
with constant velocity, changes in the quantity of money change nominal GNP

How is monetary policy set?

The **quantity theory of money** relates changes in the money supply to changes in prices and output. If the money supply (*M*) increases and velocity (*V*) is constant, then nominal GNP *(PY)* must increase. If the economy is operating at maximum capacity (producing at the potential level of output), an increase in *M* causes an increase in *P*. And if there is substantial unemployment, the increase in *M* may mean a higher price level (*Y*) as well as higher real GNP (*P*).

The Fed attempts to set money growth targets that are consistent with rising output and low inflation. In terms of the quantity theory of money, the Fed wants to increase *M* at a rate that supports steadily rising *Y* with slow and steady increases in *P*. The assumption that there is a reasonably stable relationship among *M, P,* and *Y* is what motivates the Fed to use money growth rates as an intermediate target to achieve its ultimate goal—higher *Y* with slow increases in *P*.

The FOMC defines upper and lower bounds to describe its intermediate targets. Figure 7 shows that range and the actual growth of the M2 money supply in 1989. The targeted growth of the M2 money supply was between 3 and 7 percent. The broken lines at these growth rates create a cone that represents the region of growth targeted by the Fed. The solid line plots the actual path of the M2 money supply in 1989. If the M2 money supply grew at a rate of 7 percent over the year, the solid line would be up at the top of the cone. If it grew at 3 percent, the solid line would be at the bottom of the cone. By specifying an acceptable range of growth, the Fed gave itself more room to maneuver in dealing with unexpected events that might make managing the money supply difficult.

Figure 8
Velocity of the M1, M2, and M3 Money Supplies, 1959–1989
The velocity of money is the ratio of gross national product to the money supply. The narrower the definition of money, the higher its velocity. So M1, the narrowest definition, has a higher velocity than M2 or M3. In recent years, the velocity of M1 has been much less stable than the velocity of the broader money definitions.

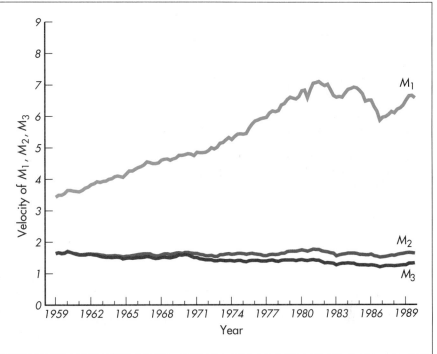

From the late 1950s to the mid-1970s, the velocity of the M1 money supply grew at a steady pace, from 3.5 in 1959 to 5.5 in 1975. Knowing that *V* was growing at a steady pace, the Fed was able to set a target growth rate for the M1 money supply, confident that it would produce a fairly predictable growth in nominal GNP. But when velocity is not constant, there can be problems using money growth rates as an intermediate target. This is exactly what happened in the late 1970s and early 1980s. Figure 8 plots the velocity of the M1, M2, and M3 money supplies from 1959 to 1989. Although the M2 and M3 velocities continued to indicate a stable pattern of growth, M1 velocity behaved erratically. With the breakdown of the relationship between the M1 money supply and GNP, the Fed shifted its emphasis from the M1 money supply, concentrating instead on achieving targeted growth in the M2 and M3 money supplies.

Economists are still debating the reason for the fluctuations in the velocity of the M1 money supply. Some argue that new deposits and innovations in banking led to fluctuations in the money held in traditional demand deposits. These changes would affect the M1 supply because its definition is so narrow. They would not affect the M2 and M3 supplies because their broader definitions include many of the new types of financial products available to the public.

In addition to targeting money growth, the Fed monitors other key variables that are used to indicate the future course of the economy. These include commodity prices, interest rates, and foreign exchange rates. Notice that the Fed simply *monitors* these variables. It does not set formal targets for them; but considers them in setting policy.

3.b. Operating Procedures

The FOMC sets monetary targets and then implements them through the Federal Reserve Bank of New York. The mechanism for translating policy into action is an **FOMC directive**. Each directive outlines the conduct of monetary policy over the six- to eight-week period until the FOMC meets again to adjust monetary targets and specify policy tools.

▼ What are the tools of
monetary policy?
▲

3.b.1. Tools of Monetary Policy

The Fed controls the money supply by changing bank reserves. There are three tools the Fed can use to change reserves: the reserve requirement, the discount rate, and open market operations. In the last chapter, you saw that banks can expand the money supply by a multiple of their excess reserves—the deposit expansion multiplier, the reciprocal of the reserve requirement.

Reserve requirement The Fed requires banks to hold a fraction of their deposits on reserve. This fraction is the reserve requirement. Table 2 lists the reserve requirements in effect in February 1990. Notice that the requirements are different for different types and sizes of deposits. *Transaction deposits* are checking accounts and other deposits that can be used to pay third parties. Large banks hold a greater percentage of deposits in reserve than do small banks (the reserve requirement increases from 3 to 12 percent for deposits in excess of $40.5 million). *Nonpersonal time deposits* are time deposits held by business firms. In February 1990, these deposits had a 3 percent reserve requirement if they matured in less than 18 months. For longer-term deposits, there was no reserve requirement. This is because it is unlikely that banks would face surprising changes in long-term deposits that would leave them short of reserves. Finally, Eurocurrency deposits—time deposits offered by U.S. international banking facilities—had a 3 percent reserve requirement.

Remember that required reserves are the dollar amount of reserves that a bank must hold to meet its reserve requirement. The sum of a bank's *vault cash* (coin and currency in the bank's vault) and deposit in the Fed is called its **legal reserves**. When legal reserves equal required reserves, the bank has no excess reserves and can make no new loans. When legal reserves exceed required reserves, the bank has excess reserves available for lending.

legal reserves:
the cash a bank holds in its vault plus its deposit in the Fed

Table 2 Reserve Requirements for U.S. Depository Institutions, February 1990

Type of Deposit	Percent of Deposits
Transaction deposits	
0–$40.5 million	3
over $40.5 million	12
Nonpersonal time deposits	
Mature in less than 1½ years	3
Mature in 1½ years or more	0
Eurocurrency deposits	3

Source: *Federal Reserve Bulletin* (Washington, D.C.), February 1990, p. A8.

As bank reserves change, the lending and money-creating potential of the banking system changes. One way the Fed can alter bank reserves is by changing the reserve requirement. If it lowers the reserve requirement, a portion of what was previously required reserves becomes excess reserves, which can be used to make loans and expand the money supply. By raising the reserve requirement, the Fed reduces the money-creating potential of the banking system and tends to reduce the money supply.

Consider the example in Table 3. If First National Bank's balance sheet shows vault cash of $100,000 and a deposit in the Fed of $200,000, the bank has legal reserves of $300,000. The amount of money that the bank can loan is determined by its excess reserves. Excess reserves (ER) equal legal reserves (LR) minus required reserves (RR):

$$ER = LR - RR$$

If the reserve requirement (r) is 10 percent (.10), the bank must keep 10 percent of its deposits (D) as required reserves:

$$RR = rD$$
$$= .10 \ (\$1,000,000)$$
$$= \$100,000$$

In this case, the bank has excess reserves of $200,000 ($300,000 − $100,000). The bank can make a maximum loan of $200,000. The banking system can expand the money supply by the deposit expansion multiplier ($1/r$) times the excess reserves of the bank, or $2,000,000 ($1/.10 \times$ $200,000).

If the reserve requirement goes up to 20 percent (.20), required reserves are 20 percent of $1,000,000, or $200,000. Excess reserves are now $100,000, which is the maximum loan the bank can make. The banking system can expand the money supply by $500,000:

$$\frac{1}{.20}(\$100,000) = 5(\$100,000)$$
$$= \$500,000$$

By raising the reserve requirement, the Fed can reduce the money-creating potential of the banking system and the money supply. And by lowering the reserve requirement, the Fed can increase the money-creating potential of the banking system and the money supply.

Discount rate   If a bank needs more reserves in order to make new loans, it typically borrows from other banks in the federal funds market. (The market is called the *federal funds market* because the funds are being loaned from one commercial bank's excess reserves on deposit with the Federal Reserve to another commercial bank's deposit account at the Fed.) When a bank borrows in the federal funds market, it pays a rate of interest called the **federal funds rate**.

At times, however, banks borrow directly from the Fed, although the Fed restricts access to such funds. The **discount rate** is the rate of interest the Fed charges banks. (In other countries, the rate of interest the central bank charges commercial banks often is called the *bank rate*.) Another way the Fed controls the level of bank reserves and the money supply is by changing the discount rate.

federal funds rate:
the interest rate a bank charges when it lends excess reserves to another bank

discount rate:
the interest rate the Fed charges commercial banks

Table 3 The Effect of a Change in the Reserve Requirement

Balance Sheet of First National Bank			

Assets		**Liabilities**	
Vault cash	$ 100,000	Deposits	$1,000,000
Deposit in Fed	200,000		
Loans	700,000		
Total	$1,000,000	Total	$1,000,000

Legal reserves (LR) equal vault cash plus the deposit in the Fed, or $300,000:

$LR = \$100,000 + \$200,000$
  $= \$300,000$

Excess reserves (ER) equal legal reserves minus required reserves (RR):

$ER = LR - RR$

Required reserves equal the reserve requirement (r) times deposits (D):

$RR = rD$

If the reserve requirement is 10 percent:

$RR = (.10)(\$1,000,000)$
  $= \$100,000$

$ER = \$300,000 - \$100,000$
  $= \$200,000$

First National Bank can make a maximum loan of $200,000.

The banking system can expand the money supply by the deposit expansion multiplier ($1/r$) times the excess reserves of the bank or $2,000,000:

$(1/.10)(\$200,000) = 10(\$200,000)$
                  $= \$2,000,000$

If the reserve requirement is 20 percent:

$RR = (.20)(\$1,000,000)$
  $= \$200,000$

$ER = \$300,000 - \$200,000$
  $= \$100,000$

First National Bank can make a maximum loan of $100,000.

The banking system can expand the money supply by the deposit expansion multiplier ($1/r$) times the excess reserves of the bank or $500,000:

$(1/.20)(\$100,000) = 5(\$100,000)$
                  $= \$500,000$

Table 4 Federal Reserve Discount Rates, January 1978–February 1989

Date	Discount Rate (percent)	Date	Discount Rate (percent)
January 9, 1978	6.50	November 2, 1981	13.00
May 11, 1978	7.00	December 4, 1981	12.00
July 3, 1978	7.25	July 20, 1982	11.50
August 21, 1978	7.75	August 2, 1982	11.50
September 22, 1978	8.00	August 16, 1982	10.50
October 16, 1978	8.50	August 27, 1982	10.00
November 1, 1978	9.50	October 12, 1982	9.50
July 20, 1979	10.00	November 22, 1982	9.00
August 17, 1979	10.50	December 15, 1982	8.50
September 19, 1979	11.00	April 9, 1984	9.00
October 8, 1979	12.00	November 21, 1984	8.50
February 15, 1980	13.00	December 24, 1984	8.00
May 30, 1980	12.00	May 20, 1985	7.50
June 13, 1980	11.00	March 7, 1986	7.00
July 28, 1980	10.00	April 21, 1986	6.50
September 26, 1980	11.00	July 11, 1986	6.00
November 17, 1980	12.00	August 21, 1986	5.50
December 5, 1980	13.00	September 4, 1987	6.00
May 5, 1981	14.00	August 9, 1988	6.50
		February 24, 1989	7.00

Source: *Federal Reserve Bulletin* (Washington, D.C.), February 1990, p. A7.

When the Fed raises the discount rate, it raises the cost of borrowing reserves, reducing the amount of reserves borrowed. Lower levels of reserves limit bank lending and the expansion of the money supply. When the Fed lowers the discount rate, it lowers the cost of borrowing reserves, increasing the amount of borrowing. As bank reserves increase, so do loans and the money supply.

The discount rate is relatively stable. While other interest rates can fluctuate daily, the discount rate usually remains fixed for months at a time. Table 4 lists the discount rate over recent years. At most the rate has changed seven times in a year.

open market operations:
the buying and selling of government bonds by the Fed to control bank reserves and the money supply

Open market operations The major tool of monetary policy is the Fed's **open market operations**, the buying and selling of government bonds. Suppose the FOMC wants to increase bank reserves to stimulate the growth of money. The committee issues a directive to the bond-trading desk at the Federal Reserve Bank of New York to buy bonds. The bonds are purchased from private bond dealers. The dealers are paid with checks drawn on the Federal Reserve, which then are deposited in the dealers' accounts at commercial banks. What happens? As bank deposits and reserves increase, banks are able to make new loans, which in turn expand the money supply through the deposit expansion multiplier process.

Table 5 The Effect of an Open Market Operation

Balance Sheet of First National Bank				
Assets			**Liabilities**	
Vault cash	$ 100,000		Deposits	$1,000,000
Deposit in Fed	200,000			
Loans	700,000			
Total	$1,000,000		Total	$1,000,000

Initially legal reserves (LR) equal vault cash plus the deposit in the Fed, or $300,000:

$$LR = \$100,000 + \$200,000$$
$$= \$300,000$$

If the reserve requirement (r) is 20 percent (.20), required reserves (RR) equal $200,000:

$$.20(\$1,000,000) = \$200,000$$

Excess reserves (ER), then, equal $100,000 ($300,000 − $200,000). The bank can make a maximum loan of $100,000. The banking system can expand the money supply by the deposit expansion multiplier (1/r) times the excess reserves of the bank, or $500,000:

$$(1/.20)(\$100,000) = 5(\$100,000)$$
$$= \$500,000$$

Open market purchase:

The Fed purchases $100,000 worth of bonds from a dealer, who deposits the $100,000 in an account at First National. At this point the bank has legal reserves of $400,000, required reserves of $220,000, and excess reserves of $180,000. It can make a maximum loan of $180,000, which can expand the money supply by $900,000 [(1/.20)($180,000)].

Open market sale:

The Fed sells $100,000 worth of bonds to a dealer, who pays with a check drawn on an account at First National. At this point, the bank has legal reserves of $200,000, required reserves of $180,000 (its deposits now equal $900,000), and excess reserves of $20,000. It can make a maximum loan of $20,000, which can expand the money supply by $100,000 [(1/.20)($20,000)].

To increase the money supply, the Fed buys bonds. To decrease the money supply, it sells bonds.

If the Fed wants to decrease the money supply, it sells bonds. Private bond dealers pay for the bonds with checks drawn on commercial banks. Commercial bank deposits and reserves drop, and the money supply decreases through the deposit expansion multiplier process.

Its open market operations allow the Fed to control the money supply. To increase the money supply, the Fed buys bonds. To decrease the money supply, it sells bonds.

The effect of open market operations assumes that there are no excess reserves in the banking system. If there are excess reserves, the money supply does not necessarily decrease when the Fed sells bonds. The open market sale may simply reduce the level of excess reserves, reducing the rate at which the money supply increases.

Table 5 shows how open market operations change bank reserves and the money-creating power of the banking system. First National Bank's initial balance sheet shows excess reserves of $100,000 with a 20 percent reserve requirement. Therefore the bank can make a maximum loan of $100,000. Based on the bank's reserve position, the banking system can increase the money supply by a maximum of $500,000.

If the Fed purchases $100,000 worth of bonds from a private dealer, who deposits the $100,000 in an account at First National Bank, the excess reserves of First National Bank increase to $180,000. These reserves can generate a maximum increase in the money supply of $900,000. The open market purchase increases the excess reserves of the banking system, stimulating the growth of money and, eventually, nominal GNP.

What happens when an open market sale takes place? If the Fed sells $100,000 worth of bonds to a private bond dealer, the dealer pays for the bonds using a check drawn on First National Bank. First National's deposits drop from $1,000,000 to $900,000, and its legal reserves drop from $300,000 to $200,000. With excess reserves of $20,000, the banking system can only increase the money supply by $100,000. The open market sale reduces the money-creating potential of the banking system from $500,000 initially to $100,000.

3.b.2. FOMC Directives

When it sets monetary policy, the FOMC begins with its *ultimate goal:* economic growth at stable prices. It defines that goal in terms of GNP. Then it works backwards to identify its *intermediate target,* the rate at which the money supply must grow to achieve the wanted growth in GNP. Then it must decide how to achieve its intermediate target. In Figure 9, as is usually the case in real life, the Fed uses open market operations. But to know whether it should buy or sell bonds, the FOMC must have some indication of whether the money supply is growing too fast or too slow. The committee relies on a *short-run operating target* for this information. The short-run target indicates how the money supply should react to a change in the short-run target. Both the quantity of excess reserves in the banking system and the federal funds rate can serve as short-run operating targets.

Figure 9
Monetary Policy: Tools, Targets, and Goals
The Fed primarily uses open market operations to implement monetary policy. The decision to buy or sell bonds is based on a short-run operating target, like the level of reserves held by commercial banks. The short-run operating target is set to achieve an intermediate target, a certain level of money supply. The intermediate target is set to achieve the ultimate goal, a certain level of gross national product.

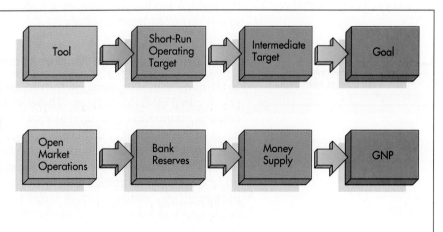

The FOMC carries out its policies through directives to the bond-trading desk at the Federal Reserve Bank of New York. The directives specify a short-run operating target that the trading desk must use in its day-to-day operations. When the FOMC first began setting intermediate monetary targets in 1970, it attempted to prescribe very specific target ranges for the federal funds rate. The committee chose the federal funds rate as the short-run target because it believed the rate was the best indicator of the status of reserves. Because the federal funds rate is the interest rate one bank charges another when the second bank borrows reserves from the first, the federal funds rate rises when there are few excess reserves and falls when the banking system has a large amount of excess reserves. The Fed believed that if the federal funds rate rose above the FOMC's target, it would indicate that there were not enough reserves in the banking system, that the money supply was not growing fast enough. The bond-trading desk would then purchase bonds from bond dealers.

In the 1970s, the federal funds rate worked well to stabilize interest rates, but it caused the money supply to fluctuate a great deal more than the FOMC wanted. For example, when people were spending at a rapid pace and so borrowing increasing amounts of money, the banking system's reserves fell and the federal funds rate rose. The rising rate signalled the trading desk to purchase bonds and increase reserves. These reserves were immediately lent, and the money supply grew more quickly. As long as the federal funds rate continued to go up, new reserves were being pumped into the banking system and the money supply grew faster and faster. Conversely, when people were not spending and excess reserves accumulated, the trading desk sold bonds, the money supply fell and continued to fall as long as the federal funds rate was below the target range.

By the fall of 1979, the FOMC had decided that it needed a better indicator of money supply growth for its short-run operating target. The committee chose bank reserves. FOMC directives now phrase their short-run operating targets in terms of the level of bank reserves.

The nature of the Fed's policy regarding reserve targeting has changed over time. In addition, the Fed takes other factors into account. For example, FOMC directives still cite a wanted range for the federal funds rate, but the range is much broader than it was in the days of targeting interest rates. The directives also cite real GNP growth, the rate of inflation, and the foreign exchange value of the dollar, factors that could affect the FOMC-targeted bank reserves.

3.c. Foreign Exchange Market Intervention

What role do central banks play in the foreign exchange market?

In the mid-1980s, conditions in the foreign exchange market took on a high priority in FOMC directives. There was concern that the value of the dollar in relation to other currencies was contributing to a large U.S. international trade deficit. Furthermore, the governments of the major industrial countries decided to work together to maintain more stable exchange rates. This meant that the Federal Reserve and the central banks of the other developed countries had to devote more attention to maintaining exchange rates within a certain target band of values, much as the federal funds rate had been targeted in the 1970s.

Figure 10
The Dollar-Yen Foreign Exchange Market
The demand is the demand for dollars arising out of the Japanese demand for U.S. goods and services. The supply is the supply of dollars arising out of the U.S. demand for Japanese goods and services. Initially, the equilibrium exchange rate is at the intersection of the demand curve (D_1) and the supply curve (S_1), where the exchange rate is ¥150 = $1. An increase in the U.S. demand for Japanese goods increases S_1 to S_2 and pushes the equilibrium exchange rate down to point B, where ¥130 = $1. If the Fed's target exchange rate is ¥150 = $1, the Fed must intervene, buying dollars in the foreign exchange market. This increases demand to D_2 and raises the equilibrium exchange rate to point C, where ¥150 = $1.

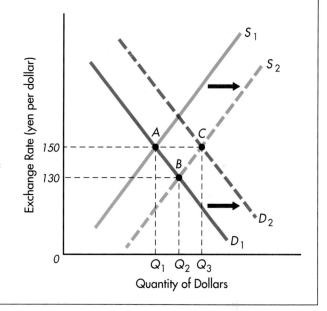

foreign exchange market intervention: the buying and selling of foreign exchange by a central bank to move exchange rates up or down to a targeted level

3.c.1. Mechanics of Intervention Foreign exchange market intervention is the buying and selling of foreign exchange by a central bank in order to move exchange rates up or down. We can use a simple supply and demand diagram to illustrate the role of intervention. Figure 10 shows the U.S. dollar–Japanese yen exchange market. The demand curve is the demand for dollars produced by the demand for U.S. goods and financial assets. The supply curve is the supply of dollars generated by U.S. residents' demand for the products and financial assets of other countries. Here, the supply of dollars to the dollar-yen market comes from the U.S. demand to buy Japanese products.

The initial equilibrium exchange rate is at point A, where the demand curve (D_1) and the supply curve (S_1) intersect. At point A, the exchange rate is ¥150 = $1 and Q_1 dollars are exchanged for yen. Suppose that over time, U.S. residents buy more from Japan than Japanese residents buy from the United States. As the supply of dollars increases in relation to the demand for dollars, equilibrium shifts to point B. At point B, Q_2 dollars are exchanged at a rate of ¥130 = $1. The dollar has *depreciated* against the yen, or, conversely, the yen has *appreciated* against the dollar.

When the dollar depreciates, U.S. goods are cheaper to Japanese buyers (it takes fewer yen to buy each dollar). The depreciated dollar stimulates U.S. exports to Japan. It also raises the price of Japanese goods to U.S. buyers, reducing U.S. imports from Japan. Rather than allow exchange rates to change with the subsequent changes in trade, central banks often seek to maintain fixed exchange rates because of international agreements or desired trade in goods or financial assets.

Suppose the Fed sets a target range for the dollar at a minimum exchange rate of ¥150 = $1. If the exchange rate falls below the minimum, the Fed must intervene in the foreign exchange market to increase the

An FOMC Directive

At the conclusion of the FOMC meeting held November 14, 1989, the following policy directive was issued to the Federal Reserve Bank of New York:

The information reviewed at this meeting suggests continuing expansion in economic activity, though at a somewhat slower pace than earlier in the year. . . .

Most interest rates have declined appreciably since the Committee meeting on October 3. In foreign exchange markets, the trade-weighted value of the dollar in terms of the other G–10 currencies declined slightly on balance over the intermeeting period.

M2 continued to grow fairly briskly in October, largely reflecting strength in its M1 and other liquid components; thus far this year M2 has expanded at a pace somewhat below the midpoint of the Committee's annual range. Growth of M3 picked up in October but has remained much more restrained than that of M2, as assets of thrift institutions and their associated funding needs apparently continued to contract; for the year to date, M3 has grown at a rate around the lower bound of the Committee's annual range.

The Federal Open Market Committee seeks monetary and financial conditions that will foster price stability, promote growth in output on a sustainable basis, and contribute to an improved pattern of international transactions. In furtherance of these objectives, the Committee at its meeting in July reaffirmed the ranges it had established in February for growth of M2 and M3 of 3 to 7 percent and 3½ to 7½ percent, respectively, measured from the fourth quarter of 1988 to the fourth quarter of 1989. . . .

In the implementation of policy for the immediate future, the Committee seeks to maintain the existing degree of pressure on reserve positions. Taking account of progress toward price stability, the strength of the business expansion, the behavior of the monetary aggregates, and developments in foreign exchange and domestic financial markets, slightly greater reserve restraint might or slightly lesser reserve restraint would be acceptable in the intermeeting period. The contemplated reserve conditions are expected to be consistent with growth of M2 and M3 over the period from September through December at annual rates of about 7½ and 4½ percent, respectively. The Chairman may call for Committee consultation if it appears to the Manager for Domestic Operations that reserve conditions during the period before the next meeting are likely to be associated with a federal funds rate persistently outside a range of 7 to 11 percent. . . .

Notice that the directive sets targets for money growth and "seeks to maintain the existing degree of pressure on reserve positions," taking account of inflation, business expansion, money growth, and foreign exchange and domestic financial markets — all factors that could affect the growth of bank reserves. Notice also that if the federal funds rate should move outside the 7 to 11 percent range, the FOMC may be consulted.

■ Source: Excerpted from *Federal Reserve Bulletin* (Washington, D.C.), February 1990, pp. 59–60.

value of the dollar. In Figure 10, you can see that the only way to increase the dollar's value is to increase the demand for dollars. The Fed intervenes in the foreign exchange market by buying dollars in exchange for yen. It uses its holdings of Japanese yen to purchase $Q_3 - Q_1$ dollars, shifting the demand curve to D_2. Now equilibrium is at point C, where Q_3 dollars are exchanged at the rate of ¥150 = $1.

The kind of intervention shown in Figure 10 is only temporary because the Fed has a limited supply of yen. Under another intervention plan, the Bank of Japan would support the ¥150 = $1 exchange rate by using yen to buy dollars. The Bank of Japan could carry on this kind of policy indefinitely because it has the power to create yen. A third alternative is *coor-*

Coordinated intervention involves more than one central bank in attempts to shift the equilibrium exchange rate.

dinated intervention, in which both the Fed and the Bank of Japan sell yen in exchange for dollars to support the minimum yen-dollar exchange rate.

A famous example of coordinated intervention occurred in September 1985. The "Group of 5" or G–5 countries—the United States, France, Japan, the United Kingdom, and West Germany—issued a joint policy statement aimed at reducing the foreign exchange value of the dollar in the face of mounting concern over the size of the U.S. trade deficit. Even before official sales of the dollar began, the dollar started to depreciate as participants in the foreign exchange market reacted to the announcement. In other words, the free market supply of dollars increased and the free market demand for dollars decreased because traders did not want to be holding dollars when the central banks started selling. The Federal Reserve (along with the U.S. Treasury) sold more than $3 billion during the period of intervention that followed. The central banks of France, Japan, the United Kingdom, and West Germany, combined, sold approximately $5 billion.

3.c.2. Effects of Intervention Intervention can be used to shift the demand and supply for currency and thereby change the exchange rate. Foreign exchange market intervention also has effects on the money supply. If the Federal Reserve wanted to increase the dollar price of the French franc, it would create dollars to purchase francs. When foreign exchange market intervention involves the use of domestic currency to buy foreign currency, it increases the domestic money supply. The expansionary effect of the intervention can be offset by a domestic open market operation, in a process called **sterilization**. If the Fed creates dollars to buy French francs, it increases the money supply. To reduce the money supply, the Fed can direct an open market bond sale. The bond sale sterilizes the effect of the intervention on the domestic money supply.

sterilization:
the use of domestic open market operations to offset the effects of a foreign exchange market intervention on the domestic money supply

RECAP

1. The ultimate goal of monetary policy is economic growth with stable prices.

2. The Fed controls GNP indirectly, through its control of the money supply.

3. The equation of exchange ($MV = PY$) relates the quantity of money to nominal GNP.

4. The quantity theory of money states that with constant velocity, changes in the quantity of money change nominal GNP.

5. Every six to eight weeks, the Federal Open Market Committee issues a directive to the Federal Reserve Bank of New York that defines the FOMC's monetary targets and policy tools.

6. The Fed controls the nation's money supply by changing bank reserves.

7. The tools of monetary policy are reserve requirements, the discount rate, and open market operations.

8. The money supply tends to increase (decrease) as the reserve requirement falls (rises), the discount rate falls (rises), and the Fed buys (sells) bonds.

9. Each FOMC directive defines its short-run operating target in terms of bank reserves, but also considers the federal funds rate, the growth of real GNP, the rate of inflation, and the foreign exchange rate of the dollar.

10. Foreign exchange market intervention is the buying and selling of foreign exchange by a central bank to achieve a targeted exchange rate.

11. Sterilization is the use of domestic open market operations to offset the money supply effects of foreign exchange market intervention.

SUMMARY

▼▲ What are the determinants of the demand for money?

1. The demand for money stems from the need to buy goods and services, to prepare for and to retain a store of value. § 1.a

2. The money demand function is a negative function of the interest rate. § 1.a.1

3. The greater nominal income, the greater the demand for money. § 1.a.1

4. Because the Fed sets the money supply, the money supply function is independent of the interest rate and national income. § 1.a.2

▼▲ How does monetary policy affect the equilibrium level of national income?

5. By altering the money supply, the Fed changes the interest rate and the level of investment, shifting aggregate demand and the equilibrium level of national income. § 1.b

6. The Federal Reserve is the central bank of the United States. § 2

7. The Federal Reserve System is operated by 12 district banks and a Board of Governors in Washington, D.C. § 2.a

▼▲ What does the Federal Reserve do?

8. The Fed services and supervises the banking system, acts as the banker of the U.S. Treasury, and controls the money supply. § 2.b

9. The Fed's primary responsibility is controlling the nation's money supply. § 2.b.2

10. The Fed controls nominal GNP indirectly by controlling the quantity of money in the nation's economy. § 3.a.1

11. The Fed uses the growth of the money supply as an intermediate target, to help it achieve its ultimate goal—economic growth with stable prices. § 3.a.1

▼▲ How is monetary policy set?

12. The Federal Open Market Committee (FOMC) issues directives to the Federal Reserve Bank of New York outlining the conduct of monetary policy. § 3.b

▼▲ What are the tools of monetary policy?

13. The three tools of monetary policy are the reserve requirement, the discount rate, and open market operations. § 3.b.1

14. The Fed buys bonds to increase the money supply and sells bonds to decrease the money supply. § 3.b.1

▼▲ What role do central banks play in the foreign exchange market?

15. Central banks intervene in the foreign exchange market when it is necessary to maintain a targeted exchange rate. § 3.c

KEY TERMS

transactions demand for money § 1.a

precautionary demand for money § 1.a

speculative demand for money § 1.a

Federal Open Market Committee (FOMC) § 2.a.3

intermediate target § 3.a.1

equation of exchange § 3.a.1

velocity of money § 3.a.1

quantity theory of money § 3.a.1

FOMC directive § 3.b

legal reserves § 3.b.1

federal funds rate § 3.b.1

discount rate § 3.b.1

open market operations § 3.b.1

foreign exchange market intervention § 3.c.1

sterilization § 3.c.2

EXERCISES

Basic terms and concepts

1. Draw a graph showing equilibrium in the money market.

2. Using the graph you prepared for Exercise 1, illustrate and explain what happens when the Fed decreases the money supply.

3. When the Fed decreases the money supply, the equilibrium level of income changes. Illustrate and explain how.

4. The Federal Reserve System divides the nation into 12 districts.

   a. List the 12 cities where the district banks are located.

   b. Which Federal Reserve district do you live in?

5. Briefly describe the functions the Fed performs for the banking community.

6. Explain the quantity theory of money.

7. There are three tools the Fed uses to implement monetary policy.

   a. Briefly describe these tools.

   b. Explain how the Fed would use each tool in order to increase the money supply.

8. First Bank has total deposits of $2,000,000 and legal reserves of $220,000.

   a. If the reserve requirement is 10 percent, what is the maximum loan that First Bank can make and what is the maximum increase in the money supply based on First Bank's reserve position?

   b. If the reserve requirement is changed to 5 percent, how much can First Bank loan and how much can the money supply be expanded?

Extended concepts

9. Suppose you are a member of the FOMC. Write a directive to the New York Fed about the conduct of monetary policy over the next two months. Your directive should address targets for the rate of growth of the M2 and M3 money supplies, the federal funds rate, the rate of inflation, and the foreign exchange value of the dollar versus the Japanese yen and German mark. You may refer to the *Federal Reserve Bulletin* for examples, since this publication reports FOMC directives.

10. Suppose the Fed has a target range for the yen-dollar exchange rate. How would it keep the exchange rate within the target range if free market forces push the exchange rate out of the range? Use a graph to help explain your answer.

Federal Reserve Sees a Way to Gauge Long-Run Inflation

When the Federal Reserve lowered interest rates last week, after having pushed them up for a year, it felt free to act in part because of reassurances provided by a new theory for predicting inflation over the long run.

The Fed has never had such a tool, and if the theory proves itself over time, it will help the Fed avoid overreacting in the face of big economic surprises like a surge in oil prices or a drought that drives up food prices.

The theory is something that the Fed chairman, Alan Greenspan, has sought for 30 years. It rests on a new calculation of . . . velocity — the speed with which money changes hands in the economy. It provides a means of measuring the long-term impact on inflation of changes the Fed makes in the nation's money supply — the amount of money in everything from checking accounts to money market mutual funds.

The Fed is constantly adjusting the money supply in an attempt to keep inflation at bay and the economy growing. Changing the money supply affects interest rates. Raising rates, in turn, tends to slow the economy, reducing inflation. Lowering rates encourages economic growth but can mean higher inflation.

Fed officials call the new theory "P-Star," for the P, with an asterisk, that they use in an algebraic equation that illustrates the theory; P* stands for expected future prices. The Fed regards the discovery as important enough to consider reporting its P* figures every quarter, officials there say. . . .

The equation rests on the notion of a school of conservative economists, the monetarists, who say that inflation

occurs when the Fed pumps too much money into the economy. They say that by adding a rigidly fixed amount year by year, the Fed can prevent inflation and the economy will grow at a steady pace.

But for the Fed, this has not been a very practical insight. Although the Fed can control the amount of money that enters the economy, it cannot control the number of times that money changes hands . . . what economists call velocity. A hundred dollars that the Fed puts into the economy might sit under someone's mattress all year, or it might be spent repeatedly, in effect multiplying itself. That makes it hard to say just how much money to pump to keep the economy growing without causing an increase in inflation.

The P* theory is a partial solution, Mr. Greenspan and his economists suspect. It was made possible by a new calculation of the velocity of the money supply, or the rate at which money changes hands. The Fed economists found that over 33 years the velocity of one of the Fed's main measures of the money supply, called M2, works out to 1.6527. . . .

This means that $100 the Fed puts into the economy becomes $165.27 before the year ends. The velocity can vary considerably from month to month or from one year to another, but over several years the velocity is constant at 1.6527, the research showed.

The Fed economists are betting that the figure will remain true in the future. This made it easy for the Fed to write an equation to predict the level of prices in the future — P*. . . .

Economists noted that Fed policy

makers, including Mr. Greenspan, still respect shorter-term gauges of inflation like the Producer Price Index, and could consider it prudent to delay for a month or so before deciding whether to let interest rates decline some more.

For Mr. Greenspan, the equation represents the solution to a problem he had pondered for years, and people at the Fed say he is its No. 1 patron. . . .

The P* equation is derived from another, MV = PQ [written as MV = PY in the text], that economists have long accepted as a statement of a simple and obvious fact — that the amount of money that washes through the economy each year is invariably the same as the amount that everybody spends. . . .

The three economists found Mr. Greenspan's answer in a modification of the old quantity equation of exchange, which they wrote this way:

$$P^* = \frac{M2 \times V^*}{Q^*}$$

. . . Because Q* is predictable and V* is constant, the Fed is left with just two variables — the eventual price level, P*, and the money supply, M-2. Since the Fed controls the money supply, it can try to predict what will happen to prices on the basis of its manipulation of the money supply.

■ Source: Peter T. Kilborn, *New York Times*, June 13, 1989. Copyright © 1989 by the New York Times Company. Reprinted by permission.

Commentary

The central policy-making arm of the nation's monetary authority is the Board of Governors of the Federal Reserve in Washington, D.C. Economists at the Board of Governors attempt to apply monetary policy in a manner that keeps inflation under control while maintaining economic growth. There is no shortage of theories that suggest ways to do this. The theory discussed in this article, called the P* theory, is a new version of an old approach to this problem. So far, the results of the P* theory are encouraging.

The central problem facing the Federal Reserve is to determine the proper quantity of money to supply to the economy. If the Fed supplies too much money, inflation will result. If, on the other hand, the Fed fails to supply sufficient funds, interest rates will rise and increase the threat of a recession. In order for the economists at the Fed to know whether they should supply more or less money, they must know whether there are underlying inflationary pressures in the economy. The P* theory is an attempt to provide this information.

The basis of the P* theory is the equation of exchange, which is expressed in the formula $MV = PY$, where M represents the money supply, V represents velocity, P is the price level, and Y (stated as Q in the article) is the real value of national income. This equation is true by definition, and thus is not a theory. The equation changes from a tautological expression to a theory of the determination of price level if we make some assumptions about the variables in the equation. If we assume that V is constant and that Y grows at a predictable rate, then this equation of exchange becomes a theory, specifically the quantity theory of money.

This is not a new theory. It has been known to economists for over 200 years. What is new about the P* version of the quantity theory is that it attempts to calculate a price that can be used to determine the *underlying* rate of inflation in an economy. The actual current price level and the actual rate of inflation may reflect one-time blips in the price level along with the underlying rate of inflation. Suppose the price figures for one month are high because of an increase in food prices that results from a bad harvest. This does not necessarily reflect an increase in the underlying rate of inflation since there could be a normal harvest next season that would not lead to a rise in prices. The best response of the Fed to a rise in prices due to a bad harvest differs from their best response to a rise in prices due to an increase in the underlying rate of inflation.

A numerical example may be helpful. Suppose that both the Consumer Price Index (CPI) and P* were equal to 1.00 last year and that this year the CPI is equal to 1.07, reflecting a 7-percent rate of inflation. If the Fed has a target rate of inflation below 7 percent, it may be led to contract the money supply in response to this news. But it is important to know whether this rise in the CPI reflects an underlying rate of inflation of 7 percent or just a temporary upward increase in prices. The P* theory enables us to determine the otherwise unobservable underlying rate of inflation. If the money supply this year is $2,000 billion, potential GNP is $3,200 billion, and velocity is the constant 1.6527, then this year's value of P* is approximately 1.03, which is equal to ($2,000 billion $\times$ 1.6527)/$3,200 billion). This reflects an underlying rate of inflation of 3 percent. Thus, a strongly contractionary response by the Fed based on calculations from actual prices rather than P* would not be warranted and could cause a recession.

The article mentions an actual incident in which the P* theory was used in the manner discussed above. One month, the Producer Price Index (PPI) increased at an annual rate of over 10 percent (0.9 percent in one month). The calculation of inflation using the P* equation suggested that this increase did not reflect an increase in the underlying rate of inflation. Federal Reserve policy reflected the information and guidance provided by the P* approach.

The key to the usefulness of the P* theory is whether velocity is stable. We have seen that velocity has been quite volatile when we calculate its historical behavior using actual prices and actual GNP. The P* version of the quantity equation differs from the standard version, however, since it includes potential GNP rather than actual GNP and since the underlying price level (the P* measure) is not the actual price level.

If the P* theory proves to provide a stable relationship among money, potential output, and the underlying price level, it represents an important advance for the conduct of monetary policy. Time and experience will tell how brightly this star will shine.

15

Macroeconomic Policy: Trade-offs, Expectations, Credibility, and Sources of Business Cycles

1. What is the Phillips curve?

2. Why does the Phillips curve vary from the short to the long run?

3. What is the relationship between unexpected inflation and the unemployment rate?

4. How are macroeconomic expectations formed?

5. What makes government policies credible?

6. How are business cycles related to political elections?

7. How do real shocks to the economy affect business cycles?

8. How is inflationary monetary policy related to government fiscal policy?

PREVIEW   Macroeconomics is a dynamic discipline. Monetary and fiscal policies change over time. And so does our understanding of those policies. Economists continue to debate the nature of business cycles—what causes them and what government can do about them. In this chapter we examine current thinking about key variables, like inflation, unemployment, and national income, and the role of government policy in determining these variables.

Some economists argue that policies that lower the unemployment rate tend to raise the rate of inflation. Others insist that only unexpected inflation can influence real national income and employment. If they are right, does government always have to fool the public in order to improve economic conditions?

Do politicians manipulate the business cycle to increase their chances of re-election? Some economists claim they do. If they are right, we should expect economic growth just before national elections. But what happens after the elections? What are the long-term effects of political business cycles?

In earlier chapters we have talked about the determinants of equilibrium national income and the effects of fiscal and monetary policies. Here we combine that information to understand the sources of business cycles and what government can do to moderate large swings in employment and national income.

1. THE PHILLIPS CURVE

▼ What is the Phillips curve? ▲

Phillips curve:
a graph that illustrates the relationship between inflation and the unemployment rate

In 1958 a New Zealand economist, A. W. Phillips, published a study of the relationship between the unemployment rate and the rate of change in wages in England. He found that over the period from 1826 to 1957 there had been an inverse relationship between the unemployment rate and the rate of change in wages. The unemployment rate fell in years when there were relatively large increases in wages, and rose in years when wages increased relatively little. Phillips's study started other economists searching for similar relationships in other countries. In those studies, it became common to substitute the rate of inflation for the rate of change in wages.

Early studies in the United States found an inverse relationship between inflation and the unemployment rate. The graph that illustrates this relationship is called a **Phillips curve**. Figure 1 shows a Phillips curve

Figure 1
A Phillips Curve, United States, 1961–1969
In the 1960s, as the rate of inflation rose, the unemployment rate fell. This inverse relationship suggests a trade-off between the rate of inflation and the unemployment rate. Source: Data are from *Economic Report of the President, 1989* (Washington, D.C.: U.S. Government Printing Office, 1989).

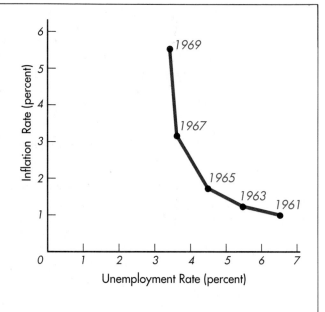

Figure 2
Unemployment and Inflation in the United States, 1955–1989
The data on inflation and unemployment rates in the United States between 1955 and 1989 show no particular relationship between inflation and unemployment over the long run. There is no evidence here of a downward-sloping Phillips curve. Source: Data are from *Economic Report of the President*, 1990 (Washington, D.C.: U.S. Government Printing Office).

for the United States in the 1960s. Over this period, lower inflation rates were associated with higher unemployment rates, so the curve slopes down.

The slope of the curve in Figure 1 depicts an inverse relationship between the rate of inflation and the unemployment rate: as the inflation rate falls, the unemployment rate rises. In 1969 the inflation rate was relatively high, at 5.5 percent, while the unemployment rate was relatively low, at 3.4 percent. In 1967 an inflation rate of 3.1 percent was consistent with an unemployment rate of 3.7 percent; and in 1961, 1 percent inflation occurred with 6.5 percent unemployment.

The downward-sloping Phillips curve seems to indicate a trade-off between unemployment and inflation. A country could have a lower unemployment rate by accepting higher inflation, or a lower rate of inflation by accepting higher unemployment. Certainly this was the case in the United States in the 1960s. But is the curve depicted in Figure 1 representative over long periods of time?

1.a. An Inflation-Unemployment Trade-off?

Figure 2 shows unemployment and inflation rates in the United States for several years from 1955 to 1989. The points in the figure do not lie along a downward-sloping curve like the one shown in Figure 1. For example, in 1955 the unemployment rate was 4.4 percent and the inflation rate was −.4 percent. In 1960 the unemployment rate was 5.5 percent and the inflation rate was 1.6 percent. Both unemployment and inflation rates had increased since 1955. Moving through time, you can see that the inflation rate tended to increase along with the unemployment rate through the

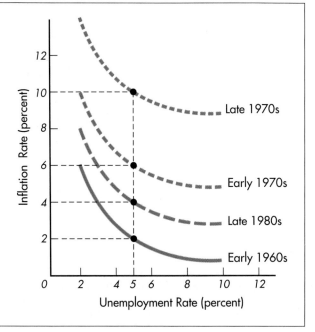

Figure 3
The Shifting Phillips Curve
We can reconcile the long-run data on unemployment and inflation with the downward-sloping Phillips curve by using a series of Phillips curves. (In effect, we treat the long run as a series of short-run curves.) The Phillips curve for the early 1960s shows 5 percent unemployment and 2 percent inflation. Over time, the short-run curve shifted out to the right. The early 1970s curve shows 5 percent unemployment and 6 percent inflation. And the short-run curve for the late 1970s shows 5 percent unemployment and 10 percent inflation. In the early 1980s, the short-run Phillips curve began to shift down toward the origin. By the late 1980s, 5 percent unemployment was consistent with 4 percent inflation.

1960s and 1970s. By 1980, the unemployment rate was 7.1 percent and the inflation rate was 13.5 percent.

The scattered points in Figure 2 show no evidence of a trade-off between unemployment and inflation. Clearly a downward-sloping Phillips curve does not exist over the long term.

The downward-sloping Phillips curve and the trade-off it implies between inflation and unemployment are short-term phenomena. Think of a series of Phillips curves, one for each of the points in Figure 2. From 1955 to 1980, the curves shifted out to the right. In the early 1980s, they shifted in to the left.

1.b. Short-Run Versus Long-Run Trade-offs

Figure 3 shows a series of Phillips curves that could account for the data in Figure 2. At any point in time, a downward-sloping Phillips curve indicates a trade-off between inflation and unemployment. But this kind of trade-off is a short-term phenomenon. Over time the Phillips curve shifts: the short-run trade-off between inflation and unemployment disappears in the long run.

> Why does the Phillips curve vary from the short to the long run?

On the early 1960s curve in Figure 3, 5 percent unemployment is consistent with 2 percent inflation. By the early 1970s, the curve had shifted up. Here 5 percent unemployment is associated with 6 percent inflation. On the late 1970s curve, 5 percent unemployment is consistent with 10 percent inflation. For more than two decades, the trade-off between inflation and unemployment worsened as the Phillips curves shifted up so that higher and higher inflation rates were associated with any given level of unemployment. Then in the 1980s, the trade-off seemed to improve as the Phillips curve shifted down. On the late 1980s curve, 5 percent unemployment is consistent with 4 percent inflation.

The Phillips curves in Figure 3 represent changes that took place over time in the United States. We cannot be sure of the actual shape of a Phillips curve at any time, but an outward shift of the curve in the 1960s and 1970s and an inward shift during the 1980s are consistent with the data. Later in this chapter we describe how changing government policy and the public's expectations about that policy may have produced these shifts in the Phillips curves.

1.b.1. In the Short Run Figure 4 uses the aggregate demand and supply analysis we developed in Chapter 11 to explain the Phillips curve. Initially

---

Figure 4
Aggregate Demand and Supply and the Phillips Curve
The movement from point 1 to point 2 to point 3 traces the adjustment of the economy to an increase in aggregate demand. Point 1 is initial equilibrium in both diagrams. At this point potential national income is Y_P and the price level is P_1 in the aggregate demand and supply diagram, and the inflation rate is 3 percent with an unemployment rate of 5 percent (the natural rate) along short-run curve I in the Phillips curve diagram.

If the aggregate demand curve shifts from AD_1 to AD_2, equilibrium income goes up to Y_2 and the price level rises to P_2 in the aggregate demand and supply diagram. The increase in aggregate demand pushes the inflation rate up to 6 percent and the unemployment rate down to 3 percent along Phillips curve I. The movement from point 1

to point 2 along the curve indicates a trade-off between inflation and the unemployment rate.

Over time the AS curve shifts in response to rising production costs at the higher rate of inflation. Along AS_2, equilibrium is at point 3, where national income falls back to Y_P and the price level rises to P_3. As we move from point 2 to point 3 in part (b), we shift to short-run Phillips curve II. Here the inflation rate remains high (at 6 percent), while the unemployment rate goes back up to 5 percent, the rate consistent with production at Y_P. In the long run, then, there is no trade-off between inflation and unemployment. The vertical long-run aggregate supply curve at the potential level of national income is associated with the vertical long-run Phillips curve at the natural rate of unemployment.

(a) Aggregate Demand and Supply

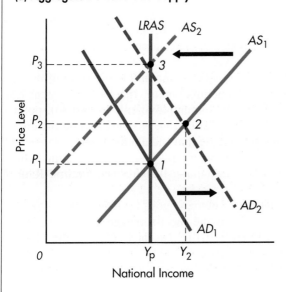

(b) Phillips Curve

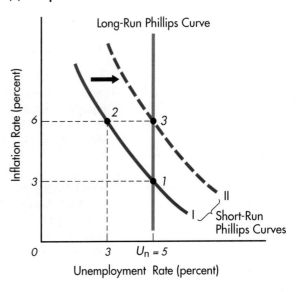

The Natural Rate of Unemployment

The natural rate of unemployment is the unemployment rate that exists in the absence of cyclical unemployment. As we discussed in Chapter 8, the natural rate of unemployment reflects the normal amount of frictional unemployment (people temporarily between jobs) and structural unemployment (people who lost jobs because of technological change). What factors determine the normal amount of frictional and structural unemployment?

One of the most important factors is demographic change. As the age, gender, and racial makeup of the labor force change, the natural rate of unemployment also changes. For instance, when the baby boom generation entered the labor force, the natural rate of unemployment increased because new workers typically have the highest unemployment rates. Between 1956 and 1979, the pro-

portion of young adults (ages 16 to 24) in the labor force increased, increasing the natural rate of unemployment. Since 1979, the fraction of young adults in the labor force has fallen, tending to lower the natural rate of unemployment.

In addition to the composition of the labor force, several other factors affect the natural rate of unemployment:

- Increases in the legal minimum wage tend to raise the natural rate of unemployment. When the government mandates that employers pay some workers a higher wage than a freely competitive labor market would pay, fewer workers are employed.

- The more generous the unemployment benefits, the higher the natural rate of unemployment. Increased benefits reduce the cost of being out of work and allow unemployed

workers to take their time finding a new job.

- Income taxes also can affect the natural rate of unemployment. Higher taxes mean that workers keep less of their earned income and so have less incentive to work.

The effect of these factors on the unemployment rate is complex, so it is difficult to state what the natural rate of unemployment is exactly. But as these factors change over time, the natural rate of unemployment also changes.

One last thing. It is not clear that minimizing the natural rate of unemployment is a universal goal. Minimum wages, unemployment benefits, and taxes have other important implications besides their effect on the natural rate of unemployment. We cannot expect these variables to be set solely in terms of their effect on unemployment.

the economy is operating at point 1 in both diagrams. In part (a), the aggregate demand curve (AD_1) and aggregate supply curve (AS_1) intersect at price level P_1 and income level Y_P, the level of potential national income. Remember that potential national income is the level of income generated at the natural rate of unemployment, the unemployment rate that exists in the absence of cyclical unemployment. In part (b), point 1 lies on Phillips curve I, where the inflation rate is 3 percent and the unemployment rate is 5 percent. We assume that the unemployment rate at the level of potential national income is 5 percent, that 5 percent is the natural rate of unemployment (U_n) (see Economic Insight: The Natural Rate of Unemployment).

What happens when aggregate demand goes up from AD_1 to AD_2? A new equilibrium is established along the short-run aggregate supply curve (AS_1) at point 2. Here the price level (P_2) is higher, as is the level of national income (Y_2). In part (b), the increase in price and income is reflected in the movement along Phillips curve I to point 2. At point 2, the inflation rate is 6 percent and the unemployment rate is 3 percent. The increase in expenditures raises the inflation rate and lowers the unemployment rate (because national output has surpassed potential output).

Notice that there appears to be a trade-off between inflation and unemployment on Phillips curve I. The increase in spending increases output and stimulates employment, so that the unemployment rate falls. And the higher spending pushes the rate of inflation up. But this trade-off is only temporary. Point 2 in both diagrams is only a short-run equilibrium.

1.b.2. In the Long Run   As we discussed in Chapter 11, the short-run aggregate supply curve shifts over time as production costs rise in response to higher prices. Once the aggregate supply curve shifts to AS_2, long-run equilibrium occurs at point 3, where AS_2 intersects AD_2. Here, the price level is P_3 and national income returns to its potential level, Y_P.

The shift in aggregate supply lowers national income. As income falls, the unemployment rate goes up. The decrease in aggregate supply is reflected in the movement from point 2 on Phillips curve I to point 3 on Phillips curve II. As national income returns to its potential level (Y_P), unemployment returns to the natural rate (U_n), 5 percent. In the long run, as the economy adjusts to an increase in aggregate demand, there is a period in which national income falls and output rises.

The data indicate that the Phillips curve may have shifted out in the 1960s and 1970s and shifted in during the 1980s.

The long-run Phillips curve is a vertical line at the natural rate of unemployment.

Over time there is no relationship between the price level and the level of real national income or output. You can see this in the aggregate demand and supply diagram. Points 1 and 3 both lie along the long-run aggregate supply curve (*LRAS*) at potential national income. The *LRAS* curve has its analogue in the long-run Phillips curve, a vertical line at the natural rate of unemployment. Points 1 and 3 both lie along this curve.

RECAP

1. The Phillips curve shows an inverse relationship between inflation and unemployment.
2. The downward slope of the Phillips curve indicates a trade-off between inflation and unemployment.
3. Over the long run that trade-off disappears.
4. The long-run Phillips curve is a vertical line at the natural rate of unemployment, analogous to the long-run aggregate supply curve at potential income.

2. THE ROLE OF EXPECTATIONS

The data and analysis in the previous section indicate that there is no long-run trade-off between inflation and unemployment. But they do not

Figure 5
Expectations and the Phillips Curve
Short-run Phillips curve I shows the trade-off between in-flation and the unemployment rate as long as people ex-pect 3 percent inflation. When the actual rate of inflation is 3 percent, the natural rate of unemployment (U_n) is 5 percent (point 1). Short-run Phillips curve II shows the trade-off as long as people expect 6 percent inflation. When the actual rate of inflation is 6 percent, the unem-ployment rate is 5 percent (point 3).

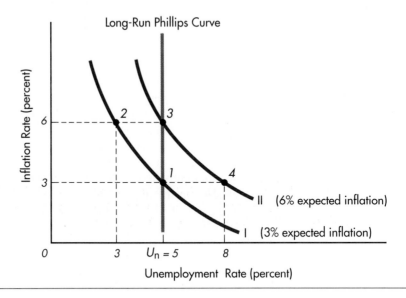

explain the movement of the Phillips curve in the 1960s, 1970s, and 1980s. To understand why the short-run curve shifts, you must understand the role that unexpected inflation plays in the economy.

2.a. Expected Versus Unexpected Inflation

Figure 5 shows two short-run Phillips curves like those in Figure 4. Each curve is drawn for a particular expected rate of inflation. Curve I shows the trade-off between inflation and unemployment when the inflation rate is expected to be 3 percent. If the actual rate of inflation (measured along the vertical axis) is 3 percent, the economy is operating at point 1, with an unemployment rate of 5 percent (the natural rate). If the inflation rate unexpectedly increases to 6 percent, the economy moves from point 1 to point 2 along Phillips curve I. Obviously unexpected inflation can affect the unemployment rate. There are three factors at work here: wage expec-tations, inventory fluctuations, and wage contracts.

> What is the relationship between unexpected inflation and the unemployment rate?

reservation wage:
the minimum wage a worker is willing to accept

2.a.1. Wage Expectations and Unemployment Unemployed workers who are looking for a job choose a **reservation wage**, the minimum wage they are willing to accept. They continue to look for work until they receive an offer that equals or exceeds their reservation wage.

Wages are not the only factor that workers take into consideration before accepting a job offer. A firm that offers good working conditions

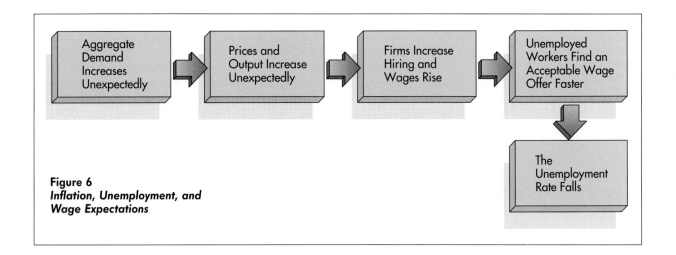

Figure 6
Inflation, Unemployment, and Wage Expectations

and fringe benefits can pay a lower wage than a firm that does not offer these advantages. But other things being equal, workers choose higher wages over lower wages. We simplify our analysis here by assuming that the only variable that affects the unemployed worker who is looking for a job is the reservation wage.

The link between unexpected inflation and the unemployment rate stems from the fact that wage offers are surprisingly high when the rate of inflation is surprisingly high. An unexpected increase in inflation means that prices are higher than anticipated, as are nominal income and wages. If aggregate demand increases unexpectedly, then, prices, outputs, employment, and wages go up. Unemployed workers with a constant reservation wage find it easier to obtain a satisfactory wage offer during a period when wages are rising faster than the workers expected. This means that more unemployed workers find jobs, and that they find those jobs quicker than they do in a period when the rate of inflation is expected. So the unemployment rate falls during a period of unexpectedly high inflation (Figure 6).

An example. Suppose an accountant named Cathy decides that she must find a job that pays at least $105 a day. Cathy's reservation wage is $105. Furthermore, Cathy expects prices and wages to be fairly stable across the economy; she expects no inflation. Cathy looks for a job and finds that the jobs she qualifies for are only offering wages of $100 a day. Because her job offers are all paying less than her reservation wage, she keeps on looking. Let's say that aggregate demand rises unexpectedly. Firms increase production and raise prices. To hire more workers, they increase the wages they offer. Suppose wages go up 5 percent. Now the jobs that Cathy qualifies for are offering 5 percent higher wages, $105 a day instead of $100 a day. At this higher wage rate, Cathy quickly accepts a job and starts working. This example explains why the move from point 1 to point 2 in Figure 5 occurs.

The short-run Phillips curve assumes a constant *expected* rate of inflation. It also assumes that every unemployed worker who is looking for a job has a constant reservation wage. When inflation rises unexpectedly,

If the reservation wage goes up with the rate of inflation, there is no trade-off between inflation and the unemployment rate.

then, wages rise faster than expected and the unemployment rate falls. The element of "surprise" is critical here. If the increase in inflation is *expected*, unemployed workers who are looking for a job will revise their reservation wage to match the expected change in the level of prices. If reservation wages go up with the rate of inflation, there is no trade-off between inflation and the unemployment rate. Higher inflation is associated with the original unemployment rate.

Let's go back to Cathy, the accountant who wants a job that pays $105 a day. Above we said that if wages increased to $105 unexpectedly because of an increase in aggregate demand, she would quickly find an acceptable job. However, if Cathy knows that the price level is going to go up 5 percent, then she knows that a wage increase from $100 to $105 is not a real wage increase because she needs $105 in order to buy what $100 would buy before. The *nominal wage* is the number of dollars earned; the *real wage* is the purchasing power of those dollars. If the nominal wage increases 5 percent at the same time that prices have gone up 5 percent, it takes 5 percent more money to buy the same goods and services. The real wage has not changed. What happens? Cathy revises her reservation wage to account for the higher price level. If she wants a 5 percent higher real wage, her reservation wage goes up to $110.25 (5 percent more than $105). Now if employers offer her $105, she refuses and keeps searching.

In Figure 5 expected inflation moves us from point 1 on curve I to point 3 on curve II. When increased inflation is expected, the reservation wage reflects the higher rate of inflation and there is no trade-off between inflation and the unemployment rate. Instead the economy moves along the long-run Phillips curve, with unemployment at its natural rate. The clockwise movement from point 1 to point 2 to point 3 is the pattern that follows an unexpected increase in aggregate demand.

What if the inflation rate is lower than expected? Here we find a reservation wage that reflects higher expected inflation. This means that those people who are looking for jobs are going to have a difficult time finding acceptable wage offers, the number of unemployed workers is going to increase, and the unemployment rate is going to rise. This sequence is shown in Figure 5, as the economy moves from point 3 to point 4. When the actual inflation rate is 6 percent and the expected inflation rate is also 6 percent, the economy is operating at the natural rate of unemployment. When the inflation rate falls to 3 percent but workers still expect 6 percent inflation, the unemployment rate rises (at point 4 along curve II). Eventually, if the inflation rate remains at 3 percent, workers adjust their expectations to the lower rate and the economy moves to point 1 on curve I. The short-run effect of *disinflation* is rising unemployment. Over time the short-run increase in the unemployment rate is eliminated.

As long as the actual rate of inflation equals the expected rate, the economy operates at the natural rate of unemployment.

As long as the actual rate of inflation equals the expected rate, the economy remains at the natural rate of unemployment. The trade-off between inflation and the unemployment rate comes from unexpected inflation.

2.a.2. Inventory Fluctuations and Unemployment Businesses hold inventories based on what they expect their sales to be. When aggregate demand is greater than expected, inventories fall below targeted levels. To restore inventories to the levels wanted, production is increased.

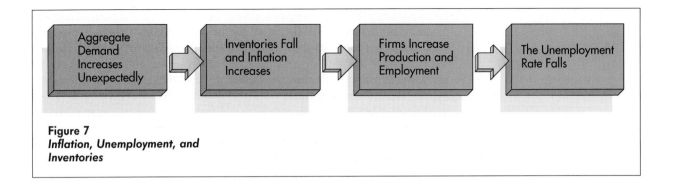

Figure 7
Inflation, Unemployment, and Inventories

When aggregate demand is higher than expected, inventories are lower than expected and prices are higher than expected, so the unemployment rate falls. When aggregate demand is lower than expected, inventories are higher than expected and prices are lower than expected, so the unemployment rate rises.

Increased production leads to increased employment. If aggregate demand is lower than expected, inventories rise above targeted levels. To reduce inventories, production is cut back and workers are laid off from their jobs until sales have lowered unwanted inventories. Once production increases, employment rises again.

Inventory, production, and employment all play a part in the Phillips curve analysis (Figure 7). Expected sales and inventory levels are based on an expected level of aggregate demand. If aggregate demand is greater than expected, inventories fall and prices rise on the remaining goods in stock. With the unexpected increase in inflation, the unemployment rate falls as businesses hire more workers to increase output to offset falling inventories. This sequence represents movement along a short-run Phillips curve because there is a trade-off between inflation and the unemployment rate. We find the same trade-off if aggregate demand is lower than expected. Here inventories increase and prices are lower than anticipated. With the unexpected decrease in inflation, the unemployment rate goes up as workers are laid off to reduce output until inventory levels fall.

2.a.3. Wage Contracts and Unemployment Another factor that explains the short-run trade-off between inflation and unemployment is labor contracts that fix wages for an extended period of time. When an existing contract expires, management must renegotiate with labor. A firm facing lower demand for its products may negotiate lower wages in order to keep as many workers employed as before. If the demand for a firm's products falls while a wage contract is in force, the firm must maintain wages, which means it is going to have to lay off workers.

For example, a pizza restaurant with $1,000 a day in revenues employs 4 workers at $40 a day. The firm's total labor costs are $160 a day. Suppose revenues fall to $500 a day. If the firm wants to cut its labor costs in half, to $80, it has two choices: it can maintain wages at $40 a day and lay off 2 workers, or it can lower wages to $20 a day and keep all 4 workers. If the restaurant has a contract with the employees that sets wages at $40 a day, it must lay off 2 workers.

If demand increases while a wage contract is in force, a business hires more workers at the fixed wage. Once the contract expires, the firm's workers will negotiate higher wages, to reflect increased demand. For instance, suppose prices in the economy, including the price of pizzas go up 10 percent. If the pizza restaurant can raise its prices 10 percent and sell as many pizzas as before (because the price of every other food also has gone up 10 percent), its daily revenues increase from $1,000 to $1,100. If the restaurant has a labor contract that fixes wages at $40 a day, its profits are going to go up, reflecting the higher price of pizzas. With its increased profits, the restaurant may be willing to hire more workers. Once the labor contract expires, the workers ask for a 10 percent wage increase to match the price level increase. If wages go up to $44 a day (10 percent higher than $40), the firm cannot hire more workers because wages have gone up in proportion to the increase in prices. If the costs of doing business rise at the same rate as prices, both profits and employment remain the same.

Wage contracts are staggered; they expire at different times. Each year only 30 to 40 percent of all contracts expire across the entire economy. As economic conditions change, firms with expiring wage contracts can adjust *wages* to those conditions; firms with existing contracts must adjust *employment* to those conditions.

How do long-term wage contracts tie into the Phillips curve analysis? The expected rate of inflation is based on expected aggregate demand and reflected in the wage that is agreed on in the contract. When the actual rate of inflation equals the expected rate, businesses retain the same number of workers they had planned on when they signed the contract. For the economy overall, when actual and expected inflation rates are the same, the economy is operating at the natural rate of unemployment. That is, businesses are not hiring new workers because of an unexpected increase in aggregate demand, and they are not laying off workers because of an unexpected decrease in aggregate demand.

When aggregate demand is higher than expected, those firms with unexpired wage contracts hire more workers at the fixed wage, reducing unemployment (Figure 8). Those firms with expiring contracts have to offer higher wages in order to maintain the existing level of employment at the new demand condition. When aggregate demand is lower than expected, those firms with unexpired contracts have to lay off workers because they cannot lower the wage, while those firms with expiring contracts negotiate lower wages in order to keep their workers.

If wages were always flexible, unexpected changes in aggregate demand would be reflected in *wage* rather than *employment* adjustments. Wage contracts force businesses to adjust employment when aggregate demand changes unexpectedly.

Wage contracts force businesses to adjust employment rather than wages in response to an unexpected change in aggregate demand.

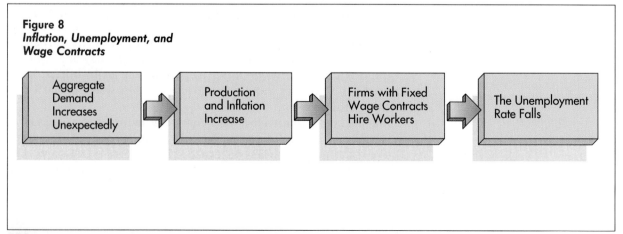

Figure 8
Inflation, Unemployment, and Wage Contracts

Aggregate Demand Increases Unexpectedly → Production and Inflation Increase → Firms with Fixed Wage Contracts Hire Workers → The Unemployment Rate Falls

2.b. Forming Expectations

▼
How are macroeconomic
expectations formed?
▲

Expectations play a key role in explaining the short-run Phillips curve, the trade-off between inflation and the unemployment rate. How are these expectations formed?

adaptive expectation:
an expectation formed on the basis of information collected in the past

2.b.1. Adaptive Expectations Expectations can be formed solely on the basis of experience. **Adaptive expectations** are expectations that are determined by what has happened in the recent past.

People learn from their experiences. For example, suppose the inflation rate has been 3 percent for the past few years. Based on past experience, then, people expect the inflation rate in the future to remain at 3 percent. If the central bank increases the growth of the money supply to a rate that produces 6 percent inflation, the public will be surprised by the higher rate of inflation. This unexpected inflation creates a short-run trade-off between inflation and the unemployment rate along a short-run Phillips curve. Over time, if the inflation rate remains at 6 percent, the public will learn that the 3 percent rate is too low and will adapt its expectations to the actual, higher inflation rate. Once public expectations have adapted to the new rate of inflation, the economy returns to the natural rate of unemployment along the long-run Phillips curve.

rational expectation:
an expectation that is formed using all available relevant information

2.b.2. Rational Expectations Many economists believe that adaptive expectations are too narrow. If people look only at past information, they are ignoring what could be important information in the current period. **Rational expectations** are based on all available relevant information.

We are not saying that people have to know everything in order to form expectations. Rational expectations require only that people consider the information they believe to be relevant. This information includes their past experience along with what is currently happening and what they expect to happen in the future. For instance, in forming expectations about inflation, they consider rates in the recent past, current policy, and anticipated shifts in aggregate demand and supply that could affect the future rate of inflation.

If the inflation rate has been 3 percent over the past few years, adaptive expectations suggest that the future inflation rate will be 3 percent. No other information is considered. Rational expectations are based on more than the historical rate. Suppose the Fed announces a new policy that everyone believes will increase inflation in the future. Rational expectations consider the effect of this announcement. Here, when the actual rate of inflation turns out to be more than 3 percent, there is no short-run trade-off between inflation and the unemployment rate. The economy moves directly along the long-run Phillips curve to the higher inflation rate, while unemployment remains at the natural rate.

If we believe that people have rational expectations, we do not expect them to make the same mistakes over and over. We expect them to learn and react quickly to new information.

1. Wage expectations, inventory fluctuations, and wage contracts help explain the short-run trade-off between inflation and the unemployment rate.

2. The reservation wage is the minimum wage a worker is willing to accept.

3. Because wage expectations reflect expected inflation, when the inflation rate is surprisingly high, unemployed workers find jobs faster and the unemployment rate falls.

4. Unexpected increases in aggregate demand lower inventories and raise prices. To increase output (to replenish shrinking inventories), businesses hire more workers, which reduces the unemployment rate.

5. When aggregate demand is higher than expected, those businesses with wage contracts hire more workers at the fixed wage, lowering unemployment.

6. If wages were always flexible, unexpected changes in aggregate demand would be reflected in wage adjustments rather than employment adjustments.

7. Adaptive expectations are formed on the basis of information about the past.

8. Rational expectations are formed using all available relevant information.

3. CREDIBILITY AND TIME INCONSISTENCY

The rate of inflation is a product of growth in the money supply. That growth is controlled by the country's central bank. If the Federal Reserve follows a policy of rapidly increasing the money supply, one consequence is rapid inflation. If it follows a policy of slow growth, it keeps inflation down.

To help the public predict the future course of monetary policy, Congress passed the Federal Reserve Reform Act (1977) and Full Employment and Balanced Growth Act (1978). The Full Employment act requires that the chairman of the Board of Governors of the Federal Reserve System testify before Congress annually, presenting the Fed's targets for money growth along with other policy plans.

time inconsistent:
a characteristic of a policy or plan that changes over time in response to changing conditions

Of course, the Fed's plans are only plans. There is no requirement that the central bank actually follow the plans announced to Congress. During the course of the year, the Fed may decide that a new policy is necessary in light of economic developments. Changing conditions mean that plans can be **time inconsistent**.

3.a. The Policymaker's Problem

Time inconsistency gives the Fed a credibility problem and the public the problem of guessing where monetary policy and the inflation rate are actually heading.

Figure 9 shows an example of how announced monetary policy can turn out to be time inconsistent. The Fed, like all central banks, always announces that it plans to follow a low-money-growth policy to promote a low rate of inflation. (It is unlikely that a central bank would ever state that it intends to follow an inflationary monetary policy.) Yet we know that the

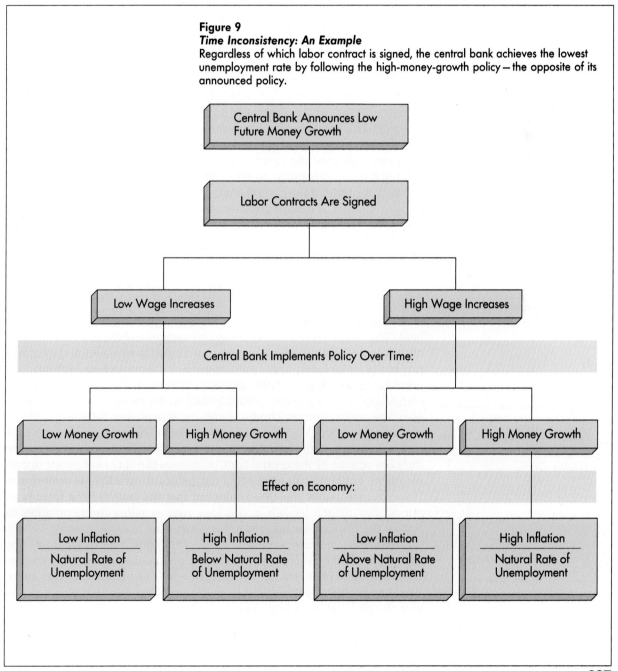

Figure 9
Time Inconsistency: An Example
Regardless of which labor contract is signed, the central bank achieves the lowest unemployment rate by following the high-money-growth policy — the opposite of its announced policy.

world often is characterized by higher rates of inflation. Because the actual inflation rate often ends up being higher than the intended inflation rate, low-inflation plans often are time inconsistent.

In Figure 9, labor contracts are signed following the central bank's announcement. The contracts call for either low wage increases or high wage increases. If everyone believes that the money supply is going to grow at the announced low rate, then the low-wage contracts are signed. However, if there is reason to believe that the announced policy is time inconsistent, the high-wage contracts are signed.

Over time, the central bank either follows the announced low-money-growth policy or implements a high-money-growth policy. If the low-wage contract is in force and the central bank follows the low-money-growth policy, the actual inflation rate will match the low rate that people expected and the unemployment rate will equal the natural rate. If the central bank follows a high-money-growth policy, the rate of inflation will be higher than expected and the unemployment rate will fall below the natural rate.

If the high-wage contract is in force and the low-money-growth policy is followed, the inflation rate will be lower than expected and the unemployment rate will exceed the natural rate. If the high-money-growth policy is followed, the inflation rate will be as expected and the unemployment rate will be at the natural rate.

Look at what happens to unemployment. Regardless of which labor contract is signed, if the central bank wants to keep unemployment as low as possible, it must deviate from its announced plan. The plan turns out to be time inconsistent. Because the public knows that unemployment, like the rate of inflation, is a factor in the Fed's policy making, the central bank's announced plan is not credible.

3.b. Credibility

What makes government policies credible?

If the public does not believe the low-money-growth plans of the central bank, high-wage contracts will always be signed, and the central bank will always have to follow a high-money-growth policy to maintain the natural rate of unemployment. This cycle creates an economy where high inflation persists year after year. If the central bank always follows its announced plan of low money growth and low inflation, the public would believe the plan, low-wage contracts would always be signed, and the natural rate of unemployment would exist at the low rate of inflation. In either case, high or low inflation, if the inflation rate is expected, the unemployment rate does not change. If the central bank eliminates the goal of reducing unemployment below the natural rate, the problem of inflation disappears. However, the public must be convinced that the central bank intends to pursue low money growth in the long run, avoiding the temptation to reduce the unemployment rate in the short run.

How does the central bank achieve credibility? One way is to fix the growth rate of the money supply by law. Congress could pass a law requiring that the Fed maintain a growth rate of, say, 3 to 5 percent a year. There would be problems defining the money supply, but this kind of law would give the Fed's policies credibility.

The short-run Phillips curve indicates a trade-off between unexpected inflation and the unemployment rate. If a government tries to change the rate of inflation significantly in a short time, much of that change is unexpected, which means the unemployment rate is going to be affected.

After World War I, hyperinflation was a critical problem in Austria, Hungary, Poland, and Germany. Each of these countries ran huge fiscal deficits financed by government-issued money. Austrian inflation was over 10,000 percent between January 1921 and August 1922. The price level in Hungary was 263 times higher in April 1924 than it was in January 1922. Polish inflation was 2,402 percent between January 1922 and December 1923. And the wholesale price index in Germany went from 96 in January 1914 to 115.9 trillion in June 1924.

In each of these countries, inflation ended abruptly with little or no recession. The reason was a credible change in economic policy. Each country created an independent central bank that was required by law to refuse any demands by government for unsecured credit. The central bank could no longer finance the fiscal deficit. At the same time, fiscal reforms were introduced that required the governments to sell their debt to private parties and foreign governments.

Once people knew that their government could not rely on the creation of money to finance deficits, the inflation ended. The constraints imposed on the central banks and the new fiscal policies convinced the public that the inflation rate would fall. Their credibility made the policies work. Because the public expected inflation to fall, it did fall. And it fell with no significant recession.

Another way to establish credibility is to create incentives for monetary authorities to take a long-term view of monetary policy. In the long run, the economy is better off if policymakers do not try to exploit the short-run trade-off between inflation and the unemployment rate. The central bank can achieve a lower rate of inflation at the natural rate of unemployment by avoiding unexpected increases in the rate at which money and inflation grow.

Reputation is a key factor here. If the central bank considers the effects of its actual policy on public expectations, it will find it easier to achieve low inflation by establishing a reputation for low-inflation policies. A central bank with a reputation for time-consistent plans will find labor contracts calling for low wage increases because people believe that the bank is going to follow its announced plans and generate a low rate of inflation. In other words, by maintaining a reputation for following through on announced policy, the Fed can earn the public confidence necessary to produce a low rate of inflation in the long run.

RECAP

1. A plan is time inconsistent when it changes over time in response to changing conditions.

2. If the public believes that an announced policy is time inconsistent, policymakers have a credibility problem that can limit the success of their plans.

3. Credibility can be achieved by fixing the growth rate of the money supply by law or by creating incentives for policymakers to follow through on announced plans.

4. SOURCES OF BUSINESS CYCLES

In Chapter 12 we examined the effect of fiscal policy on the equilibrium level of national income. Changes in government spending and taxes can expand or contract the economy. In Chapter 14 we described how monetary policy affects the equilibrium level of national income. Changes in the money supply also produce booms and recessions. Here we begin by looking at the *political business cycle,* macroeconomic policy used to promote the re-election of incumbent politicians. Then we examine a business cycle that is not related to discretionary policy actions, the *real business cycle.*

4.a. The Political Business Cycle

If a short-run trade-off exists between inflation and unemployment, an incumbent administration could stimulate the economy just before an election to lower the unemployment rate, making voters happy and increasing the probability of re-election. Of course after the election, the long-run adjustment to the expansionary policy would lead to higher inflation and move unemployment back to the natural rate.

▼ How are business cycles related to political elections? ▲

Figure 10 illustrates the pattern. Before the election, the economy is initially at point 1 in parts (a) and (b). The incumbent administration stimulates the economy by increasing government spending or increasing the growth of the money supply. Aggregate demand shifts from AD_1 to AD_2 in part (a). In the short run, the increase in aggregate demand is unexpected, so the economy moves along the initial aggregate supply curve (AS_1) to point 2. This movement is reflected in part (b) of the figure, in the movement from point 1 to point 2 along short-run Phillips curve I. The pre-election expansionary policy increases national income and lowers the unemployment rate. Once the public adjusts its expectations to the higher inflation rate, the economy experiences a recession. National income falls back to its potential level (Y_P) and the unemployment rate goes back up to the natural rate (U_n), as shown by the movement from point 2 to point 3 in both parts of the figure.

An unexpected increase in government spending or money growth temporarily stimulates the economy. If an election comes during the period of expansion, higher incomes and lower unemployment may increase support for the incumbent administration. The long-run adjustment back to potential national income and the natural rate of unemployment comes after the election.

Figure 10
The Political Business Cycle
Before the election, the government stimulates the economy, unexpectedly increasing aggregate demand. The economy moves from point 1 to point 2, pushing equilibrium national income above Y_P (part [a]) and the unemployment rate below U_n (part [b]). The incumbent politicians hope that rising incomes and lower unemployment will translate into votes. After the election comes adjustment to the higher aggregate demand, as the economy moves from point 2 to point 3. The aggregate supply curve shifts to the left, and equilibrium national income falls back to Y_P. Unemployment goes back up to U_n, and the rate of inflation rises.

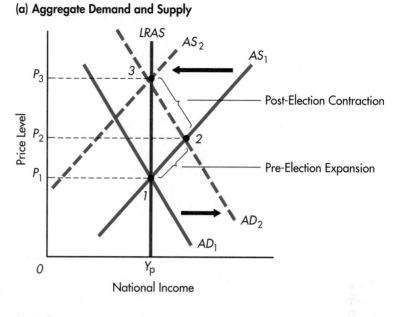

(a) Aggregate Demand and Supply

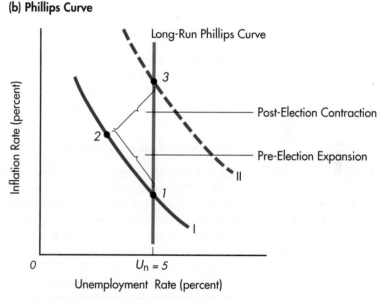

(b) Phillips Curve

Economists do not agree on whether a political business cycle exists in the United States. But they do agree that an effort to exploit the short-run trade-off between inflation and the unemployment rate would shift the short-run Phillips curve out as shown in part (b) of Figure 10.

The evidence of a political business cycle is not clear. If government macroeconomic policy is designed to stimulate the economy before elections and to bear the costs of rising unemployment and inflation after elec-

Table 1 Presidential Elections and U.S. Recessions, 1948–1988

Presidential Election (Winner)	Next Recession
November 1948 (Truman)	November 1948–October 1949
November 1952 (Eisenhower)	June 1953–May 1954
November 1956 (Eisenhower)	June 1957–April 1958
November 1960 (Kennedy)	(April 1960)–February 1961
November 1964 (Johnson)	
November 1968 (Nixon)	October 1969–November 1970
November 1972 (Nixon)	December 1973–March 1975
November 1976 (Carter)	January 1980–July 1980
November 1980 (Reagan)	May 1981–November 1982
November 1984 (Reagan)	
November 1988 (Bush)	

tions, we should see recessions regularly following national elections. Table 1 lists the presidential elections since 1948 along with the recessions that followed them. In five cases, a recession occurred the year after an election. A recession began before President Kennedy's election, and there was no recession during the Johnson and second Reagan administrations, or the Bush administration. Of course just because recessions do not follow every election, there is no guarantee that some business cycles have not stemmed from political manipulation. If a short-run Phillips curve exists, the potential for a political business cycle exists as long as the public does not expect the government to stimulate the economy before elections.

4.b. Real Business Cycles

shock:
an unexpected change in a variable

▼ How do real shocks to the economy affect business cycles? ▲

In recent years economists have paid increasing attention to real **shocks**—unexpected changes—in the economy as a source of business cycles. Many believe that it is not only fiscal or monetary policy that triggers expansion or contraction in the economy, but technological change, change in tastes, labor strikes, weather, or other real changes. A real business cycle is one that is generated by a change in one of those real variables.

Interest in the real business cycle was stimulated by the oil price shocks in the early 1970s and the important role they played in triggering the recession of 1973–1975. At that time, many economists were focusing on the role of unexpected changes in monetary policy in generating business cycles. They argued that these kinds of policy changes (changes in a nominal variable, the money supply) were responsible for the shifts in aggregate demand that led to expansions and contractions. When OPEC raised oil prices, it caused major shifts in aggregate supply. (In Chapter 11 we discussed OPEC and aggregate supply.) Higher oil prices in 1973 and 1974, and in 1979 and 1980, reduced aggregate supply, pushing the equilibrium level of national income down. Lower oil prices in 1986 raised aggregate supply and equilibrium national income.

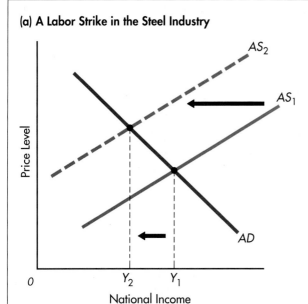

(a) A Labor Strike in the Steel Industry

AS_2

AS_1

Price Level

AD

0   Y_2 Y_1

National Income

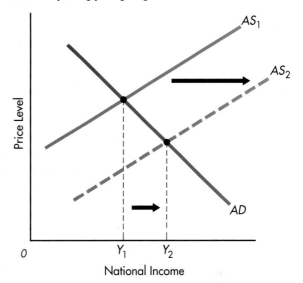

(b) A Surprisingly Large Agricultural Harvest

AS_1

AS_2

Price Level

AD

0   Y_1 Y_2

National Income

Figure 11
The Impact of Real Shocks on Equilibrium National Income
A labor strike in a key industry can shift the aggregate supply curve to the left, like the shift from AS_1 to AS_2. This pushes equilibrium national income down from Y_1 to Y_2.

If good weather leads to a banner harvest, the aggregate supply curve shifts to the right, like the shift from AS_1 to AS_2, raising equilibrium national income from Y_1 to Y_2.

An economywide real shock, like a substantial change in the price of oil, can affect output and employment across all sectors of the economy. Even an industry-specific shock can generate a recession or expansion in the entire economy if the industry produces a substantial amount of the nation's output. For example, a labor strike in the steel industry would have major recessionary implications for the economy as a whole. If the output of steel fell, the price of steel would be bid up by all the industries that use steel as an input. This would shift the aggregate supply curve to the left, as shown in part (a) of Figure 11, and would move equilibrium national income from Y_1 down to Y_2.

Real shocks also can have expansionary effects on the economy. Suppose that the weather is particularly good one year, that harvests are surprisingly large. What happens? The price of food, cotton and other agricultural output tends to fall, and the aggregate supply curve shifts to the right, as shown in Figure 11(b), raising equilibrium national income from Y_1 to Y_2.

Real business cycles explain why national output can expand or contract in the absence of a discretionary macroeconomic policy that would shift aggregate demand. To fully understand business cycles, we must consider both policy-induced changes in national income and real shocks that occur independent of government actions.

A business cycle can be the product of discretionary government policy or of real shocks that occur independent of government actions.

RECAP

1. The political business cycle is a short-term expansion stimulated by an administration before an election to earn votes. After the election comes the long-term adjustment (rising unemployment and inflation).

2. A real business cycle is an expansion and contraction caused by a change in tastes or technology, strikes, weather, or other real factors.

5. THE LINK BETWEEN MONETARY AND FISCAL POLICIES

In earlier chapters we have described how monetary and fiscal policies determine the equilibrium level of prices and national income. In our discussions we have talked about monetary policy and fiscal policy individually. Here we consider the relationship between them.

In some countries, monetary and fiscal policies are carried out by a single central authority. Even in the United States, where the Federal Reserve was created as an independent agency, monetary policy and fiscal policy are always related. The actions of the central bank have an impact on the proper role for fiscal policy, and the actions of fiscal policymakers have an impact on the proper role for monetary policy.

For example, suppose the central bank follows a monetary policy that raises interest rates. That policy raises the interest cost of new government debt, in the process increasing government expenditures. On the other hand, a fiscal policy that generates large fiscal deficits could contribute to higher interest rates. If the central bank has targeted an interest rate that lies below the current rate, the central bank could be drawn into an expansionary monetary policy.

5.a. The Government Budget Constraint

The *government budget constraint* clarifies the relationship between monetary and fiscal policies:

$$G = T + B + \Delta M^1$$

where

$$G = \text{government spending}$$
$$T = \text{tax revenue}$$
$$B = \text{government borrowing}$$
$$\Delta M = \text{the change in the money supply}$$

---

[1]The M in the government budget constraint is government-issued money (*base money* or *high-powered money*). It is easiest to think of this kind of money as currency, although in practice base money is more than currency.

The government budget constraint always holds because there are only three ways for the government to finance its spending: by taxing, by borrowing, and by creating money.

We can rewrite the government budget constraint with the change in M on the left-hand side of the equation:

$$\Delta M = (G - T) - B$$

In this form you can see that the change in government-issued money equals the government fiscal deficit $(G - T)$ minus borrowing. This equation is always true.

5.b. Monetary Reforms

In the United States and other industrial nations, monetary and fiscal policies are conducted by separate, independent agencies. Fiscal authorities (Congress and the president in the U.S.) cannot impose monetary policy on the central bank. But in typical developing countries, monetary and fiscal policies are controlled by a central political authority. Here monetary policy often is an extension of fiscal policy. Fiscal policy can impose an inflationary burden on monetary policy. If a country is running a large fiscal deficit, and much of this deficit cannot be financed by government borrowing, monetary authorities must create money to finance the deficit.

Using money to finance fiscal deficits has produced very rapid rates of inflation in several countries. As prices reach astronomical levels, currency must be issued with very large face values. For instance, when Bolivia faced a sharp drop in the availability of willing lenders, the government began to create money to finance its fiscal deficit. As the money supply increased in relation to the output of goods and services, prices rose. In 1985 the government was creating money so fast that the rate of inflation reached 8,170 percent. Lunch in a La Paz hotel could cost 10 million Bolivian pesos. You can imagine the problem of counting money and recording money values with cash registers and calculators. As the rate of inflation increased, Bolivians had to carry stacks of currency to pay for goods and services. Eventually the government issued a 1 million peso note, then 5 million and 10 million peso notes.

This extremely high inflation, or hyperinflation, ended when a new government introduced its economic program in August 1985. The program reduced government spending dramatically, which slowed the growth of the fiscal deficit. At the same time, a monetary reform was introduced. A **monetary reform** is a new monetary policy that includes the introduction of a new monetary unit. The central bank of Bolivia announced that it would restrict money creation and introduced a new currency, the Boliviano. It set 1 Boliviano equal to 1 million Bolivian pesos.

The new monetary unit, the Boliviano, did not lower prices; it lowered the units in which prices were quoted. Lunch now cost 10 Bolivianos instead of 10 million pesos. More important, the rate of inflation dropped abruptly.

How is inflationary monetary policy related to government fiscal policy?

monetary reform:
a new monetary policy that includes the introduction of a new monetary unit

Argentina's economy was one of those seriously injured by hyperinflation in the 1980s. In both 1983 and 1985, Argentina's central bank issued new units of currency in an effort to combat spiraling expansion. When no reform in fiscal policy accompanies a monetary change, however, no permanent decrease in the inflation rate can result. Thus Argentina's economy continued to "overheat" with double-digit inflation.

The introduction of a new monetary unit without a change in fiscal policy has no lasting effect on the rate of inflation.

Did the new unit of currency end the hyperinflation? No. The rate of inflation dropped because the new fiscal policy controls introduced by the government relieved the pressure on the central bank to create money in order to finance government spending. Remember the government budget constraint. The only way to reduce the amount of money being created is to reduce the fiscal deficit $(G - T)$ minus borrowing (B). Once fiscal policy is under control, monetary reform is possible. If a government introduces a new monetary unit without changing its fiscal policy, the monetary unit by itself has no lasting effect on the rate of inflation.

Table 2 lists monetary reforms enacted in recent years. Argentina had a monetary reform in June 1983. Yet by June 1985, another reform was needed. The inflationary problems Argentina faced could not be solved just by issuing a new unit of currency. Fiscal reform also was needed, and none was made. In any circumstances of inflationary monetary policy, monetary reform by itself is not enough. It must be coupled with a reduction in the fiscal deficit or an increase in government borrowing to produce a permanent change in the rate of inflation.

Monetary policy is tied to fiscal policy through the government budget constraint. Although money creation is not an important source of deficit financing in developed countries, it has been and still is a significant source of revenue for developing countries, where taxes are difficult to collect and borrowing is limited.

Country	Old Currency	New Currency	Date of Change	Nature of Change
Argentina	Peso	Peso Argentino	June 1983	1 peso Argentino = 10,000 pesos
	Peso Argentino	Austral	June 1985	1 austral = 1,000 pesos Argentino
Bolivia	Peso	Boliviano	January 1987	1 Boliviano = 1,000,000 pesos
Brazil	Cruzeiro	Cruzado	February 1986	1 cruzado = 1,000 cruzeiros
Chile	Peso	Escudo	January 1969	1 escudo = 1,000 pesos
	Escudo	Peso	September 1975	1 peso = 1,000 escudos
Israel	Pound	Shekel	February 1980	1 shekel = 10 pounds
	Old shekel	New shekel	September 1985	1 new shekel = 1,000 old shekels
Peru	Sol	Inti	February 1985	1 inti = 1,000 soles
Uruguay	Old peso	New peso	July 1975	1 new peso = 1,000 old pesos

RECAP

1. The government budget constraint $(G = T + B + \Delta M)$ defines the relationship between fiscal and monetary policies.

2. The implications of fiscal policy for the growth of the money supply can be seen by rewriting the government budget constraint this way: $\Delta M = (G - T) - B$.

3. A monetary reform is a new monetary policy that includes the introduction of a new unit of currency.

4. A government can end an inflationary monetary policy only by introducing a fiscal reform that lowers the fiscal deficit $(G - T)$ minus borrowing (B).

SUMMARY

▼▲ **What is the Phillips curve?**

1. The Phillips curve illustrates the relationship between inflation and the unemployment rate. § 1

▼▲ **Why does the Phillips curve vary from the short to the long run?**

2. In the long run, the trade-off between inflation and the unemployment rate disappears. § 1.b

3. The long-run Phillips curve is a vertical line at the natural rate of unemployment. § 1.b.2

▼▲ **What is the relationship between unexpected inflation and the unemployment rate?**

4. Unexpected inflation can affect the unemployment rate through wage expectations, inventory fluctuations, and wage contracts. § 2.a

▼▲ **How are macroeconomic expectations formed?**

5. Adaptive expectations are formed on the basis of past experience; rational expectations are formed on the basis of all available relevant information. §§ 2.b.1 and 2.b.2

▼▲ **What makes government policies credible?**

6. A policy is credible only if it is time consistent. § 3.b

▼▲ **How are business cycles related to political elections?**

7. A political business cycle is created by politicians who want to improve their chances of re-election by stimulating the economy just before an election. § 4.a

▼▲ **How do real shocks to the economy affect business cycles?**

8. Real business cycles are a product of unexpected change in technology, weather, or some other real variable. § 4.b

▼▲ **How is inflationary monetary policy related to government fiscal policy?**

9. The government budget constraint defines the relationship between monetary and fiscal policies. § 5.a

10. When government-issued money is used to finance fiscal deficits, inflationary monetary policy can be a product of fiscal policy. § 5.b

KEY TERMS

Phillips curve § 1
reservation wage § 2.a.1
adaptive expectation § 2.b.1
rational expectation § 2.b.2

time inconsistent § 3
shock § 4.b
monetary reform § 5.b

EXERCISES

Basic Terms and Concepts

1. What is the difference between the short-run Phillips curve and the long-run Phillips curve? Use an aggregate supply and demand diagram to explain why there is a difference between them.

2. Give two reasons why there may be a short-run trade-off between unexpected inflation and the unemployment rate.

3. "Unexpected increases in the money supply cause clockwise movements in the Phillips curve diagram; unexpected decreases in the money supply cause counterclockwise movements in the Phillips curve diagram." Evaluate this statement using a graph to illustrate your answer.

4. Economists have identified two kinds of macroeconomic expectations.
   a. Define them.
   b. What are the implications for macroeconomic policy of these two forms of expectations?

5. Write down the government budget constraint and explain how it can be used to understand the relationship between fiscal and monetary policies.

6. Using the government budget constraint, explain

   a. why some countries experience hyperinflation.

   b. how fiscal policy must change in order to implement a noninflationary monetary policy.

Extended Concepts

7. Parents, like governments, establish credibility by seeing to it that their "policies" (the rules they outline for their children) are time consistent. Analyze the potential for time consistency of these rules:

   a. If you don't eat the squash, you'll go to bed 30 minutes early tonight!

   b. If you get any grades below a C, you won't be allowed to watch television on school nights!

   c. If you don't go to my alma mater, I won't pay for your college education!

   d. If you marry that disgusting person, I'll disinherit you!

8. Suppose an economy has witnessed an 8 percent rate of growth in its money supply and prices over the last few years. How do you think the public will respond to an announced plan to increase the money supply by 4 percent over the next year if

   a. the central bank has a reputation for always meeting its announced policy goals.

   b. the central bank rarely does what it says it will do.

9. What are the implications for the timing of business-cycle fluctuations over the years if all business cycles are

   a. manipulated by incumbent administrations?

   b. a product of real shocks to the economy?

Teetering on the High Wire in Brazil

Two months after taking office, President Fernando Collor de Mello is fast approaching the moment of truth for his plan to integrate Brazil into the world economy.

At stake is a radical economic blueprint to end hyperinflation, remove barriers to imports and encourage foreign investment. Among other things, the plan would open Latin America's largest economy to private ownership in highway construction, telephone service and electric power generation, sectors that are now tightly controlled by the state.

Two crucial elements of the plan will soon come into play. By June 18, Brazil's ministers are to submit plans to cut payrolls by 20 to 25 percent — a total cut of up to 400,000 state workers. And by August, Mr. Collor, a staunch free-marketeer, is to start a quick-march privatization that is designed to put two-thirds of Brazil's 190 state companies into investor hands by 1995.

The goal is to attack the root cause of Brazil's chronic inflation — a Government deficit papered over during the 1980's by printing money. By trimming administrative costs and selling off companies — and by raising taxes and cracking down on tax cheats — Mr. Collor hopes to convert Brazil's 1989 budget deficit of $28 billion into a 1990 surplus of $7 billion. . . .

Whatever its ultimate fate, the Collor program began with a paradox: in the name of a free-market revolution, Brazil experienced the greatest state intervention in decades when the Government sought to stop inflation literally overnight by freezing

most of the money in circulation. For those doing business here, that set off a period of chaos that they are only now emerging from.

The "shock therapy" started on March 16, a day after the 40-year-old Mr. Collor was inaugurated as Brazil's first freely elected President in three decades. On that day, the Government froze for 18 months roughly 80 percent of savings and money market funds — about $90 billion — including the cash balances of businesses. It also imposed across-the-board wage and price controls.

And, to push its program to sell off state-owned companies, it announced that banks, insurers and pension plans would be required to buy "privatization certificates" that would be used to purchase shares in state companies. . . .

The sharp, unexpected liquidity freeze snapped this nation of 140 million people into the sharpest recession in a decade.

But the hard times have already begun to ease a bit. For example, in São Paulo, the nation's economic powerhouse, energy use is up and so are retail sales. Polls of business leaders indicate that the economy is recovering to a no-growth level.

The squeeze on money is at the heart of the economy's volatility. Liquidity was reduced March 16 from 40 percent of Brazil's $350 billion gross national product to 9 percent, according to Zélia Cardoso de Mello, the new economy minister. But today it is back up to 14 percent — partly through Government infusions to various sectors and partly through the knack that Brazilians have for knock-

ing illegal loopholes in barriers. . . .

For the moment, at least, the Government is enjoying a budget surplus — largely due to a 50 percent increase in tax collection and a series of new, one-time taxes on ownership of stocks, gold and savings accounts. . . .

The money squeeze, the wage and price freeze and the tax hikes allowed Mr. Collor to crow victory last month as Brazil's official monthly inflation rate plummeted to 3 percent, from 84 percent in March [1990].

But Mr. Collor inherited massive governmental obligations from his predecessor, obligations that could greedily — and quickly — devour the new tax collections.

"It's a two-month surplus — April and May," Roberto Campos, a Congressman and former Government minister, said in an interview here. "If spending is not cut and the deficit comes back, everything goes down the drain. . . ."

If Mr. Collor succeeds in curbing the deficit and hence inflation it would give him the political power to continue with the long-term goal of opening Brazil to more foreign investment and imports. . . .

But everything depends on the deficit, experts agree. "Either Collor does away with the deficit or the deficit does away with his plan," Antonio Delfim Netto, a Congressman, recently told a newspaper here. "Everything else is 'economese.'"

■ Source: James Brooke, "Teetering on the High Wire in Brazil," *The New York Times*, May 20, 1990, p. F12.

Commentary

There's an old saying that it is a curse to live in interesting times. A corollary of this expression, that it is a curse to live in interesting countries, may also be true, especially if the country is one in which the interest is provided by an economy gone awry. The case of Brazil, where inflation reached an annual rate of 34,000 percent in early 1990, has proven very interesting to economists. Unfortunately for the people of Brazil, serving as the "mice" in this economic "laboratory experiment" has been a painful experience as hyperinflation has decimated the national economy. The accompanying article describes the most recent attempt to bring economic stability to Brazil.

Four different economic plans in the last half of the 1980s failed to bring down inflation in Brazil. The poor performance of these programs, undertaken during the tenure of President José Sarney, can be attributed to their failure to cut government spending sufficiently. The importance of getting the government's budget under control in order to stop inflation reflects the link between fiscal policy and monetary policy and thus between fiscal policy and inflation. A government can finance a budget deficit by selling bonds or by printing money. If it chooses the latter option, the money creation will contribute to inflation, as was the case in Brazil in the late 1980s.

Fernando Collor de Mello, who was elected president of Brazil in December 1989, has undertaken a more radical therapy, one that involves deep cuts in government spending, attempts to increase the efficiency of tax collection, privatization, control of the money supply through freezing bank assets, and wage and price controls. Important aspects of this program are aimed at reducing the budget deficit; as one congressman put it, "Either Collor does away with the deficit or the deficit does away with his plan." Initially, at least, the increase in tax collection has raised government revenues. Auctioning off large government enterprises (privatizing these companies) will both raise revenues for the government and cut its costs of supporting industries that may have been run inefficiently. Cuts in the government payroll will further reduce the government's budget and with it the requirement for printing money.

Another aspect of Collor's plan involves freezing bank assets in excess of 50,000 cruzados (about $1,200). These assets will be repaid with interest by the government, but they cannot be withdrawn for 18 months. This policy has shrunk the money supply from 40 percent of GNP to 14 percent of GNP, a monetary contraction necessary for curbing inflation.

While this policy has reduced the rate of inflation, it has also caused a deep recession. In theory, it is possible to stop a hyperinflation without a recession, but this result depends upon a credible government policy. Recent history has provided the Brazilian public with four examples of failed stabilization plans. Collor's government has therefore instituted temporary wage and price controls to provide stability until the credibility of the new economic policy is established. To be effective, such controls must not be in place for long, which is why Collor intends that his disinflation plan take the form of a sudden "shock treatment" rather than a more gradual approach.

The results of President Collor's disinflation program will be closely watched by economists and non-economists alike. The outcome of Brazil's experience will provide economists with important information about stabilization policies in countries suffering from high inflation. More critically, the well-being of the people of the world's sixth most populous country rides on the success of this policy.

16

Macroeconomic Viewpoints: New Keynesian, Monetarist, and New Classical

FUNDAMENTAL QUESTIONS

1. What do Keynesian economists believe today?
2. What role do monetarists believe the government should play in the economy?
3. What is new classical economics?
4. How do new theories of economics develop over time?

PREVIEW Economists do not all agree on macroeconomic policy. Sometimes disagreements are due to normative differences, or differences in personal values, regarding what the truly pressing needs are that should be addressed. Other disagreements are based on different views of how the economy operates and what determines the equilibrium level of national income.

It would be very easy to classify economists, to call them liberals or conservatives, for example. But an economist who believes the government should not intervene in social decisions (abortion, censorship) may favor an active role for government in economic decisions (minimum wages, unemployment insurance, welfare benefits). Another economist may support an active role for government in regulating the social behavior of individuals, yet believe that government should allow free markets to operate without interference.

In this chapter we give you an overview of important differences among schools of macroeconomic thought. Most economists probably do not align themselves with any one theory of macroeconomics. But the three approaches we discuss in this chapter—Keynesian, monetarist, and new classical—have had enormous impact on macroeconomic thinking and policy in recent decades.

1. KEYNESIAN ECONOMICS

1.a. Economic Model

In Chapter 10 we described the Keynesian model of macroeconomic equilibrium. That simple model assumes that prices are constant and that changes in aggregate expenditures determine equilibrium national income. In an aggregate demand and supply analysis, the simple Keynesian model looks like the graph in Figure 1. The aggregate supply curve is a horizontal line at a fixed level of prices, P_1. Changes in aggregate demand cause changes in real national income with no change in the price level.

Figure 1 reflects the traditional Keynesian emphasis on aggregate demand as a determinant of equilibrium income. But no economist today would argue that the aggregate supply curve is always horizontal at every level of national income. More representative of Keynesian economics today is the aggregate supply curve shown in Figure 2. At low levels of national income, the curve is flat. In this region (the Keynesian region), increases in aggregate demand are associated with increases in output but not increases in prices. This flat region of the aggregate supply curve reflects the Keynesian belief that inflation is not a problem when unemployment is high. As the level of national income increases, approaching potential national income (Y_P), the aggregate supply curve grows steeper.

What do Keynesian economists believe today?

Keynesian economics:
a school of thought that emphasizes the role government plays in stabilizing the economy by managing aggregate demand

New Keynesian macroeconomists argue that wages and prices are not flexible in the short run.

The economic theories John Maynard Keynes proposed in the 1930s have given way to new theories. Today **Keynesian economics** focuses on the role the government plays in stabilizing the economy by managing aggregate demand. *New Keynesians* believe that wages and prices are not flexible in the short run. They use their analysis of business behavior to explain the Keynesian region on the aggregate supply curve. They believe that the economy is not always in equilibrium. For instance, if the demand for labor falls, we would expect the equilibrium price of labor (the wage) to fall and, because fewer people want to work at a lower wage, the number of people employed to fall. New Keynesians argue that wages do not tend to fall because firms choose to lay off workers rather than lower wages. They retain high wages for their remaining employees in order to maintain morale and productivity. The wage rigidity of New Keynesian economics is reflected in price rigidity in goods markets.

Figure 1
The Fixed-Price Keynesian Model
In the simple Keynesian model, prices are fixed at P_1 by the horizontal aggregate supply curve, so that changes in aggregate expenditures determine equilibrium national income.

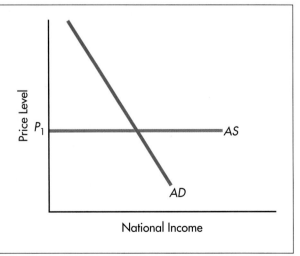

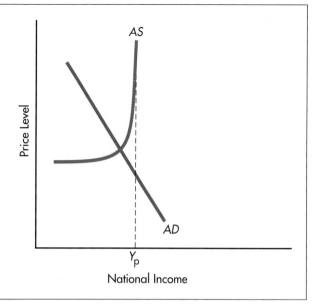

Figure 2
The Modern Keynesian Model
Modern Keynesians typically believe that the aggregate supply curve is horizontal only at relatively low levels of national income. As national income moves up toward potential income (Y_P), the aggregate supply curve becomes steeper.

1.b. The Policymaker's Problem

Because they believe that the economy is subject to disequilibrium in labor and goods markets, Keynesians believe the government must take an active role in the economy to restore equilibrium. Traditional Keynesians identified the private sector as an important source of shifts in aggregate demand. For example, they argued that investment is susceptible to sudden changes. If business spending falls, the argument continued, monetary and fiscal policies should be used to stimulate spending and offset the drop in business spending. Government intervention is necessary to stabilize aggregate demand and avoid recession. And if private spending increases, creating inflationary pressure, then monetary and fiscal policies should restrain spending, again to maintain aggregate demand.

New Keynesian macroeconomics does not focus on fluctuations in aggregate demand as the primary source of the problems facing policymakers. Keynesian economists realize that aggregate supply shocks can be substantial. But whatever the source of the instability—aggregate demand or aggregate supply—they tend to look to active government policy to return the economy to equilibrium.

RECAP

1. Keynesian economists today reject the simple fixed-price model in favor of a model in which the aggregate supply curve is relatively flat at low levels of national income, sloping upward as national income approaches its potential level.

2. Keynesians believe that the tendency for the economy to experience disequilibrium in labor and goods markets forces the government to intervene in the economy.

2. MONETARIST ECONOMICS

monetarist economics:
a school of thought that emphasizes
the role changes in the money supply
play in determining equilibrium
national income and price level

The Keynesian view dominated macroeconomics in the 1940s, 1950s, and most of the 1960s. In the late 1960s and the 1970s, Keynesian economics faced a challenge from **monetarist economics**, a school of thought that emphasizes the role changes in the money supply play in determining equilibrium income and prices. The leading monetarist, Milton Friedman, had been developing monetarist theory since the 1940s. But it would be several decades before his ideas became popular. In part the shift was a product of the forcefulness of Friedman's arguments, but the relatively poor macroeconomic performance of the United States in the 1970s probably contributed to a growing disenchantment with Keynesian economics, creating an environment ripe for new ideas. Economic Insight: "Milton Friedman" describes how Friedman's monetarist theories became popular.

2.a. Economic Model

Monetarists focus on the role of the money supply in determining the equilibrium level of national income and prices. In Chapter 14 we discussed monetary policy and equilibrium income. We showed that monetary policy is linked to changes in the equilibrium level of national income through changes in investment (and consumption). Keynesians traditionally assumed that monetary policy affects aggregate demand by changing the interest rate and, consequently, investment spending. Monetarists believe that changes in the money supply have broad effects on expenditures through both investment and consumption. An increase in the money supply pushes aggregate demand up by increasing both business and household spending, and raises the equilibrium level of national income. A decrease in the money supply does the opposite.

Monetarists believe that accelerating inflation is a product of efforts to increase real income through expansionary monetary policy.

Monetarists believe that changes in monetary policy (or fiscal policy, for that matter) have only a short-term effect on real national income. In the long run, they expect national income to be at a level consistent with the natural rate of unemployment. As a result, the long-run effect of a change in the money supply is fully reflected in a change in the price level. Attempts to exploit the short-run effects of expansionary monetary policy produce an inflationary spiral, in which the level of income increases temporarily then falls back to the potential level while prices rise. This is the rightward shift of the Phillips curve we described in Chapter 15.

2.b. The Policymaker's Problem

What role do monetarists believe the government should play in the economy?

Unlike Keynesian economists, monetarists do not believe that the economy is subject to a disequilibrium that must be offset by government action. Most monetarists believe that the economy tends toward equilibrium at the level of potential national income. Their faith in the free market (price) system leads them to favor minimal government intervention.

Monetarists often argue that government policy heightens the effects of the business cycle. This is especially true of monetary policy. To prove their point, monetarists link changes in the growth of the money supply to business cycle fluctuations. Specifically they suggest that periods of relatively fast money growth are followed by booms and inflation, and that periods of relatively slow money growth are followed by recessions.

Figure 3 shows the rate at which the money supply, consumer prices, and real GNP grew in the United States between 1957 and 1989. The inflation rate (consumer prices) seems to follow changes in the growth rate of the money supply with a lag of one or two years; GNP typically follows a change in the growth rate of the money supply by a year. The links between money growth and inflation, and money growth and GNP are by no means perfect. Sometimes there seem to be closer relationships than at other times. This makes it difficult to predict the effect of a particular change in monetary policy on prices or real GNP. In addition, a number of other variables influence GNP.

Monetarists favor nonactivist government policy because they believe that the government's attempts to make the economy better off by aiming monetary and fiscal policies at low inflation and low unemployment often make things worse. Why? Because economic policy, which is very powerful, operates with a long and variable lag. First policymakers have to recognize that a problem exists. This is the *recognition lag*. Then they

Economic policy operates with a long and variable lag.

Figure 3
The Growth Rate of the Money Supply, Consumer Prices, and Real GNP, United States, 1957–1989
In general, the inflation rate follows the rate at which the money supply grows with a lag of one or two years. Growth in real GNP follows growth in the money supply with a lag of about one year. Data from Economic Report of the President.

(a) Growth Rate of U.S. Money and Consumer Prices: 1957-1989

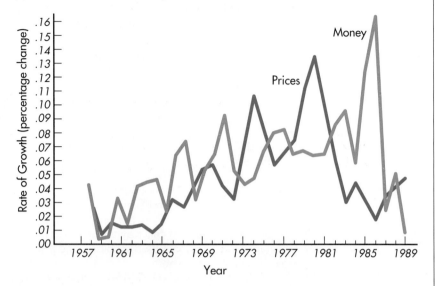

(b) Growth Rate of U.S. Money and Real GNP: 1957-1989

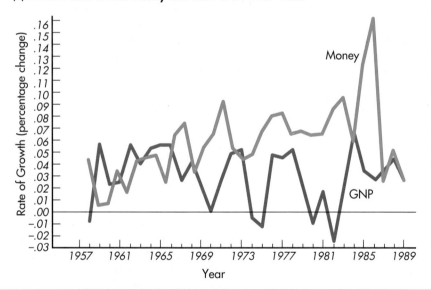

must formulate an appropriate policy. This is the *reaction lag*. Then the effects of the policy must work through the economy. This is the *effect lag*.

When the Federal Reserve changes the rate of growth of the money supply, real national income and inflation do not change immediately. In fact studies show that as much as two years can pass between a change in policy and the effect of that change on national income. This means that when policymakers institute a change targeted at a particular level of national income or rate of inflation, the effect of the policy is not felt for a long time. And it is possible that the economy could be facing an entirely different set of problems in a year or two than those policymakers are addressing today. But today's policy will still have effects next year, and those effects may aggravate next year's problems.

Because of the long and variable lag in the effect of fiscal and monetary policies, monetarists argue that policymakers should set policy according to rules that do not change from month to month or even year to year. What kinds of rules? A fiscal policy rule might be to balance the budget annually; a monetary policy rule might be to require that the money supply grow at a fixed rate over time. These kinds of rules restrict policymakers from formulating discretionary policy. Monetarists believe that by reducing discretionary shifts in policy, economic growth is steadier than it is when government consciously sets out to achieve full employment and low inflation.

RECAP

1. Monetarists emphasize the role changes in the money supply play in determining equilibrium national income and the level of prices.

2. Monetarists do not believe that the economy is subject to disequilibrium in the labor and goods markets or that government should take an active role in the economy.

3. Because economic policy operates with a long and variable lag, attempts by government to stabilize the economy, in fact, may make matters worse.

4. Monetarists believe that formal rules should govern economic policy making.

3. NEW CLASSICAL ECONOMICS

In the 1970s an alternative to Keynesian and monetarist economics was developed: new classical economics. But before we discuss the new classical theory, let's look at the old one.

classical economics:
a school of thought that assumes that real national income is determined by aggregate supply, while the equilibrium price level is determined by aggregate demand

Classical economics is the theory that was popular before Keynes changed the face of economics in the 1930s. Figure 4, the classical aggregate demand and supply diagram, shows the classical economist's view of the world. The vertical aggregate supply curve means that the equilibrium level of output (income) is a product only of the determinants of aggregate supply: the price of resources, technology, and expectations (Chapter 11).

If the aggregate supply curve is vertical, then changes in aggregate demand change only the price level; they do not affect the equilibrium level of output. Classical economics assumes that prices and wages are perfectly flexible. This rules out contracts that fix prices or wages for periods of time. It also rules out the possibility that people are not aware of all prices and wages. They know when prices have gone up and ask for wage increases to compensate.

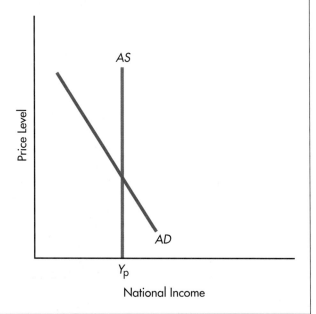

Figure 4
The Classical Model
The vertical aggregate supply curve indicates that equilibrium national income is determined strictly by the determinants of aggregate supply.

Keynesians and monetarists would argue that information about the economy, including prices and wages, is not perfect. When workers and businesses negotiate wages, they may not know what current prices are, but they certainly do not know what future prices will be. Furthermore, many labor contracts fix wages for long periods of time. This means that wages are not flexible, that they cannot adjust to new price levels.

3.a. Economic Model

new classical economics:
a school of thought that holds that changes in real national income are a product of unexpected changes in the level of prices

▼ What is new classical economics?
▲

New classical economics was a response to the problems of meeting economic policy goals in the 1970s. New classical economists questioned some of the assumptions on which Keynesian economics was based. For instance, new classical economists believe wages are flexible, while both traditional Keynesian and New Keynesian economists assume wages can be fixed in the short run.

New classical economics does not assume that people know everything that is happening, as the old theory did. People make mistakes because their expectations of prices or some other critical variable are different from the future reality. New classical economists emphasize rational expectations. As defined in Chapter 15, *rational expectations* are based on all available relevant information. This was a new way of thinking about expectations. Earlier theories assumed that people formed adaptive expectations—that their expectations were based only on their past experience. With rational expectations, people learn, not only from their past experience, but also from any other information that helps them predict the future.

Suppose the chairman of the Federal Reserve Board announces a new monetary policy. Price level expectations that are formed rationally take this announcement into consideration; those formed adaptively do not. It is much easier for policymakers to make unexpected changes in policy if expectations are formed adaptively rather than rationally.

Another element of new classical economics is the belief that markets are in equilibrium. Keynesian economics argues that disequilibrium in markets demands government intervention. For instance, Keynesian economists define a recession as a disequilibrium in the labor market—a surplus of labor. New classical economists believe that because real wages are lower during a recession, people are more willing to substitute nonlabor activities (going back to school, early retirement, work at home, or leisure) for work. As the economy recovers and wages go up, people substitute away from nonlabor activities toward more working hours. The substitution of labor for leisure and leisure for labor, over time, suggests that much of observed unemployment is voluntary in the sense that those who are unemployed choose not to take a job at a wage below their reservation wage (see Chapter 15).

3.b. The Policymaker's Problem

New classical economics emphasizes expectations. Its basic tenet is that changes in monetary policy can change the equilibrium level of real national income only if those changes are *unexpected*. Fiscal policy can change equilibrium national income only if it *unexpectedly* changes the level of prices or one of the determinants of aggregate supply.

Figure 5 (which is the same as Figure 4 in Chapter 15) illustrates the new classical view of the effect of an unexpected increase in the money supply. Suppose initially the expected rate of inflation is 3 percent and the actual rate of inflation is also 3 percent. The economy is operating at point 1 in part (b), the Phillips curve diagram, with unemployment at 5 percent, which is assumed to be the natural rate of unemployment. At the natural rate of unemployment, the economy is producing the potential level of national income (Y_P), at price level P_1. If the central bank unexpectedly increases the money supply, pushing the inflation rate up from 3 percent to 6 percent, the economy moves from point 1 to point 2 along short-run Phillips curve I, which is based on 3 percent expected inflation. The unemployment rate is now 3 percent, which is less than the natural rate. In part (a), national income rises above potential income to Y_2.

Over time, people come to expect 6 percent inflation. They adjust to the higher inflation rate, and the economy moves back to the natural rate of unemployment. At the expected rate of inflation, 6 percent, the economy is operating at point 3 on short-run Phillips curve II. As the expected rate of inflation increases from 3 percent to 6 percent, workers negotiate higher wages and the aggregate supply curve shifts to the left, from AS_1 to AS_2. A new equilibrium exists at point 3 in the aggregate demand and supply diagram, and national income drops back to its potential level.

The analysis changes dramatically if the change in the money supply is expected. Now the economy moves, not from point 1 to point 2 to point 3,

(a) Aggregate Demand and Supply

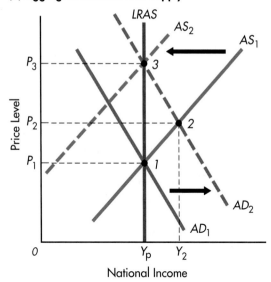

(b) The Phillips Curve

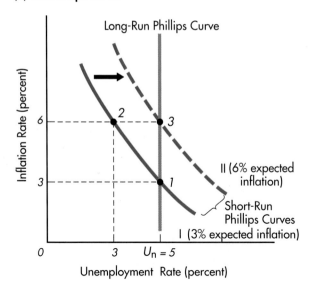

Figure 5
New Classical Economics

New classical economists believe that government-induced shifts in aggregate demand affect national income only if they are unexpected. In part (a), the economy initially is operating at point 1, with national income at Y_P, the potential level. An unexpected increase in aggregate demand shifts the economy to point 2, where both national income (Y_2) and prices (P_2) are higher. Over time, as sellers adjust to higher prices and costs of doing business, aggregate supply shifts from AS_1 to AS_2. This shift moves the economy to point 3. Here income is back at the potential level and prices are even higher. In the long run, an increase in aggregate demand does not increase output. The long-run aggregate supply curve (LRAS) is a vertical line at the potential level of national income.

If the expected rate of inflation is 3 percent and actual inflation is 3 percent, the economy is operating at point 1, at the natural rate of unemployment (U_n). If aggregate demand increases, there is an unexpected increase in inflation from 3 percent to 6 percent. This moves the economy from point 1 to point 2 along short-run Phillips curve I. Here the unemployment rate is 3 percent. As people learn to expect 6 percent inflation, they adjust to the higher rate and the economy moves back to the natural rate of unemployment, at point 3. If the increase in inflation is expected, then the economy moves from point 1 to point 3 directly with no temporary decrease in the unemployment rate.

New classical economists believe that wages and prices are flexible and that people form expectations rationally, so that only unexpected changes in the price level can affect real national income.

but from 1 directly to point 3. This is because the shift from point 1 to point 2 is temporary, based on unexpected inflation. If the inflation is expected, the economy is on short-run Phillips curve II, where inflation is 6 percent, unemployment is at the natural rate, and national income is at the potential level.

The lesson of new classical economics for policymakers is that managing aggregate demand has an effect on real national income only if change is unexpected. Any predictable policy simply affects prices. As a result, new classical economists argue that monetary and fiscal policies should be aimed at maintaining a low, stable rate of inflation, that they should not attempt to alter real national income and unemployment. This brings new classical economists close to the monetarists, who would choose policy rules over discretionary policy.

RECAP

1. New classical economics holds that wages are flexible and that expectations are formed rationally, so that only unexpected changes in prices have an effect on real national income.

2. New classical economists believe that markets are always in equilibrium.

3. According to new classical economic theory, any predictable macroeconomic policy has an effect only on prices.

4. New classical economists argue that monetary and fiscal policies should try to achieve a low, stable rate of inflation rather than changes in real national income or unemployment.

4. COMPARISON AND INFLUENCE

The three theories of macroeconomics we have been talking about often are treated as though they are different in every way. Yet at times they overlap and even share conclusions. Moreover, as we mentioned at the beginning of the chapter, it is an oversimplification to categorize economists by a single school of thought. Many if not most economists do not classify themselves by economic theory. Typically they take elements of each so that their approach to macroeconomics is more a synthesis of the various theories than strict adherence to any one theory.

▼ How do new theories of economics develop over time? ▲

Macroeconomic theories have developed over time in response to the economy's performance and the shortcomings of existing theories. Keynesian economics became popular in the 1930s because classical economics did not explain or help resolve the Great Depression. Monetarist economics offered an explanation for rising unemployment and rising inflation in the United States in the 1960s and 1970s. New classical economics suggested an alternative explanation for rising unemployment and inflation that the static Phillips curve analysis used by traditional Keynesians could not explain. Each of these theories, then, was developed or became popular because an existing theory did not answer pressing new questions.

All of these theories have influenced government policy. A by-product of Keynes's work in the 1930s was the wide acceptance and practice of activist government fiscal policy. Monetarist influence was dramatically apparent in the change in monetary policy announced by the Federal Reserve in 1979. Monetarists had criticized the Fed's policy of targeting interest rates. They argued that money-growth targets would stabilize income and prices. In October 1979, Chairman Paul Volcker announced that the Fed would concentrate more on achieving money-growth targets and less on controlling interest rates. This change in policy reflected the Fed's concern over rising inflation and the belief that the monetarists were right, that a low rate of money growth would bring about a low rate of

Table 1 Major Approaches to Macroeconomic Policy

Approach	Major Source of Problems	Proper Role for Government
New Keynesian	Disequilibrium in private labor and goods markets	Active management of monetary and fiscal policies to restore equilibrium
Monetarist	Government's discretionary policies increase and decrease aggregate demand	Follow fixed rules for money growth and minimize fiscal policy shocks
New classical	Government policies have effect on real income only if unexpected, yet government tries to manipulate aggregate demand.	Follow predictable monetary and fiscal policies for long-run stability

inflation. The new policy led to an abrupt drop in the rate of inflation, from more than 13 percent in 1979 to less than 4 percent in 1982.

The new classical economists' emphasis on expectations calls for more information from policymakers to allow private citizens to incorporate government plans in their outlook for the future. The Federal Reserve Reform Act (1977) and the Full Employment and Balanced Growth Act (1978) require the Board of Governors to report to Congress semiannually on its goals and money targets for the next twelve months. New classical economists also believe that only credible government policies can affect expectations. In the last chapter we discussed the time consistency of plans. For plans to be credible, to influence private expectations, they must be time consistent.

Table 1 summarizes the three approaches to macroeconomics, describing the major source of problems facing policymakers and the proper role of government policy according to each view. Only Keynesian economics supports an active role for government; the other two theories suggest that government should not intervene in the economy.

RECAP

1. Different economic theories developed over time as changing economic conditions pointed out the shortcomings of existing theories.

2. Keynesian, monetarist, and new classical economics have each influenced macroeconomic policy.

3. Only Keynesian economists believe that government should actively intervene to stabilize the economy.

SUMMARY

1. All economists do not agree on the determinants of economic equilibrium or the appropriate role of government policy. Preview

▼▲ **What do Keynesian economists believe today?**

2. Keynesian economists believe the government should take an active role in stabilizing the economy by managing aggregate demand. § 1.a

▼▲ **What role do monetarists believe the government should play in the economy?**

3. Monetarists do not believe that the economy is subject to serious disequilibrium, which means they favor minimal government intervention in the economy. § 2.b

4. Monetarists believe that a government that takes an active role in the economy may do more harm than good because economic policy operates with a long and variable lag. § 2.b

▼▲ **What is new classical economics?**

5. New classical economics holds that only unexpected changes in policy can influence real national income, so government policy should target a low, stable rate of inflation. § 3.b

▼▲ **How do new theories of economics develop over time?**

6. New economic theories are a response to changing economic conditions that point out the shortcomings of existing theories. § 4

KEY TERMS

Keynesian economics § 1.a
monetarist economics § 2

classical economics § 3
new classical economics 3.a

EXERCISES

Basic Terms and Concepts

1. What is the difference between traditional Keynesian and new Keynesian economics?

2. Why does monetary policy operate with a long and variable lag? Give an example to illustrate your explanation.

3. What is the difference between old classical and new classical economics?

4. Draw an aggregate demand and supply diagram for each theory of macroeconomics. Use the diagrams to explain how the government can influence equilibrium national income and prices.

Extended Concepts

5. What, if any, similarities are there among the theories of economics discussed in this chapter regarding the use of fiscal and monetary policies to stimulate national income?

6. If unexpected increases in the growth rate of the money supply can increase real national income, why doesn't the Fed follow a policy of unexpectedly increasing the money supply to increase the growth of real national income?

7. "The popular macroeconomic theories have evolved over time as economic conditions have changed to reveal shortcomings of existing theory." Evaluate this quote in terms of the emergence of the three theories discussed in this chapter.

'Fresh Water' Economists Gain

— To tinker or not to tinker? For decades most politicians and professors of economics have taken it for granted that the Government must adjust the engines of the economy to avoid recessions and create jobs. But lately, a long-belittled school of skeptics who think the Government usually just gums things up is gaining attention and influence.

The skeptics are known as "fresh water" economists, less for the purity of their thought than for their origins at universities along the shores of the Great Lakes.

The school's views are filtering into such lofty citadels of mainstream "salt water" economics as Harvard, [M.I.T.], Princeton and Stanford. . . .

The fresh-water people build their case for minimal intervention on the view that workers, consumers, business executives and investors anticipate changes in the economy faster than the Government and can adjust to them better on their own.

While acknowledging that their theories have disclosed some flaws, this school maintains that people also anticipate the effects of changes in Government policy and sometimes blunt the Government's objectives in devising ways to accommodate the changes.

These are jolting thoughts for the older school of economists, which has dominated policy making since the Presidency of Franklin D. Roosevelt. Salt-water scholars are mostly liberal and conservative Keynesians, who maintain that the economy needs a Government pilot who manipulates taxes, spending and interest rates to try to keep the economy out of a slump. . . .

Robert E. Lucas, the undisputed dean of the fresh-water school and chairman of the economics department at the University of Chicago, said, "What we're turning against is the idea that you can fine-tune the economy with any policy at all." The university has long been the home of monetarist economics . . . of which the newer theory is an offshoot. . .

Doubt about Government intrusion in the economy is hardly new. Conservatives of many stripes seek smaller Government, including President Reagan's tax-cutting corps of supply-siders. But at places like M.I.T. and Harvard, which have produced scores of the Government's top economists, the current debate has displaced one that raged for decades between pure monetarists and Keynesians. . . .

Robert Hall, a Stanford professor and a more mainstream economist, conceived the fresh-water, salt-water distinction a decade ago upon noting the workplaces of the new group's leaders — Mr. Lucas in Chicago, Thomas J. Sargent, formerly at the University of Minnesota and now at the Hoover Institution at Stanford, and Robert J. Barro, then at the University of Rochester and now at Harvard. They are also known as "rational expectationists" and as "neoclassical macroeconomists," a term reflecting the school's roots in the classical economics of Adam Smith and David Ricardo. . . .

The salt-water view arises from an eclectic compromise that has settled some earlier battles among competing theories. Keynesians said the economy could be driven out of a recession by the budget — by cutting taxes, increasing spending and letting deficits grow.

Pure monetarists said it could be driven out of a recession by keeping the growth of the nation's money supply unwaveringly steady. Less pure monetarists said the Government could fiddle with the money supply to let interest rates decline. These groups have found that no single approach really does the job, so they have combined elements of all the approaches.

In view of the record of faulty forecasts, many of these economists have come around to acknowledging that the fresh-water crowd might have a point in maintaining that people adjust to an ailing economy, by building up their savings, for example. But that does not mean the Government should walk away from the economy, they say.

The debate translates into policy making when, for example, the Government becomes alarmed about rising unemployment in a recession. Invariably, when recessions develop, the Government looks for ways to expand its aid to those who lose jobs. . .

"The fresh-water group says you can rely on supply and demand," said Mr. Hall of Stanford. "The salt-water group says it's a little more complicated than that." Olivier Blanchard, an economics professor at Harvard, said, "The debate is among people who believe that free markets work and people who are less sure."

■ Source: Peter T. Kilborn, " 'Fresh Water' Economists Gain," *The New York Times*, July 23, 1988, pp. 35, 37.

Commentary

Macroeconomics has always been a lively field, filled with controversy over the proper approach to modeling the economy, the correct interpretation of experience, and the role government policy can and should play. Indeed, debate in macroeconomics is as old as the field itself. The views of John Maynard Keynes, the founder of macroeconomics, were challenged by his colleague at Cambridge University, Arthur Pigou. The focus of this debate was the importance of the "real balance effect," whereby a fall in the price level raises real money balances (or the purchasing power of the money supply), increases wealth, and thus increases consumption. Like most debates in macroeconomics, this was more than an ivory-tower exercise since the real balance effect provides a channel for the economy to bring itself out of a slump without government intervention.

The debate between the Keynesians and the monetarists dominated macroeconomic discourse of the 1950s and 1960s. During this period, those who identified themselves as Keynesians gave primacy to the role of fiscal policy and to the issue of unemployment; these economists had great faith in the ability of the government to "fine-tune" the economy through the proper application of policy, thereby ensuring stability and growth. Keynesians of this vintage also believe that changes in the money supply had little effect on the economy. In contrast, monetarists were very concerned about inflation, which they believed to be a purely monetary phenomenon. These economists also doubted that active government intervention could stabilize the economy, for they believed that policy operated only with long and variable lags.

The shape of the Phillips curve prompted a great deal of theoretical debate in the late 1960s. The prevailing Keynesian view was that policymakers could choose any mix of inflation and unemployment through the proper application of fiscal or monetary policy. Milton Friedman of the University of Chicago and Edmund Phelps of Columbia University countered this idea, proposing that unemployment, in the long run, would be at its "natural" rate. In their view, attempts to keep unemployment below this natural rate would only result in ever-increasing rates of inflation.

A view even more at odds with the traditional Phillips-curve analysis was proposed in the 1970s by Thomas Sargent and Neil Wallace, both then of the University of Minnesota. They showed that in a model of an economy in which people used all information efficiently, attempts by the government to raise employment by increasing the money supply would have *no* effect on employment and would only lead to an increase in the price level. This analysis was an early neoclassical (also called rational expectationist) approach to modeling the economy. As discussed in the article, this approach has evolved into the "fresh-water" school.

Many economists take issue with the "fresh-water" approach to macroeconomics, which is characterized by well-functioning markets, the efficient use of information, and the consequent ineffectiveness of government policy. In criticizing the "fresh-water" approach, economists consider why prices may not clear markets, why people may not be able to use information efficiently, and thus how government policy affects the economy. Many of the most influential economists who take this "Neo-Keynesian" view are found at universities on either coast—hence the "salt-water" label.

While outside observers may view the debate within macroeconomics as evidence of confusion, a more accurate appraisal is that the debate is a healthy intellectual response to a world in which few things are certain and much is unknown, and perhaps unknowable. The well-publicized debate masks the fact that there is a great deal of consensus about a number of issues in macroeconomics. This consensus is a product of lessons learned from past debates. In a similar fashion, the controversies of today will yield tomorrow's consensus and our knowledge of the real workings of the economy will grow.

17

Macroeconomic Links
Between Countries

1. How does change in the exchange rate affect the price of goods traded between countries?

2. Why don't similar goods sell for the same price all over the world?

3. What is the relationship between inflation and changes in the exchange rate?

4. What is the domestic currency return from a foreign bond?

5. What is the relationship between domestic and foreign interest rates and changes in the exchange rate?

6. Why don't similar financial assets yield the same return all over the world?

7. How does fiscal policy affect exchange rates?

8. How does monetary policy affect exchange rates?

9. What can countries gain by coordinating their macroeconomic policies?

PREVIEW   In every chapter we have talked about the international aspects of the topics discussed. But we have yet to explicitly consider how individual economies are linked together in a global economy. At a basic level, the economic ties between nations are much like the economic ties between any two markets in different locations. For example, when Mazda introduced the Miata sports car to the United States, there were not enough cars to meet the initial demand. So car dealers began charging thousands of dollars more than the $13,000 sticker price. In some states the cars sold for almost double the sticker price; in others the surcharge was relatively small. In California the price reached approximately $25,000; in Michigan, about $15,000. What happened? Enterprising individuals were buying Miatas in Michigan and reselling them in California. This purchase and resale activity raised the price of the car in Michigan and lowered the price in California until the price in California exceeded the Michigan price only by an amount equal to shipping and other transaction costs.

arbitrage:
simultaneously buying in a market where the price is low and selling in a market where the price is high to profit from the price differential

The California and Michigan markets were linked by **arbitrage**, the act of buying in a market where the price is low and selling in a market where the price is high to profit from the price differential. Arbitrageurs equalize prices in different markets. When they buy in the low-price market, prices there go up. And when they sell in the high-price market, prices there fall.

We are talking about California and Michigan and the market for sports cars. We could be talking about Japan and Canada and the market for sheet steel, or Israel and Brazil and the market for diamonds, or any number of different countries and different goods. Arbitrage produces similar prices for similar goods and generates similar returns from similar financial assets wherever they are traded. Arbitrage links economies to each other.

open economy:
an economy that trades goods and financial assets with the rest of the world

In this chapter we discuss the ties among national economies. Our discussion applies to **open economies**, economies that trade goods and financial assets with the rest of the world. A closed economy is isolated economically from the rest of the world; it does not trade with other nations. Although no economy is absolutely closed, there are different degrees of openness. Table 1 ranks 18 countries in order of the value of international trade as a fraction of gross national product. Nations with a large domestic market in relation to the value of international trade, like Japan and the United States, are relatively closed. Nations where the value of international trade is large in relation to the size of the domestic market, like Malaysia and Jamaica, are relatively open. The more open the

Table 1   A Sample of Countries Ranked in Order of Openness

Country	(Exports + Imports) /GNP	Country	(Exports + Imports) /GNP
Malaysia	1.33	Germany	.63
Jamaica	1.23	Kenya	.51
Israel	.90	Philippines	.51
Korea	.74	United Kingdom	.50
Thailand	.72	Egypt	.37
Austria	.71	Australia	.36
Paraguay	.71	Pakistan	.30
Sweden	.65	Japan	.27
Sri Lanka	.64	United States	.20

Source: International Monetary Fund, *International Financial Statistics* (Washington, D.C., 1990). Used by permission.

economy, the more sensitive prices and interest rates in the country to changes in international economic conditions.

1. PRICES AND EXCHANGE RATES

An exchange rate is the price of one money in terms of another. The exchange rate doesn't enter into the purchase and sale of Miatas in Michigan and California because each state uses the U.S. dollar. But for goods and services traded across national borders, the exchange rate is an important part of the total price. In later chapters we discuss some of the ways nations restrict free trade in their currencies, the ways they "manage" exchange rates. Here we assume that currencies are traded freely for each other and that foreign exchange markets respond to supply and demand without government intervention.

Let's look at an example: a U.S. wine importer purchases 1,000,000 French francs (FF1,000,000) worth of wine from France. The importer demands francs in order to pay the French wine seller. Suppose the initial equilibrium exchange rate is $.15 = FF1. At this rate, the U.S. importer needs 1,000,000 francs at $.15 apiece, or $150,000:

$$\$.15 \times 1,000,000 = \$150,000$$

1.a. Appreciation and Depreciation

When the exchange rate between two currencies changes, we say that one currency *depreciates* while the other *appreciates*. Suppose the exchange rate goes from $.15 = FF1 to $.20 = FF1. The French franc is now worth $.20 instead of $.15. The dollar has *depreciated* in value in relation to the franc; dollars are worth less in terms of francs. At the new equilibrium exchange rate, the U.S. importer needs $200,000 ($.20 × 1,000,000) to buy FF1,000,000 worth of wine.

Instead of saying that the dollar has depreciated against the franc, we can say that the franc has *appreciated* against the dollar. If the dollar is depreciating against the franc, the franc must be appreciating against the dollar. Whichever way we describe the change in the exchange rate, the result is that francs are now worth more in terms of dollars. The price of a franc has gone from $.15 to $.20.

As exchange rates change, the prices of goods and services traded in international markets also change. Suppose the dollar appreciates against the franc. This means that a franc costs fewer dollars; it also means that French goods cost U.S. buyers less. If the exchange rate falls to $.10 = FF1, FF1,000,000 costs $100,000 ($.10 × 1,000,000). The French wine has become less expensive to the U.S. importer.

How does change in the exchange rate affect the price of goods traded between countries?

☐ When the domestic (home) currency *depreciates,* foreign goods become *more expensive* to domestic buyers.

☐ When the domestic currency *appreciates,* foreign goods become *less expensive* to domestic buyers.

Let's look at the problem from the French side. When the dollar price of the franc rises, the franc price of the dollar falls; and when the dollar price of the franc falls, the franc price of the dollar rises. If the dollar price of the franc ($/FF) is originally $.15, the franc price of the dollar (FF/$) is the reciprocal (1/.15), or FF6.67. If the dollar depreciates against the franc to $.20, then the franc appreciates against the dollar to 1/.20, or FF5. As the franc appreciates, U.S. goods become less expensive to French buyers. If the dollar appreciates against the franc to $.10, then the franc depreciates against the dollar to 1/.10, or FF10. As the franc depreciates, U.S. goods become more expensive to French buyers.

□ When the domestic currency *depreciates,* domestic goods become *less expensive* to foreign buyers.

□ When the domestic currency *appreciates,* domestic goods become *more expensive* to foreign buyers.

When the dollar depreciates, U.S. goods become less expensive to foreign buyers; as the dollar appreciates, those goods become more expensive.

The exchange rate is just one determinant of the demand for goods and services. Income, tastes, the prices of substitutes and complements, expectations, and the exchange rate, all determine the demand for U.S. wheat. As the dollar depreciates in relation to other currencies, the demand for U.S. wheat increases (along with foreign demand for all other U.S. goods) even if all the other determinants do not change. Conversely, as the dollar appreciates, the demand for U.S. wheat falls (along with foreign demand for all other U.S. goods) even if all the other determinants do not change.

1.b. Purchasing Power Parity

Within a country, where prices are quoted in terms of a single currency, all we need to know is the price in the domestic currency of an item in two different locations to determine where our money buys more. If Joe's bookstore charges $20 for a book and Pete's bookstore charges $40 for the same book, the purchasing power of our money is twice as great at Joe's as it is at Pete's.

International comparisons of prices must be made using exchange rates because different countries use different monies. Once we cross national borders, prices are quoted in different currencies. Suppose Joe's bookstore in New York City charges $20 for a book and Pierre's bookstore in Paris charges FF40. To compare the prices, we must know the exchange rate between dollars and francs.

purchasing power parity (PPP): the condition under which monies have the same purchasing power in different markets

If we find that goods sell for the same price in different markets, our money has the same purchasing power in those markets, which means that we have **purchasing power parity (PPP)**. PPP reflects a relationship among the domestic price level, the exchange rate, and the foreign price level:

$$P = EP^F$$

where

P = the domestic price
E = the exchange rate (units of domestic currency per unit of foreign currency)
P^F = the foreign price

If the dollar-franc exchange rate is .50 ($.50 = FF1), then a book priced at FF40 in Pierre's store in Paris costs the same as a book priced at $20 in Joe's store in New York:

$$P = EP^F$$
$$= \$.50 \times 40$$
$$= \$20$$

To determine the domestic currency value of a foreign currency price, multiply the exchange rate times the foreign price.

The domestic price (we are assuming that the U.S. dollar is the domestic currency) equals the exchange rate times the foreign price. Because the domestic price of the book in Paris is $20 and the price at home is $20, PPP holds. The purchasing power (value) of the dollar is the same in both places.

▼
Why don't similar goods sell for the same price all over the world?
▲

Why don't similar goods sell for the same price everywhere? Actually they don't even sell for the same price within a country. If the same textbook is priced differently at different bookstores, it is unrealistic to expect the price of the book to be identical worldwide. There are several reasons why PPP does not hold. The most important are that goods are not identical, that information is costly, that shipping costs affect prices, and that tariffs and legal restrictions on trade affect prices. If these factors did not exist, we would expect that any time a price was lower in one market than another, arbitragers would buy in the low-price market (pushing prices up) and simultaneously sell in the high price market (pushing prices down). This arbitrage activity would ensure that PPP holds; however, there are several reasons why this arbitrage does not occur.

Purchasing power parity does not hold perfectly for differentiated products. The photo shows a Hungarian-made bus used in Portland, Oregon. Busses are not all alike. Just as busses made by two different firms in the United States will differ, so will busses made by other nations. There is no reason why similar, but nonidentical products must sell for the same price worldwide.

Deluxe Hotel Single Room
(average price incl. any tax and service charges)

Paris (Georges V)	320.46
Tokyo (Okura)	316.00
London (Hilton)	295.00
New York (Vista)	231.33
Hong Kong (Hilton)	187.40
Rio (Caesar Park)	186.00
Bonn (Bristol)	151.00
Kansas City, Mo.	124.00 (Alameda Plaza)

McDonald's Big Mac

Paris	2.97
Tokyo	2.80
Bonn	2.50
New York	2.19
London	2.09
Kansas City, Mo.	1.45
Rio	1.18
Hong Kong	.98

One Mile Metered Taxi Ride

Tokyo	3.50
Paris	2.31
New York	2.20
London	2.18
Kansas City, Mo.	1.90
Bonn	1.21
Rio	.90
Hong Kong	.71

Man's Haircut in Hotel Barbershop

Tokyo (Okura)	36.40
London (Meridien)	30.03
New York (Waldorf)	21.00
Rio (Caesar Park)	18.70
Paris (Georges V)	17.80
Kansas City, Mo.	14.50 (Alameda Plaza)
Bonn (Bristol)	12.00
Hong Kong (Hilton)	4.50

Local Telephone Call from Pay Phone

Kansas City, Mo.	.25
New York	.25
London	.18
Paris	.18
Rio	.15
Hong Kong	.13
Bonn	.12
Tokyo	.08

First – Run Movie

Tokyo	11.40
Bonn	7.25
New York	7.00
London	6.37
Paris	6.23
Kansas City, Mo.	4.50
Hong Kong	2.96
Rio	1.57

Figure 1
What the Dollar Won't Buy
The charts compare the prices of eight common items in eight major cities: two in the United States and six abroad. All prices were converted to U.S. dollars at the current exchange rates in December 1987. Obviously prices differ considerably across cities, which means that PPP does not hold. Source: *Wall Street Journal*, December 4, 1987, p. 37.

Goods are not identical　We would expect PPP to hold for identical goods, but few goods sold around the world are exactly the same in every country. In December 1987, the *Wall Street Journal* published a comparison of the dollar value of eight goods and services in eight major cities of the world (Figure 1). Several of the products listed here are similar but not identical. Certainly a deluxe room in one hotel is not the same as a deluxe room in another hotel, even in the same city. To compare the price of a hotel room in Paris with a hotel room in Kansas City is to compare different goods. The fact that the Paris hotel costs much more than the Kansas City hotel may reflect quality differences or differences in the local market in each city. But even if the rooms were identical, it would be difficult to profit from the price difference through arbitrage because hotel services are not easy to transfer. You cannot buy hotel rooms where they appear to be relatively inexpensive and then resell them where they appear to be relatively expensive. Hotel rooms are not like sports cars.

Several of the goods described in Figure 1 are identical goods and transportable, but they sell for very different prices. A Big Mac in Paris costs $2.97; a Big Mac in Hong Kong is just $.98. Why? This is where the costs of information, shipping costs, and tariffs and legal restrictions come into play.

Information is costly　People do not know everything about everything. To learn about the quality or prices of a product offered by different stores takes time and effort. It is in this sense that information is costly. Goods may sell for different prices in different countries in part because of information costs. When we pay $2.97 for a Big Mac in Paris, we may not know that a Big Mac is selling for $.98 in Hong Kong. Furthermore, the price in Hong Kong may be irrelevant to our decision to buy a Big Mac in Paris. The Big Mac is such a small part of our total budget that it would not be worth our time to find out what the item costs in other countries. However, for automobiles and other expensive items, international price differences may determine where goods are bought. When prices are high, the value of information about differences in international prices may be worth the cost of obtaining that information.

Shipping costs after prices　It is costly to ship goods from one country to another. Shipping costs are reflected in price differentials across countries. If prices differ by no more than the costs of shipping, then it is not profitable to buy in the cheap country and sell in the more expensive country. The price difference simply reflects the cost of moving the goods.

Tariffs and legal restrictions on trade affect prices.　No country permits the free movement of all goods and services across its borders. Nations erect barriers to international trade for different reasons. These barriers may take the form of a *tariff*, a tax on goods that are traded internationally. Prices may differ across countries because of different tax structures. Other barriers to trade place limits on the quantity of a good that can be bought or sold, or simply prohibit the

The Overvalued Dollar

The text describes several reasons why purchasing power parity does not hold. Yet people often look to inflation differentials between countries as an indicator of what exchange rates should be doing. When changes in exchange rates are different from what PPP seems to indicate they should be, currencies are said to be *overvalued* or *undervalued*. In the early 1980s there was much talk of the overvalued dollar. The foreign exchange value of the dollar seemed too high relative to the inflation differentials between the United States and other developed countries. The graph shows the deviation from PPP for the dollar-mark exchange rate. It plots the actual dollar-mark exchange rate along with the exchange rate that would have been consistent with PPP in terms

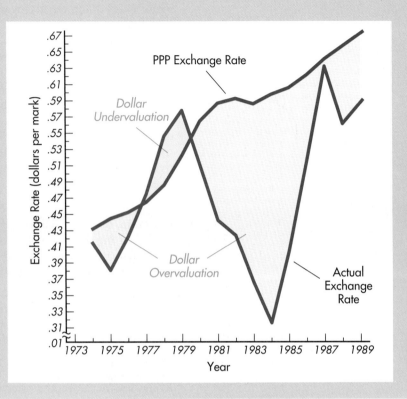

import of some goods. All of these restrictions on the free movement of goods and services contribute to different prices for the same good in different countries. Big Macs cost more in countries with high tariffs on beef imports than they do in countries that allow beef to move freely into them.

Arbitrage, the act of profiting from international price differences, brings prices closer together. If there were no information costs, shipping costs, or tariffs, PPP would hold for similar goods.

Even though PPP does not hold for most goods, it is a useful concept. It points out an important link between national economies. Exchange rates tend to change as prices change in order to move the world toward PPP. In the next section we describe the impact of purchasing power parity on the relationship between inflation and exchange rates.

1.c. Inflation and Exchange Rate Changes

The idea of purchasing power parity reflects a tendency for exchange rates to adjust to offset price level differences in different currencies. Goods

of consumer price inflation in each country (the PPP exchange rate).

In the late 1970s, the dollar seemed to be undervalued: the actual exchange rate was higher than the PPP exchange rate, the rate that would have offset the inflation differential between Germany and the United States. Beginning in 1980, the actual exchange rate was below the PPP rate. It took fewer dollars to buy a mark than the PPP rate implied, so the value of the dollar seemed too high. And the dollar was appreciating against the mark at a faster rate than the inflation differential leading to the dollar overvaluation. By 1985 the dollar began to depreciate against the mark, moving toward its PPP value.

Because PPP does not hold perfectly for any pair of countries, we are always going to have currencies that seem to be overvalued or undervalued. Economists do not agree on the effects of these deviations, but some argue that the issue becomes important when a deviation persists over time. For example, the apparent overvaluation of the dollar in the early 1980s became a major political issue in the United States because it was argued that the overvalued dollar was hurting export-oriented industries in the country. As the dollar appreciated, U.S. goods were becoming more expensive to foreign buyers, and foreign prices did not rise faster than U.S. prices to offset the change in the exchange rate.

Consider the actual price levels and exchange rates in the United States and Germany. Between 1980 and 1984, the price level in the United States increased by approximately 26 percent; in Germany the price level increased by just 18 percent. Yet during this same period, the dollar price of the mark fell by approximately 36 percent. With prices rising faster in the United States than Germany, we normally would expect the dollar to depreciate against the mark so that dollars become cheaper to German residents. Cheaper dollars offset the higher prices of U.S. goods, so that U.S. exports remain stable. But instead of depreciating, the dollar appreciated against the mark. It appeared to be overvalued in terms of the prices of goods. Highlighting the problem was a large balance of trade deficit that became a major political issue in the middle and late 1980s. In response, U.S. economic policy focused on reducing the apparent overvaluation (by depreciating the dollar) and stimulating the country's net exports.

tend to sell for equal prices all over the world. Price differences are smallest the more similar the goods being sold in different countries, the easier it is to gather information about prices, the lower the shipping costs, and the less restrictive the government barriers to trade. Even if PPP does not hold exactly, we expect the exchange rate to change in a manner roughly consistent with PPP. Because we usually measure price level changes by inflation rates, we can relate changes in exchange rates to inflation differentials between countries.

To see how inflation differences are reflected in exchange rates, let's go back to the book selling for $20 in New York and FF40 in Paris. When the exchange rate is $.50 = FF1, FF40 equals $20, so PPP holds. Now suppose that there is 100 percent inflation in France and zero inflation in the United States. If all prices double in France, the book sells for FF80. With no inflation in the United States, the book still sells for $20 there.

How much must the exchange rate change to maintain PPP? We can find out by rewriting the PPP equation this way:

$$E = \frac{P}{P^F}$$

What is the relationship between inflation and changes in the exchange rate?

The exchange rate consistent with PPP equals the ratio of the domestic price to the foreign price. If the book sells for $20 in New York and FF80 in Paris, then the PPP exchange rate is .25 (20/80). Notice what's happened. Because the price level in France doubled while the price level in the United States was constant, the dollar price of the franc was halved. Generally the dollar appreciates against currencies that have a higher inflation rate than the dollar and depreciates against currencies that have a lower inflation rate.

Generally the dollar appreciates against currencies that have a higher inflation rate than the dollar and depreciates against currencies with a lower inflation rate.

RECAP

1. When the exchange rate between two currencies changes, one currency depreciates while the other appreciates.

2. Purchasing power parity means that money has the same purchasing power in different markets.

3. Similar goods do not sell for the same price all over the world because goods are not identical, information is costly, shipping costs affect prices, and tariffs and legal restrictions on international trade affect prices.

4. The exchange rate tends to change to affect differences in the rate of inflation between two countries.

2. INTEREST RATES AND EXCHANGE RATES

Exchange rates are used to compare international prices of goods and services. They also are used to compare the return on foreign currency–denominated stocks and bonds to the return on domestic assets. For example, suppose you have a choice of buying a U.S. or a U.K. bond. The U.S. bond is denominated in dollars and pays 15 percent interest; the U.K. bond is denominated in British pounds and pays 10 percent interest. Because you are a U.S. resident and ultimately want dollars for household spending, you must compare the dollar return from holding each bond.

2.a. The Domestic Currency Return from Foreign Bonds

The U.S. bond is denominated in dollars, so the 15 percent interest is a dollar return. The U.K. bond, on the other hand, promises to pay 10 percent in terms of British pounds. If you buy the U.K. bond, you exchange dollars for pounds at the time the bond is purchased. When the bond matures, you exchange the principal and interest (the proceeds), trading pounds for dollars. If the exchange rate remains the same, the return on the U.K. bond is 10 percent. But if the exchange rate changes between the time you buy the bond and the time it matures, your return may be more or less than 10 percent.

When deciding whether to buy a bond denominated in the domestic currency or in a foreign currency, the buyer must take expected changes in the exchange rate into account.

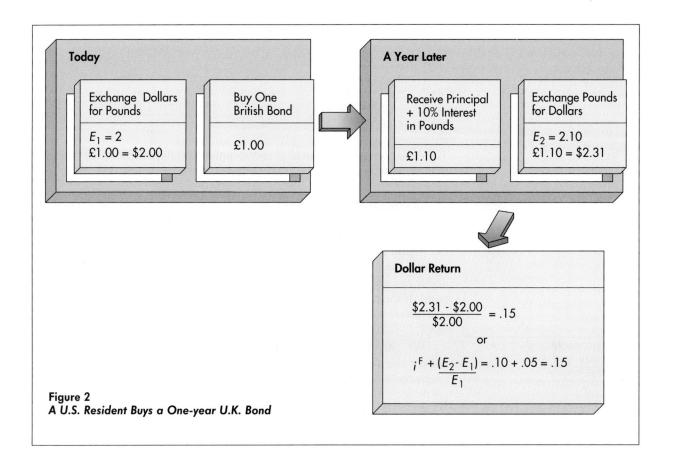

Figure 2
A U.S. Resident Buys a One-year U.K. Bond

Figure 2 shows what happens when a U.S. resident buys a one-year U.K. bond. Suppose the exchange rate is $2 = £1 when the bond is purchased, and the bond sells for £1. The U.S. resident needs $2 to buy the bond. A year later the bond matures. The bondholder receives the principal of (£1) plus 10 percent interest (£.10). Now the U.S. resident wants to convert the pounds into dollars. If the exchange rate has gone up from $2 = £1 to $2.10 = £1, the £1.10 proceeds from the bond are converted into dollars at the rate of 2.10 dollars per pound. The *dollar value* of the proceeds is $2.31 [the exchange rate (2.10) multiplied by the pound proceeds (£1.10)]. The *dollar return* from the U.K. bond is the percentage difference between the dollar proceeds received after one year, and the initial dollar amount invested, approximately 15 percent:

$$\text{Dollar return} = \frac{\$2.31 - \$2}{\$2}$$

$$= \frac{\$.31}{\$2}$$

$$= .15$$

We also can determine the dollar return from the U.K. bond by adding the U.K. interest rate to the percentage change in the exchange rate. The percentage change in the exchange rate is 5 percent:

$$\text{Percentage change in exchange rate} = \frac{\$2.10 - \$2}{\$2}$$

$$= \frac{\$.10}{\$2}$$

$$= .05$$

The dollar return from the U.K. bond equals the 10 percent interest paid in British pounds plus the 5 percent change in the exchange rate, or 15 percent.

In our example, the pound appreciates against the dollar. When the pound increases in value, foreign residents holding pound-denominated bonds earn a higher return on those bonds than the pound interest rate. If the pound depreciates against the dollar, so that the pounds received at maturity are worth less than the pounds originally purchased, then the dollar return from the U.K. bond is lower than the interest rate on the bond. If the pound depreciates 5 percent, the dollar return is just 5 percent [the interest rate (10 percent) *minus* the exchange rate change (5 percent)].

We calculate the domestic currency return from a foreign bond by adding the foreign interest rate (i^F) plus the percentage change in the exchange rate [$(E_2 - E_1)/E_1$]:

Domestic currency return = foreign interest rate + percentage change in

$$\text{exchange rate} = i^F + \frac{E_2 - E_1}{E_1}$$

▼ What is the domestic currency return from a foreign bond? ▲

2.b. Interest Rate Parity

Because U.S. residents can hold U.S. bonds, U.K. bonds, or the bonds or other securities of any country they choose, they compare the returns from the different alternatives when deciding what assets to buy. Foreign investors do the same thing. One product of the process is a close relationship among international interest rates. Specifically, the return or interest rate tends to be the same on similar bonds when returns are measured in terms of the domestic currency. This is called **interest rate parity (IRP)**.

Purchasing power parity exists when similar goods sell for the same price (quoted in a single currency) in different countries. Interest rate parity is the financial-asset version of purchasing power parity: similar financial assets have the same percentage return when that return is computed in terms of one currency. Interest rate parity defines a relationship among the domestic interest rates, the foreign interest rate, and the expected change in the exchange rate:

interest rate parity (IRP): the condition under which similar financial assets have the same interest rate when measured in the same currency

▼ What is the relationship between domestic and foreign interest rates and changes in the exchange rate? ▲

Domestic interest rate = foreign interest rate +

expected change in exchange rate

In our example, the U.S. bond pays 15 percent interest; the U.K. bond offers 10 percent interest in pounds. If the pound appreciates 5 percent, the U.K. bond offers U.S. residents a dollar return of 15 percent. Interest rate parity holds in this case. The domestic interest rate is 15 percent, which equals the foreign interest rate (10 percent) plus the change in the exchange rate (5 percent).

Interest rate parity is the product of arbitrage in financial markets. If U.S. bonds and U.K. bonds are similar in every respect except the currency used to pay the principal and interest, then they should yield similar returns to bondholders. If U.S. investors can earn a higher return from buying U.K. bonds, they are going to buy more U.K. bonds and fewer U.S. bonds. This tends to raise the price of U.K. bonds, pushing U.K. interest rates down. At the same time, the price of U.S. bonds drops, raising U.S. interest rates. The initial higher return on U.K. bonds and resulting greater demand for U.K. bonds increases the demand for pounds, increasing the value of the pound versus the dollar today. As the pound appreciates today, the expected appreciation over the future falls. The change in the exchange rate and interest rates equalizes the dollar return from holding a U.S. bond or a U.K. bond. U.K. bonds originally offered a higher return than U.S. bonds, but the increase in demand for U.K. bonds relative to U.S. bonds lowers U.K. interest rates and the expected appreciation of the pound so that the bond returns are equalized.

2.c. Deviations from Interest Rate Parity

Interest rate parity does not hold for all financial assets. Like PPP, which applies only to similar goods, IRP applies only to similar assets. We do not expect the interest rate on a 90-day U.S. Treasury bill to equal the dollar return on a one-year U.K. Treasury bill because the maturity dates are different, 90 days versus a year. Financial assets with different terms to maturity typically pay different interest rates. We also do not expect different kinds of assets to offer the same return. A 90-day Japanese yen bank deposit in a Tokyo bank should not offer the same dollar return as a 90-day U.S. Treasury bill. The bank deposit and the Treasury bill are different assets.

▼ Why don't similar financial assets yield the same return all over the world? ▲

Even with what seem to be similar assets, we can find deviations from interest rate parity. For instance, a 90-day peso certificate of deposit in a Mexico City bank does not offer a U.S. resident the same dollar return as a 90-day certificate of deposit denominated in U.S. dollars in a New York City bank. The reasons for the difference include government controls, political risk, and taxes.

> *Government controls* Certain government controls erect barriers to the free flow of money between countries. These controls can take the form of quotas on the amount of foreign exchange that can be bought or sold, high reserve requirements on foreign-owned bank deposits, or other controls designed to change the pattern in which financial assets flow between countries. These controls are called **capital controls**. Where *capital* means "financial capital," not a resource used in producing other goods and services (the usual macroeconomic sense of the word).

Political risk   Political risk is the risk associated with holding a financial asset issued in a foreign country. This risk arises from uncertainty. In 1982 the Mexican government imposed capital controls that restricted the flow of foreign exchange out of Mexico. U.S. residents who owned bank deposits or other financial assets in Mexico found that the controls substantially reduced the return on their assets. If U.S. residents believe that a foreign government may impose restrictions that reduce the return on assets issued in that country, those foreign-issued assets must offer a higher return than that offered on similar domestic assets. That extra return is called a **risk premium**. A risk premium offsets the higher risk associated with buying a foreign asset.

risk premium:
the extra return required to offset the higher risk associated with investing in a foreign asset

If political risk exists, IRP does not hold because the return on the foreign asset exceeds the return on the domestic asset by the amount of the risk premium.

Taxes   Taxes also can account for deviations from IRP. Tax rates affect after-tax returns on investments. Different countries have different tax rates, so the same financial asset can yield a different after-tax return for residents of different countries. Because nominal interest rates (the rates observed in the market) are quoted without regard to taxes, some apparent deviations from IRP are just before-tax deviations. After taxes are taken into account, similar assets should yield a similar return in the absence of capital controls and political risk.

If there are no government controls, political risk, or different tax rates, IRP should hold exactly for financial assets that differ only in the currency of denomination. That IRP is a powerful reality for financial assets traded internationally is evident from the many studies of the returns on those assets.

RECAP

1. The domestic currency return from a foreign bond equals the foreign interest rate plus the percentage change in the exchange rate.

2. Interest rate parity exists when similar financial assets have the same interest rate when measured in the same currency.

3. Interest rate parity holds when the domestic interest rate equals the foreign interest rate plus the expected change in the exchange rate.

4. Deviations from interest rate parity are a product of government controls, political risk, and different tax structures.

3. POLICY EFFECTS

The government budget constraint we described in Chapter 15 links fiscal and monetary policies. It states that government spending is financed by taxes, borrowing, and changes in the money supply. This means that when government spending exceeds tax revenues, the budget deficit must be financed by borrowing or issuing money. Both methods of financing can affect exchange rates and interest rates. Here we look first at borrowing; then we turn to monetary policy and change in the money supply.

3.a. Government Borrowing

An increase in government borrowing increases the supply of government bonds. As the supply of bonds increases, bond prices fall and interest rates go up. In Chapter 14 we defined the current interest rate (yield) this way:

$$\text{Current interest rate} = \frac{\text{annual interest payment}}{\text{bond price}}$$

Because the annual interest payment is fixed, only the bond price changes. As the price of a bond increases, the interest rate falls; and as the price falls, the interest rate rises.

Let's continue with our bond example to illustrate the probable effect of financing an increased budget deficit by borrowing. Initially the U.S. bond interest rate is 15 percent, the U.K. bond interest rate is 10 percent, and the expected change in the exchange rate is 5 percent. Remember that when interest rate parity holds, the domestic interest rate equals the foreign interest rate plus the expected change in the exchange rate.

$$i_\$ = i_£ + \frac{E_2 - E_1}{E_1}$$

In our example, interest rate parity holds:

$$i_\$ = .10 + \frac{\$2.10 - \$2}{\$2}$$

$$= .10 + \frac{\$.10}{\$2}$$

$$= .10 + .05$$

$$= .15$$

How does fiscal policy affect exchange rates?

Suppose that to finance its higher deficit, the government increases the supply of bonds, pushing the interest rate on U.S. bonds up to 20 percent. The higher rate of interest attracts foreign investors, who demand dollars to purchase U.S. bonds. As the demand for dollars increases, the dollar appreciates. Let's say the dollar appreciates today to 1.91 dollars per pound. If the future expected exchange rate is still $2.10 = £1, the expected change in the exchange rate is 10 percent:

$$\frac{E_2 - E_1}{E_1} = \frac{\$2.10 - \$1.91}{\$1.91}$$

$$= \frac{\$ .19}{\$1.91}$$

$$= .10$$

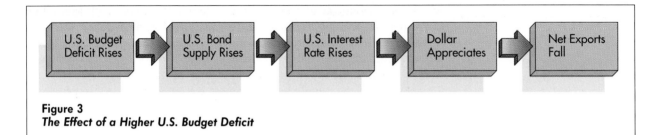

Figure 3
The Effect of a Higher U.S. Budget Deficit

Notice that the interest-rate-parity equation holds true:

$$i_\$ = i_\pounds + \frac{E_2 - E_1}{E_1}$$
$$= .10 + .10$$
$$= .20$$

Fiscal policy affects the exchange rate by changing interest rates, which changes the foreign demand for bonds.

Borrowing to finance the higher budget deficit raises the rate of interest in the United States and causes the dollar to appreciate against foreign currencies.

The appreciation of the dollar also affects the international trade of goods and services. As the dollar appreciates on the foreign exchange market, U.S. goods become more expensive to foreign buyers and foreign goods become less expensive to U.S. buyers. What happens? U.S. exports decrease and U.S. imports increase. The foreign demand for U.S. bonds created by borrowing to finance the higher budget deficit pushes U.S. net exports down (Figure 3). A change in policy that lowers the budget deficit (reducing government borrowing) has the opposite effect.

3.b. Monetary Policy

In Chapter 8 we said that the actual interest rate observed in the economy, the *nominal interest rate,* has two components: the real interest rate and the rate of inflation. Of course at the time a bond is purchased, no one knows what the actual rate of inflation is going to be over the life of the bond. This means the expected rate of inflation, not the actual rate of inflation, is reflected in the nominal interest rate:

Nominal interest rate = real interest rate + expected inflation

The greater the rate at which money grows, the greater the expected rate of inflation and the higher the nominal interest rate. So the process of financing government budget deficits by creating money pushes nominal interest rates up.

In the last section we saw that government borrowing to finance budget deficits also raises the nominal interest rate, but there the increase was a product of an increase in the real interest rate. The government must offer higher real interest rates on government bonds to induce domestic and foreign residents to buy the greater quantity of bonds supplied. In the case of monetary policy, higher nominal interest rates are a product of higher expected inflation; the real interest rate does not change.

As the nominal interest rate on domestic bonds increases, the exchange rate must change in order to maintain IRP. Let's go back to our earlier example, in which the U.S. interest rate is 15 percent, the U.K. interest rate is 10 percent, the expected future exchange rate is $2.10 = £1, and the current exchange rate is $2 = £1. Interest rate parity holds because the dollar interest rate equals the foreign interest rate plus the expected change in the exchange rate:

$$i_\$ = i_£ + \frac{E_2 - E_1}{E_1}$$

$$= .10 + \frac{\$2.10 - \$2}{\$2}$$

$$= .10 + \frac{\$.10}{\$2}$$

$$= .10 + .05$$

$$= .15$$

The dollar is expected to depreciate against the pound (or the pound is expected to appreciate against the dollar) by 5 percent, so the U.K. interest rate (10 percent) plus the higher value of U.K. currency (5 percent) equals the U.S. interest rate (15 percent).

Suppose the United States adopts an inflationary monetary policy, pushing the U.S. interest rate up to 20 percent. If the U.K. interest rate is still 10 percent, the dollar must depreciate by 10 percent for the expected return on holding a U.K. bond to equal the return on holding a U.S. bond. The dollar depreciates because the inflation rate in the United States is expected to be higher than that in the United Kingdom.

When a nation is expected to have higher inflation because of some new policy, people want to hold less of that nation's currency. If a new monetary policy raises the expected inflation rate in the United States, the nominal interest rate goes up. As a result, people sell dollars on the foreign exchange market, causing the dollar to depreciate. Continuing with our example, the U.S. interest rate is now 20 percent, the U.K. interest rate is 10 percent, and the exchange rate is $2.10 = £1. With the higher expected inflation and higher interest rate in the United States, the dollar is expected to depreciate to 2.31 dollars per pound in one year. Interest rate parity still holds:

$$i_\$ = i_£ + \frac{E_2 - E_1}{E_1}$$

$$= .10 + \frac{\$2.31 - \$2.10}{\$2.10}$$

$$= .10 + \frac{\$.21}{\$2.10}$$

$$= .10 + .10$$

$$= .20$$

The depreciation of the dollar has no effect on international trade if the depreciation simply offsets rising prices in the United States. Here purchasing power parity holds: the relative prices of goods in each country stay the same. Even though prices in the United States are rising faster, the depreciation of the dollar lowers the cost of dollars to foreigners, compensating for the higher dollar price of goods. U.S. goods continue to sell for the same foreign currency price they did before the change in monetary policy. So there is no incentive to alter the quantities of goods bought and sold internationally.

If the growth of the money supply slows, other things being equal, the expected inflation rate falls. As a result, the nominal interest rate falls and the domestic currency appreciates. Assuming that appreciation maintains purchasing power parity, the monetary policy has no effect on international trade and investment.

3.c. Linking IRP and PPP

As you have just seen, changes in government policy can affect both the exchange rate and the price level. Both PPP and IRP are relevant to the analysis. In fact now we can link the two together to demonstrate the relationship among inflation differentials between countries, interest rate differentials between countries, and changes in exchange rates.

IRP holds when the domestic interest rate equals the foreign interest rate plus the expected change in the exchange rate:

$$i = i_F + \frac{E_2 - E_1}{E_1}$$

We can rewrite the equation with the interest differential (the difference between the domestic and foreign interest rate) equal to the expected change in the exchange rate:

$$\frac{E_2 - E_1}{E_1} = i - i_F$$

PPP holds when the change in the exchange rate equals the inflation differential between countries. Inflation is the percentage change in the price level:

$$\text{Inflation} = \frac{P_2 - P_1}{P_1}$$

So PPP holds when

$$\frac{E_2 - E_1}{E_1} = \frac{P_2 - P_1}{P_1} - \frac{P_2^F - P_1^F}{P_1^F}$$

Let's use the data from our bond example to illustrate the link between IRP and PPP. Initially the U.S. interest rate is 15 percent and the U.K. interest rate is 10 percent. For IRP to hold, the dollar is expected to depreciate against the pound by 5 percent:

$$i_\$ - i_£ = \frac{E_2 - E_1}{E_1}$$

or

$$.15 - .10 = .05$$

If IRP and PPP hold, the expected change in the exchange rate equals the interest differential between domestic and foreign bonds, which equals the expected inflation differential between the domestic and foreign countries.

For PPP to hold, the change in the exchange rate must match the expected inflation differential between the United States and the United Kingdom (assuming the U.S. inflation rate is 12 percent and the U.K. inflation rate is 7 percent):

$$\frac{E_2 - E_1}{E_1} = \frac{P_2{}^\$ - P_1{}^\$}{P_1{}^\$} - \frac{P_2{}^£ - P_1{}^£}{P_1{}^£}$$

By combining the IRP and PPP conditions, we can see that a change in government policy is reflected in a new interest differential, a new expected change in the exchange rate, and a new expected inflation differential.

RECAP

1. An increase in U.S. government spending financed by borrowing tends to raise the real interest rate in the United States and cause the dollar to appreciate.

2. Changes in the rate of growth of the money supply tend to change the exchange rate; but may not affect international trade if PPP holds.

3. If PPP and IRP both hold, then the expected change in the exchange rate equals the interest differential between domestic and foreign bonds, which equals the expected inflation differential between the domestic and foreign countries.

4. INTERNATIONAL POLICY COORDINATION

Economies are linked globally by trade in goods, services, and financial assets. This means the policies of one nation can have important implications for other nations. In Chapter 10 we defined the spending multiplier as the reciprocal of the marginal propensity to save plus the marginal propensity to import:

$$\text{Spending multiplier} = \frac{1}{\text{MPS} + \text{MPI}}$$

But at the end of the chapter we said that the simple multiplier understates the effects of increases in autonomous spending because of the foreign repercussions of domestic spending. That is, some spending on imports comes back to the domestic economy in the form of exports. An increase in U.S. government expenditures of $1 increases U.S. national income by the simple multiplier. As income increases, U.S. imports increase, pushing foreign income up. As foreign income rises, so do foreign imports of goods produced in the United States. Ultimately, then, U.S. income rises by more than the simple multiplier. Since one country's economic policy can cause changes that affect other nations, there are potential gains from having economic policy formulated with a view toward the international effects.

Because countries are linked through their trade in goods, services, and financial assets, business cycles tend to follow similar trends across countries. When the U.S. economy is booming, income in countries that depend on exports to the U.S. market increases. When the United States is in a recession, income in other countries tends to fall. Because the nations of the world are linked by their common interests in trade, every country's domestic macroeconomic policy affects more than its domestic economy. And because every country has the potential to affect the economies of other nations, setting macroeconomic policy cooperatively may improve overall macroeconomic performance.

Macroeconomic policy in the United States traditionally has been formulated with little attention to the rest of the world. But in recent years, the potential gains from coordinating economic policies across countries have become increasingly apparent. Large fluctuations in exchange rates and net exports in the 1980s showed the interdependencies among nations. Over time, technological improvements in transportation and communication have created opportunities for substitution in international goods and services markets.

To coordinate economic policies, governments must communicate. Senior economic officials of the leading industrial countries come together regularly at meetings of the International Monetary Fund (IMF) and the Organization for Economic Cooperation and Development (OECD). Since 1975 the leaders of the seven largest industrial nations have held annual economic summit meetings. These seven nations (Canada, France, Germany, Italy, Japan, the United Kingdom, and the United States), known as the *Group of 7* (*G7*) countries, have made a commitment to monitor one another's economic policies. Over the 1980s, their monetary policies began to converge as they worked together coordinating those policies. Economic Insight: ''The OECD'' explains how the OECD operates.

The G7 countries are Canada, France, Germany, Italy, Japan, the United Kingdom, and the United States.

4.a. Potential Gains

Coordination here can take several directions. Countries can coordinate their goals, targeting inflation or unemployment, for example. They also can coordinate their information, exchanging forecasts of key macroeconomic variables based on their economic plans. Finally, they can coordinate the policy-making and implementation processes. The potential gains of coordination are a product of the form that coordination takes.

▼ What can countries gain by coordinating their macroeconomic policies? ▲

Setting joint goals could induce policy changes that make those goals attainable. For example, let's say that all countries set a goal of reducing the unemployment rate. To meet that goal, the countries would have to set expansionary monetary policies. Even if the countries do not explicitly discuss their future policies, the goals they set guide those policies. Of course, this assumes that policymakers target the agreed-on goals when they formulate their domestic economic policy.

The OECD

The Organisation for Economic Co-operation and Development (OECD) is an association of industrial countries with three goals: to attain the highest sustainable rate of growth while maintaining financial stability, to promote free trade, and to support development in non-OECD countries. The OECD is headquartered in Paris. The secretary general, traditionally a European, is appointed to a five-year term and chairs all meetings of the full council.

The OECD was established in 1961 and now has 24 member countries (see the table). Together they account for one-sixth of the world's population but produce two-thirds of the world's output. As the table shows, the member countries differ greatly in terms of gross domestic product (GDP), importance of agriculture, and emphasis on international trade. Given this diversity, it is not surprising that the countries often disagree on economic policy.

The OECD, unlike the IMF and the World Bank, makes no loans and has no authority to make economic policy. It serves as a meeting place where policymakers can discuss problems and points of view. Although the output of meetings is seldom concrete, the process is an important step on the road to international collaboration.

Member Country	GDP (billion dollars)*	GDP per Head (dollars)*	Employment in Agriculture (percent)	Exports as a Percentage of GDP†
United States	4,195	17,360	3.1	7.1
Japan	1,963	16,160	8.8	14.6
West Germany	892	14,610	5.5	32.5
France	724	13,070	7.6	25.1
Italy	600	10,490	11.2	27.9
Britain	548	9,650	2.6	29.4
Canada	367	14,200	5.2	28.8
Spain	229	5,920	17.6	23.3
Holland	175	12,040	4.9	64.2
Australia	168	10,540	6.2	16.4
Switzerland	135	20,830	6.6	39.1
Sweden	131	15,700	4.8	35.2
Belgium	114	11,540	2.9	77.8
Austria	94	12,480	8.2	40.3
Denmark	82	15,990	6.7	36.9
Finland	71	14,320	11.5	29.8
Norway	70	16,730	7.2	47.2
Turkey	58	1,150	57.1	21.5
Greece	40	3,990	28.9	21.6
Portugal	29	2,830	23.2	38.5
New Zealand	26	7,900	11.1	31.2
Ireland	25	6,910	16.0	62.2
Luxembourg	5	13,243	4.2	104.0
Iceland	4	16,170	10.5	45.1

*1986 data.
†Exports of goods and services.
Source: Organisation for Economic Co-operation and Development.

The coordination of information regarding the current state of the economy and forecasts of future changes can take place both informally and through formal meetings of key policymakers. Central bank and treasury staff members may regularly talk to compare notes on the world economy.

Coordination of the policy-making process offers the hope of making every country better off. For instance, in the mid-1980s, the United States experienced a large international trade deficit, while Japan and Germany had trade surpluses. At several international conferences, leading policy-makers proposed that the United States reduce its fiscal deficit to reduce domestic spending and improve its international balance of trade. Simultaneously, Japan and Germany were going to increase their fiscal deficits to stimulate spending in those countries in order to increase their imports from the United States and to avoid recessions if exports to the United States fell.

The proposed fiscal policy was not implemented at the time, but future policy actions may very well reflect this kind of multinational decision making. For example, suppose the United States wants to stimulate the domestic economy but is concerned about increasing its international trade deficit (rising income increases imports). If U.S. expansionary policies could be coordinated with expansionary policies in other large countries, so that income rises in all the countries simultaneously, the balance of trade might not change even though all the countries are increasing their national income. This is a potential benefit of international cooperation: by acting together, nations can achieve better outcomes than would be possible if they acted individually.

4.b. Obstacles

Obviously international coordination of macroeconomic policy makes sense. In practice, however, several problems stand in the way of designing and implementing economic policy across countries. First, countries may not agree on goals. Some countries may be willing to exploit the short-run trade-off between inflation and the unemployment rate, while other countries choose to follow passive policies, refusing to manipulate aggregate demand. The politicians who are involved in international agreements tend to make policies aimed at short-term political gains rather than long-term economic stability.

Second, even if countries can agree on goals, they may disagree on the current economic situation. GNP and other key macroeconomic variables are measured with a lag and often are revised substantially after their values are initially announced. At any point in time, policymakers cannot be sure whether the economy is expanding or contracting. Eventually, as official data are collected, the economic health of the nation is known, but only several months later. This means that the economic policymakers of the major developed countries could disagree on an appropriate course of action because they do not agree on current economic conditions.

An example. In 1974, President Ford declared that inflation was Public Enemy Number One. So the administration implemented a restrictive economic policy, one aimed at slowing the growth of aggregate demand. By the time the announcement was made, however, a recession had already begun. Once the data on the recession were available, the administration reversed its policy, to stimulate the economy. Had the United States led the major developed countries in a coordinated effort to restrict aggregate demand, international policy would have turned out to be just the opposite of what was needed once it was known that a recession had started.

Finally, even if countries can agree on goals and current conditions, they still may disagree on appropriate policy because they adhere to different theories of macroeconomics. Some policymakers believe that a New Keynesian fixed-price model (with a horizontal aggregate supply curve) best describes current economic conditions, that by increasing aggregate demand they can increase output and employment. Others believe that the new classical model (with a vertical aggregate supply curve) best describes the current economic situation, that increasing aggregate demand has just a temporary effect on output and employment but causes the price level to rise. These very basic disagreements make it difficult to reach a consensus on economic policy.

These obstacles may make it impossible to coordinate international economic policy. But at least international economic meetings and discussions help each country understand the views of other nations and the likely course of policy in the rest of the world. This sharing of information allows each nation to formulate its own policy in light of what policy in the rest of the world is likely to be.

RECAP

1. Because every country has the potential to affect the economies of other nations, coordinating macroeconomic policy may improve overall economic performance.
2. Coordination here means setting joint goals, exchanging information, and forming and executing policy cooperatively.
3. Obstacles to the international coordination of economic policy are disagreements over goals, current economic conditions, and macroeconomic theory.

SUMMARY

1. Arbitrage equalizes the prices of similar goods in different markets. Preview section

2. An open economy trades goods and financial assets with the rest of the world. Preview section

▼▲ **How does change in the exchange rate affect the price of goods traded between countries?**

3. When the domestic currency depreciates against other currencies, foreign goods become more expensive to domestic buyers and domestic goods become less expensive to foreign buyers. § 1.a

4. When the domestic currency appreciates against other currencies, foreign goods become less expensive to domestic buyers and domestic goods become more expensive to foreign buyers. § 1.a

5. Purchasing power parity exists when monies have the same value in different markets. § 1.b

---

▼▲ **Why don't similar goods sell for the same price all over the world?**

6. Deviations from PPP arise because goods are not identical in different countries, information is costly, shipping costs affect prices, and tariffs and restrictions on trade affect prices. § 1.b

▼▲ **What is the relationship between inflation and changes in the exchange rate?**

7. Exchange rates tend to change to offset inflation differentials between countries. § 1.c

▼▲ **What is the domestic currency return from a foreign bond?**

8. The domestic currency return from holding a foreign bond equals the foreign interest rate plus the percentage change in the exchange rate. § 2.a

▼▲ **What is the relationship between domestic and foreign interest rates and changes in the exchange rate?**

9. Interest rate parity exists when the domestic interest rate equals the foreign interest rate plus the expected change in the exchange rate, so that similar financial assets yield the same return when measured in the same currency. § 2.b

▼▲ **Why don't similar financial assets yield the same return all over the world?**

10. Deviations from IRP are a product of government controls, political risk, and taxes. § 2.c

▼▲ **How does fiscal policy affect exchange rates?**

11. Financing a government budget deficit by selling bonds (borrowing) tends to raise domestic interest rates, which attracts foreign investors and causes the domestic currency to appreciate. Ultimately, increased government borrowing tends to reduce net exports. § 3.a

▼▲ **How does monetary policy affect exchange rates?**

12. Higher expected inflation, a product of increasing the rate at which the money supply grows, tends to increase nominal interest rates. The domestic currency depreciates to offset rising prices but has no effect on net exports. § 3.b

13. If IRP and PPP hold, the expected change in the exchange rate equals the interest differential between domestic and foreign bonds, which equals the expected inflation differential between the domestic and foreign economies. § 3.c

▼▲ **What can countries gain by coordinating their macroeconomic policies?**

14. By coordinating macroeconomic policies, the goals of those policies become more attainable, nations have greater access to economic information, and the end product of those policies is improved. § 4.a

15. Obstacles to the international coordination of macroeconomic policy are disagreements over policy goals, the current economic situation, and macroeconomic theory. § 4.b

KEY TERMS

arbitrage Preview section
open economy Preview section
purchasing power parity (PPP) § 1.b

interest rate parity (IRP) § 2.b
capital control § 2.c
risk premium § 2.c

EXERCISES

Basic Terms and Concepts

1. Find the U.S. dollar value of each of the following currencies at the given exchange rates:

   a. $1 = c$1.20 (Canadian dollars)

   b. $1 = ¥140 (Japanese yen)

   c. $1 = FL2 (Netherlands guilder)

   d. $1 = SKr6 (Swedish krona)

   e. $1 = SF1.5 (Swiss franc)

2. You are a U.S. importer who buys goods from many different countries. How many U.S. dollars do you need to settle each of the following invoices?

   a. 1,000,000 Australian dollars for wool blankets (exchange rate: $A1 = $.769)

   b. 500,000 British pounds for dishes (exchange rate: £1 = $1.5855)

   c. 100,000 Indian rupees for baskets (exchange rate: Rs1 = $.0602)

   d. 150 million Japanese yen for stereo components (exchange rate: ¥1 = $0.0069?

   e. 825,000 German marks for wine (exchange rate: DM1 = $.5515)

3. What is the dollar value of the invoices in exercise 2 if the dollar

   a. depreciates 10 percent against the Australian dollar?

   b. appreciates 10 percent against the British pound?

   c. depreciates 10 percent against the Indian rupee?

   d. appreciates 20 percent against the Japanese yen?

   e. depreciates 100 percent against the German mark?

4. Explain purchasing power parity and why it does not hold perfectly in the real world.

5. Write an equation that describes purchasing power parity and explain the equation.

6. Write an equation that describes interest rate parity and explain the equation.

7. Use the equation in exercise 6 to describe the effects of an increase in domestic government spending financed by

   a. borrowing.

   b. money creation.

8. If the interest rate on one-year government bonds is 5 percent in Germany and 8 percent in the United States, what do you think is expected to happen to the dollar value of the mark? Explain your answer.

Extended Concepts

9. Suppose that on January 1, the yen price of the dollar is 120. Over the year, the Japanese inflation rate is 5 percent and the U.S. inflation rate is 10 percent. If the exchange rate is $1 = ¥130 at the end of the year, does the yen appear to be overvalued, undervalued, or at the PPP level? Explain your answer.

10. In 1960 a U.S. dollar sold for 620 Italian lire. If PPP held in 1960, what would the PPP value of the exchange rate have been in 1987 if Italian prices rose 12 times and U.S. prices rose 4 times between 1960 and 1987?

The Hamburger Standard

Four years ago *The Economist* launched its Big Mac index, a medium-rare guide to whether currencies are at their "correct" exchange rate. It is time for an annual update.

The McDonald's standard is based on the theory of purchasing-power parity (PPP), which argues that in the long run the exchange rate between two currencies should equate the price of an identical basket of goods and services in the respective countries. Our "basket" is simply a Big Mac. . .

In America the average price of a Big Mac (including tax) is about $2.20. In Tokyo our correspondent had to fork out ¥370 for this gastronomic delight. Dividing the yen price by the dollar price gives an implied PPP for the dollar of ¥168, compared with the current exchange rate of ¥159. So even after the recent slide in the yen, the dollar still looks to be 5% undervalued against the yen on PPP grounds. It also looks 14% undervalued against the D-mark, with a Mac-PPP of DM1.95.

Economists who have calculated PPPs by more sophisticated means come up with remarkably similar results. Professor Ronald McKinnon of Stanford University, one of the leading proponents of the theory of purchasing-power parity, comes up with mid-point estimates for the dollar's PPP of ¥164 and DM2.00.

The dollar's current rate against the pound ($0.61) is close to its Mac-PPP of $0.64. But that, in turn, means that the pound is undervalued by 10% against the D-mark, giving British manufacturers a competitive edge. On the other hand most EMS currencies, especially the French franc and the lira, are still overvalued against the D-mark on PPP grounds.

Mac-currencies are now becoming truly global: the opening of the first McDonald's in Moscow has allowed us to add the rouble to our sample. Muscovites have to pay the equivalent of $6.25 (converting at the official exchange rate) for a Big Mac, which makes it the most expensive hamburger in our sample. In other words, the rouble is overvalued against the dollar to a greater degree than any other currency, with an implied PPP of 1.70 roubles, compared with an official rate against the dollar of 0.60 roubles.

Yet this overlooks one crucial fact: in Moscow fast food comes slow, with two-to-three hour queues. If this time is valued at average Soviet hourly wages, then the true cost of gorging on a Big Mac is roughly double the cash price. This implies a "queue-adjusted" Mac-PPP of 3.40 roubles. Indigestion, Mikhail?

■ Source: "The Hamburger Standard," *The Economist*, May 5, 1990, p. 92.

Big MacCurrencies (Hamburger prices)

Country	Price* in local currency	Implied PPP† of the dollar	Actual exchange rate 30.4.90	% over (+) or under (−) valuation of the dollar
Australia	A$ 2.30	1.05	1.32	+26
Belgium	BFr 97	44.00	34.65	−21
Britain	£ 1.40	0.64	0.61	−5
Canada	C$ 2.19	1.00	1.16	+16
Denmark	DKr 25.50	11.60	6.39	−45
France	FFr 17.70	8.05	5.63	−30
Holland	FL 5.25	2.39	1.88	−21
Hongkong	HK$ 8.60	3.90	7.79	+100
Ireland	IR£ 1.30	0.59	0.63	+7
Italy	Lire 3900	1773	1230	−31
Japan	¥ 370	168	159	−5
Singapore	S$ 2.60	1.18	1.88	+59
S. Korea	Won 2100	955	707	−26
Soviet Union	Rouble 3.75	1.70	0.60	−65
Spain	Ptas 295	134	106	−21
Sweden	SKr 24	10.90	6.10	−44
United States††	$ 2.20	-	-	-
W. Germany	DM 4.30	1.95	1.68	−14
Yugoslavia	Dinar 16	7.27	11.72	+61

*Prices may vary between branches †Purchasing-power parity: foreign price divided by dollar price ††Average of New York, Chicago, San Francisco and Atlanta
Source: McDonald's; *Economist* correspondents

Commentary

The golden arches of McDonald's span the globe, and Big Macs can be found in Stuttgart, Sydney, Stockholm, Singapore, and Seoul. The theory of purchasing-power parity (PPP) would lead us to believe that the prices of Big Macs, when expressed in a common currency, should be very similar no matter where the burgers are sold. This article provides data that allow us to consider the theory of purchasing-power parity in light of the prices of Big Macs in 19 countries. We see that, contrary to PPP, there is a great deal of variability in the prices of Big Macs sold around the world.

The local-currency prices of Big Macs in the 19 countries listed in the table cannot be directly compared since these prices are expressed in different units for each country. Exchange-rate data are needed to convert the prices of Big Macs into a common currency. The table contains this information, providing data on the exchange rate between the U.S. dollar and the currency of 18 other countries (the exchange rates are expressed as the amount of foreign currency it takes to purchase one U.S. dollar). For example, we see that it took 4.30 deutsche marks (DM) to purchase a Big Mac in West Germany on the same day that it took DM1.68 to purchase $1.00. This means that the dollar price of a Big Mac in West Germany is DM4.30 divided by 1.68 deutsche marks per dollar, which equals $2.56. In a similar fashion, we find the U.S. dollar price of a Big Mac to be $1.74 in Australia, $2.06 in Ireland, $3.17 in Italy, and $3.93 in Sweden. (To make sure you understand how to translate the prices of Big Macs sold overseas into U.S. dollar terms, figure out the dollar price of Big Macs in some other countries listed in the table.)

We can use the data presented in this article to examine the validity of the law of one price as it pertains to Big Macs. The law of one price states that similar goods will sell for the same price, when that price is expressed in a common currency, no matter where the goods are sold. This theory is very similar to the PPP theory, which compares the price of a basket of goods across countries. Does the price of Big Macs appear to be the same across countries, as PPP theory predicts?

The data in this article do not seem to support the law of one price. The average price of a Big Mac in the United States is $2.20 (although this price varies quite a bit within the United States). The second column in the table computes the exchange rate at which PPP holds for Big Macs. For instance, the value of 1.05 for Australia is found by dividing the price in Australian dollars of 2.30 by the U.S. price of $2.20: 2.30/2.20 = 1.05. If the exchange rate were 1.05 Australian dollars per U.S. dollar, PPP would hold. Since the actual exchange rate was 1.32 Australian dollars per U.S. dollar, the U.S. dollar was overvalued in the foreign-exchange market relative to Big Mac prices in Australia. The extent of over- or undervaluation of other currencies is determined in the same way.

When purchasing-power parity is violated, the prices of similar goods will differ across countries. This has implications for the competitiveness of a country's products on the world market. The article uses the prices of Big Macs in various countries to calculate an index of the relative overvaluation or undervaluation of local currencies. For example, if the actual foreign-currency price of a dollar exceeds the ratio of the price of a Big Mac in that country divided by the price of a Big Mac in the United States ($2.20), then the dollar is overvalued. The U.S. dollar is undervalued when the foreign-currency price of a dollar is less than the ratio of the Big Mac price in a foreign country divided by its price in the United States.

This article presents a novel approach to determining whether currencies are overvalued or undervalued relative to other currencies. While the consumer price index, representing the price of a market basket of goods, is usually employed for determining real exchange rates, the hamburger standard provides us with food for thought.

Economic Growth and Development

18

Economic Growth

1. What is economic growth?
2. How are economic growth rates determined?
3. What is productivity?
4. Why has U.S. productivity changed?

PREVIEW

Why has Japanese GNP grown at a faster rate in recent decades than U.S. GNP? Is it because Japanese workers are more diligent or more highly motivated than U.S. workers? Is it because Japanese students study more and so are better educated than U.S. students? Is it because Japanese firms are more concerned with developing new products and new production techniques than U.S. firms? Understanding why and how economic growth happens is a very important part of macroeconomics.

Although much of macroeconomics is aimed at understanding business cycles—recurring periods of prosperity and recession—the fact is that over the long run, most economies do grow wealthier. The long-run trend of national income in the United States and most other countries is positive. Yet the rate at which national income grows is very different across countries. Why? What factors cause economies to grow and living standards to rise?

In this chapter we focus on the long-term picture. We begin by defining economic growth and discussing how very important long-run growth is. Then we examine the determinants of economic growth, to understand what accounts for the different rates of growth across countries. The role of productivity in sustaining growth and the recent U.S. record of productivity changes are reviewed.

1. DEFINING ECONOMIC GROWTH

▼ What is economic growth? ▲

What do we mean by economic growth? Economists use two measures of growth—real national income and per capita real national income—to compare how economies grow over time.

1.a. Real National Income

economic growth:
an increase in real national income, usually measured as the percentage change in gross national product or gross domestic product per year

Basically, **economic growth** is an increase in real national income. As more goods and services are produced, the real income of a nation (usually measured in terms of gross national product or gross domestic product) increases and people are able to consume more. We describe the growth of national income as an annual rate of percentage change in real GNP or GDP per year.

To calculate the percentage change in national income over a year, we simply divide the change in national income by the value of national income at the beginning of the year, and then multiply the quotient by 100. For instance, the GNP of the Netherlands was approximately 400 billion guilders in 1984 and approximately 420 billion guilders in 1985. So the economy grew 5 percent in 1985:

$$\text{Percentage change in national income} = \frac{\text{change over year}}{\text{beginning value}} \times 100$$

$$= \frac{420 - 400}{400} \times 100$$

$$= \frac{20}{400} \times 100$$

$$= .05 \times 100$$

$$= 5$$

1.a.1. Compound Growth From 1980 to 1987, the industrial countries of the world showed an average annual growth rate of GDP of 2.6 percent. Over the same period, the average annual growth rate of GDP for developing countries was 4 percent. The difference between a growth rate of 4 percent and one of 2.6 percent may not seem substantial, but in fact it is. Growth is compounded over time. This means that any given rate of growth is applied every year to a growing base of national income, so any difference is magnified over time.

Figure 1 shows the effects of compounding growth rates. The upper line in the figure represents the path of GDP if the economy grows at a rate of 4 percent a year. The lower line shows GDP growing at a rate of 2.6 percent a year.

Suppose in each case the economy originally is producing a GDP of $1 billion. After five years, there is not much difference: a GDP of $1.137 billion at 2.6 percent growth versus $1.217 billion at 4 percent growth. The effect of compounding becomes more visible over long periods of time. After 40 years, the difference between 2.6 and 4 percent growth, a seemingly small difference, represents a huge difference in output. A 2.6 per-

Figure 1
Comparing GDP Growth Rates of 2.6% and 4%
Between 1980 and 1987, GDP in the industrial countries grew at an average annual rate of 2.6 percent, while GDP in developing countries grew at an average annual rate of 4 percent. The difference seems small, but the graph shows how even a small difference is compounded over time, producing a substantial difference in GDP.

Small changes in rates of growth produce big changes in national income over a period of many years.

cent rate of growth yields an output of $2.792 billion; at 4 percent, output is $4.801 billion. After 40 years, the level of output is almost twice as large at the high growth rate.

1.a.2. The Rule of 72 Compound growth explains why countries are so concerned about maintaining positive high rates of growth. If growth is maintained at a constant rate, we can estimate the number of years required for output to double using the **rule of 72**. If we divide 72 by the growth rate, we find the approximate time it takes for any value to double.

rule of 72:
the number of years required for an amount to double in value is 72 divided by the annual rate of growth

Suppose you deposit $100 in a bank account that pays a constant 6 percent interest. If you allow the interest to accumulate over time, the amount of money in the account grows at a rate of 6 percent. At this rate of interest, the rule of 72 tells us that your account will have a value of approximately $200 (double its initial value) after 12 years:

$$\frac{72}{6} = 12$$

The interest rate gives the rate of growth of the amount deposited if earned interest is allowed to accumulate in the account. If the interest rate is 3 percent, the amount would double in 24 (72/3) years.

The rule of 72 applies to any value. If GNP is growing at a rate of 6 percent a year, GNP doubles every 12 years. At a 3 percent annual rate, GNP doubles every 24 years.

Table 1 lists the average annual rate of growth of GDP between 1980 and 1987 and approximate doubling times for ten countries. The countries listed range from a high growth rate of 8.6 percent in Korea to a low rate of

Table 1 GDP Growth Rates and Doubling Times

Country	Average Annual Growth Rate (percent)*	Doubling Time (years)
Korea	8.6	8
India	4.6	16
Bangladesh	3.8	19
Japan	3.8	19
Australia	3.2	23
United States	3.1	23
Canada	2.9	25
Colombia	2.9	25
Dominican Republic	1.6	45
Germany	1.6	45

*Average annual growth rates from 1980 to 1987.
Source: World Bank, *World Development Report* (Washington, D.C., 1989), pp. 166–167.

1.6 percent in the Dominican Republic and Germany. If these growth rates are maintained over time, it would take just 8 years for GDP in Korea to double and 45 years for the GDP in the Dominican Republic or Germany to double.

1.b. Per Capita Real National Income

Economic growth sometimes is defined as an increase in per capita real national income.

per capita real national income: real national income divided by the population

We've defined economic growth as an increase in real national income. But, if growth is supposed to be associated with higher standards of living, our definition may be misleading. A country could show positive growth in real GNP or GDP, but if the population is growing at an even higher rate, output per person actually can fall. Economists often adjust the growth rate of output for changes in population. **Per capita real national income** is real national income divided by the population. If we define economic growth as rising per capita real GNP or per capita real GDP, then a nation's output of goods and services must increase faster than its population.

From 1980 to 1987, per capita real GDP grew at an average annual rate of 1.8 percent in developing countries and 1.9 percent in industrial countries. The difference in per capita real GDP growth between developing and industrial countries is much smaller than the difference in real GDP. Remember that real GDP grew at a rate of 4 percent in developing countries over the same period, compared to a rate of 2.6 percent in industrial countries. The fact that real GDP grew at a faster rate in developing countries while per capita real GDP grew at a slower rate points out the dangers of just looking at real GDP as an indicator of change in the economic well-being of the citizens in developing countries. Population growth rates are considerably higher in developing countries than they are in industrial countries, so real GDP must grow at a faster rate in developing countries than they do in industrial countries just to maintain a similar growth rate in per capita real GDP.

1.c. The Problems with Definitions of Growth

We believe that economic growth is good because it allows people to have a higher standard of living, to have more material goods. But an increase in real national income or per capita real national income does not tell us whether the average citizen is better off. The problem is that these measures say nothing about how income is distributed. The national economy may be growing, yet the poor may be staying poor while the rich get richer.

We have to be careful about using per capita real national income as an indicator of standard of living. Table 2 shows why. The table lists the percentage share of household income in Sri Lanka. In 1969–1970, the poorest 20 percent of households received 7.5 percent of the nation's total income; the next 20 percent received 11.7 percent; the third 20 percent received 15.7 percent; 21.7 percent went to the next group; and, finally, the wealthiest 20 percent of households received 43.4 percent. The richest 20 percent of households received over 40 percent of all household income, while the poorest 20 percent of households received just 7.5 percent of that income.

Although per capita real GDP did grow in Sri Lanka from 1970 to 1980, we cannot say that all households benefited from that growth. Between 1969–1970 and 1980–1981, the share of household income going to each of the four poorest groups of households in Sri Lanka fell. The wealthiest group not only had a disproportionate share of national income, but saw that share increase.

The lesson here is simple. Economic growth may benefit some groups more than others. And it is entirely possible that despite national economic growth, some groups can be worse off than they were before. Clearly, real per capita GDP does not measure people's standard of living.

Another reason per capita real national income is misleading is that it says nothing about the quality of life. People have nonmonetary needs; they care about personal freedom, the environment, their leisure time. If a rising per capita GDP goes hand in hand with a repressive political regime or rapidly deteriorating environmental quality, people are not going to feel better off. By the same token, a country could have no economic growth,

Table 2   Income Distribution, Sri Lanka

	Percentage Share of Household Income Going to				
	Lowest 20 Percent	Second 20 Percent	Third 20 Percent	Fourth 20 Percent	Highest 20 Percent
1969–1970	7.5	11.7	15.7	21.7	43.4
1980–1981	5.8	10.1	14.1	20.3	49.8

Source: World Bank, *World Development Report* (Washington, D.C., 1988), p. 272.

yet reduce the hours worked each week. More leisure time could make workers feel better off, even though per capita GDP has not changed.

Once again, be careful in interpreting per capita national income. Don't allow it to represent more than it does. Per capita national income is simply a measure of the output produced divided by the population. It is a useful measure of economic activity in a country; it is a questionable measure of the typical citizen's standard of living or quality of life.

Per capita national income is a questionable indicator of the typical citizen's standard of living or quality of life.

RECAP

1. Economic growth is an increase in real national income, usually measured as a percentage change in GNP or GDP.
2. Because growth is compounded over time, small differences in rates of growth are magnified over time.
3. For any constant rate of growth, the time required for real national income to double is 72 divided by the growth rate.
4. Per capita real national income is real national income divided by the population.
5. Per capita real national income says nothing about the distribution of income in a country or the nonmonetary quality of life there.

2. THE DETERMINANTS OF GROWTH

Economic growth raises the potential level of national income, shifting the long-run aggregate supply curve to the right.

▼ _____
How are economic growth rates determined?
_____ ▲

The long-run aggregate supply curve is a vertical line at the potential level of national income (Y_P). As the economy grows, the potential output of the economy rises. Figure 2 shows the increase in potential output as a rightward shift in the long-run aggregate supply curve. The higher the rate of growth, the faster the aggregate supply curve moves to the right. To illustrate several years' growth, we would show several curves shifting to the right.

To find the determinants of economic growth, we must turn to the determinants of aggregate supply. In Chapter 11, we identified three determinants of aggregate supply: resource prices, technology, and expectations. Changes in expectations can shift the aggregate supply curve, but changing expectations are not a basis for long-run growth in the sense of continuous rightward movements in aggregate supply. The long-run growth of the economy rests on growth in productive resources (labor, capital, and land) and technological advances.

2.a. Labor

Economic growth depends on the size and quality of the labor force. The size of the labor force is a function of the size of the working-age population (16 and older in the United States) and the percentage of that popu-

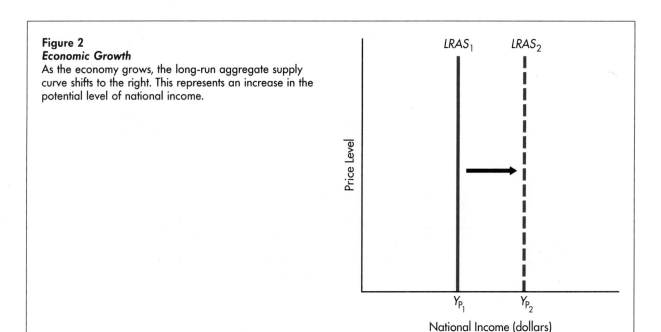

Figure 2
Economic Growth
As the economy grows, the long-run aggregate supply curve shifts to the right. This represents an increase in the potential level of national income.

lation in the labor force. The labor force typically grows more rapidly in developing countries than in industrial countries because birthrates are higher in developing countries. Figure 3 shows actual and predicted average annual growth of the population for selected developing and industrial countries, as well as average growth rates for all developing countries and all industrial countries. Between 1980 and 1987, the population grew at an average annual rate of 2 percent across developing countries and .7 percent across industrial countries. The World Bank forecasts that between 1987 and 2000, the population will grow at an average annual rate of 1.9 percent in developing countries and .5 percent in industrial countries.

Based solely on growth in the labor force, it seems that developing countries are growing faster than industrial countries. But the size of the labor force is not all that matters; changes in productivity can compensate for lower growth in the labor force, as we discuss in Section 3.

The U.S. labor force has changed considerably in recent decades. The most notable event of the post–World War II period was the baby boom. The children born between the late 1940s and the early 1960s made up more than a third of the total U.S. population in the early 1960s and have significantly altered the age structure of the population. In 1950 the largest percentage of males and females in the population was in the category of young children. By 1970 the largest percentage of the U.S. population was in the 5- to 29-year range. By 1980 this bulge in the age distribution had moved to the 20- to 44-year range.

The initial pressure of the baby boom fell on school systems faced with rapidly expanding enrollments. Over time, as these children aged and entered the labor market, they had a large impact on potential output. The U.S. labor force grew at an average rate of about 2.5 percent a year in the

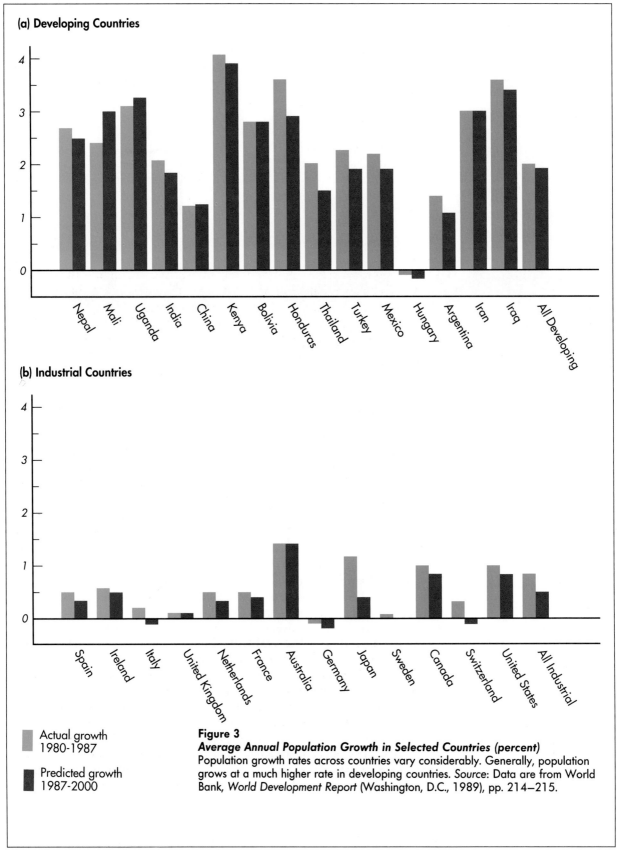

(a) Developing Countries

(b) Industrial Countries

Actual growth
1980-1987

Predicted growth
1987-2000

Figure 3
Average Annual Population Growth in Selected Countries (percent)
Population growth rates across countries vary considerably. Generally, population grows at a much higher rate in developing countries. *Source:* Data are from World Bank, *World Development Report* (Washington, D.C., 1989), pp. 214–215.

1970s, approximately twice the rate of growth in the 1950s. The growth of the labor force slowed in the 1980s, as the baby boom population moved into its twenties and thirties. Based on the size of the labor force, the 1970s should have been a time of greater economic growth than the 1950s, 1960s, or 1980s. It was not. More important than the size of the labor force is its productivity. We will discuss U.S. productivity changes later.

2.b. Capital

Labor is combined with capital to produce goods and services. A rapidly growing labor force by itself is no guarantee of economic growth. Workers need machines, tools, and factories to work. If a country has lots of workers but few machines, then the typical worker cannot be very productive. Capital is a critical resource in growing economies.

The ability of a country to invest in capital goods is tied to its ability to save. A lack of current saving can be offset by borrowing, but the availability of borrowing is limited by the prospects for future saving. Debt incurred today must be repaid by not consuming all output in the future. If lenders believe that a nation is going to consume all of its output in the future, they do not make loans today.

The lower the standard of living in a country, the harder it is to forgo current consumption in order to save. It is difficult for a population living at or near subsistence level to do without current consumption. This in large part explains the low level of saving in the poorest countries.

2.c. Land

Abundant natural resources are not a necessary condition for economic growth.

Land surface, water, forests, minerals, and other natural resources are called *land*. Land can be combined with labor and capital to produce goods and services. Abundant natural resources can contribute to economic growth, but natural resources alone do not generate growth. Several developing countries are relatively rich in natural resources but have not been very successful in exploiting these resources to produce goods and services. Japan, on the other hand, has relatively few natural resources but has shown dramatic economic growth in recent decades. The experience of Japan makes it clear that abundant natural resources are not a necessary condition for economic growth.

2.d. Technology

technology:
ways of combining resources to produce output

Technological advances allow the production of more output from a given amount of resources.

A key determinant of economic growth is **technology**, ways of combining resources to produce goods and services. New management techniques, scientific discoveries, and other innovations improve technology. Technological advances allow the production of more output from a given amount of resources. This means that technological progress accelerates economic growth for any given rate of growth in the labor force and the capital stock.

Technological change depends on the scientific community. The more educated a population, the greater its potential for technological advances. Industrial countries have better-educated populations than do developing countries. Education gives industrial countries a substantial advantage over developing countries in creating and implementing innovations. In addition, the richest industrial countries traditionally have spent 2 to 3 percent of their GNP on research and development, an investment developing countries cannot afford. The greater the funding for research and development, the greater the likelihood of technological advances.

Impeded by low levels of education and limited funds for research and development, the developing countries lag behind the industrial countries in developing and implementing new technology. Typically these countries follow the lead of the industrial world, adopting new technology developed in that world once it is affordable and feasible given their capital and labor resources. In the next chapter we discuss the role of foreign aid, including technological assistance, in promoting economic growth in developing countries.

RECAP

1. Economic growth raises the potential level of national income, shifting the long-run aggregate supply curve to the right.

2. The long-run growth of the economy is a product of growth in labor, capital, and natural resources, and advances in technology.

3. The size of the labor force is determined by the working-age population and the rate at which that population participates.

4. The post–World War II baby boom has created a bulge in the age distribution of the U.S. population.

5. Growth in capital stock is tied to current and future saving.

6. Abundant natural resources contribute to economic growth but are not essential to that growth.

7. Technology is ways of combining resources to produce output.

8. Hampered by low levels of education and limited financial resources, developing countries lag behind the industrial nations in developing and implementing new technology.

3. PRODUCTIVITY

▼ What is productivity? ▲

total factor productivity (TFP): the ratio of the economy's output to its stock of labor and capital

In the last section we described how output depends on resource inputs like labor and capital. One way to assess the contribution a resource makes to output is its productivity. *Productivity* is the ratio of output produced to the amount of input. We could measure the productivity of a single resource—say labor or capital—or the overall productivity of all resources. **Total factor productivity (TFP)** is the term economists use to describe the overall productivity of an economy. It is the ratio of the economy's output to its stock of labor and capital.

3.a. Productivity and Economic Growth

Economic growth depends on both the growth of resources and technological progress. Advances in technology allow resources to be more productive. If the quantity of resources is growing and each resource is more productive, then output grows even faster than the quantity of resources. Economic growth, then, is the sum of the growth rate of total factor productivity and the growth rate of resources:

Economic growth = growth rate of TFP + growth rate of resources

The amount that output grows because the labor force is growing depends on how much labor contributes to the production of output. Similarly, the amount that output grows because capital is growing depends on how much capital contributes to the production of output. To relate the growth of labor and capital to the growth of output (we assume no change in natural resources), then, the growth of labor and the growth of capital must be multiplied by their relative contributions to the production of output. The most straightforward way to measure those contributions is to use the share of national income received by each resource. For instance, in the United States, labor receives about 70 percent (.70) of national income and capital receives about 30 percent (.30). So we can determine the growth of output using this formula:

$$\% \, \Delta Y = \% \, \Delta TFP + .70(\% \, \Delta L) + .30(\% \, \Delta K)$$

where

Y = real national income (usually measured as GNP or GDP)
TFP = total factor productivity
L = size of the labor force
K = capital stock

The equation shows how economic growth depends on changes in productivity ($\% \, \Delta TFP$) as well as changes in resources ($\% \, \Delta L$ and $\% \, \Delta K$). Even if labor (L) and capital stock (K) are constant, technological innovation would generate economic growth through changes in total factor productivity (TFP).

For example, suppose TFP is growing at a rate of 2 percent a year. Even with labor and capital stock held constant, the economy grows at a rate of 2 percent a year. If labor and capital stock also grow at a rate of 2 percent a year, output grows by the sum of the growth rates of all three components (TFP, .70 times labor, and .30 times the capital stock), or 4 percent.

How do we account for differences in growth rates across countries? Because almost all countries have experienced growth in the labor force, the percentage change in the labor force generally has supported economic growth. Growth in the capital stock has been steadier in the industrial countries than in the developing countries, so differences in capital growth rates may explain some of the differences in economic growth across countries. But resource growth rates cannot explain the major differences we find across countries. In recent years, those differences seem to be related to productivity. In the United States, for example, there is concern that productivity has been growing too slowly. We use U.S. productivity to illustrate the determinants of total factor productivity and to show how changes in these determinants affect a country's economic growth.

3.b. The U.S. Productivity Slowdown

U.S. productivity became a major topic of discussion in the late 1970s as the growth of total factor productivity fell dramatically. From 1948 to 1965, TFP grew at an annual average rate of 2.02 percent. From 1965 to 1973, annual growth slowed to an average of 1.04 percent. And from 1973 to 1987, the growth rate was just .21 percent. If the pre-1965 rate of growth had been maintained, output in the United States would be an estimated 39 percent higher today than it actually is. What happened? What caused this dramatic change in productivity?

Several factors may be at work here. They include a drop in the quality of the U.S. labor force, fewer technological innovations, higher energy prices, and a shift from manufacturing to service industries.

Why has U.S. productivity changed?

3.b.1. Labor Quality Labor productivity is measured as output per hour of labor. Figure 4 shows how the productivity of labor changed in the United States between 1948 and 1988. Although changes in the productivity of labor can stem from technological innovation and changes in the capital stock, we focus here on changes in the quality of labor. These changes may be a product of the level and quality of education in the United States, demographic change, and changing attitudes toward work.

Education level The average level of education in the United States has gone up over time. Table 3 lists three measures of education level. The first, median school years completed, increased from 8.6 years in 1940 to

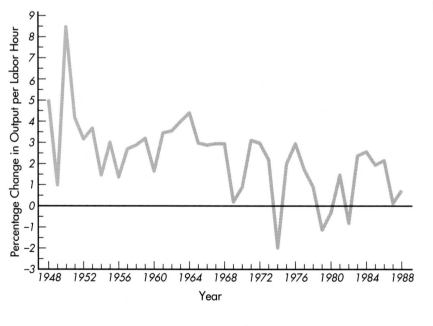

Figure 4
Percentage Change in Output per Hour of Labor, United States, 1948–1988
Output per labor hour is a measure of productivity. The graph shows the percentage change in productivity. Notice the large fluctuations from one year to the next. *Source*: Data taken from *Economic Report of the President* (Washington, D.C., 1990).

Table 3   The Average Level of Education, United States, 1940–1987*

	1940	1950	1960	1970	1980	1987
Median school years completed	8.6	9.3	10.6	12.1	12.5	12.7
People with at least a high school education (percent)	24.5	34.3	41.1	52.3	66.5	75.6
People with at least four years of college (percent)	4.6	6.2	7.7	10.7	16.2	19.9

*People 25 years of age and over.
Source: U.S. Department of Commerce, *Statistical Abstract of the United States, 1989* (Washington, D.C.: U.S. Government Printing Office, 1989), p. 130.

12.7 years in 1987. In the same period, the percentage of adults with at least a high school education rose from 24.5 to 75.6, and the percentage of those with a college education rose from 4.6 to 19.9. The figures seem to indicate that the level of education is not responsible for the slowdown in U.S. productivity.

Quality of education   Some economists argue that it is not the level of education but the quality of education that has declined in the United States. They point to the change in college entrance examination scores to support their thinking. For instance, students born in 1945 who took their SATs in 1963 scored an average of 478 on the verbal test and 502 on the math test. Students born in 1962 and tested in 1980 scored an average of 424 on the verbal test and an average of 466 on the math. Figure 5 shows the drop in test scores from the 1960s to the 1980s.

Figure 5
Average Scholastic Aptitude Test (SAT) Scores, 1967–1987
Both the math and verbal scores on the SAT fell between the late 1960s and early 1980s. This trend may have reflected a decline in the average quality of education or of students taking the test. *Source:* U.S. Department of Commerce, *Statistical Abstract of the United States, 1989* (Washington, D.C.: U.S. Government Printing Office, 1989), p. 144.

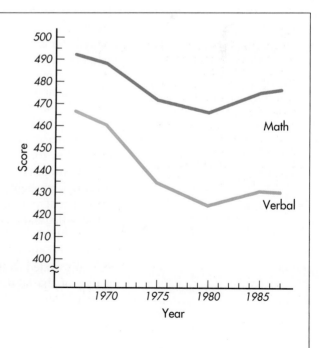

The influx of women to the labor force in the 1980s meant an increase in the number of unskilled workers, possibly contributing to a decline in overall labor productivity. Over time the numbers of new female workers should level off and those already working will become increasingly skilled and experienced, resulting in a higher quality workforce.

Test scores started to drop in 1967 (Figure 5). This decline may have had a significant effect on the productivity of the nation by the early 1970s, as this group of students entered the labor market. By the mid-1980s, test scores started to rise again, signaling a turnaround in the quality of education. By the early 1990s, this change should be reflected in an increase in the productivity of labor.

Demographic change Changes in the size and composition of the population have an impact on the labor market. As the baby boom generation entered the labor force in the late 1960s and early 1970s, a large pool of inexperienced, unskilled workers was created. The average quality of the labor force may have fallen at this time, as reflected in some large drops in output per hour of labor. In the 1980s, the baby boom segment of the labor force had more experience and was working in better jobs, pushing the quality of the labor force up.

Another important demographic change that has affected the quality of the labor force is the participation rates of women. As more and more women entered the labor force in the 1980s, the pool of untrained workers increased, probably reducing the average quality of labor. Over time, as female participation rates stabilize, the average quality of labor should rise as the skills and experience of female workers rise.

Finally, the 1970s and 1980s saw a change in the pattern of U.S. immigration. Recent immigrants to the United States, both legal and illegal, generally added to the supply of unskilled labor and reduced the average quality of the labor force. Many immigrants from developing countries come with few work skills and little knowledge of English.

Economic Insight

Culture and Productivity in Japan

Japanese culture appears to be more supportive of positive work attitudes than Western cultures are. The degree to which cultural differences contribute to greater growth of productivity in Japan is difficult if not impossible to measure. However, to many observers it seems clear that Japan's social values play an important role in the country's high rate of economic growth.

Japanese workers have a sense of loyalty and duty to their firm and society that is remarkable to Western observers. The Japanese typically consider a job to be a job for life. In addition, cultural traditions encourage people to seek fulfillment by belonging to a group and working toward the success of the group. As a result, labor-management relations are less likely to involve conflict than they are in Western societies. Workers and managers are part of a team that cooperates and works diligently to maximize the sales and profitability of the

team. This tendency to put the interests of the group above the interests of the individual has increased productivity in the industrial sector. The typical Japanese worker would face enormous social pressure if he or she asked for a raise. Rather than ask for higher wages, it is more common for workers to accept management's decisions about wages.

Some analysts argue that the selflessness of Japanese workers has its origins in the period from 1600 to the mid-1800s, when the shoguns, or military governors, established a strict social order to preserve their rule. Under the rigid class system they established, status was derived from performing service for one's superior. Workers followed orders from higher authorities without question, and citizens of each region worked for the common good. Many of these attributes can be found in modern Japan. For example, the emphasis on the group, rather

than the individual, may account for the fact that Japanese workers and managers typically are paid lower salaries than their Western counterparts. Because salaries are lower, Japanese firms are able to reinvest a larger share of their revenues, to further improve productivity.

The values that exist in Japanese society are not uniquely Japanese. It is the dominance of these values that sets the Japanese apart. Over time, as the country grows wealthier, Japanese attitudes toward work may move closer to those in Western countries. If they do, the quality of labor in Japan is likely to fall.

■ Source: Information taken from Stephen D. Cohen, *Uneasy Partnership* (Cambridge, Mass.: Ballinger, 1985); Kanji Haitani, *The Japanese Economic System* (Lexington, Mass.: Lexington Books, 1976); and Urban C. Lehner, "Japanese May Be Rich, But Are They Satisfied with Quality of Life?" *The Wall Street Journal*, January 9, 1990, p. A1.

Attitudes toward work Some economists argue that the slowdown in productivity in the United States reflects a loss of traditional values. They assert that education and hard work are not as important to Americans as they once were. As a result, the level of effort in school and on the job has fallen, and so has the quality of labor. One product of this thinking is an interest in Japanese culture. Some observations of Japanese culture are given in Economic Insight: "Culture and Productivity in Japan."

Japan has experienced a dramatic increase in labor productivity since the early 1970s, growing substantially faster than other industrial countries. Many analysts have studied the Japanese economy to understand the source of this growth. One important finding is that Japan has a relatively high saving rate, which allows a relatively high rate of growth of capital goods. The popular press in the United States regularly reports on the

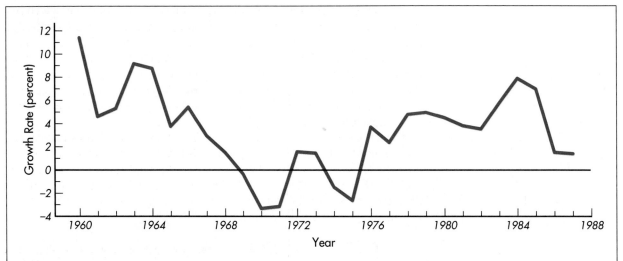

Figure 6
Annual Percentage Change in Real Spending on Research and Development, United States, 1960– 1987

Expenditures on research and development reflect a country's commitment to developing new technology. Expenditures in the United States grew rapidly in the early 1960s and 1980s but grew slowly (and in some years fell) in the late 1960s and 1970s. *Source:* U.S. Department of Commerce, *Statistical Abstract of the United States, 1989* (Washington, D.C.: U.S. Government Printing Office, 1989), p. 576.

diligence of Japanese students and the dedication of Japanese workers. Many believe that this effort accounts for the different rates of productivity in Japan and the United States. They argue that Americans should rethink their values, focusing on productivity. Unfortunately things like diligence and dedication are difficult to identify and measure. If in fact a change in attitudes about work has lowered the level of effort U.S. workers are willing to expend, then the quality of labor has fallen.

3.b.2. Technological Innovation New technology alters total factor productivity. Innovations increase productivity, so when productivity falls, it is natural to look at technological developments to see whether they are a factor in the change. Like diligence and dedication, the pace of technological innovation is difficult to measure. Expenditures on research and development are related to the discovery of new knowledge, but actual changes in technology do not proceed as evenly as those expenditures. We expect a long lag between funding and operating a laboratory and the discovery of useful technology. Still a decline in spending on research and development may indicate less of a commitment to increasing productivity.

Figure 6 shows how real expenditures on research and development changed in the United States over recent decades. Notice that these expenditures grew at a relatively rapid rate in the early 1960s and 1980s, but grew at a relatively slow rate (they actually fell in five separate years) in the late 1960s and early 1970s. This period of reduced expenditures may have been a contributing factor in the U.S. productivity slump.

patent:
a legal document that gives an inventor the legal rights to an invention

Research and development are the source of innovation. To determine if a decline in innovation has contributed to a decline in productivity, economists must be able to measure the pace of technological innovation. Some economists look at the record of new patents as an indicator of technological progress. A **patent** is a document issued by the government that gives an inventor the legal right to develop and profit from an invention. Individuals and business firms seek patents to protect themselves from those who would copy their innovations.

The number of patents issued to U.S. firms serves as a crude measure of technological innovation. Figure 7 shows that the number of patents issued peaked in 1971 and then began to fall. This pattern is consistent with the idea that a decline in technological innovation was responsible for the decline in U.S. productivity in the 1970s (see Economic Insight: "U.S. Dominance in Technology Threatened").

3.b.3. Other Factors We have seen how changing labor quality and technological innovation are related to changes in productivity. Other reasons have been offered to explain the decline in the growth of U.S. productivity in the 1970s. We examine two of them: the increased cost of energy and the shift from a manufacturing- to a service-oriented economy.

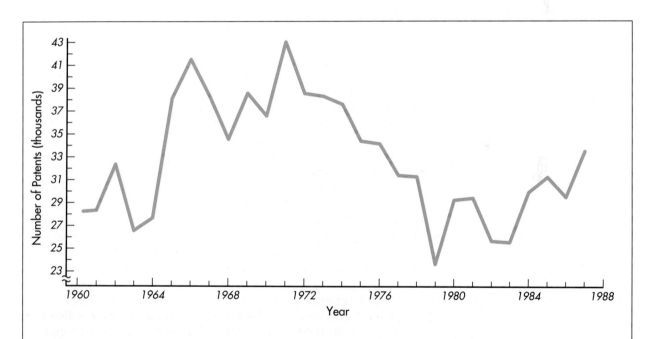

Figure 7
Number of Patents Issued to U.S. Corporations, 1960–1987.
The number of patents issued is a rough indicator of technological progress. From a peak in 1971, the number of patents issued in the United States has fallen. Some economists argue that this decline in patent activity signals a slower rate of technological progress that could be related to the slowdown in U.S. productivity. *Source:* Data are from U.S. Department of Commerce, *Statistical Abstract of the United States, 1989* (Washington, D.C.: U.S. Government Printing Office, 1989), p. 530.

Energy prices   OPEC succeeded in raising the price of oil substantially in 1973, 1974, and 1979. The timing of the dramatic increase in oil prices coincided with the drop in productivity growth in the United States. A look back at Figure 4 shows that output per labor hour actually fell in 1974 and 1979. Higher energy prices should directly decrease aggregate supply because energy is an important input across industries. As the price of energy increases, the costs of production rise and aggregate supply decreases.

Higher energy prices can affect productivity through their impact on the capital stock. As energy prices go up, energy-inefficient capital goods become obsolete. Like any other decline in the value of the capital stock, this change reduces economic growth. Standard measures of capital stock do not account for energy obsolescence, so they suggest that total factor productivity fell in the 1970s. However, if the stock of usable capital actually did go down, it was the growth rate of capital, not TFP, that fell.

Manufacturing versus services   The United States has seen a shift away from manufacturing toward services. Some economists believe that productivity grows more slowly in service industries than in manufacturing, so the movement into services reduces the overall growth rate of the economy.

Be careful with this kind of generalization. In fact, labor productivity in communications and some other service industries has grown faster than in manufacturing industries. Also it is more difficult to measure changes in the quality of services than changes in the quality of goods. If prices in an industry rise with no change in the quantity of output, it makes sense to conclude that the real level of output in the industry has fallen. However, if prices have gone up because the quality of the service has increased, then output actually has changed. Suppose a hotel remodels its rooms. In effect it is improving the quality of its service. Increased prices here would reflect this change in output.

Service industries—fast-food restaurants, airlines, hotels, banks—are not all alike. One way service firms compete is on the basis of the quality of service they provide. Because productivity is measured by the amount of output per unit of input, if we don't adjust for quality changes, we may underestimate the amount of output and so underestimate the productivity of the industry.

3.c. Growth and Development

Economic growth depends on the growth of productivity and resources. Productivity grows unevenly, and its rate of growth is reflected in economic growth. Although the labor force seems to grow faster in developing countries than in industrial countries, lower rates of saving have limited the growth of the capital stock in developing countries. Without capital, workers cannot be very productive. This means that the relatively high rate of growth in the labor force in the developing world does not translate into a high rate of economic growth. We use this information on economic growth in Chapter 19 to explain and analyze the strategies used by developing countries to stimulate output and increase standards of living.

RECAP

1. Productivity is the ratio of output produced to the amount of input.
2. Total factor productivity is the nation's income (output) divided by its stock of labor and capital.
3. Economic growth is the sum of the growth of total factor productivity and the growth rate of resources (labor and capital).
4. The decline of U.S. productivity may be a product of a drop in the quality of the labor force, fewer technological innovations, higher energy prices, and a shift from manufacturing to service industries.

SUMMARY

▼▲ **What is economic growth?**

1. Economic growth is an increase in real national income, usually measured as the percentage change in GNP or GDP per year. § 1.a

2. Economic growth is compounded over time. § 1.a.1

3. Per capita real national income is real national income divided by the population. § 1.b

4. The definitions of economic growth are misleading because they do not indicate anything about the distribution of income or the quality of life. § 1.c

▼▲ How are economic growth rates determined?

5. The growth of the economy is tied to the growth of productive resources and technological advances. § 2

6. Because their population tends to grow more rapidly, developing countries typically experience faster growth in the labor force than do industrial countries. § 2.a

7. The inability to save limits the growth of capital stock in developing countries. § 2.b

8. Abundant natural resources are not necessary for rapid economic growth. § 2.c

9. Technology is ways of combining resources to produce goods and services. § 2.d

▼▲ What is productivity?

10. Productivity is the ratio of output produced to the amount of input. § 3

11. Total factor productivity is the overall productivity of an economy. § 3

12. The percentage change in national income equals the percentage change in total factor productivity plus the percentage changes in labor and capital multiplied by the share of national income taken by labor and capital. § 3.a

▼▲ Why has U.S. productivity changed?

13. The slowdown in U.S. productivity may be a product of a change in the quality of the labor force, fewer technological innovations, higher energy prices, and a shift away from manufacturing to service industries. § 3.b

KEY TERMS

economic growth § 1.a
rule of 72 § 1.a.2
per capita real national income § 1.b

technology § 2.d
total factor productivity (TFP) § 3
patent § 3.b.2

EXERCISES

Basic Terms and Concepts

1. Why is the growth of per capita real national income a better measure of economic growth than the growth of real national income?

2. What is the level of output after four years if initial output equals $1,000 and the economy grows at a rate of 10 percent a year?

3. Use the data in the table to determine the average annual growth rate for each country in terms of real GDP growth and per capita real GDP growth (real GDP is in millions of units of domestic currency, and population is in millions of people). Which country grew at the fastest rate?

Country (currency)	1982		1987	
	Real GDP	Population	Real GDP	Population
Ghana (cedi)	315,826	11.47	378,207	13.70
Nigeria (naira)	102,957	86.13	79,556	101.90
Panama (balboa)	4,682	2.04	5,188	2.27
Sri Lanka (rupee)	140,308	15.19	171,788	16.36

4. Suppose real national income is growing at a rate of 4 percent a year, the labor force is growing at 2 percent, and the capital stock is growing at 3 percent. What is the growth rate of total factor productivity?

5. Suppose total factor productivity is growing at an annual rate of 2 percent, the labor force is growing at a rate of 1 percent, and the capital stock is growing at a rate of 3 percent. What is the annual growth rate of real national income?

6. Discuss the possible reasons for the slowdown in U.S. productivity and relate each reason to the equation for economic growth. (Does the growth of TFP or resources change?)

Extended Concepts

7. How did the post-World War II baby boom affect the growth of the U.S. labor force? What effect is this baby boom likely to have on the future U.S. labor force?

8. How do developing and industrial countries differ in their use of technological change, labor, capital, and natural resources to produce economic growth? Why do these differences exist?

9. How would an aging population affect economic growth?

Government Policy, Real Interest Rates, and Growth

In many developing countries, governments fix interest rates at levels below those a free market would have. These artificially low interest rates have resulted in repressed financial markets — *repressed* because government policies discourage citizens from using domestic financial institutions, such as banks, as a place to deposit their savings. In countries with low rates of saving, investment will also tend to be low.

The accompanying figure illustrates the relationship between growth of GDP and investment as a fraction of GDP for several developing countries. The interest-rate policy followed in each country is indicated by the color of the square representing that country. The cluster of squares for all countries suggests that a positive relationship exists between investment as a fraction of GDP and GDP growth.

Interest-rate policy is identified by the history of real interest rates. The real interest rate is equal to the nominal interest rate minus the rate of inflation. The green squares identify countries with positive real interest rates, the red squares identify those with moderately negative rates, and the gold squares identify those with strongly negative rates. Investments in all countries with positive real rates of interest were more productive than average. Investments were generally less productive than average in countries with strongly negative real rates; four of these countries actually had negative growth rates over the period studied.

■ Source: Based on "Real Interest Rates and Growth," *World Development Report*, World Bank, 1989, p. 32.

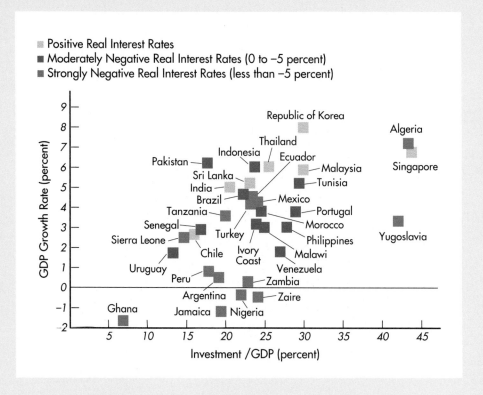

- Positive Real Interest Rates
- Moderately Negative Real Interest Rates (0 to −5 percent)
- Strongly Negative Real Interest Rates (less than −5 percent)

Commentary

If investment was equally productive in different countries, then the differences in GDP growth could be fully explained by the differences in the rate of investment. However, we see that for similar rates of investment, GDP growth varies considerably. For instance, Zaire, Malawi, and Thailand all had investment of approximately 25 percent of GDP, yet their GDP growth varied from −1 percent in Zaire to 6 percent in Thailand. Why do countries with positive real rates of interest have more productive investment than do countries with negative real rates of interest?

If the government fixes nominal interest rates at levels below the rate of inflation so that the real rate of interest is negative, then domestic financial institutions will not be widely used as a depository for savings or as a source of lending for investment funds. Rather than deposit money in an account yielding a negative real rate of interest, savers (both individuals and firms) will deposit their money in other countries that allow higher interest rates or will avoid the use of financial intermediaries altogether. Savers will lend directly to borrowers with no bank or financial institution acting as a middleman. Since savers will not know all potential uses for their funds and will not be able to judge effectively the credit risks of potential borrowers, savings will tend to go to less than their most productive use.

Financial intermediaries such as banks are typically better at selecting the most productive use for funds, so that the use of intermediaries generally results in better investments that will yield greater output of goods and services. Nations that discourage financial market development with negative real interest rates tend to have less productive investment, as seen in the gold squares in the figure. This is an important example of how government policy can affect economic growth.

19

Development Economics

1. How is poverty measured?

2. Why are some countries poorer than others?

3. What strategies can a nation use to increase its economic growth?

4. How are savings in one nation used to speed development in other nations?

PREVIEW There is an enormous difference between the standards of living in the poorest and richest countries in the world. In Bolivia the average life expectancy at birth is 53 years, more than 20 years less than in the United States. In Burma only an estimated 25 percent of the population has access to safe water. In Burundi only 23 percent of urban houses have electricity. And in Chad only 29 percent of students reach the sixth grade.

The plight of developing countries is our focus in this chapter. We begin by discussing the extent of poverty and how it is measured across countries. Then we turn to the reasons why developing countries are poor and look at strategies for stimulating growth and development. The reasons for poverty are many, and the remedies often are rooted more in politics than economics. Still economics has much to say about ways of improving the living standards of the world's poorest citizens.

1. THE DEVELOPING WORLD

Three-fourths of the world's population lives in developing countries. These countries often are called *less developed countries (LDCs)* or *Third World countries*. First World countries are the industrialized nations of Western Europe and North America, along with Australia, Japan, and New Zealand. Second World countries are the communist countries. The Third World is made up of noncommunist developing countries, although people commonly use the term to refer to all developing countries.

The common link among developing countries is low per capita GNP, which implies a relatively low standard of living for the typical citizen. Otherwise the LDCs are a diverse group—their cultures, politics, even their geography varying enormously.

Figure 1
The World by Stage of Development
This map of the world is colored to show each country's income group. For example, all low-income economies (those with a per capita GNP of $480 or less in 1987) are colored gold. *Source:* World Bank, *World Development Report, 1989* (Washington, D.C., 1989), pp. 160–161.

Low-income economies

Middle-income economies

High-income economies

Countries that do not belong to the World Bank

The developing countries are located primarily in Southeast Asia, Africa, the Middle East, and Latin America (Figure 1). In terms of population, poverty is concentrated in a few regions. The total population of developing countries is approaching 4 billion people. Of this population, 28 percent live in China and 21 percent live in India. The next largest concentration of people is in Indonesia (4 percent), followed by Brazil, Bangladesh, Nigeria, and Pakistan. Except for Latin America, where 40 percent of the population lives in cities, the poor live in rural areas and are largely dependent on agriculture.

1.a. Measuring Poverty

▼ How is poverty measured? ▲

Poverty is not easy to measure. Typically poverty is defined in an *absolute* sense: a family is poor if its income falls below a certain level. For exam-

ple, the poverty level for a family of four in the United States in 1988 was an income of $12,675. The government sets the poverty level, basing it on the estimated cost of feeding a family a minimally adequate amount of food. Once the cost of an adequate diet is estimated, it is multiplied by 3 (the assumption is that one-third of income is spent on food) to determine the poverty level income. The World Bank uses per capita GNP of less than $480 as its criterion of poverty. The countries in gold in Figure 1 meet this absolute definition of poverty.

Poverty is also a *relative* concept. Family income in relation to other incomes in the country or region is important in determining whether or not a family feels poor. The poverty level in the United States would represent a substantial increase in the living standard of most of the people in the world. Yet a poor family in the United States does not feel less poor because it has more money than the poor in other countries. In a nation where the median income of all families was over $34,000 in 1989, a family with an income of $12,675 clearly is disadvantaged.

Because poverty is also a relative concept, using a particular level of income to distinguish the poor from the not poor is often controversial. Besides the obvious problem of where to draw the poverty line, there is the more difficult problem of comparing poverty across countries with different currencies, customs, and living arrangements. Also data often are limited and difficult to obtain because many of the poor in developing countries live in isolated areas. This makes it difficult to draw a comprehensive picture of the standard of living of the typical household.

1.b. Basic Human Needs

Some economists and other social scientists, recognizing the limitations of an absolute definition of poverty (like the per capita GNP measure most commonly used), suggest using indicators of how basic human needs are being met. Although they disagree on an exact definition of *basic human needs*, the general idea is to set minimal levels of caloric intake, health care, clothing, and shelter.

An alternative to per capita GNP is a physical *quality-of-life index* to evaluate living standards. One approach uses life expectancy, infant mortality, and literacy as indicators. This very narrow definition of the quality of life ignores elements like justice, personal freedom, environmental quality, and employment opportunities. Why? Because the indicators should be measures of social progress that allow meaningful comparisons across countries whatever their social or political orientation.

A quality-of-life index assigns a value to each indicator in each country according to where it ranks among all countries. A value of zero indicates that a country has the worst performance in one of the indicators; a value of 100 indicates that the country has the best performance in one of the indicators. The values assigned to each country for each indicator then are averaged to arrive at the national quality-of-life index.

Table 1 lists per capita GNP and the indicators of basic human needs for selected countries. The table shows the actual data for the indicators along with the overall index value for each country. The countries are

Table 1 Quality-of-Life Measures, Selected Countries

Country	Per Capita GNP*	Life Expectancy at Birth (years)	Infant Mortality†	Literacy Rate‡	Quality Index
Ethiopia	120	46	155	8%	7
Bangladesh	160	50	121	33	27
India	290	57	86	44	44
China	300	69	34	69	75
Philippines	560	63	46	86	73
El Salvador	820	61	61	72	63
Turkey	1,110	65	79	74	63
Mexico	1,860	68	48	90	78
Yugoslavia	2,300	71	27	92	86
United States	17,480	75	10	99	96

Sources: World Bank, *World Development Report, 1988* (Washington, D.C., 1988), various pages, and the *United Nations Handbook of International Trade and Development Statistics* (New York 1988), various pages.
*1986 data measured in terms of U.S. dollars.
†The number of infants who die per 1,000 live births.
‡Percentage of the population that is literate.

listed by per capita GNP, beginning with the smallest. Generally there is a strong positive relationship between per capita GNP and the quality-of-life index. But there are cases where higher per capita GNP does not mean higher quality of life. For instance, El Salvador and Turkey both have a higher per capita GNP than China or the Philippines, but the quality-of-life index is higher in China and the Philippines than it is in El Salvador and Turkey. Remember the limitations of per capita national income: it is not a measure of standard of living. However, as the table shows, it is a fairly reliable indicator of differences across countries in living standards. Ethiopia has the lowest per capita GNP and is clearly one of the world's poorest nations. Usually as per capita GNP increases, living standards increase as well.

Per capita GNP and quality-of-life indexes are not the only measures used to determine a country's level of economic development—we could consider the number of households with running water, televisions, or any other good that varies with living standards. Recognizing that there is no perfect measure of economic development, economists and other social scientists often use several indicators to assess economic progress.

RECAP

1. Usually poverty is defined in an absolute sense, as a specific level of family income or per capita GNP.
2. Within a country or region, poverty is a relative concept.

3. Quality-of-life indexes based on indicators of basic human needs are an alternative to per capita GNP for measuring economic development.

2. OBSTACLES TO GROWTH

▼
Why are some countries poorer than others?
▲

Every country is unique. Each nation's history, both political and cultural, helps economists understand why poor nations have not developed and what policies offer the best hope for their development. Generally the factors that impede development are political or social. The political factors include a lack of administrative skills, instability, and the ability of special interest groups to block changes in economic policy. The social obstacles include a lack of entrepreneurs and rapid population growth.

2.a. Political Obstacles

2.a.1. Lack of Administrative Skills
Government support is essential to economic development. Whether support means allowing private enterprise to flourish and develop, or actively managing the allocation of resources, a poorly organized or corrupt government can present an obstacle to economic growth. Some developing countries have suffered from well-meaning but inept government management. This is most obvious in countries with a long history of colonialization. For example, when Zaire won independence from Belgium, few of its native citizens were college educated. Moreover, Belgians had run most of the important government offices. Independence brought a large group of inexperienced and unskilled workers to important positions of power. And at first there was a period of "learning by doing."

2.a.2. Political Instability and Risk
One of the most important functions a government performs in stimulating economic growth is providing a political environment that encourages saving and investment. People do not want to do business in an economy weakened by wars, demonstrations, or uncertainty. For instance, since becoming an independent nation in 1825, Bolivia has had more than 150 changes in government. This kind of instability forces citizens to take a short-run view of the economy. Long-term planning is impossible without knowing the attitudes and policies of the government that is going to be in power next year or even next month.

The key issue here is *property rights*. A country that guarantees the rights of private property encourages private investment and development. Where ownership rights may be changed by revolution or political decree, there is little incentive for private investment and development. People do not start new businesses or build new factories if they believe that a change in government or a change in the political will of the current government could result in the confiscation of their property.

This confiscation is called **expropriation**. Countries with a history of expropriating foreign-owned property without compensating the owners

A country must be able to guarantee the rights of private property if it is going to create an environment that encourages private investment.

expropriation:
the government seizure of assets, typically without adequate compensation to the owners

(paying them its market value) have difficulty encouraging foreign investment. An example is Uganda. In 1973 a successful revolution by Idi Amin was followed by the expropriation of over 500 foreign-owned (mostly British) firms. Foreign and domestic investment in Uganda fell dramatically as a result.

The loss of foreign investment is particularly important in developing countries. In Chapter 18 we said that developing countries suffer from a lack of saving. If domestic residents are not able to save because they are living at or below subsistence level, foreign saving is a crucial source of investment. Without that investment, the economies of developing countries cannot grow.

2.a.3. Good Economics as Bad Politics Every Third World politician wants to maximize economic growth, all things being equal. But all things are rarely equal. Political pressures may force a government to work toward more immediate objectives than economic growth.

For example, maximizing growth may mean reducing the size of government in order to lower taxes and increase investment. However, in many developing countries, the strongest supporters of the political leaders are those working for the current government. Obviously it's not good political strategy to fire those workers. So the government stays overstaffed and inefficient, and the potential for economic growth falls. The governments in LDCs often subsidize purchases of food and other basic necessities.

Reducing government expenditures and moving toward free market pricing of food, energy, and other items make good economic sense. But the citizens who depend on those subsidies are not going to be happy if they stop.

In 1977 the Egyptian government lowered its food subsidies in order to use those funds for development. What happened? There was widespread rioting that ended only when the government reinstituted the subsidies. In 1989, Venezuela lowered government subsidies on public transportation and petroleum products. Public transit fares went up 30 percent, to the equivalent of 7 U.S. cents, and gasoline prices went from 16 cents to 26 cents a gallon. (One official said that the prices were raised "from the cheapest in the world to the cheapest in the world."[1]) The resulting rioting in Caracas led to 50 deaths, over 500 injuries, and more than 1,000 arrests. Lowering government expenditures and reducing the role of government in the economy can be politically and physically dangerous.

What we are saying here is that seemingly good economics can make for bad politics. Because some group is going to be hurt in the short run by any change in policy aimed at increasing growth, there always is opposition to change. Often the continued rule of the existing regime depends on not alienating a certain group. Only a government stabilized by military force (a dictatorship), popular support (a democracy), or party support (a communist or socialist country) has the power to implement needed economic change. A government that lacks this power is handicapped by political constraints in its efforts to stimulate economic growth.

---

[1]See "Venezuela Rumblings: Riots and Debt Crisis," *The New York Times*, March 2, 1989, p. A13.

2.b. Social Obstacles

Cultural traditions and attitudes can work against economic development. In traditional societies, children follow in their parents' footsteps. If your father is a carpenter, there is a good chance that you will be a carpenter. Moreover, production is carried out in the same way generation after generation. For an economy to grow, it must be willing to change.

2.b.1. Lack of Entrepreneurs

A society that answers the questions What to produce? How to produce? and For whom to produce? by doing things as they were done by the previous generation lacks a key ingredient for economic growth: entrepreneurs. Entrepreneurs are risk-takers; they bring innovation and new technology into use. Understanding why some societies are better at producing entrepreneurs than others may help explain why some nations have remained poor while others have grown rapidly.

Entrepreneurs are more likely to develop among minority groups that have been blocked from traditional high-paying jobs.

One theory is that entrepreneurs often come from *blocked minorities*. Some individuals in the traditional society are blocked from holding prestigious jobs or political office because of discrimination. This discrimination can be based on race, religion, or immigrant status. Because discrimination keeps them from the best traditional occupations, these minority groups can achieve wealth and status only through entrepreneurship. The Chinese in Southeast Asia, the Jews in Europe, and the Indians in Africa were all blocked minorities, forced to turn to entrepreneurship to advance themselves.

Immigrants provide a pool of entrepreneurs who have skills and knowledge that often are lacking in the developing country.

In developing countries, entrepreneurship tends to be concentrated among immigrants, who have skills and experience that do not exist in poor countries. Many leaders of industry in Latin America, for example, are Italian, German, Arab, or Basque immigrants or the descendants of immigrants; they are not part of the dominant Spanish or native Indian population. The success of these immigrants is less a product of their being discriminated against than of their expertise in commerce. They know the foreign suppliers of goods. They have business skills that are lacking in developing regions. And they have the traditions—among them, the work ethic—and training instilled in their home country.

Motivation also plays a role in the level of entrepreneurship that exists in developing countries. In some societies, traditional values may be an obstacle to development because they do not encourage high achievement and view poverty as a virtue. Societies in which the culture supports individual achievement produce more entrepreneurs. It is difficult to identify the specific values in a society that account for a lack of motivation. In the past, researchers have pointed to factors that are not always valid across different societies. For instance, at one time many argued that the Protestant work ethic was responsible for the large number of entrepreneurs in the industrial world. According to this argument, some religions are more supportive of the accumulation of wealth than others. If poverty is a virtue, then working hard to make money is not an objective of the society. Today this argument is difficult to make because we find economic development in nations with vastly different cultures and religions.

Figure 2
Average Timing of Reproductive Events in Developed and Developing Countries
Women in developing countries tend to marry younger and have more children at a faster rate than do women in developed countries. *Source:* World Bank, *World Development Report, 1984* (Washington, D.C., 1984), p. 113.

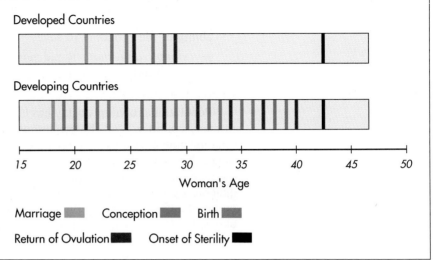

2.b.2. Rapid Population Growth

Per capita GNP is GNP divided by the population. When population rises faster than GNP, the standard of living of the average citizen does not improve. One very real problem for many developing countries is controlling the growth of their population. With the exception of China (where population growth is very much controlled), population growth in the developing countries is proceeding at a pace that will double the Third World population every 28 years. In large part the rate at which the population of the Third World is growing is a product of lower death rates. As death rates have fallen, birthrates have not.

Figure 2 shows why birthrates are different in the typical developed country and the typical developing country. The chart illustrates the average age of women at marriage, conception, birth of children, return of ovulation (fertility) following childbirth, and the onset of sterility. There are some fundamental differences here. First, women marry at a much younger age in developing countries, in their late teens versus their early twenties in developed countries. The World Fertility Study found that women in Bangladesh marry at the youngest average age, 16 years. Other things being equal, the younger women marry, the more children they have. Second, the time between the birth of one child and the conception of another is typically shorter in developing countries. Third, the average family in a developed country is likely to have no more than two children; the average family in a developing country is likely to have seven children.

Social scientists do not all agree on the effect of population growth on development. But most believe that population growth has a negative effect. They cite three reasons:

Capital shallowing Rapid population growth reduces the amount of capital per worker, lowering the productivity of labor.

Age dependency   Rapid population growth produces a large number of dependent children, whose consumption requirements lower the ability of the economy to save.

Investment diversion   Rapid population growth shifts government expenditures from the country's infrastructure (roads, communication systems) to education and health care.

Population growth probably has had a negative effect on development in many countries, but the magnitude of the effect is difficult to assess. And in some cases, population growth probably has stimulated development. The harmful effect of population growth should be most pronounced in countries where usable land and water are relatively scarce. Although generalizations about acceptable levels of population growth do not fit all circumstances, the World Bank has stated that population growth rates above 2 percent a year act as a brake on economic development.

GNP can grow steadily year after year, but if the population grows at a faster rate, the standard of living of the average individual falls. The simple answer to reducing population growth seems to be education: programs that teach methods of birth control and family planning. But here, too, governments are hampered by social custom and religion. Reducing birthrates is not simply a matter of education. People have to choose to limit the size of their families. It must be socially acceptable and economically advantageous for families to use birth control, and for many families it is neither.

Remember that what is good for society as a whole may not be good for the individual. Children are a source of labor in rural families and a support for parents in their old age. How many children are enough? That depends on the expected infant mortality rate. Although infant mortality rates in developing countries have fallen in recent years, families still tend to follow tradition, to keep having lots of children.

RECAP

1. In some countries, especially those that have been colonies, economic growth has been slow because government officials lack necessary skills.

2. Countries that are unable to protect the rights of private property have difficulty attracting investors.

3. Expropriation is the seizure by government of assets without adequate compensation.

4. Often government officials know the right economic policies to follow but are constrained by political considerations from implementing those policies.

5. Immigrants often are the entrepreneurs in developing countries.

6. Rapid population growth may slow development because of the effects of capital shallowing, age dependency, and investment diversion.

China's One-Child Family Policy

Birth control has been a national priority in China since 1971 when the government launched a new program to promote later marriage, longer spacing between births, and fewer children. In the late 1970s it became clear that, with the large number of women entering childbearing age as a result of past high fertility and falling mortality, even compliance with a two-child family norm would not reduce the rate of population growth enough to meet the national goal of 1.2 billion people by the year 2000. In 1979 Sichuan Province instituted a policy designed to persuade married couples to have no more than one child. This policy was backed by a system of economic rewards to parents with more than one child who committed themselves to have no more, and penalties for those who had more than two. This soon became a national policy and individual provinces were all expected to implement such systems. In 1980 the vice premier stated as specific goals that 95 percent of married couples in the cities and 90 percent in the countryside should have only one child. By 1982 most provinces and municipalities had introduced incentives and disincentives to promote the one-child norm.

Early results of the one-child campaign seem striking. The proportion of first births out of total births increased from 21 percent in 1970 to 42 percent in 1980 and 47 percent in 1981. By 1982 the proportion of first births exceeded 80 percent in each of the three large urban municipalities — Beijing, Shanghai, and Tianjin — and in five other provinces.

But several factors are working against the one-child policy.

- Old-age security. A compulsory pension system applies only to employees of state enterprises in urban areas, who constitute at most 15 percent of the labor force. A 1982 survey of rural production brigades in eleven provinces and municipalities found that only 1 percent of men over sixty-five and women over sixty received monthly pensions paid by welfare funds. For the rural majority, children remain the main source of old-age security.

- The responsibility system. The widespread introduction of the production responsibility system has given families a direct economic incentive to have more children, for two reasons. In some areas land for household use is allocated on a per capita basis, so more children ensures access to more land. In addition, whatever security for the elderly is provided on a collective basis will be reduced as collective income declines. In an effort to combat this, some brigades have introduced a double contracting system under which households are required both to deliver their quota of farm output to the state and to refrain from having an unauthorized birth.

- Persistent male preference. A preference for sons is a strong cultural impediment to having only one child. A 1980 survey of one-child families in Anhui Province found that 61 percent of the children of one-child certificate holders were boys. The pressure to have one child (and the desire for a boy) may have led to a revival of the practice of female infanticide, about which the Chinese government has expressed considerable concern. The 1982 census data on births in 1981 showed that there were 108.5 boys for every 100 girls at birth, an abnormally high figure.

- Financing incentives. Responsibility for financing incentives falls on local areas, not the central government. As a result there is great variation in the type and value of incentives. In a model county in Jilin Province in 1981 families pledging to have only one child were granted annual bonuses of almost fifty yuan — equivalent to 7 percent of average rural income — to last for fifteen years, and received a double-size private plot. For their single child they received an adult grain allowance and a special health care allowance. Yet in Hofei city in Anhui Province, bonuses paid to parents were much lower — a one-time payment of ten or twenty yuan, a few towels, a thermos bottle, some toys, a wash basin, or even nothing at all.

■ Source: World Bank, *World Development Report, 1984* (Washington, D.C., 1984), p. 178.

3. DEVELOPMENT STRATEGIES

▼ What strategies can a nation use to increase its economic growth?

Different countries follow different strategies to stimulate economic development. There are two basic types of development strategies: inward oriented and outward oriented.

3.a. Inward-Oriented Strategies

Inward-oriented development strategies focus on production for the domestic market rather than exports of goods and services. The typical developing country has a comparative advantage over other countries in the production of certain primary products. Having a comparative advantage means that a country has the lowest opportunity cost of producing a good (we talked about comparative advantage in Chapter 2). A **primary product** is a product in the first stage of production, which often serves as input in the production of some other good. Agricultural produce and minerals are examples of primary products. In the absence of a conscious government policy that directs production, we expect countries to concentrate on the production of that thing in which they have a comparative advantage. For example, we expect Cuba to focus on sugar production, Colombia to focus on coffee production, and the Ivory Coast to focus on cocoa production—each country selling its output of its primary product to the rest of the world.

primary product:
a product in the first stage of production, which often serves as input in the production of another product

Today many developing countries have shifted their resources away from producing primary products for export. For these countries, development means industrialization. The objective of this kind of inward-oriented strategy is **import substitution**, replacing imported manufactured goods with domestic goods.

Import-substitution policies dominate the strategies of the developing world. The basic idea is to identify domestic markets that are being supplied in large part by imports. Those markets that require a level of technology available to the domestic economy are candidates for import substitution. Industrialization goes hand in hand with tariffs or quotas on imports that protect the newly developing domestic industry from its more efficient foreign competition. As a result, production and international trade will not occur solely on the basis of comparative advantages but are also affected by some developing economies' efforts at import substitution.

import substitution:
the substitution of domestically produced manufactured goods for imported manufactured goods

Because the domestic industry can survive only with protection from foreign competition, import substitution policies typically raise the price of the domestically produced goods over the imported goods. In addition, quality may not be as good (at least at first) as the quality of the imported goods. Ideally, as the industry grows and becomes more experienced, price and quality become competitive with foreign goods. Once this happens, the import barriers are no longer needed, and the domestic industry may even become an export industry. Unfortunately the ideal is seldom realized. The Third World is full of inefficient manufacturing companies that are unlikely ever to improve enough to be able to survive without protection from foreign competitors.

3.b. Outward-Oriented Strategies

The inward-oriented strategy of developing domestic industry to supply domestic markets is the most popular development strategy, but it is not the only one. A small group of countries (notably South Korea, Hong Kong, Singapore, and Taiwan) choose to focus on the growth of exports. These countries follow an outward-oriented strategy, utilizing their most abundant resource to produce those products that they can produce better than others.

The abundant resource in these countries is labor, and the goods they produce are labor-intensive products. This kind of outward-oriented policy is called **export substitution**. The countries use labor to produce manufactured goods for export rather than agricultural products for domestic use.

Outward-oriented development strategies are based on efficient, low-cost production. Their success depends on being able to compete effectively with producers in the rest of the world. Here most governments attempt to stimulate exports. This can mean subsidizing domestic producers to produce goods for export as well as domestic consumption. International competition is often more intense than the competition at home—producers face stiffer price competition, higher quality standards, and greater marketing expertise in the global marketplace. This means domestic producers may have to be induced to compete internationally. Inducements can take the form of government assistance in international marketing, tax reductions, low-interest-rate loans, or cash payments.

export substitution:
the use of resources to produce manufactured products for export rather than agricultural products for the domestic market

Korea is one of the newly industrialized countries that has emphasized an outward-oriented strategy for development. The photo shows a team of women sewing clothes for export. By producing for export markets, Korean industry has grown rapidly and the nation serves as a popular example of successful development strategy.

Four Asian nations — Hong Kong, Singapore, South Korea, and Taiwan — are now called NICs, newly industrialized countries. Their new status is a product of outward-oriented development strategies.

In the 1950s and 1960s, the governments of the four countries followed the import-substitution strategy that was popular in the Third World. They protected domestic markets from foreign competition to stimulate domestic production for domestic consumption. The resulting lack of incentive to produce efficiently ruled out domestic production for exports of any significant magnitude. One problem was that domestic producers utilizing foreign inputs faced restrictions on many imported inputs and bureaucratic delays in obtaining permission to bring in other inputs. The growth of industry was limited by the growth of domestic demand, and because domestic demand was growing slowly, industrial development lagged.

Taiwan was the first to replace an inward-oriented policy with an outward-oriented policy. The other three countries followed closely behind. The results were soon evident; each country experienced rapid growth in exports and domestic national income.

Hong Kong essentially operates a free market economy, with little restriction on business operations. Korea, Singapore, and Taiwan maintain some restrictions on the domestic economy, but operate with another set of rules for exporting firms. Basically production for export occurs in a free market setting, with no taxes or restrictions on imports of the materials needed to manufacture goods for export. The goal is to rapidly increase exports by allowing domestic producers to seek foreign markets for their output.

Along with revisions in regulations for manufacturers, the governments have developed banking and financial institutions that can finance export production and sales. These nations had a history of severely limited sources of loans for industry, so guaranteeing exporters access to credit has given a big boost to export production.

The experience of Hong Kong, Singapore, South Korea, and Taiwan often is held as a lesson for other developing countries. But it is important to remember that other countries do not share certain key characteristics with the four NICs. For example, in the four Asian nations, wages basically are set by supply and demand; government seldom intervenes in the labor force. Also the countries are homogeneous in terms of their culture and have had a history of political stability. Finally, the governments have been willing to incur the political and economic costs of moving from an inward-oriented policy to an outward-oriented policy. This kind of shift hurts those who benefit from protection against foreign competition. In many developing countries, special interests would bring down the government if a policy of import substitution was implemented. Apparently, learning the lesson and being able to use that knowledge are two very different things.

Another inducement of sorts is to make domestic sales less attractive. This means implementing just the opposite policies of import substitution. The government reduces or eliminates domestic tariffs that keep domestic price levels above international levels. As profits from domestic sales fall, domestic industry turns to producing goods for export.

3.c. Comparing Strategies

Import-substitution policies are enacted in countries that believe industrialization is the key to economic development. In the 1950s and 1960s economists argued that specializing in the production and export of primary products does not encourage the rapid growth rates developing countries are looking for. This argument—*the deteriorating-terms-of-trade argument*—was based on the real value of primary products falling over time. If the prices of primary products fall in relation to the prices of manufactured products, then countries that export primary products and import manufactured goods find the cost of manufactured goods rising in terms of the primary products required to buy them. The amount of exports that must be exchanged for some quantity of imports often is called the **terms of trade**.

The deteriorating-terms-of-trade argument in the 1950s and 1960s led policymakers in developing countries to fear that the terms of trade would become increasingly unfavorable. One product of that fear was inward-oriented strategy, a focus on domestic industrialization rather than production for export.

At the root of the pessimism about the export of primary products was the belief that technological change would slow the growth of demand for primary products over time. That theory ignored the fact that if the supply of natural resources is fixed, those resources could become more valuable over time, even if demand grows slowly or not at all. And if the real value of primary products does fall over time, it does not necessarily mean that inward-oriented policy is required. Critics of inward-oriented policies argue that nations should exploit their comparative advantage, that resources should be free to move to their highest-valued use. And they argue that market-driven resource allocation is unlikely to occur in an inward-oriented economy where government has imposed restrictions aimed at maximizing the rate of growth of industrial output.

Other economists believe that developing countries have unique problems that call for active government intervention and regulation of economic activity. These economists often favor inward-oriented strategies. They focus on the structure of developing countries in terms of uneven industrial development. Some countries have modern manufacturing industries paying relatively high wages and traditional agricultural industries paying low wages. A single economy with industries at very different levels of development is called a **dual economy**. Some insist that in a dual economy, the markets for goods and resources do not work well. If resources could move freely between industries, then wages would not differ by the huge amounts observed in certain developing countries. Where markets are not functioning well, these economists support active government direction of the economy, believing that resources are unlikely to move freely to their highest-valued use if free markets are allowed.

The World Bank classifies developing countries according to their trade strategy. The countries are assigned to one of four categories: strongly outward oriented, moderately outward oriented, moderately inward oriented, and strongly inward oriented.

> *Strongly outward oriented*   Few or no controls on international trade. Any restrictions on imports that could limit exports are offset by export incentives.

terms of trade:
the amount of exports that must be exchanged for some amount of imports

dual economy:
an economy in which two sectors (typically manufacturing and agriculture) show very different levels of development

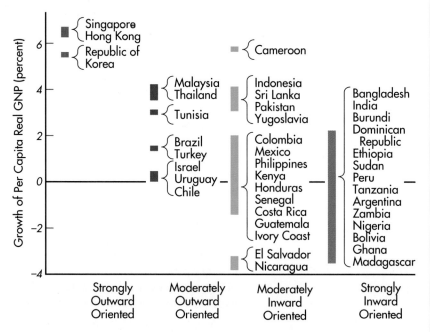

Moderately outward oriented Restrictions biased toward import
substitution rather than export promotion. Incentives for exports are
more than offset by protection against imports, so the net effect is
slightly against export promotion.

Moderately inward oriented Relatively high import-substitution restrictions. There may be some incentives for exports, but they are
weakened by inward-oriented policies.

Strongly inward oriented Exports are clearly discouraged by controls to isolate and protect the domestic market.

Figure 3 lists 41 countries by classification. Notice that Hong Kong,
Korea, and Singapore are the only countries listed with strong outward-
oriented policies. (Taiwan is not in the table because mainland China is the
only Chinese nation recognized by the World Bank and the IMF.)

As shown in the figure, the evidence suggests that the growth rates of
the outward-oriented economies are significantly higher than the growth
rates of the inward-oriented economies. Growth rates of individual countries ranged from over 6 percent per year for Singapore and Hong Kong to
almost −4 percent for Madagascar and Nicaragua. On average, per capita
income grew at a rate of 5.9 percent for the three strongly outward-
oriented economies; it fell at an average rate of .1 percent for the strongly
inward-oriented economies.

The success of the outward-oriented economies is likely to continue in
light of a strong increase in saving in those economies. In 1963, domestic
saving as a fraction of GDP was only 13 percent in the strongly outward-
oriented economies. After more than two decades of economic growth

*The growth rates of outward-oriented
economies are significantly higher
than the growth rates of
inward-oriented economies.*

driven by export-promotion policies, the rate of saving in these countries had increased to 31.4 percent of GDP. This high rate of saving increases investment expenditures, which increase the productivity of labor, further stimulating the growth of per capita GDP.

Why are outward-oriented strategies more successful than inward-oriented strategies? The primary advantage of an outward orientation is the efficient utilization of resources. Import-substitution policies do not allocate resources on the basis of cost minimization or profit maximization. In addition, an outward-oriented strategy allows the economy to grow beyond the scale of the domestic market. Foreign demand creates additional markets for exports, beyond the domestic market.

RECAP

1. Inward-oriented strategies concentrate on building a domestic industrial sector.
2. Outward-oriented strategies utilize a country's comparative advantage in exporting.
3. The deteriorating-terms-of-trade argument has been used to justify import-substitution policies.
4. Evidence indicates that outward-oriented policies have been more successful than inward-oriented policies at generating economic growth.

4. FOREIGN INVESTMENT AND AID

Developing countries rely on savings in the rest of the world to finance much of their investment needs. Foreign savings may come through commercial loans or gifts from industrial countries. In this section we describe the ways that savings are transferred from industrial to developing countries and the benefits of foreign investment and aid to developing countries.

4.a. Foreign Savings Flows

Poor countries that are unable to save enough to invest in capital stock must rely on the savings of other countries to help them develop economically. Foreign savings come from private sources as well as official government sources.

foreign direct investment:
the purchase of a physical operating unit in a foreign country

portfolio investment:
the purchase of securities

Private sources of foreign savings can take the form of direct investment, portfolio investment, commercial bank loans, and trade credit. **Foreign direct investment** is the purchase of a physical operating unit, like a factory, in a foreign country. This is different from **portfolio investment**, which is the purchase of securities, like stocks and bonds. In the case of

commercial bank loan:
a bank loan at market rates of interest, often involving a bank syndicate

trade credit:
the extension of a period of time before an importer must pay for goods or services purchased

foreign aid:
gifts or low-cost loans made to developing countries from official sources

How are savings in one nation used to speed development in other nations?

direct investment, the foreign investor may actually operate the business. Portfolio investment helps finance a business, but host-country managers operate the firm; foreign investors simply hold pieces of paper that represent a share of the ownership or the debt of the firm. **Commercial bank loans** are loans made at market rates of interest to either foreign governments or business firms. These loans often are made by a *bank syndicate*, a group of several banks, to share the risk associated with lending to a single country. Finally, exporting firms and commercial banks offer **trade credit**, allowing importers a period of time before payment is due on the goods or services purchased. Extension of trade credit usually involves payment in 30 days (or some other term) after the goods are received.

Direct investment and bank lending have changed over time. In 1970, direct investment in developing countries was greater than bank loans. By the late 1970s and early 1980s, however, bank loans were far in excess of direct investment. Bank lending gives the borrowing country greater flexibility in deciding how to use funds. Direct investment carries with it an element of foreign control over domestic resources. Nationalist sentiment combined with the fear of exploitation by foreign owners and managers has led many developing countries to pass laws restricting direct investment. In Chapter 39 we examine national debt and the problems that have arisen with bank loans to developing countries.

Official foreign savings are usually available as either outright gifts or low-interest-rate loans. These funds are called **foreign aid**. Figure 4 shows the foreign aid commitments of the major developed countries and of some oil-exporting developing countries. The figure shows both the U.S. dollar value of the development assistance and the percentage of each nation's GNP devoted to foreign aid. Large countries, like the United States, provide much more funding in terms of the dollar value of aid than do small countries. However, some small countries—for example, the Netherlands and Norway—commit a much larger percentage to their GNP to foreign aid.

4.b. Benefits of Foreign Investment

Not all developing countries discourage foreign direct investment. In fact many countries have benefited from foreign investment. Those benefits fall into three categories: new jobs, new technology, and foreign exchange earnings.

4.b.1. New Jobs
Foreign investment should stimulate growth and create new jobs in developing countries. But the number of new jobs created directly by foreign investment often is limited by the nature of the industries in which foreign investment is allowed.

Usually foreign investment is invited in capital-intensive industries, like chemicals or mineral extraction. Because capital goods are expensive and often require advanced technology to operate, foreign firms can build a capital-intensive industry faster than the developing country. One product of the emphasis on capital-intensive industries is that foreign

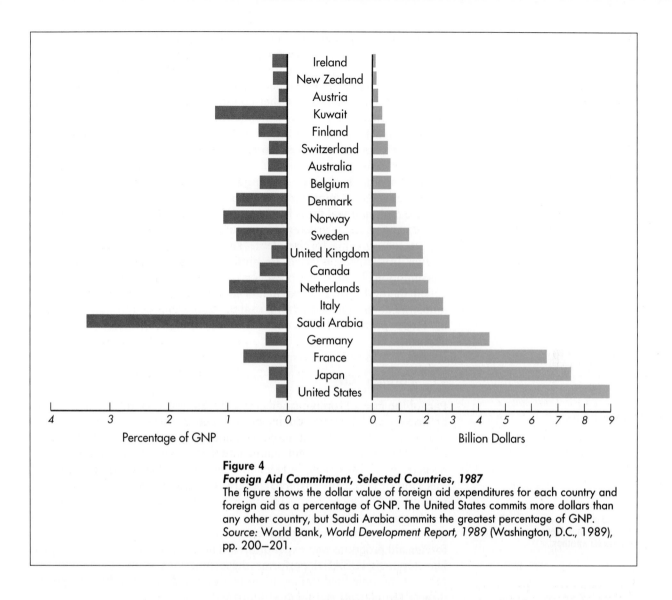

Figure 4
Foreign Aid Commitment, Selected Countries, 1987
The figure shows the dollar value of foreign aid expenditures for each country and foreign aid as a percentage of GNP. The United States commits more dollars than any other country, but Saudi Arabia commits the greatest percentage of GNP.
Source: World Bank, *World Development Report, 1989* (Washington, D.C., 1989), pp. 200–201.

investment often has little effect on employment in developing countries. A \$.5-billion oil refinery may employ just a few hundred workers; yet the creation of these few hundred jobs, along with other expenditures by the refinery, will stimulate domestic income by raising incomes across the economy, through the multiplier effect.

4.b.2. Technology Transfer In Chapter 18 we said that economic growth depends on the growth of resources and technological change. Most expenditures on research and development are made in the major industrial countries. These also are the countries that develop most of the innovations that make production more efficient. For the Third World country with limited scientific resources, the industrial nations are a critical source of information, technology, and expertise.

The ability of foreign firms to utilize modern technology in a developing country depends in part on having a supply of engineers and technical personnel in the host country. India and Mexico have a fairly large number of technical personnel, which means new technology can be adapted relatively quickly. Other countries, where a large fraction of the population has less than an elementary-level education, must train workers and then keep those workers from migrating to industrial countries where their salaries are likely to be much higher.

4.b.3. Foreign Exchange Earnings Developing countries expect foreign investment to improve their balance of payments. The assumption is that the multinational firms located inside the developing country increase exports and generate greater foreign currency earnings that can be used for imports or repaying foreign debt. This scenario does not unfold if the foreign investment is used to produce goods primarily for domestic consumption. In fact, the presence of a foreign firm can create a larger deficit in the balance of payments if the firm sends profits back to its industrial country headquarters from the developing country and the value of those profits exceeds the value of foreign exchange earned by exports.

4.c. Foreign Aid

Part of the flow of foreign savings into developing countries is in the form of foreign aid. Foreign aid itself can take the form of cash grants or transfers of goods or technology, with nothing given in return by the developing country. Often foreign aid is used to "reward" political allies, particularly when those allies hold a strategic military location. Examples of this kind of politically inspired aid are Soviet support of Cuba and U.S. support of Turkey.

bilateral aid:
foreign aid that flows from one country to another

Foreign aid that flows from one country to another is called **bilateral aid**. Governments typically have an agency that coordinates and plans foreign aid programs and expenditures. The U.S. Agency for International Development (USAID) performs these functions in the United States. Most of the time bilateral aid is project oriented, given to fund a specific project (an educational facility, an irrigation project).

Food makes up a substantial portion of bilateral aid. After a bad harvest or a natural disaster (drought in the Sudan, floods in Bangladesh), major food-producing nations help feed the hungry. Egypt and Bangladesh were the leading recipients of food aid during the late 1980s. The major recipients of food aid change over time, as nature and political events combine to change the pattern of hunger and need in the world.

The economics of food aid illustrates a major problem with many kinds of charity. Aid is intended to help those who need it without interfering with domestic production. But when food flows into a developing country, food prices tend to fall, pushing farm income down and discouraging local production. Ideally food aid should go to the very poor, who are less likely to have the income necessary to purchase domestic production anyway.

Foreign aid does not flow directly from the donors to the needy. It goes through the government of the recipient country. Here we find another problem: the inefficient and sometimes corrupt bureaucracies in recipient nations. There have been cases where recipient governments have sold products that were intended for free distribution to the poor. In other cases, food aid was not distributed because the recipient government had created the conditions leading to starvation. In still other cases, a well-intentioned recipient government simply did not have the resources to distribute the aid, so the products ended up largely going to waste. One response to these problems is to rely on voluntary agencies to distribute aid. Another is to rely on multilateral agencies.

multilateral aid:
aid provided by international organizations supported by many nations

Multilateral aid is provided by international organizations that are supported by many nations. The largest and most important multilateral aid institution is the World Bank. The World Bank makes loans to developing countries at below-market rates of interest and oversees projects it has funded in developing countries. As an international organization, the World Bank is not controlled by any single country. This allows the organization to advise and help developing countries in a nonpolitical way that usually is not possible with bilateral aid.

RECAP

1. Private sources of foreign savings include direct investment, portfolio investment, commercial bank loans, and trade credit.

2. Foreign aid is gifts or low-cost loans made available to developing countries by official sources.

3. Developing countries can benefit from foreign investment through new jobs, the transfer of technology, and foreign exchange earnings.

4. Foreign aid can be provided bilaterally or multilaterally.

SUMMARY

▼▲ **How is poverty measured?**

1. Poverty usually is defined in an absolute sense and measured by per capita GNP or GDP. § 1.a

2. Some economists and social scientists use a quality-of-life index to evaluate standards of living. § 1.b

▼▲ **Why are some countries poorer than others?**

3. There are both political obstacles (lack of skilled officials, instability, constraints imposed by special interest groups) and social obstacles (cultural attitudes that discourage entrepreneurial activity and encourage rapid population growth) that limit economic growth in developing countries. §§ 2.a and 2.b

▼▲ **What strategies can a nation use to increase its economic growth?**

4. Inward-oriented development strategies focus on developing a domestic manufacturing sector to produce goods that can substitute for imported manufactured goods. § 3.a

5. Outward-oriented development strategies focus on producing manufactured goods for export. § 3.b

6. The growth rates of outward-oriented economies are significantly higher than those of inward-oriented economies. § 3.c

7. Private sources of foreign savings include direct investment, portfolio investment, commercial bank loans, and trade credit. § 4.a

8. Official gifts or low-cost loans made to developing countries by official sources are called foreign aid. § 4.a

▼▲ **How are savings in one nation used to speed development in other nations?**

9. Foreign investment in developing countries can increase their economic growth by creating jobs, transferring modern technology, and stimulating exports to increase foreign exchange earnings. § 4.b

10. Foreign aid can be distributed bilaterally or multilaterally. § 4.c

KEY TERMS

expropriation § 2.a.2

primary product § 3.a

import substitution § 3.a

export substitution § 3.b

terms of trade § 3.c

dual economy § 3.c.

foreign direct investment § 4.a

portfolio investment § 4.a

commercial bank loan § 4.a

trade credit § 4.a

foreign aid § 4.a

bilateral aid § 4.c

multilateral aid § 4.c

EXERCISES

Basic Terms and Concepts

1. What are basic human needs?

2. Per capita GNP is used as an absolute measure of poverty.

   a. What are some criticisms of using per capita GNP as a measure of standard of living?

   b. Do any of these criticisms also apply to a quality-of-life index?

3. In many developing countries there are economists and politicians who were educated in industrial countries. These individuals know the policies that would maximize the growth of their countries, but they do not implement them. Why not?

4. Suppose you are a benevolent dictator who can impose any policy you choose in your country. If your goal is to accelerate economic development, how would you respond to the following problems?

   a. Foreign firms are afraid to invest in your country because your predecessor expropriated many foreign-owned factories.

   b. There are few entrepreneurs in the country.

   c. The dominant domestic religion teaches that the accumulation of wealth is sinful.

   d. It is customary for families to have at least six children.

5. What effect does population growth have on economic development?

6. Why have most developing countries followed inward-oriented development strategies?

7. Why is an outward-oriented development strategy likely to allocate resources more efficiently than an inward-oriented strategy?

8. Who benefits from an import-substitution strategy? Who is harmed?

Extended Concepts

9. If poverty is a relative concept, why don't we define it in relative terms?

10. "The poor will always be with us." Does this statement have different meanings depending on whether poverty is interpreted as an absolute or relative concept?

11. How do traditional societies answer the questions What to produce? How to produce? and For whom to produce?

12. What are the most important sources of foreign savings for developing countries? Why don't developing countries save more so that they don't have to rely on foreign savings for investment?

13. Private foreign investment and foreign aid are sources of savings to developing countries. Yet each has been controversial at times. What are the potential negative effects of private foreign investment and foreign aid for developing countries?

Economically Speaking

Not by Bread Alone

The impending famine in northern Ethiopia threatens the lives of as many as 2 million people. If it happens, it will be one of many famines that have struck in the past 20 years. In 1973 close to 200,000 died in the Wollo province of Ethiopia, and around 500,000 in the Sahel region in Africa. In 1974 as many as 1 million died in Bangladesh. Five years ago between 500,000 and 1 million people died in Ethiopia and Sudan.

Governments and international agencies responded to these famines by distributing food to those in need. They undoubtedly saved millions of lives. But as the death tolls show, food aid usually arrives too late to save everyone. When it does come, it harms farmers still able to sell their crops or livestock and can make a country even more dependent on western aid in the event of a future drought.

A better approach, argue [Messrs] Amartya Sen of Harvard University and Jean Dreze of the London School of Economics in a new book, would often be to give money to the hungry. Cash aid should push up food prices, thereby encouraging food imports and greater domestic production of food. With the money, those facing starvation could buy food from those who have enough. Unlike food aid, cash can be dispatched quickly to the famine area and is less disruptive to the economy.

Cash aid will work only if there is already enough food in a famine-stricken country to feed everyone, and only if food can be bought and sold relatively freely. These conditions, say [Messrs] Sen and Dreze, exist more often than is usually supposed. In a previous book Mr. Sen

examined most of the big famines since the second world war. In every case famine was caused not by an overall shortage of food, but by how food was distributed.

Consider the Ethiopian famine of 1973. The country as a whole produced roughly as much food as in previous years. But there was a big decline in output in Wollo, the province that saw the worst of the famine. Most of the victims were subsistence farmers, living off food they produced themselves. When their crops failed they had no income to buy food from elsewhere. If they had had money, they could have done so. There was enough food in the rest of Ethiopia; trade was possible because the roads into Wollo were open. Indeed, some of Wollo's farmers had surplus food and sold it outside the province. In just the same way, food was exported from Ireland to England during the Irish famine of 1848.

In the 1974 Bangladesh famine 1 million people died even though food output that year was higher than in any of the previous four. The floods of 1974 came too late to affect the harvests, but they caused unemployment and cut the incomes of farm workers. Also, the threat of a bad crop in the next year had pushed up rice prices. So rural workers, who received no income support, could not afford to buy rice. Bangladesh's famine thus happened not because there was too little food, but because so many people could not afford to buy any.

Bolstering the incomes of the starving can thus prevent some famines just as effectively as directly increasing the supply of food. In countries where private trade is better than

public distribution at getting food to those in need, cash aid will actually work better. However, where a major civil war (like the one now going on in Ethiopia) causes trade between districts to break down, cash aid may fail altogether. In countries where corruption is a problem, cash aid has another drawback: money is even easier to steal than food.

In practice, cash aid has often succeeded where food aid has failed. India, for example, relies heavily on cash-for-work programmes when food shortages threaten. It has avoided a major famine since independence — even though food output and incomes in some provinces are lower than anywhere in the world. In the Indian province of Maharashtra, grain output dropped by 60% in the early 1970s — a much bigger drop than in Africa's Sahel, where around 500,000 died in the famines of 1973. Cash-for-work schemes in Maharashtra employed 5 million. These schemes provided enough income to encourage imports into the province from other Indian regions. Average food consumption fell by only 10%; there was no widespread starvation. . . .

The clear moral for the next famine is this: if internal trade looks feasible, prefer cash aid to food aid. This prescription will not help today's war-torn Ethiopia, but in many other countries it could save thousands of lives.

■ Source: "Not by Bread Alone," *Economist*, January 13, 1990, p. 65. COPYRIGHT Economist Newspaper Ltd. (England) 1990

Commentary

Though efforts to combat famines often take the form of food aid, famines do not necessarily imply a shortage of food. Instead, famines represent shortfalls in purchasing power of the poorest sectors of society. In many cases, grants of income are a better means of alleviating famines than grants of food.

We can understand this argument using demand and supply analysis. In the following two diagrams we represent the demand for food and the supply of food in a famine-stricken country receiving aid. In each diagram, the demand curve D_1 intersects the supply curve S_1 at an equilibrium quantity of food Q_1, which represents a subsistence level of food consumption. The equilibrium depicted in each graph is one in which, in the absence of aid, a famine would occur.

The first graph illustrates the effects of providing aid in the form of food. The food aid increases the available supply of food, which is shown by an outward shift of the supply curve to S_2. The effect of this aid is to increase the equilibrium quantity of food (Q_2) and lower the equilibrium price (P_2). The lower price of food will adversely affect the income of domestic producers. Domestic producers will also attempt to grow other crops, or to search for sources of income other than growing food, if they cannot receive enough money for their produce. As the amount of domestic food production falls, a country becomes more dependent upon imports of food.

The second graph illustrates the effect of income aid for the famine-stricken country. The aid is depicted by a shift in the demand curve to D_2. As with food aid, this relief allows consumption to rise to a point above the subsistence level. The effects of this aid on domestic food producers, however, are quite different. The price of food rises, and thus domestic food producers are not hurt by the aid package. As a result, aid in the form of income does not cause disincentives for production. An increase in domestic food production also serves to make a country less dependent upon food imports.

In this analysis we have assumed that markets and food distribution channels work. In Ethiopia, where civil war has disrupted regular trade paths, we cannot make such assumptions. Starvation there is unlikely to be allieviated by simply sending income aid and not worrying about food distribution. Nevertheless, the importance of recognizing the effects of different types of aids can save lives.

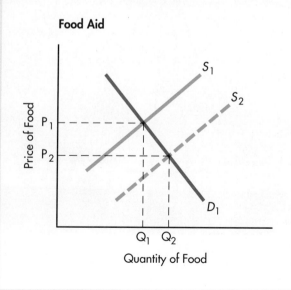

Food Aid

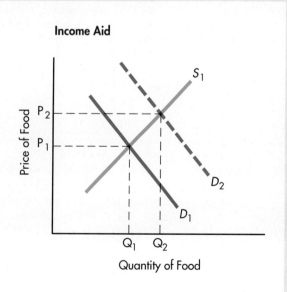

Income Aid

V

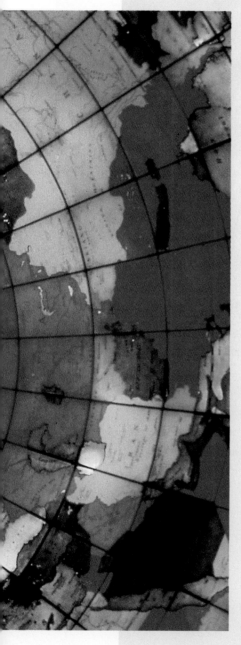

Issues in International Trade and Finance

20

World Trade Equilibrium

1. What are the prevailing patterns of trade between countries? What goods are traded?

2. What determines the goods a nation will export?

3. How are the equilibrium price and the quantity of goods traded determined?

4. What are the sources of comparative advantage?

PREVIEW The United States' once-dominant position as an exporter of color television sets has since been claimed by nations like Japan and Taiwan. What caused this change? If countries tend to specialize in the export of particular kinds of goods, why does the United States import Heineken beer at the same time it exports Budweiser? This chapter will examine the volume of world trade and the nature of trade linkages between countries. As we have seen, trade occurs because of specialization in production. No single individual or country can produce everything better than others can. The result is specialization of production based on comparative advantage. Remember that comparative advantage is in turn based on relative opportunity costs: a country will specialize in the production of those goods for which its opportunity costs of production are lower than costs in other countries. Nations then trade what they produce in excess of their own consumption to acquire other things they want to consume. In this chapter, we will go a step further to discuss the sources of comparative advantage. We will look at why one country has a comparative advantage in, say, automobile production while another country has a comparative advantage in wheat production.

The world equilibrium price and quantity traded are derived from individual countries' demand and supply curves. This relationship between the world trade equilibrium and individual country markets will be utilized in Chapter 21 to discuss the ways that countries can interfere with free international trade to achieve their own economic or political goals.

1. AN OVERVIEW OF WORLD TRADE

Trade occurs because it makes people better off. International trade occurs because it makes people better off than they would be if they could consume only domestically-produced products. This section will consider the direction of international trade, who trades with whom, and what sorts of goods are traded.

1.a. The Direction of Trade

> What are the prevailing patterns of trade between countries? What goods are traded?

Table 1 shows patterns of trade between three large groups of countries: the industrial countries, developing countries, and the Eastern trading area. The industrial countries include all of Western Europe, Japan, Australia, New Zealand, Canada, and the United States. The Eastern trading area includes the USSR, Eastern Europe, China, North Korea, and Vietnam. The developing countries are, essentially, the rest of the world. The table shows the dollar value and percent of total trade between these groups of countries. The vertical column at the left lists the origin of exports, and the horizontal row at the top lists the destination of imports.

Trade between industrial countries accounts for the majority of international trade.

As Table 1 shows, trade between industrial countries accounts for the bulk of international trade. Trade between industrial countries exceeds $1 trillion in value, and amounts to 54.8 percent of world trade. Exports from industrial countries to developing countries represent 12.6 percent of total

Table 1   The Direction of Trade (in billions of dollars and percentages of world trade, 1987)

Destination:	Industrial Countries	Developing Countries	Eastern Trading Area
Origin:			
Industrial Countries	$1,360 54.8%	$312 12.6%	$61 2.5%
Developing Countries	$321 13.0%	$125 5.1%	$38 1.5%
Eastern Trading Area	$61 2.5%	$42 1.7%	$132 5.3%

Source: Data from *United Nations Conference on Trade and Development Handbook of International Trade and Development Statistics 1988*, (New York: 1989), pp. 60–61.

world trade, and exports from industrial countries to the Eastern area only 2.5 percent. Exports from developing countries to industrial countries account for 13 percent of total trade, while exports from the Eastern trading area to industrial countries currently represent only 2.5 percent of international trade. Clearly, the Eastern-trading-area countries have participated least in international trade, but this pattern should change now that the Eastern European countries are replacing communist regimes with new market-oriented leadership.

Table 2 lists the major trading partners of selected countries, and the percentage of total exports and imports accounted for by each country's top ten trading partners. For instance, 22.9 percent of U.S. exports went to Canada, and 20.8 percent of U.S. imports came from Japan. From a glance at the other countries listed in Table 2, it is clear that the United States is a major trading partner for many nations. This is true because of the size of the U.S. economy and the nation's relatively high level of income. It is also apparent that Canada and Mexico are very dependent on trade with the United States: about two-thirds of Canadian exports and imports, and well over half of Mexican exports and imports, involve the

Table 2   Major Trading Partners of Selected Countries

United States				Canada			
Exports		**Imports**		**Exports**		**Imports**	
Canada	22.9%	Japan	20.8%	U.S.	72.8%	U.S.	65.9%
Japan	11.3	Canada	19.9	Japan	5.4	Japan	6.3
Mexico	5.8	Germany	6.6	U.K.	2.3	U.K.	3.6
U.K.	5.6	Mexico	4.8	Germany	1.3	Germany	2.9
Germany	4.7	U.K.	4.2	China	1.1	Korea	1.5

Germany				Mexico			
Exports		**Imports**		**Exports**		**Imports**	
France	12.1%	France	11.6%	U.S.	69.6%	U.S.	73.5%
U.S.	9.5	Netherlands	11.0	Japan	5.6	Japan	7.1
U.K.	8.8	Italy	9.6	Spain	4.9	Germany	4.2
Netherlands	8.7	U.K.	7.1	Canada	3.3	Canada	2.0
Italy	8.7	Belgium	7.1	France	2.3	France	1.8

Japan				USSR			
Exports		**Imports**		**Exports**		**Imports**	
U.S.	36.8%	U.S.	21.2%	East Germany	11.5%	East Germany	11.4%
Korea	5.8	Indonesia	6.1	Czechoslovakia	10.2	Czechoslovakia	10.5
Germany	5.6	Korea	5.4	Poland	10.0	Bulgaria	9.9
Hong Kong	3.9	Australia	5.3	Bulgaria	9.9	Poland	9.8
U.K.	3.7	United Arab Em.	5.0	Hungary	6.8	Hungary	7.8

Source: Data for all countries but the USSR from International Monetary Fund, *Direction of Trade Statistics Yearbook,* 1988. USSR data from United Nations, *International Trade Statistics Yearbook,* 1986.

The Eastern European Business Climate

The countries of Eastern Europe underwent radical political and economic change in 1989–1990, when they began to move from rigid state control of the economy to free markets. In response, firms in the rest of the world began searching for new opportunities in Eastern Europe. *USA Today* commissioned an expert on Eastern Europe to rate the various countries on the current opportunities they offer for foreign firms. The ratings were based on: availability of existing firms offering good growth opportunities, government attitudes toward foreign investors, quality of the labor force, and macroeconomic prospects for growth and price stability. The Eastern European countries were graded in the following order.

Hungary: A−

The government has actively recruited foreign investors. Foreigners can purchase a less-than-50-percent interest in a firm with no government approval. With approval, foreigners can own 100 percent. The labor force is productive. Good opportunities exist in telecommunications, tourism, construc-

tion, pharmaceuticals, and computer software.

Czechoslovakia: B

The government has been slow to attract foreign investors, and there are many limits on investment, but the economy is relatively sound compared to other East-bloc nations. The labor force should adapt easily to Western work ethics. Best opportunities are in food-storage facilities, textiles, and chemicals.

U.S.S.R.: B−

Abundance of natural resources and investment opportunities make the U.S.S.R. the nation with the greatest ultimate potential for foreign investors. Recent political and ethnic conflicts and a slow-moving bureaucracy create greater risks and lower the grade. Best opportunities are in energy, food processing, tourism, road construction, ceramics, and medicine.

Poland: C+

Labor is inexpensive and the government has welcomed foreign investors, allowing 100-percent ownership and the same rights as Polish citizens. The

weak macroeconomic condition of the economy lowers the grade. Best opportunities are in food processing, small agricultural machinery, medical equipment, medicine, chemicals, textiles, and steel.

Bulgaria: C+

Political and economic reform are slow to take hold, and there are still many uncertainties regarding future policies. Labor is capable, and foreign-investment laws are expected to be liberalized in the future. Best opportunities are in consumer products, electronics, energy, pollution-control technology, and minerals.

Romania: C−

There are substantial restrictions on foreign investment, though changes are promised. The slow pace of new legislation will cause most firms to wait and see what actually occurs. Best opportunities are in energy, chemicals, textiles, agricultural equipment, furniture, and food processing.

■ Source: Based on "East Bloc Business," *USA Today*, March 19, 1990, p. 6B.

United States. The dollar value of trade among the three North American nations is shown in Figure 1.

1.b. What Goods Are Traded

Because countries differ in their comparative advantages, they will tend to export different goods. Countries also have different tastes and technological needs, and thus tend to differ in what they will import. Some goods are more widely traded than others, as Table 3 shows. Crude petroleum is by far the most heavily traded good in the world, accounting for 10.8 percent of the total volume of world trade. Crude petroleum is followed by motor

The volume of trade in crude petroleum exceeds that of any other good.

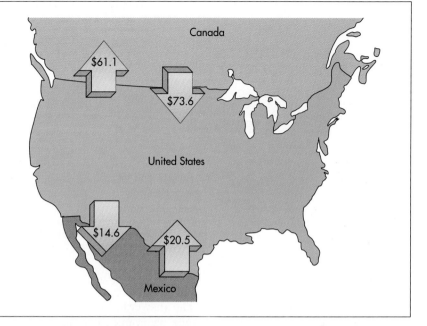

Figure 1
Merchandise Trade Flows in North America (billions of 1987 dollars)
In 1987, the United States exported $61.1 billion worth of goods to Canada and imported $73.6 billion of goods from Canada. The same year, U.S. merchandise exports to Mexico were $14.6 billion while merchandise imports from Mexico were $20.5 billion. Data from International Monetary Fund, *Direction of Trade Statistics Yearbook*, 1988, various pages.

vehicles, petroleum products, nonelectrical machinery, and electrical machinery. The top ten exported products, however, represent only 40 percent of world trade. The remaining 60 percent is distributed among a great variety of products. The importance of petroleum, motor vehicles, and machinery in international trade should not obscure the fact that international trade involves all sorts of products from all over the world.

RECAP

1. Trade between industrial countries accounts for the bulk of international trade.
2. The most important trading partners of the United States are Canada (for U.S. exports) and Japan (for U.S. imports).
3. Crude petroleum is the most heavily traded good in the world, in terms of value of exports.
4. World trade is distributed across a great variety of products.

2. AN EXAMPLE OF INTERNATIONAL TRADE EQUILIBRIUM

The international economy is very complex. Each country has a unique pattern of trade, in terms both of trading partners and of goods traded. Some countries trade a great deal and others trade very little. We already know that countries specialize and trade according to comparative advan-

Table 3   The Top Ten Exported Products (in millions of dollars and percentages of world exports)

Product Category	Value	Percent of World Trade
Crude petroleum	$205,260	10.8%
Motor vehicles	148,900	7.8
Petroleum products	91,233	4.8
Machinery, nonelectrical	71,053	3.7
Machinery, electrical	52,634	2.8
Office machines	46,930	2.5
Clothing	39,927	2.1
Gas, natural and mfg.	38,537	2.0
Organic chemicals	36,156	1.9
Telecommunications	35,260	1.9

Source: Data from *United Nations Conference on Trade and Development Handbook of International Trade and Development Statistics,* 1989, p. 180.

tage, but what are the fundamental determinants of international trade that explain the pattern of comparative advantage?

The answer to this question will in turn provide a better understanding of some basic questions about how international trade functions: What goods will be traded? How much will be traded? What prices will prevail for traded goods?

2.a. Comparative Advantage

What determines the goods a nation will export?

Comparative advantage is found by comparing the relative costs of production in each country. We measure the cost of producing a particular good in two countries in terms of opportunity costs—what other goods must be given up in order to produce more of the good in question.

Table 4 presents a hypothetical example of two countries, the United States and India, that both produce two goods, wheat and cloth. The table lists the hours of labor required to produce one unit of each good. This example assumes that labor productivity differences alone determine comparative advantage. In the United States, 1 unit of wheat requires 3 hours of labor and 1 unit of cloth requires 6 hours of labor. In India, 1 unit of wheat requires 6 hours of labor and 1 unit of cloth requires 8 hours of labor.

The United States has an **absolute advantage** in producing both wheat and cloth. Absolute advantage is determined by comparing the absolute cost in different countries of producing each good. Since it requires fewer hours of labor to produce either good in the United States than in India, the United States is the most efficient producer of both goods in terms of the domestic labor hours required.

It might seem that, since the United States is the most efficient producer of both goods, this country cannot gain from trading with India. But absolute advantage is not the critical consideration. As we saw with regard to trade in general in Chapter 2, what matters in international trade is comparative advantage. To find the **comparative advantage**, we must compare the opportunity cost of producing each good in each country. Since

Table 4 An Example of Comparative Advantage

	Labor hours required to produce 1 unit each of two goods	
	U.S.	**India**
Wheat	3	6
Cloth	6	8

Opportunity cost of producing 1 unit of wheat:

U.S. 1 W = 1/2 C

India 1 W = 3/4 C

The United States has the comparative advantage in wheat.

Opportunity cost of producing 1 unit of cloth:

U.S. 1 C = 2 W

India 1 C = 1 1/3 W

India has the comparative advantage in cloth.

wheat requires 3 labor hours while cloth requires 6, the opportunity cost in the United States of producing a unit of wheat is 1/2 unit of cloth. In other words, to produce an extra unit of wheat, we must shift 3 hours of labor away from cloth production. Since 1 unit of cloth requires 6 hours of labor, the loss of 3 hours of labor would lower cloth output by 1/2 unit. So the extra unit of wheat costs 1/2 unit of cloth in the United States. It is assumed here that labor can move freely between industries but does not move between countries.

In India, producing one more unit of wheat would require shifting 6 hours of labor from cloth to wheat production. Since one unit of cloth takes 8 hours of labor, the loss of 6 hours of labor from cloth production means a reduction in cloth output of 6/8, or 3/4. So the opportunity cost of producing an additional unit of wheat in India is 3/4 units of cloth.

A comparison of the domestic opportunity costs in each country will reveal which one has the comparative advantage in producing each good. The U.S. opportunity cost of producing one unit of wheat is 1/2 unit of cloth; the Indian opportunity cost is 3/4 unit of cloth. Because the United States has a lower domestic opportunity cost, it has the comparative advantage in wheat production and will export wheat.

The comparative advantage in cloth is found the same way. One unit of cloth requires 6 hours of labor in the United States. Since a unit of wheat requires 3 hours of labor, producing one more unit of cloth costs 2 units of wheat. In India, one unit of cloth requires 8 hours of labor. Since a unit of wheat requires 6 hours of labor, shifting 8 hours of labor from wheat production to cloth production means a loss of 8/6 or 1 1/3 units of wheat. Comparing the U.S. opportunity cost of 2 units of wheat with the Indian opportunity cost of 1 1/3 units, we see that India has the comparative advantage in cloth production and will therefore export cloth.

Every country has a comparative advantage in something, and one good Holland has long been known for is its tulips. Countries that are associated with flower cultivation have been innovators in horticulture or have favorable growing conditions. The source of comparative advantage may be based in technology, resource availability, or other factors economists have identified as important.

Countries export goods in which they have a comparative advantage.

In international trade, as in other areas of economic decision making, it is opportunity cost that matters—and opportunity costs are reflected in comparative advantage. Absolute advantage is irrelevant, because knowing the absolute number of labor hours required to produce a good does not tell us if we can benefit from trade. We benefit from trade if we are able to obtain a good from a foreign country by giving up less than we would have to give up to obtain the good at home. Because only opportunity cost can allow us to make such comparisons, international trade proceeds on the basis of comparative advantage.

2.b. Terms of Trade

Based on comparative advantage, India will specialize in cloth production and the United States will specialize in wheat production. The two countries will then trade with each other to satisfy the domestic demand for both goods. International trade permits greater consumption than would be possible from domestic production alone. Since countries trade when they can obtain a good more cheaply from a foreign producer than they can at home, international trade allows all traders to consume more. This is evident when we examine the terms of trade.

terms of trade:
the amount of an export good that must be given up to obtain one unit of an imported good

The **terms of trade** are the amount of an export good that must be given up to obtain one unit of an imported good. As we saw earlier, comparative advantage dictates that the United States will specialize in wheat production and export wheat to India in exchange for Indian cloth. But the amount of wheat that the United States will exchange for a unit of cloth is limited by the domestic tradeoffs. If a unit of cloth can be obtained domestically for 2 units of wheat, the United States will only be willing to trade with India if the terms of trade are less than 2 units of wheat for a unit of cloth.

The terms of trade are the amount of an export that must be given up for a certain quantity of an import. The price of an import will be equal to its price in the foreign country of origin multiplied by the exchange rate (the domestic-currency price of foreign currency). As the exchange rate changes, the terms of trade will change. This can have important consequences for international trade.

A problem can arise when one export industry in an economy is booming relative to others. In the 1970s, for instance,

the Netherlands experienced a boom in its natural-gas industry. The dramatic energy price increases of the 1970s resulted in large Dutch exports of natural gas. Increased demand for exports from the Netherlands caused the Dutch currency to appreciate, making Dutch goods more expensive for foreign buyers. This situation caused the terms of trade to worsen for the Netherlands. While the natural-gas sector boomed, Dutch manufacturing was finding it difficult to compete in the world market.

The phenomenon of a boom in one industry causing declines in the rest of the economy is popularly called the Dutch Disease. It is usually associated with dramatic increases in the demand for a primary commodity, and could afflict any nation experiencing such a boom. For instance, a rapid rise in the demand for coffee could lead to a Dutch-disease problem for Colombia, where a coffee boom is accompanied by decline in other sectors of the economy.

India in turn will be willing to trade its cloth for U.S. wheat if it can receive a better price than its domestic opportunity costs. Since a unit of cloth in India costs 1 1/3 units of wheat, India will gain from trade if it can obtain more than 1 1/3 units of wheat for its cloth.

The limits of the terms of trade are determined by the opportunity costs in each country. In this example, the limits of the terms of trade are:

1 unit of cloth for more than 1 1/3 but less than 2 units of wheat

Within this range, the actual terms of trade will be decided by the bargaining power of the two countries. The closer the United States can come to giving up only 1 1/3 units of wheat for cloth, the better the terms of trade for the United States. The closer India can come to receiving 2 units of wheat for its cloth, the better the terms of trade for India.

The gain from trade is increased consumption.

Though each country would like to push the other as close to the limits of the terms of trade as possible, any terms within the limits set by domestic opportunity costs will be mutually beneficial. Both countries benefit because they are able to consume goods at a cost less than their domestic opportunity costs. To illustrate the *gains from trade,* let us assume that the actual terms of trade are 1 unit of cloth for 1 1/2 units of wheat.

Suppose the United States has 60 hours of labor, half of which goes to wheat production and the other half to cloth production. Since a unit of wheat requires 3 labor hours, 10 units of wheat are produced. Cloth requires 6 labor hours, so 5 units of cloth are produced. Without international trade, the United States can produce and consume 10 units of wheat and 5 units of cloth. If the United States, with its comparative advantage in wheat production, chooses to produce only wheat, it can use all 60 labor hours to produce 20 units. If the terms of trade are 1 1/2 units of wheat per unit of cloth, the United States can keep 10 units of wheat and trade the other 10 for 6 2/3 units of cloth (10 divided by 1 1/2). By trading U.S. wheat for Indian cloth, the United States is able to consume more than it could without trade. With no trade, and half its labor hours devoted to each good, the United States could consume 10 units of wheat and 5 units of cloth. After trade, the United States consumes 10 units of wheat and 6 2/3 units of cloth. By devoting all its labor hours to wheat production and trading wheat for cloth, the United States gains 1 1/3 units of cloth. This is the gain from trade—an increase in consumption.

2.c. Export Supply and Import Demand

The preceding example suggests that countries all benefit from specialization and trade. Realistically, however, countries do not completely specialize. Typically, domestic industries satisfy part of the domestic demand for goods that are also imported. To understand how the quantity of goods traded is determined, we must construct demand and supply curves for each country, and use them to create export supply and import demand curves.

The proportion of domestic demand for a good that is satisfied by domestic production, and the proportion that will be satisfied by imports, are determined by the domestic supply and demand curves and the international equilibrium price of a good. The international equilibrium price and quantity may be determined once we know the export supply and import demand curves for each country. These curves are derived from the domestic supply and demand in each country. Figure 2 illustrates the derivation of the export supply and import demand curves.

Figure 2(a) shows the domestic supply and demand curves for the U.S. wheat market. The domestic equilibrium price is $6 and the domestic equilibrium quantity is 200 million bushels. (The domestic "no-trade" equilibrium price is the price that exists prior to international trade.) A price above $6 will yield a U.S. wheat surplus. For instance, at a price of $9, the U.S. surplus will be 200 million bushels. A price below equilibrium will produce a wheat shortage: at a price of $3, the shortage will be 200 million bushels. The key point here is that the world price of a good may be quite different than the domestic "no-trade" equilibrium price. And once international trade occurs, the world price will prevail in the domestic economy.

If the world price of wheat is different than a country's domestic "no-trade" equilibrium price, the country will become an exporter or importer. For instance, if the world price is above the domestic "no-trade" equilibrium price, the domestic surplus can be exported to the rest of the world. Figure 2(b) shows the U.S. **export supply curve.** This curve illustrates the U.S. domestic surplus of wheat for prices above the domestic "no-trade" equilibrium price of $6. At a world price of $9, the United States would supply 200 million bushels of wheat to the rest of the world. The export supply is equal to the domestic surplus. The higher the world price above the domestic "no-trade" equilibrium, the greater the quantity of wheat exported by the United States.

If the world price of wheat is below the domestic "no-trade" equilib-

export supply curve:
a curve showing the relationship between the world price of a good and the amount that a country will export

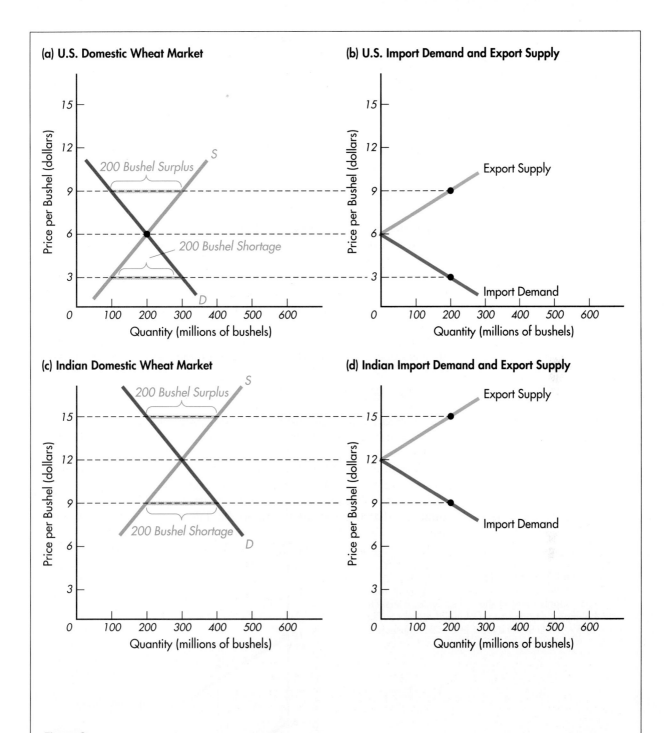

Figure 2
The Import Demand and Export Supply Curves
Figures 2(a) and 2(c) show the domestic demand and supply curves for wheat in the United States and India respectively. The domestic "no-trade" equilibrium price is $6 in the United States and $12 in India. Any price above the domestic "no-trade" equilibrium prices will create do- mestic surpluses, which are reflected in the export supply curves in Figures 2(b) and (d). Any price below the domestic "no-trade" equilibrium prices will create domestic shortages, which are reflected in the import demand curves in Figures 2(b) and (d).

rium price, the United States will import wheat. The **import demand curve** is the amount of the U.S. shortage at various prices below the "no-trade" equilibrium. In Figure 2(b), the import demand curve is a downward-sloping line, indicating that the lower the price below the domestic "no-trade" equilibrium of $6, the greater the quantity of wheat imported by the United States. At a price of $3, the United States will import 200 million bushels.

The export supply and import demand curves for India appear as parts (c) and (d) of Figure 2. The domestic "no-trade" equilibrium price in India is $12. At this price, India would neither import nor export any wheat because the domestic demand would be satisfied by domestic supply. The export supply curve for India is shown in Figure 2(d) as an upward-sloping line that measures the amount of the domestic surplus as the price level rises above the domestic "no-trade" equilibrium price of $12. According to Figure 2(c), if the world price of wheat is $15, the domestic surplus in India is equal to 200 million bushels. The corresponding point on the export supply curve indicates that, at a price of $15, 200 million bushels will be exported. The import demand curve for India reflects the domestic shortage at a price below the domestic "no-trade" equilibrium price. At $9, the domestic shortage is equal to 200 million bushels: the import demand curve indicates that, at $9, 200 million bushels will be imported.

2.d. The World Equilibrium Price and Quantity Traded

How are the equilibrium price and the quantity of goods traded determined?

International equilibrium occurs at the point where the quantity of imports demanded by one country is equal to the quantity of exports supplied by the other country.

The international equilibrium price of wheat and quantity traded are found by combining the import demand and export supply curves for the United States and India, as in Figure 3. International equilibrium occurs if the quantity of imports demanded by one country is equal to the quantity of exports supplied by the other country. In Figure 3, this equilibrium occurs at the point labeled *e*. At this point, the import demand curve for India indicates that India wants to import 200 million bushels at a price of $9.

Figure 3
International Equilibrium Price and Quantity
The international equilibrium price is the point at which the export supply curve of the United States intersects with the import demand curve of India. At the equilibrium price of $9, the U.S. will export 200 million bushels to India.

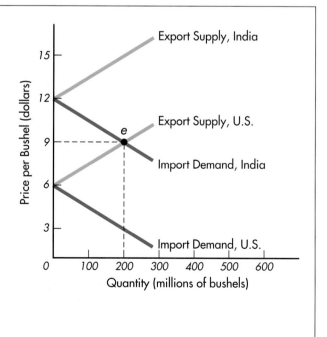

The export supply curve for the United States indicates that the United States wants to export 200 million bushels at a price of $9. Only at $9 will the quantity of wheat demanded by the importing nation equal the quantity of wheat supplied by the exporting nation. So the equilibrium world price of wheat is $9 and the equilibrium quantity of wheat traded is 200 million bushels.

RECAP

1. Comparative advantage is based on the relative opportunity costs of producing goods in different countries.
2. A country has an absolute advantage when it can produce a good for a lower input cost than can other nations.
3. A country has a comparative advantage when the opportunity cost of producing a good, in terms of forgone output of other goods, is lower than that of other nations.
4. The terms of trade are the amount of an export good that must be given up to obtain one unit of an import good.
5. The limits of the terms of trade are determined by the domestic opportunity costs of production in each country.
6. The export supply and import demand curves measure the domestic surplus and shortage, respectively, at different world prices.
7. International equilibrium occurs at the point where one country's import demand curve intersects with the export supply curve of another country.

3. SOURCES OF COMPARATIVE ADVANTAGE

What are the sources of comparative advantage?

We know that countries specialize and trade in accordance with comparative advantage, but what gives a country a comparative advantage? Economists have suggested several theories of the source of comparative advantage. Let us review these theories.

3.a. Productivity Differences

The example of comparative advantage earlier in this chapter showed the United States to have a comparative advantage in wheat production, and India to have a comparative advantage in cloth production. Comparative advantage was determined by differences in the labor hours required to produce each good. In this example, differences in the *productivity* of labor accounted for comparative advantage.

For over 200 years, economists have argued that productivity differences account for comparative advantage. In fact, this theory of compar-

Comparative advantage due to productivity differences between countries is often called the Ricardian model of comparative advantage.

ative advantage is often called the *Ricardian model,* after David Ricardo, an eighteenth-century English economist who explained and analyzed the idea of productivity-based comparative advantage. Variation in the productivity of labor can explain many observed trade patterns in the world.

Workers in industrial countries earn much higher wages than workers in developing countries because of the higher productivity of labor in industrial countries. While we know that labor productivity differs across countries—and that this can help explain why countries produce the goods they do—there are factors other than labor productivity that determine comparative advantage. Furthermore, even if labor productivity were all that mattered, we would still want to know why some countries have more productive workers than others. The standard interpretation of the Ricardian model is that technological differences between countries account for differences in labor productivity. The countries with the most advanced technology would have a comparative advantage with regard to those goods that can be produced most efficiently with modern technology.

3.b. Factor Abundance

Goods differ in terms of the resources, or factors of production, required for their production. Countries differ in terms of the abundance of different factors of production: land, labor, capital, and entrepreneurial ability. It seems self-evident that countries would have an advantage in producing those goods that use relatively large amounts of their most abundant factor of production. Certainly countries with a relatively large amount of farmland would have a comparative advantage in agriculture, and countries with a relatively large amount of capital would tend to specialize in the production of manufactured goods.

Comparative advantage based on differences in the abundance of factors of production across countries is described in the Heckscher-Ohlin model.

The idea that comparative advantage is based on the relative abundance of factors of production is sometimes called the *Heckscher-Ohlin model,* after the two Swedish economists, Eli Heckscher and Bertil Ohlin, who developed the original argument. The original model assumed that countries possess only two factors of production: labor and capital. Thus, researchers have examined the labor and capital requirements of various industries to see whether labor-abundant countries export goods whose production is relatively labor-intensive, and capital-intensive countries export goods that are relatively capital intensive. In many cases, factor abundance has served well as an explanation of observed trade patterns. However, there remain cases in which comparative advantage seems to run counter to the predictions of the factor-abundance theory. In response, economists have suggested other explanations for comparative advantage.

3.c. Other Theories of Comparative Advantage

New theories of comparative advantage have typically come about in an effort to explain the trade pattern in some narrow category of products. They are not intended to serve as general explanations of comparative advantage, as do factor abundance and productivity. These supplementary theories emphasize human skills, product cycles, and preferences.

Human Skills This approach emphasizes differences across countries in the availability of skilled and unskilled labor. The basic idea is that countries with a relatively abundant stock of highly-skilled labor will have a comparative advantage in producing goods that require relatively large amounts of skilled labor. This theory is similar to the factor-abundance theory, except that here the analysis rests on two segments (skilled and unskilled) of the labor factor.

The human-skills argument is consistent with the observation that most U.S. exports are produced in high-wage (skilled-labor) industries, and most U.S. imports are of products produced in relatively low-wage industries. Since the United States has a well-educated labor force, relative to many other countries, we would expect the United States to have a comparative advantage in industries requiring a large amount of skilled labor. Developing countries would be expected to have a comparative advantage in industries requiring a relatively large amount of unskilled labor.

Manufactured goods have life cycles. At first they are produced by the firm that invented them. Later, they may be produced by firms in other countries that copy the technology of the innovator.

Product Life Cycles This theory explains how comparative advantage in a specific good can shift over time from one country to another. This occurs because goods experience a *product life cycle*. At the outset, development and testing are required to conceptualize and design the product. For this reason, the early production will be undertaken by an innovative firm. Over time, however, a successful product tends to become standardized, in the sense that many manufacturers can produce it. The mature product may be produced by firms that do little or no research and development, specializing instead in copying successful products invented and developed by others.

The product-life-cycle theory is related to international comparative advantage in that a new product will be first produced and exported by the nation in which it was invented. As the product is exported elsewhere and foreign firms become familiar with it, the technology is copied in other countries by foreign firms seeking to produce a competing version. As the product matures, comparative advantage shifts away from the country of origin if other countries have lower manufacturing costs using the now-standardized technology.

The history of color-television production shows how comparative advantage can shift over the product life cycle. Color television was invented in the United States, and U.S. firms initially produced and exported color TVs. Over time, as the technology of color-television manufacturing became well known, countries like Japan and Taiwan came to dominate the business. Firms in these countries had a comparative advantage over U.S. firms in the manufacture of color televisions. Once the technology is widely available, countries with cheaper assembly lines, due to lower wages, can compete effectively against the higher-wage nation that developed the technology.

Preferences The theories of comparative advantage we have looked at so far have all been based on supply factors. It may be, though, that the demand side of the market can explain some of the patterns observed in international trade. Seldom are different producers' goods exactly identical. Consumers may prefer the goods of one firm to those of another firm.

Domestic firms usually produce goods to satisfy domestic consumers. But since different consumers have different preferences, some consumers will prefer goods produced by foreign firms. International trade allows consumers to expand their consumption opportunities.

Consumers who live in countries with similar levels of development can be expected to have similar consumption patterns. The consumption patterns of consumers in countries at much different levels of development are much less similar. This would suggest that firms in industrial countries will find a larger market for their goods in other industrial countries than in developing countries.

As we saw earlier in this chapter, industrial countries tend to trade with other industrial countries. This pattern runs counter to the factor-abundance theory of comparative advantage, which would suggest that countries with the most dissimilar endowments of resources would find trade most beneficial. Yet rich countries, with large supplies of capital and skilled labor forces, trade more actively with other rich countries than they do with poor countries. Firms in industrial countries tend to produce goods that relatively wealthy consumers will buy. The key point here is that we do not live in a world based on simple comparative advantage, in which all cloth is identical, regardless of the producer. We inhabit a world of differentiated products, and consumers want choices between different brands or styles of a seemingly similar good.

intraindustry trade:
simultaneous import and export of goods in the same industry by a particular country

Another feature of international trade that may be explained by consumer preference is **intraindustry trade**, a circumstance in which a country both exports and imports goods in the same industry. The fact that the United States exports Budweiser beer and imports Heineken beer is not surprising when preferences are taken into account. Supply-side theories of comparative advantage rarely provide an explanation of intraindustry trade, since they would expect each country to export only those goods produced in industries in which a comparative advantage exists. Yet the real world is characterized by a great deal of intraindustry trade.

We have discussed several potential sources of comparative advantage: labor productivity, factor abundance, human skills, product cycles, and preferences. Each of these theories, summarized in Figure 4, has proven useful in understanding certain trade patterns. Each has also been shown to have limitations as a general theory applicable to all cases. Once again we are reminded that the world is a very complicated place. Theories are simpler than reality. Nevertheless, they help us to understand how comparative advantage arises.

RECAP

1. Comparative advantage can arise because of differences in labor productivity.

2. Countries differ in their resource endowments, and a given country may enjoy a comparative advantage in products that intensively use its most abundant factor of production.

3. Industrial countries may have a comparative advantage in products requiring a large amount of skilled labor. Developing countries may

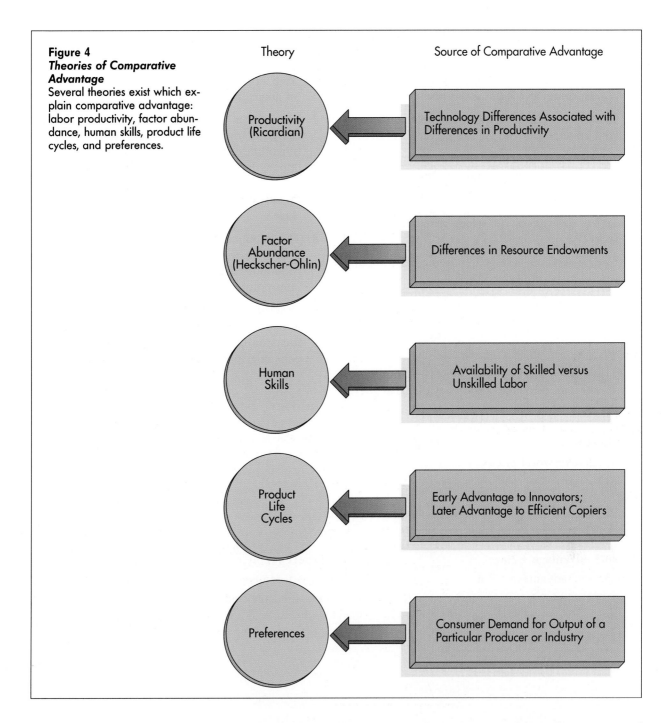

Figure 4
Theories of Comparative Advantage
Several theories exist which explain comparative advantage: labor productivity, factor abundance, human skills, product life cycles, and preferences.

Theory

Source of Comparative Advantage

Productivity (Ricardian) — Technology Differences Associated with Differences in Productivity

Factor Abundance (Heckscher-Ohlin) — Differences in Resource Endowments

Human Skills — Availability of Skilled versus Unskilled Labor

Product Life Cycles — Early Advantage to Innovators; Later Advantage to Efficient Copiers

Preferences — Consumer Demand for Output of a Particular Producer or Industry

have a comparative advantage in products requiring a large amount of unskilled labor.

4. Comparative advantage in a new good initially resides in the country that invented the good. Over time, other nations learn the technology and may gain a comparative advantage in producing the good.

5. In some industries, consumer preferences for differentiated goods may explain international trade flows, including intraindustry trade.

▼▲ **What are the prevailing patterns of trade between countries? What goods are traded?**

1. International trade flows largely between industrial countries. § 1.a.

2. International trade involves many diverse products, but crude petroleum accounts for more than 10 percent of its total value. § 1.b.

▼▲ **What determines the goods a nation will export?**

3. Comparative advantage is based on the opportunity costs of production. § 2.a.

4. Domestic opportunity costs determine the limits of the terms of trade between two countries—that is, the amount of exports that must be given up to obtain imports. § 2.b.

5. The export supply curve shows the domestic surplus and amount of exports available at alternative world prices. § 2.c.

6. The import demand curve shows the domestic shortage and amount of imports demanded at alternative world prices. § 2.c.

▼▲ **How are the equilibrium price and the quantity of goods traded determined?**

7. The international equilibrium price and quantity of a good traded are determined by the intersection of the export supply of one country with the import demand of another country. § 2.d.

▼▲ **What are the sources of comparative advantage?**

8. The productivity-differences and factor-abundance theories of comparative advantage are general theories that seek to explain patterns of international trade flow. § 3.a and § 3.b.

9. Other theories of comparative advantage aimed at explaining trade in particular kinds of goods focus on human skills, product life cycles, and consumer preferences. § 3.c.

KEY TERMS

absolute advantage § 2.a.
comparative advantage § 2.a.
terms of trade § 2.b.

export supply curve § 2.c.
import demand curve § 2.c.
intraindustry trade § 3.c.

Basic Terms and Concepts

1. Why must voluntary trade between two countries be mutually beneficial?

2. Use this table to answer the following questions.

Labor hours required to produce 1 unit of each good

	Canada	*Japan*
Beef	2	4
Computers	6	5

a. Which country has the absolute advantage in beef production?

b. Which country has the absolute advantage in computer production?

c. Which country has the comparative advantage in beef production?

d. Which country has the comparative advantage in computer production?

e. What are the limits of the terms of trade? Specifically, when is Canada willing to trade with Japan, and when is Japan willing to trade with Canada?

3. Consider this supply and demand schedule for two countries.

Demand and Supply of Shoes (1000s)

| | Mexico | | Chile | |
Price	*Qty. demanded*	*Qty. supplied*	*Qty. demanded*	*Qty. supplied*
$10	40	0	50	0
$20	35	20	40	10
$30	30	40	30	20
$40	25	60	20	30
$50	20	80	10	40

What is the international equilibrium price of shoes? How many shoes will be traded?

4. How would each of the following theories of comparative advantage explain the fact that the United States exports computers?

   a. productivity differences

   b. factor abundance

   c. human skills

   d. product life cycle

   e. preferences

5. Which of the theories of competitive advantage could explain why the United States exports computers to Japan at the same time that it imports computers from Japan? Explain.

Extended Concepts

6. Developing countries have complained that the terms of trade they face are unfavorable. If they voluntarily engage in international trade, what do you suppose they mean by "unfavorable terms of trade"?

7. If two countries reach equilibrium in their domestic markets at the same price, what can be said about their export supply and import demand curves and about the international trade equilibrium?

Economically Speaking

Believe It or Not, Japan is Changing

Japan's colossal trade imbalance with the U.S. is making it America's least favorite nation. Pollsters report deepening public distrust. Alarmists warn that a trade war will soon supplant the fading cold war. Ironically, the trade hawks may be gearing up to fight a battle that's all but over.

True, last week's trade report showed that in December Japan sold the United States $3.5 billion more in merchandise than it bought. And, as trade hard-liners like to point out, Japan's economy remains relatively closed...

But Japan is starting to act more like other rich countries, argues trade expert Robert Lawrence of the Brookings Institution in a recent study, "How Open Is Japan?" And Tokyo's towering trade surpluses could soon be history...

Signs of a sea change abound. Japan's rocklike trade surplus with the rest of the world is crumbling fast. In a year, Japan's monthly current-account balance has plunged from a high of $8 billion to a low last December of $1 billion (see chart)...

Japan is behaving more like an insatiable yuppie than an ascetic samurai, sucking in goods and services from abroad like never before. Sales of foreign consumer goods ... have tripled since 1986. The pull? Purchasing power multiplied by the mighty yen, a booming economy and burgeoning consumerism.

Japanese salaried men now crave Arrow shirts, Marlboros and souped-up BMW's. Their working wives show up at the office in Estée Lauder lip gloss. Savvy shoppers are circumventing pricey Japanese middlemen. Foreign-catalog sales are rocketing. So is direct buying abroad by ... consumer co-ops....

Meanwhile, Japan's powerful export engine is idling. Real growth has throttled back to less than 5 percent a year. Japan has large and growing deficits in food, oil, industrial materials and consumer nondurables. Its lofty surpluses in cars, machinery and electronics are falling. One reason: Japanese manufacturers are building most of their new plants overseas and sending Hondas and Sonys back home. Domestic capacity for cranking out more exports is tight and not growing much.

Until Tokyo opens up more, Japanophobes will hurl fighting words about unfair trade. But with Japanese consumers handing the U.S. one bloodless victory after another, who needs calls to arms?

■ Source: Sylvia Nasar, "Believe It or Not, Japan Is Changing," *U.S. News & World Report*, February 26, 1990, p. 49.

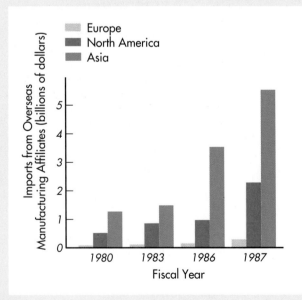

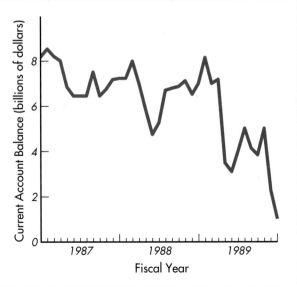

Commentary

There is no lack of stories in the American press on the purported threat of Japanese economic domination. The main piece of evidence used in arguing that the United States will soon become an economic vassal state of Japan is the large bilateral trade imbalance between the two countries. The article points out that economic forces are working to diminish Japan's trade surpluses with other countries as the income generated by its exports is beginning to be channeled into greater consumption by Japanese citizens.

An even more fundamental point, however, is that bilateral trade accounts provide little, if any, information on relative economic strengths. Indeed, it is easy to think of an example in which a country has a persistent trade deficit with one of its trading partners but has its overall trade account in balance. Suppose there are three countries that trade among themselves, which we will call countries A, B, and C. The people of each country produce only one type of good and consume only one other type of good. The people of country A produce apples and consume bananas, the people of country B produce bananas and consume cucumbers, and the people of country C produce cucumbers and consume apples. Even when the trade account of each country is balanced, each has a deficit with one of its trading partners and a surplus with the other. Furthermore, a larger trade deficit between countries A and B (with each country retaining balanced trade) implies that the people of country A are better off since they are consuming more. If the government of country A tried to impose a law forcing bilateral trade balance with country B, citizens of country A could not consume as many bananas as before and would be forced to attempt to sell apples to the uninterested citizens of country B.

This simple example demonstrates that the U.S. trade deficit with Japan should not in itself be a cause for concern, especially if the overall trade surplus is shrinking. The United States could have a persistent trade deficit with Japan and yet maintain an overall balanced trade account. In fact, any country would be expected to have a trade deficit with some countries and a trade surplus with others. This reflects comparative advantage. Trade between countries makes both the exporting and the importing countries better off.

This is not to say that concern about the *overall* trade deficit is not well founded. An overall trade deficit indicates that a country is consuming more than it is producing. Just as an individual can do this through borrowing (as you may very well be borrowing to finance your college education), a country can run a trade deficit by borrowing from the rest of the world. The money lent to a country must be repaid. Borrowing may not be a problem if the loans are used to finance investment that will enable the country to become more productive (just as you may be willing to take out college loans since you expect higher future income because of your college degree). If, on the other hand, the loans only finance consumption, the future repayment of the debt will not be possible because any potential future income will have been consumed in the present.

At any particular time, a country may want to run a trade deficit or a trade surplus, depending on the circumstances it faces. But regardless of the overall trade account of a country, we should expect bilateral trade imbalances among trading partners.

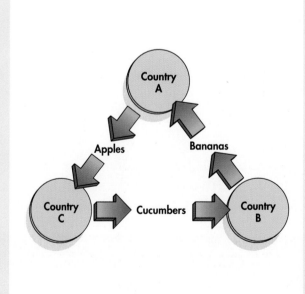

21

Commercial Policy

1. Why do countries restrict international trade?

2. How do countries restrict the entry of foreign goods and promote the export of domestic goods?

3. What sorts of agreements do countries enter into to reduce barriers to international trade?

PREVIEW

The Japanese government once announced that foreign-made skis would not be allowed into Japan because they were unsafe. Japanese ski manufacturers were active supporters of the ban. The U.S. government once imposed a tax of almost 50 percent on imports of motorcycles with engines larger than 700cc. The only U.S.-owned motorcycle manufacturer, Harley-Davidson, produced no motorcycles with engines smaller than 1000cc, and so did not care about the small-engine market. There are many other examples of government policy influencing the prices and quantities of goods traded internationally.

International trade is rarely determined solely by comparative advantage and the free-market forces of supply and demand. Governments often find that political pressures favor policies that at least partially offset the prevailing comparative advantages. Government policy aimed at influencing international trade flows is called **commercial policy**. This chapter first examines the arguments in support of commercial policy, and then discusses the various tools of commercial policy employed by governments.

commercial policy:
government policy that influences international trade flows

1. ARGUMENTS FOR PROTECTION

▼ Why do countries restrict international trade? ▲

Governments restrict foreign trade to protect domestic producers from foreign competition. In some cases the protection may be justified; in most cases it harms consumers. Of the arguments used to promote such protection, only a few are valid. We will look first at arguments widely considered to have little or no merit, and then at those that may sometimes be valid.

International trade on the basis of comparative advantage maximizes world output and allows consumers access to better-quality products at lower prices than would be available in the domestic market alone. If trade is restricted, consumers pay higher prices for lower-quality goods and world output declines. Protection from foreign competition imposes costs on the domestic economy, as well as on foreign producers. When production does not proceed on the basis of comparative advantage, resources are not expended on their most efficient uses. Whenever government restrictions alter the pattern of trade, we should expect someone to benefit and someone else to suffer. Generally speaking, protection from foreign competition benefits domestic producers at the expense of domestic consumers.

Protection from foreign competition generally benefits domestic producers at the expense of domestic consumers.

1.a. Creation of Domestic Jobs

If foreign goods are kept out of the domestic economy, it is often argued, jobs will be created at home. This argument holds that domestic firms will produce the goods that otherwise would have been produced abroad, thus employing domestic workers instead of foreign workers. The weakness of this argument is that only the protected industry would benefit in terms of employment. Since domestic consumers will pay higher prices to buy the output of the protected industry, they will have less to spend on other goods and services, which could cause employment in other industries to drop. If other countries retaliate by restricting entry of U.S. exports, the output of U.S. firms that produce for export will fall as well. Typically, restrictions to "save domestic jobs" simply redistribute jobs by creating employment in the protected industry and reducing employment elsewhere.

Table 1 shows estimates of consumer costs and producer gains associated with protection in certain U.S. industries. The first column lists the total cost to U.S. consumers, in terms of higher prices paid, for each industry. For instance, the consumer cost of protecting U.S. book manufacturing is $500 million. The second column lists the cost to consumers of saving one job in each industry (found by dividing the total consumer cost by the number of jobs saved by protection). In book manufacturing, each job saved costs U.S. consumers $100,000. The gain to U.S. producers appears in the third column. Government protection of book manufacturers allowed them to gain $305 million. This gain is less than the costs to consumers of $500 million.

Saving domestic jobs from foreign competition may cost domestic consumers more than it benefits the protected industries.

Table 1 demonstrates the very high cost per job saved by protection. If the costs to consumers are greater than the benefits to protected indus-

Table 1 Benefits and Costs of Protection from Foreign Competition: Some U.S. Case Histories

Case	Consumer Losses Totals (million dollars)	Consumer Losses Per job saved[1] (dollars)	Producer Gains Totals (million dollars)
Manufacturing			
Book manufacturing	$ 500	$ 100,000	$ 305
Benzenoid chemicals	2,650	over 1 million	2,250
Glassware	200	200,000	130
Rubber footwear	230	30,000	90
Ceramic articles	95	47,500	25
Ceramic tiles	116	135,000	62
Orange juice	525	240,000	390
Canned tuna	91	76,000	74
Textiles and apparel: Phase I	9,400	22,000	8,700
Textiles and apparel: Phase II	20,000	37,000	18,000
Textiles and apparel: Phase III	27,000	42,000	22,000
Carbon steel: Phase I	1,970	240,000	1,330
Carbon steel: Phase II	4,350	620,000	2,770
Carbon steel: Phase III	6,800	750,000	3,800
Ball bearings	45	90,000	21
Specialty steel	520	1,000,000	420
Nonrubber footwear	700	55,000	250
Color televisions	420	420,000	190
CB radios	55	93,000	14
Bolts, nuts, large screws	110	550,000	60
Prepared mushrooms	35	117,000	13
Automobiles	5,800	105,000	2,600
Motorcycles	104	150,000	67
Services			
Maritime industries	3,000	270,000	2,000
Agriculture and fisheries			
Sugar	930	60,000 690/acre	550
Dairy products	5,500	220,000 1,800/cow	5,000
Peanuts	170	1,000/acre	170
Meat	1,800	160,000 225/head	1,600
Fish	560	21,000	200
Mining			
Petroleum	6,900	160,000	4,800
Lead and zinc	67	30,000	46

[1]Unless otherwise specified, figures are per worker.
Source: Data from Cletus C. Coughlin, et al., "Protectionist Trade Policies: A Survey of Theory, Evidence, and Rationale," *Federal Reserve Bank of St. Louis Review*, January/February 1988, p. 18. Based on data reported in Gary Clyde Hufbauer, et al., *Trade Protection in the United States: 31 Case Studies*, Institute for International Economics, Washington, D.C., 1986.

tries, you may wonder why government provides any protection aimed at saving jobs. The answer, in a word, is politics. Protection of book manufacturing means that all consumers pay a higher price for books. But the individual consumer does not know how much of the book's price is due to protection, and consumers rarely lobby their political representatives to eliminate protection and reduce prices. Meanwhile, there is a great deal of pressure for protection. Employers and workers in the industry know the benefits of protection: higher prices for their output, higher profits for owners, and higher wages for workers. As a result, there will be active lobbying for protection against foreign competition.

1.b. Creation of a "Level Playing Field"

Special-interest groups sometimes claim that other nations that export successfully to the home market have unfair advantages over domestic producers. Fairness, however, is often in the eye of the beholder. People who call for creating a "level playing field" believe that the domestic government should take steps to offset the perceived advantage of the foreign firm. They often claim that foreign firms have an unfair advantage because foreign workers are willing to work for very low wages. "Fair trade, not free trade" is the cry that this claim generates. But advocates of fair trade are really claiming that production in accordance with comparative advantage is unfair. Such statements are clearly wrong. A country with relatively low wages is typically a country with an abundance of low-skilled labor. Such a country will have a comparative advantage in products that use low-skilled labor most intensively. To create a "level playing field" by imposing restrictions that eliminate the comparative advantage of foreign firms will make domestic consumers worse off and undermine the basis for specialization and economic efficiency.

Calls for "fair trade" are typically aimed at imposing restrictions to match those imposed by other nations.

Some calls for "fair trade" are based on the notion of reciprocity. If a country imposes import restrictions on goods from a country that does not have similar restrictions, reciprocal tariffs and quotas may be called for in the latter country in order to stimulate a reduction of trade restrictions in the former country. For instance, it has been claimed that U.S. construction firms are discriminated against in Japan, because no U.S. firm has had a major construction project in Japan since the 1960s. Yet Japanese construction firms do billions of dollars' worth of business in the United States each year. Advocates of fair trade could argue that U.S. restrictions should be imposed on Japanese construction firms. Reciprocity is generally considered a more valid reason for restrictions on free trade than is protection of domestic jobs.

Calls for fairness based on reciprocity are becoming more common. One danger is that calls for fair trade may be invoked in cases where, in fact, foreign restrictions on U.S. imports do not exist. For instance, suppose the U.S. auto industry wanted to restrict the entry of imported autos to help stimulate sales of domestically-produced cars. One strategy might be to point out that U.S. auto sales abroad had fallen and to claim that this was due to unfair treatment of U.S. auto exports in other countries. Of course, there are many other possible reasons why foreign sales of U.S.

Table 2 Tariffs as a Percent of Total Government Revenue

Country Category	Tariffs as Percent of Government Revenue
Industrial countries	3.0%
African developing countries	32.4
Asian developing countries	24.3
European developing countries	12.9
Middle Eastern developing countries	14.7
Western Hemisphere developing countries	22.7

Source: International Monetary Fund, *Government Finance Statistics Yearbook*, Washington, D.C., 1987, p. 32–33. Used by permission.

autos might have fallen. But blaming foreign trade restrictions might win political support for restricting imports of foreign cars into the United States.

1.c. Government Revenue Creation

Developing countries often justify tariffs as an important source of government revenue.

Tariffs on trade generate government revenue. Industrial countries, which find income taxes easy to collect, rarely justify tariffs on the basis of the revenue they generate for government spending. But many developing countries find income taxes difficult to levy and collect, while tariffs are easy to collect. Customs agents can be positioned at ports of entry to examine all goods that enter and leave the country. The observability of trade flows makes tariffs a popular tax in developing countries, whose revenue requirements may provide a valid justification for their existence. Table 2 shows that tariffs account for a relatively large fraction of government revenue in many developing countries, and only a small fraction in industrial countries.

1.d. National Defense

Industries that are truly critical to the national defense should be protected from foreign competition if that is the only way to ensure their existence.

It has long been argued that industries crucial to the national defense, like shipbuilding, should be protected from foreign competition. Even though the United States does not have a comparative advantage in shipbuilding, a domestic shipbuilding industry is necessary since foreign-made ships may not be available during war. This is a valid argument as long as the protected industry is genuinely critical to the national defense. In some industries, like copper or other basic metals, it might make more sense to import the crucial products during peacetime and store them for use in the event of war; these products do not require domestic production to be useful. Care must be taken to ensure that the national-defense argument is not used to protect industries other than those truly crucial to the nation's defense.

1.e. Infant Industries

If a nation sees an opportunity to develop a new industry to compete with established foreign firms, it may want to ensure that industry adequate

National defense is often used to justify protecting a domestic industry. This U.S. Navy submarine is built in the United States. Other nations have shipbuilding industries but in times of war, a nation cannot rely on foreign sources of defense-related goods.

Countries sometimes justify protecting new industries that need time to become competitive with the rest of the world.

time to develop. The new industry will need time to establish itself, and to become efficient enough that its costs are no higher than those of its foreign rivals. An alternative to protecting young and/or critical domestic industry with tariffs and quotas is to subsidize them. Subsidies allow such firms to charge lower prices, and to compete with more efficient foreign producers, while permitting consumers to pay the world price rather than the higher prices associated with tariffs or quotas on foreign goods.

Protecting an infant industry from foreign competition may make sense, but only until the industry matures. Once the infant achieves sufficient size, protection should be withdrawn, and the industry should be made to compete with its foreign counterparts. Unfortunately, such protection is rarely withdrawn, because the larger and more successful the industry becomes, the more political power it wields. In fact, if an infant industry truly has a good chance to become competitive and produce profitably once it is well established, it is not at all clear that government should even offer protection to reduce short-run losses. New firms typically incur losses, but they are only temporary if the firm is successful.

1.f. Strategic Trade Policy

There is a new view of international trade that regards as misleading the simple formula of comparative advantage presented in the previous chapter. According to this new outlook, which advocates what it calls strategic trade policy, international trade largely involves firms that pursue economies of scale—that is, firms that achieve lower costs per unit of production the more they produce. In contrast to the constant opportunity costs illustrated in the example of wheat and cloth in Chapter 20, opportunity costs in some industries may fall with the level of output. Such **decreasing-cost industries** will tend to concentrate production in the hands of a few very large firms, rather than many competitive firms. Proponents of strategic trade policy contend that government can use tariffs or subsidies to allow domestic firms with decreasing costs an advantage over their foreign rivals.

decreasing-cost industry:
an industry in which the costs of producing a unit of output fall as more output is produced

Government can use trade policy as a strategy to stimulate production by a domestic industry capable of achieving decreasing costs as output rises.

Decreasing-cost industries are sometimes called natural monopolies. A monopoly exists when there is only one producer in an industry, and no close substitutes for the product exist. If the average costs of production decline with increases in output, then the larger a firm is, the lower its per-unit costs will be. One large producer will be more efficient than many small ones. A simple example of a natural-monopoly industry will indicate how strategic trade policy can make a country better off. Suppose that the production of buses is a decreasing-cost industry, and that there are only two firms capable of producing buses: Mercedes-Benz in Germany and General Motors in the United States. If both firms produce buses, their costs will be so high that both will experience losses. If only one of the two produces buses, however, it will be able to sell buses at home and abroad, creating a level of output that allows the firm to earn a profit.

Assume further that a monopoly producer will earn $100 million and that if both firms produce, they will each lose $5 million. Obviously, a firm that doesn't produce earns nothing. Which firm will produce? Because of the decreasing-cost nature of the industry, the firm that is the first to produce will realize lower costs and be able to preclude the other firm from entering the market. But strategic trade policy can alter the market in favor of the domestic firm.

Suppose Mercedes-Benz is the world's only producer of buses. General Motors does not produce them. The U.S. government could offer General Motors an $8 million subsidy to produce buses. General Motors would then enter the bus market, since the $8 million subsidy would more than offset the $5 million loss it would suffer by entering the market. Mercedes-Benz would sustain losses of $5 million once General Motors entered. Ultimately, Mercedes-Benz would stop producing buses to avoid the loss, and General Motors would have the entire market and earn $100 million plus the subsidy of $8 million.

Strategic trade policy is aimed at offsetting the decreasing-cost advantage enjoyed by foreign producers, and at stimulating production in domestic industries capable of realizing decreasing costs. One practical problem for government is the need to understand the technology of different industries and to forecast accurately the subsidy needed to induce domestic firms to produce new products. A second problem is the likelihood of retaliation by the foreign government. If the U.S. government subsidizes General Motors in its attack on the bus market, the German government is likely to subsidize Mercedes-Benz rather than lose the entire bus market to a U.S. producer. As a result, taxpayers in both nations will be subsidizing two firms each producing too few buses to earn a profit.

RECAP

1. Government restrictions on foreign trade are usually aimed at protecting domestic producers from foreign competition.

2. Import restrictions may save domestic jobs, but the costs to consumers may be greater than the benefits to those who retain their jobs.

3. Advocates of "fair trade," or the creation of a level playing field, call for import restrictions as a means of lowering foreign restrictions on markets for domestic exports.

4. Tariffs are an important source of revenue in many developing countries.

5. The national-defense argument in favor of trade restrictions is that protection from foreign competition is necessary to ensure that certain key defense-related industries continue to produce.

6. The infant-industries argument in favor of trade restriction is to allow a new industry a period of time in which to become competitive with its foreign counterparts.

7. Strategic trade policy is intended to provide domestic decreasing-cost industries an advantage over their foreign competitors.

2. TOOLS OF POLICY

How do countries restrict the entry of foreign goods and promote the export of domestic goods?

Commercial policy makes use of several tools, including tariffs, quotas, subsidies, and nontariff barriers like health-and-safety regulations that restrict the entry of foreign products. Since 1945, barriers to trade have been reduced. Much of the progress toward free trade may be linked to the *General Agreement on Tariffs and Trade*, or *GATT*, that began in 1947. The Economic Insight: GATT describes how this document and the continuing negotiations under its auspices have worked to eliminate quotas on manufactured goods and lower tariffs (see Economic Insight: "The GATT").

2.a. Tariffs

tariffs:
taxes on imports or exports

A **tariff** is a tax on imports or exports. Every country imposes tariffs on at least some imports. Some countries also impose tariffs on selected exports as a means of raising government revenue. Brazil, for instance, taxes coffee exports. The United States does not employ export tariffs, which are forbidden by the U.S. Constitution.

Tariffs are frequently imposed in order to protect domestic producers from foreign competition (see Economic Insight: Smoot-Hawley Tariff). The effect of a tariff is illustrated in Figure 1, which shows the domestic market for oranges. Without international trade, the domestic equilibrium price P_d and quantity demanded Q_d are determined by the intersection of the domestic demand and supply curves. If the world price of oranges, P_w, is lower than the domestic equilibrium price, this country will import oranges. The quantity imported will be the difference between the quantity Q_1 produced domestically at a price of P_w, and the quantity Q_2 demanded domestically at the world price of oranges.

When the world price of the traded good is lower than the domestic equilibrium price without international trade, free trade causes domestic production to fall and domestic consumption to rise. The domestic shortage at the world price is met by imports. Domestic consumers are better off, since they can buy more at a lower price. But domestic producers are worse off, since they now sell fewer oranges and receive a lower price.

Suppose a tariff of T (the dollar value of the tariff) is imposed on orange imports. The price paid by consumers is now $P_w + T$, rather than P_w. At this higher price, domestic producers will produce Q_3 and domestic consumers will purchase Q_4. The tariff has the effect of increasing domestic production and reducing domestic consumption, relative to the free-trade equilibrium. Imports fall accordingly, from $(Q_2 - Q_1)$ to $(Q_4 - Q_3)$.

Domestic producers are better off, since the tariff has increased their sales of oranges and raised the price they receive. Domestic consumers pay higher prices for fewer oranges than they would with free trade, but they are still better off than they would be without trade. If the tariff had raised the price paid by consumers to P_d, there would be no trade and the domestic equilibrium quantity Q_d would prevail.

Smoot-Hawley Tariff

Many economists believe that the Great Depression of the 1930s was at least partly due to the Smoot-Hawley Tariff Act, signed into law by President Herbert Hoover in 1930. Hoover had promised that, if elected, he would raise tariffs on agricultural products to raise U.S. farm income. Congress began work on the tariff increases in 1928. Congressman Willis Hawley and Senator Reed Smoot conducted the hearings.

In testimony before Congress, manufacturers and other special-interest groups also sought protection from foreign competition. The resulting bill increased tariffs on over 12,000 products. Tariffs reached their highest levels ever, about 60 percent of average import values. Only twice before in U.S. history had

tariffs approached the levels of the Smoot-Hawley era.

Before President Hoover signed the bill, 38 foreign governments made formal protests, warning that they would retaliate with high tariffs on U.S. products. A petition signed by 1,028 economists warned of the harmful effects of the bill. Nevertheless, Hoover signed the bill into law.

World trade collapsed as other countries raised their tariffs in response. Between 1930 and 1931, U.S. imports fell 29 percent, but U.S. exports fell by 33 percent. By 1933, world trade was about one-third of the 1929 level. As the level of trade fell, so did income and prices. In 1934, in an effort to correct the mistakes of Smoot-Hawley, Congress passed the Reciprocal

Trade Agreements Act, which allowed the president to lower U.S. tariffs in return for reductions in foreign tariffs on U.S. goods. This act ushered in the modern era of relatively low tariffs. In the United States today, tariffs are about 5 percent of the average value of imports.

Many economists believe the collapse of world trade and the Depression to be linked by a decrease in real income caused by abandoning production based on comparative advantage. Few economists argue that the Great Depression was caused solely by the Smoot-Hawley tariff, but the experience serves as a lesson to those who support higher tariffs to protect domestic producers.

Figure 1
The Effects of a Tariff
The domestic equilibrium price and quantity with no trade are P_d and Q_d respectively. The world price is P_w. With free trade, therefore, imports will equal $(Q_2 - Q_1)$. A tariff added to the world price reduces imports to $(Q_4 - Q_3)$.

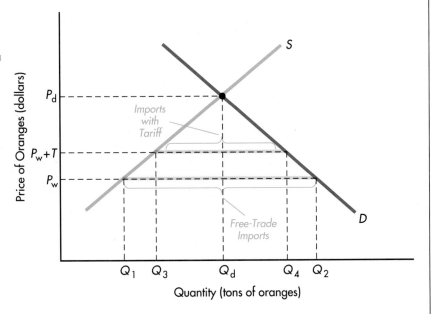

Figure 2
The Effects of a Quota
The domestic equilibrium price with no international trade is P_d. At this price, 250 tons of oranges would be produced and consumed at home. With free trade, the price is P_w and 300 tons will be imported. An import quota of 100 tons will cause the price to be P_q, where the domestic shortage equals the 100 tons allowed by the quota.

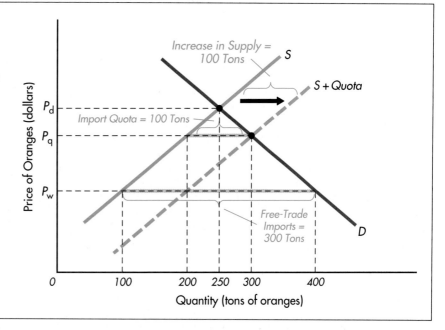

The government earns revenue from imports of oranges. If each ton of oranges generates tariff revenue of T, the total tariff revenue to the government is found by multiplying the tariff by the quantity of oranges imported. In Figure 1, this amount is $T \times (Q_4 - Q_3)$. As the tariff changes, so does the quantity of imports and the government revenue.

2.b. Quotas

Quotas are limits on the quantity or value of goods imported and exported. A **quantity quota** restricts the physical amount of a good. For instance, in 1987 the United States allowed only 1 million tons of sugar to be imported. A **value quota** restricts the monetary value of a good that may be traded. Instead of a physical quota on sugar, the United States could have limited the dollar value of sugar imports.

Quotas are used to protect domestic producers from foreign competition. By restricting the amount of a good that may be imported, they increase its price and allow domestic producers to sell more at a higher price than they would with free trade. Figure 2 illustrates the effect of a quota on the domestic orange market. The domestic equilibrium supply and demand curves determine the equilibrium price and quantity without trade to be P_d and 250 tons respectively. The world price of oranges is P_w. Since P_w lies below P_d, this country will import oranges. The quantity of imports is equal to the amount of the domestic shortage at P_w. The quantity demanded at P_w is 400 tons, and the quantity supplied domestically is 100 tons, so imports will equal 300 tons of oranges. With free trade, domestic producers sell 100 tons at a price of P_w.

But suppose domestic orange growers convince the government to restrict orange imports. The government then imposes a quota of 100 tons

quantity quota:
a limit on the amount of a good that may be imported

value quota:
a limit on the monetary value of a good that may be imported

on imported oranges. The effect of the quota on consumers is to shift the supply curve to the right by the amount of the quota, 100 tons. Since the quota is less than the quantity of imports with free trade, the quantity of imports will equal the quota. The domestic equilibrium price with the quota occurs at the point where the domestic shortage equals the quota. At price P_q, the domestic quantity demanded (300 tons) is 100 tons more than the domestic quantity supplied (200 tons).

Quotas benefit domestic producers in the same way that tariffs do. Domestic producers receive a higher price (P_q instead of P_w) for a greater quantity (200 instead of 100) than they do under free trade. The effect on domestic consumers is also similar to that of a tariff: they pay a higher price for a smaller quantity than they would with free trade. A tariff generates government tax revenue; quotas do not. Furthermore, a tariff only raises the price of the product in the domestic market. Foreign producers receive the world price, P_w. With a quota, both domestic and foreign producers receive the higher price, P_q, for the goods sold in the domestic market. So foreign producers are hurt by the reduction in the quantity of imports permitted, but they do receive a higher price for the amount they sell.

In some cases, countries negotiate *voluntary export restraints* rather than imposing quotas. A voluntary export restraint limits the quantity of goods shipped from the exporting country to an importing country. For instance, in the 1980s the United States negotiated voluntary export restraints on Japanese auto exports to the United States, limiting such exports to 1.62 million autos in 1981. The agreement lasted until 1985, with the quantity of exports rising over time.

2.c. Other Barriers to Trade

Voluntary export restraints are a substitute for quotas. They limit the amount exporters ship to an importing country.

Tariffs and quotas are not the only barriers to the free flow of goods across international borders. There are three additional sources of restrictions on free trade: subsidies, government procurement, and health-and-safety standards. Though often enacted for reasons other than protection from foreign competition, a careful analysis reveals their import-reducing effect.

Before discussing these three types of barriers, let us note in passing the cultural or institutional barriers to trade that also exist in many countries. Such barriers may exist independently of any conscious government policy. For instance, Japan has frequently been criticized by U.S. officials for informal business practices that discriminate against foreigners. Under the Japanese distribution system, goods typically pass through several layers of middlemen before appearing in a retail store. A foreign firm faces the difficult task of gaining entry to this system to supply goods to the retailer. Furthermore, a foreigner cannot easily open a retail store. Japanese law requires a new retail firm to receive permission from other retailers in the area in order to open a business. A firm that lacks contacts and knowledge of the system cannot penetrate the Japanese market.

In the fall of 1989, the U.S. toy firm Toys "R" Us announced its intent to open several large discount toy stores in Japan. However, local toy stores in each area objected to locating a Toys "R" Us store nearby. The U.S. government has argued that the laws favoring existing firms are an important factor in keeping Japan closed to foreign firms that would like to enter the Japanese market.

subsidies:
payments made by government to domestic firms to encourage exports

2.c.1. Subsidies Subsidies are payments by a government to an exporter. Subsidies are paid to stimulate exports by allowing the exporter to charge a lower price. The amount of a subsidy is determined by the international price of a product relative to the domestic price in the absence of trade. Domestic consumers are harmed by subsidies in that their taxes finance the subsidies. Also, since the subsidy diverts resources from the domestic market toward export production, the increase in the supply of export goods could be associated with a decrease in the supply of domestic goods, causing domestic prices to rise.

Subsidies may take forms other than direct cash payments. These include tax reductions, low-interest loans, low-cost insurance, government-sponsored research funding, and other devices. The U.S. government subsidizes export activity through the U.S. Export-Import Bank, which provides loans and insurance to help U.S. exporters sell their goods to foreign buyers. Subsidies are more commonplace in Europe than in Japan or the United States.

2.c.2. Government Procurement Governments are often required by law to buy only from local producers. In the United States, a "buy American" act passed in 1933 requires U.S. government agencies to buy U.S. goods and services unless the domestic price is more than 12 percent above the foreign price. This kind of policy allows domestic firms to charge the government a higher price for their products than they charge consumers; the taxpayers bear the burden. The United States is by no means alone in requiring the federal government to purchase domestic goods. Many other nations also use such policies to create larger markets for domestic goods.

2.c.3. Health and Safety Standards Government serves as a guardian of the public health and welfare by requiring that products offered to the public are safe and fulfill the use for which they are intended. Government standards for products sold in the domestic marketplace can have the effect (intentional or not) of protecting domestic producers from foreign competition. These effects should be considered in evaluating the full impact of such standards.

The government of Japan once prohibited foreign-made snow skis from entering the country for reasons of safety. Only Japanese-made skis were determined to be suitable for Japanese snow. Several Western European nations announced that U.S. beef would not be allowed into Europe because hormones approved by the U.S. government are fed to U.S. beef cattle. In the late 1960s, France required tractors sold there to have a maximum speed of 17 miles per hour; in Germany, the permissible speed was 13 m.p.h., and in the Netherlands it was 10 m.p.h. Tractors produced in one country had to be modified to meet the requirements of the other countries. Such modifications raise the price of goods and discourage international trade.

Product standards may not eliminate foreign competition, but standards different from those of the rest of the world do provide an element of protection to domestic firms.

RECAP

1. A tariff is a tax on imports or exports. Tariffs protect domestic firms by raising the prices of foreign goods.

2. Quotas are government-imposed limits on the quantity or value of an imported good. Quotas protect domestic firms by restricting the entry of foreign products to a level less than the quantity demanded.

3. Subsidies are payments by the government to domestic producers. Subsidies lower the price of domestic goods.

4. Governments are often required by law to buy only domestic products.

3. PREFERENTIAL TRADE AGREEMENTS

▼ What sorts of agreements do countries enter into to reduce barriers to international trade?
▲

In an effort to stimulate international trade, groups of countries sometimes enter into agreements to abolish most barriers to trade among themselves. Such arrangements between countries are known as preferential trading agreements. The European Economic Community and the Canada-U.S. Free Trade Agreement are examples of preferential trading agreements.

3.a. Free Trade Areas and Customs Unions

free trade area:
an organization of nations whose members have no trade barriers among themselves but are free to fashion their own trade policies toward nonmembers

customs union:
an organization of nations whose members have no trade barriers among themselves but impose common trade barriers on nonmembers

Two common forms of preferential trade agreements are **free trade areas** (FTAs) and **customs unions** (CUs). These two approaches differ with regard to treatment of countries outside the agreement. In an FTA, member countries eliminate trade barriers among themselves, but each member country chooses its own trade policies toward nonmember countries. Members of a CU agree to eliminate trade barriers among themselves and to maintain common trade barriers against nonmembers.

The best-known CU is the European Economic Community (EEC), created in 1957 by France, West Germany, Italy, Belgium, the Netherlands, and Luxembourg. The United Kingdom, Ireland, and Denmark joined in 1973, followed by Greece in 1981 and Spain and Portugal in 1986. The EEC agreement has eliminated most tariffs within the CU, but full-fledged free trade within the union has been slow in coming due to the presence of nontariff barriers. The EEC nations plan to have achieved a barrier-free Europe by 1992. Besides free trade in goods, European financial markets and institutions will operate across national boundaries.

Economic Insight

The U.S.–Canada Free Trade Agreement

The U.S.–Canada Free Trade Agreement, which became effective on January 1, 1989, will lower trade barriers between the two nations over time. By the end of the century, nearly all barriers to trade in goods and financial assets will have been eliminated. The purpose of the agreement is to stimulate economic growth and improve living standards in both countries, by allowing for greater specialization and trade in keeping with comparative advantage.

Tariffs will be eliminated over a ten-year period. By January 1, 1999, there will be no more tariffs between the two nations. Restrictions on investment across the border will be relaxed, and Canada will allow U.S. investors to establish new businesses without government approval. By 1992, government approval will be required only for investments in the 600 largest existing Canadian businesses. A notable exception is Canada's insistence on maintaining exclusive Canadian ownership of energy industries and "cultural" industries like broadcasting, newspapers, and films.

The stakes involved in Canada–U.S. trade are large. The United States accounts for three-fourths of Canadian exports, and Canada accounts for one-fifth of U.S. exports. The creation of a free trade area will allow resources in both countries to be more efficiently employed, better satisfying consumer wants on both sides of the border.

For instance, a bank in any EEC country will be permitted to operate in any or all other EEC countries.

The United States and Canada established a free trade area in 1987. All tariffs between the two countries were to be eliminated either on January 1, 1989, or in annual steps over a ten-year period, depending on the product in question. The U.S.–Canada Free Trade Agreement also eliminated most quotas between the two nations and established rules limiting nontariff barriers. Economic Insight: "The U.S.–Canada Free Trade Agreement" discusses the provisions of this agreement and what their effect is likely to be.

3.b. Trade Creation and Diversion

Free trade agreements provide for free trade among a group of countries, not worldwide. As a result, a customs union or free trade area may make a nation better off or worse off compared to the free-trade equilibrium.

Figure 3 illustrates the effect of a free trade area. With no international trade, the U.S. supply and demand curves for oranges would result in an equilibrium price of $500 per ton and an equilibrium quantity of 425 tons. Suppose there are two other orange-producing countries, Israel and Brazil. Israel, the low-cost producer of oranges, is willing to sell all the oranges the United States can buy for $150 per ton, as represented by the horizontal supply curve S_I. Brazil will supply oranges for a price of $200 per ton, represented by the horizontal supply curve S_B.

With free trade, the United States would import oranges from Israel. The quantity demanded at $150 is 750 tons, and the domestic quantity supplied at this price is 100 tons. The shortage of 650 tons is met by imports from Israel.

Figure 3
Trade Creation and Trade Diversion with a Free Trade Area
With no trade, the domestic equilibrium price is $500 and the equilibrium quantity is 425 tons. With free trade, the price is $150; and 650 tons would be imported, as indicated by the supply curve for Israel, S_I. A 100-percent tariff on imports would result in imports of 350 tons from Israel, according to the supply curve S_I + Tariff. A free-trade agreement that eliminates tariffs on Brazilian oranges only would result in a new equilibrium price of $200 and imports of 550 tons from Brazil, according to supply curve S_B.

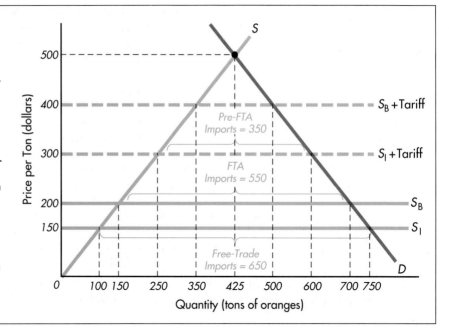

trade diversion:
an effect of a preferential trade agreement, reducing economic efficiency by shifting production to a higher-cost producer

Now suppose a 100-percent tariff is imposed on orange imports. The price domestic consumers pay for foreign oranges is twice as high as before. For oranges from Israel the new price is $300, twice the old price of $150. The new supply curve for Israel is represented as S_I + Tariff. Oranges from Brazil now sell for $400, twice the old price of $200; the new supply curve for Brazil is shown as S_B + Tariff. After the 100-percent tariff is imposed, oranges are still imported from Israel. But at the new price of $300, the domestic quantity demanded is 600 tons and the domestic quantity supplied is 250 tons. Thus only 350 tons will be imported. The tariff reduces the volume of trade relative to the free-trade equilibrium, at which 650 tons were imported.

Now suppose that this country negotiates a free-trade agreement with Brazil, eliminating tariffs on imports from Brazil. Israel is not a member of the free-trade agreement, so imports from Israel are still covered by the 100-percent tariff. The relevant supply curve for Brazil is now S_B, so oranges may be imported from Brazil for $200, a lower price than Israel's price including the tariff. At a price of $200, the domestic quantity demanded is 700 tons and the domestic quantity supplied is 150 tons; 550 tons will be imported.

The effects of the free-trade agreement are twofold. First, trade was diverted away from the lowest-cost producer, Israel, to the FTA partner, Brazil. This **trade diversion** effect of an FTA reduces worldwide economic efficiency, since production is diverted from the country with the comparative advantage. Oranges are not being produced as efficiently as possible.

The other effect of the FTA is that the quantity of imports increases relative to the effect of a tariff applicable to all imports. Imports rise from

350 tons (the quantity imported from Israel with the tariff) to 550 tons. The FTA thus has a **trade creation** effect, resulting from the lower price available after the tariff reduction. Trade creation is a beneficial aspect of the FTA: the expansion of international trade allows this country to realize greater benefits from trade than would be possible without trade.

Countries form preferential trade agreements because they believe they will be better off. They view the trade-creation effects of such agreements as benefiting their exporters by increasing exports to member countries, and as benefiting consumers by making a wider variety of goods available at a lower price. From the point of view of the world as a whole, preferential trade agreements are more desirable the more they stimulate trade creation to allow the benefits of trade to be realized, and the less they emphasize trade diversion, so that production occurs on the basis of comparative advantage. This principle suggests that the most successful FTAs or CUs are those that increase trade volume but do not change the patterns of trade in terms of who specializes and exports each good. In the case of Figure 3, a more successful FTA would reduce tariffs on Israeli as well as Brazilian oranges, so that oranges would be imported from the lowest-cost producer, Israel.

RECAP

1. Countries form preferential trade agreements in order to stimulate trade among themselves.
2. The most common forms of preferential trade agreement are free trade areas (FTAs) and customs unions (CUs).
3. Preferential trade agreements have a harmful trade-diversion effect when they cause production to shift from the nation with a comparative advantage to a higher-cost producer.
4. Preferential trade agreements have a beneficial trade-creation effect when they reduce prices for traded goods and stimulate the volume of international trade.

SUMMARY

1. Commercial policy is government policy that influences the direction and volume of international trade. § 1

2. Protecting domestic producers from foreign competition usually imposes costs on domestic consumers. § 1

▼▲ **Why do countries restrict international trade?**

3. Rationales for commercial policy include saving domestic jobs, creating a fair-trade relationship with other countries, raising tariff revenue, ensuring a domestic supply of key defense goods, allowing new industries a chance to become internationally competitive, and giving decreasing-cost domestic industries an advantage over foreign competitors. § 1

▼▲ **How do countries restrict the entry of foreign goods and promote the export of domestic goods?**

4. Tariffs protect domestic industry by increasing the price of foreign goods. § 2.a

5. Quotas protect domestic industry by limiting the quantity of foreign goods allowed into the country. § 2.b

6. Subsidies allow relatively inefficient domestic producers to compete with foreign firms. § 2.c.1

7. Government procurement practices and health-and-safety regulations can protect domestic industry from foreign competition. § 2.c.2 and § 2.c.3

▼▲ **What sorts of agreements do countries enter into to reduce barriers to international trade?**

8. Customs unions and free trade areas are two types of preferential trade agreement that reduce trade restrictions among member countries. § 3.a

9. Preferential trade agreements have harmful trade-diversion effects and beneficial trade-creation effects. § 3.b

KEY TERMS

commercial policy § preview
decreasing-cost industry § 1.f
tariffs § 2.a
quantity quota § 2.b
value quota § 2.b

subsidies § 2.c.1
free trade area § 3.a
customs union § 3.a
trade diversion § 3.b
trade creation § 3.b

EXERCISES

Basic Terms and Concepts

1. State the potential benefits and costs of a commercial policy designed to pursue each of the following goals.

   a. save domestic jobs

   b. create a level playing field

   c. increase government revenue

   d. provide a strong national defense

   e. protect an infant industry

   f. stimulate exports of a decreasing-cost industry

2. For each of the goals listed in Question 1, discuss what the appropriate commercial policy is likely to be (in terms of tariffs, quotas, subsidies, etc.).

3. Tariffs and quotas both raise the price of foreign goods to domestic consumers. What is the difference between the effects of a tariff and a quota on:

   a. the domestic government?

   b. foreign producers?

   c. domestic producers?

4. Would trade-diversion and trade-creation effects occur if the whole world became a free trade area? Explain.

5. What is the difference between a customs union and a free trade area?

6. Draw a graph of the U.S. automobile market in which the domestic equilibrium price without trade is P_d and the equilibrium quantity is Q_d.

Use this graph to illustrate and explain the effects of a tariff if the United States were an auto importer with free trade. Then use the graph to illustrate and explain the effects of a quota.

Extended Concepts

7. If commercial policy can benefit U.S. industry, why would any U.S. resident oppose such policies?

8. Suppose you were asked to assess U.S. commercial policy to determine whether the benefits of protection for U.S. industries are worth the costs. Does Table 1 provide all the information you need? If not, what else would you want to know?

9. How would the effects of international trade on the domestic orange market change if the world price of oranges were above the domestic equilibrium price? Draw a graph to help explain your answer.

Economically Speaking

Textile Makers Demanding More Protection Threaten Hopes for Seamless U.S. Trade Policy

—When a powerful group of U.S. textile manufacturers invited White House Trade Representative Carla Hills to speak at their annual meeting here, they promised to treat her "like a queen."

"Which queen?" Ambassador Hills asked upon her arrival. "Mary Queen of Scots? Marie Antoinette?"

Both monarchs, of course, were beheaded, and Mrs. Hills has reason to think the textile industry may be planning a similar fate for her. She has staked the Bush administration's trade policy, as well as her own success as trade representative, on the so-called Uruguay round of talks under the international trade treaty known as the General Agreement on Tariffs and Trade. But the textile industry, with its powerful ties to Congress, could ruin those plans. . . .

Mrs. Hills and her counterparts from almost 100 other nations in the GATT talks are committed to eliminating the need for special trade rules for textiles and replacing the 29-year-old Multi-Fiber Arrangement, a complex set of quotas among the main textile consuming and producing nations. The resulting freer trade in textiles would offer greater opportunities to the more competitive U.S. companies and reduce prices for U.S. consumers, but it would also result in some less-competitive companies having to adjust or fail.

But the trade treaty, scheduled to be completed in December, must eventually be approved by the Senate, and there the textile industry has the upper hand. Its saber-rattling political backers are claiming they already have the power to block any trade treaty they don't like. As a result, Mrs. Hills may be forced to back down from her free-trade stance. She has tried to be conciliatory, even proposing a 10-year transition period while the U.S. abandons its current textile quotas. . . .

Indonesia, Bangladesh, Mexico, India and a host of other developing countries are clamoring for better access to Western markets for their textiles. They see this as a trade for opening up their markets to Western services, investment and intellectual property.

"Textiles and agriculture seem to be the two areas that are potential deal-makers or deal-breakers," for the GATT round, says William Cline, a senior fellow at the Institute for International Economics who is currently preparing a new study of the textile industry.

Mr. Cline estimates that protection of the industry now costs the U.S. $25 billion a year, or $238 for every U.S. family. If the textile industry's bill is adopted — with its 1%-a-year allowable growth in quotas — the costs of protection would rise to about $85 billion a year in the year 2000, he estimates.

Many expect compromise and a transition period that effectively allows textile protection to tighten. It remains to be seen "if the administration is prepared to commit to liberalization and whether the transition will be credible," says Mr. Cline. . .

There are also obvious inconsistencies in the textile industry's approach to trade policy that are likely to become more apparent. It is ironic, for instance, that the textile industry ardently favors open trade when it comes to duty-free access for foreign textile machinery.

The industry also isn't in bad shape, contrary to its claims. In fact, industry shipments of man-made fibers increased 17.8% between 1987 and 1989, while exports of these same items jumped 59%, according to the Commerce Department. And in 1989 the industry had after-tax profit of $1.32 billion, which represented 2.5% of net sales and a 10.3% return on equity.

The industry's campaign is certainly crafted to play on people's fears of an ailing national textile business. The new textile act "is essential to halt further erosion of this major American industry," says the manufacturers association. . .

Retailers, people in the apparel industry and free-trade advocates hope that the Bush administration will face down the textile industry. The ability to destroy the GATT round is "clearly the underlying threat (the textile industry) is trying to portray," says Joseph O'Neill, president of the National Retail Federation, which is seeking freer trade in textiles. "I'd hope textiles wouldn't be given such an inordinate amount of leverage."

■ Source: Peter Truell, "Textile Makers Demanding More Protection Threaten Hopes for Seamless U.S. Trade Policy," *The Wall Street Journal*, May 16, 1990, p. A22.

Commentary

Consider the following hypothetical situation: The legislature of the state of Maine considers a tax to support the pineapple farmers of the state. Of course, Maine's climate is not conducive to growing pineapples, but it is possible, at great cost, to grow a few pineapples in greenhouses. The tax on pineapples brought into the state raises the price of Hawaiian pineapples by enough to make pineapples grown in Maine competitive. Thus Maine's pineapple industry is saved from competitors whose price reflects their unfair climatic advantage, though the consumers of the state must pay exorbitant prices for their pineapples.

This scenario, with its absurd distortion of the workings of the market, differs in degree but not in kind from the description of the textile industry in the accompanying article. The protectionist measure of imposing quotas on foreign textile imports saves jobs in the domestic textile industry, but at a great cost to the U.S. consumer. William Cline estimates that the cost of protecting the domestic textile industry is $238 per family in the United States.

The effect of the textile quotas can be understood using supply-and-demand analysis. S_1 is the domestic supply of textiles, S_2 is the sum of the domestic supply and the foreign supply allowed in by the quotas, and D is the demand for textiles. Under the quota system, the price of textiles in the United States is represented by P_q and the quantity of textiles consumed is Q_q. If the quotas were removed, the price of textiles in the United States would equal the world price of P_w, and this lower price would be associated with an increase in the consumption of textiles to Q_w. The quota represents a cost to society in terms of a loss of consumer welfare as well as a loss from the inefficient use of resources in an industry in which this country has no comparative advantage, just as Maine has no comparative advantage in the production of pineapples.

Given the costs to society of these quotas, why is there such strong support for them in Congress? An important political aspect of protectionist policies is that their benefits are concentrated among a relatively small number of people while their costs are diffuse and spread across all consumers. Each individual textile producer faces very large losses from free trade while the cost to each consumer of a protectionist policy is less dramatic. It is also easier to organize a relatively small number of manufacturers than to mobilize a vast population of consumers. These factors explain the strong lobby for the protection of the textile industry and the absence of a legislative lobby that operates specifically in the interest of textile consumers.

It is possible to patch together a case for the protection of the textile industry, just as it is possible to concoct an argument for the protection of the hypothetical Maine pineapple industry. But these arguments should be seen for what they are: an attempt by an industry to increase its profits at the expense of the general public.

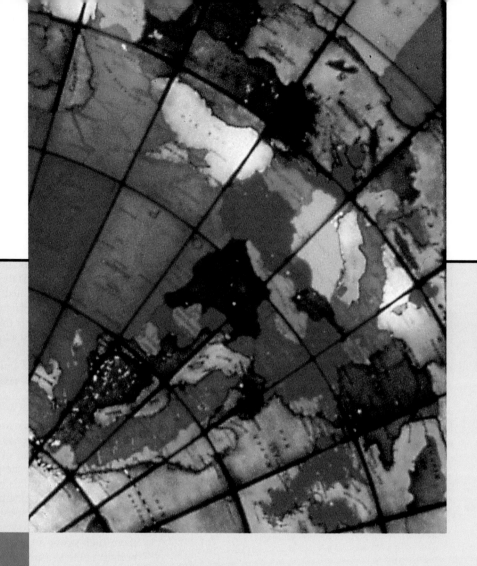

22

Exchange-Rate Systems and Practices

1. How does a commodity standard fix exchange rates between countries?

2. What kinds of exchange-rate arrangements exist today?

3. How is equilibrium determined in the foreign-exchange market?

4. How do fixed and floating exchange rates differ in their adjustment to shifts in supply and demand for currencies?

5. What are the advantages and disadvantages of fixed and floating exchange rates?

6. What determines the kind of exchange-rate system a country adopts?

PREVIEW

Exchange-rate policy is an important element of macroeconomic policy. An exchange rate is the link between two nations' monies. The value of a U.S. dollar in terms of Japanese yen or German marks determines how many dollars a U.S. resident will need to buy goods priced in yen or marks. Thus changes in the exchange rate can have far-reaching implications. Exchange rates may be determined in free markets, or through government intervention in the foreign-exchange market, or even by law.

At the beginning of 1989, one U.S. dollar was worth 123.8 Japanese yen and 1.77 German marks. By mid-June of that year, the dollar was worth 151.8 yen and 2.05 marks. Why did the dollar rise in value relative to the yen and the mark? What are the effects of such changes? Should governments permit exchange rates to change?

What can governments do to discourage changing exchange rates? These are all important questions, which this chapter will help to answer.

This chapter begins with a review of the history of exchange-rate systems. Then follows an overview of exchange-rate practices in the world today, and an analysis of the benefits and costs of alternative exchange-rate arrangements. Along the way, we will introduce terminology and institutions that play a major role in the evolution of exchange rates.

1. PAST AND CURRENT EXCHANGE-RATE ARRANGEMENTS

1.a. The Gold Standard

▼ How does a commodity standard fix exchange rates between countries? ▲

gold standard:
a system whereby national currencies are fixed in terms of their value in gold, thus creating fixed exchange rates between currencies

In ancient times, government-produced monies were made of precious metals like gold. Later, when governments began to issue paper money, it was usually convertible into a fixed amount of gold. Ensuring the convertibility of paper money into gold was a way to maintain confidence in the currency's value, at home and abroad. If a unit of currency was worth a fixed amount of gold, its value could be stated in terms of its gold value. The countries that maintained a constant gold value for their currencies were said to be on a **gold standard**.

Some countries had backed their currencies with gold long before 1880; however, the practice became widespread around 1880 so that economists typically date the beginning of the gold standard around this period. From roughly 1880 to 1914, currencies had fixed values in terms of gold. For instance, the U.S. dollar's value was fixed at $20.67 per ounce of gold. Any other currency that was fixed in terms of gold also had a fixed exchange rate against the dollar. A simple example will illustrate how this works.

Suppose the price of an ounce of gold is $20 in the United States and £4 in the United Kingdom. The pound is worth five times the value of a dollar, since it takes five times as many dollars as pounds to buy one ounce of gold. Because one pound buys five times as much gold as one dollar, the exchange rate is £1 = $5. Since currency values are linked by gold values, as the supply of gold fluctuates, there will be pressure to alter prices of goods and services. The gold standard only fixes the current price of gold. As the stock of gold increases, ceteris paribus, the gold and currency prices of goods and services will tend to rise (as would occur when the money supply increases).

A commodity money standard exists when exchange rates are fixed based on the values of different currencies in terms of some commodity.

A gold standard is only one possible *commodity money standard*. Any other highly-valued commodity (silver, for instance) could serve as a standard linking monies in a fixed exchange-rate system.

The gold standard ended with the outbreak of World War I. War financing was partially funded by increases in the money supplies of the hostile nations. A gold standard would not permit such a rapid increase in the money supply unless the stock of gold increased dramatically, which it did not. As money supplies grew faster than gold supplies, the link between money and gold had to be broken. During the war years and the Great Depression of the 1930s, and on through World War II, there was no organized system for setting exchange rates. Foreign trade and investment shrunk as a result of the war, obviating the need for a well-functioning method of determining exchange rates.

1.b. The Bretton Woods System

At the end of World War II, there was widespread political support for an exchange-rate system linking all monies in much the same way as the gold standard had. It was believed that a system of fixed exchange rates would promote the growth of world trade. In 1944, delegates from 44 nations met in Bretton Woods, New Hampshire, to discuss such a system. The agreement reached at this conference has had a profound impact on the world.

The Bretton Woods agreement established a system of fixed exchange rates.

The exchange-rate arrangement that emerged from the Bretton Woods conference is often called a **gold exchange standard**. Each country was to fix the value of its currency in terms of gold, just as it had under the gold standard. The U.S.-dollar price of gold, for instance, was $35 an ounce. However, there were fundamental differences between this system and the old gold standard. The U.S. dollar, rather than gold, served as the focal point of the system. Instead of buying and selling gold, countries bought and sold U.S. dollars to maintain a fixed exchange rate with the dollar. Since the United States was the major victor nation, its currency was the dominant world currency. The United States had the productive capacity to supply much needed goods to the rest of the world, and these goods were priced in dollars.

gold exchange standard:
an exchange-rate system in which each nation fixes the value of its currency in terms of gold, but buys and sells the U.S. dollar rather than gold to maintain fixed exchange rates

The U.S. dollar was the **reserve currency** of the system. International debts were settled with dollars, and international trade contracts were often denominated in dollars. In effect, the world was on a dollar standard following World War II.

reserve currency:
a currency that is used to settle international debts and is held by governments to use in foreign-exchange market interventions

1.c. The International Monetary Fund and the World Bank

Two new organizations also emerged from the Bretton Woods conference: the International Monetary Fund and the World Bank. The **International Monetary Fund**, or **IMF**, was created to supervise the exchange-rate practices of member countries, and to encourage the free convertibility of any national money into the monies of other countries. The IMF also lends money to countries that are experiencing problems meeting their international payments obligations. The funds available to the IMF come from the annual membership fees (called *quotas*) of the 151 member countries of the IMF. The U.S. quota, for instance, is almost $23 billion. (The term *quota* has a different meaning in this context than it does in international trade.)

International Monetary Fund (IMF):
an international organization that supervises exchange-rate arrangements and lends money to member countries experiencing problems meeting their external financial obligations

The **World Bank** was created to help finance economic development in poor countries. It provides loans to developing countries at more favorable terms than are available from commercial lenders, and also offers technical expertise. The World Bank obtains the funds it lends by selling

World Bank:
an international organization that makes loans and provides technical expertise to developing countries

Economic Insight   The IMF and the World Bank

The International Monetary Fund (IMF) and the World Bank were both created at the Bretton Woods conference in 1944. The IMF oversees the international monetary system, promoting stable exchange rates and macroeconomic policies. The World Bank promotes the economic development of the poor nations. Both organizations are owned and directed by their 151 member countries. Except for the Soviet Union, some of its Eastern European allies, and a few other small countries, every nation on earth is a member of both organizations.

The IMF provides loans to nations having trouble repaying their foreign debts. Before the IMF lends any money, however,

the borrower must agree to certain conditions. IMF *conditionality* usually requires that the country meet targets for key macroeconomic variables like money-supply growth, inflation, tax collections, and subsidies. The conditions attached to IMF loans are aimed at promoting stable economic growth.

The World Bank assists developing countries by providing long-term financing for development projects and programs. The Bank also provides expertise in many areas in which poor nations lack expert knowledge: agriculture, medicine, construction, and education, as well as economics. The IMF primarily employs economists to carry out its mission.

The diversity of World Bank activities results in the employment of about 6,500 people. The IMF has a staff of approximately 1,700. Both organizations post employees around the world, but most work at the headquarters in Washington, D.C.

World Bank funds are largely acquired by borrowing on the international bond market. The IMF receives its funding from member-country subscription fees, called *quotas*. A member's quota determines its voting power in setting IMF policies. The United States, whose quota accounts for the largest fraction of the total, has the most votes.

bonds. It is one of the world's major borrowers. See Economic Insight: "The IMF and the World Bank" for an explanation of how these institutions work.

1.d. The Transition Years

The Bretton Woods system of fixed exchange rates required countries to actively buy and sell dollars to maintain fixed exchange rates when the *free-market equilibrium* in the foreign-exchange market differed from the fixed rate. The free-market equilibrium exchange rate is the rate that would be established in the absence of government intervention. Governmental buying and selling of currencies to achieve a target exchange rate is called **foreign-exchange market intervention.** The effectiveness of such intervention was limited to situations in which free-market pressure to deviate from the fixed exchange rate was temporary. For instance, suppose a country has a bad harvest and earns less foreign exchange than usual. This may only be a temporary situation if the next harvest is plentiful and the country resumes its typical export sales. During the period of reduced exports, it will be necessary for the government of this country to intervene to avoid a depreciation of its domestic currency. In the 1960s, however, there were several episodes of permanent rather than temporary changes that called for changes in exchange rates rather than government

foreign-exchange market intervention: buying or selling of currencies by a government or central bank to achieve a specified exchange rate

foreign-exchange market intervention. The problems that arise in response to permanent pressures to change the exchange rate will be discussed further in Section 2, when we analyze the benefits and costs of alternative exchange-rate systems.

The Bretton Woods system officially dissolved in 1971, at a meeting of the finance ministers of the leading world powers at the Smithsonian Institution in Washington, D.C. The Smithsonian agreement changed the exchange rates set during the Bretton Woods era. One result was a **devaluation** of the U.S. dollar. (A currency is said to be devalued when its value is officially lowered.) The official gold value of the dollar dropped from $35 an ounce to $38 an ounce.

Under the Smithsonian agreement, countries were to maintain fixed exchange rates at newly defined values. It soon became clear, however, that the new exchange rates were not **equilibrium exchange rates** that could be maintained without government intervention, and that government intervention could not maintain the disequilibrium fixed exchange rates forever. The U.S. dollar was devalued again in February 1973, when the dollar price of gold was raised to $42.22. This new exchange rate was still not an equilibrium rate, and in March 1973 the major industrial countries abandoned fixed exchange rates.

1.e. Floating Exchange Rates

When the major industrial countries abandoned fixed exchange rates in March 1973, they did not move to freely-floating exchange rates determined by the forces of free-market supply and demand alone. Under the system in existence since that time, the major industrial countries intervene to keep their currencies within acceptable ranges while many smaller countries maintain fixed exchange rates.

The world today consists of some countries with fixed exchange rates, whose governments keep the exchange rates between two or more currencies constant over time; other countries with floating exchange rates, which shift on a daily basis according to the forces of supply and demand; and still others whose exchange-rate systems lie somewhere in between. Table 1, which lists the exchange-rate arrangements of over 100 countries, illustrates the diversity of exchange-rate arrangements currently in effect. We will focus here on the differences between fixed and floating exchange rates. All of the other exchange-rate arrangements listed in Table 1 are special versions of these two general exchange-rate systems.

As Table 1 shows, the major industrial countries maintain **managed floating exchange rates.** Although Table 1 lists countries like Japan and the United States as "independently floating," in fact their central banks, such as the Federal Reserve in the United States, intervene from time to time in the foreign exchange market. Since exchange-rate variations can alter the prices of goods traded internationally, governments often attempt to push exchange rates to values consistent with some target value of international trade or investment. For example, in late summer 1989, the U.S. Treasury and the Federal Reserve were concerned that a rise in the value of the dollar would hurt the competitiveness of U.S. goods. As a result, the Fed sold $1,452 million in exchange for German marks and

devaluation:
a deliberate decrease in the official value of a currency

equilibrium exchange rates:
the exchange rates that are established in the absence of government foreign-exchange market intervention

In March 1973, the major industrial countries abandoned fixed exchange rates for floating rates.

▼ What kinds of exchange-rate arrangements exist today? ▲

managed floating exchange rates:
the system whereby central banks intervene in the floating foreign-exchange market to influence exchange rates; also referred to as *dirty float*

Table 1 Exchange-Rate Arrangements

| Currency Pegged to | | | | | Flexibility Limited in Terms of a Single Currency or Group of Currencies | | More Flexible | | |
U.S. Dollar	French Franc	Other currency	SDR	Other composite[1]	Single currency[2]	Cooperative arrangements[3]	Adjusted according to a set of indicators[4]	Other managed floating	Independently floating
Afghanistan	Benin	Bhutan (Indian Rupee)	Burundi	Algeria	Bahrain	Belgium	Brazil	Argentina	Australia
Angola	Burkina Faso	Kiribati (Australian Dollar)	Iran, I. R. of	Austria	Qatar	Denmark	Chile	China, P.R.	Bolivia
Antigua and Barbuda	Cameroon	Lesotho (South African Rand)	Libya	Bangladesh	Saudi Arabia	France	Colombia	Costa Rica	Canada
Bahamas, The	C. African Rep.	Swaziland (South African Rand)	Myanmar	Botswana	United Arab Emirates	Germany	Madagascar	Dominican Rep.	Gambia, The
Barbados	Chad	Tonga (Australian Dollar)	Rwanda	Cape Verde		Ireland	Portugal	Ecuador	Ghana
Belize	Comoros		Seychelles	Cyprus		Italy		Egypt	Japan
Djibouti	Congo		Zambia	Fiji		Luxembourg		Greece	Lebanon
Dominica	Côte d'Ivoire			Finland		Netherlands		Guinea	Maldives
El Salvador	Equatorial Guinea			Hungary		Spain		Guinea-Bissau	New Zealand
Ethiopia	Gabon			Iceland				India	Nigeria
Grenada	Mali			Israel				Indonesia	Paraguay
Guatemala	Niger			Jordan				Jamaica	Philippines
Guyana	Senegal			Kenya				Korea	South Africa
Haiti	Togo			Kuwait				Lao P.D. Rep.	United Kingdom
Honduras				Malawi				Mauritania	United States
Iraq				Malaysia				Mexico	Uruguay
Liberia				Malta				Morocco	Venezuela
Nicaragua				Mauritius				Mozambique	Zaïre
Oman				Nepal				Pakistan	
Panama				Norway				Singapore	
Peru				Papua New Guinea				Sri Lanka	
St. Kitts and Nevis				Poland				Tunisia	
St. Lucia				Romania				Turkey	
St. Vincent				Sao Tome and Principe				Yugoslavia	
Sierra Leone				Solomon Islands					
Sudan				Somalia					
Suriname				Sweden					
Syrian Arab Rep.				Tanzania					
Trinidad and Tobago				Thailand					
Uganda				Vanuatu					
Vietnam				Western Samoa					
Yemen Arab Rep.				Zimbabwe					
Yemen, P.D. Rep.									

[1] Comprises currencies which are pegged to various "baskets" of currencies of the members' own choice, as distinct from the SDR basket.
[2] Exchange rates of all currencies have shown limited flexibility in terms of the U.S. dollar.
[3] Refers to the cooperative arrangement maintained under the European Monetary System.
[4] Includes exchange arrangements under which the exchange rate is adjusted at relatively frequent intervals, on the basis of indicators determined by the respective member countries.
Source: International Monetary Fund, International Financial Statistics, Washington, D.C., January 1990, p. 22.

**Table 2 Exchange Rates of Selected Countries
(Currency units per U.S. dollar)**

Year	Canadian Dollar	Japanese Yen	French Franc	German Mark	Italian Lira	British Pound
1950	1.06	361	3.50	4.20	625	.36
1955	1.00	361	3.50	4.22	625	.36
1960	1.00	358	4.90	4.17	621	.36
1965	1.08	361	4.90	4.01	625	.36
1970	1.01	358	5.52	3.65	623	.42
1975	1.02	305	4.49	2.62	684	.50
1980	1.19	203	4.52	1.96	931	.42
1985	1.40	201	7.56	2.46	1,679	.69
1989	1.16	143	5.79	1.70	1,271	.62

Source: Data are end-of-year exchange rates from International Monetary Fund, *International Financial Statistics*, Washington, D.C., various issues.

Fixed (pegged) exchange rates are held constant over time.

special drawing right:
an artificial unit of account created by averaging the values of the U.S. dollar, German mark, Japanese yen, French franc, and British pound

European Monetary System (EMS):
an organization composed of Western European nations that maintain fixed exchange rates among themselves and floating exchange rates with the rest of the world

$1,699 million in exchange for Japanese yen. This intervention in the foreign exchange market caused the dollar to fall lower in value than private-market pressures would have done.

Some countries, like Afghanistan and Benin, maintain a fixed value (or peg) relative to a single currency such as the dollar or French franc. Fixed exchange rates are often called *pegged* exchange rates. Other countries, like Algeria and Austria, peg to a composite of currencies by setting the value of their currency at the average value of several foreign currencies.

Some currencies are pegged to the *SDR*. The SDR, which stands for **special drawing right**, is an artificial unit of account. Its value is determined by combining the values of the U.S. dollar, German mark, Japanese yen, French franc, and British pound. A country that pegs to the SDR determines its currency's value in terms of an average of the five currencies that make up the SDR.

The column entitled "Cooperative arrangements" in Table 1 lists the countries that belong to the **European Monetary System**, or **EMS**. These countries maintain fixed exchange rates against each other, but allow their currencies to float jointly against the rest of the world. In other words, the values of currencies in the EMS all shift together relative to currencies outside the EMS.

Table 2 lists the end-of-year exchange rates for several currencies versus the U.S. dollar from the 1950s to 1989. For most of the currencies, there was little movement in the 1950s and 1960s, the era of the Bretton Woods agreement. In the early 1970s, exchange rates began to fluctuate. More recently, there has been considerable change in the foreign-exchange value of a dollar, as Table 2 illustrates.

RECAP

1. Under a gold standard, each currency has a fixed value in terms of gold. This arrangement provides for fixed exchange rates between countries.

2. At the end of World War II, the Bretton Woods agreement established a new system of fixed exchange rates. Two new organizations—the International Monetary Fund (IMF) and the World Bank—also emerged from the Bretton Woods conference.

3. Fixed exchange rates are maintained by government intervention in the foreign-exchange market; governments or central banks buy and sell currencies to keep the equilibrium exchange rate steady.

4. The governments of the major industrial countries adopted floating exchange rates in 1973. In fact, the prevailing system is characterized by ''managed floating''—that is, by occasional government intervention rather than a pure free-market-determined exchange-rate system.

5. Some countries choose independently floating exchange rates; others peg their currencies to a single currency or a composite.

6. The European Monetary System maintains fixed exchange rates among several Western European currencies, which then float jointly against the rest of the world.

2. FIXED OR FLOATING EXCHANGE RATES

Is the United States better off today, with floating exchange rates, than it was with the fixed exchange rates of the post–World–War–II period? This question is difficult to answer, since much else has changed along with the exchange-rate system.

The choice of an exchange-rate system has multiple implications for the performance of a nation's economy and, therefore, for the conduct of macroeconomic policy. Economists often debate the merits of fixed versus flexible exchange rates. As is true of many policy issues in economics, such disagreements are difficult to settle. Let us look at the characteristics of the different exchange-rate systems.

2.a. Equilibrium in the Foreign-Exchange Market

▼ How is equilibrium determined in the foreign-exchange market? ▲

Equilibrium in the foreign-exchange market occurs at the point where the foreign-exchange demand and supply curves intersect.

An exchange rate is the price of one money in terms of another. Equilibrium is determined by the supply of and demand for the two currencies in the foreign exchange market. Figure 1 contains two supply-and-demand diagrams for the U.S. dollar–French franc foreign-exchange market. The downward-sloping demand curve indicates that the higher the dollar price of French francs, the fewer francs will be demanded. The upward-sloping supply curve indicates that the higher the dollar price of French francs, the more francs will be supplied.

In Figure 1(a), the initial equilibrium occurs at the point where the demand curve D_1 intersects the supply curve. At this point, the equilibrium exchange rate is .15 (1 franc costs $.15) and the quantity of francs bought and sold is Q_1.

Suppose U.S. residents increase their demand for French wine. Because francs are needed to pay for the wine, the greater U.S. demand

(a) A Change in the U.S. Demand for French Wine

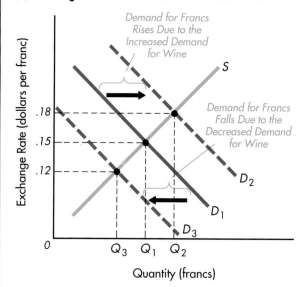

(b) A Change in the French Demand for U.S. Tractors

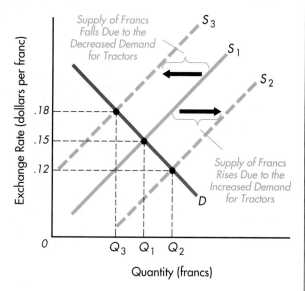

Figure 1
The Supply of and Demand for Foreign Exchange
Figure 1 represents the foreign exchange market for francs traded for dollars. The demand curve for francs is based on the U.S. demand for French products, and the supply curve of francs is based on the French demand for U.S. products. An increase in demand for French wine causes demand for francs to increase from D_1 to D_2. This shift causes an increase from Q_1 to Q_2 in the equilibrium quantity of francs traded, and causes the franc to appreciate to .18 from the initial equilibrium exchange rate of .15. A decrease in demand for French wine causes the

demand for francs to fall from D_1 to D_3. This shift leads to a fall in the equilibrium quantity traded to Q_3 and a depreciation of the franc to .12. If the French demand for U.S. tractors falls, fewer francs are supplied for exchange for dollars, as illustrated by the fall in supply from S_1 to S_3. This shift causes the franc to appreciate to .18 and the equilibrium quantity of francs traded to fall to Q_3. If the French demand for U.S. tractors rises, then more francs are supplied for dollars and the supply curve increases from S_1 to S_2. This causes the franc to depreciate and the equilibrium quantity of francs traded to rise to Q_2.

for French wine generates a greater demand for francs by U.S. citizens, who hold dollars. The demand curve in Figure 1(a) thus shifts from D_1 to D_2. This increased demand for francs causes the franc to appreciate relative to the dollar. The new exchange rate is .18, and a greater quantity of francs, Q_2, is bought and sold.

If the U.S. demand for French wine falls, the demand for francs also falls, as illustrated by the shift from D_1 to D_3 in Figure 1(a). The decreased demand for francs causes the franc to depreciate relative to the dollar, so that the exchange rate falls to .12.

So far, we have considered how shifts in the U.S. demand for French goods affect the dollar–franc exchange rate. We can also use the same supply-and-demand diagram to analyze how changes in the French demand for U.S. goods affect the equilibrium exchange rate. The supply of francs to the foreign-exchange market originates with French residents who buy goods from the rest of the world. If a French importer buys a tractor from a U.S. firm, the importer must exchange francs for dollars to pay for the tractor. As French residents' demand for foreign goods and services rises and falls, the supply of francs to the foreign-exchange market changes.

Figure 2
Foreign-Exchange Market Equilibrium Under Fixed and Flexible Exchange Rates
Initially, equilibrium is at point A; the exchange rate is .15 and Q_1 francs are traded. An increase in demand for French wine causes the demand for francs to increase from D_1 to D_2. With flexible exchange rates, the franc appreciates in value to .18 and Q_2 francs are traded; equilibrium is at point B. If the government is committed to maintaining a fixed exchange rate of .15, the supply of francs must be increased to S_2 so that a new equilibrium can occur at point C. The government must intervene in the foreign-exchange market and sell francs to shift the supply curve to S_2.

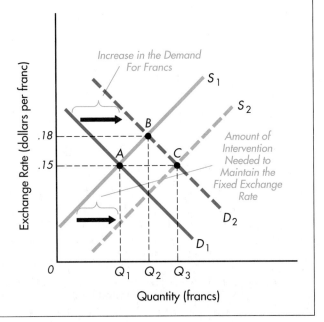

Suppose the French demand for U.S. tractors increases. This brings about a shift of the supply curve: as francs are exchanged for dollars to buy the U.S. tractors, the supply of francs increases. In Figure 1(b), the supply of francs curve shifts from S_1 to S_2. The greater supply of francs causes the franc to depreciate relative to the dollar, and the exchange rate falls from .15 to .12. If the French demand for U.S. tractors decreases, the supply of francs decreases from S_1 to S_2, and the franc appreciates to .18 dollars.

Foreign-exchange supply and demand curves are affected by changes in tastes and technology, and by changing government policy. As demand and supply change, the equilibrium exchange rate changes. In fact, continuous shifts in supply and demand cause the exchange rate to change as often as every day, based on free-market forces. Now let us consider how fixed exchange rates differ from floating exchange rates.

2.b. Adjustment Mechanisms Under Fixed and Flexible Exchange Rates

How do fixed and floating exchange rates differ in their adjustment to shifts in supply and demand for currencies?

appreciate:
increase in the value of a currency under floating exchange rates—that is, exchange rates determined by supply and demand

Figure 2 shows the dollar–franc foreign-exchange market. The exchange rate is the number of dollars required to buy one franc; the quantity is the quantity of francs bought and sold. Suppose that, initially, the equilibrium is at point A, with quantity Q_1 francs traded at .15 dollars per franc.

Suppose French wine becomes more popular in the United States, and the demand for francs increases from D_1 to D_2. With flexible exchange rates (as in Figure 1), a new equilibrium is established at point B. The exchange rate rises to $.18 per franc, and the quantity of francs bought and sold is Q_2. The increased demand for francs has caused the franc to appre-

In September 1985, representatives of the United States, Germany, Japan, the United Kingdom, and France (the so-called *Group of 5* or *G5* countries) met at the Plaza Hotel in New York City to plan coordinated foreign-exchange-market interventions aimed at bringing about a depreciation of the dollar. Although the meeting was secret, the participants announced their plan immediately after they adjourned. The dollar had appreciated throughout the early 1980s, and it was widely believed that this appreciation was causing U.S. exports to drop; U.S. goods were becoming too expensive for foreign buyers. The dollar had begun to depreciate in early 1985, and

this turn of events was welcomed as a means of stimulating U.S. exports. By late summer, however, the dollar began again to appreciate. The G5 leaders considered further dollar appreciation undesirable (the U.S. Congress was threatening to impose restrictions on imports, in order to reduce the U.S. international trade deficit), so they agreed to sell dollars simultaneously. The resulting sudden increase in supply was intended to drive down the value of the dollar.

The intervention succeeded in pushing down the value of the dollar against other currencies, just as the G5 officials desired. It is important to realize that governments intervene in foreign

exchange markets not only to maintain fixed exchange rates, but also to manage floating exchange rates. The Plaza Agreement was a notable attempt at *coordinated intervention* involving several countries — notable both for the effect on exchange rates and for the public nature of the agreement. Central banks rarely hold press conferences to discuss their plans. The public announcement was considered a major shift in the foreign exchange policy of the previously noninterventionist Reagan Administration, signaling a new desire for international coordination of policy among the G5.

---

depreciate:
decrease in the value of a currency under floating exchange rates

An increase in demand for a currency will cause an appreciation of its exchange rate, unless governments intervene in the foreign-exchange market to increase the supply of that currency.

fundamental disequilibrium:
a permanent shift in the foreign-exchange-market supply and demand curves, such that the fixed exchange rate is no longer an equilibrium rate

ciate (to rise in value against the dollar) and the dollar to **depreciate** (to fall in value against the franc). This is an example of a freely-floating exchange rate, determined by the free-market forces of supply and demand.

Now suppose the Federal Reserve is committed to maintaining a fixed exchange rate of $.15 per franc. The increase in demand for francs causes a shortage of francs at the exchange rate of $.15. According to the new demand curve D_2, the quantity of francs demanded at $.15 is Q_3. The quantity supplied is found on the original supply curve S_1, at Q_1. The only way to maintain the exchange rate of $.15 is for the Federal Reserve to supply francs to meet the shortage of $Q_3 - Q_1$. In other words, the Fed must sell $Q_3 - Q_1$ francs to shift the supply curve to S_2 and thus maintain the fixed exchange rate.

If the increased demand for francs is temporary, the Fed can continue to supply francs for the short time necessary. However, if the increased demand for francs is permanent, the Fed's intervention will eventually end when it runs out of francs. This situation—a permanent change in demand—is referred to as a **fundamental disequilibrium**. Under the Bretton Woods agreement, a country was supposed to devalue its currency in such cases.

Suppose that the shift to D_2 in Figure 2 is permanent. In this case, the dollar should be devalued. A devaluation to $.18 per franc would restore equilibrium in the foreign-exchange market without requiring further intervention by the government. Sometimes, however, governments try to maintain the old exchange rate ($.15 per franc, in this case) even though most people believe the shift in demand to be permanent. When this happens, **speculators** buy the currency that is in greater demand (francs, in our example) in anticipation of the eventual devaluation of the other currency (dollars, in Figure 2). A speculator who purchases francs for $.15 prior to the devaluation and sells them for $.18 after the devaluation earns $.03 per franc purchased—a 20-percent profit.

Speculation puts greater devaluation pressure on the dollar: the speculators sell dollars and buy francs, causing the demand for francs to increase even further. Such speculative activity contributed to the breakdown of the Bretton Woods system of fixed exchange rates. Several countries intervened to support exchange rates that were far out of line with free-market forces. The longer a devaluation was put off, the more obvious it became that devaluation was forthcoming and the more speculators entered the market. In 1971 and 1973, speculators sold dollars for yen and German marks. They were betting that the dollar would be devalued; both times they were correct. The speculative activity of the early 1970s drew attention to the folly of efforts to maintain fixed exchange rates in the face of a change in the fundamental equilibrium exchange rate.

2.c. Constraints on Economic Policy

▼ What are the advantages and disadvantages of fixed and floating exchange rates? ▲

Fixed exchange rates can be maintained over time only between countries with similar economic policies and similar underlying economic conditions. As prices rise within a country, the domestic value of a unit of its currency falls, since the currency buys fewer goods and services. In the foreign-exchange market too, the value of a unit of domestic currency falls, since it buys relatively fewer goods and services than the foreign currency does. A fixed exchange rate thus requires that the purchasing power of the two currencies change at roughly the same rate over time. Only if two nations have approximately the same inflation experience will they be able to maintain a fixed exchange rate. This condition was a frequent source of problems in the Bretton Woods era of fixed exchange rates. In the late 1960s, for instance, the U.S. government was following a more expansionary macroeconomic policy than was Germany. U.S. government expenditures on the war in Vietnam and domestic antipoverty initiatives led to inflationary pressures that were not matched in Germany. Between 1965 and 1970, price levels rose by 23.2 percent in the United States but only 12.8 percent in Germany. Since the purchasing power of a dollar was falling faster than that of the mark, the fixed exchange rate could not be maintained. The dollar had to be devalued.

One of the advantages of floating exchange rates is that countries are free to pursue their own macroeconomic policies without worrying about maintaining an exchange-rate commitment. If U.S. policy produces a higher inflation rate than Japanese policy, the dollar will automatically depreciate in value against the yen. The United States can choose the macroeconomic policy it wants, independent of other nations, and let the exchange rate adjust if its inflation rate differs markedly from that of other

If the money price is below equilibrium, then some other means of rationing goods is used. Centrally-planned economies, like that of the Soviet Union, are traditionally characterized by a heavy reliance on non-price means of rationing goods and services. As a result, it is common for people to wait in long lines, such as this one at a Moscow appliance store, to obtain goods. Such a state-directed distribution system is reflected in international monetary affairs. Centrally-planned economies have *inconvertible* currencies. Neither Soviet citizens nor foreigners are allowed to freely buy and sell Soviet rubles for U.S. dollars, or other currencies. All foreign exchange trading involving rubles is carried out by the government.

nations. If the dollar were fixed in value relative to the yen, the two nations couldn't follow independent policies and expect to maintain the exchange rate.

It became obvious in the late 1960s that many governments considered other issues more important than maintenance of a fixed exchange rate. A nation that puts a high priority on reducing unemployment will typically stimulate the economy to try to increase income and create jobs. This initiative may cause the domestic inflation rate to rise and the domestic currency to depreciate relative to other currencies. If one goal or the other—lower unemployment or a fixed exchange rate—must be given up, it is likely that the exchange-rate goal will be sacrificed.

Floating exchange rates allow countries to formulate their macroeconomic policies independently of other nations. Fixed exchange rates require the economic policies of countries linked by the exchange rate to be similar.

Floating exchange rates allow countries to formulate domestic economic policy solely in response to domestic issues; attention need not be paid to the exchange rate of the rest of the world. For residents of some countries, this freedom may be more of a problem than a benefit. The freedom to choose a rate of inflation and let the exchange rate adjust itself can have undesirable consequences in countries whose politicians, for whatever reason, follow highly inflationary policies. A fixed-exchange-rate system would impose discipline, since maintenance of the exchange rate would not permit policies that diverged sharply from those of its trading partner.

RECAP

1. Under a fixed-exchange-rate system, governments must intervene in the foreign-exchange market to maintain the exchange rate. A fundamental disequilibrium requires a currency devaluation.

2. Fixed exchange rates can only be maintained between countries with similar macroeconomic policies and similar underlying economic conditions.

3. Fixed exchange rates serve as a constraint on inflationary government policies.

3. THE CHOICE OF AN EXCHANGE-RATE SYSTEM

▼ What determines the kind of exchange-rate system a country adopts? ▲

Different countries choose different exchange-rate arrangements. Why does the United States choose floating exchange rates while Guatemala adopts a fixed exchange rate? Let us compare the characteristics of countries that choose to float with those of countries that choose to fix their exchange rates.

3.a. Country Characteristics

The choice of an exchange-rate system is an important element of the macroeconomic policy of any country. The choice seems to be related to country size, openness, inflation, and diversification of trade.

3.a.1 Size Large countries (measured by economic output or GNP) tend to be both independent and relatively unwilling to forgo domestic policy goals in order to maintain a fixed exchange rate. Because large countries have large domestic markets, international issues are less crucial to everyday business than they are in a small country.

3.a.2 Openness Closely related to size is the relative openness of the economy. By openness, we mean the degree to which the country depends on international trade. Because every country is involved in international trade, openness is very much a matter of degree. An **open economy**, according to economists, is one in which a relatively large fraction of the GNP is devoted to internationally tradable goods. In a closed economy, a relatively small fraction of the GNP is devoted to internationally tradable goods. The more open an economy, the greater the impact of variations in the exchange rate on the domestic economy. The more open the economy, therefore, the greater the tendency to establish fixed exchange rates.

open economy:
an economy in which a relatively large fraction of the GNP is devoted to internationally tradable goods

3.a.3 Inflation Countries whose policies produce inflation rates much higher or lower than those of other countries tend to choose floating exchange rates. A fixed exchange rate cannot be maintained when a country experiences inflation much different from that of the rest of the world.

3.a.4 Trade Diversification Countries that trade largely with a single foreign country tend to peg their currencies' value to that of the trading partner. For instance, the United States accounts for 60 percent of total Haitian trade. By pegging its currency, the gourde, to the U.S. dollar,

Table 3 Characteristics of Countries with Fixed and Floating Exchange Rates

Fixed-Rate Countries	Floating-Rate Countries
Small size	Large size
Open economy	Closed economy
Harmonious inflation rate	Divergent inflation rate
Concentrated trade	Diversified trade

Haiti enjoys more stable gourde prices of goods than it would with floating exchange rates. Trade with the United States is such a dominant feature of the Haitian economy that a fluctuating gourde price of the dollar would be reflected in a fluctuating price level in Haiti. If the gourde depreciated against the dollar, the gourde prices of imports from the United States would rise: this would bring about a rise in the Haitian price level. Exchange-rate depreciation tends to affect the domestic price level in all countries, but the effect is magnified if a single foreign country accounts for much of a nation's trade. Countries with diversified trading patterns find fixed exchange rates less desirable, because price stability would only prevail in trade with a single country. With all other trading partners, prices would still fluctuate.

Table 3 summarizes the national characteristics associated with alternative exchange-rate systems. Many countries do not fit into the neat categorization of Table 3, but it is nonetheless useful for understanding the great majority of countries' choices.

3.b. Multiple Exchange Rates

multiple exchange rates:
a system whereby a government fixes different exchange rates for different types of transactions

Most countries conduct all their foreign-exchange transactions at a single exchange rate. For instance, if the dollar–pound exchange rate is $1.80, residents of the United States can purchase British pounds at $1.80, no matter what use they make of the pounds. At the end of 1989, however, the 21 countries listed in Table 4 had **multiple exchange rates**—different

Table 4 Countries with Multiple Exchange Rates (as of December 31, 1989)

Afghanistan	Lesotho
The Bahamas	Luxembourg
Bangladesh	Mexico
Belgium	Nicaragua
China	Peru
Costa Rica	Poland
Egypt	South Africa
El Salvador	Syrian Arab Republic
Ghana	Vietnam
Honduras	Zambia
Jordan	

Source: International Monetary Fund, *IMF Survey*, Washington, D.C., February 19, 1990, p. 63. Used by permission.

exchange rates for different types of transactions. A typical arrangement is a dual exchange-rate system, consisting of a free-market-determined floating exchange rate for financial transactions, and a fixed exchange rate that overvalues the domestic currency for transactions in goods and services. Some countries adopt even more elaborate arrangements, with special exchange rates for a variety of different transactions. For example, at the end of 1985, Venezuela had a four-tier system. The central bank traded dollars for bolivars (symbol Bs) at the following rates: sell dollars for Bs4.30 for interest payments on foreign debt; sell dollars for Bs6.00 for national petroleum and iron-ore companies; and sell dollars for Bs7.50 for other government agencies. All other transactions took place at the free-market floating exchange rate of Bs14.40.

Countries with multiple exchange rates use them as an alternative to taxes and subsidies. Activities that the policymakers want to encourage are subsidized by allowing participants in them to buy foreign exchange at an artificially low price or sell foreign exchange at an artificially high price. Participants in activities that policymakers want to discourage are forced to pay an artificially high price to buy foreign exchange and an artificially low price to sell foreign exchange. For instance, firms that manufacture goods for export, but import some of the resources used in production, may be permitted to buy foreign exchange at an artificially low price. This allows them to pay a lower domestic-currency price for their imported resources, and consequently to charge a lower price for their output, which increases exports. In Venezuela, as we saw above, petroleum companies could buy dollars from the Central Bank for Bs6.00 even though the free-market rate was Bs14.40. In order to encourage greater production and export of Venezuelan petroleum, the Central Bank subsidized the dollars the petroleum companies needed for imports.

In an effort to discourage imports, developing countries often charge an artificially high price for foreign exchange that will be used to import consumer goods. Such multiple-exchange-rate systems have the same effects as direct government subsidies to exporting manufacturers and taxes on the importation of consumer goods: exports are stimulated and consumer-goods imports are reduced.

The IMF has tried to discourage multiple exchange rates, because they cause the domestic prices of internationally traded goods to differ from the international prices. The result is inefficient resource utilization in consumption and production, since domestic residents respond to the contrived relative prices rather than the true prices set on world markets. Monitoring and administering compliance with multiple exchange rates create additional costs, and people devote resources to avoiding the unfavorable aspects of multiple exchange rates (for example, by getting their transactions classified to the most favorable exchange rate).

3.c. Overvalued Exchange Rates

Developing countries often establish an official exchange rate—the exchange rate set by law—that differs from the equilibrium exchange rate. Figure 3 illustrates an overvalued exchange rate. Assume that a develop-

Figure 3
Overvalued Exchange Rate
The official exchange rate is 150 pesos per dollar, while the free-market equilibrium exchange rate is 200 pesos per dollar. Since the official peso price of a dollar is below the equilibrium, the peso is said to be overvalued.

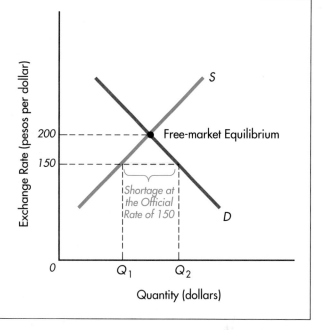

ing country whose currency is called the peso fixes an official peso–dollar exchange rate of 150 pesos per dollar, while the free-market equilibrium exchange rate is 200 pesos per dollar. Since the official rate is less than the equilibrium rate, a dollar shortage results. Q_2 dollars are demanded at 150 pesos per dollar, but only Q_1 are supplied.

When the official peso–dollar rate is less than the free-market rate, the peso is overvalued. To support the official rate, the country must impose tariffs or other restrictions on trade to reduce the demand for dollars. Overvaluing the domestic currency subsidizes favored activities or groups: if everyone had access to the official rate, there would be a dollar shortage. In addition to imposing quotas or tariffs on international trade in goods or financial assets, the country can use multiple exchange rates to ensure that only favored groups buy dollars at the official rate. In fact, a typical feature of multiple-exchange-rate regimes is the availability of an overvalued domestic-currency rate for favored transactions. Other residents are forced into the free market, where in this case they pay 200 pesos for their dollars.

Overvalued exchange rates are used to subsidize favored transactions.

RECAP

1. Countries with fixed exchange rates tend to be small open economies with inflation rates similar to those of their trading partners. Their currencies are typically pegged to that of their main trading partner.
2. Some countries adopt multiple exchange rates for different kinds of transactions.

3. Multiple exchange rates resemble a system of subsidies for favored activities and taxes for activities that are discouraged.

4. An exchange rate is overvalued when the official domestic-currency price of foreign currency is lower than the equilibrium price.

SUMMARY

▼▲ **How does a commodity standard fix exchange rates between countries?**

1. Between 1880 and 1914, a gold standard provided for fixed exchange rates among countries. § 1.a

2. The gold standard ended with World War I, and no established international monetary system replaced it until after World War II, when the Bretton Woods agreement created a fixed-exchange-rate system. § 1.b

▼▲ **What kinds of exchange-rate arrangements exist today?**

3. Today some countries have fixed exchange rates, others have floating exchange rates, and still others have managed floats or other types of systems. § 1.e

▼▲ **How is equilibrium determined in the foreign-exchange market?**

4. Foreign-exchange-market equilibrium is determined by the intersection of the demand and supply curves for foreign exchange. § 2.a

▼▲ **How do fixed and floating exchange rates differ in their adjustment to shifts in supply and demand for currencies?**

5. Under fixed exchange rates, central banks must intervene in the foreign-exchange market to keep the exchange rate from shifting. § 2.b

▼▲ **What are the advantages and disadvantages of fixed and floating exchange rates?**

6. Floating exchange rates permit countries to pursue independent economic policies. A fixed exchange rate requires a country to adopt policies similar to those of the country whose currency it pegs to. A fixed exchange rate may serve to prevent a country from pursuing inflationary policies. § 2.c

▼▲ **What determines the kind of exchange-rate system a country adopts?**

7. The choice of an exchange-rate system is related to the size and openness of a country, its inflation experience, and the diversification of its international trade. § 3.a

8. Multiple exchange rates are used to subsidize favored activities and raise costs for other activities. § 3.b

KEY TERMS

gold standard § 1.a

gold exchange standard § 1.b

reserve currency §1.b

International Monetary Fund (IMF) § 1.c

World Bank § 1.c

foreign-exchange market intervention § 1.d

equilibrium exchange rates § 1.d

devaluation § 1.d

managed floating exchange rates § 1.e

special drawing right § 1.e

European Monetary System (EMS) § 1.e
appreciate § 2.b
depreciate § 2.b
fundamental disequilibrium § 2.b

speculators § 2.b
open economy § 3.a.2
multiple exchange rates § 3.b

EXERCISES

Basic Terms and Concepts

1. Under a gold standard, if the price of an ounce of gold is 400 U.S. dollars and 500 Canadian dollars, what is the exchange rate between U.S. and Canadian dollars?

2. What were the three major results of the Bretton Woods conference?

3. What is the difference between the IMF and the World Bank?

4. How can Mexico fix the value of the peso relative to the dollar, when the demand for and supply of dollars and pesos changes continuously? Illustrate your explanation with a graph.

5. Draw a foreign-exchange-market supply-and-demand diagram to show how the mark–dollar exchange rate is determined. Set the initial equilibrium at a rate of 2.5 marks per dollar.

   a. Illustrate the effect of a change in tastes prompting German residents to buy more goods from the United States. If the exchange rate is floating, what will happen to the foreign-exchange-market equilibrium?

   b. Illustrate the effect of the change in German tastes if exchange rates are fixed. What will happen to the foreign-exchange-market equilibrium?

6. When and why should exchange rates change under a fixed exchange-rate system?

7. Other things being equal, what kind of an exchange-rate system would you expect each of the following countries to adopt?

   a. A small country that conducts all of its trade with the United States

   b. A country that has no international trade

   c. A country whose policies have led to a 300 percent annual rate of inflation

   d. A country that wants to offer exporters cheap access to the imported inputs they need, but to discourage other domestic residents from importing goods

   e. A large country like the United States or Japan

Extended Concepts

8. Illustrate and explain the meaning and likely effects of an overvalued exchange rate.

9. The countries listed as pegging to the French franc in Table 1 have a characteristic in common that helps to explain why they maintain fixed exchange rates with the franc. Explain what that characteristic is.

Pound's Link to Europe

With the first phase of European economic and monetary union set to begin on July 1, the anticipation is rising in the British financial markets that Prime Minister Margaret Thatcher will soon let the pound join the European exchange rate mechanism.

By agreeing a year ago to participate in the first phase, Mrs. Thatcher committed Britain to joining the currency system, which would require the Government to hold the value of the pound within set exchange rate bands. While the West German mark, the French franc and the other major Western European currencies are already full members, the pound is not.

But Mrs. Thatcher refused to say precisely when Britain would come aboard the European currency system. She said then that Britain could join only after all the other member countries had liberalized free movement of capital, as Britain had done, and after Britain got its inflation rate down closer to the level of the other European countries.

European economic and monetary union is envisioned as a three-step process. The first phase requires the 12 nations of the European Community to eliminate most restrictions on currency movement, closely coordinate their economic policies and agree to join the European Monetary System. Stages two and three remain sketchy, but would presumably require the countries first to cede some sovereignty over monetary policy, and then agree to a single European central bank and a single currency. Not only the timing but also whether all 12 nations will approve the later phases is uncertain.

Italy, Belgium and France recently lifted most of their restrictions. And even though British inflation has continued to rise, to a current level of 9.4 percent, Mrs. Thatcher said last weekend that when the effects of a new local tax and of high interest rates were taken out of the figures, British inflation was not that much higher than the European Community average, which was 4.8 percent last year.

To British pundits, this sounded less like "no, until" than "yes, when." But Mrs. Thatcher's aides insisted that though her tone might have changed, her basic policy had not, nor had she dropped her fundamental skepticism about government-controlled exchange rates and a common European currency in the later stages of a monetary union.

Her Chancellor of the Exchequer, John Major, has reflected this line in public statements, including an interview in *The Wall Street Journal* Thursday. But when the newspaper put it under a headline suggesting that he was easing Britain's stand against a single currency and a single European central bank, the London stock market and the value of the pound surged.

The stock market and the pound fell somewhat today, after Mr. Major made clear that there were still important obstacles ahead. "I am sure we will benefit from joining" the exchange rate mechanism, "and join it we most certainly will when our conditions are met," he told a group of British business leaders, who are generally in favor of a closer monetary union, in a speech in May, 1990....

It is generally believed that Mr. Major will take the pound into the exchange rate mechanism sooner rather than later. Doing so early next year, when the Government hopes that it will have inflation under better control, would allow Mrs. Thatcher to deprive the opposition Labor Party of a political issue before the general elections she must call by mid-1992....

What happens after Britain does join the exchange rate mechanism is far less clear. The second stage of a European economic and monetary union, according to the ... blueprint suggested by the president of the European Community's Executive Commission, Jacques Delors, would involve fixed exchange rates among the 12 currencies, moving toward a common currency in the third stage....

Stage two would require, by universal agreement, such closely coordinated monetary policies among the 12 European Community countries that, in effect, each would have to cede sovereignty on the money supply to the others. A single European currency in the third stage would require them to cede it to a single central bank, like the Federal Reserve in the United States, which would hold the monopoly on the issuance of European money....

[A] conference will be convened at the end of this year, and will try to work out a plan that can be ratified by all 12 members by the end of 1992, when they have pledged to eliminate most of the remaining barriers to trade among them and create a single European market of 320 million people.

■ Source: "Pound's Link to Europe," Craig R. Whitney, *The New York Times*, May 19, 1990, pp. 31, 43.

Commentary

Great Britain's decision to let the pound join the exchange-rate mechanism (ERM) of the European Monetary System (EMS) may seem like an economic technicality, but it is an issue that has important political as well as economic ramifications. These ramifications involve the costs and benefits to Britain of closer macroeconomic ties to the rest of Europe. National economic policy in Britain will be affected in significant ways when the pound is subject to the (partially) fixed exchange-rate system of the EMS.

A fixed exchange-rate system represents an agreement among countries to convert their individual currencies into another at a given rate. The exchange-rate system of the EMS is a bit looser than this since it allows its members' currencies to fluctuate within a 4.5-percent band rather than remain rigidly fixed. While in theory either fiscal or monetary policy could be used to control exchange rates, in practice monetary policy is the method that countries use to maintain their exchange rates within the band. This means that individual countries must subjugate their monetary policies to the goal of maintaining exchange rates within the permissible band. This loss of autonomy of monetary policy is viewed by some British politicians as too large a cost of membership in the ERM.

For most of the 1980s there were eight European countries that participated in the ERM. This means that there were only seven independent exchange rates within the ERM and that one country could have played the role of "leader" in terms of monetary policy. Much evidence points to the fact that Germany has served as the leader of the EMS with other member nations following its monetary policy. Germany's monetary policy in the 1980s was geared toward keeping inflation low. From the beginning of the EMS in 1979 until 1987, the inflation rate in Germany averaged 3.2 percent. The inflation rates of other countries in the EMS, which were generally higher than the inflation rate in Germany in 1979, have all decreased toward the German rate during the 1980s.

This convergence in inflation rates is necessary for the smooth operation of the EMS. Persistent inflation differentials across the members of a fixed exchange-rate system affect the competitiveness of each member's exports in the world market. Though a fixed exchange-rate system maintains stable *nominal exchange rates* (the rate observed in the foreign-exchange market), the competitiveness of a currency is represented by the *real exchange rate*. The real exchange rate is the nominal exchange rate adjusted for the price level at home compared to the price level abroad. It is calculated as follows:

Real exchange rate =

$$\frac{(\text{Nominal exchange rate})(\text{Foreign price level})}{\text{Domestic price level}}$$

The disruptive changes in competitiveness caused by persistent inflation differentials require a *realignment* of a fixed exchange-rate system that adjusts nominal exchange rates to keep real exchange rates from drifting too far from their correct value. For instance, if the U.S. price level starts to rise faster than foreign prices, U.S. goods will be priced out of the world market unless the dollar depreciates on the foreign-exchange market. According to the above equation, if the United States is the domestic country and its price level rises, the real exchange rate falls and U.S. goods are less competitive unless the nominal exchange rate rises to offset the higher domestic price level. The need for similar inflation rates within a fixed exchange-rate system lies behind Mrs. Thatcher's statement that Britain would only join the ERM when its inflation rate fell to a level closer to that of other European countries.

Plans have been put forward for the evolution of the EMS toward greater exchange-rate convergence, culminating in a single European currency. This plan would force individual countries to abandon completely any control over monetary policy. Proponents of the plan argue that one currency in Europe would facilitate international trade and investment. Opponents of the plan think that the cost of giving up national control over monetary policy is too high relative to the benefits of a single currency. This issue is far from settled, and we can expect to continue to read about the debate over European integration well into the 1990s.

23

Foreign-Exchange Risk and International Lending

1. What is foreign-exchange risk, and how does it affect international traders?

2. How do the forward, futures, and option markets in foreign exchange allow a firm to eliminate foreign-exchange risk?

3. What caused the international debt crisis?

4. What solutions have been proposed for the debt crisis?

PREVIEW

Suppose you are a manufacturer of toys, located in Los Angeles. You have sold $100,000 worth of toys to a Mexico City department store and have agreed to accept payment in Mexican pesos. Suppose the current exchange rate is 2,000 pesos per dollar. Based on today's exchange rate, you agree to accept 200 million pesos in payment for the toys (2,000 times $100,000). However, the Mexican firm has 30 days before payment is due. This presents a problem that you have never faced in your dealings with U.S. toy stores: you will receive payment in a currency that could change in dollar value.

Ultimately, you want dollars. When you receive the 200 million pesos, you will exchange them for dollars. But what will the exchange rate between pesos and dollars be in 30 days? As the exchange rate changes, the dollar value of the transaction changes.

▼ What is foreign exchange risk, and how does it affect international traders? ▲

Foreign-exchange market risk of this kind arises only in international transactions. Any firm that buys and sells across international borders has to deal with the issue of foreign-exchange risk. Similarly, firms that lend money across international borders face risks that are missing from domestic loans.

International trade involves foreign exchange risk. The French vineyard in this photo conducts business at home in French francs. A U.S. wine importer uses U.S. dollars for its domestic business. Yet if the U.S. firm buys wine from the French producer, dollars must ultimately be exchanged for francs, and the fluctuating exchange rate between the dollar and the franc will add an element of uncertainty that is missing in purely domestic transactions.

Another risk in international finance is the risk of lending to developing countries. The international debts of the developing countries emerged as a major economic issue in the 1980s. Banks in the industrial countries found themselves holding loans to developing countries that were not being repaid. This chapter will examine the international debt crisis, and the efforts of banks and governments to reduce the debt burden of developing countries and improve the prospects of repayment. We will see that international lending creates problems that domestic loans do not.

1. FOREIGN-EXCHANGE TRANSACTIONS

Delayed payment adds an element of uncertainty to international transactions, since exchange rates tend to fluctuate over time. A firm receiving payment in a foreign currency faces the risk that the foreign currency will depreciate in value, reducing the domestic-currency value of the payment.

A firm making a payment in a foreign currency faces the risk that the foreign currency will appreciate in value, increasing the domestic-currency cost of the payment.

1.a. An Importer's Problem

The effect of exchange-rate changes on the value of international transactions is well illustrated by the example of a U.S. wine importer, Vine Brothers, Inc. Suppose Vine Brothers has contracted to receive a shipment of wine from a German exporter, Rhine Wines. Rhine Wines wants payment in German marks. The contract between Rhine Wines and Vine Brothers calls for payment of DM1 million (DM stands for *Deutsche mark,* or German mark). Vine Brothers has to purchase marks in the foreign-exchange market in order to pay Rhine Wines.

The dollar value of the DM1 million contract is determined by the exchange rate between the dollar and the mark. Figure 1 lists the foreign-exchange rates for a particular day, as published in *The Wall Street Journal.* The dollar value of 1 German mark is .5986. If one mark sells for $0.5986, the dollar value of 1 million marks is: $0.5986 × 1,000,000 = $598,600.

spot exchange rate:
the exchange rate for delivery of a currency immediately, or "on the spot"

The exchange rate of .5986 dollars per mark is called the **spot exchange rate**. This is the price of marks purchased today for delivery now, or "on the spot." When foreign currency is needed immediately, the spot rate is the price paid. If Vine Brothers is to pay for the wine shipment today, it will pay the spot exchange rate times DM1,000,000, or $598,600, to buy the marks needed to settle the contract.

But what if the contract signed today calls for delivery of the wine and payment of the contract in three months? One alternative is for Vine Brothers to wait and buy marks at the spot rate existing three months from now. The risk of this strategy is that the exchange rate could change in a way that would make the transaction less profitable. If the dollar depreciates against the mark over the next three months, marks will cost more in dollars. For instance, if the exchange rate moves to .6000, then DM1,000,000 costs $600,000, instead of $598,600. The dollar depreciation thus raises the cost of the transaction for Vine Brothers by $1400.

On the other hand, if the dollar appreciates against the mark, the dollar cost of the wine will fall. If the exchange rate moves to .5900, then DM1,000,000 will cost only $590,000. The dollar appreciation thus lowers the dollar cost of the transaction for Vine Brothers by $8600.

foreign-exchange risk:
the threat that future foreign currency payments or receipts will have a different domestic currency value than expected

open position:
the situation of a firm waiting to buy foreign currency at a future spot rate

Waiting to buy marks at the future spot rate is risky. The gamble could be rewarded with a lower dollar cost, but it could also result in a higher dollar cost. Since future spot rates are not known today, transactions payable in a foreign currency at some future date are said to involve **foreign-exchange risk**. The strategy of waiting to buy foreign currency at a future spot rate is called taking an **open position** in a currency. A firm that takes an open position leaves itself open to foreign-exchange risk and the potential impact on its profits of future changes in exchange rates.

One way for Vine Brothers to eliminate the foreign-exchange risk associated with the DM1 million contract due in three months is to buy marks now and hold them until payment is due. In reality, Vine Brothers would not let the marks sit idle for three months, but would invest them in

Figure 1
Exchange Rates
Source: *The Wall Street Journal*, February 22, 1990, p. C10.

EXCHANGE RATES

Wednesday, February 21, 1990

The New York foreign exchange selling rates below apply to trading among banks in amounts of $1 million and more, as quoted at 3 p.m. Eastern time by Bankers Trust Co. Retail transactions provide fewer units of foreign currency per dollar.

	U.S. $ equiv.		Currency per U.S. $	
Country	Wed.	Tues.	Wed.	Tues.
Argentina (Austral) ...	.0002381	.0002381	4200.09	4200.09
Australia (Dollar)	.7665	.7590	1.3046	1.3175
Austria (Schilling)	.08511	.08505	11.75	11.76
Bahrain (Dinar)	2.6522	2.6522	.3771	.3771
Belgium (Franc)				
Commercial rate	.02872	.02867	34.82	34.88
Financial rate	.02872	.02867	34.82	34.88
Brazil (Cruzado)	.03749	.03732	26.68	26.80
Britain (Pound)	1.7130	1.7110	.5838	.5845
30-Day Forward ...	1.7044	1.7023	.5867	.5874
90-Day Forward ...	1.6862	1.6840	.5930	.5938
180-Day Forward ...	1.6605	1.6582	.6022	.6031
Canada (Dollar)	.8342	.8330	1.1987	1.2005
30-Day Forward ...	.8313	.8300	1.2030	1.2048
90-Day Forward ...	.8250	.8236	1.2121	1.2142
180-Day Forward ...	.8174	.8163	1.2234	1.2251
Chile (Official rate) ...	.003439	.003439	290.80	290.80
China (Yuan)	.211752	.211752	4.7225	4.7225
Colombia (Peso)	.002252	.002252	444.09	444.09
Denmark (Krone)	.1555	.1552	6.4315	6.4440
Ecuador (Sucre)				
Floating rate	.001458	.001458	686.07	686.07
Finland (Markka)	.25419	.25361	3.9340	3.9430
France (Franc)	.17646	.17635	5.6670	5.6704
30-Day Forward ...	.17616	.17602	5.6767	5.6811
90-Day Forward ...	.17535	.17510	5.7030	5.7109
180-Day Forward ...	.17402	.17376	5.7465	5.7549
Greece (Drachma)	.006337	.006341	157.80	157.70
Hong Kong (Dollar) ...	.12807	.12806	7.8080	7.8090
India (Rupee)	.05910	.05910	16.92	16.92
Indonesia (Rupiah)	.0005562	.0005562	1798.01	1798.01
Ireland (Punt)	1.5887	1.5825	.6294	.6319
Israel (Shekel)	.5383	.5383	1.8578	1.8578
Italy (Lira)	.0008092	.0008071	1235.76	1239.00
Japan (Yen)	.006873	.006892	145.50	145.10
30-Day Forward ...	.006881	.006899	145.33	144.94
90-Day Forward ...	.006891	.006910	145.12	144.71
180-Day Forward ...	.006903	.006932	144.87	144.25
Jordan (Dinar)	1.5053	1.5053	.6643	.6643
Kuwait (Dinar)	3.4632	3.4632	.2888	.2888
Lebanon (Pound)	.001807	.001807	553.50	553.50
Malaysia (Ringgit)	.3702	.3702	2.7010	2.7010
Malta (Lira)	3.0628	3.0628	.3265	.3265
Mexico (Peso)				
Floating rate	.0003662	.0003662	2731.05	2731.05
Netherland (Guilder) .	.5312	.5311	1.8825	1.8830
New Zealand (Dollar)	.5895	.5890	1.6964	1.6978
Norway (Krone)	.1549	.1551	6.4550	6.4475
Pakistan (Rupee)	.0472	.0472	21.18	21.18
Peru (Inti)	.00007931	.00007931	12608.75	12608.75
Philippines (Peso)	.04593	.04593	21.77	21.77
Portugal (Escudo)	.006813	.006813	146.78	146.78
Saudi Arabia (Riyal) ..	.26681	.26681	3.7480	3.7480
Singapore (Dollar)	.5376	.5379	1.8600	1.8590
South Africa (Rand)				
Commercial rate	.3946	.3940	2.5342	2.5381
Financial rate	.2853	.2861	3.5051	3.4953
South Korea (Won) ...	.0014584	.0014584	685.70	685.70
Spain (Peseta)	.009276	.009268	107.80	107.90
Sweden (Krona)	.1642	.1638	6.0900	6.1050
Switzerland (Franc) ...	.6768	.6764	1.4775	1.4785
30-Day Forward ...	.6764	.6759	1.4785	1.4795
90-Day Forward ...	.6754	.6750	1.4805	1.4815
180-Day Forward ...	.6732	.6725	1.4855	1.4870
Taiwan (Dollar)	.038565	.038580	25.93	25.92
Thailand (Baht)	.03766	.03766	26.55	26.55
Turkey (Lira)	.0004234	.0004234	2362.00	2362.00
United Arab (Dirham)	.2723	.2723	3.6725	3.6725
Uruguay (New Peso)				
Financial	.001245	.001245	803.00	803.00
Venezuela (Bolivar)				
Floating rate	.02299	.02299	43.50	43.50
W. Germany (Mark) ..	.5986	.5993	1.6705	1.6685
30-Day Forward ...	.5987	.5994	1.6704	1.6684
90-Day Forward ...	.5983	.5997	1.6713	1.6675
180-Day Forward ...	.5973	.6010	1.6742	1.6640
SDR	1.33175	1.32898	.75089	.75246
ECU	1.22635	1.22026	....	....

Special Drawing Rights (SDR) are based on exchange rates for the U.S., West German, British, French and Japanese curren-cies. Source: International Monetary Fund.

European Currency Unit (ECU) is based on a basket of community currencies. Source: European Community Commission.

an interest-earning asset, such as a bank deposit. This approach would eliminate foreign-exchange risk, since Vine Brothers would know the exact dollar cost of the DM1 million. The disadvantage of buying marks in the current spot market is that Vine Brothers must spend dollars today, and the marks must be invested for three months. The firm may not want to spend the dollars today, or may not have the dollars to spend. Also, the need to invest the marks is a new problem that Vine Brothers probably wants to avoid. They are in the business of importing wine, not investing in German-mark-denominated securities. As a result, immediate purchase of marks in the spot market may not be the best way to eliminate the open position in marks.

There are other ways to eliminate Vine Brothers' foreign-exchange risk. Organized markets exist to provide firms like Vine Brothers with what are called **covered positions**. A firm is said to have a covered position when the foreign-exchange risk of a future transaction is eliminated. The next section will discuss the forward, futures, and option markets in foreign exchange.

covered position:
the situation of a firm whose foreign exchange risk from a future transaction has been eliminated

1.b. The Forward Exchange Market

▼ How do the forward, futures, and option markets in foreign exchange allow a firm to eliminate its foreign exchange risk? ▲

forward exchange rate:
the price established today for delivery of a foreign currency at a future date

The forward exchange market is a market in which foreign currencies are traded for delivery at some future date. The participants in this market are large commercial banks, governments, and corporations. In this market, the price of one currency in another currency is known as the **forward exchange rate**. A forward exchange rate is the price established today for delivery of a foreign currency at a future date.

Figure 1 lists the forward exchange rates in dollars for the major traded currencies: the British pound, Canadian dollar, French franc, Japanese yen, Swiss franc, and West German mark. Forward rates are given for 30, 90, and 180 days forward. Since Vine Brothers has to pay DM1 million in three months, the 90-day forward rate is the relevant rate. The 90-day forward rate for the mark in Figure 1 is .5983. That is, one mark to be delivered in 90 days sells for $0.5983. So DM1 million costs $598,300, which is $300 less than the cost of marks at the spot rate.

The advantage of the forward market is that the exchange rate between the dollar and mark is set today, but the marks are not received or paid for until 90 days from now. In practice, a corporation buys foreign exchange in the forward market from a bank. Vine Brothers calls its bank and receives a forward-exchange quote for the marks desired in 90 days. If they agree to buy the marks, in 90 days they pay the bank $598,300 and the bank sends the DM1 million to Rhine Wines.

In real life, however, the $598,300 transaction is too small for the forward exchange market, which is a market for very large-scale transactions only. The introduction to Figure 1 states that its quotes apply to trades of $1 million or more. Only the largest banks and corporations, engaged in multimillion-dollar deals, trade in the forward exchange market. But foreign-exchange risk exists for small transactions as well as large. How do smaller firms and banks deal with foreign-exchange risk? They can use the futures or options markets. Let us now turn to these markets.

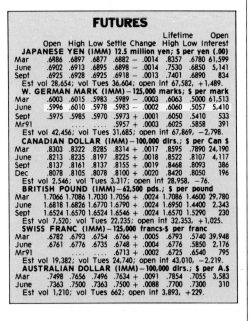

Figure 2
Futures
Source: *The Wall Street Journal,*
February 22, 1990, p. C10.

1.c. Foreign-Exchange Futures

The foreign-exchange spot and forward markets have no physical location. Telephones and electronic mail enable commercial banks, business firms, and governments all over the world to buy and sell currencies. By contrast, the futures and options markets have actual physical locations where trading occurs.

In the foreign-exchange futures market, foreign currencies are bought and sold for delivery at a future date. The futures market differs from the forward market in that only a few currencies are traded; trading proceeds by means of contracts, for standardized amounts of currency and specific maturity dates; and trading occurs in a specific location, such as the International Monetary Market (IMM) of the Chicago Mercantile Exchange, the largest currency-futures market. (In the forward market, by contrast, a bank can quote a rate on any currency it is willing to offer, for whatever amount and date the buyer and seller agree to.)

IMM futures are traded in the Japanese yen, German mark, Canadian dollar, British pound, Swiss franc, and Australian dollar. Futures contracts are for a specific amount of currency to be delivered at specific maturity dates. Figure 2 shows futures quotes as listed in *The Wall Street Journal*. Contracts mature on the third Wednesday of March, June, September, and December. The amount of currency covered by each contract is listed in Figure 2: 12.5 million yen, 125,000 marks, 100,000 Canadian dollars, 62,500 British pounds, 125,000 Swiss francs, and 100,000 Australian dollars.

The first column of Figure 2 lists the month when the contract matures; the remaining columns yield the following information:

The spot and forward markets in foreign exchange have no geographic locale; they are global markets. The futures markets trade at specific locations.

open: price of the contract at the start of business that day

high: high price of the contract on that day

low: low price of the contract on that day

settle: price at which contracts are settled at the close of trading that day

change: change in the settlement price from the previous day

lifetime high: highest price at which this contract has ever traded

lifetime low: lowest price at which this contract has ever traded

open interest: number of outstanding contracts on the previous trading day

Suppose Vine Brothers is interested in the June mark contract. According to Figure 2, the contract began trading on this particular day at $0.5996 per mark. At this price, DM1 million would cost $599,600. During the day, the price rose to a high of $.6010, fell to a low of $.5978, and settled at $.5983. The settlement price was down $.0002 from the previous day. Over the life of this contract, the highest price ever was $.6060 and the lowest ever was $.5057. On the previous day, 5,410 contracts for June mark futures were outstanding.

Vine Brothers is interested in using the June futures contract for marks to eliminate its foreign-exchange risk on the DM1 million it owes. Since each contract is for 125,000 marks, they must buy eight contracts in order to purchase 1 million marks. Assuming that the contracts are purchased at the low price of $.5978, then DM1 million for June delivery in the futures market will sell for 1 million times $.5978, or $597,800. Vine Brothers has eliminated the foreign-exchange risk associated with the DM1 million contract it must settle in three months by fixing the dollar value of the contract at $597,800.

A money dealer makes a face during another hectic trading day at a foreign-exchange merchant's office in Tokyo. The buying and selling of different currencies determines the value of a nation's money compared to those of other nations.

Figure 3
Options
Source: *The Wall Street Journal,*
February 22, 1990, p. C12.

OPTIONS
PHILADELPHIA EXCHANGE

Option & Underlying	Strike Price	Calls—Last Mar	Apr	Jun	Puts—Last Mar	Apr	Jun
50,000 Australian Dollars-cents per unit.							
ADollr	...70	r	r	r	r	r	0.58
76.69	...72	r	r	r	r	r	1.03
76.69	...73	r	r	r	r	0.67	1.32
76.69	...74	r	r	r	0.32	0.85	1.86
76.69	...76	r	r	r	r	1.86	r
76.69	...77	0.35	0.57	1.00	r	r	r
76.69	...78	r	r	0.75	r	r	r
50,000 Australian Dollars-European Style.							
76.69	...72	r	r	r	r	r	0.99
31,250 British Pounds-cents per unit.							
BPound	160	r	r	r	r	r	1.20
171.13	162½	r	r	8.80	r	0.50	1.88
171.13	.165	r	r	r	r	0.96	r
171.13	167½	4.13	r	r	0.63	r	r
171.13	.170	2.25	2.80	r	1.40	r	5.00
171.13	172½	1.10	1.60	r	r	r	r
171.13	.175	0.43	r	1.60	r	r	r
50,000 Canadian Dollars-cents per unit.							
CDollr	.81½	r	r	r	r	0.24	r
83.48	...82	r	r	r	r	0.42	r
83.48	.82½	r	r	r	0.20	r	r
83.48	...83	0.47	0.53	0.62	r	0.78	1.38
83.48	.83½	0.25	0.40	0.53	r	1.12	r
83.48	...84	r	r	r	1.10	1.50	r
83.48	.84½	r	r	r	r	r	2.56
50,000 Canadian Dollars-European Style.							
CDollar	...81	r	r	r	r	r	0.55
83.48	...82	r	r	r	0.11	r	r
83.48	.82½	r	r	r	0.24	r	r
83.48	.83½	r	0.30	r	r	r	r
83.48	...84	0.10	r	r	r	r	r
62,500 West German Marks-cents per unit.							
DMark	..53	r	s	r	r	s	0.06
59.87	...54	r	r	r	r	r	0.11
59.87	...56	3.91	r	r	0.01	0.10	0.34
59.87	...57	r	r	r	r	0.17	0.46
59.87	.57½	r	s	s	0.07	s	s
59.87	...58	2.05	r	r	0.11	0.33	0.76
59.87	...59	1.26	1.55	2.10	0.32	0.65	1.13
59.87	.59½	0.94	r	s	0.45	r	s
59.87	...60	0.63	r	1.45	r	1.01	1.60
59.87	.60½	r	0.79	s	r	r	s
59.87	...61	0.28	0.61	1.11	r	r	r
59.87	.61½	0.21	r	s	r	r	s
59.87	...62	0.10	0.33	0.75	r	r	r
59.87	...63	r	r	0.53	r	r	r
59.87	...64	r	r	r	4.12	r	r
6,250,000 Japanese Yen-100ths of a cent per unit.							
JYen	...64	r	r	r	r	r	0.12
68.79	...65	r	r	r	r	r	0.16
68.79	...66	r	r	r	r	r	0.27
68.79	...67	r	r	r	0.08	r	0.47
68.79	...68	r	r	r	0.24	r	0.76
68.79	.68½	r	r	s	0.36	r	s
68.79	...69	0.47	0.76	1.23	0.60	r	1.18
68.79	.69½	0.27	r	s	r	r	s
68.79	...70	0.16	0.38	0.83	r	r	r
68.79	...71	0.05	r	0.53	r	r	r
68.79	...72	r	0.09	0.32	r	r	r
68.79	...73	r	0.09	0.21	r	r	r
68.79	...74	r	0.04	r	r	r	r
68.79	...76	r	r	0.05	r	r	r
68.79	...87	4.85	s	s	r	s	s
6,250,000 Japanese Yen-European Style.							
68.79	...69	0.44	r	r	r	r	r
62,500 Swiss Francs-cents per unit.							
SFranc	.63	r	r	r	0.03	r	r
67.70	...64	r	r	r	r	r	0.55
67.70	...65	r	r	r	r	0.28	0.70
67.70	...66	r	r	r	0.22	r	r
67.70	...67	1.18	r	r	r	r	r
67.70	.67½	0.86	r	s	r	r	s
67.70	...68	0.71	r	r	r	r	r
67.70	.68½	0.48	r	s	r	r	s
67.70	...69	0.30	0.65	r	r	r	r
67.70	...70	0.14	r	r	r	r	r

Total call vol. 38,441   Call open int. 287,429
Total put vol. 20,585   Put open int. 336,417
r—Not traded. s—No option offered.
Last is premium (purchase price).

1.d. Foreign-Currency Options

There is a third market where Vine Brothers could reduce or eliminate the foreign-exchange risk on its wine contract. It is called the options market. A foreign-currency option is a contract that provides the right to buy or sell a given amount of currency at a fixed exchange rate on or before the maturity date. (This is an American option: a European option gives the right to buy or sell only at maturity.) A **call** option is the right to buy currency, and a **put** option gives the right to sell. The price at which currency can be bought or sold is the **striking price**.

The first currency options market was created in 1982 by the Philadelphia Stock Exchange. The Philadelphia exchange offers contracts for 50,000 Australian dollars, 31,250 British pounds, 50,000 Canadian dollars, 62,500 German marks, 6,250,000 Japanese yen, and 62,500 Swiss francs. Figure 3 lists foreign-currency options prices for a particular day. The first column lists the currency traded and its current spot exchange rate. The next column lists the alternative striking prices available. The next three columns list the call option prices (often called *premiums*) existing at the close of business for three different maturity months. The final three columns list the put option prices, or premiums, for three maturity months.

Let's assume that Vine Brothers is interested in a June option on the mark. In Figure 3, we see in the first column that the current spot exchange rate is 59.87 cents per mark, or $0.5987. The next column lists the alternative striking prices available, which range from 53 to 64 cents per mark. The next three columns list the premium to buy a call option. This is what Vine Brothers is interested in.

Suppose Vine Brothers decides that it wants to pay no more than 60 cents per mark. A striking price of 60 for a June call option sells for 1.45 cents per mark, or $0.0145. One option contract covers only 62,500 marks, so Vine Brothers must buy 16 option contracts to cover DM1 million. The option price of a single mark of $0.0145 times the number of marks, 1 million, gives the dollar cost of the options, $14,500.

The 16 option contracts give Vine Brothers the right to buy DM1 million for $0.60 per mark, or $600,000, on or before the expiration of the option in June. Vine Brothers pays $14,500 for this right. If the dollar price of a mark rises above $0.60, the firm will exercise the option. If the dollar price of the mark is below $0.60, the firm will buy marks in the spot market instead of exercising the option. In essence, it is paying $14,500 for an insurance policy. The option insures Vine Brothers that it will pay no more than $600,000 to buy the German wine.

If Vine Brothers knew what the future exchange rate would be, it would have no interest in options, futures, or forward contracts. But in an uncertain world, firms and individuals willingly pay to avoid the possible losses that could arise from changes in exchange rates.

RECAP

1. The current price of a currency to be delivered immediately is called the spot exchange rate.

call:
the right to buy currency at a certain price

put:
the right to sell currency at a certain price

striking price:
the fixed price at which you may buy or sell in an option contract

2. Since future exchange rates cannot be known with certainty, transactions denominated in a foreign currency to be settled at a future date involve foreign-exchange risk.

3. Foreign-exchange risk may be eliminated in the forward, futures, or options markets.

4. The forward market is for large-scale buying and selling of foreign exchange, in any quantity agreed to by buyer and seller, for future delivery at a price set today.

5. The futures market trades in standardized contracts to buy or sell foreign currency for delivery at a future date.

6. The options market trades the rights to buy or sell foreign exchange for a specific price on or before a certain future date.

2. THE INTERNATIONAL DEBT PROBLEM

Individuals and firms involved in trading foreign exchange face a great deal of uncertainty generated by fluctuations in exchange rates. International lending and borrowing also give rise to foreign-currency purchases and sales, and thus also involve foreign-exchange risk. An additional uncertainty involved in any loan, including international loans, is the question of whether the debt will be repaid. Commercial banks in the industrial countries must assess the economic outlook for borrowing countries to determine their ability to repay. Political turmoil or recession in a debtor country could affect lenders' likelihood of receiving full payment of the interest and principal due on their loans.

2.a. A Brief History

The international debt problem began in August 1982, when Mexico announced that it could not pay its debts as promised.

▼
What caused the
international debt crisis?
▲

In August 1982, Mexico announced that it was unable to meet its debt obligations to foreign creditors. This event is widely regarded as the beginning of the international debt crisis, which eventually touched most developing countries. If Mexico alone, or some other single country, had had problems repaying its debt, there would have been no crisis. But the fact that most developing nations were having debt-repayment problems by the early 1980s created a crisis for the creditor banks, all located in the industrial countries. These banks had made large loans to developing countries during the previous decade, in the belief that the borrowers would be able to repay their debts when due.

Table 1 lists the external public debt of several large debtor countries. Brazil has the largest debts among the developing countries, followed by Mexico. To measure the burden of such debts, Table 1 indicates their magnitude relative to GNP. Chile's external debt is 89.4 percent of its GNP. Thus debt to foreign creditors is more burdensome in Chile than in Argentina, whose debt is equal to 61.7 percent of GNP.

The last column presents another measure of the burden of debt, the ratio of debt service to exports. *Debt service* is the cost of the debt, in

Table 1 International Debts of Selected Countries

Country	External Public Debt (million dollars)	Percent of GNP	Ratio of Debt Service to Exports
Argentina	47,451	61.7	45.3
Brazil	91,653	29.1	26.7
Chile	15,536	89.4	21.1
Mexico	82,771	59.5	30.1
Peru	12,485	28.0	12.5
Philippines	22,321	65.0	23.2
Venezuela	25,245	52.3	22.6

Source: Data from World Bank, *World Development Report* (Washington, D.C., 1989), p. 211.

terms of interest and principal repayment. Since the debt is owed largely to creditors in industrial countries, the debtors must earn dollars and other industrial-country currencies in order to repay the debt. The ratio of debt service to exports indicates how difficult it is to service the debt. The higher the ratio, the more burdensome the debt; in other words, a greater fraction of export revenues is used for debt repayment. The data in Table 1 indicate that the burden of debt is greater in Argentina, whose debt-service ratio is 45.3 percent, than in Chile, where the debt-service ratio is 21.1 percent. There is no universally recognized indicator of the burden of foreign debt to a country, and different measures sometimes point to different conclusions.

Many analysts of the international-debt situation point to the oil-price increases of the 1970s as an important factor in understanding how the debt crisis came about. Oil prices increased dramatically in 1973–1974 and again in 1979, thus increasing the revenues of the oil-exporting nations. These nations deposited their earnings in international banks, which gave the banks large supplies of loanable funds. The large inflow of dollar deposits (oil is priced in dollars worldwide) was loaned to developing countries.

Before the large inflow of deposits from the oil-exporting nations, bank loans to developing countries were usually earmarked for specific projects or purposes. A government could borrow to finance a particular new factory or a new dam, but general-purpose loans—to be used for whatever the government chose—were considered too risky. But the large deposits from the oil-exporting nations prompted banks to seek out new uses for the available funds. They began making general-purpose loans to developing-country governments.

Initially, the loans appeared to be sound. Income growth in many large developing countries exceeded the growth of debt, so it was not an obvious mistake to extend loans. A combination of events led to the initial problems. A global recession in the early 1980s caused interest rates to increase dramatically. Recession in the industrial countries also reduced demand for the exports of developing countries. As exports fell, it became more difficult for the borrowers to repay. Meanwhile, rising interest rates in the late 1970s and early 1980s added greatly to the debt burden of the debtor countries. The interest cost of new borrowing rose as interest rates

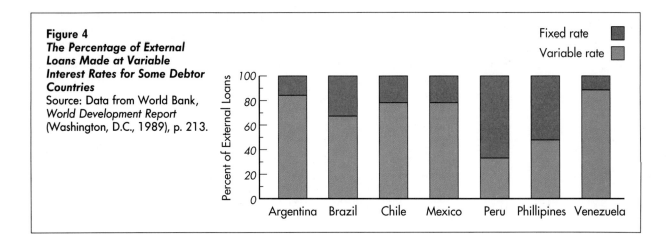

Figure 4
The Percentage of External Loans Made at Variable Interest Rates for Some Debtor Countries
Source: Data from World Bank, *World Development Report* (Washington, D.C., 1989), p. 213.

rose, but even old borrowing was not immune to increased costs. Many of the existing loans were at *variable interest rates*, which rise and fall with current interest rates. Figure 4 shows the percentage of several debtor countries' external debt that is at variable interest rates. As the figure shows, 89.1 percent of Venezuela's debt has a variable interest rate. All of the other countries listed, except Peru, have most of their debt at variable interest rates.

Variable-interest-rate loans typically tie the interest rate to some key indicator of the cost of money to lending institutions. Two indicators frequently used to price international loans are the U.S. prime rate and LIBOR. The *prime rate* is the rate that U.S. banks charge their best customers. It is usually identical at the major banks in the United States. **LIBOR**, which stands for London Interbank Offer Rate, is the rate charged for loans between major banks in London. A variable-interest-rate loan stipulates that the interest rate is adjusted periodically, often quarterly, to some specified level above the U.S. prime rate or LIBOR. For instance, a developing-country government may borrow at 2 percentage points above LIBOR. As the interest rate in the London interbank market changes, the interest rate on the loan also changes. When interest rates rose in the industrial countries in the late 1970s and early 1980s, the burden of developing-country debt increased as the interest payments on variable-interest-rate loans increased. The prime rate in the United States, which peaked at 20.5 percent in August 1981, was at 15 percent in August 1982, when the debt crisis first became apparent. Both were extremely high rates by historical standards.

The greater burden of debt resulting from higher interest rates and lower export revenues was not foreseen. Commercial banks loaned Mexico $6.4 billion in the first half of 1982, and a syndicate of banks was seeking additional lenders to offer a new $100 million loan in July 1982, just before Mexico's announcement that it could not afford to repay its debts. Commercial banks were as surprised by the debt crisis as were international agencies like the International Monetary Fund.

After Mexico's problems surfaced, every Latin American country except Colombia and Paraguay experienced debt-repayment problems.

LIBOR:
the London interbank offer rate; the interest rate charged for loans between major London banks

The 1982–1985 period was a time of **debt reschedulings**. When it became apparent that a given country could not adequately meet its external-debt obligations, creditor groups met with government officials to work out a new repayment schedule. The typical agreement extends the repayment period and offers a grace period during which no interest payments are due and no principal is repaid.

These debt reschedulings were usually conducted with the assistance of the IMF. Bank creditors have an interest in IMF participation because, when the IMF offers a country new loans, it imposes conditions aimed at increasing the growth of the debtor country while reducing the government fiscal deficit. Debt reschedulings typically include new loans, to help the debtor maintain its interest payments during the difficult process of cutting government subsidies and raising taxes to reduce the deficit.

2.b. Debt-Reduction Strategies

Debt is normally reduced in the course of scheduled repayments. In the case of the developing-country debtors, scheduled repayments have not been met. Debts have risen rather than fallen, since new loans have been necessary to support debtor-country policy changes associated with debt-rescheduling agreements.

▼ What solutions have been proposed for the debt crisis? ▲

Several strategies for reducing developing-country debts or improving the prospects for repayment have been proposed and enacted in recent years. Let us look at some of these plans and their effects on the debtor countries and their creditors.

The Baker Plan called for new bank lending to developing countries, which would enact market-oriented reforms and reduce the role of government in the economy.

2.b.1. The Baker Plan In October 1985, James Baker, then Secretary of the U.S. Treasury, announced what has come to be known as the *Baker Plan* for dealing with the debt crisis in the developing countries. The essence of the plan was that commercial banks would keep lending money to developing countries in order to stimulate economic growth. The recipients of the new loans were to restructure their economies to emphasize free markets and de-emphasize government intervention in markets, government subsidies, and government-operated enterprises. The rationale for the plan was that market-oriented reforms would provide a foundation for greater efficiency and long-term growth, which would enable the debtors to repay their debts.

Secretary Baker identified 15 debtor nations that would benefit from his plan. The 15 countries are listed in Table 2. The second column of the table lists the dollar amount of new commercial bank loans made to each country over the three years following announcement of the Baker Plan. The total of new loans to all 15 countries was approximately $20 billion. The remaining three columns list real GDP growth in each country over the three years following the announcement of the Baker Plan. Their growth rates have varied considerably. One problem has been the inability of the governments to carry out their end of the Baker Plan. Political realities in each country have favored continued government subsidies and state-owned enterprises, rather than an emphasis on privately-owned business to promote free markets and economic growth, as called for by Secretary Baker.

Table 2 New Lending and Growth in Baker Plan Countries

Country	New Bank Loans Since Sept. 1985 (billion dollars)	Real GDP Growth		
		1985–86	1987	1988
Argentina	$2.0	0.5%	2.0%	2.2%
Bolivia	0	−1.6	2.2	2.5
Brazil	5.9	8.2	2.9	0
Chile	1.5	4.1	5.7	6.3
Colombia	2.0	4.1	5.4	4.5
Ecuador	.2	3.9	−5.2	4.0
Ivory Coast	.4	3.5	−1.5	.5
Mexico	7.7	− .7	1.4	− .5
Morocco	.0	5.0	1.0	5.0
Nigeria	.3	1.0	−2.0	0
Peru	.0	5.2	6.9	−3.0
Philippines	.3	−1.1	5.7	6.0
Uruguay	.1	3.5	4.9	2.5
Venezuela	.0	4.1	3.0	1.8
Yugoslavia	.3	1.8	− .5	1.0

Source: Data from Morgan Guaranty Bank, *World Financial Markets*, New York, 1988, pp. 4–5. Copyright: J.P. Morgan & Co Incorporated. Used by permission.

2.b.2. Debt Buy-Backs Some countries' external debt has been reduced by purchasing the debt back from creditors. Private firms and state-owned enterprises in Brazil, Mexico, and Chile have been the most active repurchasers of debt from banks. The debtor negotiates with creditor banks to accept payment for outstanding debts at less than the face value of the debt. For instance, a Mexican firm may owe a U.S. bank $1 million. Suppose the firm and the bank agree to a debt buy-back at a discount of 50 percent. The firm pays the bank $500,000 to wipe out the debt.

A debt buy-back is an agreement that the creditor bank will eliminate the debt for an immediate payment of less than the face value of the debt.

Why would the bank accept half the face value of the loan? Because the bank believes that this amount is worth more than what it will receive by holding the debt until it is fully payable. A debt buy-back allows the bank to receive an early settlement of the debt, rather than risk that the debt will be tied up for years in a debt-rescheduling scheme, with small return to the bank.

Data on privately negotiated debt buy-backs are not widely available, so it is not known how much developing-country debt has been eliminated by such agreements. Morgan Guaranty Bank has estimated that, between 1982 and 1988, debt buy-backs reduced developing-country debts by $8 to $10 billion. There have been few debt buy-backs directly involving loans to sovereign governments. Bolivia was the first government to negotiate a debt buy-back; its negotiations are discussed in Economic Insight: ''Buying Back Bolivian Government Debt.''

2.b.3. Debt-for-Equity Swaps One approach to reducing the debts of developing countries has been to swap debt for equity in or ownership of business firms in debtor countries. Consider the following example of a debt-for-equity swap involving Mexico and Nissan Motor Company.

Economic Insight

Buying Back Bolivian Government Debt

In 1986, the government of Bolivia owed about $670 million to commercial banks. To reduce the size of its debt, the government proposed to negotiate a debt-buy-back agreement with the creditor banks. Bolivia's 131 creditor banks agreed to allow Bolivia to buy back some of its debt, subject to the following qualifications: Bolivia could not use its own holdings of dollars or other major currencies to buy the debt. Only donations of dollars from other countries could be used. The donations would be placed in a trust fund controlled by the IMF. Any donations unused in the buy-back would be returned to the donor nations.

In January 1988, Bolivia announced that it would pay 11 cents for each dollar of debt it purchased. Fifty-three banks offered to sell $270 million of debt for cash. Why would banks be willing to exchange Bolivian debt for 11 percent of its face value? Bolivia had made no payments on the debt for four years, and was unlikely to make payments any time soon. The banks realized that the money for the buy-back was coming from industrial-country foreign-aid support for Bolivia and would not reduce living standards below their already low level. Finally, Bolivia stated that any future buy-backs would occur at less than 11 cents on the dollar. The prospect of receiving a certain 11 percent was more attractive to 53 banks than the prospect of receiving nothing or less than 11 percent several years in the future.

■ For more information see Ruben Lamdany, "Voluntary Debt Reduction Operations: Bolivia, Mexico, and Beyond," *Contemporary Policy Issues*, April 1989, pp. 66–82.

In a debt-for-equity swap, a firm purchases a country's debt for less than its face value. The firm then trades the debt to the debtor government for currency, in order to purchase or increase an ownership position in a firm in the debtor country.

In 1986, Nissan wanted to expand its Mexican subsidiary and needed to acquire Mexican pesos to spend on the expansion. Nissan bought $60 million of Mexican government debt from U.S. commercial banks and other industrial countries for approximately $40 million. The Mexican government accepted the debt from Nissan in exchange for $54 million in pesos. Nissan used the pesos to expand its Mexican subsidiary.

How did each of the parties to the debt-for-equity swap benefit from the transaction? Mexico benefited by paying off some of its dollar-denominated debt at a discount from the face value ($54 million to wipe out $60 million of debt). Mexico was also able to wipe out this debt using pesos rather than dollars. An additional benefit to Mexico was that foreign investment in Mexican industry may stimulate growth of Mexican income, employment, and exports.

Nissan benefited by acquiring Mexican currency at a discount. This is the advantage of the debt-equity swap to the investor. The amount of the discount varies from country to country. The greater the risk of nonpayment associated with a country's debt, the greater the discount offered on the debt to prospective buyers. The bank benefits because the amount it receives—though less than the face value of the debt—is greater than what it will probably receive if it continues to hold the debt.

Table 3 lists the dollar amounts of debt-for-equity swaps by the major debtor nations. The amount of debt swapped ranges from $5.89 billion for Brazil to $0.04 billion for Nigeria. As a fraction of the debt owed to commercial banks, debt-for-equity swaps have been insignificant. Chile has been the most successful at reducing its bank debt, swapping 16 percent of its debt for equity.

Table 3 Debt-for-Equity Swaps, 1983–1988

Country	Amount of Debt Swapped	Percent of Bank Debt Swapped
Argentina	$ 1.32 billion	5 percent
Bolivia	.06	10
Brazil	5.89	8
Chile	2.35	16
Mexico	2.40	3
Nigeria	0.04	1
Philippines	0.53	4
Venezuela	0.35	1
Total	12.94	5

Bank debt owed is as of the end of 1985.
Source: From *World Financial Markets 7*, 1988, with permission of J.P. Morgan & Co Incorporated, copyright owner.

A debt-for-bonds swap is an exchange of new debtor-country bonds for existing commercial-bank debt.

2.b.4. Debt-for-Bonds Swaps   Another approach to reducing the bank debt of developing countries is a debt-for-bonds swap. The idea is that the developing country offers new long-term bonds in exchange for existing debt.

Mexico was the first country to attempt such a swap. In 1987 the Mexican government announced its offer to exchange twenty-year bonds for Mexican debt held by banks. The principal on the Mexican bonds was protected by U.S. Treasury bonds, which Mexico offered as collateral to any bank that participated. (*Collateral* is what stands behind the debt. If you take out a car loan and fail to repay it, the lender can seize your car. Home mortgages are backed by the real estate they finance. Often there are problems with collateral when lending to a foreign country. If a government can't repay its debt, how can the bank take back a highway or a dam?)

It might appear that a debt-for-bonds swap would not reduce a country's indebtedness, but simply change the composition of the debt from bank loans to long-term bonds. However, the debts owed to commercial banks are sold at a discount from the face value, due to the poor prospects of timely repayment. A debtor country can swap a dollar of bank debt for less than a dollar of bonds.

In the Mexican debt-for-bonds swap, commercial banks agreed to swap $3.7 billion of their Mexican loans for the new Mexican bonds at a rate of 69.77 cents per dollar. Mexico swapped $3.7 billion of commercial bank debt for $2.6 billion of new bonds, thereby lowering its outstanding external debt by $1.1 billion.

RECAP

1. The developing-country debt crisis first became apparent when Mexico announced its inability to meet its foreign loan obligations in 1982.

Country Risk

International lending involves risks that are absent from domestic transactions. There are no international courts to enforce contracts, and there is typically no collateral for a lender to repossess in case of a default. As a result, it is important for commercial banks to assess carefully the risks involved in lending to a particular country.

Country risk is the term for the overall political and financial situation in a country, and the extent to which these conditions may affect its ability to repay its debts. Political factors that may be important in assessing risk include: tensions between ethnic and religious groups that could lead to conflict; extreme nationalism and dislike for foreigners, which could lead to nationalization of foreign assets in the country; social conflicts that could give rise to demonstrations, violence, and guerrilla war; and the organization and strength of radical groups.

Economic and financial factors that are often considered in assessing country risk include: the amount of debt owed to foreigners; holdings of major currencies, like the dollar, that can be used to finance short-term needs if exports fall; diversification of exports, since a country heavily dependent on a single export commodity will be more subject to wide swings in export revenues; and GNP growth, which serves as a crude indicator of general economic conditions in a country.

Institutional Investor magazine surveys international bankers twice a year, seeking their evaluations of the credit worthiness of different countries. The bankers rate each country on a scale of zero (for worst risk) to 100 (for best risk). The accompanying table lists a recent ranking of the 25 most credit-worthy countries. The United States was always the top-ranked country until September 1986, when Japan moved to the top. All of the countries at the top of the list are good risks, to whom banks readily lend money. Those at the bottom of the list (not shown here) would find new commercial bank lending almost impossible to obtain.

Rank Sept. 1988	Country	Institutional Investor Credit Rating
1	Japan	94.8
2	Switzerland	93.9
3	West Germany	93.1
4	United States	89.7
5	United Kingdom	86.9
6	Netherlands	86.7
7	Canada	85.4
8	France	84.7
9	Austria	82.9
10	Sweden	79.7
11	Norway	79.2
12	Finland	78.3
13	Italy	77.5
14	Belgium	77.3
15	Taiwan	76.8
16	Singapore	74.8
17	Spain	73.4
18	Denmark	71.7
19	Australia	69.2
20	Hongkong	69.0
21	U.S.S.R.	64.7
22	New Zealand	63.9
23	South Korea	63.7
24	China	63.3
25	Ireland	62.3
Global average rating		38.7

Source: Data from *Institutional Investor*, September 1988, p. 226. Used by permission.

2. The debt crisis was brought on by a combination of rising interest rates and worldwide recession.

3. The Baker Plan called for commercial banks to lend new money to debtors, enabling them to restructure their economies to promote free enterprise.

4. Some countries have been able to reduce their external debt by buying back the debt they owe to commercial banks at a discount from face value.

5. In a debt-for-equity swap, a firm acquires a country's debt at a discount from face value and then swaps this debt for the debtors' domestic currency. The firm then uses this currency to buy equity in a debtor-country firm.

6. In a debt-for-bonds swap, a debtor country issues bonds which it offers to its creditor banks in exchange for existing debt at a discount.

SUMMARY

▼▲ **What is foreign-exchange risk, and how does it affect international traders?**

1. An amount of foreign currency to be paid or received in the future has an uncertain domestic-currency value, since future exchange rates are not known. § 1.a

▼▲ **How do the forward, futures, and option markets in foreign exchange allow a firm to eliminate foreign-exchange risk?**

2. The foreign-exchange risk associated with foreign-currency-denominated transactions may be reduced or eliminated in the forward, futures, or option market. § 1

3. The forward exchange market is a global telephone market in which foreign currencies in amounts of $1 million or more are bought and sold for delivery at some future date. § 1.b

4. The foreign-exchange futures market is an organized market where certain currencies are

bought and sold, by means of contracts standardized as to amount and duration, for delivery at a future date. § 1.c

5. Foreign-currency options provide the right to buy or sell a specified amount of currency at a set price on or before a particular date. § 1.d

▼▲ **What caused the international debt crisis?**

6. The developing-country debt crisis was partly a result of the global recession and record high interest rates that occurred in the early 1980s. § 2.a

▼▲ **What solutions have been proposed for the debt crisis?**

7. Plans to reduce the burden of developing-country debt include the Baker Plan, which called for new loans in return for greater reliance on free markets, debt buy-backs, debt-for-equity swaps, and debt-for-bond swaps. § 2.b

spot exchange rate § 1.a

foreign-exchange risk § 1.a

open position § 1.a

covered position § 1.a

forward exchange rate § 1.b

call § 1.d

put § 1.d

striking price § 1.d

LIBOR § 2.a

debt rescheduling § 2.a

EXERCISES

Basic Terms and Concepts

1. A U.S. importer has agreed to purchase £1 million worth of books from a British publisher. Payment is to be made in 30 days. Use Figures 1–3 to determine the dollar cost of the books on the forward, futures, and options markets.

2. In question 1, under what circumstances would the importer benefit by waiting 30 days and buying the pounds in the spot market?

3. How do the forward, futures, and options markets for foreign exchange differ?

4. The fact that many developing-country loans are made at variable interest rates is important in understanding the debt crisis. Why?

5. What was the Baker Plan? Why did it have limited success?

6. Describe each of the following and explain how it can reduce a country's debt burden: (a) debt buy-backs, (b) debt-for-equity swaps, (c) debt-for-bonds swaps. Why would creditors accept less than the face value of a loan in repayment?

Extended Concepts

7. Suppose the current spot price of French francs is $.15. Vine Brothers wine importers is buying French wine, to be paid for in six months. At the time the contract is signed, John Vine predicts that the exchange rate in six months will be $.14. Jack Vine predicts that the exchange rate will be $.18. Suppose the actual spot exchange rate in six months turns out to be $.155. Which of the Vine Brothers made the best forecast of the future spot rate? (Hint: the best forecast is the one that would have led the Vine Brothers to choose a strategy that maximized its profits.)

8. If you were a bank loan officer considering a loan of $1 million to the government of a small developing country, what economic and political data would be useful in deciding whether or not to make the loan?

The Dirty Little Debt Secret

In all the hand wringing over Latin America's economic problems, one dirty little secret is often overlooked: the countries with the largest debts also have some of the world's biggest savers. The problem is that rich Latins smuggle much of what they own to places like the United States and Switzerland. The "flight capital" sits in foreign bank accounts or is invested in foreign real estate. Repatriated, it would go a long way toward easing the debt crisis. Mexico, which owes foreigners about $100 billion, has an estimated $84 billion in assets overseas; Venezuela's flight-capital assets equal nearly twice its foreign debt . . . In private, Treasury Secretary Nicholas Brady has called the situation "outrageous." Publicly, he says the return of flight capital is crucial to the success of his plan for cutting Third World debt.

Getting the money to flow back in the other direction is no small task. Latins have good reasons for shipping their riches overseas. If they keep money in savings accounts at home, its value can be wiped out by triple-digit and even quadruple-digit inflation. If they invest in local businesses, the profits may be taxed at steep rates. Decades of economic mismanagement and political instability have caused many Latins simply to lose faith in their governments. . .

American banks that have lent huge sums to Latin America complain that flight capital is keeping them from getting the money back. But ironically, the banks sometimes contribute to the problem. They not only accept expatriated deposits, they solicit them. In February Citibank's Argentine operation mailed a letter to its local clients saying it could increase

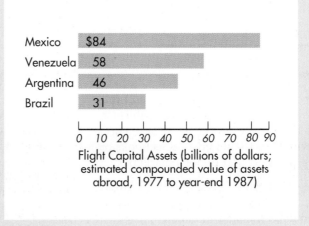

Mexico	$84
Venezuela	58
Argentina	46
Brazil	31

0 10 20 30 40 50 60 70 80 90

Flight Capital Assets (billions of dollars; estimated compounded value of assets abroad, 1977 to year-end 1987)

their capital "through investments in liquid assets, local as well as foreign." An Argentine banker calls the letter a "discreet invitation" to send money abroad. Some critics of the banks say they haven't been hurt by the debt crisis as much as they protest, since much of the money they lent to the Latin countries has made it back to them in private bank accounts.

Latin countries could reduce the incentives to stash capital abroad by taxing the funds their citizens keep overseas. For that to work, rich nations would have to force their banks to reveal the identities of foreign depositors and assist their governments in withholding taxes. But expatriated capital won't really get put to work unless it's returned home. The world's leading bankers are determined to start making that happen. In April, 1989 the International Monetary Fund and the World Bank tentatively earmarked $25 billion to support Brady's plan on condition that Latin debtors be pressured to adopt policies that would slow capital flight.

To bring the money back home,

international banks will have to lean harder on Latin countries, forcing them to make their economies good investments. It's long been a condition of debt renegotiation that nations adopt austerity measures that will lower inflation rates and stabilize growth. Under the new plan, the banks may monitor capital flight to gauge how well the countries are doing — and refuse new loans if the money keeps hemorrhaging. That's tough stuff, since countries that do shape up have no guarantee that skeptical citizens will start repatriating their cash. Says William Cline of the Institute for International Economics, "It will probably be later rather than sooner that you start getting that capital back from abroad and out from under floorboards and mattresses." Given the record so far, even getting the money back "later" would be a small miracle.

■ Source: David Pauly with Rich Thomas and Judith Evans, "The Dirty Little Debt Secret: Searching for Ways to Stem Latin 'Capital Flight,'" Newsweek, April 17, 1989, p. 46.

Commentary

The developing-country debt crisis arose from a number of causes. High interest rates in the early 1980s (see figure below) raised the debt payments owed to creditors. A global recession caused the exports of developing countries to fall, making it more difficult for these countries to earn the dollars, yen, and deutsche marks required to service their debt. Much of the borrowed money was used for consumption, which does not add to the capital stock of a country, rather than investment, which would have increased the productive capacity of countries and thus their ability to export. Finally, some of the borrowed money that entered the country simply flowed out again to private bank accounts in Europe or the United States. The debt crisis faced by governments of developing countries would be eased at least somewhat if the private funds that left their countries through capital flight were brought back home for domestic investment.

Capital flight occurs when people expect that the return from investing money abroad is higher or safer than the return from keeping money in a domestic account. A government's financial policies may cause domestic interest rates to fall below those offered in other countries. In some developing countries, these policies resulted in negative real interest rates during periods of rapid inflation. There is also a political dimension to capital flight. People will attempt to take their wealth out of a country when there is a perceived threat of expropriation of their assets or when there are fears of political instability.

Another important cause of capital flight is an overvalued exchange rate. Foreign assets (such as a foreign savings account) can be purchased cheaply when the exchange rate is strong. Also, if the exchange rate's strength is thought to be temporary, there will be high returns in terms of the domestic currency on purchasing foreign assets before the exchange rate weakens. In the late 1970s, there was a significant overvaluation of the currency in Argentina, Uruguay, and Chile, the "Southern Cone" countries of Latin America. The strength of the exchange rate in these countries was seen as temporary, leading to a surge in capital flight.

Actual data on the magnitude of capital flight are very difficult to obtain since the process is necessarily surreptitious. Economists at the World Bank have constructed estimates of capital flight as a percentage of gross capital inflows (*World Development Report*, 1985). The estimates show that, for the period 1979–1982, capital flight represented 27 percent of gross capital inflows for Uruguay, 48 percent for Mexico, 65 percent for Argentina, and 137 percent for Venezuela. Capital flight is not just a Latin American phenomenon. There was also significant capital flight in the Philippines and Nigeria, for example, in the early 1980s.

Capital flight benefits some sectors of society at the expense of others. Typically, the wealthier sectors of society engage in capital flight and benefit from higher returns than they would otherwise have obtained. The increased indebtedness of a country due to capital flight necessitates painful adjustment policies. The burden of these policies falls disproportionately on the poorer sectors of society. Thus capital flight often generates a redistribution of income from the poor to the rich.

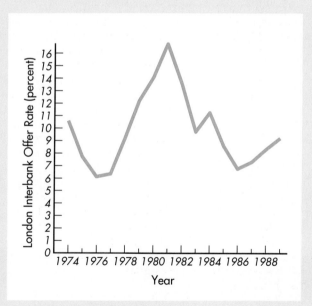

Glossary

absolute advantage   the ability to produce a good or service with fewer resources than others use

adaptive expectation   an expectation formed on the basis of information collected in the past

aggregate demand curve   a curve that shows the different equilibrium levels of expenditures at different price levels

aggregate supply curve   a curve that shows the amount of production at different price levels

allocative efficiency   the efficiency that occurs when no resources are wasted; when no one can be made better off without making someone worse off

antitrust policy   government policies and programs designed to control the growth of monopoly and enhance competition

appreciate   to increase the value of a currency under floating exchange rates—that is, exchange rates determined by supply and demand

arbitrage   simultaneously buying in a market where the price is low and selling in a market where the price is high to profit from the price differential

association as causation   the mistaken assumption that because two events seem to occur together, one causes the other

assumptions   statements that are taken for granted without justification

automatic stabilizer   an element of fiscal policy that changes automatically as income changes

autonomous consumption   consumption that is independent of income

average propensity to consume (APC)   the proportion of disposable income spent for consumption

average propensity to save (APS)   the proportion of disposable income saved

bad   any item for which we would pay to have less

balance of payments   a record of a country's trade in goods, services, and financial assets with the rest of the world

balanced-budget multiplier   a measure of how much equilibrium income changes if government spending and taxes both increase or decrease by the same amount

barter   the direct exchange of goods and services without the use of money

base year   the year against which other years are measured

bilateral aid   foreign aid that flows from one country to another

black market   illegal exchanges

budget deficit   the shortage that results when government spending is greater than revenue

budget surplus   the excess that results when government spending is less than revenue

business cycle   the recurrent pattern of rising real GNP followed by falling real GNP

business firm   a business organization controlled by a single management

call   the right to buy currency at a certain price

capital   products such as machinery and equipment that are used in production

capital account   the record in the balance of payments of the flow of financial assets into and out of a country

capital consumption allowance   the estimated value of depreciation plus the value of accidental damage to capital stock

capital control   a government-imposed restriction on the free movement of financial assets between nations

capitalism   an economic system in which most economic decisions are made by private owners and most property is privately owned

cash transfers   money allocated away from one group in society to another

centrally planned system   an economic system in which the government determines what goods and services are produced and the prices at which they are sold

ceteris paribus   other things being equal, or everything else held constant

circular flow diagram   a model showing the flow of output and income from one sector of the economy to another

classical economics   a school of thought that assumes that real national income is determined by aggregate supply, while the equilibrium price level is determined by aggregate demand

coincident indicator   a variable that changes at the same time that real output changes

commercial bank loan   a bank loan at market rates of interest, often involving a bank syndicate

commercial policy government policy that influences international trade flows

communism an economic system characterized by collective ownership of all resources and centrally planned economic decision making

comparative advantage the ability to produce a good or service at a lower opportunity cost than someone else

complementary goods goods that are used together (as the price of one rises, the demand for the other falls)

composite currency an artificial unit of account that is an average of the values of several national currencies

constant marginal opportunity cost an unchanging amount of one good or service that must be given up to obtain one additional unit of another good or service, no matter how many units are being produced

consumer price index (CPI) a measure of the average price of goods and services purchased by the typical household

consumer sovereignty the supreme authority of consumers to determine, by means of their purchases, what is produced

consumption household spending

consumption function the relationship between disposable income and consumption

corporation a legal entity owned by shareholders whose liability for the firm's losses is limited to the value of the stock they own

cost of living adjustment (COLA) an increase in wages that is designed to match increases in prices of items purchased by the typical household

covered position the situation of a firm whose foreign exchange risk from a future transaction has been eliminated

credit available savings that are lent to borrowers to spend

crowd out a drop in consumption or investment spending caused by government spending

currency substitution the use of foreign money as a substitute for domestic money when the domestic money has a high rate of inflation

current account the sum of the merchandise, services, and unilateral transfers accounts in the balance of payments

customs union an organization of nations whose members have no trade barriers among themselves but impose common trade barriers on nonmembers

debt rescheduling an agreement that offers debtors a longer repayment period and, usually, a short grace period during which no payments, or only small payments, are required

decreasing-cost industry an industry in which the costs of producing a unit of output fall as more output is produced

decreasing marginal opportunity cost a falling amount of one good or service that must be given up to obtain one additional unit of another good or service, no matter how many units are being produced

deficit in a balance of payments account, the amount by which debits exceed credits

demand the quantities of a well-defined commodity that consumers are willing and able to buy at each possible price during a given period of time, ceteris paribus

demand curve a graph of a demand schedule that measures price on the vertical axis and quantity demanded on the horizontal axis

demand schedule a list or table of the prices and the corresponding quantities demanded of a particular good or service

deposit expansion multiplier the reciprocal of the reserve requirement

depreciation (of capital) a reduction in the value of capital goods over time due to their use in production

depreciate (a currency) to decrease in the value of a currency under floating exchange rates

depression a severe, prolonged economic contraction

derived demand demand stemming from what a good or service can produce, not demand for the good or service itself

determinants of demand factors other than the price of the good that influence demand—income, tastes, prices of related goods and services, expectations, and number of buyers

determinants of supply factors other than the price of the good that influence supply—prices of resources, technology and productivity, expectations of producers, number of producers, and the prices of related goods and services

devaluation a deliberate decrease in the official value of a currency

differentiated products products that consumers perceive to be different from one another

discount rate the interest rate the Fed charges commercial banks

discouraged workers workers who have stopped looking for work because they believe no one will offer them a job

discretionary fiscal policy changes in government spending and taxation aimed at achieving a policy goal

discrimination prejudice that occurs when factors unrelated to marginal productivity affect the wages or jobs that are obtained

disequilibrium a point at which quantity demanded and quantity supplied are not equal at a particular price

disposable personal income (DPI) personal income minus personal taxes

dissaving spending financed by borrowing or using savings

double coincidence of wants the situation that exists when A has what B wants and B has what A wants

double-entry bookkeeping a system of accounting in which every transaction is recorded in at least two accounts and in which the debit total must equal the credit total for the transaction as a whole

dual economy an economy in which two sectors (typically manufacturing and agriculture) show very different levels of development

dumping selling goods at a lower price in foreign markets than at home

durables goods that are used over a period of one or more years

economic costs total costs including explicit costs and the full opportunity costs of the resources that the producer does not buy or hire but already owns

economic efficiency the employment of resources in their highest-valued use to maximize the value of the output

economic good any good that is scarce

economic growth an increase in real national income, usually measured as the percentage change in gross national product or gross domestic product per year

economic profit total revenue less total costs including opportunity costs

economies of scale the decrease of unit costs as the quantity of production increases and all resources are variable

entrepreneur someone who recognizes an opportunity for earning economic profit and is able to collect and organize the resources and undertake the risk necessary to obtain this profit

entrepreneurial ability the ability to recognize a profitable opportunity and the willingness and ability to organize land, labor, and capital and assume the risk associated with the opportunity

equation of exchange an equation that relates the quantity of money to nominal GNP

equilibrium the point at which quantity demanded and quantity supplied are equal at a particular price

equilibrium exchange rates the exchange rates that are established in the absence of government foreign exchange market intervention

Eurocurrency market the market for deposits and loans generally denominated in a currency other than the currency of the country in which the transaction occurs; also called offshore banking

European Currency Unit (ECU) a unit of account used by western European nations as their official reserve asset

European Monetary System (EMS) an organization composed of Western European nations that maintain fixed exchange rates among themselves and floating exchange rates with the rest of the world

excess reserves the cash reserves beyond those required, which can be loaned

exchange rate the price of one country's money in terms of another country's money

excise tax a tax on the sale of a particular commodity

export substitution the use of labor to produce manufactured products for export rather than agricultural products for the domestic market

export supply curve a curve showing the relationship between the world price of a good and the amount that a country will export

exports products that a country sells to other countries

expropriation the government seizure of assets, typically without adequate compensation to the owners

external costs costs not borne by the direct participants in a transaction

externalities costs or benefits of a transaction that are borne by someone not directly involved in the transaction

factors of production land, labor, capital, and entrepreneurial activity

fallacy of composition the mistaken assumption that what applies in the case of one applies to the case of many

Federal Deposit Insurance Corporation (FDIC) a federal agency that insures deposits in commercial banks

federal funds rate the interest rate a bank charges when it lends excess reserves to another bank

Federal Open Market Committee (FOMC) the official policy-making body of the Federal Reserve System

Federal Reserve the central bank of the United States

fiscal policy policy directed toward government spending and taxation

FOMC directive instructions issued by the FOMC to the Federal Reserve bank in New York to implement monetary policy

foreign aid gifts or low-cost loans made to developing countries from official sources

foreign direct investment the purchase of a physical operating unit in a foreign country

foreign exchange foreign currency and bank deposits that are denominated in foreign money

foreign exchange market a global market in which people trade one currency for another

foreign exchange market intervention buying or selling of currencies by a government or central bank to achieve a specified exchange rate

foreign exchange risk the threat that future foreign currency payments or receipts will have a different domestic currency value than expected

forward exchange rate the price established today for delivery of a foreign currency at a future date

fractional reserve banking system a system in which banks keep less than 100 percent of the deposits available for withdrawal

free good a good for which there is no scarcity

free ride the enjoyment of the benefits of a good by a producer or consumer without having to pay for it

free rider a consumer or producer who enjoys the benefits of a good without paying for it

free trade area an organization of nations whose members have no trade barriers among themselves but are free to fashion their own trade policies toward nonmembers

fundamental disequilibrium a permanent shift in the foreign-exchange-market supply and demand curves, such that the fixed exchange rate is no longer an equilibrium rate

future value the equivalent value in the future of some amount received today

gold exchange standard an exchange-rate system in which each nation fixes the value of its currency in terms of gold, but buys and sells the U.S. dollar rather than gold to maintain fixed exchange rates

gold standard a system whereby national currencies are fixed in terms of their value in gold, thus creating fixed exchange rates between currencies

gross domestic product (GDP) gross national product minus net factor income from abroad

gross investment total investment, including investment expenditures required to replace capital goods consumed in current production

gross national product (GNP) the market value of all final goods and services produced in a year by domestic resources

household one or more persons who occupy a unit of housing

human capital skills, training, and personal health acquired through education and on-the-job training

hyperinflation an extremely high rate of inflation

hypothesis an explanation that accounts for a set of facts

implicit GNP deflator a broad measure of the prices of goods and services included in the gross national product

import demand curve a curve showing the relationship between the world price of a good and the amount that a country will import

import substitution the substitution of domestically produced manufactured goods for imported manufactured goods

imports products that a country buys from other countries

in-kind transfers the allocation of goods and services from one group in society to another

income effect the change in quantity demanded that occurs when the purchasing power of income is altered as a result of a price change

increasing marginal opportunity cost a rising amount of one good or service that must be given up to obtain one additional unit of any good or service, no matter how many units are being produced

indirect business tax a tax that is collected by businesses for a government agency

inflation a sustained rise in the average level of prices

interest rate effect a change in interest rates that causes investment and therefore aggregate expenditures to change as the level of prices changes

interest rate parity (IRP) the condition under which similar financial assets have the same interest rate when measured in the same currency

intermediate good a good that is used in the production of final goods and services

intermediate target an objective used to achieve some ultimate policy goal

international banking facility (IBF) a division of a U.S. bank that is allowed to receive deposits from and make loans to nonresidents of the United States without the restrictions that apply to domestic U.S. banks

International Monetary Fund (IMF) an international organization that supervises exchange-rate arrangements and lends money to member countries experiencing problems meeting their external financial obligations

international reserve asset an asset used to settle debts between governments

international reserve currency a currency held by a government to settle international debts

international trade effect the change in aggregate expenditures resulting from a change in the domestic price level that changes the price of domestic goods in relation to foreign goods

intraindustry trade simultaneous import and export of goods in the same industry by a particular country

intrapreneurial ability an ability to act as an entrepreneur within an existing institution or firm

inventory the stock of unsold goods held by a firm

investment spending on capital goods to be used in producing goods and services

Keynesian economics a school of thought that emphasizes the role government plays in stabilizing the economy by managing aggregate demand

Keynesian region the portion of the aggregate supply curve at which prices are fixed because of unemployment and excess capacity

labor the physical and intellectual services of people, including the training, education, and abilities of the individuals in a society

labor force participation entering the work force

lagging indicator a variable that changes after real output changes

laissez faire total reliance on the market system, with no government intervention

land all natural resources, such as minerals, timber, and water, as well as the land itself

law of demand as the price of a good or service rises (falls), the quantity of that good or service that people are willing and able to purchase during a particular period of time falls (rises), ceteris paribus

law of supply as the price of a good or service that producers are willing and able to offer for sale during a particular period of time rises (falls), the quantity of that good or service supplied rises (falls), ceteris paribus

leading indicator a variable that changes before real output changes

legal reserves the cash a bank holds in its vault plus its deposit in the Fed

LIBOR the London interbank offer rate; the interest rate charged for loans between major London banks

liquid asset an asset that can easily be exchanged for goods and services

long run a period of time just long enough that the quantities of all resources can be varied

long-run aggregate supply curve (LRAS) a vertical line at potential level of national income

macroeconomics the study of the economy as a whole

managed floating exchange rates the system whereby central banks intervene in the floating foreign-exchange market to influence exchange rates; also referred to as dirty float

marginal opportunity cost the amount of one good or service that must be given up to obtain one additional unit of another good or service

marginal propensity to consume (MPC) change in consumption as a proportion of change in disposable income

marginal propensity to import (MPI) change in imports as a proportion of change in income

marginal propensity to save (MPS) change in saving as a proportion of change in disposable income

market a place or service that enables buyers and sellers to exchange goods and services

market price the equilibrium price

market price system an economic system in which supply and demand determine what goods and services are produced and the prices at which they are sold

microeconomics the study of economics at the level of the individual

mixed economies economies that have characteristics of more than one economic system

monetarist economics a school of thought that emphasizes the role changes in the money supply play in determining equilibrium national income and price level

monetary policy policy directed toward control of the money supply

monetary reform a new monetary policy that includes the introduction of a new monetary unit

money anything that is generally acceptable to sellers in exchange for goods and services

money supply financial assets that are immediately available for spending

multilateral aid aid provided by international organizations supported by many nations

multinational business a firm that owns and operates producing units in foreign countries

multiple exchange rates a system whereby a government fixes different exchange rates for different types of transactions

multiplier a measure of the change in income produced by a change in autonomous expenditures

national income (NI) net national product minus indirect business taxes

national income accounting the process that summarized the level of production in an economy over a specific period of time, typically a year

natural rate of unemployment the unemployment rate that would exist in the absence of cyclical unemployment

net exports exports minus imports

net investment gross investment minus capital consumption allowance

net national product (NNP) gross national product minus capital consumption allowance

new classical economics a school of thought that holds that changes in real national income are a product of unexpected changes in the level of prices

nominal GNP a measure of national output based on the current prices of goods and services

nominal interest rate the observed interest rate in the market

nominal price the money price of a good

nondurables goods that are used over a short period of time

nonexhaustible natural resources resources that can be replaced or renewed

normal goods goods for which the income elasticity of demand is positive

normative analysis analysis of what ought to be

occupational segregation the separation of jobs by sex

open economy an economy in which a relatively large fraction of the GNP is devoted to internationally tradable goods

open market operations the buying and selling of government bonds by the Fed to control bank reserves and the money supply

open position the situation of a firm waiting to buy foreign currency at a future spot rate

opportunity cost the highest-valued alternative that must be forgone when a choice is made

opportunity cost of capital the forgone return on an entrepreneur's funds used in business

partnership a business with two or more owners who share the firm's profits and losses

patent a legal document that gives an inventor the legal rights to an invention

per capita real national income real national income divided by the population

personal income (PI) national income plus income currently received but not earned, minus income currently earned but not received

Phillips curve a graph that illustrates the relationship between inflation and the unemployment rate

portfolio investment the purchase of securities

positive analysis analysis of what is

potential GNP the output produced at the natural rate of unemployment

precautionary demand for money the demand for money to cover unplanned transactions or emergencies

predatory dumping dumping to drive competitors out of business

price index a measure of the average price level in an economy

primary product a product in the first stage of production, which often serves as input in the production of another product

principle of mutual exclusivity the owner of private property is entitled to enjoy the consumption of the property privately

private costs costs borne by the individual in the transaction that created the costs

private property right the limitation of ownership to an individual

privatization transferring a publicly owned enterprise to private ownership

producer price index (PPI) a measure of average prices received by producers

production possibilities curve (PPC) a graphical representation showing the maximum quantity of goods and services that can be produced using limited resources to the fullest extent possible

productivity the quantity of output produced per unit of resource

progressive tax a tax whose rate rises as income rises

proportional tax a tax whose rate does not change as the tax base changes

public goods goods whose consumption cannot be limited only to the person who purchased the good

purchasing power the quantity of goods and services that a given quantity of income can buy

purchasing power parity (PPP) the condition under which monies have the same purchasing power in different countries

put the right to sell currency at a certain price

quantity quota a limit on the amount of a good that may be imported

quantity theory of money with constant velocity, changes in the quantity of money change nominal GNP

rate of return profit as a percentage of the cost of an investment

rational expectation an expectation that is formed using all available relevant information

rational self-interest the term economists use to describe how people make choices

real GNP a measure of the quantity of goods and services produced, adjusted for price changes

real interest rate the nominal interest rate minus the rate of inflation

recession a period in which real GNP falls

recessionary gap the increase in expenditures required to reach potential GNP

regressive tax a tax whose rate decreases as the tax base changes

relative price the price of one good expressed in terms of another good

required reserves the cash reserves (a percentage of deposits) a bank must keep on hand or on deposit with the Federal Reserve

reservation wage the minimum wage a worker is willing to accept

reserve currency a currency that is used to settle international debts and is held by governments to use in foreign exchange market interventions

residual claimants entrepreneurs who acquire profit or the revenue remaining after all other resources have been paid

risk premium the extra return required to offset the higher risk associated with investing in a foreign asset

rule of 72 the number of years required for an amount to double in value is 72 divided by the annual rate of growth

saving not consuming all current production

saving function the relationship between disposable income and saving

scarcity the shortage that exists when less of something is available than is wanted at a zero price

scientific method a manner of analyzing issues that involves five steps: recognition of the problem, making assumptions, model building, hypothesis formation, and hypothesis testing

services work done for others that does not involve the production of goods

shock an unexpected change in a variable

short run a period of time just short enough that the quantities of all resources cannot be varied

shortage a quantity supplied that is smaller than the quantity demanded at a given price

social benefits the private and external benefits of a transaction

social costs the private and external costs of a transaction

socialism an economic system characterized by government ownership of resources other than labor and centralized economic decision making

sole proprietorship a business owned by one person who receives all the profits and is responsible for all the debts incurred by the business

special drawing right (SDR) an artificial unit of account created by averaging the values of the U.S. dollar, German mark, Japanese yen, French franc, and British pound

specialist someone whose opportunity costs of switching to an activity other than the one he or she specializes in is very high relative to the opportunity cost of the activity in which he or she specializes

speculative demand for money the demand for money created by uncertainty about the value of other assets

speculators people who seek to profit from an expected shift in an exchange rate by selling the currency expected to depreciate and buying the currency expected to appreciate, then exchanging the appreciated currency for the depreciated currency after the rate adjustment

spending multiplier the reciprocal of the sum of the MPS and the MPI

spot exchange rate the exchange rate for delivery of a currency immediately, or ''on the spot''

sterilization the use of domestic open market operations to offset the effects of a foreign exchange market intervention on the domestic money supply

striking price the fixed price at which you may buy or sell in an option contract

subsidies payments made by government to domestic firms to encourage exports

substitute goods goods that can be used in place of each other (as the price of one rises, the demand for the other rises)

substitution effect the tendency of people to purchase less expensive goods that serve the same purpose as a good whose price has risen

supply the amount of a good or service that producers are willing and able to offer for sale at each possible price during a period of time, ceteris paribus

supply curve a graph of a supply schedule that measures price on the vertical axis and quantity supplied on the horizontal axis

supply schedule a list or table of prices and corresponding quantities supplied of a particular good or service

surplus a quantity supplied that is larger than the quantity demanded at a given price

surplus (in a balance of payments account) the amount by which credits exceed debits

tariffs taxes on imports or exports

tax multiplier a measure of the effect of a change in taxes on the equilibrium level of income

technical efficiency the combination of inputs that results in the lowest cost

technology ways of combining resources to produce output

terms of trade the amount of exports that must be exchanged for some amount of imports

tests trials or measurements used to determine whether a theory is consistent with the facts

theory (or model) a simplified, logical story based on positive analysis that is used to explain an event

time inconsistent a characteristic of a policy or plan that changes over time in response to changing conditions

trade creation an effect of a preferential trade agreement, allowing a country to obtain goods at a lower cost than is available at home

trade credit the extension of a period of time before an importer must pay for goods or services purchased

trade diversion an effect of a preferential trade agreement, reducing economic efficiency by shifting production to a higher-cost producer

trade off to give up one good or activity in order to obtain some good or activity

trade surplus (deficit) exists when imports are less than (exceed) exports

traditional economies economic systems in which economic decisions are based on customs, beliefs, and practices handed down from one generation to another

transaction costs the costs involved in making an exchange

transactions account a checking account at a bank or other financial institution that can be drawn on to make payments

transactions demand for money the demand to hold money to buy goods and services

transfer payment income transferred from one citizen, who is earning income, to another citizen, who may not be

underemployment the employment of workers in jobs that do not utilize their productive potential

underground market unreported exchanges of goods and services

unemployment rate the percentage of the labor force that is not working

unlimited wants boundless desires for goods and services

value added the difference between the value of output and the value of the intermediate goods used in the production of that output

value-added tax (VAT) a general sales tax collected at each stage of production

value quota a limit on the monetary value of a good that may be imported

velocity of money the average number of times each dollar is spent on final goods and services in a year

venture capital funds provided by a firm or individual that specializes in lending to new, unproven firms

wealth the value of all assets owned by a household

wealth effect a change in the real value of wealth that causes spending to change when the price level changes

World Bank an international organization that makes loans and provides technical expertise to developing countries

X-inefficiency the tendency of a firm not faced with competition to become inefficient

Credits *(continued from p. ii)*

Macroeconomics photo essay: 1 © Bob Daemmrich/Stock, Boston; 2 © 1987 Peter Menzel/Stock, Boston; 3 © David R. Frazier Photolibrary; 4 Michael Gluck; 5 © J. L. Atlan/Sygman; 6 © Bob Daemmrich/The Image Works; 7 courtesy of Matsushita; 8 © Bob Daemmrich/The Image Works; 9 © Francis de Richemond/The Image Works; 10 © 1990 Louis Psihoyos/Matrix; 11 (top) © Cameramann International, Ltd.; 12 (bottom) © Cameramann International, Ltd.;

In-text photos: 1.1 © David R. Frazier Photolibrary; 2.1 © 1988 Penn/Reflex/Picture Group; 2.2 Terry Husebye; 2.3 Howard Grey/Tony Stone Worldwide; 3.1 © Chris Andrews/Stock, Boston; 4.1 AP/Wide World Photos; 4.2 © David R. Frazier Photolibrary; 5.1 © 1988 Andrew Popper/Picture Group; 5.2 Haruyoshi Yamaguchi; 5.3 ©1988 Reginald Parker/Images Unlimited; 6.1 © 1989 Robert D. Tonsing/Picture Group; 7.1 © Dr. Jeffrey Aranita 1989/courtesy Bank of Tokyo New York Group; 7.2 ©1990 Arthur Meyerson; 8.1 Margaret Bourke-White, Life Magazine © Time Warner Inc.; 9.1 © Kennedy/TexaStock; 10.1 Nina Barnett; 10.2 Thomas W. Parkin/VALAN; 11.1 © David R. Frazier Photolibrary; 12.1 Katherine Lambert; 13.1 © David R. Frazier Photolibrary; 14.1 UPI/Bettmann Newsphotos; 15.1 Gilabert/J.B. Pictures; 17.1 C. Bruce Forster; 18.1 © David R. Frazier Photolibrary; 18.2 © Mark Antman/The Image Works; 19.1 © Cameramann International, Ltd.; 20.1 © 1979 Farrell Grehan/Photo Researchers; 21.1 courtesy General Dynamics; 22.1 © F. Hibon/Sygma; 23.1 © Gayard/REA/Picture Group; 23.2 AP/Wide World Photos.

Text: Chapter 2: Economically Speaking, "Selling Your Firm May Hike Your Pay." Reprinted by permission, Nation's Business, September 1989. Copyright 1989, U.S. Chamber of Commerce. Chapter 4: Economically Speaking, "Travel Industry Is Out of Touch, Customers Say." Reprinted by permission of *The Wall Street Journal*, © 1989 Dow Jones & Company, Inc. All Rights Reserved Worldwide. Chapter 5: Figure 5, "The World's Ten Largest Public Companies." Reprinted by permission of *The Wall Street Journal*, © 1989 Dow Jones & Company, Inc. All Rights Reserved Worldwide. Economically Speaking, "Student Entrepreneurs Find Road to Riches on Campus." Reprinted by permission of *The Wall Street Journal*, © 1989 Dow Jones & Company, Inc. All Rights Reserved Worldwide. Chapter 6: Economically Speaking, "Shaky Numbers: U.S. Statistics Mills Grind Out More Data That Are Then Revised." Reprinted by permission of *The Wall Street Journal*, © 1989 Dow Jones & Company, Inc. All Rights Reserved Worldwide. Chapter 8: Economic Insight, "Living with Hyperinflation in Argentina." Copyright, 1989, Los Angeles Times. Reprinted by permission. Chapter 9: Economic Insight, "The Great Ice Cream War." Reprinted by permission of *The Wall Street Journal*, and the author. Economically Speaking, "Saving, Not the American Way." From NEWSWEEK, 1/8/90, © 1990, Newsweek, Inc. All rights reserved. Reprinted by permission. Graph accompanying article in Economically Speaking. NEWSWEEK, 1/8/90, Blumrich. Chapter 11: Economically Speaking, "What Crisis in Productivity?" Copyright © 1989 by The New York Times Company. Reprinted by permission. Chapter 12: Economically Speaking, "Fantasy and Facts About the Budget Deficit." Copyright, Feb. 5, 1990, U.S. News & World Report. Chapter 13: Table 6, "The World's 25 Largest Companies." Reprinted by permission of *The Wall Street Journal, World Business Supplement*, © 1989 Dow Jones & Company, Inc. All Rights Reserved Worldwide. Chapter 20: Economically Speaking, "Believe It or Not, Japan Is Changing." Copyright, Feb. 26, 1990, U.S. News & World Report. Chapter 21: Economically Speaking, "Textile Makers Demanding More Protection Threaten Hopes for Seamless U.S. Trade Policy." Reprinted by permission of *The Wall Street Journal*, © 1990 Dow Jones & Company, Inc. All Rights Reserved Worldwide. Chapter 22: Table 1, "Exchange-Rate Arrangements." Used by permission. Chapter 23: Figure 1, "Exchange Rates." Reprinted by permission of *The Wall Street Journal*, © 1990 Dow Jones & Company, Inc. All Rights Reserved Worldwide. Figure 2, "Futures." Reprinted by permission of *The Wall Street Journal*, © 1990 Dow Jones & Company, Inc. All Rights Reserved Worldwide. Figure 3, "Options." Reprinted by permission of *The Wall Street Journal*, © 1990 Dow Jones & Company, Inc. All Rights Reserved Worldwide.

Index